The Wine Dictionary

ROSEMARY GEORGE

The Wine Dictionary

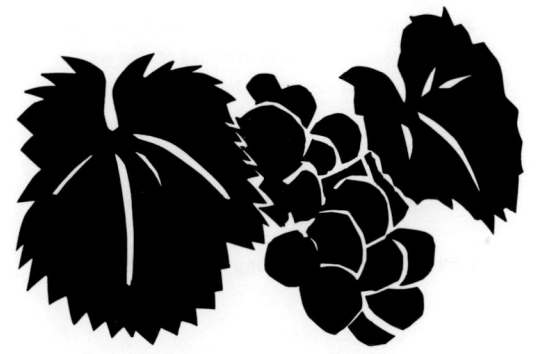

Longman

LONGMAN GROUP UK LIMITED
Longman House
Burnt Mill, Harlow, Essex CM20 2JE, England
and Associated Companies throughout the World

© Rosemary George 1989

All rights reserved. No part of this publication
may be reproduced, stored in a retrieval system,
or transmitted in any form or by any means, electronic,
mechanical, photocopying, recording or otherwise,
without the prior written permission of the copyright owner.

First published 1989

Designed and illustrated by Roy Trevelion

British Library Cataloguing in Publication Data

George, Rosemary
 The wine dictionary.
 1. Wines – Encyclopaedias
 I. Title
 641.2'2'0321

ISBN 0–582–89302–X

Set in 9/12 Novarese, Linotron 202 by Quorn Selective Repro
Queens Road, Loughborough, Leics.

Produced by Longman Group (FE) Ltd.
Printed in Hong Kong

Introduction

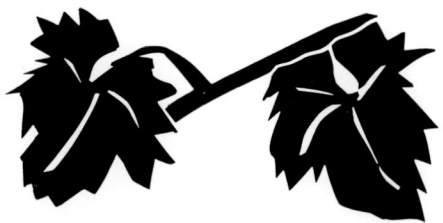

This was conceived as an easy reference book with an answer to all those questions to which I, for one, always forget the answer; how many bottles in a Salmanazar? what are the grape varieties of Pacherenc de Vic Bihl? is Chateau Kirwan in St. Julien or Margaux? and so on. My editor asked for 'fact-packed' entries; that is what I have tried to give. The objective of this dictionary is to supply information, as succinctly and as accurately as possible, to convey a brief impression of a wine, a grape variety or a region and an explanation of tasting terms and the terms used in viticulture and wine-making. If every single wine estate of any significance was to be included, this book would be unusable on grounds of weight – the Cocks & Feret directory of Bordeaux alone nearly broke my kitchen scales – so inevitably a personal selection has been made and I apologise for omissions of favourite producers.

Several people, more expert in particular areas than I am, checked my text for accuracy. I am very grateful to the following for all their comments and help, who allowed me to call upon their individual expertise in the compilation of this work: Maureen Ashley M.W.; Elizabeth Robertson M.W.; Elizabeth Berry M.W.; Jane Hunt M.W.; John Walter; David Hunter; Jaspar Morris M.W.; John Lipitch; Emmanuel de Kadt; Sheila Cavenagh Bradbury; Jo Hawkins; Joao Henriques; David Balls; Maggie McNie M.W.; Margarit Todorov. It goes without saying that any errors are mine alone.

ROSEMARY GEORGE   *May 1989*

A

A.C. See Appellation Contrôlée.

A.O.C. See Appellation Contrôlée.

A.P. NUMBER See Amtliche Prüfungsnummer.

AVA

The common abbreviation for the Californian equivalent of an appellation, an Approved Viticultural Area.

ABBOCCATO

An Italian term meaning between sweet and dry, lightly honeyed rather than very sweet and corresponding to medium dry on a label.

ABOURIOU

One of the several grape varieties used in the red wine of the Côtes du Marmandais, a local variety peculiar to that region, which gives the wine its distinctive flavour.

ABRUZZI ITALY

With some of the wilder, more mountainous countryside of southern Italy, this region has two DOCs: Montepulciano d'Abruzzo and Trebbiano d'Abruzzo. Other grape varieties are grown in the region, such as Riesling Renano, Pinot Grigio and Moscato, but only in tiny quantities.

ABYMES Savoie: FRANCE

One of the better crus of Vin de Savoie, producing crisp white wine from the Jacquère grape, grown on vineyards to the south of Chambéry.

ACACIA WINERY California: USA

One of the successful wineries of the Carneros region of the Napa and Sonoma Valleys, making excellent Pinor Noir and Chardonnay from this cool vineyard region.

ACESCENCE

An ailment resulting from a prolonged exposure to oxygen, with the formation of a grey film, caused by acetobacter attacking the alcohol in the wine, so that it eventually turns to vinegar.

ACETALDEHYDE

The principal aldehyde in all wines, and especially in sherry. In table wines, a large amount of acetaldehydes is undesirable as it means that the wine is beginning to oxidise, and may even have a sherry-like smell.

ACETIC

Describes a wine with a small amount of vinegar. A wine that is exposed to air, fermented at too high a temperature or carelessly bottled, is liable to turn acetic.

ACETOBACTER

The bacteria which can develop on the surface of the wine if it is subjected to a prolonged exposure to oxygen. Eventually they transform the ethyl alcohol into acetic acid and vinegar. The ailment is called *acescence*.

ACHAIA CLAUSS   GREECE

The largest and most important Greek wine house, with cellars in Patras and vineyards in the Peloponnese and Crete. Their wines include several brands: red and white Demestica, Castel Danielis, Château Clauss, as well as Mavrodaphne from Patras.

ACIDITY

This, in the form of various acids, mainly tartaric, citric, lactic and malic, is a vital constituent of wine. Without acidity, the wine would taste dull and flabby; with too much it is sharp and green. Acidity comes from the grapes and also from the fermentation process. Acetic acid is to be avoided. Three types of acidity are recognised: volatile acidity, fixed acidity and total acidity. Acetic acid is the main type of volatile acidity; tartaric, malic and citric acid are the main constituents of fixed acidity and the two make up the total acidity of the wine.

ACQUIT

The official document which accompanies all movements of wines and spirits in France, destined for export, on which domestic taxes have not been paid. The colour varies according to the type of wine or spirit. An *acquit vert* is needed for *Appellation Contrôlée* table wines.

ADEGA

The Portuguese term for a building where wine is made.

ADELMANN   Württemberg: GERMANY

Weingut Graf Adelmann 'Brüssele' is an important Württemberg property near Stuttgart. The vineyards are said to have Roman origins and have belonged to the Adelmann family since 1914. Brüssele was a former owner. Nearly half their vines are red.

ADGESTONE   ENGLAND

A successful vineyard on the Isle of Wight. The first vines were planted in 1968 and a white wine is made from 50% Müller-Thurgau, 25% Reichensteiner and 25% Seyval Blanc grapes, with a tiny amount of Kerner.

ACKERMAN LAURANCE   Loire: FRANCE

The original producers of sparkling wine in Saumur. The company was founded in 1811 when Jean Ackerman, a Belgian, introduced the champagne method of producing a sparkling wine to the region and married a Mademoiselle Laurance, the daughter of a wealthy vineyard owner.

AEROBIC

Means 'in the presence of air.' Oxygen can play a detrimental part in winemaking, but sometimes it is necessary for a procedure. For example, the development of *flor* on *fino* sherry only occurs in aerobic conditions.

ACONCAGUA VALLEY   CHILE

Part of the central vineyard area of Chile where some of the country's best wines are produced. Aconcagua is also the name of the highest peak of the Andes.

AFAMES   CYPRUS

Sodap's brand name for their best red wine, and also a wine village in the Troodos mountains where the Mavron grape is reputedly at its best.

AFFENTAL   Baden: GERMANY

Means, literally, 'monkey valley', a village south of Baden-Baden where Affentaler Spätburgunder Rotwein is made. This is a red wine from the Spätburgunder grape, distinguished by a monkey embossed on the side of the bottle.

AFTERTASTE

Describes the flavour a wine leaves in the mouth after it has been swallowed or spat out. A great wine will have a long lingering aftertaste.

D'AGASSAC   Bordeaux: FRANCE

D'Agassac is a Cru Grand Bourgeois Exceptionnel of Ludon in the Haut-Médoc. There is a medieval castle with a moat.

AGIORGITIKO

Agiorgitiko, or the vine of St. George, is a red grape grown in Greece in the Nemea valley of the Peloponnese for robust red wines.

AGLIANICO

A red grape of southern Italy, at its best in Taurasi and Aglianico del Vulture, where it produces rich, concentrated heady wines.

AGLIANICO DEL VULTURE
Basilicata: ITALY

A heady red DOC wine from the Basilicata region, made from Aglianico grapes grown on vineyards dominated by the volcanic Monte Vulture. Fratelli d'Angelo are the best producers, ageing their wine in wood for a minimum of one year. *Riserva* indicates five years of ageing in both barrel and bottle.

AGRAFE

The metal clip that was used to secure a champagne cork during the second fermentation. With the advent of crown corks, it is now rarely found.

AGUARDIENTE

The neutral grape spirit used for fortifying port.

DOMAINE D'AHÉRA   CYPRUS

Keo's best red wine, an estate wine produced in small quantities from a mixture of grapes including Cabernet Franc and Grenache, as well as Cyprus varieties.

AHR   GERMANY

The northernmost wine region of Germany and illogically, known for its red rather than its white wine. The Ahr is a small tributary of the Rhine, joining the main river below Bonn. The principal grape varieties are Spätburgunder and Portugieser, which can be vinified dry or to retain some residual sugar to cater for the traditional German taste. Often, with the climatic problems of a northern vineyard, the colour is closer to pink than to red. There is one *Grosslage*, Klosterberg and much of the wine is produced by local cooperatives. In addition, some white wine is made from Riesling and Müller-Thurgau.

AÏN BESSEM BOUIRA   ALGERIA

In the province of Alger, this is the most easterly of Algeria's quality zones, known for light reds and some good rosés.

AÏN MERANE   ALGERIA

Part of the combined quality zone of Tanghrite, Aîn Merane and Mazouna. Originally called Rabelais, under the French VDQS system, it is situated in the hills near Dahra and known for full-bodied red wines.

AIRÉN

Spain's most widely planted grape variety, accounting for the vast production of white wine of La Mancha. Methods of vinification have improved enormously so that Airén can now make fresh, fruity white wines.

AJACCIO
Corsica

A separate appellation which covers the hills around the city of Ajaccio. The local Sciacarello is the dominant grape variety for red and rosé wine; it is usually blended with Grenache and other Midi varieties to produce wines with a distinctive flavour. The dry white wines are made from the local Malvoisie de Corse and should be drunk young. Domaine Peraldi is the best producer.

ALAMBRADO

The Spanish term to describe the wire netting that covers Rioja bottles and sometimes bottles from other areas. It was originally designed to prevent the fraudulent replacement of the wine of particularly fine bottles.

ALAMEDA
California: USA

A wine growing county to the east of San Francisco and part of the Central Coast area. The Livermore Valley is its most important AVA, noted for white wines, especially Gray Riesling, Sémillon, Chardonnay, Chenin Blanc and Sauvignon Blanc.

ALBALONGA

A German crossing of the Riesling and Silvaner grape varieties grown mainly in the Rheinhessen, producing good must weights.

ALBAN

Was a wine of ancient Rome, described by Pliny as sweet or dry, and good for the stomach.

ALBANA

A white grape cultivated mainly in Emilia Romagna for the neutral DOCG of Albana di Romagna.

ALBANA DI ROMAGNA
Emilia-Romagna: ITALY

From the Albana grape, grown between Bologna and Rimini, this is a new addition to the ranks of DOCG. White, it is either dry or medium sweet and may also be *spumante*.

ALBARINO see Alvarinho

ALBARIZA

The best of the three types of soil in the sherry vineyards of Spain. It is very chalky, almost 40%, with sand and clay. Vineyards on albariza soil are highly prized.

The main areas in descending order of quality are Macharnudo, Carrascal, Balbaina and Anina.

ALBERELLO

An Italian term for a traditional method of pruning and training the vine, similar to the *gobelet* system with low bushes.

ALBERO

The name used in Jerez to describe the chalky *albariza* soil where it occurs in the immediate subsoil of the vineyards to the south of Jerez de la Frontera in Spain.

ALCAMO
Sicily: ITALY

Also called Bianco Alcamo, this is a dry white DOC wine made in the western half of the island around the town of Alcamo, mainly from Catarratto Bianco grapes.

ALCOBACA
PORTUGAL

This region of western Portugal has a tradition of wine-making dating back to the monks of the 12th century. A mixture of grape varieties produce both red and white wines in the cool Atlantic climate.

ALCOHOL

Namely ethyl alcohol, this is a vital ingredient of wine. It comes from the sugar in the grapes which has been converted by the enzymes created by the yeast cells. The alcoholic content of a wine is usually expressed as a percentage of the volume.

ALCOHOLIC FERMENTATION

A term used to describe the main fermentation that transforms grape sugar into alcohol, to distinguish it from the malo-lactic fermentation.

ALDEHYDES

Produced in wine by oxidation of alcohol, they have an important effect on the development of the bouquet of a wine.

ALENQUER PORTUGAL

An undemarcated wine region of western Portugal, important mainly for its bulk wine. The whites were imported to England in the 14th century and today Quinta de Porto Franco is making some interesting wines.

ALENTEJO PORTUGAL

A large province south of the River Tagus, recently determined for wine production with five sub-regions: Vidigueira, Reguerngos de Monsaraz, Redondo, Borba and Portalegre. An area of untapped potential for easy to drink reds.

ALEATICO

A red grape grown in Italy, distinguished by its almost Muscat-like perfume. Its importance is diminishing; it is planted mainly in Apulia and Latium, for Aleatico di Puglia and Aleatico di Gradoli.

ALEXANDER VALLEY California: USA

An important wine region and AVA of Sonoma County, between Geyersville and Healdsburg.

ALEZIO Apulia: ITALY

A red and *rosato* DOC made around the village of the same name to the east of Gallipoli on the Salento peninsula. The grape varieties are Negroamaro and Malvasia Rosso. The red is warming and becomes *riserva* after two years. The *rosato* can also be called Lacrima di Terra d'Otranto.

ALEATICO DI GRADOLI Latium: ITALY

A little-known dessert DOC wine from near lake Bolsena, made from the Aleatico grape. Unfortified, it is light and fragrant; fortified at 17.5° minimum alcohol, it is more port-like.

ALEATICO DI PUGLIA Apulia: ITALY

A red DOC dessert wine made from Aleatico grapes in two versions: *dolce naturale* at 15° minimum alcohol and fortified *liquoroso dolce naturale* at 18.5°. *Riserva* denotes three years' ageing.

ALELLA SPAIN

A D.O. wine from one of the smallest wine regions of Spain, to the north of Barcelona, with Roman origins. Today its vineyards are threatened by the expanding suburbs of Barcelona. The small town of Alella is at the centre of the area. The wines are white, dry or sweet, red and rosé. The grape varieties are those of northern Spain, Xarel-lo and Garnacha Blanca for whites; Tempranillo, Garnacha Tinta and Garnacha Peluda for red and rosé. All wines must be aged for at least two years, including one in wood.

ALGARVE PORTUGAL

A recently demarcated wine area of Portugal, known for a traditional white wine, drunk as an aperitif for it is aged in wood and develops a flor as in Jerez. However the greater volume of wine from this narrow strip of vineyards between the Atlantic coast and the mountains is undistinguished red, made from a mixture of grape varieties.

ALGERIA

The largest of the wine-producing countries of North Africa, as a result of the strong French colonising influence. The subsequent exodus of *pieds noirs* caused a decline in the industry. Once there were twelve VDQS areas, today the Office Nationale de la Commercialisation des Produits Vinicoles, or ONCV, has defined seven quality zones in the provinces of Alger and Oran, namely: Côteaux de Tlemcen, Monts du Tessalah, Côteaux du Mascara, the combined areas of Tanghrite, Aïne Merane and Mazouna, Côtes du Zaccar, Medea and Aïne Bessem Bouira. All are within a hundred miles of the Mediterranean and the best vineyards are those on hillsides. The grape varieties are those of Southern France: Carignan, Cinsaut, Alicante Bouschet, Mourvèdre, Grenache and Syrah. Reds are generally rich and full-bodied; *rosés* quite dry and fresh and whites, from Clairette and Ugni Blanc, less successful.

CAVES ALIANÇA

One of the main wine producers of Portugal, both for still and sparkling wine, dealing in the full range of Portuguese table wines, and based in the Bairrada region. One of their best wines is a red Bairrada.

ALICANTE SPAIN

A D.O. wine of the Levante. The vineyards are in the hills behind the seaside resort, and produce a delicate rosé, a full-bodied *vino de doble pasto* for blending and a heady red, mainly from the Monastrell grape. There is a small amount of dry white too, coming principally from the Verdil grape. The main villages are Villena, Pinosa and Monóvar.

ALICANTE BOUSCHET

A *teinturier* grape, used in the south of France to boost the colour of rather paler grapes like Aramon. It was developed by Henri Bouschet in 1886, a crossing between Petit Bouschet (a crossing of Aramon and Teinturier du Cher) and Grenache. It is prolific, colourful and characterless and grown mainly for *vin de table* and to a lesser extent for *vin de pays*.

It is also found in California, mainly in the Central Valley for jug wine.

ALICE SPRINGS AUSTRALIA

An unlikely site for a vineyard, with its semi desert conditions. However Château Hornsby combats the extreme climatic conditions with a drip irrigation system for the vineyards, a vintage during the first week of January and refrigerated fermentation tanks in an air conditioned underground cellar. Cabernet Sauvignon, Shiraz, Sémillon and Rhine Riesling have been produced since 1979, the winery's first commercial vintage.

ALIGOTÉ

Aligoté is a white grape found most commonly in Burgundy, but considered something of a poor relation to Chardonnay. In the Côte d'Or it is grown on less good sites and tends to produce a rather thin acidic wine. The appellation is Bourgogne Aligoté; it is only in the village of Bouzeron in the Côte Chalonnaise that it is allowed the separate appellation of Bourgogne Aligoté de Bouzeron. Further north in the Yonne at St-Bris le Vineux and Chitry-le-Fort it is planted on better sites and has more flavour. Outside France Aligoté can be found in Eastern Europe, Bulgaria, Roumania and the Soviet Union, and also a little in California.

ALLANDALE WINERY AUSTRALIA

A small estate in the Hunter Valley concentrating on Sémillon, Chardonnay, Gewürztraminer and Chenin Blanc grapes for whites and Shiraz, Cabernet Sauvignon and Pinot Noir for reds. Each wine is made from the grapes of a single vineyard mentioned on the label, with varietal and regional descriptions.

ALLESVERLOREN SOUTH AFRICA

An important estate in Swartland, South Africa, specialising in red table wines, notably Cabernet Sauvignon and Tinta Barocca as well as port, from Tinta Barocca and Souzao.

ALLIER

One of the types of French oak widely used for wine barrels. It comes from forests near those of Nevers and has similar characteristics, with dense tightly grained wood, so that the wine absorbs less oak character.

ALMACENISTA

The Spanish term for the man who has a *bodega* where he holds sherry for sale to larger shippers. Sometimes they are sold unblended as almacenista sherries and can be very fine indeed.

ALMADEN VINEYARDS California: USA

One of California's oldest and largest wineries, founded by two Frenchmen, Etienne Thee and Charles Lefranc in 1852, with extensive vineyards and vinification plants in the Central Coast area, producing a wide range of wines, from jug wine to varietal. The better varietals come under the Charles Lefranc label.

ALMANSA SPAIN

A D.O. of south west Spain, centred upon the town of Almansa. The wines are mainly warm, full-bodied reds made from Monastrell, with some Garnacha tinta and Tintorera grapes. There is also a little white made from Airén.

ALMUDE

Part of a port pipe, the traditional cask used for storing port. An almude holds 25.4 litres, 21 almudes make one pipe. Apparently an almude was the quantity that could be carried on a man's head.

ALOXE-CORTON Burgundy: FRANCE

The village of Aloxe took on the name of its most famous vineyard, Corton. Vines have been grown here since the 9th century; Dukes of Burgundy, Knights Templars and kings of France have owned vineyards here. The village shares two Grands Crus with the neighbouring villages of Ladoix Serrigny and Pernand Vergelesses, namely Corton and Corton Charlemagne.

The Premiers Crus of the village are la Maréchaude, la Toppe-au-Vert, la Coutière, les Grandes Lolières, les Petites Lalières, les Basses Mourettes, Valozières (part), Chaillots (part), Pauland (part), les Vercots (part) and Guèrets (part).

ALSACE

ALSACE
FRANCE

A wine producing region of north east France covering the *départements* of the Haut-Rhin and Bas-Rhin. Her vineyards form a logical continuation of the German vineyards of the Rhine and indeed between 1870 and 1919 they were German. Consequently the wines of Alsace still have certain affinities with Germany; they are certainly unlike any other French wines. With the exception of the blend Edelzwicker, all Alsace wines are pure grape varieties and labelled accordingly; Sylvaner, Pinot Blanc, Pinot Gris or Tokay d'Alsace, Muscat, Riesling, Gewürztraminer and the red grape Pinot Noir. In addition you occasionally find Chasselas and Pinot Auxerrois, Pinot Blanc, which is also called Klevner and can include Pinot Auxerrois and even Pinot Noir vinified white, which is very rare.

This is one of the most beautiful wine regions of France. The Vosges mountains form a backdrop to picturesque villages such as Riquewihr and Eguisheim. Alsace wines, unlike German wines, are basically dry, but in especially fine years when the grapes are particularly ripe, wines are made in which some sugar can remain, called *Vendange Tardive* and *Sélection de Grains Nobles*. Alternatively they can be fermented dry. The wines of Alsace were given Appellation Contrôlée status in 1962 and it has been compulsory for all Alsace wine to be bottled in Alsace since 1972.

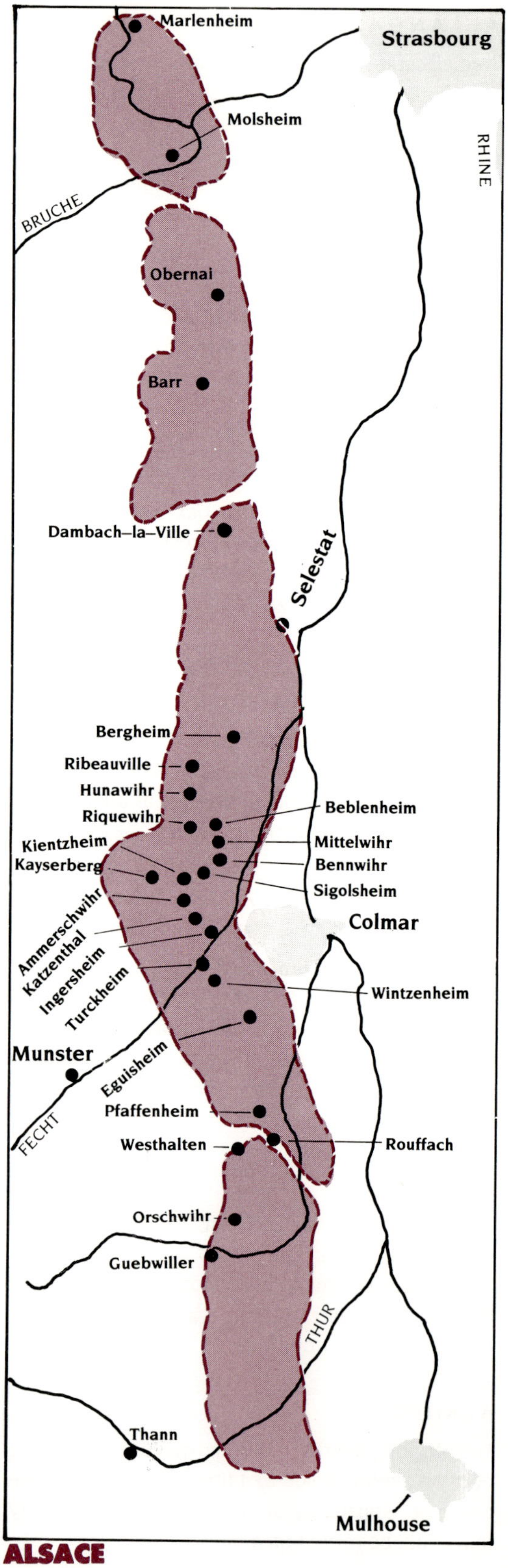

ALSACE GRAND CRU

Like many vineyard areas, Alsace recognises certain sites as better than others; twenty five sites were classified as Grand Cru in 1985 and a further twenty-two in 1987. Only four grape varieties are permitted, Riesling, Muscat, Pinot Gris and Gewürztraminer. The Grand Cru vineyards must have a historic reputation and a special soil character. Yields are lower than for the basic appellation, 70 hl/ha as opposed to 100 hl/ha and the minimum alcohol level is higher, 10° or more for Riesling and Muscat and a minimum of 11° for Gewürztraminer and Pinot Gris. The name of the vineyard must be stated on the label and the wine can be *Vendange Tardive* or *Sélection de Grains Nobles*. The wines undergo a blind tasting each year.

ALSHEIM   *Rheinhessen*: GERMANY

A growing village within the *Grosslagen* of Krötenbrunnen for the flat land and Rheinblick for the hillsides and better vineyards. The development of new crossings has helped the growth of this village. Frühmesse is the best-known *Einzellage*.

ALTAR WINE

A loose term to describe wine used for the eucharist. It is usually a sweet fortified wine. Wineries in California survived Prohibition by making it; Tarragona is another source.

ALTENBAMBERG   *Nahe*: GERMANY

A small village within the *Grosslage* of Burgweg with some good Riesling wines.

ALTESSE

A white grape grown in the Savoie, where it is the main variety for sparkling Seyssel. Sometimes it is called Roussette but, confusingly, a Roussette de Savoie can also include a large amount of Chardonnay as well as Altesse.

ALTITUDE

An important aspect in determining the quality of a vineyard, for altitude affects temperature and susceptibility to frost. The lowest vineyards are just above sea-level; the highest in Europe are in Switzerland and in the Alto Adige in Italy at about 1000 metres. Temperatures vary significantly with altitude; essentially, the higher the cooler.

ALTO   SOUTH AFRICA

A fine wine estate in the Stellenbosch area of South Africa, which specialises in red wines, notably Cabernet Sauvignon and Alto Rouge, a lighter blend of Shiraz and Cinsaut.

ALTO ADIGE   ITALY

The most northern part of Italy, just south of the Austrian border, it is more Germanic than Italian. The Sudtirol is the other name for the region. The vineyards are on steep hillsides. The cool mountainous climate results in fragrant whites and light reds. The Alto Adige or Südtirol DOC covers most of the province and eighteen bilingual types of wine. In addition there are other smaller DOCs in the region: Lago di Caldaro, Santa Maddalena, Valle Isarco, Meranese di Collina, Colli di Bolzano and Terlano. The eighteen varieties are: Cabernet, Franc and/or Sauvignon, becoming *riserva* after two years' ageing; Chardonnay; Lagrein Rosato or Kretzer, a *rosato* wine from the Lagrein grape, as opposed to Lagrein Scuro or Dunkel, a red wine; Malvasia Nera, a scented red wine; Merlot, a herbal red wine, becoming *riserva* after one year; Moscato Giallo, or Goldenmuskateller, an aromatic white; Moscato Rosa, or Rosenmuskateller, a rare, perfumed pinky-red; Müller Thurgau, a flowery white; Pinot Bianco or Weissburgunder, often with a touch of Chardonnay; Pinot Grigio or Rülander, a light dry white; Pinot Nero or Blauburgunder, a light red becoming *riserva* after one year; Riesling Italico or Welschriesling, little of which is made; Riesling Renano or Rheinriesling, at its best in this part of Italy; Sauvignon, of which, as yet, little is produced; Schiava or Vernatsch, a soft red; Sylvaner, a lively white, made in small quantities; Traminer Aromatico or Gewürztraminer, at its best in its home town, Tramin.

ALVARELHÃO

A Portuguese red grape, grown mainly in Tras-os-Montes, the Minho and the Douro, but not allowed as a port grape. The wines are light and balanced.

ALVARINHO
One of the best grapes for white Vinho Verde and the only grape in Portugal which can be vinified as a single variety. It is also grown in Galicia in Spain where it is called Albarino and produces similar wines.

ALZEY Rheinhessen: GERMANY
Was important as the home of the viticultural institute where Dr. Scheu developed the Scheurebe and Faber grape varieties, which today are planted in most of the town's vineyards. Its *Einzellagen* are little-known; its wines are sold either as Bereich Wonnegau or under the *Grosslage* name of Sybillenstein, or they go into Liebfraumilch.

AMABILE
An Italian term to describe a wine with some sweetness, without being very sweet and corresponding to medium sweet on a label, such as Frascati Amabile.

AMADOR California: USA
The most important wine producing county of the Sierra Foothills in eastern California. Zinfandel is the dominant grape variety, grown mainly in the AVAs of Shenandoah Valley and Fiddletown.

AMARO
Means 'bitter' in Italian. An *amaro* is a bitter drink like Fernet Branca or Barolo Chinato with a quinine base.

AMARONE See Recioto della Valpolicella Amarone.

AMBONNAY Champagne: FRANCE
An important champagne village on the Montagne de Reims.

AMBRATO DI COMISO Sicily: ITALY
An obscure amber-coloured dessert wine made from black grapes grown around Comiso. It can be medium dry or sweet, has 17° alcohol and is very aromatic.

AMERICAN OAK
American oak, in contrast to French oak, has less subtle characteristics when used to age fine wines, giving the wine a strong flavour of vanilla, as in Rioja. It comes from a different species of oak, *quercus alba* from the two main forest areas of Tennessee and Kentucky. American oak has the advantage of being considerably cheaper than French oak, but can give too strong a taste to the wine.

AMERICAN VINES
A general term for the other species of vines, other than *vitis vinifera*, which are grown in the United States and which are used for grafting European vines, as they are resistant to phylloxera. They also produce wine in the eastern United States and Canada, which is distinguished by its foxy flavour.

AMERINE
Maynard Amerine is one of the great names of the Californian wine world. Once a professor at U.C. Davis specialising in tasting techniques and fermentation methods and now a consultant and author.

AMONTILLADO SPAIN
The name Amontillado comes from Montilla, meaning 'in the style of Montilla'. It loosely describes any medium sherry. However, the real thing is a *fino* sherry which has been further aged after the elimination of the flor so that it develops a dry nutty flavour, with 16.5° to 18° alcohol.

AMOROSO
Amoroso, meaning loving in Spain, is used to describe a smooth, sweet *oloroso* made by adding Pedro Ximénez and *vino de color*. It is less common now than previously.

ROBERT AMPEAU — Burgundy: FRANCE

One of the great names of Meursault. His 10-hectare estate includes vineyards in Puligny-Montrachet, les Combettes, Meursault les Perrières and les Charmes for whites, and Volnay les Santenots and Pommard for reds.

AMPELOGRAPHY

The study of vine varieties and their characteristics in the vineyard.

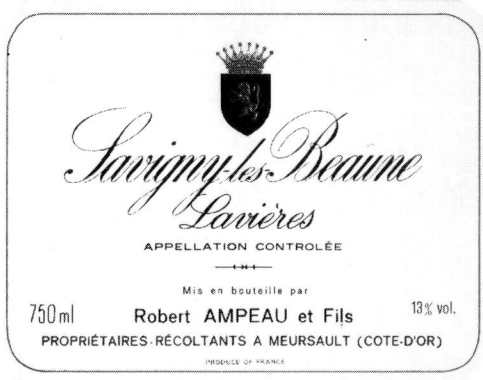

AMPHORA

A fat earthenware two-handled jar used by the Greeks and Romans to store wine. Today the shape of the Italian Verdicchio bottle bears a resemblance to an *amphora*.

AMPUIS — Rhône: FRANCE

The village at the foot of the Côte Rôtie on the west bank of the Rhône, where most of the producers of Côte Rôtie have their cellars.

AMPURDAN-COSTA BRAVA — SPAIN

A relatively new D.O. The vineyards are inland from the coast in northern Catalonia in the province of Gerona. Most of the wine is rosé, made from Garnacha Tinta and Cariñena. The most important producer of the region is Cavas del Ampurdán, for sparkling as well as still wine.

AMSELFELDER — YUGOSLAVIA

A successful Pinot Noir wine made in Kosmet in a sweet style for the German market.

AMTLICHE PRÜFUNGSNUMMER

All quality German wine is submitted to a chemical analysis and tasting, an *Amtliche Prüfung*. If successful, the wine will be given an *Amtliche Prüfungsnummer*, or A.P. number for short, which is displayed on the label. This system of quality control, run through nine centres, is not without its loopholes.

AMYNTEION — GREECE

An astringent red wine produced in the mountains of Macedonia near the Albanian and Yugoslav borders, from the Xynomavro grape.

AÑADA

The term used in sherry production for a young wine of a single year that has not yet been added to a *criadera*.

ANAEROBIC

Means 'in the absence of air.' Most wine-making operations are carried out in anaerobic conditions.

ANATOLIA — TURKEY

One of Turkey's main wine regions, covering a large area for white Urgüp, sweet white Narbag and red Buzbag.

ANBAUGEBIET   See *Qualitätswein*.

ANDALUSIA — SOUTH AFRICA

Andalusia, in the Orange River area, originally called the Ward of Vaalharts, is now a Wine of Origin district in its own right. Production is concentrated on dessert wines from vineyards in the Vaalharts irrigation scheme. It is also a brand name of the Vaalharts cooperative, South Africa's most northerly cooperative.

ANDERSON VALLEY — California: USA

A part of Mendocino County, a recently developed vineyard area and AVA near the Pacific Ocean and especially successful for white varietals.

ANDRES WINES — CANADA

One of the largest wineries in Canada with plants in both British Columbia and Ontario. They are especially known for their Baby Duck brand, and have vineyards in British Columbia called Inkameep for hybrids and varietals.

ANDRON-BLANQUET
Bordeaux: FRANCE

A Cru Grand Bourgeois Exceptionnel of St-Estèphe.

ANGELICA

A Californian originality, a sweet wine created by the Spanish missionaries and made by fortifying fresh grape juice, usually from the Mission grape, and letting it age in cask. Angelica is now accepted as a generic wine name and is still sometimes found, slightly modified in that the grape juice must ferment a little before fortification.

L'ANGÉLUS
Bordeaux: FRANCE

A Grand Cru Classé St-Émilion and one of the largest vineyards of the *côtes*, making sound wine with modern methods.

MARQUIS D'ANGERVILLE
Burgundy: FRANCE

A fine estate with vineyards, notably in Volnay Champans, as well as Volnay Clos des Ducs, and the unusual white Meursault les Santenots.

ANGHELU RUJU
Sardinia: ITALY

A dessert wine made by Sella & Mosca from semi-dried Cannonau grapes. It ages well after two or three years in barrel and is warm and alcoholic at 18°.

D'ANGLUDET
Bordeaux: FRANCE

A *château* generally considered to merit classed growth status, since the Margaux vineyards have been reconstructed by its English owner, Peter Sichel.

ANHEUSER
Nahe: GERMANY

Weingut Ökonomierat August E. Anheuser is the largest estate in the Nahe, founded in 1869. They are also owners of the merchant company, Anheuser & Fehrs. Vineyards include sites in Bad Kreuznach, Norheim, Niederhausen and Schlossböckelheim.

Weingut Paul Anheuser with the same origins as August Anheuser became a separate estate in 1888 under Rudolf Anheuser who introduced Riesling to the Nahe. Today the company specialises in Riesling Kabinett halbtrocken.

AÑINA
SPAIN

One of the districts with *albariza* soil, between Jerez de la Frontera and Sanlúcar de Barrameda and rated fourth in order of quality.

ANJOU
Loire: FRANCE

Anjou is a province and an appellation. Anjou Blanc is made from Chenin Blanc and is often slightly sweet. Dry versions may include some Sauvignon or Chardonnay. The best known Anjou Blanc is Moulin Touchais. Rosé d'Anjou is a slightly sweet, pale pink wine, usually made from the Groslot grape. Red Anjou, made either from Gamay, in which case it is called Anjou Gamay, or from Cabernet Franc and/or Cabernet Sauvignon, is becoming increasingly popular. It is also possible to find Anjou Mousseux in white and rosé and Anjou Pétillant.

The other wines of the province include Quarts de Chaume, Bonnezeaux, Savennières, Coteaux de l'Aubance, Anjou Coteaux de la Loire, Coteaux du Layon, Saumur, Coteaux de Saumur and Saumur Champigny, as well as wines like Rosé de Loire and Crémant de la Loire which are also made in Touraine.

ANJOU COTEAUX DE LA LOIRE
Loire: FRANCE

A small appellation to the west of Angers on the right bank of the Loire. The wine is made from the Chenin Blanc grape and is very similar to Coteaux de l'Aubance.

ANNATA

An Italian term meaning the year or vintage.

ANREICHERUNG   see Chaptalization.

ANTHOCYANS

An important constituent of wine, giving red wine its colour. They are present in the skins of grapes and pass into the must during the early stages of fermentation if the grapes are squashed. Anthocyans disappear from wine after two or three years' ageing, after which time the tannins supply colour.

ANTHRACNOSE

A vine disease. It develops in warm humid conditions; stains appear on the grapes and shoots. It is treated with copper sulphate.

ANTINORI   Tuscany: ITALY

A leading producer of Chianti, a six hundred year old family company with estates in Chianti Classico where they make not only Villa Antinori Riserva and Santa Cristina Chianti, but also experiment with Cabernet Sauvignon and ageing in French barrels to produce Tignanello, Solaia and, most recently, Seicentenario. They also own the Orvieto estate, Castello della Sala, where they are applying the same innovative principles to white wine.

APETLON   AUSTRIA

One of the principal Burgenland villages, where Lenz Moser have extensive vineyards.

APHRODITE   CYPRUS

Keo's brand name for their standard dry white wine. Legend has it that the goddess Aphrodite came out of the sea at Cyprus.

APPELLATION CONTRÔLÉE

Appellation Contrôlée is part of a system of laws that protect and define French wines. The wines are placed into four categories, of which *Appellation Contrôlée* is the highest quality. An appellation may be as small as one tiny vineyard like Château Grillet, or a village like Pommard, or it may cover parts of a large area like Bordeaux and, for each appellation, the regulations define the precise vineyard area determined according to soil and aspect, the permitted grape varieties, maximum yields and the minimum alcohol level of the wine. They often cover vineyard and cellar practices, too. Annual compulsory tastings ensure that the wine reaches the required standard.

APPELLATION D'ORIGINE CONTRÔLÉE
See Appellation Contrôlée.

APPELLATION SIMPLE

Was a lower category of wine than *Appellation Contrôlée*, often used to describe what is now *vin de pays*.

APPLES

A characteristic smell of young immature wine, coming from malic acid.

APPROVED VITICULTURAL AREA   California: USA

Approved Viticultural Area or AVA is the North American equivalent of an appellation, a precise viticultural area, defined by the Federal Government. The system was only instigated in 1980 and many potential AVAs are still seeking recognition.

APREMONT   Savoie: FRANCE

One of the better crus of Vin de Savoie, producing mainly crisp white wine from the Jacquère grape, grown on vineyards to the south of Chambéry.

APRILIA   Latium: ITALY

A DOC wine in three versions from vineyards around the town of Aprilia. The best is Merlot di Aprilia; Sangiovese is an insipid red and Trebbiano a bland white.

APULIA   ITALY

The wine region in the heel of Italy. There is a dense concentration of vines, many of which are for table grapes and, of the wine grapes, most are destined for the vermouth factories in the north or contribute to the European wine lake. The 18 DOCs represent just 2% of the region's production and many of the better wines are not DOC. A red table

wine made by one producer in the region from Primitivo, Negroamaro and Malvasia Nera grapes also goes under the name Apulia.

AQUILEA   Friuli-Venezia Giulia: ITALY

A DOC from Friuli-Venezia Giulia on the Adriatic coast, covering seven varieties: Cabernet Franc and Sauvignon; Merlot, the most popular as well as red; Pinot Bianco; Pinot Grigio in limited quantity and the best white; Refosco; Riesling Renano and Tocai Friuliano.

ARAMON

A feeble red grape that was planted extensively in southern France, mainly in the Hérault, after the *phylloxera* crisis, on account of its prolific yields. It needs a *teinturier* grape like Alicante Bouschet to boost its pale colour. Plantings are now beginning to decline though it is still found in *vin ordinaire* and *vin de pays*.

ARBANE

Or Arbanne, one of the permitted grape varieties for champagne, which is disappearing from the area as it is sensitive to mildew and gives low yields.

ARBIN   Savoie: FRANCE

One of the crus of Vin de Savoie, with a reputation for red wine from the Mondeuse grape.

ARBOIS

A white grape variety grown at the eastern end of the Loire valley around Orléans, but now of little importance.

ARBOIS   Jura: FRANCE

One of the four appellations of the Jura and the town where Louis Pasteur did much of his research on vinification. The wine can be red, white or rosé; *vin jaune* and sparkling wines are made too. The principal grape varieties are Chardonnay and Savagnin for white wine; Pinot Noir, Poulsard and Trousseau for red and rosé wine. The Trousseau, peculiar to the Jura, does particularly well in this area and produces some distinctive perfumed wines. Most wines spend a minimum of twelve months in large or small oak barrels.

ARCHANES   GREECE

A full-bodied sweet red wine from Crete made from indigenous Cretan grape varieties, including Romeiko, Kotsifali and Liatiko.

D'ARCHE   Bordeaux: FRANCE

A second growth Sauternes in the commune of Sauternes. D'Arche Lafaurie was once part of the same property, but is now separate, although under the same ownership. In effect, d'Arche Lafaurie is the second wine of Château d'Arche.

ARCINS   Bordeaux: FRANCE

A commune of the Médoc. The best-known *château* is D'Arcins, with the appellation Haut-Médoc.

ARE

One hundredth of a hectare. In regions where the vineyards are split into very small parcels, a grower will often say that he or she has so many *ares* of a Grand Cru.

ARENA

One of the three soil types of Jerez in Spain, the other two being albariza and barro. It is a red sandy soil with about 10% chalk, on which the Moscatel grape grows well. Otherwise it is the least good of the three.

ARGANDA-COLEMENAR DE OREJA   SPAIN

An undemarcated wine area within Tierra de Madrid to the north of the capital, producing both red and white wines, which were at the height of their popularity in the 17th century.

ARGENTINA

The world's fifth largest wine-producing country, but her wines are relatively unknown abroad as most are consumed at home. The climate is influenced by the Andes; the summers are very dry so the vineyards have to be irrigated with the melted snows from the mountains. The province of Mendoza is the biggest wine region; San Juan, Salta and the valley of Rio Negro in the south are important, too. The dry climate results in healthy grapes. Criolla is the most widely-grown indigenous grape. Malbec has been successfully introduced from Europe, as well as Cabernet Sauvignon, Merlot, Lambrusco, Nebbiolo, Barbera and Tempranillo. White wine represents the smaller part of the production and there is untapped potential with Sémillon, Chenin Blanc, Chardonnay and grapes for sherry styles, Palomino and Pedro Ximenez. Argentina currently produces enormous quantities of reliable wines, without attaining any great heights of distinction. This is yet to come, encouraged by foreign investment from Seagrams and Moët & Chandon.

ARINTO

A white grape variety noted in Portugal for its high acidity, even in a hot climate. It is the principal variety of Bucellas but, sadly, is disappearing elsewhere.

ARKANSAS   USA

Arkansas has one small pocket of *vitis vinifera* vines, which were planted in the 1870s at Altus, which is on a 1000–2000 foot plateau and benefits from a particular microclimate. Hybrids are grown too at Wiederkehr Cellars, a family winery entirely responsible for the wine of Arkansas.

ARLAY   Jura: FRANCE

An important village within the appellation of the Côtes du Jura. The Château d'Arlay, which has associations with William of Orange, is an estate making the range of Côtes de Jura wines. Jean Bourdy is another good producer in the village.

ARMENIA   USSR

This part of the Soviet Union, bordering Turkey, lies within sight of Mount Ararat, where Noah may have planted a vineyard – the region's viticultural origins are certainly very old. A mixture of local grape varieties are grown, including Voskheat for a sherry-type wine called Ashtarak. Port and madeira styles are made, too.

ARMIGNE   SWITZERLAND

A white wine from the Valais, an old grape variety that makes an almost sweet wine.

ARNEIS DEI ROERI   Piedmont: ITALY

A little-known dry white wine of fine potential made from a native vine, the Arneis, which has been recently revived and planted in the Roeri hills, north of Alba.

AROMA

Another word for smell, usually describing a young wine with a nose very reminiscent of the grape variety, that has not yet developed a mature bouquet.

AROMATIC

A descriptive term for the smell and flavour of particularly spicey grape varieties like Muscat and Gewürztraminer.

ARROPE   SPAIN

A dark syrup, made by evaporating unfermented grape must. This is then mixed with more must and fermented to become *vino de color*, the colouring wine in sweet brown sherry.

L'ARROSÉE
Bordeaux: FRANCE

A Grand Cru Classé, St-Émilion, an old established estate on the *côtes*.

ARROYO SECO
California: USA

An AVA in Monterey County in the Salinas Valley.

ARRUDA DOS VINHOS
PORTUGAL

One of the undemarcated wine regions of western Portugal, important for its bulk table wine production and beginning to produce red and white table wine in bottle.

ARRUFIAT   See Raffiat de Moncade.

ARSAC
Bordeaux: FRANCE

One of the villages near the village of Margaux and included in the appellation.

ARSINOE
CYPRUS

Sodap's brand name for their best white wine.

ARVE-ET-LAC
SWITZERLAND

A small wine-producing region in the canton of Geneva.

ARVE-ET-RHÔNE
SWITZERLAND

A small wine-producing region in the canton of Geneva.

ARVINE
SWITZERLAND

Or Petite Arvine, this is a white wine from the Valais, an old grape variety that makes an almost sweet wine.

GEHEIMRAT ASCHROTT'SCHE ERBEN
Rheingau: GERMANY

One of the leading estates of Hochheim, planted mainly with Riesling vines.

ASCORBIC ACID

More commonly known as Vitamin C. An anti-oxidant which can be added to wine just before bottling to prevent oxidation.

ASENOVGROD
BULGARIA

Asenovgrod, in the Upper Maritsa Valley of Bulgaria, has a reputation for Mavrud wines as well as Cabernet Sauvignon and Merlot.

ASHTARAK   See Armenia.

ASPECT

A significant factor in the quality of a vineyard. This is the way the vineyard is facing in relation to the sun. In cool climates, a southwest-facing vineyard is best for it will have the longest hours of sunshine. In a hotter climate, a northern aspect may be preferable. Most of the best vineyards are on slopes which gives them a better exposure to sunshine.

ASPERSION

A method of protecting the vines against frost damage. The vines are sprayed with water from the moment the temperature drops to freezing point, so that a protective coating of ice is formed round the young buds. Vines are not normally damaged by frost until the temperature drops below −5°C. To be effective, spraying must continue all the while the temperature is at or below 0°C. Although not as expensive as lighting *chaufferettes*, aspersion tends to be less efficient as it can be affected by wind and cracked pipes.

ASPRINO
Basilicata/Campania: ITALY

Also called Asprinio, this is an acidic *frizzante* white wine made in the regions of Basilicata and Campania from the Asprinio grape. It is mostly drunk in Naples.

ASSAGGIO

The Italian term for a tasting.

ASSEMBLAGE

The French term for blending. In Bordeaux it is particularly used to describe the process of blending together the *cuvées* of different grape varieties. Some wines may be rejected altogether or possibly used for the second wine of the property. In Champagne a blend of still wines is made from an *assemblage* of grape varieties, vineyards and years. This blend will then be turned into champagne.

ASSMANNSHAUSEN Rheingau: GERMANY

A village situated at the point where the Rhine turns north towards Koblenz. Unusually, it is known for its red rather than white wine. The grape variety is the Spätburgunder; the same categories of sweetness apply for red as for white wine and, while they are greatly appreciated in Germany, have less appeal abroad. The village comes within the *Grosslage* of Steil; the principal vineyard of Spätburgunder is Höllenberg; Hinterkirch and Frankenthal are important sites too. The best producer is the State Domain at Eltville.

ASSOCIAÇAO DOS EXPORTADORES DO VINHO DO PORTO

Alternatively, the Port Wine Shippers' Association, or AEVP for short, represents the Portuguese port shippers, but it is not obligatory for a shipper to be a member. The AEVP is responsible to the Instituto do Vinho do Porto for all matters concerning the blending, maturing and shipping of port in Vila Nova da Gaia. Before the 1974 Revolution it was called the Gremio dos Exportadores and membership was compulsory.

ASSOCIATED VINTNERS   USA

One of the leading wineries of Washington State, set up by a pioneering group of university professors who planted vines in 1962 and in 1976 it became a commercial operation. White wines are particularly successful with Chardonnay, Gewürztraminer and Sémillon.

ASSYRTIKO

A white Greek grape variety which retains its acidity in a hot climate, and is used for Retsina and fortified wine.

ASTI SPUMANTE   Piedmont: ITALY

Italy's best known sparkling wine, made from the aromatic Muscat grape in and around the town of Asti. The production process is a variation of the *cuve close* method. The first fermentation is stopped by chilling the juice when it contains only 5° of alcohol. After filtration and the addition of more yeast, the wine is allowed to referment and is then bottled under pressure. Good Asti is low in alcohol and retains the natural sweetness and flavour of the grape. Reputable producers include Fontanafredda, Cinzano and Martini.

ASTRINGENT

A dry, mouth-puckering sensation, caused by tannin and acidity, which often fades as a wine matures. Chianti is often characterised by astringency, which should be balanced with fruit.

ASZÚ   see Tokay.

ATESINO

An *indicazione geografica* covering wine from the regions of both the Alto Adige and Trentino.

ATMOSPHERE

The means of measuring pressure in sparkling wine, at a temperature of 20°C. Champagne is usually 5 or 6 atmospheres, with a legal minimum of 3.5 atmospheres, or 3 for half bottles. One atmosphere equals 15 lbs per square inch.

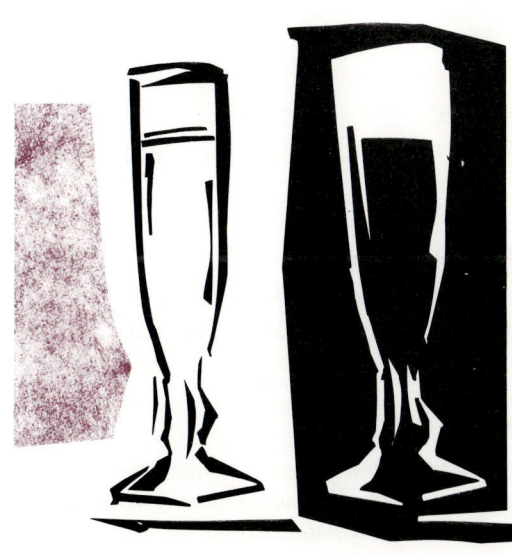

CONTI ATTEMS
Friuli-Venezia Giulia: ITALY

A family company of many generations making a fine range of Collio and Isonzo wines.

ATTENUATED

Describes a wine that is losing its fruit and flavour and becoming thin on the palate.

ATTICA
GREECE

The vineyards of Attica around Athens produce predominantly white Savatiano grapes for Retsina – Retsina from Attica is said to be the best in Greece – as well as a little rosé from the Rhoditis grape, light red wine from the Mavroudi grape grown near Delphi and dry white Hymettus from vineyards on the slopes of Mount Hymettus. White Kanza of Attica from the Savatiano grape is an appellation of origin.

AUBE
Champagne: FRANCE

There are vineyards in the *département* of the Aube near Bar-sur-Seine and Bar-sur-Aube that form part of the vineyards of Champagne.

AUBUN

A red grape variety similar to Carignan, that is planted in the Southern Rhône, where it is also called Counoise. As Counoise it is allowed in Châteauneuf-du-Pape.

AUME

The name of an Alsace barrel; it holds 114 litres.

AURORA

Also called Seibel 5279. A French white hybrid grape and popular in the eastern United States.

AUSBRUCH
AUSTRIA

An Austrian wine category, coming between *Beerenauslese* and *Trockenbeerenauslese* in must weight, a wine made from nobly-rotten grapes.

AUSLESE

The third category of German *Prädikat* wines, meaning literally 'selected harvest'. They are not necessarily late picked, but are a choice of bunches that are especially ripe or more than averagely affected with noble rot, so the resulting wine will be rich and honeyed. The statutory sugar content, measured as the oechsle degree, which varies according to grape

AUSONE
Bordeaux: FRANCE

One of the great names of St-Émilion, it was classified as one of the two Premiers Grands Crus Classés A in 1954. Cheval Blanc is the other. The vineyard, associated with the Roman poet Ausonius, is a mere five hectares, almost inside the town of St-Émilion itself. Ausone went through a period of neglect but, with the arrival of a new manager, the wine is taking its proper place in the classification once again. The wine is made equally from Merlot and Cabernet Franc grapes; new barrels are used for each vintage.

AUSSCHANKWEIN   See Schoppenwein.

AUSTERE

Describes a tough, ungiving wine, which may be immature and lacking in charm.

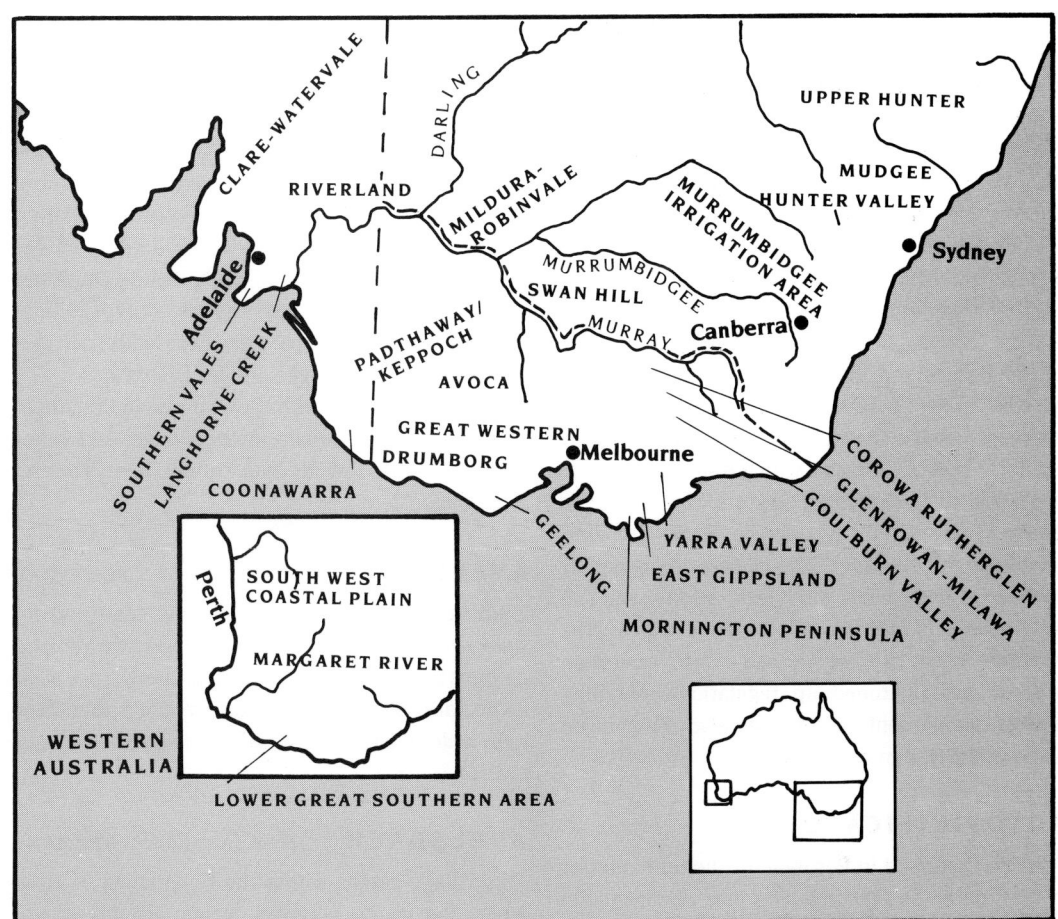

AUSTRALIA

AUSTRALIA

The first vines were brought to Australia by British colonists at the end of the 18th century. James Busby takes some credit for establishing viticulture more soundly in the Hunter Valley. However, until about 1960 the Australian wine industry concentrated on port and sherry style wine, or strong red wines, full of sugar and low in acidity. Then things changed; there was a switch to lighter wines and a vast improvement in expertise and equipment. Australia has the beginnings of a system of appellations, but many of the large wineries prefer to blend wines from different areas, according to their requirements. In New South Wales the Hunter Valley, Lower and Upper and Mudgee are the main areas. Victoria has vineyards around Great Western, Yarra Valley, Geelong, Milawa, Rutherglen and the Goulburn Valley. The principal vineyards of South Australia are Clare-Watervale, Southern Vales, Padthaway-Keppoch, the Barossa Valley and Coonawarra. Queensland has just two vineyards, for climatic conditions are generally unsuitable. Tasmania is showing potential with its cooler climate and Western Australia is developing her wine industry in the Margaret River, Swan Valley and Mount Barker and now producing some of the country's best wines. Grape varieties are those of Europe; Cabernet Sauvignon and Chardonnay are widely and successfully planted; Sémillon produces good results in the Hunter Valley, Victoria and Western Australia; Rhine Riesling is appreciated by the German immigrants of the Barossa Valley while Shiraz or Hermitage is the most individual Australian grape variety, with some superb red wine, at its best in Penfold's Grange Hermitage.

AUSTRIA
Wine is only produced in the eastern part of the country, in the regions of Niederösterreich (or Lower Austria), Burgenland, Steiermark (or Styria) and Vienna. Over three-quarters of the production is white. Grüner Veltliner is the most common grape variety. Welschriesling, Neuburger, Muscat-Ottonel, Thurgau, Weissburgunder, Rhine Riesling, Zierfandler, and Gewürztraminer are grown, too. Red wines, little-known outside the country, are made mainly from Blauer Portugieser, Rotgipfler, Blaufränkisch and Zweigelt. The wines north of Vienna tend to be light and flowery and those of the Burgenland are contrastingly sweeter and heavier, while those of the Steiermark come in between. Austria has a classification of quality similar to that of Germany, with the same categories of *Kabinett* to *Trockenbeerenauslese* and the additional *Ausbruch*, measured in degrees KMW (Klosterneuburger Mostwaage). The wines are generally sweeter and heavier with less acidity and no Süssreserve is allowed for *Prädikat* wines. The Austrian Wine Law which came into operation in 1986 has tightened up regulations, entailing stricter quality controls and has also reorganised some of the designated areas.

AUTOVINIFICATOR
A special vat used in Portugal for the fermentation of port grapes and some table wines which ensures that the cap of grape skins is continually submerged. The fermenting must is at intervals forced by the pressure of carbon dioxide up a pipe into an open reservoir at the top of the vat. A valve then opens to release the gas, allowing the must to flow back into the vat and over the cap. The aim is to extract the maximum amount of colour and tannin from the grape skins.

AUXERROIS
A synonym, used in Cahors, for the Malbec grape and not to be confused with white Auxerrois, which is grown in Alsace and is similar to and usually blended with and sold as Pinot Blanc.

AUXERROIS Burgundy: FRANCE
A general term for the vineyards around Auxerre and Chablis. Before the phylloxera crisis, the *département* of the Yonne was an important vineyard area supplying the cafés of Paris. Since then it has declined significantly. However, the villages of Irancy, Épineuil, Coulanges-la-Vineuse, St-Bris-le-Vineux and Chitry-le-Fort continue to produce a variety of red and white wines.

AUXEY DURESSES Burgundy: FRANCE
A lesser village of the Côte de Beaune. Two thirds of its production is red wine and is sold more often under the name Côtes de Beaune-Villages. The best known Premier Cru vineyard of the village is les Duresses; there is also les Bas de Duresses, Reugne (dit la Chapelle) les Grands Champs, Climat du Val dit Clos du Val (part), les Ecusseaux (part) les Bretterins dit la Chapelle and les Bretterins.

Leroy, co-proprietors of Domaine de la Romanée-Conti, have their cellars in the village, and other growers' names include Jean Prunier, René Roy and F. Lafouge-Clerc.

AVELEDA PORTUGAL
Quinta da Aveleda is the most famous estate making *vinho verde* and it is a beautiful property with exotic gardens that belongs to the Guedes family. They have 24 hectares of vines; Quinta da Aveleda is their best *vinho verde*; Aveleda and Casal Garcia are their bigger brands.

AVELSBACH Mosel-Saar-Ruwer: GERMANY
This village comes within the boundaries of Trier, where the largest vineyard owners are the Staatsweingut and Hohe Domkirche, which sells its wines as Dom Avelsbach. The *Grosslage* is Römerlay and the best *Einzellagen* Herrenberg, Altenberg, Hammerstein and Rotlay

AVENSAN Bordeaux: FRANCE
One of the communes of the Médoc, but without its own appellation. Its tiny production is very similar to adjoining Moulis.

AVIZE Champagne: FRANCE
The village of Avize in Champagne has some of the best vineyards on the Côtes des Blancs.

AY Champagne: FRANCE
The village of Ay in Champagne has some of the best vineyards of the Montagne de Reims. Some red wine is also made and the village is the home of the company of Bollinger.

AYALA   *Champagne*: FRANCE

A traditional champagne house and, although a *grande marque*, it is better-known in France than in England.

AYL   *Mosel-Saar-Ruwer*: GERMANY

A small village on the Saar which owes its reputation to a south facing hillside, planted with vines in two vineyards, Kupp and Herrenberg. Bischöfliche Weingüter make excellent wine, as does the village cooperative. Scharzberg is the *Grosslage*.

AYMAVILLE   *Valle d'Aosta*: ITALY

A non-DOC red wine from the Valle d'Aosta.

AYZE   *Savoie*: FRANCE

Ayze is a tiny cru of Savoie, making *méthode champenoise* wine from Altesse and Gringet grapes, from vineyards around the town of Bonneville in Haute-Savoie.

AZÉ   See Mâcon Villages.

AZERBAIJAN   USSR

In the southeastern part of the Soviet Union, this area concentrates on dessert wines made mainly from Rkatiseli grapes.

AZIENDA

An Italian term for business or firm. The word often precedes the name of a company; it may be, more specifically, an agricultural company e.g. Azienda Agricola X which would have its own vineyards as well as making the wine; or Azienda Vinicola Y which would not own vineyards, but would buy grapes or must to make wine, or wine to blend.

AZORES   PORTUGAL

Two islands of the Azores produce wine, Pico and Graciosa. Production is small, mainly from the Verdelho grape and the wine is drunk locally.

B.A.T.F.
The Bureau of Alcohol, Tobacco and Firearms, which is the American body controlling the official aspects of wine in the United States. Incongruously, wine is lumped with cigarettes and guns.

B.G.O.   See Bourgogne Grand Ordinaire.

B.O.B.
The common abbreviation for 'Buyer's Own Brand' in connection with champagne.

BABIČ   YUGOSLAVIA
A red wine made in the Dalmatian peninsular from the grape of the same name. It usually benefits from a little bottle age.

BABICH   NEW ZEALAND
A sixty year old family winery in the Henderson area of New Zealand's North Island. They make good white wine, especially Sauvignon and Chardonnay but have a better reputation for red wines.

BABY DUCK   CANADA
Baby Duck is one of the more common of the many Canadian sparkling wines, made from Labrusca grapes. It is artificially carbonated, sweet and low in alcohol. Canada Duck, Daddy Duck and Cold Turkey are other names.

BACCHUS
Bacchus is the Latin name for Dionysus, the God of wine but in Germany it is a grape variety, not a god, a crossing of Silvaner X Riesling with Müller Thurgau. It is planted mainly in the Rheinhessen, produces a large quantity of grapes with low acidity and features in Liebfraumilch.

BACHARACH   Mittelrhein: GERMANY
One of the three *Bereichs* of the Mittelrhein and the principal wine town of the region.

BACKSBERG   SOUTH AFRICA
An outstanding estate in Paarl which made its reputation on red wine, notably Cabernet Sauvignon, Shiraz and Pinotage. It has always been an innovative estate, abreast of any important developments and over the last five years has grown to include white wines, especially Sauvignon Blanc and Chardonnay.

BACKWARD
Describes a wine that is undeveloped for its age and vintage.

BACO NOIR
An American hybrid grape, a crossing of Folle Blanche with *Vitis Riparia*, producing red wine in the eastern United States. Baco Blanc is a hybrid variety, grown extensively in Armagnac, but now giving way to Ugni Blanc.

BAD DÜRKHEIM   Rheinpfalz: GERMANY
One of the important wine centres of the Rheinpfalz. As the name implies, it is also a spa town. Its vineyards are in three *Grosslagen*: Feuerberg with Steinberg and Nonnengarten; Hochmess with Michelsberg, Spielberg, Rittergarten and Hochbenn, and Schenkenböhl with Abtsfronhof, Fuchsmantel and Fronhof.

BAD KREUZNACH Nahe: GERMANY

Bad Kreuznach is the commercial centre of the Nahe, the home of most of the region's best producers and an attractive spa town. It comes within the *Grosslagen* of Kronenberg and its best Einzellagen include Kahlenberg, Brückes, Steinweg and Krötenpfuhl.

BAD MÜNSTER AM STEIN-EBERNBERG Nahe: GERMANY

Bad Münster is a small spa town on the Nahe, coming within the Grosslage of Burgweg, with some good but little known Einzellagen.

BADACSONY HUNGARY

This district of extinct volcanos, including Mount Badacsony, on the northern shores of Lake Balaton, produces fine white wine from Szürkebarát and Kéknyelü grapes.

BADEN GERMANY

The southernmost wine region of Germany and the warmest. It comes third in production behind the Rheinpfalz and the Rheinhessen. Most of the Baden vineyards face those of Alsace across the Rhine, running from Baden-Baden to Basel, in the foothills of the Black Forest. There is also a small area on the banks of the Bodensee, as the Germans call Lake Constance. The region is divided into seven *Bereichs* which are much more important than any individual vineyards. Cooperatives dominate the region; over 100 local ones are united into the ZBW or Zentralkellerei Badischer Winzergenossenschaft in Breisach. A selection of grape varieties are grown over the region; Müller-Thurgau accounts for the bulk of the white wine with some Ruländer, Gutedel, Riesling, Silvaner, Weissburgunder and Gewürztraminer. Spätburgunder is important too, especially for *Weissherbst*. Baden wines are generally heavier and fuller than those from more northern regions.

BADIA A COLTIBUONO Tuscany: ITALY

A 12th century abbey now owned by the Stucchi family who make fine Chianti Classico and good *rosato* and white wine too.

BAG-IN-THE-BOX

A relatively new way of buying wine in a large capacity, usually of three or ten litres, introduced from Australia. An airtight bag, made of several layers of impermeable plastic is filled with wine and protected by a cardboard box. A tap permits access to the wine, and as the wine is drunk, the bag collapses around the wine, continuing to keep it away from air

BAGA

The principal grape variety of red Bairrada and Portugal's most widely planted grape, found also in the Minho and in Dão. The black grapes are thick skinned and the wine can be deep and astringent.

BAHANS-HAUT-BRION See Haut-Brion.

BAILEYS VINEYARDS AUSTRALIA

Baileys vineyards have a long tradition of winemaking in north east Victoria with the famous Bundarra vineyard, which produces rich Liqueur Muscats from granite soils that give grapes with both high sugar and acid levels.

BAILLY-REVERDY Loire: FRANCE

A reputable Sancerre grower with vineyards in the Clos du Chêne Marchand. His other wine is called Domaine de Mercy Dieu.

BAIRRADA PORTUGAL

The rising star among Portuguese wines. The area was demarcated as recently as 1979 and covers the districts of Aveiro and Coimbra with the town of Anadia at its centre. Bairrada is predominantly red, with a little white wine, which is now usually sparkling. The main red grape is Baga, with some João de Santarém, Castelao, Tinta Pinheira and Bastardo. For the white wine, Maria Gomes is the most important grape. There are also small plantings of Pinot Noir, Pinot Blanc, Gamay and Chardonnay which are used for making sparkling wine. The Baga is a tough tannic grape and makes wines which develop beautifully with barrel and bottle ageing. Certain changes in vinification are taking place to make the red wines softer.

BAISSAGE

The tying down of the young vine shoots onto supporting wires. This is usually done in May when the shoots are long enough and the risk of damage from spring frost is over.

BAJA CALIFORNIA   MEXICO

Or lower California, this is the best wine region of Mexico. It benefits from the cooling influence of the Pacific Ocean. Bodegas de Santo Tomas are a notable producer with vineyards in the Guadalupe Valley Mantro with European grape varieties introduced from the Napa Valley. Domecq have vineyards here, too.

BAKED

Describes a rather cooked, earthy red wine made from grapes produced in a hot climate, often with insufficient rainfall, such as the hotter parts of Australia.

BALANCE

The relationship of all the component parts of wine, notably fruit, tannin, acidity, alcohol and maybe sweetness. A wine should be well-balanced.

BALATON   HUNGARY

Describes wine made on the northern shore of Lake Balaton, mainly from Olaszrizling and Sylvaner grapes.

BALATONFÜRED-CSOPAK   HUNGARY

A small region to the east of Badacsony near Lake Balaton, where Olaszrizling, Furmint and Müller-Thurgau grape varieties make dry, white wines.

BALBACH   Rheinhessen: GERMANY

Weingut Bürgermeister Anton Balbach Erben is one of the best estates of the Rheinhessen. Several Balbachs were Bürgermeisters of Nierstein: Anton cleared the woods from what is now the Pettenthal vineyard. Today their vineyards include Niersteiner Rehbach, Auflangen and Spiegelberg as well as Niersteiner Einzellagen.

BALBAINA   SPAIN

A district to the west of Jerez de la Frontera with *albariza* soil and rated third in order of quality.

BALEAU   Bordeaux: FRANCE

A lesser-known Grand Cru Classé of St-Émilion.

BALESTARD-LA-TONNELLE   Bordeaux: FRANCE

A Grand Cru Classé of St-Émilion, owned by the Capdemourlin family for five centuries, since the poet François Villon described it as *'ce divin nectar qui porte nom de Balestard'*.

BALGOWNIE   AUSTRALIA

The first new winery in the Bendigo area of Victoria for over eighty years, with its first vintage in 1972. Grape varieties include Shiraz, Cabernet Sauvignon, Chardonnay and Pinot Noir, all aged in French or American oak. It is now owned by Mildara.

BALLARAT
AUSTRALIA

A small unimportant wine region of Victoria with a relatively new, scattered wine production. Yellowglen Vineyards is the main producer.

BALLING

A scale used in the United States to measure sugar and thereby potential alcohol in grape juice. A hydrometer is used; for the Balling scale it is usually calibrated at 60°F.

BALSEIRO

A cylindrical wooden vat, tapered at the top and supported by stone legs, used for maturing port.

BALTHAZAR

A champagne bottle size, equal to sixteen ordinary bottles (1200cl).

BAN DE VENDANGE

The declaration of the official beginning of the vintage in the various wine regions of France. The date is determined by the growers of the area, in conjunction with the INAO, and announced by the *préfet* of the *département*. Picking cannot begin before that date.

BANAT
YUGOSLAVIA

A flat sandy region of Yugoslavia, adjoining Roumania and producing a variety of white wines similar to those of Fruška Gora, mainly from Laski Rizling.

BANDA AZUL

A brand name owned by Paternina in Spain for their best selling Rioja.

BANDOL
Provence: FRANCE

One of the finest wines of Provence, coming from vineyards around the town of Bandol. It can be red, white or rosé, but the production of red is most important. Mourvèdre is the grape which gives red Bandol its character, with a minimum of 50%, but often much more. Grenache, Cinsaut and occasionally Cariganan and Syrah make up the balance. The red wine must be aged for a minimum of 18 months in wood, usually in large old *foudres*, rather than small new *barriques* and merits considerable bottle age. A little white is made from Clairette, Ugni Blanc, Bourboulenc and Sauvignon. Domaine Tempier is the most traditional estate.

BANFI VINTNERS

Leading American wine importers. In 1977 they bought vineyards in Tuscany to make not only Brunello di Montalcino, but also varietal wines, especially Cabernet Sauvignon and Chardonnay, as well as *spumante* Moscadello di Montalcino and substantial amounts of ordinary table wine. The modern winery is streamlined, with space age efficiency. They have a wine-making plant at Strevi in Piedmont for Asti Spumante, dry *méthode champenoise spumante* and still Gavi. Across the Atlantic, they are producing New York State Chardonnay.

BANYULS
The Midi: FRANCE

A sweet dessert wine, a *vin doux naturel*, coming from vineyards around the seaside town of Banyuls, almost on the Spanish border in the foothills of the Pyrenees. The principal grape variety is Grenache Noir; Malvoisie, Macabéo and Muscat are also grown. The fermentation is stopped so that the finished wine has about 15–18° alcohol. Banyuls can be bottled young, or matured in cask for several years and is red or tawny in colour.

BANYULS GRAND CRU
The Midi: FRANCE

A supposedly superior version of Banyuls with a minimum of 75% Grenache and aged for three years.

BANYULS RANCIO
The Midi: FRANCE

Aged in oak barrels for several years, sometimes in a solera system, for maybe as many as ten or twenty years, so that it takes on a maderised flavour, known as *rancio*.

BARBACARLO   See Oltrepò Pavese.

ANTONIO BARBADILLO
SPAIN

The oldest and biggest of the sherry firms of Sanlúcar, producing superb *manzanillas* and other sherries from vineyards in the surrounding *albariza* areas of Balbaina, Carrascal and elsewhere. They have also developed a dry white table wine from Palomino grapes.

BARBARESCO   Piedmont: ITALY

One of the great wines of Piedmont, made from the Nebbiolo grape and grown around the villages of Barbaresco, Treiso and Neive. It became DOCG with the 1981 vintage. Barbaresco is always aged for a minimum of two years in both barrel and bottle. If it is a *riserva*, it has three years' ageing and four years' for a *riserva speciale*. Although it does not have the weight of a Barolo it is a wine that develops well with bottle age. Angelo Gaja is generally considered to be the best producer, but other notable names include Ceretto, Franco Fiorino, Giacosa, Prunotto and Oddero.

BARBAROSSA

A red grape variety grown in very limited quantities in Emilia Romagna at the Fattoria Paradiso which has saved it from extinction.

BARBERA

A red grape planted over large parts of Italy, notably in the north west, accounting for a few DOCs, such as Barbera d'Alba, Barbera d'Asti, as well as featuring in Colli Piacentini, Colli Bolognesi and the red wines of the Oltrepò Pavese. It has also spread south to Apulia and Campania.

Acidity is the dominant feature of Barbera; the wines are generally for drinking young rather than for ageing. They may now be made into still and sparkling whites.

It is also widely planted in California, especially in the Central Valley, generally for dull jug wines, and is also found in Argentina.

BARBERA D'ALBA   Piedmont: ITALY

As its name implies, this is made from the red Barbera grape grown around the town of Alba. More substantial than other Barbera wines, it has a minimum of one year's ageing and, if it is *superiore*, it requires two years' ageing and 13° alcohol as opposed to 12°. It is generally intended for drinking within two or three years.

BARBERA D'ASTI   Piedmont: ITALY

A Piedmontese wine made from the Barbera grape and grown in the province of Asti and Alessandria. It requires a minimum of 12.5° alcohol and two years' ageing. *Superiore* needs three years' ageing and 13° alcohol. It is best drunk young.

BARBERA DEL MONFERRATO   Piedmont: ITALY

A red Piedmontese wine made from the Barbera grape, but with a possible 10–15% of Freisa, Grignolino or Dolcetto. It comes from the Monferrato hills around Asti and Alessandria and is sometimes *frizzante*. It must have 12° alcohol and, if *superiore*, two years of ageing and 12.5° alcohol.

BARCO RABELO

The traditional boat used in Portugal to transport six month old port from the Douro Valley to Vila Nova de Gaia. It had a single sail with a flat bottom and a shallow draft to navigate the rapids of the Upper Douro. Such a journey would have taken three days in a race against nature.

BARDOLINO   Veneto: ITALY

A DOC wine which takes its name from a pretty village on Lake Garda. It is red, pink, called Chiaretto, or *Novello*, released early in November, made from Corvina Veronese, Rondinella, Molinara and Negrara grapes. *Classico* comes from the immediate vicinity of the village. *Superiore* denotes a year's ageing. The red should be drunk within four years and the lighter Chiaretto in two.

BARDONE   Piedmont: ITALY

The brand name for a wine produced by Fontanafredda from a mixture of Barbera, Dolcetto and Nebbiolo grapes, vinified so that it is young, light and fruity. It is best drunk within the year.

BARET
Bordeaux: FRANCE

A Graves from the commune of Villenave d'Ornon which enjoys a good reputation for both its red and white wine.

BARNES WINES
CANADA

Barnes Wines in Ontario is Canada's oldest winery, created in 1873 by George Barnes. They have links with Gilbeys and their main label is Heritage Estates. Johannisberg Riesling is their flagship.

BAROLET COLLECTION

Dr. Barolet was an eccentric physician who lived in Beaune. As well as making wine from his own vineyard, he bought wine from other growers and, by the time of his death in 1968 had amassed a collection over 100,000 bottles, which were purchased by Henri de Villamont and which have gradually been released onto the market.

BAROLO
Piedmont: ITALY

Considered by many to be the greatest Italian wine. The Piedmontese call it the King of Wine and Wine of Kings. It is made from the Nebbiolo grape in the Langhe hills southeast of Alba and takes its name from the village of Barolo. It has been DOCG since the 1980 vintage. Traditional producers age their wines in large oak barrels for several years, for the DOCG regulations dictate three years' ageing for the ordinary Barolo (including two in barrel), four years for a *riserva* and five years for a *riserva speciale*. More modern producers are tending to limit the effect of wood and emphasise the fruit. Fine Barolo is capable of a very long life. Notable producers include Ceretto, Aldo Conterno, Franco Fiorina, Bruno Giacosa, Pio Cesare, Renato Ratti and Vietti.

BAROLO CHINATO
Piedmont: ITALY

An *amaro* allowed by the DOC regulations, made by flavouring the wine with *Guina*, a bitter Peruvian bark. It used to be quite common, but is now rarely produced.

BAROQUE

An unusual grape variety peculiar to the VDQS Tursan Blanc, which must contain 90% Baroque. It makes rather heavy rustic wine without much fruit.

BAROSSA VALLEY
AUSTRALIA

The Barossa Valley in Southern Australia, north east of Adelaide is one of the best known Australian wine regions. The area was first settled by German immigrants and consequently there is a strong Germanic influence in the wines, with Rhine Riesling the most widely grown grape. The climate tends to be hot and dry; temperatures vary between hill and valley, and so far the region is phylloxera free so that some growers take the risk of planting vines on their own roots. Palomino and Pedro Ximenez are important grapes for fortified wines, while Shiraz and Grenache are the main red grapes. Barossa owes its original reputation to fortified and dessert wines; today there is an increasing emphasis on table wines, especially white.

BARREL

A wooden container of unspecified size, used to mature and store wine.

BARREYRES
Bordeaux: FRANCE

An important but little-known property in Arcins, Haut-Médoc.

BARRICA

The Spanish term for a barrel, or barrique of 225 litres, used most commonly in Rioja.

BARRIQUE

The traditional Bordeaux barrel containing 225 litres, which will yield 24 cases of 12 bottles. Four *barriques* equal one *tonneau*. This barrel size is now common in the New World where new oak barrels are increasingly used.

BARRO

One of the three soil types of Jerez in Spain, the other two being albariza and arena. It is a mud clay containing up to 10% chalk, and darker in colour than albariza as it also contains iron oxide. The wine produced on barro soil is inferior to that from albariza.

BARROS & ALMEIDA

One of the largest Portuguese port houses, owning Feuerheerd, Kopke, the Douro Wine Shippers' Association and others.

BARSAC
Bordeaux: FRANCE

One of the villages of the appellation of Sauternes and also an appellation in its own right. Wine from Barsac may call itself Sauternes, but Sauternes produced outside Barsac may not be labelled Barsac. The appellation regulations are the same. In taste, Barsac is perhaps a little lighter and more elegant, but the differences are almost imperceptible. The two best Barsac wines are Climens and Coutet.

BAS-MÉDOC
Bordeaux: FRANCE

The enormous area of the Médoc is split into two parts, the Haut-Médoc in the south and, in the north the part traditionally called the Bas-Médoc, although its wines have the appellation of Médoc. It runs from the boundary of St-Estèphe to Soulac, and the best known *château* is Loudenne.

BASILICATA
ITALY

An obscure southern region of Italy with just one DOC wine, Aglianico del Vulture.

BASSERMANN-JORDAN
Rheinpfalz: GERMANY

Weingut Geheimer Rat Dr. von Bassermann-Jordan is an important family estate in existence since 1250, and in the hands of the Jordan family since 1816. The vineyards are purely Riesling grapes, including sites in Deidesheim, Forst, Ruppertsberg, and Ungstein. The wine is made with meticulous care aged in oak and the results are excellent.

BASTARD

An Elizabethan wine, mentioned as 'brown and white bastard' by Shakespeare in 'Measure for Measure'. It was possibly sweet, mixed with something else like honey, or may have come from the island of Madeira, from the Bastardo grape.

BASTARDO

One of the main grape varieties for red port, giving sugar and quantity, rather than flavour and quality. It also features in Dão and Bairrada and in Madeira and has travelled as far as Australia for port style wines.

In Madeira, planting of the Bastardo grape declined dramatically after the *phylloxera* crisis, Bastardo was usually blended with other grapes, but occasionally found on its own as Bastardo. 1844 was a great Bastardo vintage.

BASTOR-LAMONTAGNE
Bordeaux: FRANCE

A well-made Cru Bourgeois Sauternes in the commune of Preignac, with a good reputation.

BATAILLEY
Bordeaux: FRANCE

A fifth growth Pauillac. The name of this property is said to originate from Joseph Batailhé, Charles II's wine merchant. It is a large estate making somewhat austere wines and is now owned by a branch of the Borie family.

BÂTARD-MONTRACHET
Burgundy: FRANCE

A Grand Cru vineyard in the villages of Chassagne-Montrachet and Puligny-Montrachet, producing some fine white wine.

BÂTONNAGE

Describes the process of mixing the fine lees at the bottom of a barrel with the wine. This can be done every couple of months while the wine is ageing in wood, usually by beating the barrel with a rod or bâton, and is believed to give more flavour to the wine. The term applies only to white wine, notably Burgundy and it is amusing to recall the old verse:

A dog, a woman and a walnut tree
– and also a hogshead of Puligny –
The more you beat them the better they be.

JEAN BAUMARD *Loire*: FRANCE

A serious producer in Anjou. His property includes vineyards in Quarts de Chaume; Savennières, where he owns part of Clos du Papillon and the vineyard of Clos Ste-Catherine in the Coteaux du Layon. As well as Anjou Rouge, he makes Logis de la Giraudière from Cabernet Franc and Sauvignon grapes and a Crémant de la Loire from Chardonnay.

BAUMÉ

The French system for measuring must weight to obtain an idea of the potential alcohol of the wine. 1° Baumé corresponds to between 17 and 18 grams of sugar in a litre of water.

BAY OF PLENTY NEW ZEALAND

A small wine region adjoining Waikato on North Island, historically of little importance but now enjoying a revival with the new Morton Estate Winery.

BAYAN SHIREY

A grape variety widely planted in the Soviet Union, but as it oxidises quickly it is diminishing in importance.

BEAD See Billes.

BÉARN SOUTH WEST FRANCE

An *appellation contrôlée* wine of the Pyrenees. It can be red, white or rosé, but rosé is most common as Rosé de Béarn. It is produced in three different areas, within the appellations of Madiran and Jurançon and from vineyards around the town of Salies de Béarn and Orthez. Here the production is dominated by the cave cooperative of Bellocq and this area is distinguished from the rest of the appellation by the indication Salies-Bellocq on the label. In the Salies-Bellocq area the grape varieties are Tannat, Cabernet Franc and Cabernet Sauvignon for Rouge de Béarn. Rosé de Béarn is either pure Tannat or pure Cabernet Franc. The rare Blanc de Béarn is made only from a local grape, Raffiat de Moncade. Elsewhere Gros and Petit Manseng are also used, the rosé wines are light and fruity; the reds can be aged for a year or two.

BEAU RIVAGE *Bordeaux*: FRANCE

A Bordeaux Supérieur in Macau, owned by the house of Borie Manoux. It is an interesting example of a wine from the Médoc *palus*.

BEAU-SÉJOUR BÉCOT *Bordeaux*: FRANCE

Has been demoted from Premier Grand Cru Classé to Grand Cru Classé as the owner has included wines from the Grand Cru vineyards of Chateau la Carte and Chateau les Trois Moulins under the Beau-Séjour Bécot label. The vineyards are just outside the ramparts of St-Émilion and originally formed a single property with Beau séjour Duffau-Lagarosse.

BEAU-SITE *Bordeaux*: FRANCE

A Cru Grand Bourgeois Exceptionnel of St-Estèphe, making consistent wine.

BEAUJOLAIS *Burgundy*: FRANCE

A wine and a region of Burgundy. The wine, which is usually red, but which can also be rosé or white, is produced from vineyards on the gently undulating hills to the north of the city of Lyon around the town of Villefranche. The grape variety for red Beaujolais is Gamay Noir à Jus Blanc and Chardonnay is used for white. The area is split into two parts, Haut Beaujolais and Bas Beaujolais. The latter is where the bulk of Beaujolais, Beaujolais-Villages and Beaujolais Nouveau comes from, while the former is where the ten Crus of Beaujolais are situated: Moulin-à-Vent, Chénas, Fleurie, St-Amour, Brouilly, Côte de Brouilly Regnié, Morgon, Juliénas and Chiroubles. Most Beaujolais is made by a variation of the *macération carbonique* method of vinification which gives the wine an immediately appealing fruitiness, so it is best drunk during the year following the vintage. The wines from the ten Crus are more substantial and the best vintages can benefit from ageing.

BEAUJOLAIS NOUVEAU

The new young Beaujolais, vinified by *macération carbonique* so that it is ready for release for sale on the third Thursday in November, within a very few weeks of the vintage. Nearly half the production of Beaujolais is now sold as Nouveau, such is the commercial success of the idea of drinking the young wine of the year. Beaujolais Nouveau is sold until Christmas, but the better wines will last longer, like normal Beaujolais.

BEAUJOLAIS SUPÉRIEUR
Burgundy: FRANCE

The difference between Beaujolais and Beaujolais Supérieur is one of alcoholic degree. Beaujolais Supérieur must have a minimum of 10° of alcohol, whereas in theory Beaujolais, need only have 9°, but in reality always exceeds 10°. Consequently, Beaujolais Supérieur is rarely found on a label.

BEAUJOLAIS-VILLAGES
Burgundy: FRANCE

The better villages, including some of the ten Beaujolais Crus have the right to the appellation Beaujolais-Villages. The wine is nearly always red and has a little more body than simple Beaujolais. Occasionally the village is included on the label. The villages are: Chânes, la Chapelle-de-Guinchay, Leynes, Pruzilly, Romanèche-Thorins, St-Amour, Bellevue, St-Symphorien-d'Ancelles, St-Véran, Arbuissonaz, Beaujeu, Blacé, Cercié, Charentay, Chénas, Chiroubles, Denice, Durette, Emeringes, Fleurie, Juliénas, Jullie, Lancié, Lantignié, Montmélas, Odenas, le Perréon, Quincié, Régnié, Rivolet, St-Etienne-des-Ouillères, St-Etienne-la-Varenne, St-Julien, St-Lager, Salles, Vaux, Villié-Morgon.

BEAULIEU VINEYARDS
California: USA

Beaulieu Vineyards, or B.V. for short, was one of the earliest wineries of the Napa Valley, founded by a Frenchman, Georges de Latour in the early 1900s. André Tchelistcheff, one of the great winemakers of California, was here from 1938 for nearly forty years and under his influence B.V. had an unrivalled reputation until the 1970s. Cabernet Sauvignon is the winery's best varietal, notably Georges de Latour Private Reserve Cabernet, an intensive American oak-aged wine.

BEAULIEU-SUR-LAYON
Loire: FRANCE

One of the villages of the Coteaux du Layon whose name can feature on the label as Coteaux du Layon Villages – Beaulieu-sur-Layon

BEAUMES-DE-VENISE
Rhône: FRANCE

One of the seventeen Côtes du Rhône Villages of the southern Rhône. However it is better known for its *vin doux naturel*, a Muscat de Beaumes-de-Venise. The most important producer is the Cave Cooperative of the village whose wines are sold in distinctive outsize perfume bottles. Other leading producers include Domaine Durban, Domaine des Bernardins, and Domaine de Coyeux. Most people produce Côtes du Rhône Villages as well as Muscat de Beaumes de Venise.

BEAUNE
Burgundy: FRANCE

The town of Beaune is the heart of the Côte de Beaune and the home of many famous shippers and growers. It is no exaggeration to call it the wine capital of Burgundy. The famous Hospices de Beaune which owns many vineyards in the Côte de Beaune is situated here. Their wines are sold at annual auction. There is also a wine museum. The production of the vineyards is predominantly red. The Premier Cru vineyards are les Marconnets, les Fèves, les Bressandes, les Grèves, les Teurons, le Clos des Mouches, Champs Pimont (or Champimonts), Clos du Roi (part), aux Coucherias (part), en l'Orme, en Genêt, les Perrières, à l'Écu, les Cent Vignes, les Toussaints, sur les Grèves, aux Cras (or Crais), le Clos de la Mousse, les Chouacheux, les Boucherottes, les Vignes Franches, les Aigrots, Pertuisots, le Tièlandry (or Clos Landry), les Sizies, les Avaux, les Reversèes, le Bas de Teurons, les Seurey, la Mignotte, Montée Rouge (part), les Montrevenots (part), les Blanches Fleurs (part), les Epenottes.

Growers and shippers with their headquarters in Beaune include Albert Bichot, Bouchard Ainé, Bouchard Père et Fils, Calvet, Champy Père et Fils, Paul Chanson, Chanson Père et Fils, Joseph Drouhin, Louis Jadot, Louis Latour, P. de Marcilly Frères, Patriache Père et Fils, Pierre Ponnelle, Remoissenet Père et Fils and Domaine Voiret.

BEAUNOIS

A synonym used in Chablis for the Chardonnay grape, possibly a reference to the fact that Chardonnay may have been introduced to the region from Beaune.

BEAUREGARD
Bordeaux: FRANCE

An important property in Pomerol, well run and making consistent wine. The distinctive 17th and 18th century *château* has been reproduced on Long Island for the Guggenheim family.

BEERENAUSLESE

The fourth category of German *Prädikat* wines, meaning literally a 'selection of berries', which have been affected by noble rot. *Beerenauslese* is made only in the best years and the resulting wine is richly sweet and will develop with bottle age. The necessary sugar content, measured as oechsle degree, which varies according to grape variety and region, is 125° for a Riesling in the Rheingau and 110° in the Mosel.

BEESWING

A thin light crust, resembling the wing of a bee, which forms in some old bottles of port.

BÉGADAN   *Bordeaux*: FRANCE

An important village within the Médoc appellation with several reputable *châteaux* such as Laujac, Patâche d'Aux and La Tour de By.

BEICHUN

A red hybrid grape variety developed in China to withstand low winter temperatures and also rot in the humid vineyards of the south.

BEINES   *Burgundy*: FRANCE

One of the larger villages within the vineyards of Chablis.

BEIRAS   PORTUGAL

A province between Dão and the Spanish frontier with Guardia at its centre. The best wine area is in Beira Alta where Pinhel is a determinate area, especially for its white wine. Malvasia is grown in the region of Moimenta da Beira for sparkling wines. However red wine forms the greater part of the region's production.

BEKÁA VALLEY   LEBANON

The main wine area of the Lebanon just north of Beirut. The vineyards are some 1000 metres above sea level and protected by Mount Lebanon, to give a constant microclimate. The soil is limestone with a gravel topsoil and Château Musar is the finest estate of the area.

DOMAINE DE BEAURENARD   *Rhône*: FRANCE

An important estate in Châteauneuf-du-Pape, making wine partly by *macération carbonique* and partly by using traditional methods, so that the wine is ready for drinking between three and eight years after the vintage.

BEAUROY   *Burgundy*: FRANCE

A Premier Cru Chablis vineyard. Part of the vineyard can be sold under the name of Troesmes (or Troême).

BEAUSÉJOUR DUFFAU-LAGAROSSE   *Bordeaux*: FRANCE

A Premier Grand Cru Classé St-Émilion which once formed a single property with Beau Séjour Bécot. The vineyard is planted with 55% Merlot grapes and some Cabernet Franc and Cabernet Sauvignon.

BEAUSITE-HAUT-VIGNOBLE   *Bordeaux*: FRANCE

Next to Beau-Site in St-Estèphe but the wines are tougher and less attractive than its neighbours.

BEL-AIR-MARQUIS D'ALIGRE
Bordeaux: FRANCE

An important estate in the commune of Soussans, Margaux, deemed to be Cru Bourgeois Exceptionnel.

BEL-ORME-TRONQUOY-DE-LALANDE
Bordeaux: FRANCE

A Cru Grand Bourgeois from the village of St-Seurnin de Cadourne, Haut-Médoc. This mouthful of a name is often shortened to Bel-Orme and should not be confused with the St-Estèphe property Tronquoy de Lalande. The wines are consistent.

BELAIR
Bordeaux: FRANCE

Premier Grand Cru Classé St-Émilion, it shares the owner and manager of Ausone. The vineyards are nearby. It is one of the great wines of St-Émilion.

BELGRAVE
Bordeaux: FRANCE

A fifth growth, St-Laurent in the Haut-Médoc. Has had a chequered reputation. However, since 1980, Professor Peynaud has been asked to advise and the property has been modernised. It may merit its classification once again.

BELI PINOT

The Yugoslav name for the Pinot Noir grape.

BELIC PINOT

The Yugoslav name for the Pinot Blanc grape.

BELIMINITA QUADRATA

A particular type of chalk found in the champagne region which contributes to the character of the wine. It comes from the sediment of minerals and fossils left by the sea in the Paris Basin, several million years ago. It is only on this chalk that vines are planted. It also provides ideal cellars with a constant temperature, for the maturation of the wine.

BELLAPAIS
CYPRUS

Keo's brand name for their slightly sparkling dry white wine. It takes its name from a village in the northern part of the island.

BELLE TERRE
California: USA

A vineyard situated in the Alexander Valley and owned by Château St. Jean. The label is seen for single vineyard Cabernet Sauvignon, Chardonnay and Johannisberg Riesling.

BELLET
Provence: FRANCE

A tiny appellation within the commune of Nice with just five producers who sell their wine in bottle, of which Château de Crémat and Château de Bellet are the largest. The vineyards on the hills behind Nice are planted with Braquet, Folle Noire and Grenache for red and rosé. Opinions differ as to whether Braquet or Folle Noire give the red its character. The white is made mainly from Rolle with some Chardonnay, and ages well, while the red is lighter, for early drinking.

BELLEVUE
Bordeaux: FRANCE

A Grand Cru Classé of St-Émilion. Situated on the *côtes*, it is one of the most popular names in the Gironde.

BEN EAN   see Lindeman.

BENCH GRAFTING

Describes the joining of American rootstock and *vitis vinifera* scions in a nursery, rather than in the vineyard. The vine is not planted until the graft has healed.

BENDIGO
AUSTRALIA

A small wine area of the state of Victoria, which in the 1850s was the centre of the Gold Rush. Phylloxera destroyed the industry until a gentle revival began with the creation of the Balgownie Estate in 1969. Rainfall is low so irrigation is necessary. The red wines are showing great promise.

BENEDE-ORANGE
SOUTH AFRICA

The most northerly Region of Origin of South Africa. A very hot area, with vineyards depending upon irrigation around the town of Upington on the Lower Orange River. The vineyards produce large crops mainly for distillation.

BENI M'TIR MOROCCO

An *appellation d'origine garantie* in the region of Meknès Fez, producing wines from Cinsaut, Carignan and Grenache grapes under the name of Tarik.

BENI SADDEN MOROCCO

An *appellation d'origine garantie*, in the region of Meknès Fez.

BENMARL USA

An estate in the Hudson River Valley, making some of the better wines of New York State.

BENTONITE

A type of clay used for fining wine, especially white wine, which is particularly useful for removing an excess of protein from wine.

BERBERANA SPAIN

A Rioja company founded by the Berberana family and run by them until 1970. They have recently expanded with a new *bodega* in Cenicero and nearly half their grapes come from their own vineyards, including extensive new plantings on the higher land of the Rioja Baja. Their range comprises a *sin crianza* Preferido, 3 year old Carta de Plata and 5 year old Carta de Oro. Their white wine is not aged in wood.

BEREICH

A subregion of German vineyards. Each *Anbaugebiet* is divided into *Bereichs*, which usually take their name from the most important village in the area, e.g. Bereich Nierstein. A *Bereich* is used for a *Qualitätswein* and groups vineyards of similar character.

BERGAT *Bordeaux*: FRANCE

One of the smallest Grand Crus Classés of St-Émilion and relatively unknown.

BERGERAC SOUTH WEST FRANCE

A wine which comes in a variety of guises, red, white and rosé, with smaller appellations such as Pécharmant and Saussignac within the zone of Bergerac. The attractive town of Bergerac with its associations with Cyrano de Bergerac, gave the wine its name and the vineyards stretch from near Bergerac in the east, following the Dordogne to the *départemental* boundary that separates them from the Gironde and Bordeaux. The grape varieties are those of Bordeaux, Sauvignon, Sémillon and Muscadelle for white, Cabernet Franc and Sauvignon and Merlot for reds and rosés. The taste is not unlike claret, but the wine is generally shorter-lived.

BERGERAC SEC SOUTH WEST FRANCE

The dry white wine of Bergerac; it is made from Sauvignon, Sémillon and Muscadelle and can, according to growers' personal preferences, be a pure Sauvignon. It can be produced all over the area of Bergerac and is a wine to drink young.

BERGERON See Chignin.

BERGKELDER See Oude Meester.

BADISCHE BERGSTRASSE-KRAICHGAU *Baden*: GERMANY

One of the seven Bereichs of Baden, covering two sub-regions; an extension of the Hessische Bergstrasse around Heidelberg and the Kraichgau south of Heidelberg between the Rhine and the Neckar. Müller Thurgau is the most important grape, followed by Riesling and Ruländer and an assortment of others.

BERGWEILER-PRÜM ERBEN *Mosel-Saar-Ruwer*: GERMANY

The estate of Zach. Bergweiler Prüm Erben was part of the Prüm family's original property. It consists of vineyards in Bernkastel, Wehlen and Zeltingen.

BERINGER *California*: USA

Jacob Beringer first planted vines in the Napa Valley in 1873; the winery in St. Helena was built in 1883 when Jacob was joined by his brother Frederick. Today Beringer belongs to Nestlé who have revitalised it and established a reputation, especially for white wines. Los Hermanos, meaning the brothers, is the second label.

BERKANE-OUJDA MOROCCO

A very small wine region of Morocco, near the Algerian border.

BERN
SWITZERLAND

The wines of the canton of Bern are similar to those of Neuchâtel, mainly from Chasselas and Pinot Noir grapes.

BERNKASTEL
Mosel-Saar-Ruwer: GERMANY

One of the most famous Mosel names. Bereich Bernkastel is one of the four *Bereichs* of the river, covering the Mittelmosel, while the town of Bernkastel-Kues contains many of the important cellars of the area. The vineyards of Bernkastel are covered by two *Grosslagen*, the smaller Badstube with Bernkastel's five best vineyards and the much larger Kurfürstlay. The most famous *Einzellage* is the Doktor vineyard, so called for the supposedly curative powers of the wine. Today, the principal owners are Deinhard, Thanisch and Lauerburg. The other vineyards are Bratenhöfchen, Matheisbildchen, Lay, Graben, Johannisbrünnchen, Stephanus-Rosengärtchen, Kardinalsberg, Schlossberg, Rosenberg and Weissenstein.

BERRI
AUSTRALIA

An important producer in the Riverland district of South Australia. Originally concentrating on bulk wines, Berri are now changing direction towards better quality wines. Renmano is another Riverland cooperative that has joined with Berri as Consolidated Cooperatives, but with separate products and names.

BERSANO
Piedmont: ITALY

A well-established firm, making a range of wines, including Barolo and Barbaresco. A wine museum is open five days a week.

BERTANI
Veneto: ITALY

An important family producer, making a range of Soave, Bardolino and Valpolicella, most notably Amarone.

LES BERTHIERS
Loire: FRANCE

An important village in the appellation of Pouilly Fumé.

BESSERAT DE BELLEFON
Champagne: FRANCE

A small champagne house applying modern methods with success.

BESTS WINES
AUSTRALIA

Bests Wines consists of two estates, Concongella in the Great Western region and the St. Andrew's Winery at Lake Boga in north west Victoria. These are traditional Victorian wineries, little known outside the state, producing quite different wines in each area, including Bests Great Western varietals, notably No. 0 Great Western Hermitage.

BEUGNON   See Vaillons.

BEYAZ

The Turkish word for 'white'.

BEYCHEVELLE
Bordeaux: FRANCE

A fourth growth St-Julien standing regally at the entrance to St-Julien on the road from Margaux. A former owner, the Duc d'Éperon, was an Admiral of France and required ships passing his property to lower their sails. Beychevelle is a corruption of *Baisse les voiles* and there is a sail on the label. The property has a good reputation in Britain. It is said that a good year for Beychevelle is a good year for Bordeaux. The name of the second wine has recently changed from Réserve de l'Amiral to Clos de l'Amiral.

LÉON BEYER
Alsace: FRANCE

An important Alsace house, a family company based in Eguisheim, with large vineyard holdings. Cuvée des Ecaillers for Riesling and Cuvée des Comtes d'Eguisheim are their best wines; they also make very good *Vendange Tardive* wines, while Cuvée Particulière describes a better *cuvée* that has been kept until it is mature before sale.

BIANCHELLO DEL METAURO
The Marches: ITALY

A crisp dry white DOC from the valley of the river Metauro, made from the Bianchello grape.

BIANCHI
ARGENTINA

A winery in Mendoza. Cabernet Particular is their best wine, and Don Valentin (the founder's family name) is a standard red.

BIANCO

White in Italian, referring to wine.

BIANCO CAPENA Latium: ITALY

A white DOC wine made from Trebbiano and Malvasia grapes, around the town of Capena. If it has 12° alcohol, it is *superiore*.

BIANCO DEI COLLI MACERATESI
The Marches: ITALY

A dry white DOC made from the Trebbiano Toscano and Maceratino grapes in small quantity over a large area around Macerata.

BIANCO DI CUSTOZA Veneto: ITALY

A dry white DOC wine from south of Lake Garda, made mainly from a blend of Trebbiano Toscana, Garganega and Tocai grapes. It takes its name from the village of Custoza near Verona. The still wine is an alternative to Soave; *spumante* is occasionally found.

BIANCO DI GRAVINA Apulia: ITALY

A new DOC, a dry white made from the Verdeca grape.

BIANCO DELLA LEGA Tuscany: ITALY

A neutral dry white wine made from the excess of Chianti grapes, Trebbiano and Malvasia. Production is supervised by the Chianti Classico Consorzio.

BIANCO PISANO SAN TORPE
Tuscany: ITALY

A dry white DOC wine made from Trebbiano, Canaiolo Bianco and Malvasia grapes grown south-east of Pisa.

BIANCO DI PITIGLIANO
Tuscany: ITALY

A dry neutral white DOC made from Trebbiano, Grechetto and other grapes grown around Pitigliano in southern Tuscany.

BIANCO DEI ROERI Piedmont: ITALY

An unusual white wine made from the white Arneis and red Nebbiolo grape, vinified off the skins.

BIANCO DI SCANDIANO
Emilia-Romagna: ITALY

A DOC from around the town of Scandiano, made from Sauvignon, Malvasia and Trebbiano grapes. It is usually *frizzante* and sometimes *spumante*, dry or medium dry.

BIANCO VAL D'ARBIA Tuscany: ITALY

A dry white DOC wine made from Trebbiano and Malvasia grapes, grown in the valley of the Arbia south east of Siena.

BIANCO DELLA VALDIENIEVOLE
Tuscany: ITALY

A white DOC wine produced from Trebbiano grapes grown around Montecatini Terme. Vin Santo della Valdienievole is also DOC, but rare.

BIANCO VERGINE DELLA VALDICHIANA Tuscany: ITALY

A dry white DOC wine made from Trebbiano and Malvasia grapes grown in the valley of the Chiana near Arezzo.

BICAL

A white grape grown for the tiny production of white Bairrada in Portugal.

ALBERT BICHOT Burgundy: FRANCE

Important producers in Beaune, both growers and *négociants*. They own two estates, Clos Frantin in Vosne-Romanée and Long-Depaquit in Chablis, and have taken over several other companies under whose names they trade, such as Paul Bouchard. Their estate wines are excellent; as *négociants* they are less exacting.

BIDDENDEN ENGLAND

Biddenden Vineyards near Ashford in Kent is a 16 acre vineyard growing Müller-Thurgau with some Ortega, Reichensteiner, Huxelrebe and Seyval Blanc grapes for a medium-dry white wine, and Pinot Noir for a rosé. Their first vintage was 1973.

BIENVENUES-BÂTARD-MONTRACHET

This is a 2.30 hectare Grand Cru vineyard in the village of Puligny-Montrachet, producing some of the finest white wine from the Côte d'Or. There is often amusing speculation as to the origin of vineyard names. In this instance there is an apocryphal story, dating back to the Crusades when *droit de seigneur*, or *droit de cuissage*, was generally accepted and, as the name of the vineyard suggests, it seems bastards were welcome!

BIFERNO Molise: ITALY

One of the two DOC wines from the Molise region. There are red, *rosato* and white wines, named after the river which flows through the vineyard area. For red and *rosato*, Montepulciano, Aglianico and Trebbiano Toscano grapes are the main varieties, while Trebbiano Toscano, Bombino Bianco and Malvasia Bianca account for the white. Red becomes *riserva* after three years if it has 13° alcohol.

BIG

Describes a full-bodied wine, rich in flavour as well as alcohol.

BIGI Umbria: ITALY

Now part of the Swiss Winefood group, one of the better-known producers of Orvieto. They also include Est! Est!! Est!!! and Vino Nobile di Montepulciano amongst their wines.

BIJELO

Means white on a Yugoslav wine label.

BILBAINAS SPAIN

Founded as a family firm in 1901. A third of their grape requirements are produced in their own vineyards. Their principal wines comprise a *clarete* Viña Zaco, a red Viña Pomal and a sparkling Royal Carlton, with *reservas* and dry and sweet white wine.

BILLES

or in English 'beads'. These are being developed by Moet & Chandon in their research work to facilitate the process of the second fermentation. The yeasts are mixed with alginate, which contains them within a very fine net with tiny pores. The second fermentation takes place in the normal way, but instead of the lengthy process of remuage, the 'billes' fall to the bottom of the bottle in a matter of seconds. The process needs to be perfected, but augurs well for the future.

BIN LABEL

A china label used in an old-fashioned wine cellar to indicate the contents of each bin in the cellar, when the bottles were unlabelled. Today these are collectors' items.

BINGEN Rheinhessen: GERMANY

Facing Rüdesheim across the Rhein at the junction of the Rhein and the Nahe. It gives its name to one of the three *Bereichs* of the Rheinhessen, covering the western half of the region adjoining the Nahe. The vineyards of the town come within the *Grosslage* of Sankt Rochuskapelle and its best site is the Scharlachberg. Other lesser-known vineyards include Schlossberg-Schwätzerchen, Bubenstück, Kirchberg, Rosengarten and Kapellenberg.

BIONDI-SANTI Tuscany: ITALY

The most well-known makers of Brunello di Montalcino. They make wines of immense longevity commanding a fabulous price from their Il Greppo estate. The family are credited with isolating the right Sangiovese grape clone to make fine Brunello, and hence establishing the reputation of Brunello di Montalcino.

BISCHÖFLICHES KONVIKT
Mosel-Saar-Ruwer: GERMANY

One of the three main ecclesiastical estates of the Mosel that make up the Bischöflichen Weingüter, Trier. This is the largest, going back to 1653 with vineyards in the Ruwer, Saar and Mosel. It is the sole owner of Ayler Herrenberg.

BISCHÖFLICHES PRIESTERSEMINAR
Mosel-Saar-Ruwer: GERMANY

One of the three main ecclesiastical estates of the Mosel, that make up the Bischöflichen Weingüter, Trier, with vineyards on the Mosel and Saar.

BISHOP

A mulled port drink, made with an orange, cloves and nutmeg and set alight before serving. Some recipes suggest claret rather than port.

BITE

Describes a strong element of acidity and maybe also tannin in a young wine, which will mellow with age.

BLAAUWKLIPPEN   SOUTH AFRICA

A flourishing wine estate in the Stellenbosch area of South Africa, producing a fine range of cultivars, notably Cabernet Sauvignon and Pinot Noir and, more unusually, Zinfandel, both for table wine and 'port'.

BLACK HAMBURG   see Schiava

BLACK ROT

A disease of the vine. Black stains appear on the leaves and the fruit shrivels. This occurs in hot humidity and can be treated with copper sulphate.

BLACK SPANISH

A red hybrid grape variety planted quite extensively in Madeira, having gained in importance after the *phylloxera* crisis. It is appreciated for its good colour and sugar but with the impending EEC regulations about the use of grape varieties and labelling, can no longer be used for Madeira and is now turned into table wine for local consumption. It is also called Jacquet.

BLACK TOWER

A Liebfraumilch brand owned by Hermann Kendermann in the Rheinhessen, coming in a distinctive crock shaped black bottle.

BLACK TSIMILYANSKY

A red grape variety grown extensively in the Don region of the Soviet Union, especially for sparkling wine.

BLACKCURRANT

The characteristic smell of wines made from Cabernet Sauvignon, of wines from the Médoc and also the New World.

BLADDER PRESS   See press.

BLAGNY
Burgundy: FRANCE

The hamlet of Blagny on the Côte d'Or is next to Meursault and Puligny. It gives its name to the red wines of Puligny-Montrachet, though more often these are sold as Côte de Beaune Villages. The Premiers Crus white wines of La Pièce sous-le Bois and Sous le Dos de l'Âne can be sold as Meursault Blagny.

BLANC

The French term for 'white'.

BLANC DE BLANCS

A white wine made from white grapes. Basic French table wine is sometimes described as *blanc de blancs* in an attempt to make it sound smarter than it is. When champagne is made purely from Chardonnay grapes, it can also be labelled Blanc de Blancs.

BLANC FUMÉ DE POUILLY
Loire: FRANCE

An alternative name for Pouilly Fumé.

BLANC DE MARBONNE   SOUTH AFRICA

Blanc de Marbonne is a dry white wine, made from Steen, produced by Koopmanskloof estate in Stellenbosch.

BLANC DE MORGEX   Valle d'Aosta: ITALY

A non-DOC white wine from the Valle d'Aosta, made from Blanc de Valdigue grapes grown in some of Europe's highest vineyards.

BLANC DE NOIRS

A white wine made from black grapes. Champagne is the most notable example of this. In countries where there is a shortage of white wine and an excess of red grapes, such as California, they sometimes make a white wine from red grapes.

BLANC DE LA SALLE   Valle di Aosta: ITALY

A non-DOC white wine from the Valle d'Aosta made from Blanc de Valdigue grapes grown at 1000 metres above sea level.

BLANCHOTS   Burgundy: FRANCE

One of the seven Grand Cru vineyards of Chablis.

BLANCO

The Spanish word for white.

BLANDY

An important Madeira house, founded in 1811 and now part of the Madeira Wine Company. Brand names for their wines include the Dukes of Clarence, Cambridge and Sussex.

BLANQUEFORT   Bordeaux: FRANCE

One of the riverside communes of the Médoc. It produces very little wine today in its rich alluvial soil.

BLANQUETTE

A synonym for the Mauzac grape, as in Blanquette de Limoux.

BLANQUETTE DE LIMOUX
                     The Midi: FRANCE

A sparkling wine produced from vineyards near Carcassonne around the town of Limoux. Blanquette is a local name for Mauzac, the principal grape variety of the region. Some Chenin Blanc and Chardonnay are also grown. Limoux claims an even longer history than Champagne, using the *méthode rurale* of Gaillac. Today the cooperative at Limoux, the principal producer of the area, follows the *méthode champenoise*.

WOLF BLASS   AUSTRALIA

An important South Australian wine company which takes its name from its winemaker, who is one of the personalities of the Australian wine industry. The vineyard in the Barossa Valley is called Bilyara. Wolf Blass's success is due to his talent as a négociant, buying, blending and ageing wine. His reputation was made with his red wines, but his Yellow Label (indicating the wine is ready for drinking) Rhine Riesling is now his best seller. There is also a Grey Label (drink now or lay down) and a Black Label for award winning wines, of which there are many.

BLATINA   YUGOSLAVIA

An ordinary red wine produced in Herzegovina from the grape of the same name.

BLAUBURGUNDER

Blauburgunder or Blauerburgunder is a German name for the Pinot Noir grape.

BLAUER LIMBERGER   see Blaufrankisch

BLAUER PORTUGIESER

A red Austrian grape variety, grown also in Germany and Eastern Europe, and to a much lesser extent in France. In Germany it makes Weissherbst from the Palatinate; in Austria it accounts for a large part of the red wine of the vineyards south of Vienna and it also occurs in Hungary's Bulls Blood and in Gaillac as Portugais Bleu. The unblended wine tends to be light in colour and fairly undistinguished.

BLAUFRANKISCH

A grape also known as Limberger in Austria and Czechoslovakia, and as Blauer Limberger in Germany and grown widely in Central Europe, notably in Austria and in Württemberg. In Hungary it is called Kékfrankos and is an ingredient of Bulls Blood.

BLAYAIS   Bordeaux: FRANCE

One of the three appellations of the Blaye vineyard. It is mainly for dry white wines from Sauvignon and Sémillon grapes.

BLAYE
Bordeaux: FRANCE

The town at the centre of the vineyards for the appellations of Côtes de Blaye, Blayais and Premières Côtes de Blaye. The white wine is sometimes called Blaye but, more commonly, Blayais.

BLEASDALE VINEYARDS   see Langhorne Creek.

BLEND

A mixture of different wines, from different vineyards or grapes. Often the blend of component parts is better than any single part, as in the case of claret or champagne. Sometimes a blended wine is made to ensure a consistent taste for a wine, year after year, especially in the case of branded wine like Hirondelle.

BLENDING   see *assemblage*.

BLIND TASTING

The term used to describe a wine tasting, when the label on the bottle is hidden and the name of the contents unknown. Friends may do this for fun; or it is a useful way of obtaining an objective assessment of a wine.

BLOOM   See pruina.

BLUE CASSE   See iron casse.

BLUE FININGS

A more common name for potassium ferrocyanide, which can be used in some countries to cure iron and copper *casse*. A minute amount of potassium ferrocyanide precipitates the metal in the wine. This practice is forbidden in France; where it is allowed, it is very strictly controlled.

BLUE IMPERIAL

Blue Imperial is an Australian synonym for the Cinsaut grape variety.

BLUE NUN

A leading Liebfraumilch brand produced by H. Sichel Söhne in Alzey. The brand was created in the 1930s and originally the nuns wore brown habits.

BLUSH WINE

Currently a fashionable term used especially to describe a white wine made from red grapes; in fact it is the palest shade of pink. Some European winemakers are also using it in preference to unfashionable rosé.

BOBAL

A widely grown red Spanish grape variety, producing surprisingly light red and *rosados* in Utiel Requena and Valencia. It is also grown in Alicante and Aragon.

BOBERG
SOUTH AFRICA

A Wine of Origin region, covering the districts of Paarl and Tulbagh, but is an appellation only for fortified wine.

BOBILLON

A term for a small cask in Champagne.

BOCA
Piedmont: ITALY

A sturdy wine made from between 45–70% Nebbiolo grapes, with Vespolina and Bonarda, grown in the Novara hills near the village of Boca. It needs three years' ageing, including two in barrel.

BOCKSBEUTEL

The traditional squat rounded bottle traditionally used for Franconian wine and also for some Baden wine. It also appears in Chile and Portugal. *Bock* means 'goat' in German and the shape is supposed to resemble a goat's scrotum.

BODEGA

The Spanish word for a wine cellar. It can describe a wine shop, the winery where the wine is fermented, blended and matured and the company engaged in producing the wine.

BODENHEIM
Rheinhessen: GERMANY

A small wine town on the Rhein-front within the *Grosslage* of St. Alban, producing full-bodied, rather earthy wines. The single vineyard names are unknown outside the area.

BODENSEE   Baden: GERMANY

One of the seven *Bereichs* of Baden covering a small area around the Bodensee, where the lake creates an especially warm micro-climate. The main grape varieties are Müller-Thurgau and Spätburgunder for *Weissherbst*. There is one *Grosslage*, Sonnenufer and a 60 hectare State Domain at Meersburg.

BODY

Describes the weight of a wine, as determined by the alcoholic content and extract. Wines from hotter climates tend to have more body than those from cooler areas. For example, a Californian wine will have more body than a Rhine wine.

BOGDANUŠA

A white grape variety grown on the Dalmatian islands of Hvar and Brac, making light aromatic wine.

BOHEMIA   CZECHOSLOVAKIA

Bohemia has a tiny wine production around the town of Melnik. Ludmilla is a popular brand.

BARON LE ROY DE BOISEAUMARIE

The owner of Château Fortia in Châteauneuf-du-Pape who in 1923 defined regulations to protect the quality and control the production of Châteauneuf-du-Pape that were to become the guidelines for the laws of *appellation contrôlée*. The vineyards of Châteauneuf-du-Pape were delimited, according to where lavender and thyme grow, as they like as poor soil as the vine.

BOIZEL   Champagne: FRANCE

A small, family champagne house.

BOLGHERI   Tuscany: ITALY

A recent DOC, white and *rosato*, coming from around the village of Bolgheri on the Tuscan coast south of Livorno. The white wine is made from Trebbiano and Vermentino grapes, and the *rosato*, typified by Antinori, who have large estates in the area, is made from Sangiovese and Canaiolo Sassicaia, the best-known wine of the region is red and is a *vino da tavola* as it does not conform to any regulations.

BOLLA   Veneto: ITALY

A family company with big exports of Soave especially to the United States. Bardolino and Valpolicella are also produced in their modern winery.

BOLLINGER   Champagne: FRANCE

One of the great names of Champagne, as was Madame Jacques Bollinger, who died in 1977 and who was one of the great characters of the region. Their methods are traditional, including fermentation in barrel. Of special note is Bollinger RD or *Récemment Dégorgé* and Bollinger Vieilles Vignes which comes from a small parcel of ungrafted vines in the village of Ay.

BOMBARRAL   PORTUGAL

One of the undemarcated wine regions of western Portugal, producing mainly white wine.

BOMBINO

A prolific white grape variety grown extensively in southern Italy, in Apulia and Abruzzi, for wines like San Severo and Castel del Monte. It also goes into EEC table wine, is low in alcohol and rather neutral.

BOMBONA

A traditional Spanish ageing vessel, a glass pear-shaped carboy of about 30 litres capacity, used for maturing wine out of doors.

BOMMES   Bordeaux: FRANCE

One of the villages of the Sauternes appellation.

LE BON-PASTEUR Bordeaux: FRANCE

A small but excellent Pomerol *château*, establishing a good reputation.

BONARDA

A synonym of the Croatina grape and features in the DOC of the Oltrepò Pavese. There is another distinct grape variety called Bonarda Piemontese which is grown around Turin.

BONDE

The French term for a bung in a cask. Barrels are positioned, either with the bung on top of the barrel so that it is exposed to air and the barrel consequently needs frequent topping up, or with the *bonde de côté*, the bung at the side, below the level of the wine, so that there is less evaporation and less need for *ouillage*.

LE BONHEUR SOUTH AFRICA

A small wine estate in the Simonsig-Stellenbosch district of South Africa, with an excellent reputation for the Blanc Fumé and a rosé made from Cabernet Sauvignon.

BONNEAU DE MARTRAY
Burgundy: FRANCE

One of the principal proprietors of the superb white Burgundy, Corton-Charlemagne, with vineyards in Corton as well. The cellars of the estate are in Pernand-Vergelesses, where traditional methods are used to make long-lasting wines.

BONNES MARES Burgundy: FRANCE

A Grand Cru vineyard in the village of Chambolle-Musigny, producing excellent red wine.

BONNEZEAUX Loire: FRANCE

One of the best sweet wines of the Loire valley, taking its name from the village. It is a part of the larger vineyards of the Coteaux du Layon. Only Chenin Blanc can be used and in the best years the climatic conditions allow for the development of *pourriture noble* to produce rich honeyed wines which benefit from some bottle age.

BORDEAUX

The city that gave its name to one of the most varied wine regions of France. The wines of Bordeaux range from everyday reds to some of the greatest, most prestigious and most expensive red wines, from crisp dry whites, to rich luscious sweet wines. The area was delimited in 1911 to include only wine produced within the *département* of the Gironde. There are over 3000 individual *châteaux* in Bordeaux; the humblest of these are mere farmhouses that produce a wine either of simple Bordeaux appellation, or are one of the multitude of unknown *petits châteaux* from the peripheral regions of Bordeaux, such as Côtes de Francs or Côtes de Castillon. The better red wines divide themselves between those of the softer style of St-Emilion and Pomerol, where Merlot is the dominant grape variety and the slightly more austere wines of the Médoc and Graves where Cabernet Sauvignon excels. The greatest red wines of the Médoc were classified into five categories of classed growth in 1855 and include wines like Lafite, Latour, Beychevelle and Palmer. There are four principal villages or communes in the Médoc: St-Estèphe, Pauillac, St-Julien and Margaux and less distinguished Moulis and Listrac. Red Bordeaux, or claret, as it is commonly called in English-speaking countries, is always a blend of grape varieties, namely Cabernet Sauvignon, Cabernet Franc and Merlot, with a little Malbec and Petit Verdot. White Bordeaux is made from Sauvignon, Sémillon and occasionally Muscadelle grapes. Bordeaux Blanc, the basic appellation, and Entre-Deux-Mers and the more distinctive Graves, used to be slightly sweet, but now, to meet the requirements of modern taste, tend to be dry and even made purely from the crisp Sauvignon grape.

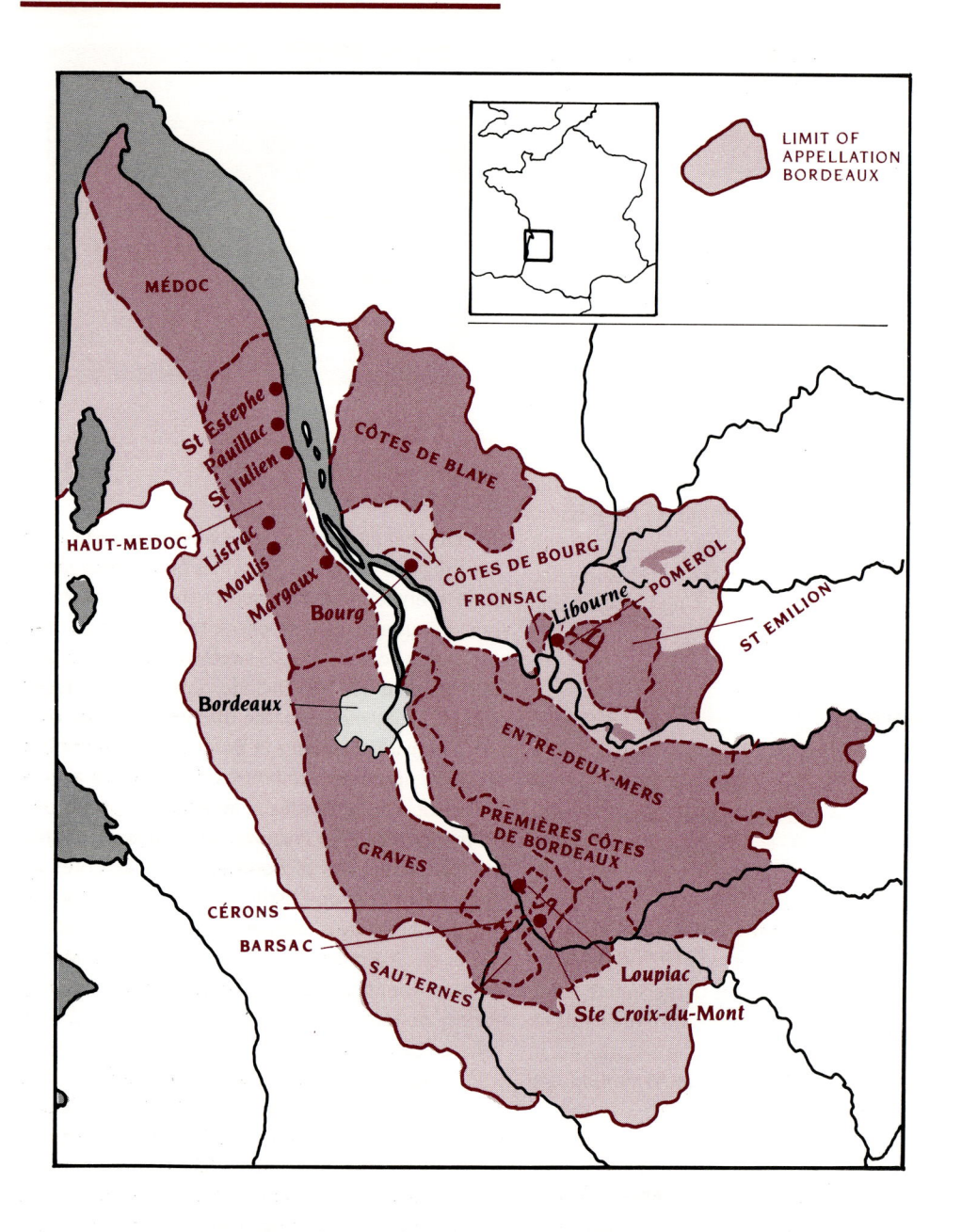

Really sweet wines come from Sauternes. In the best years, and in the right climatic conditions, the grapes are affected by noble rot so that their juice concentrates to produce rich luscious wines. The neighbouring appellation of Barsac is very similar; Ste-Croix-du-Mont and Loupiac are less luscious. Bordeaux includes the following appellations: Bordeaux Rouge and Blanc, Bordeaux Clairet, Bordeaux Supérieur, Côtes de Blaye, Blayais, Premières Côtes de Blaye, Côtes de Bourg, Côtes de Castillon, Côtes de Francs, Premières Côtes de Bordeaux, St-Emilion (and the satellites of Puisseguin, Lussac, Montagne, Ste-Georges), Pomerol, Lalande de Pomerol, Fronsac, Côtes de Canon Fronsac, Médoc, Haut Médoc, St-Estephe, St-Julien, Pauillac, Margaux, Listrac, Moulis, Graves, Graves Supérieures, Haut Benauge, Entre-Deux-Mers, Sauternes, Barsac, Ste-Croix-du-Mont, Loupiac, Graves de Vayres, Ste-Foy-Bordeaux, Côtes de Bordeaux-Ste-Macaire, Cérons, Cadillac and Néac.

BORDEAUX MIXTURE

The traditional remedy for downy mildew, a mixture of copper sulphate, chalk and water. Also called *Bouille Bordelaise*.

BORDEAUX SUPÉRIEUR

Differs from the basic appellation of Bordeaux by requiring 10.5° of alcohol for red wine as opposed to 10° and a maximum yield of 40 hl/ha as opposed to 50 hl/ha; and for white wine, 11.5° versus 10.5°, and the same yield. Consequently, both red and white Bordeaux Supérieur should be wines with more concentration and flavour than ordinary Bordeaux.

BORGES & IRMÃO

One of the older Portuguese port shippers, known for table wine as well as port.

BORJA   see Campo de Borja.

CA' DEL BOSCO   Lombardy: ITALY

A reputable Lombardy producer, making not only table wines, but excellent *méthode champenoise spumante*, Brut, Cremant and Dosage Zero from Pinot and Chardonnay.

LE BOSCQ   Bordeaux: FRANCE

A Cru Bourgeois of St-Estèphe.

BOTRYTIS CINEREA

The name of the fungus responsible for the development of noble rot, attacking the grapes so that, in the right climatic conditions, they shrivel up, the juice becomes sweet and concentrated and the yield considerably reduced, a necessary condition for all of the great sweet wines.

BOTTE

A large barrel used in an Italian wine cellar, made from Slavonic oak and holding several hectolitres. Usually they are very old as they are very expensive to replace.

BOTTICINO   Lombardy: ITALY

A red DOC wine, taking its name from the town of Botticino and made from Barbera grapes with some Marzemino, Schiava Gentile and Sangiovese. Alcohol is a minimum of 12° and after ten months' wood ageing, it improves in bottle.

BOTTLE AGE

The characteristic of maturity developed after the wine has spent some time in bottle. It is a quality factor.

BOTTLE SICKNESS

A temporary ailment from which a wine can suffer when it is first bottled. The wine has been shaken up and is in a numbed state of shock, so it needs a few weeks' rest after bottling for its true flavours to come out.

BOTTLE STINK

Describes the rather unpleasant whiff of stale air trapped between the wine and the cork. This fades very soon after the bottle has been opened.

BOTTLING

The process of transferring wine from vat to bottle. The wine must be bright, free from haze and deposits, and stable, with no danger of yeast activity. Bottling must be carried out in absolutely hygienic conditions, so that there is no risk of contamination or oxidation. Bottling lines vary in sophistication from the very simple pipe-connecting barrel and bottle to the fully-automated machine filling several hundred bottles an hour.

BOTTLING AT SOURCE

Means that the wine is bottled at the place of production, rather than by a distant merchant or *négociant*.

BOUCHARD AÎNÉ   Burgundy: FRANCE

The smaller of the two related Bouchard companies who parted ways back in 1750. Although based in Beaune, they also have vineyards on the Côte Chalonnaise in Mercurey.

BOUCHARD PÈRE ET FILS
                  Burgundy: FRANCE

Once related to Bouchard Aîné, they are not only the largest domaine in Burgundy, but also important *négociants*. Their principal vineyards include the *monopoles* of Greves Vignes de l'Enfant Jésus, Clos de la Mousse and Clos St. Landry in Beaune, as well as large parcels of Corton and Corton Charlemagne, Chevalier Montrachet and Volnay Caillerets. All their red estate wines are aged in new oak for a few months.

BOUCHET
The name used in St-Émilion for the Cabernet Franc grape.

BOUDES FRANCE
A cru of the V.D.Q.S. Côtes d'Auvergne.

BOUILLAGE
Another term for the tumultuous fermentation.

BOUILLE BORDELAISE See Bordeaux Mixture.

BOUQUET
Describes the nose or smell of a mature wine that is no longer in the first stages of youth.

BOURBOULENC
Bourboulenc is a white grape, one of the thirteen varieties of Châteauneuf-du-Pape and also producing rather neutral white wine as part of a blend in parts of the Midi and the southern Rhône. In Minervois it is called Malvoisie.

JEAN BOURDY Jura: FRANCE
A long established family estate in the village of Arlay, making the range of Côtes de Jura wines, as well as Château-Chalon. They have a fine collection of old vintages of Château-Chalon and their *vin jaune* is aged in old vaulted cellars.

BOURGNEUF-VAYRON
Bordeaux: FRANCE

A second rank Pomerol *château* in the heart of the area.

BOURGOGNE Burgundy: FRANCE
The basic appellation of Burgundy. It can be red, white or rosé and is made from Chardonnay, if white, and Pinot Noir, if rosé or red. It is usually produced from pockets of vines outside a more specific appellation. For example, in the Yonne in northern Burgundy, there are vineyards outside Chablis that produce Chardonnay where there is no specific appellation and so the wine is labelled Bourgogne Blanc, provided it meets the basic requirements of the appellation.

BOURGOGNE ALIGOTÉ
Burgundy: FRANCE

A white wine that can come from all over the Burgundy region. It is made predominantly from the Aligoté grape, though it is possible to include a small amount of Chardonnay. With the exception of Bouzeron, which has its own separate appellation of Bourgogne Aligoté de Bouzeron, the precise provenance cannot appear on the label. However, that problem can be solved by reading the grower's address. St-Bris-le-Vineux and Pernand Vergelesses have a reputation for producing good Aligoté with fresh, fruity acidity. It is a wine to drink in early youth and it goes especially well with *cassis* to make the Burgundian aperitif, Kir.

BOURGOGNE GRAND ORDINAIRE
Burgundy: FRANCE

One of the basic appellations of Burgundy. It is red white or rosé. The red and rosé wines are usually made from Gamay, or occasionally Pinot Noir. The grapes for the white are Pinot Blanc, Chardonnay, Melon de Bourgogne and, in the Yonne, Sacy. The appellation is commonly referred to as BGO, for short.

BOURGOGNE HAUTES CÔTES DE BEAUNE
Burgundy: FRANCE

The appellation covering the *arrières côtes* or back slopes of the Côte de Beaune. The wine can be red or white, usually from Pinot Noir or Chardonnay grapes, sometimes Pinot Blanc or Gris. The villages with the right to the appellation are: Baubigny, Bouze-les-Beaune, Cirey-les-Nolay, Cormot, Echevronne, Fussey, la Rochepot, Magny les Villers, Mavilly-Mandelot, Meloisey, Nantoux, Nolay, Vauchignon, Change, Créot, Epertully, Paris-l'Hopital, part of Cheilly-les-Maranges, Dezizes les Maranges and Sampigny les Maranges. These vineyards have enjoyed something of a renaissance in recent years, with some major replanting. Their distinct disadvantage is their aspect; some vineyards lack sunshine so the grapes ripen as much as ten days later than the main Côte d'Or.

BOURGOGNE HAUTES CÔTES DE NUITS
Burgundy: FRANCE

This is the appellation covering the *arrières côtes* or back slopes of the Côte de Nuits. The wine can be red or white. The following villages have the right to the appellation: Arcénant, Bévy, Chaux, Chévannes, Collonges-les-Bévy, Curtil-Vérgy, l'Etang-Vérgy, Magny-les-Villers, Marey-les-Fussey, Mesanges, Meuilley, Reule-Vérgy, Villars-Fontaine and Villers la Faye. Production has increased in recent years, so it is no longer less than the similar Hautes Côtes de Beaune. The vineyards have the disadvantage of a late ripening site.

BOURGOGNE MOUSSEUX
Burgundy: FRANCE

The basic sparkling wine appellation of Burgundy which is gradually being replaced by the higher quality Crémant de Bourgogne. Although the method is that of champagne, the regulations covering production are not as strict as for Crémant de Bourgogne.

BOURGOGNE PASSE-TOUT-GRAINS
Burgundy: FRANCE

This is a basic Burgundy produced in parts of the Yonne, the Côte d'Or and the Côte Chalonnaise. It is a blend of Gamay and Pinot Noir grapes that are fermented together. Pinot Noir must account for at least one third of the blend. When the wine is young, the character of the Gamay dominates and as it matures, the Pinot Noir takes over. However it is rare to find older PTG as it is known for short.

BOURGUEIL
Loire: FRANCE

One of the best red wines of the Loire, made from Cabernet Franc and a little Cabernet Sauvignon, grown in vineyards around the village and seven other communes. Bourgueil has more ageing potential than Chinon and the village of St. Nicholas-de-Bourgueil merits its own appellation. A rosé is also occasionally found.

BOURRUT

The new wine that has not quite finished fermenting, so that it still retains at least 10 gms per litre of sugar. It tastes slightly sweet and is deceptively drinkable!

BOUSCAUT
Bordeaux: FRANCE

A Graves from the commune of Cadaujac, a Grand Cru Classé for both its red and white wine, though its reputation lies more in its red wine. The white is modern in style.

BOUTIQUE WINERY

A Californian term which came into use in the 1970s to describe a small winery, producing only a few thousand cases per year, that concentrates on quality varietal wines.

BOUVET-LADUBAY
Loire: FRANCE

Known for their sparkling Saumur, but also *négociants* for the still wines of the Loire. The company belongs to the champagne house, Taittinger.

BOUVIER

A white grape variety grown mainly in the Burgenland area of Austria and to a lesser extent in Yugoslavia where it is called Ranina, as it is in Hungary.

BOUZERON
Burgundy: FRANCE

A village in the Côte Chalonnaise that has had its own appellation for Aligoté, Bourgogne Aligoté de Bouzeron, since 1979. The village is also the home of the estate of A. & P. de Vilaine.

BOUZY
Champagne: FRANCE

An appropriate name for a wine village, it is on the Montagne de Reims, and also has a reputation for its red (still) wine, Côteaux Champenois.

BOYD-CANTENAC
Bordeaux: FRANCE

A third growth Margaux. It had an English owner in the 19th century which accounts for its name. It is a small property producing good wine.

BOZNER LEITEN
Trentino-Alto Adige: ITALY

The German name for Colli di Bolzano.

BRACHETTO

A red grape grown for the Piedmont DOC of Brachetto d'Acqui. Its origins were probably French and it is also grown in Bellet where it is called Braquet.

BRACHETTO D'ACQUI
Piedmont: ITALY

A slightly sweet *frizzante* or *spumante* DOC wine made from the Brachetto grape in the area of Acqui Terme.

BRACHETTO D'ASTI   Piedmont: ITALY

A slightly sweet red *spumante* wine made from the Brachetto grape and a recent DOC.

BRAMATERRA   Piedmont: ITALY

A red DOC wine made from 50–70% Nebbiolo grapes, blended with Bonarda, Vespolina and Croatina, which takes its name from a village in the Vercelli hills. It requires a minimum of three years' ageing including two in barrel and develops well in the bottle.

BRANAIRE-DUCRU   Bordeaux: FRANCE

A fourth growth St-Julien owned by the Tapie family who successfully combine Algerian experience with that of a *maître de chais* from the Médoc.

BRANCO

Means white in Portuguese.

BRAND

The make of a product, for example Blue Nun is a brand of Liebfraumilch. The advantage to the consumer is being able to depend upon the consistency and reliability of a particular brand once the wine is known. A branded wine will be blended regularly to a consistent taste, and may not even be affected by vintage differences.

BRAND   Alsace: FRANCE

A Grand Cru vineyard in the village of Turckheim.

BRANE-CANTENAC   Bordeaux: FRANCE

A second growth Margaux *château* in the commune of Cantenac. It is a large property owned by the Lurton family and has a sound reputation. The second wine is Domaine de Fontarney.

BRAQUET

The French synonym for the Italian grape variety, Brachetto, and as such found only in Bellet.

BRAUNEBERG   Mosel-Saar-Ruwer: GERMANY

A Mittelmosel village of lesser importance within the *Grosslage* of Kurfürstlay. The best vineyard site belongs to Juffer, then, in descending order, Mandelgraben, Klostergarten, Juffer Sonnenuhr, Kammer and Hasenläufer.

BRAZIL

Most of her vineyards are in the southern state of Rio Grande do Sol. Hybrid varieties dominate, but *vitis vinifera* vines are slowly being established. The country's large domestic market has attracted foreign investment by Cinzano, Moët & Chandon, Martini Rossi and others.

MARC BRÉDIF   Loire: FRANCE

An important producer of Vouvray, whose company has been taken over by the Pouilly Fumé house of Patrick de Ladoucette.

BREED

The distinctive quality of a fine wine, coming from a combination of soil, grape variety, situation of the vineyard and the talent of the winemaker.

BREEDE RIVER VALLEY   SOUTH AFRICA

The Breede River Valley covers the wine regions of Worcester, Robertson and Swellendam, east of the Drakenstein mountains and provides an appellation for fortified wines.

BREEDRIVIERVALLEI   See Breede River Valley.

BREGANZE   Veneto: ITALY

Breganze, a DOC from near Vicenza, comes in seven versions: white, mainly from Tocai Friuliano, Cabernet, Sauvignon and more commonly Franc, *superiore* at 12° minimum alcohol; Pinot Bianco and Pinot Grigio, both dry and fresh; Pinot Nero, a light red and *superiore* at 12°; red, the most typical, based on Merlot; Vespaiolo, from a local white grape, and *superiore* at 12°.

BREIDECKER

A New Zealand crossing of Müller-Thurgau and Seibel 7053, designed for its resistance to rot with a flavour similar to Müller-Thurgau.

BREISGAU   Baden: GERMANY

One of the seven *Bereichs* of Baden, an area covering the foothills of the Black Forest from Freiburg to Offenburg and split into three *Grosslagen*: Schutterlindenberg, Burg Lichteneck and Burg Zähringen. Müller-Thurgau is the most important grape variety, followed by Ruländer and Spätburgunder.

BRENTANO'SCHE GUTSVERWALTUNG Rheingau: GERMANY

A large estate in Winkel planted almost exclusively with Riesling vines. It has historic associations with Goethe and Beethoven and there is a Goethe museum on the estate.

BRESTNIK   BULGARIA

A defined Controliran wine region concentrating on the production of red wine from Mavrud, Cabernet Sauvignon and Merlot grapes.

BRETON

The synonym used in the Loire Valley for the Cabernet Franc grape.

DU BREUIL   Bordeaux: FRANCE

A Cru Bourgeois of Cissas, Haut-Médoc with a ruined medieval *château*. It is also called Le Breuil.

BRICCO DEL DRAGO   Piedmont: ITALY

A non-DOC blend of mainly Dolcetto grapes with some Nebbiolo, made by Cascina Drago near Alba.

BRICCO MANZONI   Piedmont: ITALY

A superb but non-DOC blend of Nebbiolo and Barbera grapes, produced by Podere Manzoni at Monforte d'Alba.

BRIGHT

Describes a wine with a brilliant clear colour without any hint of cloudiness or haze.

BRIGHTS WINES   CANADA

One of the largest wineries in Ontario, founded in 1874 by Thomas Bright. Adhémar de Chaunac, a member or the company who gave his name to a grape, pioneered the planting of *vitis vinifera* and hybrids in Canada in the post-war years. Today, the company produces a full range of wines from Labrusca, hybrid and *vitis vinifera* grapes.

BRINDISI   Apulia: ITALY

A new Apulian DOC for red and *rosato* wines, made mainly from the Negroamaro grape grown inland from the town of Brindisi. The reds mature well and a *riserva* denotes two years' ageing.

BRISTOL CREAM

The world's biggest selling brand of sherry, a sweet sherry, produced by Harveys of Bristol.

BRISTOL MILK

A traditional dessert sherry imported to Bristol, one of the centres of the British sherry trade. Averys is the best known label.

BRITISH COLUMBIA   CANADA

One of the two main wine-producing provinces in Canada. It is a relatively new industry, started in the 1930s and based on French hybrids with some *vitis vinifera*. The climate is extreme, with heat and low humidity requiring irrigation. The nights are cool and there are long days of sunshine. The main wine area is the Okanagan Valley with the small wineries of Claremont, Sumac Ridge and Gray Monk. The small estates use their own grapes, while the larger wineries buy grapes from California, Washington and Oregon.

BRITISH WINE

British wine or British sherry describes a wine that is produced in Britain from reconstituted concentrated grape must, usually imported from Cyprus. There is the price advantage of a lower duty rate but the product is artificial and bears no relation to English wine.

BRIX

The American system for measuring must weight. It is similar to the Balling system.

BROCOL
A synonym for the Valdiguié grape.

BROKENWOOD AUSTRALIA
A small winery in the Hunter Valley, working principally with Shiraz and Cabernet grapes and since 1982 has also made award winning Sémillon and Chardonnay. Small oak barrels are an important aspect of vinification.

BROKER   See *courtier*.

BROLIO   See Ricasoli.

BROTHER TIMOTHY
One of the great figures of the California wine trade. He has been the cellarmaster of Christian Brothers at Mount la Salle for forty years. Until recently he refused to give his wines a vintage, but preferred to make a blended wine to maintain a uniform style of wine each year.

BROUILLY Burgundy: FRANCE
One of the ten and the largest of the Beaujolais Crus, with a right to a separate appellation. Some consider Brouilly to be the most typical Beaujolais wine.

BROUSTET Bordeaux: FRANCE
A second growth Sauternes in the commune of Barsac, making elegant sweet wine and a dry white called Camperos.

BROWN BROTHERS AUSTRALIA
One of the leading wine companies of Northeast Victoria at Milawa, with vineyards at Mystic Park and in the King Valley. They are very much a family firm, forward looking and experimental, with higher altitude vineyards in the Victoria Alps. Individual vineyards such as Koombahla and Meadow Creek are important. Their range of varietals is extensive, including dry and Liqueur Muscat.

BROWN MUSCAT
Sometimes describes the deeper coloured grape, Muscat Blanc à Petits Grains used to make Liqueur Muscat in Victoria, Australia.

BROWN SHERRY
The English name for dark, i.e. brown dessert sherry, of usually only average quality.

BRUNELLO
A clone of the Sangiovese grape variety, grown exclusively in Montalcino.

BRUNELLO DI MONTALCINO
Tuscany: ITALY
A fine red wine, one of the five Italian wines meriting DOCG status. It comes from the Brunello grape, a clone of Sangiovese Grosso, grown in the commune of Montalcino, an attractive hilltop town south of Siena. Four years' ageing in oak is necessary for *normale* and five for a *riserva*. The results can be outstanding and long-lived. The most notable producer, who established the reputation of the area, is Biondi Santi, but others merit recognition too.

BRUSCO DEI BARBI Tuscany: ITALY
A red *vino da tavola* made by the Fattoria dei Barbi in Montalcino from Brunello grapes using the *governo* method so that it is ready to drink earlier than Brunello di Montalcino.

BRUT
Means 'very dry'. In Champagne it is the wine with the lowest dosage.

BUAL Madeira: PORTUGAL
One of the four styles of the fortified wine, Madeira; sweeter than Sercial and Verdelho and not as sweet as Malmsey. It can be drunk as a dessert wine, or with cheese. Brandy is added to stop the fermentation and retain sufficient sugar in the wine.

BUÇACO PORTUGAL

The Palace Hotel do Buçaco, on the edge of the Bairrada region, has made its own distinctive wines from a small vineyard since the first world war. This majestic hotel was built originally for the Portuguese royal family at the turn of the century. Methods are very old-fashioned and the wine is matured in cellars under the hotel. Red, white and a little rosé wine is made. The reds spend four or five years in cask and the whites two or three. The hotel wine list has vintages going back to 1927 for red wine and 1944 for white; the wines have an amazing depth of flavour.

BUCELAS PORTUGAL

Bucelas, or Bucellas, is a white Portuguese wine coming from a small demarcated area in central Portugal near Lisbon, from vineyards along the Trancão river, planted with two grape varieties, Arinto, accounting for a minimum of 65% and Esgana Cão. The production is dominated by one company, Camilo Alves, that has acquired the firm of Caves Velhas and markets most of its wine under that label. Most Bucelas is aged in large old oak barrels for years, especially the *garrafeiras*. The younger styles for export spend less time in wood.

BUDBREAK See *débourrement*.

BUÉ Loire: FRANCE

One of the most important villages of the vineyards of Sancerre. Its best vineyard is Clos du Chêne Marchand.

BUGEY Savoie: FRANCE

A VDQS area between Savoie and Lyon, with scattered vineyards around the town of Bellay in the *département* of the Ain. Vin du Bugey can be red, white or rosé, still, sparkling or pétillant. Five communes can add their name to the appellation as a cru, namely Virieu-le-Grand, Montagnieu, Manicle, Machuraz and Cerdon. In practice Virieu-le-Grand and Machuraz are never seen and there is only one producer of Manicle. The main grape varieties are Gamay, Pinot Noir and Mondeuse for reds. Chardonnay, Altesse (also called Roussette, though today Roussette de Bugey describes a style of wine rather than a specific grape variety), Jacquère and Molette for whites. The grape name appears on the label if the wine is from that grape alone. The wines are light, attractive and individual.

BUKETTRAUBE

A peculiarly South African grape of German origins, first introduced in 1967 and now widely accepted. Buket means bouquet in German and as the name suggests, the grape provides a very perfumed wine which blends well with other white wines.

BULGARIA

Bulgaria is an important wine-producing country in eastern Europe and the one that has most successfully adapted her wines to western taste, with considerable modernisation of her industry since the Second World War.

The main wine area divides into five. In the east, there are two sub-regions along the shores of the Black Sea, with mainly white wines from Chardonnay. Riesling and Muscat Ottonel grapes in the north and local varieties like Misket, Dimiat and Tamianka in the south. The northern region between the Danube and the Balkan mountains produces mainly red wines from Cabernet Sauvignon, Merlot, Pamid and Gamza. The southern region, below the Balkan mountains is noted for its red wines from Cabernet Sauvignon and Mavrud. The smallest wine region, in the southwest bordering Yugoslavia and Greece, with a Mediterranean climate, is known for its powerful red Melnik.

Within these five regions, there are 20 defined Controliran regions of origin, with more to come, based on microclimate and local traditions and producing one or more grape varieties. Most Bulgarian wine is labelled according to grape variety. There is a strong western European influence with Cabernet Sauvignon, Merlot, Chardonnay, Rhine and Italian Riesling, as well as indigenous varieties like Dimiat, Melnik, Gamza, Mavrud, Pamid and Rkatzitelli.

A new Reserve category of wines has been introduced for the best wines of a Controliran region; they are aged in oak, two years for whites and three for reds. All grapes are grown by cooperatives; wine production is in the hands of four state organisations, of which Vinprom is the biggest, and exports are controlled by Vinimpex.

BULLAY Mosel-Saar-Ruwer: GERMANY

A little known village on the Lower Mosel, within the *Grosslage* Grafschaft. Kronenberg is the most important vineyard.

BULLS BLOOD
HUNGARY

The brand name under which Hungary's most popular red wine, Egri Bikaver, is sold. The name recalls a legendary moment in Eger's history when the Magyars were defending the town against the Turks. The wine-stained beards of the Magyars were supposedly mistaken by the Muslim non-wine drinking Turks for the blood of bulls.

BURGENLAND
AUSTRIA

One of the main wine regions of Austria, next to the Hungarian border. Indeed, it was part of Hungary until 1921. Hungarian influence is apparent with some rich dessert wines made from Furmint grapes with noble-rot, akin to Tokay. The region divides into four: Neudsiedlersee, Neudsiedlersee-Hügelland, Mittelburgenland, and Südburgenland. The dominant feature of the region is Europe's largest lake, the Neusiedlersee.

BURGERSPITAL ZUM HEILIGEN GEIST
Franken: GERMANY

An important Franconian estate and one of the largest in Germany. The property was originally a charity to support an old people's home founded in 1319. Vineyards include a large part of Würzburger Stein. Riesling, though good, is only a small part of the total with a range of grape varieties. Most wines are *trocken*.

BURGESS CELLARS
California: USA

A small Napa Valley winery that was established in its present form by the Burgess family in 1972. Red wines are best, Cabernet Sauvignon, Petite Sirah and Zinfandel.

BURGUNDAC CRNI

The Yugoslav name for the Pinot Noir grape.

BURGUNDY
FRANCE

The vineyards of Burgundy can be divided into five distinct areas, from north to south: Chablis and the surrounding vineyards of the Auxerrois; the Côte d'Or, which splits into the Côte de Nuits and the Côte de Beaune; the Côte Chalonnaise; the Mâconnais and finally Beaujolais.

The wines can range in quality from some of the greatest produced in France, the Grands Crus of the Côte d'Or with prestigious names like Chambertin and Corton, down to humble everyday Passe-Tous-Grains. The main grape varieties are Chardonnay for white wine and Pinot Noir for red, with Gamay for Beaujolais.

BURING
AUSTRALIA

Leo Buring was once one of the great figures of the Australian wine industry. After a varied career he bought Château Leonay in the Barossa Valley, which is now part of the Lindeman's empire and concentrates on the production of fine white wines.

BÜRKLIN WOLF
Rheinpfalz: GERMANY

One of the great producers of the Rheinpfalz. Their cellars are in Wachenheim with important vineyard holdings in all the best villages of the Rheinpfalz. The estates have been in the family for 400 years and there are barrels in the cellars that are 300 years old. Methods combine the modern and the traditional to produce superlative wines, predominantly from the Riesling grape.

BURMEISTER

J. W. Burmeister is a small port house of German and English origin and now Portuguese owned, producing port under the brand name of Tordiz.

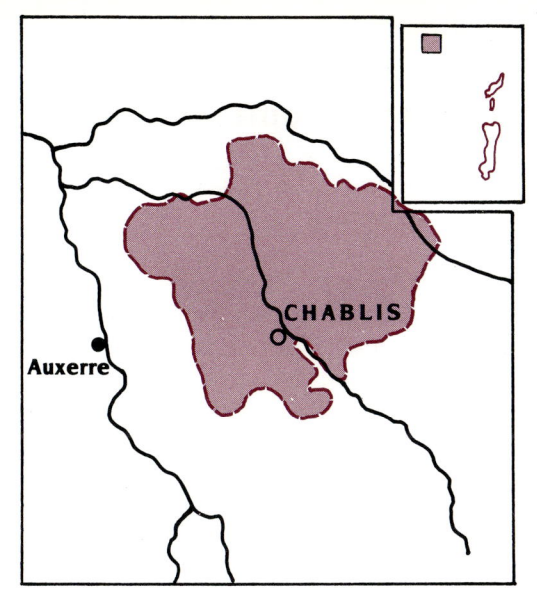

JAMES BUSBY

James Busby was one of the pioneers of the Australian wine industry and played an important, but perhaps sometimes exaggerated part in the development of viticulture in the Hunter Valley. He wrote numerous books on viticulture including 'A Treatise on the Culture of the Vine' and 'A Manual and Plan Directions for Planting and Cultivating of Vineyards and for Making Wine in New South Wales' He collected vine cuttings from Europe which were planted in the Botanical Gardens in Sydney, but these died from neglect. He also planted New Zealand's first vines at Northland on North Island in the 1830s.

BUTT

The usual name for a sherry barrel. The standard butt used for ageing sherry holds 500 litres.

BUTTAFUOCO   See Oltrepò Pavese.

BUTTEAUX   See Montmains.

BUXY   *Burgundy*: FRANCE

A village in the Côte Chalonnaise within the appellation of Montagny. It has a successful cooperative that dates back to 1929. The wine was once sold as Côte de Buxy.

BUYER'S OWN BRAND

The term used to describe a champagne sold under the wine merchant's own label, rather than a producer's label. It allows the wine merchant to choose his/her own style of champagne and market this brand.

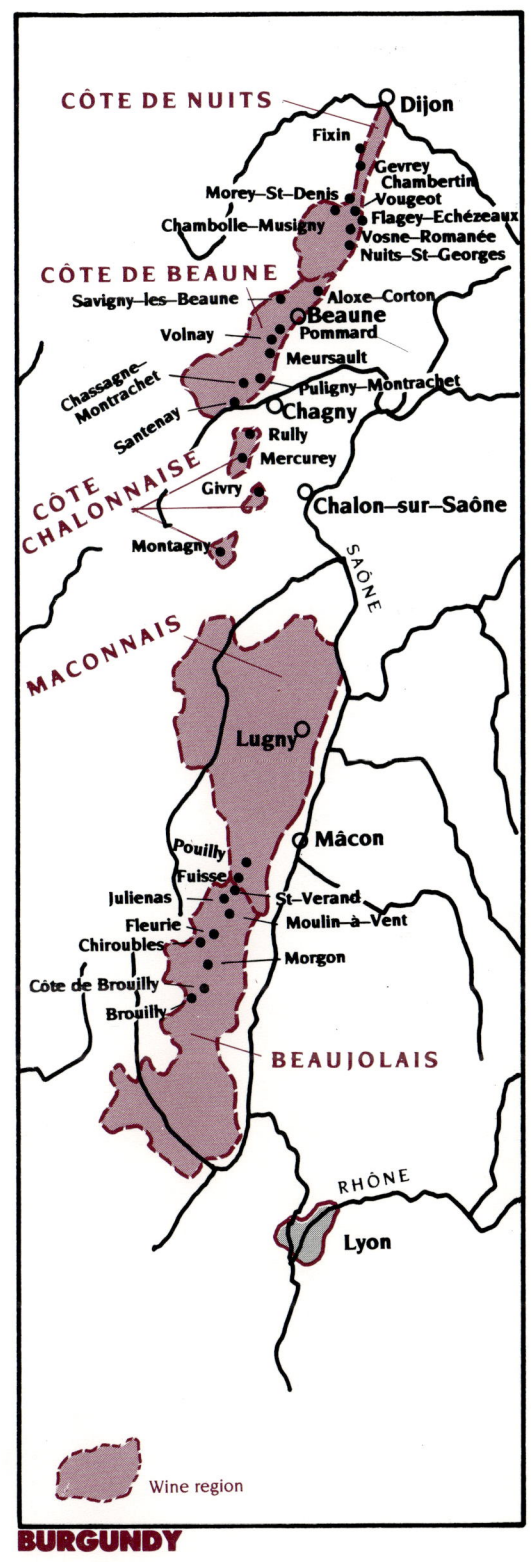

BUZBAG
TURKEY

Comes from eastern Anatolia, a full-flavoured red wine made from Bogazkarasi grapes in the Elâzig region of Turkey.

BUZET   see Côtes de Buzet.

BUZZETTO DI QUILIANO
Liguria: ITALY

A crisp white non-DOC wine, made from the Buzzetto grape and grown around Quiliano in Liguria.

BYBLINE

A wine of ancient Greece, coming from Byblos in northern Syria. It was sweet and fragrant.

C

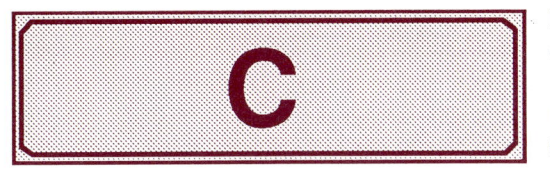

C.I.V.C.
These initials stand for the Comité Interprofessional du Vin de Champagne, the body that protects and promotes champagne. It has fought numerous court cases to prevent the illegal use of the name champagne. In conjunction with the growers and producers, it establishes a price each year for the champagne grapes.

C.M.
On a champagne label, this means that the wine has been produced by a *coopérative manipulant*.

LA CABANNE   Bordeaux: FRANCE
A little-known Pomerol *château*.

CABARDÈS   The Midi: FRANCE
A VDQS for red and rosé wine from vineyards to the north east of Carcassonne. The main grape varieties are Carignan (maximum 30%), Cinsaut, Grenache, Mourvèdre and Syrah as well as Cabernet Sauvignon, Cabernet Franc and Merlot. This is where the vineyards of the Midi meet those of the south west. The rosés are fruity and quaffable; the reds more substantial.

CABERNET D'ANJOU   Loire: FRANCE
A rosé wine of slightly better quality than Rosé d'Anjou. It is made from one or both Cabernet grapes and can be dry or slightly sweet. The production area is the same as for Rosé d'Anjou.

CABERNET FRANC
This grape produces its most characteristic wines in the Loire valley, notably Chinon, Bourgueil, St-Nicolas de Bourgueil and Saumur Champigny. Lesser versions are simple Anjou, Saumur and Touraine Rouge. In hot years these red wines with the distinctive earthy character of the grape are wines to age; otherwise they are best for early drinking.

In Cabernet d'Anjou, Cabernet Franc makes some attractive rosé wine, which is sometimes sweet.

Cabernet Franc is an important part of the Bordeaux *encépagement*, when blended with Cabernet Sauvignon and Merlot, especially in St-Émilion, where it is more important than Cabernet Sauvignon. It also features in the other wines of the south west. Cabernet Franc has not travelled as well as Cabernet Sauvignon. It is not found elsewhere in France. In Italy, Cabernet is planted widely in the north east, but without precision between Sauvignon and Franc, for the two plants are often difficult to distinguish. It has also reached Apulia and the Favonio vineyards.

In the New World the impact has been much less than with Cabernet Sauvignon; Merlot and Shiraz have been preferred for blending with Cabernet Sauvignon and little has been planted. There is some in Chile, a little in South Africa, none in New Zealand and it is scattered throughout eastern Europe.

CABERNET GROS
An Australian synonym for the Bastardo grape.

CABERNET DE SAUMUR   Loire: FRANCE
The pink wine of Saumur, made mainly from Cabernet Franc, and is lighter and drier than Cabernet d'Anjou.

CABERNET SAUVIGNON
The Cabernet Sauvignon grape, for many wine lovers, gives the world its finest wines. The great red wines of Bordeaux and the finest wines of the New World are based on Cabernet Sauvignon. In the Médoc and Graves it is the dominant grape in a blend with Merlot and Cabernet Franc, and maybe Malbec and Petit Verdot, though in St-Émilion and Pomerol, Merlot is much more important. The flavour is characterised by blackcurrants or cedarwood; it demands ageing in small oak barriques and once bottled requires bottle age for fine bottles to attain great heights. It is an easy grape to grow, buds and ripens late and is resistant to frost and disease and consequently has travelled well and adapted to conditions all over the world.

Elsewhere in France it plays an important part in the other vineyards of the south west, such as Côtes de Duras, Bergerac and so on, and in the Midi it is encouraged as one of the *améliorateur* varieties and has improved countless indifferent *vin de pays*. Mas de Daumas Gassac in the Hérault is a notable example of what can be achieved in the south. It has spread as far as Provence and is found in large amounts in some properties of the Coteaux d'Aix en Provence, such as Vignelaure and Trévallon and in others a small percentage gives the wine more backbone and character. In the Loire Valley, some Cabernet Sauvignon is grown as well as the more important Cabernet Franc. Across the Pyrenees it is planted by Miguel Torres in Penedés for Gran Coronas Black Label; Jean Léon produces a pure varietal; it is also part of the Vega Sicilia blend and some is planted on the Raimat estate. J. M. da Fonseca have some in Portugal. Cabernet Sauvignon has made great inroads into Italy too. Sassicaia sets the trend for Cabernet Sauvignon in Tuscany and now countless Tuscan estates make a *vino da tavola* with some Cabernet Sauvignon or use it to improve their Chianti. Antinori in particular have pioneered with Tignanello, Solaia and Seicentenario. Adjoining Carmignano does specifically allow for the inclusion of Cabernet Sauvignon within the DOC regulations. Cabernet is grown in north eastern Italy too, often without specifying Franc or Sauvignon, so the wine is usually a blend of both, softer and fruity without the tannin prevalent elsewhere.

Eastern Europe too has espoused Cabernet Sauvignon. There is Château Carras in Greece, experiments in Cyprus, and further afield, Château Musar in the Lebanon. It is successful and popular in Bulgaria, less so in Yugoslavia and Hungary and even the Soviet Union has some.

However if Bordeaux is rivalled anywhere, it is in California and Australia. Methods in California follow those of Bordeaux; the wines are aged in new French oak barriques and instead of the pure varietal, often blended with some Merlot. Opus One is a joint Bordeaux-Californian venture. Jo Heitz at Martha's Vineyard produces the most characteristic Californian Cabernet Sauvignon and other estates in Napa Valley and elsewhere are making some fine wine.

The best Australian region for Cabernet Sauvignon is Coonawarra in South Australia, where the vines are grown on the *terra rossa* soil and have a long ripening season. Sometimes Cabernet Sauvignon is blended with Shiraz, and occasionally with Merlot, Cabernet Franc or Malbec. A small amount of Cabernet Sauvignon is grown in New Zealand, but with little success as the climate is too cool. Some successful Cabernet Sauvignon is made in South Africa, such as Nederburg's Paarl Cabernet, and sometimes it is blended with Merlot as in Meerlust's Rubicon blend. Paarl and Stellenbosch are the better cooler areas.

Wine production in Chile has depended on Cabernet Sauvignon with a little Malbec and Merlot and there is some in Argentina too. In fact there is hardly anywhere where this versatile grape does not grow and produce exciting wine. The danger is that intrinsic regional characteristics are lost in the love affair with Cabernet Sauvignon.

CABINET

The old spelling of *Kabinett* used before the changes of the 1971 German wine law.

CABREROS   SPAIN

An undemarcated wine region in the province of Avila, west of Madrid, producing full-bodied red wines from Garnacha and Tinta Aragones grape varieties and white from Albillo.

CACC'E MMITTE DI LUCERA
Apulia: ITALY

A red DOC made from a mixture of grapes including red Uva di Troia, Montepulciano, Sangiovese and white Trebbiano and Malvasia. A possible interpretation of the dialect name is "toss it down and fill it up"; unfortunately the wine does not always encourage you to replenish your glass.

MARQUÉS DE CACERES   SPAIN

A *bodega* founded in Rioja in 1970 by Enrique Forner, whose family owns property in the Médoc so there is a strong Bordelais influence. Professor Emile Peynaud is a consultant. White Marqués de Cáceres was one of the first non oak-aged Riojas. The red wines are made by individual growers under the *bodega's* supervision and then aged as the *bodega*, but for less time than other Riojas.

CACHAPOAL   See Chile.

CADAUJAC Bordeaux: FRANCE

A commune within the Graves. Bouscaut is the only property of any importance.

CADET-BON Bordeaux: FRANCE

A little-known, tiny Grand Cru Classé of St-Émilion with a windmill in the vineyards.

CADET-PIOLA Bordeaux: FRANCE

A relatively unknown Grand Cru Classé of St-Émilion. The wines are sturdy with a low proportion of Merlot grapes.

CADILLAC Bordeaux: FRANCE

A sweet white, Bordeaux appellation. It was created in 1973 from the best communes of the southern part of the Premières Côtes de Bordeaux in an attempt to distinguish them. In practice it is little used.

CAECUBAN

Another name for the ancient wine Cecubus.

CAHORS SOUTH WEST FRANCE

One of the best red wines of south west France. It is produced mainly from the Malbec grape, or Auxerrois as it is called locally, with some Tannat and Merlot. The vineyards stretch along the Lot from just east of the town of Cahors, some 50 kilometres downstream to Fumel. The vines are planted, either on the more fertile lower slopes of the river valley, or on the arid plateau or 'causses' above. The wine was known as the black wine of Cahors in the last century; more often this was a concentrated wine, not for consumption but used to boost weaker wines from Bordeaux. Today traditional producers of Cahors age their wine in oak barrels; more modern growers have stainless steel or cement vats. The cave cooperative at Parnac dominates the production of the area but there are numerous independant growers amongst whom the best known names include Jouffreau at Clos de Gamot and Château Cayrou; Georges Vigouroux at Château Haute Serre, Baldès at Clos Triguedina and Rigal at Château St. Didier.

CAILLOU Bordeaux: FRANCE

A second growth Barsac Sauternes, making some good wine under young, enthusiastic ownership. There is also a dry white, Domaine Sarraute.

CAILLOU BLANC See Talbot.

CAIRANNE Rhône: FRANCE

Rivals Vacqueyras as the best of the 17 villages of the appellation Côtes du Rhône Villages from the southern Rhône. Vines have been grown there since at least the 14th century. It is now the home of one of the best cooperatives of the Rhône Valley. The wine is predominantly red with a little rosé, made principally from Grenache and a little white from Clairette, Marsanne, Grenache Blanc and Ugni Blanc.

CAKEBREAD CELLARS California: USA

A small Napa Valley winery, founded in 1972, which specialises in Sauvignon Blanc. Cabernet Sauvignon, Chardonnay and Zinfandel are made too.

CALABRIA ITALY

The wine region in the toe of Italy, it has eight DOC wines, of which Cirò is the best. The region's red wines are based on the Gaglioppo grape and the whites are often made from Greco.

CALCIUM

Important in soil to balance acidity. It helps in the development of a good root system, providing the base for a good soil structure. In excess it causes chlorosis, preventing the vine from extracting iron or magnesium from the soil.

CÁLEM

A. A. Cálem is one of the leading Portuguese port houses, established in 1859. They own Quinta da Foz. Their methods are a combination of the traditional and the modern.

CALIFORNIA USA

The wine industry of the Golden State has changed dramatically over the last twenty years. In 1966 Robert Mondavi opened the first new winery in the Napa Valley since Prohibition and since then new wineries and vineyards have multiplied. The early Spanish missionaries first brought the Mission grape to California from Mexico at the end of the 18th century; Jean Louis Vignes planted European vines in the 1830s; Agoston Haraszathy laid the foundations of the Californian wine industry and the first wineries, such as Almadén and Buena Vista were started in the 1850s. The period of Prohibition did considerable

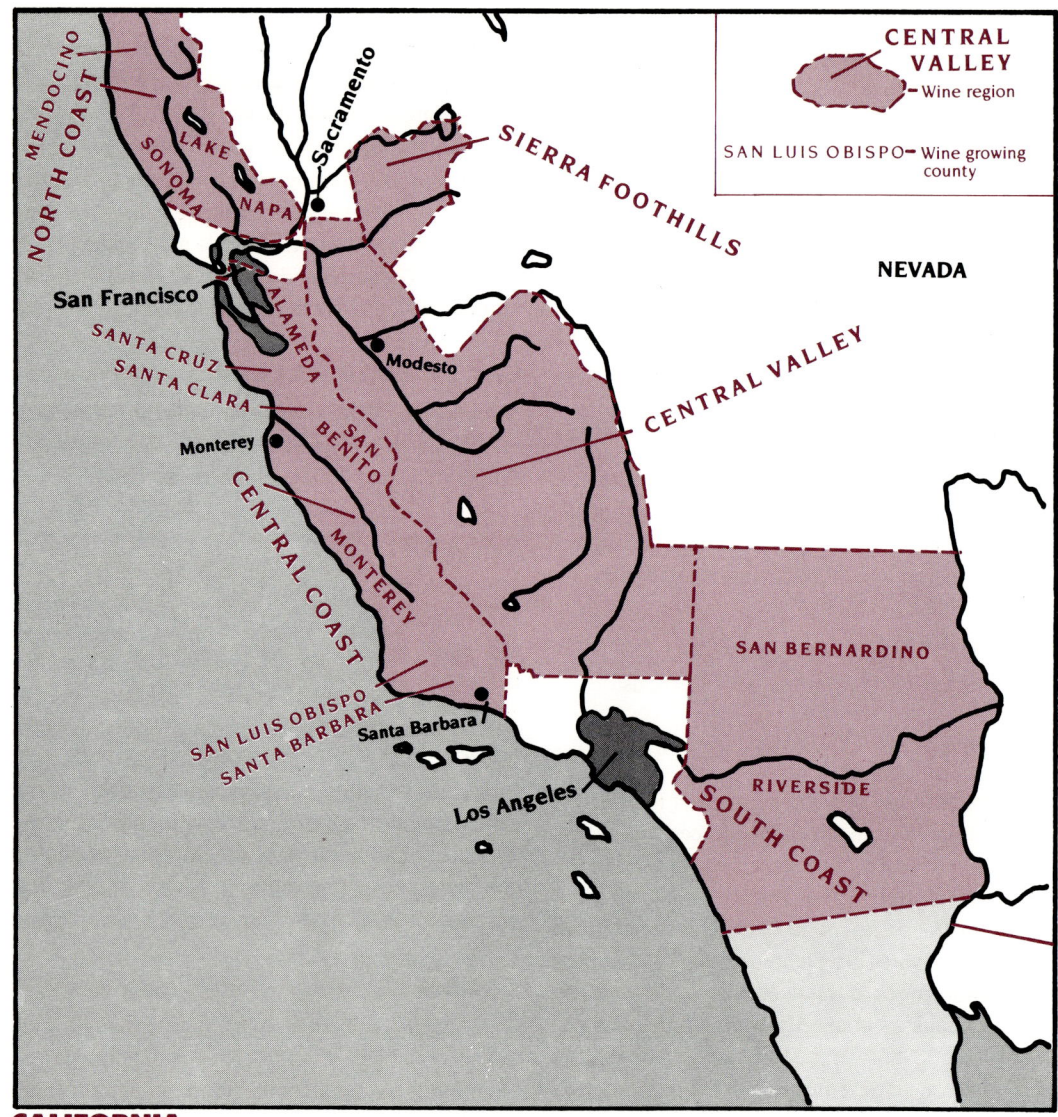

CALIFORNIA

CENTRAL VALLEY — Wine region
SAN LUIS OBISPO — Wine growing county

CALIFORNIA

damage to the California wine industry and it was not until the mid 1960s that it began to revive with any energy. Since 1980 the concept of an Approved Viticultural Area or AVA as a form of appellation has been implemented, but it only indicates that 85% of the grapes comes from that area. Not all the wineries use this system and some blend as they wish.

The main regions of California include the Napa Valley, with one of the highest reputations for quality; the parallel Sonoma Valley and the numerous AVAs of Sonoma County, Mendocino, the most northern vineyards of the state; Livermore Valley to the east of San Francisco; the Central Coast area between San Francisco and San Luis Obispo; the South Coast area extending to the Mexican border and finally Central Valley of San Joaquin and Sacramento, the provider of Californian jug wine.

European grape varieties are firmly established with the majority of fine California wine sold under a varietal name, denoting a minimum of 75% of the grape variety in the wine. Cabernet Sauvignon, Chardonnay, Sauvignon or Fumé Blanc, Rhine Riesling, known as White or Johannisberg Riesling, Pinot Noir and others have all made their mark. Zinfandel, possibly of Italian origins, is the most individual grape variety.

Technical expertise, inspired by the oenology department of the University of California at Davis is exemplary. Californians use cultured yeast, control fermentation temperatures meticulously and experiment with oak barrels. The vineyards have been divided into climatic zones, I is coolest, such as Carneros; V is hottest such as the Central Valley; most of Napa is II or III.

Reputable wineries in California are too numerous to name, though Robert Mondavi has probably done more for the reputation of the Californian wine industry than any other.

CALISTOGA   *California*: USA

A small town at the northern end of the Napa Valley, known for its mud baths as well as its wines.

CALON-SÉGUR   *Bordeaux*: FRANCE

Third growth St-Estèphe. This is the most northern of the Médoc classed growths. A former proprietor was the Marquis de Ségur, who also owned Lafite and Latour, but said that his heart was at Calon, hence the heart on the label. The *château* is now owned by the Capbern-Gasqueton family who consistently make reliable wine.

CALONA WINES   CANADA

The largest winery in British Columbia, best known for their Germanic-style Schloß Ledenheim, made from Canadian hybrids and Californian-grown Johannisberg Riesling.

CALUSO PASSITO   See Erbaluce di Caluso

CALVERAS   *California*: USA

A small, relatively unimportant vineyard and county of the Sierra Foothills in eastern California, where Zinfandel and Sauvignon are the main varietals.

CALVET

An important Bordeaux *négociant* house, dealing not only in claret, but also with Rhône and Burgundy, where they have cellars.

CALVI   CORSICA

One of the separate areas within the overall appellation Vin de Corse. The wine is also sometimes called Vin de la Balagne as the delimited appellation covers the whole of that part of western Corsica from north of Calvi, south almost as far as Porto. In practice however most of the vineyards are around Calvi. The wines are red, dry white and rosé. Malvoisie de Corse is the main grape variety for the white and the red and rosé are usually a blend of the local Nielluccio and Sciacarello as well as some Midi grape varieties. The results are quite distinctive.

CAMARATE   PORTUGAL

A fine Portuguese red wine, made by one of the country's leading wine producers, J. M. da Fonseca. It is a blend of Cabernet Sauvignon, Periquita and Merlot grown in vineyards around Azeitão in the Alentejo region and aged in wood to give it a stylish fruity flavour.

CAMENSAC   *Bordeaux*: FRANCE

A fifth growth St-Laurent in the Haut-Médoc. After a long period of obscurity, it has been bought and renovated by the Forner family of Rioja.

CAMP DE TARRAGONA   see Tarragona.

CAMPANIA   ITALY

Viticulture thrived in Campania in Roman times with Falernum being the favourite wine, but today the emphasis is on quantity more than quality. DOCs comprise, most notably, Fiano di Avellino, Greco di Tufo, Falerno and Taurasi, as well as Capri, Ischia, Solopaca and the picturesque Lacryma Christi del Vesuvio.

CAMPBELL'S EARLY
A red American hybrid grown extensively in Japan.

CAMPIDANO DI TERRALBA
Sardinia: ITALY

A soft red DOC wine made principally from Bovale grapes grown around Oristano.

CAMPO DE BORJA
SPAIN

One of the D.O.s of Aragón, taking its name from the town of Borja near Zaragoza. The wine is mainly red, principally from Garnacha Tinta, full-bodied and astringent and often blended with lighter wines from other regions.

CAMPO FIORIN
Veneto: ITALY

A non-DOC red wine made by the Valpolicella producer Masi. It would be a Valpolicella except that a second fermentation is induced by the addition of the lees from their Amarone, which are considered too good to waste! This is a *ripasso* style and the resulting wine is smooth and rich.

CAMPO VIEJO
SPAIN

One of the largest Rioja *bodegas*, an amalgamation of two old companies and owned by Savin. San Asensio, a *sin crianza* is a successful wine and Marqués de Villamagna is their *gran reserva*.

CANADA
Canada has begun to emerge in the last few years as a small but keen wine-producing country. Ontario and British Columbia are the two provinces with a considerable acreage of vineyards, but there are pockets of vineyards in other provinces. Hybrid grape varieties such as de Chaunac, Maréchal Foch, Okanagan Riesling and Seyval Blanc dominate the industry, as well as Lambrusca vines like Catawba, Concord and Niagara. There are some pioneering producers of *vitis vinifera*, notably at the Inniskillen winery, whose Chardonnay shows potential. Regulations are flexible, allowing for the blending of Californian, Washington State and Oregon wines with home-produced wines.

CANADA
Part of a port pipe, the traditional cask for storing port. A canada holds 2.1 litres and 251 canadas equals one pipe. The contents of a canada was at one time considered the optimum measure a man could drink in a day!

CANAIOLO
A red Italian grape variety, grown for Chianti, especially for *governo* wines, but now tending to decline in importance.

CANAMERO
SPAIN

A small town in southern Spain in the Extremadura which is famous for *flor* affected oak aged white wines, made from Alarije, Bonita, Airén and Marfil grapes.

CANARD DUCHÊNE
Champagne: FRANCE

A champagne house that was owned by Veuve Clicquot and is therefore now part of the Moët-Hennessy group.

CANARY ISLANDS
Although the Canaries were famous for Sack in the 16th century, wine production is now confined to the islands of Tenerife, La Palma and Lanzerote. Red Listan and white Malvasia grown on volcanic soil produce wines for holiday consumption.

CANARY WINE
Was another name for the Sack of Falstaff and the Elizabethans.

CANDIA DEI COLLI APUANI
Tuscany: ITALY

A new white DOC made from Vermentino and Malvasia grapes in the northwest of the region.

CANDIDA MYCODERMA   See mycodermi vini.

CANNELLINO
Applies only to Frascati and describes a wine with some sweetness, with between 3% and 6% residual sugar.

CANNONAU
A synonym for Grenache in Sardinia where it is grown widely.

CANNONAU DI SARDEGNA
Sardinia: ITALY

A red DOC from the Cannonau grape, which is grown all over the island. The normal dry red wine has 13.5° alcohol and is drunk after one year in barrel; two years' ageing makes it *superiore*, which can be dry or medium sweet with 15° alcohol; three years' ageing is necessary for a *riserva*. Fortified wine has 18° alcohol, whether it is dry or sweet. The subdivisions Oliena and Capo Ferrato are also allowed. In addition there are many non-DOC Cannonaus, (usually because of insufficient ageing or alcohol) in various guises, dry or sweet, usually red, but occasionally *rosato* and even white. These include some of the island's best wines, such as Anghelu Ruju, Cannonau del Goceano and Cannonau del Parteolla.

CANON
Bordeaux: FRANCE

A Premier Grand Cru Classé. One of the best wines of the *côtes* of St-Émilion. It is a traditional family estate with only oak vats. The percentage of Cabernet grapes is higher than the average St-Émilion. There is also an unknown property of the same name in the Côtes de Canon Fronsac.

CANON-LA-GAFFELIÈRE
Bordeaux: FRANCE

A Grand Cru Classé of St-Émilion. A large property making soft attractive wines on the *côtes*.

CANTEGRIL
Bordeaux: FRANCE

A Cru Bourgeois Sauternes in the commune of Barsac with a sound reputation.

CANTEMERLE
Bordeaux: FRANCE

A fifth growth Macau, a popular *château* that only just scraped into the 1855 classification as virtually its entire crop was sold to Holland and it was unknown in France. The wine has an excellent reputation, though it went through a period of the doldrums in the 1970s. The run-down property has been bought by Cordier and modernisation-work is in hand.

CANTENAC
Bordeaux: FRANCE

The most important of the villages included in the appellation of Margaux. The best properties include Palmer, Cantenac-Brown, Brane Cantenac, Kirwan and d'Issan.

CANTENAC-BROWN
Bordeaux: FRANCE

A third growth Margaux in the commune of Cantenac. After a chequered history, this now belongs to Rémy Martin. The wines today tend to be a little course and lack the elegance of fine Margaux.

CANTERBURY
NEW ZEALAND

Just north of Christchurch, Canterbury is New Zealand's most southern wine region. The climate is generally cool and rainfall low. The main grape varieties are Rhine Riesling, Müller-Thurgau, Gewürztraminer and Pinot Noir, while the experimental vineyards of Lincoln College are exploring other possibilities. So far St. Helena is the only winery of any importance.

CANTINA

Literally means 'cellar' in Italian. The word often precedes the name of an Italian wine family e.g. Cantina Fratelli Pieropan.

CANTINA SOCIALE

An Italian growers' cooperative, which takes their grapes, pays the growers according to the quantity and quality of the grapes, makes the wine (possibly several wines) and then sells it, either in bulk or more often in bottle.

CAP BON
TUNISIA

A promontory in the northeast corner of Tunisia which has the oldest vineyards in the country. It has a reputation for Muscat wines, such as Muscat de Kelibia.

CAP DE MOURLIN
Bordeaux: FRANCE

A Grand Cru Classé of St-Émilion that has belonged to the Capdemourlin family for nearly 500 years.

CAPBERN Bordeaux: FRANCE

Also called Capbern-Gasqueton, a Cru Bourgeois Exceptionnel of St-Estèphe, named after its owner. It is next to Calon-Ségur and enjoys a good reputation.

CAPE CAVENDISH

The brand name for a South African sherry style wine produced by the K.W.V.

CAPE MENTELLE AUSTRALIA

One of the first vineyards to be planted in the Margaret River. That was in 1970 and it is now the leading winery of the region. There are now 17 hectares planted with Cabernet Sauvignon, Shiraz, Zinfandel, Sémillon and Sauvignon Blanc. Cabernet Sauvignon aged in French oak is their flagship.

CAPE RIESLING

Cape Riesling bears no relation to Rhine Riesling. It is in fact the same grape as the virtually unknown French grape, Cruchen Blanc, which is very similar to Sémillon. It is widely grown in South Africa in Stellenbosch and Paarl; its most notable wine is Nederburg's Paarl Riesling, a crisp fragrant wine, with higher acidity than most Rhine Riesling.

CAPE WINE FARMERS' ASSOCIATION   see K.W.V.

CAPE MENTELLE

1986 CABERNET SAUVIGNON

PRODUCED AND BOTTLED BY CAPE MENTELLE MARGARET RIVER W.A.
750ml PRODUCE OF AUSTRALIA 12.0% ALC/VOL
PRESERVATIVE 220 ADDED

CAPEZZANA Tuscany: ITALY

A 15th century estate owned by the Bonacossi family, making not only Carmignano and Chianti Montalbano, but a range of other excellent wines, Ghiaie della Furba, Vin Ruspo and experimental white and *spumante* wines.

CAPRI Campania: ITALY

The DOC wines of the island of Capri are red, based on Piedirosso grapes and white from Falanghina and Greco grapes. They are best drunk on the island!

CAPRIANO DEL COLLE Lombardy: ITALY

A recent two-coloured DOC from vineyards near Capriano del Colle, south of Brescia. The red is made from Sangiovese and Marzemino grapes and the white from Trebbiano.

CAPSULE CONGÉ

The stamped capsule on a French bottle of wine, indicating that domestic tax has been paid on it.

CARBONIC MACERATION   See macération carbonique.

CARAFE WINE

A general term for a wine sold in a restaurant in a jug, as the house wine. In a wine region it has probably never been bottled.

CARAMANY The Midi: FRANCE

A village within the area of Côtes du Roussillon with its own appellation. The wine is similar.

CARAMAYOLE

The traditional Chilean wine bottle which is the same rounded squat shape as the German *Bocksbeutel*.

CARAMINO Piedmont: ITALY

An unusual, rather heavy, chocolatey non-DOC wine made mainly from Nebbiolo grapes in the vineyards around the castle of Caramino at Faro in the Novara hills. The producers are Luigi Dessiliani & Figli.

CARATELLO

A *caratello* is a 50 litre barrel used for Vin Santo, the Italian dessert wine.

CARBOJ
Sicily: ITALY

The brand name for a respectable Sicilian table wine from Sciacca in the southwest of the island.

CARBOJ

A large glass or occasionally terracotta container, with a wicker frame, like a Chianti *fiasco*, used for carrying wine. It can also be called a *dame-jeanne*.

CARBON DIOXIDE

One of the products of alcoholic fermentation produced by the yeasts along with alcohol. In the case of still wines, it is allowed to escape naturally, but it is a vital ingredient of sparkling wine, with bubbles originating from a second fermentation in either bottle or tank. For very cheap sparkling wine, carbon dioxide may simply be injected into the wine.

Carbon Dioxide is also used, sometimes with nitrogen, to top up a vat and thus keep wine fresh and away from any contact with oxygen. Occasionally a little CO_2 may be absorbed by the wine, giving a slight *pétillance*.

CARBONATED WINE

Wine into which carbon dioxide has been injected to give it a sparkle, which is short-lived once the bottle has been opened. Mateus Rosé is an example of carbonated wine.

CARBONNIEUX
Bordeaux: FRANCE

A Cru Classé Graves from the commune of Léognan. Known, unusually, more for its white than for its red wine. It is the largest producer of classified white Graves, a wine which was once sent to Muslim Constantinople by the monks who owned the property who labelled it *Eau Minérale de Carbonnieux*. Methods for the white are modern, and for the red still rather rustic.

CARCAVELOS
PORTUGAL

Carcavelos is an unusual white Portuguese wine, coming from vineyards near Lisbon, which are fast disappearing with the growth of the seaside resort of Estoril. It is made from Galego, Dourado, Boais Arinto and Espadeiro grapes, grown on mainly limestone soil. The taste is individual, varying from sweet to medium dry, and high in alcohol and is drunk as an aperitif or dessert wine accordingly.

LA CARDONNE
Bordeaux: FRANCE

A Cru Grand Bourgeois of the Médoc from the village of Blaignan, owned by the Rothschilds of Lafite and meriting its good reputation.

CAREMA
Piedmont: ITALY

A red DOC wine made from the Nebbiolo grape and similar in style to the adjoining DOC of Donnaz in the Valle d'Aosta. It needs a minimum of four years' ageing, including two in wood. The cold mountainous climate and rough terrain give the wine an individual taste.

CARIGNAN

The Carignan grape, also called Cariñena and Mazuelo in Spain, Carignano in Italy and Carignane in California, is widely grown in the south of France, mainly in the Aude and the Hérault as a constituent of *vin de table* and *vin de pays*. At its best it is blended with Cinsaut and Grenache, for it is a prolific producer, making astringent wines which need to be diluted with other varieties. It used to constitute 70% of Côtes de Provence but the proportion has now been reduced to 40%.

It is sometimes found in Sardinia, and Apulia, as Carignano del Sulcis. In California, Carignane is used for jug wines. In Spain around the Aragonese town of Cariñena it forms part of the D.O. of Cariñena and is also grown in Penedés and in Rioja where it is called Mazuelo.

There is a white version, Carignan Blanc, which is grown for *vin ordinaire* in the Midi.

CARIGNANO DEL SULCIS
Sardinia: ITALY

A red or *rosato* DOC wine made from Carignano grown on the islands of Sant'Antioco and San Pietro and in Sulcis, the southwest corner of the main island. The red can be drunk young or improved in bottle after ageing in barrel for a year to become *invecchiato*.

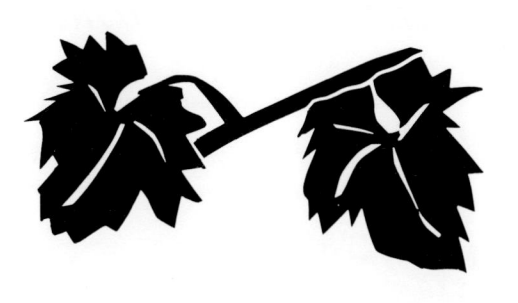

CARIÑENA — SPAIN

An important D.O. of Aragón, situated around the village of the same name to the south of Zaragoza. The wines are mainly red, and *claretes*, oak aged for at least two years, from the grape varieties, Bobal, Cariñena, which originated here and became more widely grown in France as Carignan, Juan Ibañez and Garnacha Negro. Some white wine comes from Garnacha Blanco and Viura, (called Pajarilla locally) as well as a fortified wine similar to Málaga.

CARLONET — SOUTH AFRICA

The red wine of the Uitkyk estate, made from Cabernet Sauvignon and aged in small oak barrels.

CARLOWITZ — YUGOSLAVIA

A red wine made in the Yugoslav province of Vojvodina. It once had a reputation outside the country and was appreciated in Victorian England.

CARLSHEIM — SOUTH AFRICA

A white wine made at Uitkyk from a blend of Cape Riesling and Chenin Blanc. Recent vintages have been improved with some Sauvignon Blanc.

CARMEL — *California*: USA

A tiny AVA of Monterey County, near the town of the same name and the Pacific Ocean.

CARMEL — ISRAEL

The brand name of the leading producer of Israeli wines, the Société Coopérative Vigneronne des Grandes Caves. All the wines are kosher.

CARMEL VALLEY — *California*: USA

An AVA within Monterey County, near the Pacific Ocean.

CARMENÈRE

One of the permitted grape varieties of red Bordeaux, for Graves and Médoc, where it was grown extensively before the phylloxera crisis. As it is particularly susceptible to *coulure*, it has tended to disappear from the vineyards.

LES CARMES HAUT-BRION — *Bordeaux*: FRANCE

A Graves from the commune of Pessac. A small property next to Haut-Brion, making red wine. It takes its name from the Carmelites who owned it until the Revolution.

CARMIGNANO — *Tuscany*: ITALY

A small but fine red DOC wine based on Sangiovese grapes, but including between 6% and 10% Cabernet Sauvignon. It was first recognised by the Grand Duke of Tuscany in 1716. It needs 18 months' ageing for *normale* and three years for a *riserva*. Capezzana is the most important property. *Rosato* and Vin Santo are destined for inclusion in the DOC too.

CARMINE

The Carmine grape is a Californian attempt to reproduce a Cabernet Sauvignon suitable for a hot climate, and like Centurion and Carnelian is a crossing of Carignan x Cabernet Sauvignon with Grenache. It is no more successful than the others.

CARNELIAN

A Californian grape invention, a crossing of Carignan x Cabernet Sauvignon, called F2-7 with Grenache. The object was to produce a vine with some Cabernet character in a hot climate, but so far success in the Central Valley has been limited and the wines are rather neutral.

CARNEROS *California*: USA

An important wine area and AVA at the bottom of the Napa and Sonoma Valleys, adjoining the Bay of San Francisco, which gives it a cool, often foggy climate, making it suitable for Chardonnay and Pinot Noir.

CARNEROS CREEK *California*: USA

A winery in the cooler Carneros area, south of the Napa Valley which has established a fine reputation for its Chardonnay and makes some good Pinot Noir.

CARONNE-STE-GEMME
Bordeaux: FRANCE

A Cru Grand Bourgeois Exceptionnel of St-Laurent, Haut-Médoc and one of the better wines of the commune.

CAROUSEL

A custom of the Palatinate and a way of sampling several wines. Eight to a dozen glasses are served on a wrought-iron turntable; each with a different local wine.

CARR TAYLOR VINEYARDS ENGLAND

Near Hastings in Sussex this takes its name from one of the more energetic English winemakers who runs 21 acres and makes a white wine from Müller-Thurgau, Gutenborner, Reichensteiner, Kerner, Huxelrebe and Schonburger grapes. The vines were first planted in 1974.

CARRAS GREECE

Or Château Carras, the property of a Greek tycoon, John Carras, with extensive vineyards in the Khalkidhiki peninsular, planted with Bordelais grape varieties on the advice of Professor Peynaud. Five wines are made, red, white and rosé, amongst which Château Carras, aged in oak *barriques*, has some Bordelais pretensions.

CARRASCAL SPAIN

A district to the north of Jerez de la Frontera with *albariza* soil and rated second in order of quality.

CARRUADES DE LAFITE   See Lafite.

CARTAXO PORTUGAL

One of the undemarcated wine regions of Portugal in the Ribatejo north of the Tagus. It produces mainly bulk table wine.

LA CARTE ET LE CHÂTELET
Bordeaux: FRANCE

A relatively unknown Grand Cru Classé of St-Émilion immediately next to more famous neighbours. Legionnaires of the Emperor Probus are said to have planted vines here in 276-282 A D.

CARTIZZE   See Prosecco di Conegliano.

CASA DO DOURO

The association to which all Portuguese farmers producing grapes for port belong. It authorises the planting of new vineyards and the fortification of must and checks on production processes. It also buys and stores wine for the government in years of surplus and releases wine in years of penury so as to ensure a regular supply of wine to the shippers.

CASABELLO WINES CANADA

One of the largest wineries in British Columbia, making a range of table wines from Canadian hybrids and imported Californian wines.

CASABLANCA MOROCCO

The coastal region of Casablanca contains three *appellation d'origine garantie*: Zennata, Sahel and Doukkla, which generally produce undistinguished solid red wine.

CASAL GARCIA

The brand name of one of the Vinho Verde wines produced by the Guedes family at Quinta da Avelada in Portugal.

CASAL THAULERO *Abruzzi*: ITALY

One of the few Abruzzi wineries with an international reputation, a cooperative producing sound Montepulciano and Trebbiano d'Abruzzo.

CASALINHO PORTUGAL

An important Vinho Verde brand made by Caves do Casalinho.

CASARSA

A method of pruning developed at the town of Casarsa in Friuli, Italy, entailing the high training of the vines along wires. The vines are planted at wide intervals, to allow for maximum mechanisation in the vineyard.

CASK

A wooden container, of unspecified size, used to age and store wine and spirits.

CASSE

A chemical disorder in a wine causing haziness. There are four types of *casses*, oxidasic, protein, iron and copper.

CASSIS   Provence: FRANCE

Predominantly a white wine made from Clairette, Ugni Blanc, Marsanne and a little Sauvignon. Some red and rosé are produced, but they are of less importance. The vineyards are around the sailing resort of Cassis on the Mediterranean and suffer from the town's encroaching suburbs. Good Cassis can be light and fragrant, though more often it is heavy and flat. It was one of France's first appellations in 1936, with Arbois and Châteauneuf du Pape.

CASTEL GRIFONE   See Lungarotti.

CASTEL DANIELIS   GREECE

A blended red wine produced by Achaia Clauss, improved with some bottle age.

CASTEL DEL MONTE   Apulia: ITALY

The best known Apulian DOC, a tricoloured wine named after the castle of the Emperor Frederick II. *Rosato* is most popular, made from Bombino Nero grapes. Red, which can be *riserva* after three years' ageing, is based on the Uva di Troia grape with Bombino Nero and Montepulciano. The white, made from Pampanuto, is dull.

CASTEL SAN MICHELE   Trentino-Alto Adige: ITALY

A reputable red wine; a Cabernet/Merlot blend, recently elevated to DOC status in Trentino, made by the agricultural school of San Michele all'Adige.

CASTELLER   Trentino-Alto Adige: ITALY

The everyday DOC red wine of the Trentino, made from Schiava, Merlot and Lambrusco grapes and grown along the Adige river to the north of Verona. It is best drunk within two years.

CASTELLI ROMANI   Latium: ITALY

An *indicazione geografica* covering the hills southeast of Rome. The white, made from Malvasia and Trebbiano grapes, is similar to Frascati; the red and *rosato* are mainly made from Sangiovese, Montepulciano and Cesanese. All should be drunk young.

CASTELLO

Italian term for castle. The word often precedes the name of an Italian wine estate, where there is a large house or indeed a castle, e.g. Castello della Sala.

CASTELLI MEDIOEVALI   See Colli Bolognesi.

CASTELLO DELLA SALA   See Antinori.

CATARRATTO

A white grape grown in Sicily, but nowhere else in Italy, and one of the varieties used for Marsala.

CATAWBA

A native American grape variety named after the Catawba river in North Carolina where it originated. It is grown widely in the eastern part of the United States to make a pinkish red wine with a flavour reminiscent of raspberry jelly.

CATOLOGO BOLAFFI

Or Catologo dei Vini Italiani, is an all-embracing catalogue of Italian wine, first published by Bolaffi and now by Mondadori. It is compiled with a grading system of stars by Luigi Veronelli, a great Italian wine critic. It is an indispensable book of reference for Italian wine.

CAVA

The term for Spanish sparkling D.O. wine made by the champagne method. The best *cavas* come from Penedés, where most of the producers have their cellars at San Sadurnui da Noya. The champagne method was first practised in Spain in 1872 by Don José Raventós whose family firm of Codorníu are now one of the largest producers of *cava*. Confusingly the companies that make *cava* are also themselves called cavas.

not hurt; cool, at a constant temperature of about 50°F; free of vibrations, and dark. The cellars of large wine companies may be below their offices, but more often nowadays they take the form of insulated warehouses.

CELLAR BOOK

The record of the contents of a wine cellar. It is kept by the owner to show purchases, with dates, source and prices, when the wine is drunk, maybe with whom and even tasting notes, as well as indicating remaining stocks.

CELLATICA   Lombardy: ITALY

A light red DOC wine made from the Schiava Gentile, Barbera and Marzemino grapes grown around the town of Cellatica.

CENCIBEL

A synonym, for the Tempranillo grape variety, in La Mancha and Valdepeñas.

CENICERO   SPAIN

An important centre for Rioja *bodegas* in the Rioja Alta. The name actually means ashtray in Spanish and the town was the burial or cremation ground for Roman legions stationed in the area.

CENTRAL COAST   California: USA

A general term to describe the vineyards that extend south of San Francisco as far as San Luis Obispo. They can be split into two smaller areas, the Bay Area of Alameda, Contra Costa, San Mateo and Santa Clara Counties and North Central Coast with Santa Cruz, San Benito and Monterey Counties.

CENTRAL VALLEY   California: USA

The overall name for the two valleys of San Joaquin to the south and Sacramento to the north in central California, which produces 80% of California's wine. It is mainly jug wine from French Colombard, Chenin Blanc, Barbera, Carignane, Grenache, Ruby Cabernet and Zinfandel grape varieties. Thompson Seedless is also grown, but for table grapes and raisins as well as wine. There are three AVAs; Madera in Madera County and Clarksburg and Merritt Island in Yolo County.

CAVE

The French term for a cellar.

CAVE COOPÉRATIVE

A common organisation in most French wine areas. It caters for the grape farmer who grows the grapes, but has no means of vinifying them. Usually the farmer delivers grapes, or sometimes must, to the cooperative, which is responsible for vinification, élevage, marketing and sale of the wine.

CAVISTE

The French term for a cellarman.

CECUBO   Latium: ITALY

As a wine of ancient Rome, it was sweet and syrupy. Today it is a dry red *vino da tavola* made from Abbuoto, Negroamaro and other grapes grown on the ancient site of Caccabum near Gaeta.

CECUBUS

A wine of ancient Rome, highly rated by Pliny. It was said to be a wine of breed, generous and heady, not reaching its peak for many years. Today it is a dry red *vino da tavola* called Cecubo.

CEDARWOOD

A characteristic smell for Cabernet Sauvignon grapes in fine mature clarets of the Médoc and Graves.

CELLAR

A place for storing wine, normally below ground. A cellar should be dry, although a little humidity will

CENTRAL VICTORIA — AUSTRALIA

A term to describe the vineyards around Bendigo and Ballarat, north west of Melbourne.

CENTRIFUGE

A piece of equipment used to separate the solids from must or wine, to clean and clarify the liquid. The wine or must is spun round very fast inside the centrifuge so that any solids adhere to the sides and the clear liquid is run off.

CENTURION

Like Carnelian, this is a Californian grape invention - a crossing of Carignan x Cabernet Sauvignon, called F 2 - 7 with Grenache, with the aim of producing some Cabernet character in a hot climate. It is marginally more successful than Carnelian but far from emulating Cabernet Sauvignon.

CÉPAGE

The French term for grape variety, e.g. Pinot Noir or Chardonnay, and one of the principal factors determining the taste of a wine.

CÉPAGE AMÉLIORATEUR

Describes grape varieties such as Cabernet Sauvignon, Merlot, Mourvèdre and Syrah, which are not really traditional to the area, but are being used in the Midi to improve the more common blends of Carignan, Cinsaut and Grenache.

CEPHALONIA — GREECE

An Ionian island which makes a full-bodied white, Robola of Cephalonia, as well as Muscat and Mavrodaphne.

CERASUOLO

Usually describes a light cherry-coloured red wine in Italy, as in Cerasuolo di Vittoria. See also Montepulciano d'Abruzzo.

CERASUOLO DI VITTORIA — Sicily: ITALY

A light red, almost *rosato* DOC wine made from Calabrese and Frappato grapes grown around Vittoria in southeast Sicily. Although it is good drunk young, it also develops well with age as does Stravecchio Siciliano.

CERDON — Savoie: FRANCE

Part of the Vin du Bugey and a VDQS in its own right for its red or rosé, and sometimes sweet, sparkling wine, coming from vineyards around the town of Cerdon, planted with Gamay and Pinot Noir. Two vinification methods are possible, the *méthode champenoise* and the so-called 'traditional' method of Clairette de Die, whereby some residual sugar is left in the bottle to referment the following spring.

CERETTO — Piedmont: ITALY

A family company with a fine reputation for Barolo and Barbaresco. Bricco Rocche is their trademark and also, confusingly, the name of one of their Barolo vineyards. They also own the vineyards of Prapo and Brunate in Barolo and Bricco Asili in Barbaresco. Zonchera is another label for Barolo. They are now planting vineyards for Arneis.

CÉRONS — Bordeaux: FRANCE

A small appellation next to Barsac and within the appellation of the Graves. If sweet wine is made, which depends upon the climatic conditions, it is called Cérons. If the wine is dry, or red, it is appellation Graves. Three communes make up the appellation: Cérons itself, Illats and Podensac. The best-known estates are Archambeau and Chantegrive.

CERTAN DE MAY — Bordeaux: FRANCE

A small Pomerol *château* well situated between Vieux Château Certan and Pétrus, though not of their stature.

CERTAN MAZELLE — Bordeaux: FRANCE

A Pomerol *château* next to and sharing ownership with Certan Giraud.

CERVETERI Latium: ITALY

A bi-coloured DOC from the northwest of Rome, around the town of Cerveteri. The red, from Sangiovese and Montepulciano grapes, is fruity; the white, from Trebbiano and Malvasia, can be dry or medium dry and is best drunk young.

CESANESE

A red grape grown all over Latium and the southern part of central Italy for wines like Castelli Romani, Cesanese del Piglio and Torre Ercolana.

CESANESE DI AFFILE Latium: ITALY

A red DOC similar to its neighbour, Cesanese del Piglio.

CESANESE DI OLEVANO ROMANO Latium: ITALY

A red DOC similar to its neighbours, Cesanese del Piglio and Cesanese di Affile.

CESANESE DEL PIGLIO Latium: ITALY

A red DOC wine made from Cesanese grapes grown around the village of Piglio, southeast of Rome. It comes in a variety of styles: dry, medium dry, medium sweet, sweet, *frizzante* and *spumante*. Still and dry is best.

CÉSAR

A red grape occasionally included in Irancy with Pinot Noir to give it more body, colour and tannin. It is sometimes called Romain and was reputedly brought to the region by the Roman legions.

PIO CESARE Piedmont: ITALY

A traditional family company producing long-lived Barolo, as well as Barbaresco and other Alba wines.

CHABLAIS SWITZERLAND

One of the three main wine regions in the canton of the Vaud, centred on the town of Aigle, between Villeneuve and Bex. Fendant is the dominant grape variety, grown on southwest-facing slopes above the Rhône. Clos des Murailles is a well-known vineyard here.

CHABLIS Burgundy: FRANCE

Authentic Chablis is a dry white wine from the vineyards around the town of the same name in northern France. However, in other parts of the world such as California and Australia, the name has been borrowed to mean a dry white wine of uncertain provenance. The real thing comes from the most northerly vineyards of Burgundy; they are quite isolated from the rest of the region. It is made from the Chardonnay grape grown on kimmeridgian clay, interspersed with fossilised oyster shells. The appellation is split into four categories: Grand Cru with seven named vineyards, Blanchots, Preuses, Bougros, Grenouilles, Valmur, Vaudésir and Les Clos, plus an anomaly, La Moutonne; Premier Cru with 30 possible names, now rationalised under the umbrella names, Fourchaume, Montée de Tonnerre, Mont de Milieu, Vaucoupin, les Fourneaux, Beauroy, Côte de Léchet, Vaillons, Mélinots, Montmains, Vosgros and Vaudevey, then Chablis and Petit Chablis.

The vineyards have expanded considerably over recent years as, with improved methods of frost protection, viticulture has become more viable and the production more certain. However the vineyards are still subject to the vagaries of a northern climate, resulting in annual variations in the quality and quantity of the wine.

More traditional growers age their wine in oak barrels; the modern school favours stainless steel. Good Chablis will age and traditionally develop the *goût de pierre à fusil*, or gunflint taste. It is always a wine with a firm acidity that accompanies fish well, especially oysters.

CHABLIS GRAND CRU
Burgundy: FRANCE

The best Chablis. It consists of seven vineyards grouped together on a slope outside the village: Blanchots, Preuses, Bougros, Grenouilles, Valmur, Vaudésir and Les Clos, plus an anomaly, La Moutonne.

CHABLIS PREMIER CRU
Burgundy: FRANCE

Consists of 30 possible vineyard names that have been rationalised under the umbrella names: Fourchaume, Montée de Tonnerre, Mont de Milieux, Vaucoupin, les Fourneaux, Beauroy, Côte de Léchet, Vaillons, Mélinots, Montmains, Vosgros and Vaudevey.

LA CHABLISIENNE
Burgundy: FRANCE

The cooperative which accounts for nearly a third of the total production of Chablis. Its members have vineyards all over the area. Most of its wine is sold in bulk to *négociants* in Chablis or elsewhere in Burgundy. The methods are those of a classic white wine vinification, with some oak barrels and modern equipment.

CHABROL

Or chabrot, this is a tradition in rural parts of France. A little wine is added to the dregs of the soup in the bowl and drunk.

CHACOLI
SPAIN

A fragrant light white wine made in the foothills of the Spanish Pyrenees around Guernica. It is slightly petillant, only 9° alcohol, rather acidic and should be drunk young and fresh.

CHAI

The term for a Bordeaux wine cellar, except that it is not a real cellar as a *chai* is traditionally always above ground. The *chai* is where the wine is aged in barrel; usually it is divided according to the age of the wine with first and second year *chais*.

CHALK

The dominant soil constituent of Champagne, with characteristics similar to limestone. Chalk gives wines with good acidity and flavour; it drains well and retains the heat.

CHALK HILL
California: USA

One of the many AVAs of Sonoma County.

CHALONE
California: USA

An AVA in Monterey County in the Salinas Valley. Chalone Vineyard was a pioneering vineyard in the 1960s, isolated on the limestone hills of the Santa Lucia mountains. It produces some of California's finest Pinot Noir and Chardonnay, using French oak and Burgundian methods.

CHALYBON   See Helbon.

CHAMBAVE
Valle d'Aosta: ITALY

A village in the Valle d'Aosta which produces two fine wines, Chambave Rouge and Passito di Chambave. Chambave Rouge is made from a unique mixture of Gros Vien, Dolcetto and Barbera and is given two to three years' barrel ageing. Passito di Chambave is made from semi-dried Moscato grapes. It is reputed to be very long-lived.

LE CHAMBERTIN
Burgundy: FRANCE

One of the greatest red wines in the world, made in the village of Gevrey-Chambertin on the Côte de Nuits. The name was perhaps once *Champ de Bertin*, a field belonging to a peasant called Bertin. It was alleged to be Napoleon's favourite wine.

CHAMBERTIN CLOS DE BÈZE
Burgundy: FRANCE

The neighbouring vineyard to Chambertin. Its wine can be sold as Chambertin, but never vice versa. In the 7th century, the vineyard was given to the Abbey of Bèze by the Duke of Burgundy, hence the name.

CHAMBOLLE-MUSIGNY
Burgundy: FRANCE

The village of Chambolle-Musigny on the Côte de Nuits boasts two Grands Crus; le Musigny and Bonnes Mares.

The two most notable Premiers Crus of the village are les Amoureuses and les Charmes, and in addition there are les Cras (part), les Borniques, les Baudes, les Plantes, les Haut Doix, les Châtelots, les Gruenchers, les Groseilles, les Fuées, les Lavrottes, Derrière la Grange, les Noirots, les Sentiers, les Fouselottes, aux Beaux Bruns, les Combottes and aux Combottes.

The main growers of the village are Alain Hudeot-Noëllat, Domaine Georges Roumier et ses Fils and Domaine Comte Georges de Vogüe.

CHAMBRÉ

Means 'at room temperature' and is said to be the ideal temperature at which to serve red wine. However, in these days of central heating, the average living room temperature may be too warm, so the temperature of an unheated room is better.

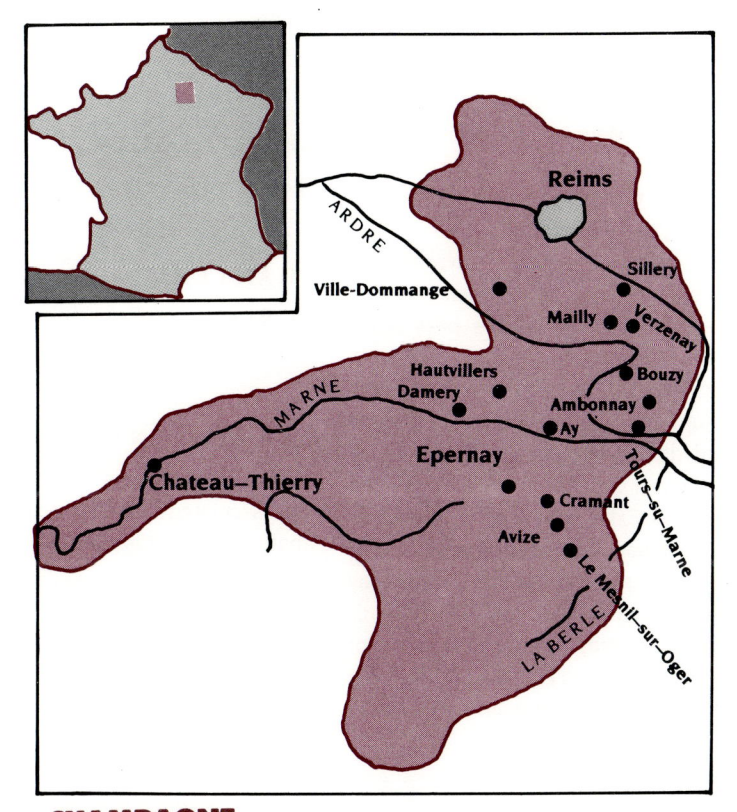

CHAMPAGNE

CHAMPAGNE
FRANCE

Indisputably the world's finest sparkling wine. It comes from a small vineyard in northern France around the city of Reims and the town of Épernay. The *méthode champenoise* of making sparkling wine, which entails a second fermentation in the bottle and the subsequent processes of *remuage* and *dégorgement*, implemented by Dom Pérignon and Veuve Clicquot, has been imitated in other parts of France as well as elsewhere in Europe and the New World. The unique quality of champagne comes from the combination of three principal grape varieties, two red: Pinot Noir and Pinot Meunier, and one white, Chardonnay (occasionally Arbanne and Petit Meslier) grown on the particular chalk soil of the region, belimnita quadrata. The Champagne region divides into five principal areas, namely the Côte des Blancs, which as the name implies, is best for Chardonnay, the Montagne de Reims which is important for Pinot Noir, the Vallée de la Marne for Pinot Meunier, the Aube and the Côte de Sézanne, which is growing in importance for Chardonnay. The villages of the first three are classified according to their quality.

Champagne is a blended wine; the main producers aim to make a uniform house style each year and a vintage wine is made only in the best years. The dosage determines the degree of sweetness, from extra brut, which is very dry, brut (very dry), extra sec (medium dry), sec (medium sweet), demi sec (sweet) and doux (very sweet). Unsweetened champagne, without a dosage, is a recent fashion and is described as Extra Brut. Blanc de Blancs describes a wine made from Chardonnay alone, while Blanc de Noirs means that no Chardonnay has been included. Champagne can also be pink, made either by adding a tiny amount of red wine, or by leaving the juice on the red grape skins for a very short time. Lightly sparkling champagnes are called Crémant.

CHAMPAGNE METHOD   See *méthode champenoise*.

CHAMPÁNA   SOUTH AMERICA
The Spanish word for 'champagne'. In South America it may describe any sparkling wine.

CHAMPET   Rhône: FRANCE
Emile Champet is a leading grower of Côte Rôtie.

CHAMPOREAU
A hot drink made by adding, usually brandy, but sometimes wine, to black coffee.

DOMAINE CHANDON   California: USA
The first French venture into California and is owned by Moet Hennessy. The streamlined winery was built in 1977 and produces sparkling Chandon Napa Valley Brut and a heavier Blanc de Noirs, as well as some still Chardonnay and Pinot Noir as white wine.

CHANSON PÈRE ET FILS
Burgundy: FRANCE
Growers and *négociants* in Beaune, with vineyards mainly in Beaune Premiers Crus, as well as in Savigny and Pernand-Vergelesses.

CHANTALOUETTE   Bordeaux: FRANCE
The second label of Château de Sales.

CHANTEPLEURE
An old French cellar instrument, used for topping up barrels, without disturbing the wine.

CHANTOVENT   The Midi: FRANCE
Important producers of sound table wine; they are associated with a property in the Minervois, Château de Gourgazaud.

CHANTURGUE   Loire: FRANCE
One of the better crus of the Côtes d'Auvergne.

CHAPEAU
The cap of stalks and skins that forms during the fermentation of red wine. It either floats on top of the fermentation vat or is broken up and submerged at regular intervals to extract colour and tannins.

CHAPELLE-CHAMBERTIN
Burgundy: FRANCE
A Grand Cru vineyard in the village of Gevrey-Chambertin.

CHAPELLE-MADELEINE
Bordeaux: FRANCE

A tiny Grand Cru Classé of St-Émilion, next to Ausone and under the ownership of Mme. Dubois-Challon.

CHAPELOT See Montée de Tonnerre.

CHAPOUTIER
Rhône: FRANCE

The house of Chapoutier is one of the leading growers and *négociants* of the Rhône Valley, with cellars in Tain l'Hermitage. The family own vineyards in several appellations: red Hermitage la Sizeranne; white Hermitage Chante Alouette; Crozes Hermitage les Meysonniers; Côte Rôtie, St. Joseph and Châteauneuf-du-Pape, Domaine de la Bernardine, as well as dealing with the other wines of the Rhône Valley. Methods are traditional and the results can be excellent.

CHAPPELLET VINEYARDS
California: USA

Donn Chappellet was one of the pioneers of the new wave of Californian winemaking, building a star-shaped winery in 1968 in the hills to the east of the Napa Valley. His wines have an excellent reputation, especially Chenin Blanc and oak-aged Cabernet Sauvignon.

CHAPTALIZATION

The process of chaptalization was the concept, at the beginning of the 19th century, of a certain Dr. Jean-Antoine Chaptal, Napoleon's Minister of Agriculture, hence its name. It is a means of increasing the alcohol level in wine by adding sugar to the must so that the yeasts have more sugar to convert into alcohol. There are precise regulations as to its use. The grapes must already have obtained a certain potential alcohol level, only so much sugar can be used per hectolitre of juice and the alcohol level can only be increased by a certain amount. In the northern vineyards of France, such as Chablis and Champagne, the use of chaptalization depends solely upon the decision of the individual winemaker, and is permitted every year. In some years, such as the hot summer of 1976, it was quite unnecessary, but in a cooler year such as 1984, it helps to make a more successful and better balanced wine. Further south, in Bordeaux and the surrounding vineyards, special authority has to be obtained, and the sugar is taxed. In the Midi and the Rhône Valley and also for table wines, including *vin de pays*, it is forbidden altogether. In Germany, where it is called Anreicherung, it is allowed in all areas except Baden but it is not allowed for the Pradikat category of wines. It is forbidden in Italy, where they use concentrated must. Nor is it allowed in the vineyards of the New World.

M. CHAPOUTIER

SAINT-JOSEPH
DESCHANTS
MARQUE DÉPOSÉE
APPELLATION St-JOSEPH CONTRÔLÉE
MIS EN BOUTEILLE PAR
M. CHAPOUTIER S.A.   e 75 cl
NÉGOCIANTS-ÉLEVEURS A TAIN L'HERMITAGE DRÔME

CHARAL
CANADA

An Ontario winery making some good Riesling, Gewürztraminer and Chardonnay. Hybrids still dominate their production.

CHARBONO

An obscure Californian red grape variety which is rarely planted now.

CHARDONNAY

The grape variety that produces some of the world's finest dry white wines, notably in Burgundy. It is part of the Champagne blend with Pinot Noir and Pinot Meunier, and is found on its own in Blanc de Blancs Champagne. It can be found elsewhere in France, in Haut Poitou and on an experimental basis in the Midi and Ardèche. In the rest of Europe it is grown in the Alto Adige in Italy, in Penedès in Spain and in Bulgaria. In the New World, it is especially successful in California, and has also been established in Australia and South America. To a lesser extent it is grown in South Africa and New Zealand.

A village of the same name in the Mâconnais may have given the grape variety its name, or vice versa. For a long time Chardonnay was believed to be the white version of Pinot Noir, but this has now been disproved and, despite the confusion over the use of the term Pinot Chardonnay, especially in California, there is no relationship between the two grape varieties.

Chardonnay is a vigorous grape variety with good resistance to low winter temperatures. It ripens early and is therefore suitable for cultivation in areas such as Champagne, with a short growing season. Its yield can vary considerably, depending on the richness of the soil and the climatic conditions, ranging from 15 to more than 100 hectolitres per hectare. Although it has some resistance to downy mildew, Chardonnay is sensitive to powdery mildew and to botrytis.

In some areas, such as the Côte de Beaune and California, it benefits considerably from ageing in wood and produces wine with a long life. Elsewhere it is vinified in stainless steel or concrete-lined vats and designed for earlier drinking.

CHARMAT   See *cuve close*.

CHARMES-CHAMBERTIN
Burgundy: FRANCE

An important Grand Cru vineyard in the village of Gevrey-Chambertin.

CHARPIGNAT
Savoie: FRANCE

One of the crus of Vin de Savoie, but in practice it is never seen on a label.

CHARTA

The Association of Charta-estates was founded in Germany 1984 and consists of Rheingau estates who are committed to the production and promotion of Rheingau wines of traditional style and quality. It sets very high quality standards, based upon the Riesling grape. Wines are bottled in the Association's special bottle.

CHARTRONNAIS

A term to describe a member of the traditional Bordeaux wine trade, whose companies have their cellars and offices on the Quai des Chartrons, with convenient access to the port.

CHASSAGNE-MONTRACHET
Burgundy: FRANCE

As with many other villages in the area, Chassagne has added the name of its most famous vineyard, Montrachet, to give the village a double-barrelled name. The village produces a little more red than white wine, but the white has the better reputation with the Grand Cru name Le Montrachet shared with the adjoining village of Puligny, as well as Bâtard-Montrachet and Criots Bâtard-Montrachet.

The Premiers Crus vineyards for red wine are: Clos Saint-Jean (part) Morgeot (part), Abbaye de Morgeot (part), La Boudriotte (part), la Maltroie (part), les Chenevottes, les Champs Gains (part), Grandes Ruchottes, la Romanée, les Brussonnes (part), les Vergers, les Macherelles en Cailleret (part) and for white wine: Morgeot (part), Abbaye de Morgeot (part), la Boudriotte (part), la Maltroie, Clos Saint-Jean, les Chenevottes, les Champs Gains, Grandes Ruchottes, la Romanée, les Brussonnes, les Vergers, les Macherelles, Chassagne (or Cailleret).

There are several growers worthy of note: Bachelet Ramonet, Delagrange-Bachelet, Jean-Noël Gagnard, Gagnard-Delagrange, Marquis de Laguiche, Domaine du Duc de Magenta, Albert Morey and Ramonet Prudhon.

CHASSE-SPLEEN
Bordeaux: FRANCE

The leading Moulis property recognised to be of classed growth quality, although it is only a Cru Grand Bourgeois Exceptionnel. The property has been recently modernised.

CHASSELAS

A relatively unexciting grape, and only of any real significance in Switzerland where it is known as Fendant and Dorin. It is planted mainly in the Valais and the Vaud where it makes fairly neutral dry white wine, with low alcohol and acidity. Once it was more important in France, with a large amount in Alsace, which has now disappeared. It is also grown a little in the Haute Savoie near the Swiss border. Elsewhere it is considered a table grape. Chasselas Doré or Chasselas Dorato is a synonym for Pinot Blanc in Italy.

CHÂTAINS   See *Vaillons*.

CHATAUQUA USA

One of the wine producing areas of New York State, with vineyards on the eastern shores of Lake Erie.

CHÂTEAU

Literally means 'castle'. The term is used especially in Bordeaux, rarely in Burgundy and sometimes in the Midi to describe a wine estate. The *château* itself may be a large mansion in the case of the classed growths of the Médoc, but is more likely to be a small farmhouse in most other parts of Bordeaux. The term is also used in the New World.

CHÂTEAU BARKER AUSTRALIA

A pioneering winery in the Great Southern area of Western Australia, planted in 1973. Grape varieties include Cabernet Sauvignon, Malbec, Merlot, Shiraz and some white varieties, Gewürztraminer and Sauvignon. Pyramup, the original name for the farm, is their red wine label, and Quondyp is used for their whites.

CHÂTEAU DE BEAUCASTEL
Rhône: FRANCE

One of the best properties of Châteauneuf-du-Pape, making long-lived wines, practising organic viticulture and using a special vinification *à chaud* to extract the maximum amount of colour and substance from the grapes.

CHÂTEAU BELLEVUE-LA-FORET SOUTH WEST FRANCE

The best known property of the Côtes du Fronton. The vineyards were first planted in 1974, principally with Négrette, as well as Cabernet Franc, Cabernet Sauvignon, Syrah and Gamay grape varieties.

CHÂTEAU BOTTLED

Indicates that the wine is bottled at the *château* rather than by a *négociant* or merchant.

CHÂTEAU DE CAYROU SOUTH WEST FRANCE

Château de Cayrou and Clos de Gamot are both owned by the patriach of Cahors, Jean Jouffreau. Château de Cayrou is a 12th century château, with vineyards planted only in 1971. Clos de Gamot has been the family property for several generations, where the *perpetuelles* are aged in barrels for many years.

CHÂTEAU DE CHAINTRE Loire: FRANCE

An excellent property in Saumur Champigny.

CHÂTEAU-CHALON Jura: FRANCE

One of the four appellations of the Jura and the only one for *vin jaune* alone. The village of Château-Chalon has a microclimate which encourages the development of the flor, which gives the wine, which is left to age untouched in oak barrels or pièces of 228 litres for at least six years, its distinctive flavour, reminiscent of fino sherry. The Savagnin grape alone is used to make Château-Chalon which is considered to be the best of the *vin jaune* of the Jura.

CHÂTEAU DES CHARMES CANADA

This winery was created by an Algerian immigrant, Paul Bosc, in Ontario in 1978. He firmly believes in the potential of *vitis vinifera*, especially Chardonnay in Canada but, for financial reasons he also produces hybrid wines.

CHÂTEAU DE FESLES Loire: FRANCE

An important estate in Bonnezeaux, owned by the Boivin family.

CHÂTEAU DES FINES ROCHES
Rhône: FRANCE

One of the old names of Châteauneuf-du-Pape with vineyards around a 19th century mock gothic château. Vinification is both traditional and by *macération carbonique*.

CHÂTEAU FONSCOLOMBE
Provence: FRANCE

One of the better known properties of the Coteaux d'Aix-en-Provence, belonging to the family of the Marquis de Saporta. They make red, white and rosé wines and are noted especially for their white wine which includes a proportion of Sauvignon. The reds, mainly from Grenache, Cinsaut and Cabernet Sauvignon, are soft and fruity and require little ageing.

CHÂTEAU FORTIA Rhône: FRANCE

An important estate in Châteauneuf-du-Pape. Its owner in the 1920s, Baron le Roy, was the instigator of the forerunner of the laws of *appellation contrôlée*. Methods are traditional and the wines intended for a long life.

CHÂTEAU GAI CANADA

An important winery in Ontario which was the first to produce *cuve close* sparkling wine in Canada in 1928. Their table wines come mainly from hybrid varieties, as well as a limited amount of Chardonnay and Johannisberg Riesling grapes.

CHÂTEAUGAY FRANCE

One of the better communes of the Côtes d'Auvergne.

CHÂTEAU DE GOURGAZAUD
The Midi: FRANCE

An important estate in the Minervois. The wine is made by *macération carbonique* and is sometimes aged in oak barrels. A Vin de Pays de l'Hérault from the same estate is called Domaine de Gourgazaud.

CHÂTEAU GRILLET Rhône: FRANCE

The smallest appellation of France with just under three hectares of vines. It is a white wine of the northern Rhône, near the village of Condrieu, made from the Viognier grape, grown in an amphitheatre of terraced vineyards under single ownership. It is a dry wine with a distinctive flavour of apricots aged in wood for several months, but best drunk when about five years old.

CHÂTEAU HORNSBY   see Alice Springs.

CHÂTEAU LEONAY   See Leo Buring.

CHÂTEAUMEILLANT Loire: FRANCE

A little known red and rosé VDQS from vineyards near the city of Bourges. The grape varieties are mainly Gamay, as well as some Pinot Noir and Pinot Gris. The *vin gris* style of rosé is particularly successful.

CHÂTEAU MONTELENA California: USA

Founded in 1882 by Alfred Tubbs, a whaling tycoon. The vineyards did not survive Prohibition and were revived in the 1960s, with an emphasis on Cabernet Sauvignon, Zinfandel, Chardonnay and Johannisberg Riesling. The French style *château* with its Chinese water garden is outside Calistoga in the Napa Valley.

Produce of France
CHATEAU LA NOË
Appellation
muscadet de sèvre et maine
contrôlée
12% VOL.   *Mise en bouteilles au château*   75 cl
COMTE DE MALESTROIT · PROPRIETAIRE VALLET (LOIRE AT.) FRANCE

CHÂTEAU MORNAG TUNISIA

A red and a rosé wine produced by the U.C.C.V.T. in the Mornag hills, east of Tunis.

CHÂTEAU MUSAR LEBANON

The pioneering wine estate owned by the Hochar family, situated in the Bekáa Valley, just north of Beirut. The vineyards are planted with a number of French grape varieties, notably Cabernet Sauvignon, Cinsaut, Syrah, as well as Chardonnay, Sauvignon and Muscat, in the proportion of three-quarters red and one-quarter white. Vinification methods follow those of Bordeaux, with ageing in *barrique*, for Serge Hochar, the winemaker, was trained in Bordeaux. Despite the hostilities of the civil war, Château Musar continues, with some interruptions, to produce fine distinctive wines.

CHÂTEAU DE LA NERTE
Rhône: FRANCE

One of the great names of Châteauneuf-du-Pape, producing a traditional heavy style of wine that has been aged in oak casks for three years.

CHÂTEAU LA NOË Loire: FRANCE

An important estate in Muscadet, owned by the Comtes de Malestroit de Bruc since 1740. They make an unusually full-bodied Muscadet.

CHÂTEAU-NEUF Bordeaux: FRANCE

A little-known unclassified Graves property in the commune of Léognan, making both red and white wine.

CHÂTEAUNEUF-DU-PAPE
Rhône: FRANCE

The best-known wine of the southern Rhône. It is usually red, but can sometimes be white. Thirteen different grape varieties can be grown within the appellation – for reds: Grenache, Syrah, Mourvèdre, Cinsaut, Counoise, Vaccarèse, Terret Noir and Muscardin and for whites: Clairette, Bourboulenc, Roussane, Picpoul, and Picardin.

The village of Châteauneuf-du-Pape takes its name from its association with papal history. One of the Avignon Popes, John XXII did much to develop the vineyards and there is a ruined château in the village.

The wine is also significant in viticultural history as in 1923 it was the subject of the regulatory laws that were to be the forerunners of *appellation contrôlée*.

Châteauneuf-du-Pape, at its best, is a rich full-bodied wine with a minimum alcoholic strength of 12.5°. Wines made in the traditional way are capable of considerable development. Other growers favour the *macération carbonique* method of vinification, resulting in a lighter, less long-lived style of wine.

There are numerous estates in Châteauneuf-du-Pape. Those worthy of note include Château Fortia, Domaine de Beaucastel, Domaine du Vieux Télégraph, Chateau de la Nerte, Clos du Mont Olivet, Domaine de Beaurenard, Domaine de Mont Redon and Domaine de Nalys and Château Rayas.

CHATEAU DU NOZET   see Patrick de Ladoucette.

CHÂTEAU RAYAS   Rhône: FRANCE

One of the outstanding wines of Chateauneuf-du-Pape under the ownership of Louis Reynaud. The family also own Château de Fonsalette in the Côtes du Rhône.

CHÂTEAU REMY   AUSTRALIA

One of the outstanding wines of Châteauneuf-du-company, Remy Martin, for the production of sparkling wine in the Pyrenees district of Victoria. The main grape variety is Ugni Blanc, enlivened with some Chardonnay.

CHÂTEAU REYNELLA   AUSTRALIA

An important estate in the Southern Vales part of South Australia. As the name indicates, the vineyards were planted by John Reynell. These were the first vineyards of South Australia. The recent history of the company includes a series of takeovers. Their original reputation was for port styles; improvements have been made in red and white table wines.

CHÂTEAU ROMASSAN   see Domaines Ott.

CHÂTEAU DE SARAN   Champagne: FRANCE

A property belonging to Moët & Chandon which they use as a guest house. The vineyards produce a white Côteaux Champenois.

CHÂTEAU DE SELLE   see Domaines Ott.

CHÂTEAU SIMONE   See Palette.

CHÂTEAU ST. JEAN   California: USA

A winery in the Sonoma Valley which has created a reputation for its single vineyard wines, notably Belle Terre, with as many as eight Johannisberg Rieslings of different provenance and sweetness. A new venture into sparkling wine is also creating an impact.

CHÂTEAU STE. MICHELLE   USA

One of the leading wineries of Washington State. André Tchelistcheff has advised since its beginning in 1967. Most of the wines are white, notably Chardonnay, Johannisberg Riesling, even an Eiswein. There is also oak aged Cabernet Sauvignon and Pinot Noir for sparkling wine.

CHÂTEAU TAHBILK   AUSTRALIA

An important winery in the Goulburn Valley district of Victoria in Australia. Since its foundation in 1860 it has had a varied history and now produces a range of table wines, notably Marsanne, Riesling, Cabernet and Shiraz of distinctive quality.

CHÂTEAU THIBAR — TUNISIA

A red wine by the Tunisian Office des Terres Domainiales in the Medjerdah Valley, west of Tunis.

CHÂTEAU DE TRACEY — Loire: FRANCE

One of the oldest estates of Pouilly, its vineyards date back to 1396.

CHÂTEAU TREUIL NAILHAC
SOUTH WEST FRANCE

Along with Château La Borderie, this property is run by Dominique Vidal, one of the most talented producers of Monbazillac.

CHÂTEAU VIGNELAURE — Provence: FRANCE

Château Vignelaure in the Coteaux d'Aix-en-Provence was created out of nothing by the former owner of Château la Lagune. The estates are planted with Cabernet Sauvignon, Syrah and Grenache. Attention to detail is meticulous, with an impeccably run cellar. The wines are aged in wood and merit further bottle age.

CHÂTILLON-EN-DIOIS — Rhône: FRANCE

A village in the southern Rhône producing red, white and rosé wines, that were elevated to *appellation contrôlée* status in 1974. The red and rosé wines are made from 75% Gamay and 25% Syrah and Pinot Noir grapes. The white is made from Aligoté and Chardonnay. All the wines are made by the cave cooperative of Die.

CHAUCHÉ GRIS

A synonym in California for the Trousseau Gris grape, where it is better known as Gray Riesling and makes rather neutral white wine.

CHAUFFERETTE

A heater used to warm the air in vineyards, such as Chablis, where there is a danger of spring frosts. Usually a *chaufferette* is filled automatically with oil, but lit manually. This is an expensive but efficient way of protecting the vines from frost damage.

CHÂTEAU DE TRACY
APPELLATION POUILLY FUMÉ CONTROLÉE

COMTESSE A. D'ESTUTT D'ASSAY
58150 POUILLY-SUR-LOIRE
(NIÈVRE) · FRANCE

MISE EN BOUTEILLE AU CHATEAU
12,5% Vol.   e 75 cl
PRODUCE OF FRANCE

CHAUME — Loire: FRANCE

One of the villages of the Coteaux du Layon and has its own separate identity as Coteaux du Layon Chaume. Chaume has a yield of only 25 hectolitres per hectare as opposed to 30 hectolitres for the other villages. The wine can be deliciously honeyed.

DE CHAUNAC

Also called Seibel 9549, a red French hybrid grape variety, grown in north America, notably in Canada. It is named after a French oenologist who worked in Ontario.

CHAUTAGNE — Savoie: FRANCE

One of the better crus of the Vin de Savoie, notably for red wines.

CHAUVIN — Bordeaux: FRANCE

A little-known Grand Cru Classé of the *graves* part of St-Émilion.

CHAVE — Rhône: FRANCE

One of the great names of Hermitage, making superlative wines with immense talent and care. Both red and white are aged in wood for several months and the reds are amongst the most long-lived of the appellation.

CHEILLY LES MARANGES   See les Maranges.

CHELLAH   See Rabat.

CHELOIS

Also called Seibel 10,878, is a white hybrid grape variety grown in the United States and once in France. It performs well in cooler climates.

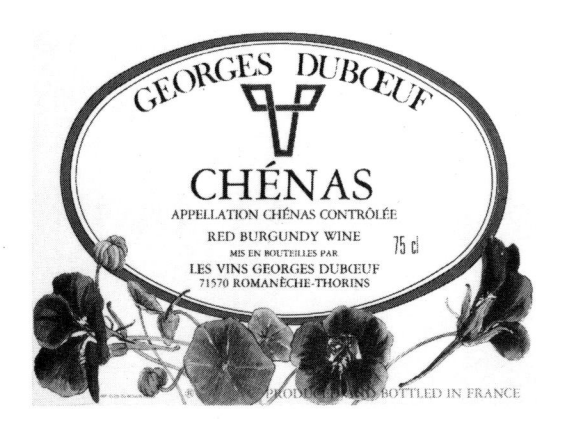

CHÉNAS   Burgundy: FRANCE

One of the ten Beaujolais Crus with the right to a separate appellation. The name comes from the forest of oaks, *chênes*, which once covered the area.

CHENIN BLANC

A white grape originating in the Anjou - Touraine area of the Loire Valley, where it is sometimes called Pineau de la Loire, and where it shows great versatility, producing not only still and sparkling wines, but the whole range of tastes from very dry to very sweet, and always with a backbone of firm acidity. It is the grape for dry Savennières and Jasnières; in Vouvray the wine can be sec, demi sec, moelleux or doux if the grapes have been affected by noble rot. Bonnezeaux, Coteaux du Layon and Quarts de Chaume are honey sweet and capable of considerable longevity. Less exciting are basic Anjou and Saumur Blanc.

Chenin Blanc has travelled to California where it is used for everyday table wines. In South Africa it is called Steen, where its quality ranges from basic varietal wine to the luscious Edelkeur of Nederburg. It is also planted in Australia and New Zealand. It is at its best in the sweet wines of the Loire, which are some of the most underrated of wines.

CHEREAU-CARRÉ   Loire: FRANCE

A company in Muscadet, linking the estates of two families, Chéreau and Carré, including Domaine de Chasseloir, Domaine du Bois Bruley, Grand Fief de Cormeraie and Château du Coing de St. Fiacre. The first to age Muscadet in new oak.

CHESTE   SPAIN

Formerly a D.O. in its own right, but has now been incorporated into the D.O. of Valencia.

CHEVAL BLANC   Bordeaux: FRANCE

One of the two Premier Grands Crus Classés, category A, of St-Émilion (the other being Ausone). It is on the *graves* part of St-Émilion, next to Pomerol. Unusually, the main grape variety is Cabernet Franc. There are imposing new *chais* in which magnificent wines are made. 1947 Cheval Blanc was a legendary vintage.

DOMAINE DE CHEVALIER   Bordeaux: FRANCE

A Graves Cru Classé from the commune of Léognan. Has a fine reputation for both its red and white wine. Unusually for Bordeaux it does not call itself a *château* and there is only a farmhouse in the middle of a wood.

CHEVALIER-MONTRACHET   Burgundy: FRANCE

A small Grand Cru vineyard, next to le Montrachet in the village of Puligny-Montrachet, with an excellent reputation for fine white wine.

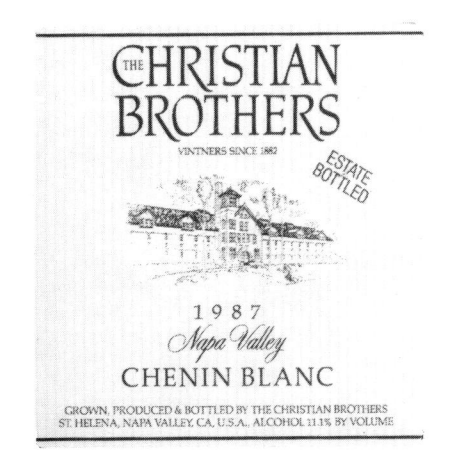

CHEVALIER DE STÉRIMBERG   Rhône: FRANCE

The brand name used by Jaboulet for their best white Hermitage and commemorates the legend of a wounded knight who settled at Hermitage on his return from the Albigensian crusade in the 13th century.

CHEVERGNY   Loire: FRANCE

A little-known VDQS of Touraine. The white wine can be made from an unusual grape variety, Romorantin, which produces very dry crisp wines. Other possible white grapes are Chenin Blanc, Sauvignon, Chardonnay and Pineau Menu (or Arbois). Red wine comes from Gamay, Cabernet Franc and

Sauvignon, Pinot Noir or Malbec. These may also make rosé wine, as may Pinot d'Aunis and Pinot Gris. There is also a little *méthode champenoise* sparkling wine.

CHEVILLE

The name given to an old champagne cork which is no longer swollen, but straight and tight when removed from the bottle. The opposite is a *juponne*.

CHIAN

Said to be one of the best wines of ancient Greece, coming from the island of Chian. It was sweet and dark and much appreciated by Horace.

CHIANTI   Tuscany: ITALY

A red wine that was promoted to DOCG status in 1984. Most of the best comes from the central area between Florence and Siena and is called Chianti Classico, with the black cockerel as its emblem; the peripheral areas, which extend all over Tuscany, are collectively called Chianti Putto and their emblem is a *putto* or fat cherub. They are Colli Aretini, Colli Fiorentini, Colli Senese, Colline Pisane, Montalbano and Rufina. Chianti is predominantly made from the Sangiovese grape, with some Canaiolo (minimum 5%) and a tiny amount of Trebbiano and Malvasia (minimum 2%) with the possibility of a small amount (maximum 10%) of traditional grapes such as Cabernet Sauvignon. Young Chianti is occasionally vinified by the *governo* method, more substantial wines are aged; *vecchio* for two years and *riserva* for three years. The taste and style of Chianti can vary enormously with a range of microclimates and producers. The advent of DOCG should reduce the danger of over-production and result in a general improvement in quality.

CHIANTI CLASSICO   Tuscany: ITALY

The heart of Chianti between Florence and Siena, including the towns of Greve, Castellina, Radda and Gaiole. The Chianti Classico Consorzio is identified by a black cockerel on the neck of the bottle. Fine wines, especially *riservas*, are made from the vines on these beautiful hills. The permitted yield is much smaller than for Chianti Putto, 75 quintals as opposed to 100 quintals.

CHIANTI PUTTO   Tuscany: ITALY

The overall term for the peripheral areas of Chianti surrounding Chianti Classico, namely Colli Aretini, Colli Fiorentini, Colline Pisane, Colli Senesi, Montalbano and Rufina. *Consorzio* members' bottles bear a pink cherub or *putto*. Yields are higher than for Chianti Classico at 100 quintals, except for Colli Fiorentini and Rufina with only 80 quintals. Ageing regulations and grape varieties are the same as for Chianti Classico, though more white grapes are allowed for Chianti Putto.

CHIANTIGIANA

A Chianti bottle size for 1.75 litres.

CHIARETTO

Describes a light pinky-red colour in Italy and is a specific style in Bardolino. It is not as long-lasting as red.

CHICLANA   SPAIN

A village on the edge of the demarcated area of sherry south of Cadiz. The wines from this area are not of the best quality and are often used for inexpensive blends.

CHIGNIN
Savoie: FRANCE

One of the more important crus of Vin de Savoie, making white wine from Jacquère and a little red from Gamay and Mondeuse. A local peculiarity is Chignin-Bergeron, a separate appellation for a white wine made from Bergeron, which is the local name for the Roussanne of the northern Rhône.

CHILE

Viticulture was introduced into Chile in the mid-16th century by Spanish missionaries. They planted the undistinguished Pais grape, which is still widely grown. French grapes arrived in the mid-19th century, before they were affected by phylloxera, which means that Chile is still one of the world's few phylloxera-free countries. The heart of Chile's wine industry is in the valleys of Maipo, Aconcagua, Cachapoal, Lontué, Rapel and Maule near Santiago. Rainfall is very low so irrigation is essential. The climate is influenced by deserts in the north, the Andes to the east and the Pacific Ocean to the west. Red wine is generally better than white: Bordelais grape varieties are the most successful while Riesling, Sauvignon and Chardonnay are planted for white wines. It is a country with enormous potential, as illustrated by the arrival of Miguel Torres from Spain. Any classification of Chilean wines, such as *reserva*, depends upon the individual producer and lacks any official status.

CHILES VALLEY
California: USA

Part of the vineyards of the Napa Valley, to the east of St. Helena but not yet a separate AVA.

CHILSDOWN VINEYARD
ENGLAND

Lies at the foot of the Sussex Downs, near Chichester, and is planted with Müller-Thurgau, Reichensteiner and Seyval Blanc grapes. 1974 was their first vintage. The winery building used to be the railway station for Goodwood race course.

CHINA

Vitis vinifera reached China during the second and third centuries B.C. brought along the caravan routes of central Asia. Today there are six distinct vineyard areas: Sinkiang in the northwest; Kiangsu, north of Shanghai; Sheris or Sharis near Sian on the Yellow River; the Shantung peninsular; Hebei, northeast of Peking and Liaoming in Manchuria near the Great Wall. Rémy Martin have an important investment in China for a white wine called Dynasty. There are some indigenous Chinese grape varieties as well as Pinot Noir, Merlot, Cabernet Franc, Riesling and Muscat.

CHINON
Loire: FRANCE

One of the best red wines of the Loire valley. The town of Chinon is also famous for its château and its associations with Rabelais and English kings. The red wine is made purely from Cabernet Franc, grown in vineyards in a large area around the town of Chinon and is generally intended to be drunk quite young. It is also possible, but unusual, to find rosé and white wine from Chinon.

CHIPIONA
SPAIN

A seaside town with *arena* vineyards, noted for the production of Moscatel for sweet sherries.

CHIROUBLES
Burgundy: FRANCE

One of the ten Beaujolais Crus with a right to a separate appellation. The vineyards have a particularly sunny aspect, resulting in vineyard names like Côte Rôtie and Grille Midi.

CHITRY-LE-FORT
Burgundy: FRANCE

A village just outside the Chablis area that produces a white wine from the Chardonnay grape which local growers would have you believe is as good as Chablis. Other grapes are also grown: Aligoté, Pinot Noir, Gamay and Sacy. The label Côtes de Chitry is sometimes found, although officially the village does not have its own appellation.

CHLOROSIS

A disease of the vine, caused by an excess of calcium in the soil, which prevents the vine from assimilating iron. The leaves of the vine tend to turn yellow. It is combated by using chalk-resistant rootstock or by adding iron to the soil or the vine.

CHOCOLATE

Can sometimes describe rich plummy Burgundies.

CHOREY LES BEAUNE
Burgundy: FRANCE

Most of the red wine of this village is sold as Côte de Beaune villages; a minute quantity of white wine is also made. Growers in the village include Domaine Germain, Château de Chorey, Tollot Beaut and Voarick.

CHRISTIAN BROTHERS California: USA

One of the largest wineries of California. They have been making wine in the Napa Valley at Mont la Salle and Greystone Cellars since the 1900s and have cellars elsewhere in the Napa and San Joaquin Valley. Brother Timothy was their famous winemaker. The Christian Brothers' range is comprehensive and reliable.

CHRISTIES

One of the two principal London auction houses, with an important department for wine, covering the sale of every type of wine from *vin ordinaire* to old and rare bottles, which reach record breaking prices. They also hold regular wine auctions in Amsterdam, Geneva and Chicago.

CHRISTWEIN

The name given, in Germany, to an E*iswein* made on 24th and 25th December.

CHURCHILL

Formed in 1982, it is the youngest port house by at least 50 years. They make no tawny or ruby port, but concentrate on Vintage Character and Crusted Port. They declared the 1982 and 1985 vintages, and in 1983 a single Quinta da Agua Alta.

CHUSCLAN Rhône: FRANCE

One of the seventeen villages of the appellation Côtes du Rhone Villages in the southern Rhône. Chusclan once had a reputation for its rosé wine, but now its wine is mainly red as rosé has gone out of fashion. As well as the usual Côtes du Rhône grapes, the local Camarèse can be included in the blend.

LA CIENEGA California: USA

An AVA within San Benito County.

CIGALES SPAIN

An undemarcated area near Vallodolid with a reputation going back to the Middle Ages for *claretes* made from a mixture of red and white grapes. Today the reputation is somewhat tarnished.

CILIEGIOLO

A red grape grown all over central Italy, mainly in Tuscany for Rosso delle Colline Lucchesi and in Umbria at Torgiano and for Colli del Trasimeno and for Velletri in Latium.

CINQUETERRE Liguria: ITALY

Literally means 'the five lands', or rather five fishing villages on the scenic Ligurian coast – Monterosso, Vernazza, Corniglia, Manarolo and Riomaggiore. Dry white Cinqueterre is made from Bosco, Albarolo and Vermentino grapes and owes its reputation more to its romantic associations than to the quality of the wine. There is a dessert or aperitif wine called Sciacchetrà, made from the same grapes which have been dried before pressing and aged in wood for a year, so it is slightly sweet.

CINSAULT   see Cinsaut

CINSAUT

A red grape variety widely planted in the Midi, and usually blended with Grenache and Carignan. It is also grown in Provence and Corsica and features as one of Châteauneuf-du-Pape's thirteen varieties. It is also popular in north Africa. In South Africa, where confusingly it is called Hermitage, it is widely planted and popular for its productivity and usefulness as a blending wine, though is occasionally found as a pure cultivar.

CINZANO

A household name for vermouth, they also make Asti Spumante, other *spumante*, Cinzano Brut and Principe di Piemonte Blanc de Blancs. They control the wine house of Florio in Marsala as well as wine houses in Tuscany.

CIRÒ Calabria: ITALY

The best DOC Calabrian wine. The full-bodied red with 13.5° alcohol, made from Gaglioppo grapes with up to 10% white Greco or Trebbiano ages well and is *riserva* after three years. R*osato* is made from the same grapes and the white comes from Greco Bianco. Wines from around the town of Cirò itself are called *classico*. Librandi is the best producer.

CISSAC Bordeaux: FRANCE

One of the communes within the appellation of the Haut-Médoc. Its best wine is Château Cissac, a Cru Grand Bourgeois Exceptionnel that enjoys a good reputation under the ownership of Louis Vialard.

CITRAN
Bordeaux: FRANCE

A Cru Grand Bourgeois Exceptionnel in Avensan, Haut-Médoc with a good reputation.

CITRIC ACID

Naturally present in grapes and in wine to a lesser extent and in some parts of the world may be added to a wine that is deficient in acidity.

DOMAINE CLAIR-DAÜ
Burgundy: FRANCE

An important estate based in Marsanny-la-Côte and now owned by the *négociant* company, Louis Jadot. The family created Rosé de Marsannay. They have a reputation for long-lasting tannic wines, with vineyards in Gevrey-Chambertin, Clos St-Jacques, Clos de Bèze, Bonnes Mares and les Amoureuses in Chambolle-Musigny.

CLAIRE RIESLING

An Australian synonym for the Cruchen Blanc grape.

CLAIREFORT
Bordeaux: FRANCE

The second label of the Prieuré-Lichine estate.

CLAIRET

Clairet describes a wine that is light red in colour and also light in body. The English word claret is said to have derived from the term clairet. Today the appellation Bordeaux Clairet exists to denote a pale red or dark pink wine from the Gironde.

CLAIRETTE DE BELLEGARD
The Midi: FRANCE

A dry white AC wine produced in the commune of Bellegard within the appellation of Costières du Gard, between Nimes and Arles from the Clairette grape.

CLAIRETTE DE DIE
Rhône: FRANCE

A sparkling wine from the southern Rhone. There are two styles, Brut and Tradition. The Brut is made purely from the Clairette grape, whereas the Tradition includes anything from 25% to 75% Muscat, which gives the wine a very distinctive grapey flavour. The method is peculiar to the appellation – the sparkle comes not from a second fermentation, but from a prolonged continuation of the first fermentation. When the wine is bottled in January there is still some unfermented sugar left which subsequently provides the bubbles without any extra yeast or sugar. A little still wine is also made.

CLAIRETTE DU LANGUEDOC
The Midi: FRANCE

A distinctive white wine made from the Clairette grape grown in the Hérault around the town of Pezenas. Improved vinification methods have greatly enhanced the flavour of this wine; it used to be rather dull, but well made is a full-bodied dry, but not acidic, white wine, with hints of aniseed and almond.

Clairette du Languedoc rancio was made when the grapes were picked particularly late, so that the wine reached 14° alcohol. It was then aged until it had an almost maderised taste. It is rarely found now.

CLAIRETTE ROUSSE

A synonym of Bourboulenc.

CLAPE
Rhône: FRANCE

One of the best growers of Cornas, making solid full-bodied wines of considerable longevity.

LA CLAPE
The Midi: FRANCE

The former VDQS of La Clape is now part of the all-embracing appellation of the Coteaux du Languedoc. The vineyards of La Clape are on a limestone promontory at the mouth of the river Aude just north of Narbonne. Carignan, Cinsaut, Grenache and some Mourvèdre and Syrah make the red wine, while white comes from Bourboulenc, Terret Blanc and Grenache Blanc. Cool sea breezes benefit the microclimate.

CLARE-WATERVALE
AUSTRALIA

The most northerly of the wine areas of South Australia, a valley with the towns of Clare and Watervale. The climate is hot and dry with unirrigated vineyards so that the red wines tend to be rich and full-bodied. Shiraz is the main red grape variety, while Clare Riesling dominates the whites.

CLAREMONT WINES   CANADA

Considered to be one of the best wineries in British Columbia, with a variety of *vitis vinifera*, as well as some hybrids. 1980 Gewürztraminer was one of their best wines; they also grow Pinot Blanc, Johannisberg Riesling and Sauvignon Blanc.

CLARET

The English term for red Bordeaux. It originates from the word *clairet* which describes a light red wine that was made around Bordeaux in the Middle Ages, in contrast to the fuller wines of the hinterland.

CLARET JUG

Attractive glassware has evolved around wine. Claret jugs can be elegant and decorative and much prized as collectors' pieces. A claret jug is used in the same way as a decanter, but traditionally used for red Bordeaux.

CLARETE

The Spanish term for a light red wine, as opposed to a fuller darker red which is called tinto.

CLARKE   Bordeaux: FRANCE

Château Clarke is a Cru Bourgeois of Listrac and a rising star of the Médoc since its purchase by Baron Edmond de Rothschild in 1973. No expense has been spared in modernising the *chais*, the wine storehouses, making it one of the best equipped *châteaux* of Bordeaux. An enormous planting programme on its 130 hectares has given it one of the largest vineyards of the Médoc.

CLARKSBURG   California: USA

An AVA on the banks of the Sacramento River in Yolo County in the Central Valley.

CLASSIC

Describes a traditional wine type; a Bordeaux or Burgundy may be classic, but not a Shiraz or a Liqueur Muscat. However the word is sometimes over-used.

CLASSICO

An Italian term meaning that the vineyards lie in the heart of the region, which is generally considered to produce the best and most typical wine of the area. For example, Chianti Classico refers to the area between Siena and Florence, as opposed to the outlying areas around Pisa or Arezzo.

CLAVELIN

The distinctive fat, square-shouldered bottle used in the Jura for Château-Chalon and *vin jaune*. It holds 62 centilitres, which is the amount of wine left from a litre of wine, after it has matured in barrel for the statutory six years of ageing necessary for *vin jaune*.

CLAY

An important soil constituent in some vineyards, often mixed with limestone which gives better drainage. The vines need to be on slopes, to improve the drainage and clay tends to be a difficult soil to work. However the wines, especially reds, are high in alcohol, tannin and colour, but tend to be a little coarse. For instance, compare the Bas-Médoc which has more clay, with the Haut-Médoc, with a higher proportion of limestone.

CLEAN

Describes a wine without any unpleasant smell.

CLEAR LAKE   California: USA

An AVA in Lake County. Cabernet Sauvignon is the main grape variety.

CLERC-MILON "MONDON"

A fifth growth Pauillac. A little-known property usually called Clerc-Milon, that was bought in 1970 by Baron Philippe de Rothschild.

RAOUL CLERGET   Burgundy: FRANCE

One of the oldest St-Aubin houses of the Côte d'Or, going back to 1270. There are several other wine-making Clerget in the area. This one is best known for his St-Aubin and Domaine de Pimont. As a *négociant*, he deals in the other Côte d'Or wines.

CLESSÉ   See Mâcon Villages.

CLEVNER

An Alsace term for the Pinot grape in general, either Noir, or more commonly Blanc. Pinot Blanc can be blended with the similar Auxerrois and sold as either Pinot Blanc or Clevner.

CLEVNER D'HEILIGENSTEIN see Savagnin

CLIMAT

The Burgundian term for a specific vineyard.

CLIMATE

One of the factors determining the quality of a wine. Rainfall and heat are the two most important aspects of climate, but frost, hail and wind all have an effect. Vines produce the most interesting wines in regions where there are the climatic variations which determine the character of each year's vintage, while vines in countries of constant sunshine generally produce bland uninteresting wine. In the temperate regions of the world's best vineyards, cool wet winters and warm dry summers with some rainfall are most desirable. Rainfall is most appreciated in the winter and spring; some is necessary in the summer to help the grapes to fill out but not in excess so as to cause rot. Enough sunshine for the grapes to ripen is essential; in cooler regions, a longer growing season is necessary and the quality of a vintage may be determined by warm weather at the harvest or spoilt by cool wet weather.

CLIMENS Bordeaux: FRANCE

A first growth Sauternes, one of the two great wines of Barsac, Coutet being the other. The vineyard is planted with a very high proportion of Sémillon grapes, which suit the chalky soil of the property. The wine has an excellent reputation with consistent quality.

CLINET Bordeaux: FRANCE

A second growth Pomerol *château* situated near the village of Pomerol. The wine has a high proportion of Cabernet Sauvignon grapes.

CLINTON

A curiosity from the Italian Veneto, an American grape variety brought to the area some 200 years ago and now producing rough, and occasionally sweet, red wine.

CLONAL SELECTION See clone.

CLONE

Most vine varieties have several different clones produced from that one variety, with different characteristics which are more or less desirable, such as productivity, colour and tannin. Much research work has been done to identify and separate the different clones of the world's main grape varieties so new vineyards in the better wine regions can be planted according to clonal selection. There should be at least three or four different clones in a vineyard so that the results are not uniform.

CLOS

Literally means 'walled vineyard' in French, though often the walls have long disappeared since the vineyard was so named. They occur especially in Burgundy; Clos de Vougeot is a notable example and Les Clos in Chablis.

LES CLOS Burgundy: FRANCE

The largest of the seven Grand Cru vineyards of Chablis. There is also a vineyard in Vouvray with the same name. The inference is that the vineyard was surrounded by a stone wall.

CLOS DE L'AMIRAL See Beychevelle.

CLOS DU BOIS California: USA

A winery in the Sonoma Valley, producing a limited range of varietals; Chardonnay, Gewürztraminer, Johannisberg Riesling, Cabernet Sauvignon and Pinot Noir, which are released for sale, only when the wines are ready for drinking.

CLOS DE LA CHAINETTE
Burgundy: FRANCE

A tiny vineyard inside the town of Auxerre in northern Burgundy. It is all that remains of the once famous Grande Côte d'Auxerre. White and a little rosé wine is produced by rustic methods.

CLOS DU CLOCHER
Bordeaux: FRANCE

A little-known Pomerol *château* making sound wine.

CLOS DE COULÉE DE SERRANT
Loire: FRANCE

An estate within the appellation of Savennières with its own appellation, Savennières Coulée de Serrant. It is owned by the Joly family, who practice organic viticulture and make the wine with meticulous care and talent.

CLOS L'EGLISE
Bordeaux FRANCE

A second growth Pomerol property, sharing ownership with Plince, where they make more successful wine.

CLOS FOURTET
Bordeaux: FRANCE

A Premier Grand Cru Classé of St-Émilion. Situated just outside the town, it has magnificent quarried cellars. The high proportion of Cabernet Franc grapes makes for a tougher wine than the average St-Émilion.

CLOS DE GAMOT See Château de Cayrou.

CLOS HAUT-PEYRAGUEY
Bordeaux: FRANCE

A first growth Sauternes in Bommes, a little-known property with little production.

CLOS DES JACOBINS
Bordeaux: FRANCE

A reputable Grand Cru Classé of St-Émilion, owned and made by the house of Cordier.

CLOS DE MARQUIS
Bordeaux: FRANCE

The second wine of the Léoville-Lascases estate.

CLOS MIREILLE   see Domaines Ott.

CLOS NAUDIN
Loire: FRANCE

One of the great estates of Vouvray, owned by the Foreau family.

CLOS DE L'ORATOIRE
Bordeaux: FRANCE

A Grand Cru Classé of St-Émilion, of average quality.

CLOS DU PAPILLON
Loire: FRANCE

A famous vineyard in Savennières, partly owned by Jean Baumard.

CLOS DE LA POUSSIE
Loire: FRANCE

The white Sancerre of the Bordeaux house, Cordier.

CLOS RENÉ
Bordeaux: FRANCE

An important second growth Pomerol *château* enjoying a good reputation.

CLOS DE LA ROCHE
Burgundy: FRANCE

The largest Grand Cru vineyard in the village of Morey St-Denis.

CLOS STE-CATHERINE
Loire: FRANCE

A famous vineyard in the Coteaux du Layon owned by Jean Baumard.

CLOS ST-DENIS
Burgundy: FRANCE

A Grand Cru vineyard in the village of Morey St-Denis.

CLOS ST-MARTIN
Bordeaux: FRANCE

One of the many little-known Grands Crus Classés of St-Émilion.

CLOS DE TART
Burgundy: FRANCE

This Grand Cru vineyard is in the village of Morey St-Denis on the Côte de Nuits and is owned by the Mommessin family.

CLOS TRIGUEDINA
SOUTH WEST FRANCE

Clos Triguedina is the property of Baldès, one of the larger growers in Cahors, with a particular reputation for their Prince Probus quality that is aged for several months in new wood.

CLOS DU VAL
California: USA

A Napa Valley winery run by a Frenchman, Bernard Portet. His father was the *régisseur* at Château Lafite; his brother makes wine at Taltarni Vineyards in Victoria. The Cabernet Sauvignon is blended with Merlot; Zinfandel and Chardonnay are made too.

CLOS DE VOUGEOT or CLOS VOUGEOT
Burgundy: FRANCE

This is the largest Grand Cru vineyard of the Côte d'Or, consisting of just over 50 hectares. In the Middle Ages, it was owned and run by the Cistercian monks as an offshoot of the Abbey of Cîteaux. Since then the vineyard has been divided and now has more than eighty owners, ranging from large shippers to local proprietors. Inevitably, the quality of the wine varies according to the name on the label. The *château* of Clos de Vougeot is now the home of the Confrérie des Chevaliers du Tastevin. The press house and cellars with their enormous wooden presses and oak vats are well worth a visit.

LA CLOSERIE GRAND POUJEAUX
Bordeaux: FRANCE

A Cru Bourgeois of Moulis in the Haut-Médoc.

LA CLOTTE
Bordeaux: FRANCE

A small, little-known Grand Cru Classé of St-Émilion on the best slopes of the *côtes* below the ramparts of the town. The wines are light and elegant.

CLOUDY BAY
NEW ZEALAND

New Zealand's newest winery, in the Marlborough district of South Island with its first vintage in 1985, and fast establishing a reputation for Sauvignon and Chardonnay. The winery takes its name from the bay named by Captain Cook in 1770. It is owned by Cape Mentelle in Western Australia.

CLOYING

Can describe a sweet, heavy wine that lacks any balancing acidity to make it fresh.

LA CLUSIÈRE
Bordeaux: FRANCE

A Grand Cru Classé of St-Émilion adjoining Pavie.

COAN

A wine of ancient Greece from the island of Cos, white in colour and usually mixed with seawater.

COARSE

Describes a rough wine that lacks elegance and style.

COASTAL REGION — SOUTH AFRICA

A large wine region of South Africa that covers the districts of the Wines of Origin of Constantia, Durbanville, Stellenbosch, Paarl, Tulbagh and Swartland.

COCHYLIS

A moth which lays its eggs on grapes, producing larvae which feed off the grapes. This can be effectively treated with various sprays.

COCKBURN SMITHES

One of the great names of port, founded by Robert Cockburn in 1815; John Smithes became a partner in 1848. Although the company is now owned by Allied Breweries, the founders' descendants still run it. They own several *quintas* in the Douro; 60% of their wines are still traditionally trodden by foot. Their best known tawny is Cockburn's Director's Reserve. Martinez Gassiot is an associate company.

COCKS ET FÉRET

Sometimes known as the Bordeaux Bible and now called simply Féret, a massive reference work, covering all the Bordeaux *châteaux* in detail. It is revised at regular intervals.

COCOCCIOLA

A white grape, a small amount of which may be used in the DOC of Trebbiano d'Abruzzo.

CODORNÍU — SPAIN

The oldest and largest *cava* house in Spain and indeed, the biggest producer of sparkling wine in the world. The Raventós family who own it have been making wine since 1551 and in 1872 began making sparkling wine following Don José Raventos' studies in Reims. They own no vineyards; the grapes are bought and carefully vinified according to the champagne method in their enormous cellars in *fin de siecle* buildings. Their best wines are Gran Codorníu Brut and Non Plus Ultra. They also own the Raimat estate.

COLARES — PORTUGAL

Colares is a Portuguese red wine, from vineyards around the town of the same name near Lisbon, where they grow the tough skinned Ramisco grape. The vines are planted in clay soil covered with sand, as deep as three to ten metres. The sand has protected the vines from phylloxera so that it is one of the few phylloxera free vineyards of Europe. Colares is matured in wood for at least two years and requires still further ageing to show its true character. A little white Colores is also made.

COLD FERMENTATION

A fermentation conducted at a lower than usual temperature, usually for white wine. The must is cooled so that it ferments, usually at about 17-18°C. If the fermentation is too cool, it can give the wine a characteristic flavour of boiled sweets. Cold fermentation is becoming increasingly common for white wines, as cellars become better-equipped, particularly in hotter climates, such as the Midi.

COLD STABILISATION TREATMENT

This entails chilling a wine to prevent the precipitation of tartrate crystals in the bottle. The temperature of the wine is lowered to about −5°C for eight to ten days, depending on alcoholic content, to allow the tartrates to precipitate in the vat, so that they can be filtered out before bottling.

COLE RANCH — *California*: USA

An AVA in Mendocino County, inland near the Russian River.

COLHEITA

Means vintage or year in Portuguese.

COLLAGE

The French term for 'fining'.

COLLE PICCHIONI — *Latium*: ITALY

One of the better reds of the Castelli Romani, though not DOC, made from Merlot, Cesanese, Sangiovese and Montepulciano grapes, to develop into a full robust wine after four years.

COLLI ALBANI — *Latium*: ITALY

A white DOC wine made from Malvasia and Trebbiano grapes grown around Lake Albano. It is usually dry, but may be medium sweet or *spumante*. *Superiore* denotes 12.5° alcohol.

COLLI ALTOTIBERINI
Umbria: ITALY

A new DOC from the upper valley of the Tiber, covering red and *rosato* wine from Sangiovese and Merlot grapes, and white from Trebbiano and sometimes other varieties like Riesling and Pinot.

COLLI ARETINI
Tuscany: ITALY

One of the Chianti Putto zones, from hills around the town of Arezzo.

COLLI ASOLANI See Montello.

COLLI BERICI
Veneto: ITALY

A DOC from hills near Vicenza which comes in seven varieties. There is Cabernet, both Franc and Sauvignon which is *riserva* after three years' ageing; Garganega, a dry white; Merlot, soft and fruity; Pinot Bianco; Sauvignon; Tocai Italico, which is not as good as Tocai Friuliano, and Tocai Rosso, a local rarity.

COLLI BOLOGNESI
Emilia-Romagna: ITALY

A DOC from the foothills of the Apennines, southwest of Bologna. Two sub-areas, Monte San Pietro and Castelli Medioevali, may also appear on a label. There are seven versions: Barbera, the most popular and *riserva* after three years; a recent addition Cabernet Sauvignon; Bianco made from Albano and Trebbiano; Merlot; Pinot Bianco; Riesling Italico, or alternatively Pignoletto, which is the name of a local clone of Riesling Italico, and finally, the best white, Sauvignon.

COLLI DI BOLZANO
Trentino-Alto Adige: ITALY

A soft red DOC wine made from Schiava grapes around the town of Bolzano.

COLLI EUGANEI
Veneto: ITALY

A DOC from a volcanic outcrop in the Po Valley near Padua, consisting of red, muscatel and white. The white comes from Garganega, Serprina, Tocai and Sauvignon grapes. It is usually dry but can be medium sweet and also *spumante*. Muscatel can be still, *frizzante* or *spumante* and is always sweet. Red is from Merlot, Cabernet, Barbera, and Rabosa grapes, can be *superiore* after one year's ageing and benefits from further maturation. Medium sweet and *spumante* versions are included in the DOC.

COLLI FIORENTINI
Tuscany: ITALY

One of the Chianti Putto zones, covering an area to the south and east of Florence. The permitted yield for this zone and for Rufina is smaller than for other Chianti Putto.

COLLI GORIZIANO
Friuli-Venezia Giulia: ITALY

Also called Collio, this is a DOC area on the Yugoslav border near Gorizia, producing fine white wines. Twelve varieties make up the DOC: Collio, the one non-varietal wine of the DOC describes a dry white made from Ribolla, a distinctive indigenous grape; Malvasia and Tocai; Cabernet Franc; Malvasia; Merlot, *rosato* as well as red; Pinot Bianco which sometimes includes Chardonnay; Pinot Grigio; Pinot Nero; Riesling Italico; Sauvignon; Tocai Friuliano and Traminer. In addition Chardonnay, Cabernet Sauvignon, Müller Thurgau and Riesling Renano produce sound *vino da tavola*.

COLLI LANUVINI
Latium: ITALY

A little-known dry white DOC wine made from Malvasia and Trebbiano grapes near Lake Nemi.

COLLI MORENICI MANTOVEANI DEL GARDE
Lombardy: ITALY

A DOC wine from the province of Mantua. There are three versions, a white from Garganega and Trebbiano grapes with a vague resemblance to Soave; a light red from Rondinella, Merlot and Rossannella grapes, which may also be called *rubino*, and a *rosato* from the same grapes which is also called *chiaretto*.

COLLI ORIENTALI DEL FRIULI
Friuli-Venezia Giulia: ITALY

One of the DOCs of Friuli Venezia Giulia on the Yugoslav border. It comes in twelve varieties, reds are *riserva* after two years: Cabernet Franc and/or Sauvignon; Merlot; Picolit, DOC only here; Pinot Bianco; Pinot Grigio; Pinot Nero; Refosco; Ribolla in tiny quantities; Riesling Renano; Sauvignon; Tocai and Verduzzo which can be dry, medium dry or sweet from slightly-dried grapes.

COLLI DI PARMA
Emilia-Romagna: ITALY

A new DOC from the region of Emilia Romagna. The red is made from Barbera, Bonarda Piemontese and Croatina grapes and there are two whites, from

Malvasia di Candia which may be dry or medium sweet, occasionally also *spumante*. There is also a crisp white made from Sauvignon grapes.

COLLI PERUGINI
Umbria: ITALY

A recent DOC from vineyards around the town of Perugia, covering red, white and *rosato* wine. Sangiovese, Merlot, Barbera and Montepulciano grapes are used for the red and *rosato*, Trebbiano, Malvasia, Verdicchio and Grechetto are used for the white.

COLLI PIACENTINI
Emilia-Romagna: ITALY

The new DOC of Colli Piacentini incorporates three existing DOCs: Gutturnio dei Colli Piacentini, Monterosso Val d'Arda and Trebbianino Val Trebbia, and creates eight further versions of the DOC, which, with one exception, are based on a single grape variety, to which up to 15% of another grape variety can be added. The exception is Colli Piacentini Val Nure, a white wine made from Malvasia di Candia Aromatica, Ortrugo and Trebbiano Romagnolo and which can be *spumante*. The single grape varieties are Barbera, Bonarda and Malvasia, which can be dry or semi-sweet and *spumante*, Ortrugo, Pinot Grigio, Pinot Nero and Sauvignon, all of which can be both *spumante* and still wines.

COLLI PISANE
Tuscany: ITALY

One of the Chianti Putto zones, covering the hills southeast of Pisa. It is the lightest Chianti.

COLLI SENESI
Tuscany: ITALY

The largest of the Chianti Putto zones, covering three areas around Montalcino, Montepulciano and near Siena between San Gimignano and Castelnuovo Berardenga. It covers a variety of styles.

COLLI DEL TRASIMENO
Umbria: ITALY

A DOC from vineyards around Lake Trasimeno. The red comes from Sangiovese, Ciliegiolo and Gamay grapes and needs three to four years' ageing; the white, from Trebbiano, Malvasia, Verdicchio and Grechetto is light and fruity.

COLLINE TORTONESI
Piedmont: ITALY

A DOC area near the town of Tortona in southeast Piedmont, with two wines, red Barbera and white Cortese. Barbera requires at least 85% Barbera grapes and, if *superiore*, has at least two years' ageing. Cortese is a dry white, usually still, but occasionally *spumante*.

COLLIO   See Colli Goriziano.

COLLIOURE
The Midi: FRANCE

A red wine which has had an appellation since 1949, coming from vineyards around the coastal resorts of Banyuls and Collioure near the Spanish border. The area is identical for both appellations. The main grape variety is Grenache (minimum 60%) with some Mourvèdre, Syrah, Cinsaut and a very little Carignan, making tough full-bodied wines.

COLOMBARD

In France the Colombard grape is grown in the Charente and the Gers for distillation into Cognac and Armagnac. It is also vinified as a light dry white table wine in Vin de Pays des Côtes de Gascogne.

Surprisingly, it has been widely planted in California in recent years for quaffable jug wine. In South Africa, as Colombar, it enjoys a similar success.

COLOMBIER MONPÉLOU
Bordeaux: FRANCE

A Cru Grand Bourgeois in Pauillac.

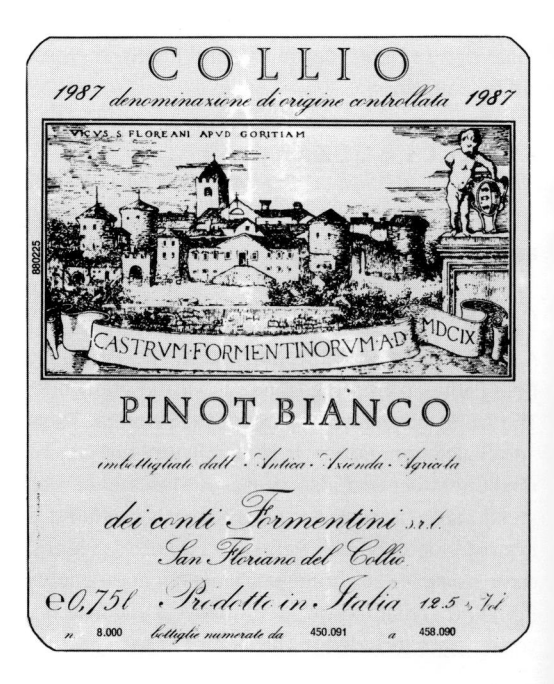

COLONY   see Italian Swiss Colony.

COLORINO

A local Tuscan grape variety which can be used in small proportions for Chianti, but now is diminishing in importance.

COLTASSALA   Tuscany: ITALY

A non-DOC wine produced by the Chianti estate of Castello di Volpaia mainly from Sangiovese grapes and aged in small oak barrels.

COMBINAT

Hungarian wine production is dominated by seven regional *combinats*, which are responsible for making their area's wine. They operate individually, but are controlled by the state. In addition there is a separate organisation running the state farms, as well as a few privately owned vineyards.

COMET YEAR

A great vintage has sometimes coincided with the appearance of a comet. 1630 was one such year and more recently 1811, which is the vintage more usually described as a comet year. 1811 Lafite was particularly praised as *le vin de la comète* and is one of the great wines of the Château. Perhaps it may be superceded by 1985 in years to come.

COMITÉ INTERPROFESSIONNEL

Most of the main wine regions of France have an organisation, the Comité Interprofessionnel, which is responsible for the promotion of the region's wines. Money is raised from the wines growers according to the size of their production.

COMMANDARIA   CYPRUS

The traditional dessert wine of Cyprus. It was given its name by the Knights Templar in the twelfth century. It can be made from pure white Xynisteri, also from red Mavron and Ophthalmo grapes. Usually, it is a deep-coloured wine, aged in barrel for at least five years. The grapes are first dried in the sun, then pressed so that the fermentation is long and slow and no fortification is necessary. The best Commandaria is made over the southern slopes of the Troodos mountains near Limassol; production is limited to eleven villages.

COMMANDERIE DU BONTEMPS DU MÉDOC ET DES GRAVES

The wine fraternity of the Médoc and the Graves in Bordeaux, a ceremonial and promotional body which organises three annual festivities: the feast of St-Vincent, the Fête de la Fleur and the Bal des Vendanges.

COMMISSIONAIRE

A variation on a *courtier*, buying wine on his/her own account and selling it at a profit, rather than putting the seller in contact with the purchaser and taking a commission like a *courtier*.

COMPLETER

A white grape grown in the village of Malans just south of Lichtenstein in German-speaking Switzerland. It ripens to a potential 15° of alcohol and makes an unusual *Auslese*.

COMPLEX

Describes a wine with many nuances and layers of flavour.

COMTE GEORGES DE VOGÜÉ   Burgundy: FRANCE

A fine estate in Chambolle-Musigny making Bonnes Mares and Chambolle-Musigny les Amoureuses, as well as some unusual white Musigny.

COMTES LAFON   Burgundy: FRANCE

Important growers, based in Meursault, but known for their share of Le Montrachet. They also have vineyards in Meursault, notably de la Barre, and in Volnay.

CON CRIANZA   see crianza.

CON RETROGUSTO

Describes, in Italian, a wine with 'aftertaste'.

CONCA DE BARBERA   SPAIN

An aspiring D.O. of Catalonia, to the west of Penedès. The vineyards are planted mainly with white grapes, Parellada and Macabeo, for everyday drinking and sparkling wine.

CONCANNON VINEYARD California: USA

Founded in 1883 in the Livermore Valley to make altar wine and thus survived Prohibition. Specialities include the first bottling of Petite Sirah in California and unusual Rkatsiteli, a grape of Russian origin.

CONCENTRATED MUST   See *concentrato*.

CONCENTRATO

Used in Italy instead of chaptalisation as a means of boosting the alcohol content of a wine. The *concentrato* should be neutral, without flavour and acidity, which is an expensive process. In practice, this does not always happen.

CONCHA Y TORO   CHILE

The largest producer in Chile, with estates near Santiago. They grow European grape varieties: Cabernet Sauvignon, Riesling, Sauvignon Blanc, Chardonnay and other white varieties. Marqués de Casa Concha describes a wine from a single vineyard; Casillero del Diablo is their best-known brand and the name Santa Emiliana is used for some of their wines.

CONCIA   See Marsala.

CONCORD

The most common grape variety of New York State, a variety of *Vitis Labrusca* with the distinctive foxy flavour, for reddish pink wine that is sometimes sweet and sometimes fizzy.

CONDADO DE TEA   SPAIN

A wine region of Galicia which can also be called the Condada de Mino or de Salvaterra. Unusually, reds are more important than whites, but both are hard to find as they are not sold commercially.

CONDRIEU   Rhône: FRANCE

A white wine from the northern Rhône, made from the Viognier grape produced from vineyards around the village of the same name. It is a small appellation and the Viognier gives tiny yields. The wine has the distinctive apricot flavour of the grape variety. The leading growers are Georges Vernay, Paul Multrier at Château de Rozay and Jean Pinchon.

CONEGLIANO

Conegliano in the Veneto, is the home of Italy's leading oenology school, as well as the Istituto Sperimentale per la Viticoltura, where they experiment on clonal selection, cross-breeding and other aspects of viticultural research.

CONFRÉRIE DES CHEVALIERS DU TASTEVIN

Founded in 1934 by Camille Rodier and Georges Faiveley to promote 'the wines of Burgundy in general and the wines of Nuits in particular'. The first banquet was held on the eve of the 1934 Hospices de Beaune sale and this event is now the first of Les Trois Glorieuses. It is one of twenty or so dinners held by the Confrérie throughout the year at Clos de Vougeot. The Confrérie also awards special labels to wines that prove to be outstanding examples of their appellation in a blind tasting.

CONFRÉRIE DES VIGNERONS DE OISLY ET THESÉE   Loire: FRANCE

A young, go-ahead growers' cooperative dealing in the appellation of Touraine and making successful whites from Sauvignon, Chenin Blanc and Chardonnay grapes and red from Cabernet Franc, Malbec and Gamay.

CONN CREEK WINERY   California: USA

A Napa Valley property, producing fine Cabernet Sauvignon, as well as Zinfandel and Chardonnay. Chateau Maja is a second label.

CONNECTICUT   USA

Connecticut has just one winery, Haight Vineyards, with *vitis vinifera* and hybrid grapes.

CONNÉTABLE TALBOT   See Talbot.

CONO

A term used in Valencia and Málaga to describe large oak storage vats which are elsewhere in Spain called *tinos*.

LA CONSEILLANTE
Bordeaux: FRANCE

Despite the lack of official classification, la Conseillante is considered to be one of the top Pomerol wines. It is next to Pétrus but the wine is different as it has more Cabernet Franc grapes in the *encépagement*. The N on the label represents the Nicolas family who have owned the *château* for several generations.

CONSEJO REGULADOR

The body that controls the production of a wine in a demarcated area of Spain. The first was set up in Rioja in 1926.

CONSORZIO

The Italian term for a consortium, describes a voluntary group of producers who work together to maintain the quality of their wine and to market it. The most important example is the Chianti Classico Consorzio which laid down the guidelines for the introduction of the DOC regulations in Italy.

CONSTANTIA
SOUTH AFRICA

The most southern Wine of Origin region of the Cape. Van Riebeeck's first vineyard was here near Table Mountain, but many of the original vineyards have now disappeared under the growing city of Cape Town. The estate of Groot Constantia remains a flourishing reminder of the past. A highly esteemed dessert or Liqueur Muscat of Constantia was produced in the early 19th century.

GIACOMO CONTERNO   Piedmont: ITALY

A 200 year old family company noted for its fine Barolo.

CONTINUOUS PRESS

May be used when quantity rather than quality is the winemaker's prime criterion. As the name implies, the pressing of the grapes is a continual operation, with grapes put in at one end of a cylindrical chamber, with an archimedes screw device, and juice flowing out at the other end. The *marc* is often damaged by the press and can produce fairly unsatisfactory results.

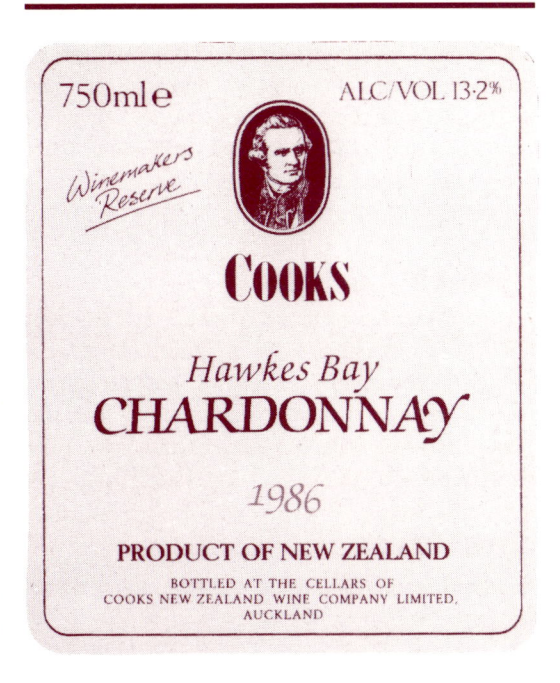

GUISEPPE CONTRATTO
Piedmont: ITALY

An important family firm, making a full range of Alba wines, including Asti Spumante and other *spumante*. It is especially noted for Contratto Brut Reserve.

COOKS
NEW ZEALAND

One of New Zealand's most important wineries, especially on the export market, which came to prominence in the 1970s. It is based at Te Kauwhata in the Waikato region, with a modern streamlined winery, handling grapes from Gisborne and Hawkes Bay growers. Their white wines, notably Chardonnay and Gewürztraminer are good. Cabernet Sauvignon has had some success.

COOLER

A fairly recent concoction, developed in the United States with the demand for low alcohol drinks. It is usually wine-based, but flavoured with fruit juice and often diluted with soda water.

COONAWARRA
AUSTRALIA

One of the most important regions of Australia; an isolated area in the state of South Australia, near the Victoria border. In Aborigine the name means wild honeysuckle. The climate is favourable to viticulture with mild summers, cool winters and less hours of sunshine than anywhere else in Australia. Vintages can vary considerably. The soil is distinctive too, with the famous terra rossa of Coonawarra. The wines are amongst the best Australia has to offer, with fine Cabernet Sauvignon and Shiraz and some elegant Rhine Riesling. There are numerous successful estates including Wynns, Redman and Rouge Homme.

COOPER

A person who makes and repairs barrels. The craft nearly died out as barrels were discarded in favour of concrete or stainless steel vats, but the current fashion for new oak barrels is maintaining the craft. Some Bordeaux *châteaux* such as Lafite have their own cooper.

COOPERAGE

A general term for the repair and manufacture of casks.

COPERTINO   Apulia: ITALY

A red and *rosato* DOC, made from Negroamaro grapes grown at Copertino. The red becomes a *riserva* after two years and improves further in the bottle.

COPITA

The traditional narrow sherry glass.

COPPER CASSE

Or *cuprous casse* occurs in wine containing a small amount of protein and copper, when it is kept in a warm light place and exposed to air. Fining with bentonite is the remedy.

CORBANS   NEW ZEALAND

An important New Zealand wine company in Henderson, dating back to 1902. More recently they have expanded to Gisborne and Marlborough. Their wines come under three names, Corbans, Riverlea and Robard & Butler. Whites are better than reds.

CORBIÈRES   The Midi: FRANCE

One of the most important wines of the Midi and promoted in 1985 to *appellation contrôlée*. It is mainly red with a little white and rosé, coming from a large area in the Aude to the south east of the town of Carcassonne. The principal grape varieties are those of the Mediterranean, Carignan, Cinsaut, Grenache and Mourvèdre but some Syrah has also been planted. The introduction of *macération carbonique* has improved the standard of wine-making and good Corbières can be a rich, solid wine, especially if it has been aged in oak. Sadly there is still an abundance of indifferent Corbières, despite a drastic reduction with the introduction of *appellation contrôlée*.

CORBIÈRES SUPÉRIEURES
The Midi: FRANCE

Used to denote a slightly better quality of wine, but the term has been discontinued.

CORBIN   Bordeaux: FRANCE

A Grand Cru Classé of St-Émilion. The property was once part of a larger domaine belonging to the Black Prince.

CORBIN-MICHOTTE   Bordeaux: FRANCE

A little-known Grand Cru Classé of the *graves* part of St-Émilion.

CORDIER

An important *négociant* house in Bordeaux and owner of several important *châteaux*: Gruaud Larose, Talbot, Meyney, Cantemerle, Lafaurie Peyraguey and Clos des Jacobins.

CORDON

A method of pruning and training the vine. The trunk of the vine is usually parallel to the ground, supported by a wire, with branches growing off the trunk. *Guyot* is the most common form of *cordon* training.

CORK

The traditional stopper of a wine bottle. It comes from the bark of the cork oak tree, which mainly grows in Spain and Portugal but is also grown in other parts of the world, such as North Africa and southern Europe. The significant characteristic of cork is its resistance to humidity and its ability to prevent air from entering a bottle, while allowing the wine to breathe and mature in the bottle. A good cork is essential as the continuing quality of a wine depends upon it. It should be as non-porous as possible, tight and springy with very few markings. It is now possible to find artificial plastic corks, and agglomerated corks, composed of tiny pieces of cork glued together.

CORKAGE

The fee charged by a restaurant for serving the customer's own bottle of wine.

CORKSCREW

The device used for extracting a cork from a wine bottle. At its simplest, it is a cylindrical screw on a handle. The coil should be wide enough to ensure that there is sufficient grip to pull the cork out of the bottle without damaging it. Corkscrews used to be much more sophisticated than they are now and old ones form important collectors' items.

CORNAS   Rhône: FRANCE

A full-bodied red wine produced in the northern Rhône from the Syrah grape, from vineyards around the village of the same name. Wine has been made in the village for over a thousand years. Today the production is very small; methods are traditional and the wine is aged for several months in oak. The best growers are Auguste Clape, Robert Michel, Guy de Barjac and Marcel Juge.

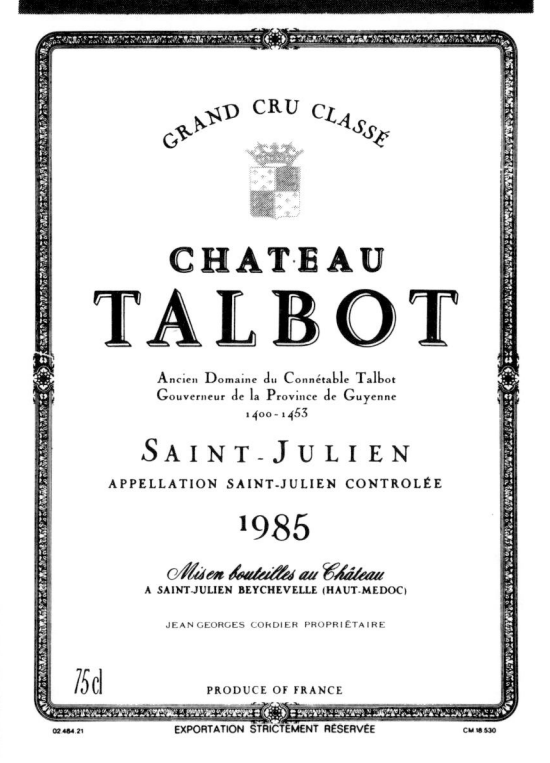

CORDON DE ROYAT

One of the methods of pruning allowed in Champagne. A single branch is trained horizontally about two feet from the ground, off which grape-bearing shoots grow.

CORENT   Loire: FRANCE

A pink crus of the Côtes d'Auvergne.

CORI   Latium: ITALY

A little-known DOC wine produced around the town of Cori. The red comes from Montepulciano, Nero Buono di Cori and Cesanese grapes. The white, from Trebbiano and Malvasia, can be dry, medium sweet or sweet.

CORIA   Sicily: ITALY

The most individual table wine maker of Sicily, with vineyards in the DOC of Cerasuolo di Vittoria. They make unique wines aged in barrel for several years, such as Stravecchio Siciliano.

CORTESE

A rather neutral grape grown in Piedmont, where it makes Gavi dei Gavi, as well as Cortese dei Colli Tortonesi and Cortese dell'Alto Monferrato. It is also found in Lombardy for white Oltrepò Pavese and in the Veneto as a part of the blend of Bianco di Custoza.

CORTESE DELL'ALTO MONFERRATO   Piedmont: ITALY

A pale dry white DOC wine from the Cortese grape grown in vineyards in the Alto Monferrato hills. It can also be *frizzante* or *spumante*.

CORTESE DI GAVI   Piedmont: ITALY

A notable white DOC wine made from the Cortese grape, which is at its most successful around the town of Gavi. It may also be *frizzante* or *spumante*.

CORTON   Burgundy: FRANCE

A vineyard situated mainly in the village of Aloxe-Corton, but also overlapping Pernand Vergelesses and Ladoix Serrigny. It is actually not one vineyard, but several, one of which is called Le Corton. All these vineyards are of Grand Cru quality, making Corton the largest Burgundy Grand Cru, and all can call their wine simply Corton, or Corton plus the name of the *climat* such as Corton Bressandes. Most of the wine is red. The full list of these wines is as follows: les Vergennes, le Rognet et Corton, le Clos du Roi, les Renardes, les Bressandes, les Maréchaudes (part), en Pauland (part), les Chaumes, la Vigne au Saint, les Meix Lallemand, les Meix (part), les Combes (part), le Charlemagne (part), les Pougets (part), les Languettes (part), les Chaumes de la Voirosse, les Frêtres, les Perrières and les Grèves.

There is a local proverb which says, 'Give a dumb man a glass of old Corton and he will chatter like a magpie.'

CORTON CHARLEMAGNE
                Burgundy: FRANCE

A Grand Cru white Burgundy, second only to Le Montrachet, produced mainly in the village of Aloxe-Corton but also in Pernand-Vergelesses and Ladoix-Serrigny. There is an apocryphal story as to the origins of the vineyard. The Emperor Charlemagne apparently took great delight in drinking the wine from his vineyard at Corton, but it tended to stain his snow-white beard, so to avoid this happening, he planted vines to produce white wine.

COROWA   AUSTRALIA

The southernmost wine region of New South Wales, adjacent to Rutherglen in Victoria and also with a reputation for sweet fortified wines. It is especially connected with Lindeman who make an excellent range of port and sherry styles and muscats.

CORSÉ

The French term for a full-bodied but immature wine.

CORSICA

The island of Corsica has an appellation to cover the whole island, Vin de Corse, including five smaller areas within the main one, namely Calvi, Coteaux du Cap Corse, Figari, Porto Vecchio and Sartène, as well as two separate appellations, Ajaccio and Patrimonio. The vin de pays de l'Ile de Beauté also covers the whole island. Grape varieties are a mixture of the traditionally Corsican Vermentino, which is also called Malvoisie de Corse, for white wine and Sciacarello and Nielluccio for red and rosé wine, as well as the grapes of the Midi, Cinsaut, Grenache and Carignan which were planted on a considerable scale by the *pied noirs* returning from Algeria. More forward looking growers are experimenting with Chardonnay, Chenin Blanc, Merlot and Cabernet Sauvignon with some success. Some good vin doux naturel is made in Cap Corse and around Patrimonio from the Muscat grape.

CORTAILLOD   SWITZERLAND

The best village name of the canton of Neuchâtel.

CORTON-GRANCEY   Burgundy: FRANCE

The name under which the house of Louis Latour sells its production of Corton. There is no vineyard with this name; Château de Grancey is the name of their property in Aloxe-Corton.

CORVINA

The most important grape for Valpolicella, accounting for up to 70% of the blend, as well as appearing in other Veneto reds such as Bardolino.

CORVO   Sicily: ITALY

The brand name of Sicily's leading wine produced by the Duca di Salaparuta company. Corvo Bianco, a fresh dry wine made from Inzolia, Trebbiano and Catarratto grapes comes in two versions: Marca Verde Prima Goccia and a more elegant Colomba Platino. Corvo Rosso, a fruity red, is made from Nerello Mascalese, Perricone and Nero d'Avola. Corvo Spumante, coming from the same grapes as Corvo Bianco, is dry or medium dry and Corvo Stravecchio di Sicilia is a fortified wine made from Inzolia, Cataratto and Grillo grapes aged in wood for several years.

COS D'ESTOURNEL   Bordeaux: FRANCE

A second growth St-Estèphe. The exotic Chinese façade of Cos d'Estournel houses not a *château* but the *chais*. The wine is generally considered to be the best of St-Estèphe with flavour and vigour. It is owned by the Prats family.

COS LABORY   Bordeaux: FRANCE

A fifth growth St-Estèphe, a small, relatively-unknown property making sound wine.

COSECHA

The Spanish term for vintage or harvest.

COSSART GORDON

One of the great names of Madeira, founded in 1745 and now part of the Madeira Wine Company. Good Company is a brand name for some of their wines.

COSTA DEL SEGRE   SPAIN

A new D.O. covering the area of Lérida in north west Catalonia. Raimat is the most important producer.

COSTIÈRES DU GARD   The Midi: FRANCE

A tricolour A.C. from the *département* of the Gard, from a large area of arid vineyards between Nimes and Montpellier. The red wines are made from Carignan (maximum 50%), with Cinsaut, and an increasing amount of Mourvèdre, Syrah and Grenache. Some rosé is made and a tiny amount of white wine from Grenache Blanc, Bourboulenc and Ugni Blanc. The regional cooperatives are the main producers, but there are an increasing number of domaines making some very good wine.

COT

A synonym for the Malbec grape.

CÔTE

Means 'hill' or 'slope' in French. Many of the better French vineyards are on slopes and the word is often incorporated into the name of the appellation, eg. Côte de Beaune, Côtes de Duras.

LA CÔTE   SWITZERLAND

One of the three main wine regions in the canton of the Vaud, covering the lakeside vineyards between Geneva and Lausanne. They are planted mainly with Gamay and Fendant grapes.

CÔTE DE BEAUNE   Burgundy: FRANCE

The southern half of the Côte d'Or. It is made up of twenty villages, most of which give their name to a wine. From north to south they are: Pernand Vergelesses, Aloxe-Corton, Chorey-les-Beaune, Savigny-les-Beaune, Beaune, Pommard, Volnay, Monthelie, Auxey-Duresses, Meursault, Blagny, Puligny-Montrachet, St-Romain, St-Aubin, Chassagne-Montrachet, Ladoix-Serrigny, Santenay, Dezizes-les-Maranges, Cheilly-les-Maranges, Sampigny-les-Maranges. The last three were rarely found under their own name and are now grouped together under one appellation, Les Maranges. Unlike the Côte de Nuits, the Côte de Beaune produces both red and white wine of equally distinguished quality. The attractive town of Beaune is the heart of the area and the home of the famous Hospices de Beaune.

There is also an appellation Côte de Beaune, which was created in 1937 at the same time as Côte de Beaune Villages in a vain attempt to clarify a confusion of names. The appellation only covers wine from the commune of Beaune, produced on the hills above the town. La Grande Châtelaine is the best-known vineyard of the appellation, but it is rarely seen.

CÔTE DE BEAUNE VILLAGES   Burgundy: FRANCE

Sixteen of the villages of the Côte de Beaune may sell their red wine under the label Côte de Beaune Villages, the four exceptions being Aloxe-Corton, Beaune, Pommard and Volnay. This system has two distinct advantages: it permits a shipper to blend the wines of two or more villages, thus combining their different qualities, say a tougher with a more elegant wine, and also enables production of a large quantity of wine with the same characteristics under the same name. It is also much easier for the less well-known villages of Dezizes-les-Maranges. Cheilly-les-Maranges and Sampigny-les-Maranges to sell their wine under the Côte de Beaune Villages label rather than as Les Maranges.

COTE DES BLANCS   Champagne: FRANCE

One of the three main areas of Champagne. As the name implies, the vineyards are planted with white grapes, namely Chardonnay. The main villages, in their respective categories, are:
Catégorie Hors Classe; Avize, Cramant
Première Catégorie; le Mesnil sur Oger, Oger, Oiry
Deuxième Catégorie; Bergères-les-Vertus, Chouilly, Vertus.

CÔTE BLONDE   Rhône: FRANCE

One of the two main slopes of the Côte Rôtie; the other being the Côte Brune. Local legend has it that in feudal times the owner of the Château d'Ampuis had two beautiful daughters, one with blond hair and the other with brown hair and when he split his property between them, the slopes were named according to the colour of the girls' hair. Most growers' Côte Rôtie is a blend of wine from both slopes.

CÔTE DE BROUILLY

One of the ten Beaujolais Crus with a right to a separate appellation. The vineyards are situated in parts of the villages of Odénas, Saint-Lagar, Cercié and Quincié.

CÔTE BRUNE   Rhône: FRANCE

One of the two main slopes of the Côte Rôtie; the other being the Côte Blonde. Local legend has it that in feudal times the owner of the Château d'Ampuis had two beautiful daughters, one with blond hair and the other with brown hair and when he split his property between them, the slopes were named according to the colour of the girls' hair. Most growers' Côte Rôtie is a blend of wine from both slopes.

CÔTE CHALONNAISE   Burgundy: FRANCE

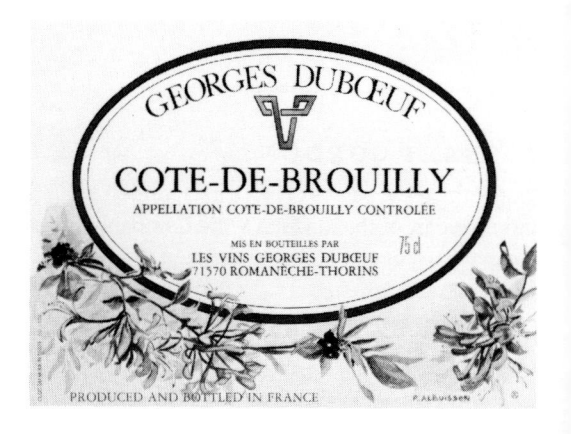

Part of Burgundy, between the Côte d'Or and the Mâconnais. The vineyards are a geographical continuation of the Côte d'Or, stretching from the village of Chagny in the north to Jully-les-Buxy in the south. Four villages give their names to the four main appellations of the area: Rully, Givry, Mercurey and Montagny. Montagny produces solely white wine; Givry and Mercurey red and very occasionally white, and Rully both red and white. The region can also be called the Région de Mercurey. This is an area that suffered particularly from the phylloxera crisis. Also, the casualties of the First World War caused considerable depopulation. It was only in the 1970s that the area was partially replanted and it now provides good alternatives to the more expensive wines of the Côte d'Or. The grape varieties are principally Chardonnay for white wine and Pinot Noir for red wine. Crémant de Bourgogne or Bourgogne Mousseux and Passe-Tous-Grains are also produced.

CÔTE DE FONTENAY   See Fourchaume.

CÔTE DE LÉCHET   Burgundy: FRANCE
A Premier Cru Chablis vineyard.

CÔTE DE NUITS   Burgundy: FRANCE
The northern half of the Côte d'Or, running from the suburbs of Dijon to the village of Corgoloin. The centre of the Côte is, not surprisingly, the town of Nuits St-Georges. The Côte de Nuits produces, almost entirely, red wines which tend to be fuller and more substantial than the elegant, lighter wines of the Côte de Beaune. The Côte de Nuits is indisputably the home of the greatest of red Burgundies, sometimes described as 'regal reds'. It is smaller than the Côte de Beaune, with a narrower strip of vineyards on steeper slopes. The villages that make up the Côte de Nuits are: Marsannay, Couchey, Fixin, Brochon, Gevrey-Chambertin, Morey St-Denis, Chambolle-Musigny, Vougeot, Flagey-Echézeaux, Vosne-Romanée, Nuits St-Georges, Prissey, Comblanchien and Corgoloin.

CÔTE DE NUITS VILLAGES   Burgundy: FRANCE
Contrary to what one might expect, this is not a parallel appellation to Côte de Beaune Villages, and although the wine is usually red, it may also be white. Seven villages used to make up the appellation: Marsannay, Couchey, Fixin and Brochon at the northern end of the Côte de Nuits, and Prissey, Comblanchien and Corgoloin at the southern end. However, as from 1987, Marsannay has its own appellation for red, white and rosé wine.

CÔTE DES PRÈS GIROTS   See Les Fourneaux.

CÔTE D'OR   Burgundy: FRANCE
Literally means 'the golden slope' where the finest red and white Burgundies are made from the Pinot Noir and Chardonnay grapes respectively. It is also the name of the *département*. The area is sub-divided into the Côte de Beaune and Côte de Nuits; in all it is a 30 mile line of hills running south from Marsannay on the outskirts of Dijon, to the village of Santenay at the bottom of the Côte de Beaune. The soil is predominantly limestone and the vines are grown on east and southeast facing slopes. The climate is continental, with hard winters and warm summers.

Vines were first brought here by the Romans; in the Middle Ages, the Cistercian Abbey of Citeaux played an important part in the development of the vineyards, notably with its ownership of Clos Vougeot. The Dukes of Burgundy also helped to establish the reputation of the Côte d'Or wines.

CÔTES ROANNAISES   Loire: FRANCE
A VDQS wine from around the town of Roanne in the upper reaches of the Loire. Light red and a little rosé are made from the Gamay grape and have a resemblance to Beaujolais.

CÔTE RÔTIE   Rhône: FRANCE
One of the finest red wines of the northern Rhône. Its name means literally "roasted slope" and the vines are grown on steep terraced slopes below the town of Vienne. The village of Ampuis is the centre of this small vineyard. The grape variety is Syrah and a small percentage of Viognier also used to be added to soften the wine, but this practice is now less usual. The main vineyard slope is split into the Côte Brune and the Côte Blonde; most growers' wines are a blend of both. Côte Rôtie well repays

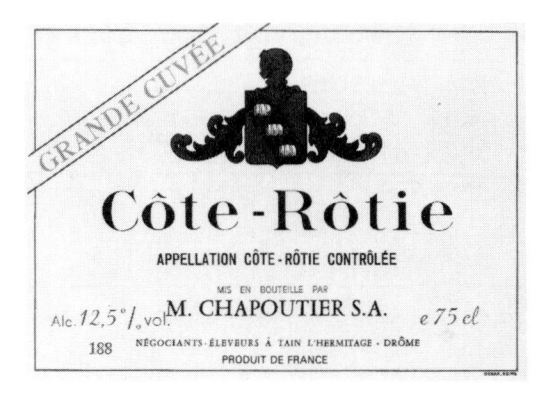

ageing in bottle. The best known growers include E. Guigal, Robert Jasmin, Marius Gentaz-Dervieux, Pierre Barge and Edmond Duclaux.

CÔTE ST-JACQUES Burgundy: FRANCE

All that remains of a once-famous vineyard at Joigny in northern Burgundy. The existing vineyard is much reduced in size. Traditionally, the vineyard produces a *vin gris* from Pinot Gris and the present owner also makes some red and white wine from Pinot Noir and Chardonnay.

CÔTE DE SÉZANNE Champagne: FRANCE

A growing area of Champagne to the south of the Côte des Blancs, which is particularly suitable for Chardonnay.

CÔTE VERMEILLE Midi: FRANCE

A recent vin de pays created in 1987 to cover wines made around Banuyls and Collioure. All three colours can be made.

COTEAU

Means 'slope' or 'hillside' in French. Many of the better French vineyards are on slopes and the word is often incorporated into their names, eg. Coteaux d'Aix en Provence, Coteaux de Tricastin.

COTEAUX D'AIX-EN-PROVENCE
Provence: FRANCE

Coteaux d'Aix-en-Provence is a recently elevated (since 1985) appellation of Provence, a red, white and rosé wine produced from vineyards covering a large area around the town of Aix-en-Provence, as far as Les Baux, where there is a separate sub-division of the appellation, with the long-winded name of Coteaux d'Aix-en-Provence – Coteaux des Baux-en-Provence. Nearly half the appellation is red, using mainly Grenache, Cinsaut, Cabernet Sauvignon and Syrah. White wine is made from Clairette, Grenache Blanc, Ugni Blanc and Sauvignon. Well vinified whites and rosés are light and fresh; reds are sometimes aged in wood and are fruity, with good structure. Château Vignelaure is the most individual estate; Domaine de Trévallon fails to conform to the appellation regulations as there is no Grenache in the vineyards. Château Fonscolombe, Château Calissanne, Château Bas and others make sound enjoyable wine.

COTEAUX D'ANCENIS Loire: FRANCE

A VDQS wine from around the town of Ancenis in the lower reaches of the Loire. It is predominantly red and rosé, made mainly from Gamay and a little Cabernet. The tiny amount of white comes from either the Chenin Blanc or Malvoisie grape.

COTEAUX DE L'AUBANCE
Loire: FRANCE

Coteaux de l'Aubance in the Loire Valley, takes its name from the Aubance river to the south of Angers. The wine is white, made only from the Chenin Blanc grape and comes in varying degrees of sweetness.

COTEAUX DES BAUX-EN-PROVENCE Provence: FRANCE

Comes within the appellation of Coteaux d'Aix-en-Provence. A small number of properties with vineyards around the dramatic Alpilles of Les Baux are allowed to put both names on their labels. The principal grape varieties are Grenache, Cinsaut, Syrah, Cabernet Sauvignon, Ugni Blanc and Sauvignon. Important producers include Domaine des Terres Blanches, Mas de la Dame, Domaine de Trévallon and Mas Gourgonnier.

COTEAUX DE CAP CORSE CORSICA

One of the separate areas within the overall appellation of Vin de Corse. The wine is mainly dry white, from the local Malvoisie de Corse and the production is now tiny, when once this northern promontory of the island was covered with vines. Some *vin doux naturel* is also made from the Muscat grape, but is not as yet entitled to an appellation. Clos Nicrosi is the best producer.

COTEAUX DE CARTHAGE   TUNISIA

A standard wine from the U.C.C.V.T., coming in three colours. Red is best.

COTEAUX DU GIENNOIS
Loire: FRANCE

A tricolour VDQS wine produced in the *départements* of the Loiret and Nièvre, mainly around the town of Gien. The white comes from Sauvignon and Chenin Blanc grapes; Gamay and Pinot Noir make the red and rosé.

COTEAUX DU LANGUEDOC
The Midi: FRANCE

A new appellation dating from 1985, and incorporating the previous VDQS of La Clape, Picpoul de Pinet, Cabrières, Coteaux de la Méjanelle, Coteaux de Vérargues, Coteaux de St-Christol, Montpeyroux, Pic St-Loup, Quatourze, St-Dézery, St-Georges d'Orques and St-Saturnin, as well as the appellations of Faugères and St-Chinian. Both names appear on the label. In addition it can include any other appellation vineyards for all three colours in this vast area of the Midi, stretching virtually from Narbonne to Nîmes. The proponents of Côteaux du Languedoc see it as a regional appellation, with several individual crus. Carignan is still the main grape variety but the wines are improving with increasing amounts of Grenache, Syrah and Mourvèdre.

COTEAUX DU LAYON   *Loire*: FRANCE

A sweet white wine from the Loire valley produced, as the name implies, on the banks of the river Layon, and mainly the north bank. The grape variety is Chenin Blanc; the permitted yield only 30 hectolitres per hectare and the growers hope for noble rot to make rich honeyed wines. Six communes have the designation Coteaux du Layon Villages, with the name of the village on the label too. They are Beaulieu sur Layon, Faye d'Anjou, Rablay sur Layon, Rochefort sur Loire, Saint Aubin de Luigné and Saint Lambert de Lattay. The seventh commune of Chaume has the separate identity of Coteaux du Layon Chaume. All must have a minimum of 12° alcohol instead of 11° for Coteaux du Layon.

COTEAUX DU LOIR   *Loire*: FRANCE

A tricolour wine from the Loire valley, produced from vineyards on the banks of the tributary river Loir. The white wine is similar to Jasnières, a dry wine from the Chenin Blanc grape. The red wine is made from Pinot d'Aunis, Cabernet, Gamay and Malbec. The rosé may include some Groslot.

COTEAUX DU LYONNAIS
Burgundy: FRANCE

An A.C. wine produced from vineyards south west of the city of Lyon in the *département* of the Rhône. Most of the wine is made from the Gamay grape and there is also a little *rosé*. Some white is produced from Chardonnay and Aligoté.

COTEAUX DU MASCARA   ALGERIA

One of the seven quality zones in the southeast of Oran, producing powerful reds, often wood-aged, and dry whites.

COTEAUX DE LA MÉJANELLE
The Midi: FRANCE

Formerly an obscure VDQS, Coteaux de la Méjanelle, or simply Méjanelle, is now part of the all-embracing appellation of Coteaux du Languedoc, coming from vineyards just east of Montpellier. Carignan, Cinsaut and Grenache grapes make a solid, heady wine.

COTEAUX DE PIERREVERT
Provence: FRANCE

A little known VDQS in the département of the Alpes-de-Haute-Provence, centred on the village of Pierrevert. The local cooperative members grow the traditional grapes of the area, Grenache, Syrah, Cinsaut, Mourvèdre, Ugni Blanc and Clairette, while a more adventurous grower at Domaine de Régusse is experimenting with other grapes, including Cabernet Sauvignon, Pinot Noir, Chardonnay and Aligoté, with some success. This is an area in transition.

COTEAUX DE SAINT-CHRISTOL
The Midi: FRANCE

Formerly a VDQS, Coteaux de St-Christol, or simply St-Christol, is now part of the new all-embracing appellation of the Coteaux du Languedoc, a red wine from vineyards around the village of the same name near Montpellier. Carignan, Cinsaut and Grenache grapes make a light fruity wine.

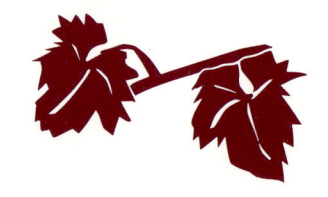

COTEAUX DE SAUMUR Loire: FRANCE

A semi-sweet white wine made only from the Chenin Blanc grape, produced in the vineyards around Saumur. The area of production is smaller than for Saumur Blanc, and the permitted yield lower at 30 hectolitres per hectare, as opposed to 45 hectolitres. The alcohol level is a minimum of 12°, compared to 10° for Saumur Blanc.

COTEAUX DE TLEMCEN MOROCCO

One of the seven quality wine zones in a region of sandstone hills close to the Moroccan border, producing strong reds, dry whites and rosés.

COTEAUX DU TRICASTIN Rhône: FRANCE

A wine of the Rhône Valley that has undergone a considerable revival since the late 1950's and was promoted to VDQS status in 1964. The vineyards are between Montélimar and Bollène. The main grape varieties are Grenache, Cinsaut, Syrah, Mourvèdre and Carignan. The production is almost entirely red, which is best drunk when it is two or three years old, and an occasional rosé or white. The best-known estate is Domaine de Grangeneuve.

COTEAUX D'UTIQUE TUNISIA

Produced near the sea north of Tunis, this is one of the better Tunisian reds, notably Domaine Karim made by the Société Lomblot and Château Feriani.

COTEAUX VAROIS Provence: FRANCE

A newly promoted VDQS from Provence, from the centre of the *département* of the Var, around the town of Brignoles. The grape varieties are those of Provence, mainly Grenache, Cinsaut, Mourvèdre and Carignan for red and rosé. No white is made. Some innovative estates are experimenting with Cabernet Sauvignon and Syrah.

COTEAUX DU VENDÔMOIS Loire: FRANCE

A VDQS wine from the Loire, from around the town of Vendôme. The whites are made from Chenin Blanc and a maximum of 20% Chardonnay, the rosé from Pinot d'Aunis and a maximum of 20% Gamay and the red from a minimum of 30% Pinot d'Aunis plus Gamay, Pinot Noir, Cabernet Franc and Cabernet Sauvignon.

COTEAUX DE VÉRARGUES The Midi: FRANCE

Formerly a VDQS, Coteaux de Vérargues is now part of the all-embracing new appellation of the Coteaux du Languedoc, red and rosé wine from around Lunel, north east of Montpellier. Carignan is the main grape variety, as well as Grenache, Cinsaut and occasionally Aramon. These are sunny, uncomplicated wines.

COTES D'AGLY The Midi: FRANCE

A *vin doux naturel* from the *département* of the Aude, rarely made now. The principal grape varieties are Grenache and Muscat.

CÔTES D'AUVERGNE Loire: FRANCE

A VDQS wine from the Upper reaches of the Loire, coming from vineyards around Clermont Ferrand. The reds, made from Gamay and a little Pinot Noir, are not dissimilar to Beaujolais. The rosés are also made from the same grapes and the white, from Chardonnay, is virtually non-existent. The better communes of the appellation have the right to add their name to the label, namely Boudes, Châteaugay, Chanturgue, Corent and Médargues as eg. Côtes d'Auvergne Boudes.

COTES DE BERGERAC SOUTH WEST FRANCE

Can be red or white. If red, the difference from simple Bergerac is one of alcoholic degree, 11° versus 10°, with a slightly lower yield permitted per hectare. Generally, Côtes de Bergerac Rouge is considered to be a slightly longer-lived wine.

Côtes de Bergerac Blanc is distinguished from Bergerac Sec by the slight amount of sugar left in the wine so that the taste is medium dry rather than dry. Côtes de Bergerac Moelleux has an even higher level of residual sugar.

CÔTES DE BLAYE
Bordeaux: FRANCE

One of the three appellations of Blaye covering white wine made from Sauvignon and Sémillon grapes. It is similar to Blayais.

CÔTES DE BORDEAUX
Bordeaux: FRANCE

Not an appellation but an umbrella name for the outlying appellations of Premières Côtes de Bordeaux, Côtes de Castillon, Côtes de Blaye, Côtes de Bourg and Côtes de Francs.

CÔTES DE BORDEAUX ST-MACAIRE
Bordeaux: FRANCE

An appellation for semi-sweet white wine in Bordeaux, covering ten villages adjoining Ste-Croix-du-Mont. It is rarely seen.

CÔTES DE BOURG
Bordeaux: FRANCE

A lesser Bordeaux appellation of mainly red wine produced in vineyards on the right bank of the Gironde opposite the Médoc. The wines are made mainly from Merlot and Cabernet Franc grapes which produce some sound quicker-maturing claret. The town of Bourg was once an important port and houses the ruins of a Vauban fortress. The best-known properties include de Barbe, de Bousquet, Eyquem, Mendoce, Mille Secousses, Plaisance, Rousset, Tayac and Falfas. Very little white wine is made under the appellation.

CÔTES DE BRULHOIS
SOUTH WEST FRANCE

Côtes de Brulhois is a predominantly red VDQS wine from around the small town of Layrac in the Lot et Garonne. The main grape varieties are Cabernet Sauvignon, Cabernet Franc and Tannat, as well as Malbec, Fer Servadou and Merlot.

CÔTES DE BUZET
SOUTH WEST FRANCE

Since 1988 called simply Buzet. A Bordelais style of wine. It is predominantly red, though can be white or rosé. The grape varieties are Cabernet Sauvignon and Franc and Merlot for red and rosé and Sauvignon, Sémillon and Muscadelle for white. The production comes mainly from the regional cave cooperative at Buzet-sur-Baise, which was responsible for the revival of the wine so that it became AC in 1973. This cave cooperative has one of the largest cellars for oak ageing of any cooperative in France, as well as its own cooper, and its wines are found under the label Cuvée Napoléon and two individual properties, Château de Bouchet and Château de Gueyze.

CÔTES DU CABARDÈS ET DE L'ORBIEL
The Midi: FRANCE

An alternative name for Cabardès.

CÔTES DE CANON-FRONSAC
Bordeaux: FRANCE

The smaller part of the vineyards of the village of Fronsac, situated on the higher slopes where the soil is thinner, with more lime. The appellation is one of the best of the minor areas of Bordeaux. Principal *châteaux* are Canon, Canon de Brem, Junayme, Vrai-Canon-Bouché and Vray-Canon-Boyer.

CÔTES DE CASTILLON
Bordeaux: FRANCE

One of the peripheral Bordelais appellations with the full title of Bordeaux Côtes de Castillon, or Bordeaux Supérieur Côtes de Castillon. It is a neighbour to St-Émilion, was once called St-Émilionais and the better wines resemble those of the satellite villages of St-Émilion. Castillon-la-Bataille, at the centre of the appellation, is where John Talbot, Earl of Shrewsbury, lost Gascony to the French in 1453. Château de Pitray is a reputable and consistent property.

CÔTES DE DURAS
SOUTH WEST FRANCE

An AC wine produced in the Lot et Garonne, just across the *départemental* boundary from the Gironde. The vineyards are a natural continuation of the Entre-Deux-Mers and are situated around the attractive town of Duras. Until recently the appellation was predominantly white. Red wine has been introduced only over the last twenty years. The grape varieties are those of Bordeaux, Sauvignon, Sémillon and a little Muscadelle for whites; Cabernet Sauvignon, Merlot, a little Cabernet Franc and Malbec for reds and rosés. The white is usually dry, but can be sweet; reds are not intended to have a long life.

CÔTES DU FOREZ   Loire: FRANCE

A red and rosé VDQS wine of the upper reaches of the Loire valley, not far from Lyon. It is made purely from the Gamay grape and is not dissimilar to a light Beaujolais.

CÔTES DE FRANCS   Bordeaux: FRANCE

As yet a little-known appellation of Bordeaux, neighbour to the Côtes de Castillon and producing similar wine.

CÔTES DE FRONTONNAIS
SOUTH WEST FRANCE

The Côtes du Frontonnais is a small but growing appellation with vineyards around the towns of Fronton and Villaudric, situated on a plateau north west of the city of Toulouse. The principal grape variety is the Négrette, which is peculiar to the area, and gives the wine its distinctive flavour. The appellation regulations dictate between 50% and 70% Negrette, which is usually blended with Syrah, Cabernet Franc, Cabernet Sauvignon, Cot, Gamay or Fer Servadou. The red wine is soft and fruity, ready to drink early; a little rosé is made but no white.

CÔTES DU JURA   Jura: FRANCE

The overall appellation of the Jura, covering all the vineyards not classified as Arbois, l'Etoile or Château-Chalon. The wines can be red, white or rosé, with *vin jaune, vin de paille* and sparkling *méthode champenoise* wine as well. The grape varieties are Chardonnay and Savagnin for white wine and Poulsard, Trousseau and Pinot Noir for red and rosé. The vineyards are around the town of Lons le Saunier; the area to the south is known as Le Sud Revermont and Arlay is an important village in the north.

CÔTES DE LUBÉRON   Rhône: FRANCE

A red, white or rosé wine produced in the *département* of the Vaucluse to the east of Avignon. The wines were once sold as Côtes du Rhône, but now have their own appellation. All three colours are best drunk young. The grape varieties are Syrah, Grenache, Cinsaut and Mourvedre for red and rosé and Clairette, Ugni Blanc, as well as Chardonnay and Sauvignon for white wine. The largest producer is the local cooperative; Château Val Joanis is a new innovatory estate.

CÔTES DE LA MALEPÈRE
The Midi: FRANCE

A red and rosé VDQS from the region of Carcassonne. Reds come mainly from the grape varieties Merlot, Malbec and Cinsaut (none more than 60% of the total) and Cabernet Sauvignon, Cabernet Franc, Grenache and Syrah (each limited to 30%). Rosés are made usually from Grenache and Cinsaut. This is the meeting point of the Midi and the south west with an unusual mixture of grape varieties.

CÔTES DU MARMENDAIS
SOUTH WEST FRANCE

A VDQS from around the town of Marmande. The red and rosé wines are made partly from Cabernet Sauvignon, Cabernet Franc and Merlot and partly from local grape varieties such as Fer Servadou and Abouriou as well as a little Syrah. The tiny production of dry white wine comes from Sauvignon with a little Sémillon and Muscadelle. All are intended for early drinking and the production is dominated by the two cave cooperatives at Cocumont and Beaupuy.

CÔTES DE MONTRAVEL
SOUTH WEST FRANCE

A white wine produced in a small area within the zone of Bergerac. It is slightly sweet, like Côtes de Bergerac, and is sometimes sold as Côtes de Bergerac, although of the Montravel appellations it is the most common.

LES CÔTES D'OLT   SOUTH WEST FRANCE

The principal brand name for the cave cooperative responsible for a third of the production of the appellation of Cahors.

CÔTES DE PROVENCE
Provence: FRANCE

The largest appellation of Provence, created in 1977, covering a considerable part of the *département* of the Var, with vineyards along the coast from west of Toulon towards St. Tropez and inland, as well as some in the Bouches du Rhône and one commune in the Alpes-Maritimes. The colour breakdown is 60% rosé, 35% red, 5% white, from 18,000 hectares of vines. A considerable variety of grapes are permitted: Grenache, Cinsaut and Tibouren for rosé; Mourvèdre, Carignan, now declining in favour of Cabernet Sauvignon and Syrah for red, and Ugni

Blanc, Clairette, Rolle and Sémillon for whites. Surprisingly Côtes de Provence has a classification of cru classé; this has more historical than quality significance and generally belongs to the early bottlers of the appellation. Quality in the appellation varies enormously; the cooperatives dominate the production, but the best wines come from individual estates, notably Domaines Ott, Château Minuty, Domaine de la Bernarde, Commanderie de Peyrassol. Château Ste. Rosaline is an old traditional estate. The wine is presented in a plethora of different bottle shapes, usually a variation on an amphora.

Rochegude, Rousset-les-Vignes, Sablet, St. Gervais, St. Maurice-sur-Eygues, St. Pantaléon-les-Vignes, Séguret, Vacqueyras, Valréas, Vinsobres, Visan.

Gigondas was elevated to an appellation of its own in 1971 and it may well be that Vacqueras will soon follow suit.

The objective of the appellation is to distinguish the wine from the sea of Côtes du Rhône by a higher alcoholic strength, lower yields and stricter regulations about production in general.

CÔTES DU RHÔNE
Rhône: FRANCE

Comes mainly from the southern Rhône Valley, from the *départements* of the Ardèche, Drôme, Gard and Vaucluse, where it accounts for 80% of the wine production of the area. It can be red, white or rosé, but most successfully red and the grape varieties may include any or all of the following: Grenache, Clairette, Syrah, Mouvèdre, Picpoul, Terret Noir, Counoise, Muscardine, Bourboulenc, Carignan, Ugni Blanc, Roussanne, Marsanne and Viognier. Much of the wine is made by village cooperatives; the *négociants* of the area produce sound wine too, but the best and more individual wines come from numerous single estates.

CÔTES DU RHÔNE VILLAGES
Rhône: FRANCE

In 1988 17 villages made up this wine in the southern Rhône. The appellation has existed since 1967. The wine can either be sold under a village name, or if the wine of two villages is blended together, it is labelled Côtes du Rhône Villages. The villages in question are: Beaumes de Venise, Cairanne, Chusclan, Laudun, Rasteau, Roaix,

CÔTES DU ROUSSILLON
The Midi: FRANCE

An appellation from the old French province of Roussillon which stretches from Perpignan to the Pyrénées. Reds and rosés are made from a mixture of 70% Carignan, plus mainly Cinsaut, Grenache, and Mourvèdre, while whites come from Maccabéo. There is some experimentation with reds, ageing in wood and vinification by *macération carbonique*. They are best drunk at two or three years when their fruit is at its peak.

CÔTES DU ROUSSILLON VILLAGES The Midi: FRANCE

A superior version of red Côtes du Roussillon from the best part of the area, with an alcohol level of at least 12° (as opposed to 11.5°) and a lower yield of 45 hectolitres per hectare, instead of 50 hectolitres.

CÔTES DE SAINT-MONT SOUTH WEST FRANCE

A VDQS wine from near the Pyrenees. The sole producer is the cave cooperative of Saint-Mont which is working to reestablish the reputation of this little-known wine. The red and rosé versions are made from Tannat, Cabernet Sauvignon and Franc grapes and the white from Gros and Petit Manseng, Petit Courbu and Arruffiac. The white is dry and fresh; the red light and fruity.

CÔTES DE TOUL NORTHEAST FRANCE

A VDQS from the hillsides around the town of Toul in the *département* of the Meurthe et Moselle in north east France. Most of the wine is vin gris or pale rosé, made mainly from the Gamay grape, plus a little Pinot Noir or Pinot Meunier. There is also some red and dry white.

CÔTES DU VENTOUX Rhône: FRANCE

A wine from the southern Rhône which takes its name from the situation of the vineyards along the southern slopes of Mont Ventoux. The wines, red white and rosé, were given their appellation in 1974, though sometimes there is little to distinguish them from the run of the mill wines of the Midi. The grape varieties are Grenache, Carignan, Cinsaut, Syrah and Mourvèdre for red and rosé and Clairette, Ugni Blanc and Bourboulenc for the tiny amount of white.

La Vieille Ferme and Domaine des Anges are the best labels.

CÔTES DU VIVARAIS Rhône: FRANCE

A wine from Ardèche *département* of the Rhône. It is usually red, but can also be rosé or white and is the only VDQS wine of the Ardèche. Grape varieties include Grenache, Cinsaut, Carignan and occasionally Syrah and Gamay. The wine is generally fruity and easy to drink.

CÔTES DE ZACCAR ALGERIA

One of the seven quality zones in the province of Alger, producing dry red wines and some well-made rosés.

COTESTI   See Fosani.

COTNARI ROMANIA

One of the most distinctive Romanian wines, a rich dessert wine made from a type of Furmint grape, grown around the town of Cotnari in north-eastern Moldavia.

COTTO   See Marsala.

COUFRAN Bordeaux: FRANCE

A Cru Grand Bourgeois in the commune of St-Seurnin and the last vineyard of the Haut-Médoc. It is made of 80% Merlot grapes and is therefore unusually soft.

COUHINS Bordeaux: FRANCE

A Graves from the commune of Villenave d'Ornon, classified only for its white wine. Some rosé is also made by its owners, the Lurton family, but no red wine.

COULANGES-LA-VINEUSE Burgundy: FRANCE

A village near Chablis in northern Burgundy producing an elegant red wine from the Pinot Noir grape. Technically, the appellation is Bourgogne Rouge, but the name Coulanges-la-Vineuse is tolerated on the label.

COULURE

A disorder of the vine, which can occur if the flowering takes place in unsatisfactory climatic conditions, usually sudden warmth, so that the sap is diverted from the tiny berries to the stalks of vine and the berries fail to develop. The resulting yield is very small.

COULY DUTHEUIL Loire: FRANCE

An important grower in Chinon and a *négociant* for other Loire wines. Their vineyards are Domaine de Turpensay, Domaine René Couly, Clos de l'Echo and Clos de l'Olive. Methods are modern.

COUNOISE

A synonym for the Aubun grape.

COUPAGE

Another term for blending wine. It has a pejorative ring, implying that the blending has been done to improve a mediocre wine and does not entail the skill of a Bordelais *assemblage*. In the Common Market, this describes the illegal blending of wine, for instance red with white wine, or across zones.

COUPÉ

Describes a wine that has been blended to render it palatable.

COURBU

A white grape grown in France. It is blended with Gros and Petit Manseng, to make Jurançon and also Pacherenc de Vic Bihl. Courbu Noir is a little known red grape variety occasionally found in Béarn and in the Pyrenees.

LA COURONNE — *Bordeaux*: FRANCE

A Cru Bourgeois Exceptionnel Pauillac belonging to the Borie family who are making wine comparable to many of the fifth growths of Pauillac.

COURT NOUÉ

Or 'fanleaf' in English, a virus causing a degeneration in the vine that is spread in the soil. There is no known remedy, apart from allowing the soil to lie fallow until the old roots die. It shortens the life of a vine, the leaves turn yellow and the yield is dramatically reduced.

COURTIER

The French term for a wine broker, who acts as a link between the small growers who may not bottle their wine, and the larger *négociants*.

COUSINO MACUL — CHILE

One of the best Chilean wine estates, near Santiago and now over a hundred years old. Its founder Don Luis Cousino was one of the first to plant French vines in the country. Antiguas Reservas Cabernet is a distinguished wine; Sémillon also comes under the Antiguas Reservas label. They have Chardonnay too, but red wines dominate the production, particularly with Cabernet, as well as Merlot and Petit Verdot grapes.

LA COUSPAUDE — *Bordeaux*: FRANCE

A little-known Grand Cru Classé of St-Émilion.

COUTET — *Bordeaux*: FRANCE

A first growth Sauternes, one of the two great wines of Barsac, Climens being the other. Methods are traditional with fermentation in wood. The vineyard is 80% Sémillon grapes and 20% Sauvignon. The results are consistently delicious. There is also a Grand Cru Classé of St-Émilion of minor stature with the same name.

COUTRAS — *Bordeaux*: FRANCE

A minor region on the northern fringe of Bordeaux towards Cognac with the basic appellation. There is one important property, Méaume.

LE COUVENT — *Bordeaux*: FRANCE

The smallest of the Grands Crus Classés of St-Émilion, with a vineyard at the foot of the medieval castle in the heart of the town. The convent was *le couvent des Ursulines*, whose nuns made the macaroons for which St-Émilion is also famous.

COUVENT-DES-JACOBINS — *Bordeaux*: FRANCE

A Grand Cru Classé of St-Émilion. It was once a religious foundation, as the name implies. The 13th century buildings are in the old town of St-Émilion and the vineyards reach the ramparts.

CRACKLING

An American term, sometimes used instead of sparkling, usually for cheap, fizzy wine.

CRADLE

A wicker or wire basket designed to hold a wine bottle at a slight angle, so that the wine can be poured with the sediment being disturbed as little as possible and remaining at the bottom of the bottle. Often it is much better to decant the wine instead.

CRAIGMOOR
AUSTRALIA

The oldest estate of Mudgee in New South Wales, established in 1858 by a German immigrant, Adam Roth. Recently the winery has experimented with varietal wines and oak-ageing. Chardonnay is proving especially successful and also a Sémillon/Chardonnay blend, as well as Rummy port, a port matured in rum casks.

CRAMANT
Champagne: FRANCE

One of the most important villages of the Côte des Blancs.

CREAM SHERRY
SPAIN

A sweet sherry made by blending dry *oloroso* with sweet Pedro Ximénez wines, as well as *vino de color* if it is to be a dark brown as opposed to a pale cream sherry.

CRÉMANT

In Alsace, Burgundy and the Loire it is a fully sparkling wine, while in Champagne it is slightly less fizzy than Champagne, for while Champagne has a pressure of five or six atmospheres, a crémant traditionally has only about 3.6 atmospheres. In the 18th century a crémant was considered superior to the fully sparkling Champagne.

CRÉMANT D'ALSACE

A sparkling wine from Alsace that was recognised as an appellation in 1976. Production has increased rapidly since then. Any of the Alsace grape varieties may be used, except Gewürztraminer, which is too spicey. However the main grape varieties are Pinot Blanc and Pinot Auxerrois, with some Riesling and Pinot Gris, and for rosé, Pinot Noir. The production method is that of Champagne.

CRÉMANT DE BOURGOGNE
Burgundy: FRANCE

Can be red, white or rosé and was introduced as an appellation for sparkling Burgundy, made by the *méthode champenoise* in 1975. Regulations controlling its production are stricter than for Bourgogne Mousseux which is gradually to disappear. The principal grape varieties are Chardonnay, Pinot Noir, Sacy, Aligoté and Gamay and the main centres of production are the SICAVA near Chablis, Nuits St-Georges on the Côte d'Or and some producers in the Côte Chalonnaise and Mâconnais. It can be a very good alternative to Champagne.

CRÉMANT DE LOIRE
Loire: FRANCE

A sparkling wine from the Loire Valley. The appellation was introduced in 1975 and covers not only Saumur, the sparkling wine capital of the region, but also Anjou and Touraine. The methods are identical to those of Champagne. The grape variety is predominantly Chenin Blanc for the white wine and it can be a very acceptable and cheaper alternative to Champagne. Some rosé and a little red wine is also made.

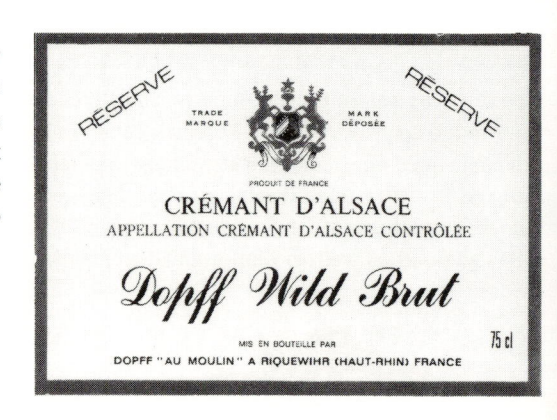

CRÉPY   Savoie: FRANCE

Crépy is an individual appellation of the region of Savoie, comprising some ninety hectares just over the border from Switzerland in the Haute Savoie, planted with the Chasselas grape. The wines are usually faintly sparkling or *perlant*, low in alcohol, with fresh acidity when young, and can age into more distinctive tastes.

CRETE   GREECE

A large wine-producing island with four appellations, all for heavy sweet red wines: Daphnes, Archanes, Sitia and Peza. They are all made from indigenous Cretan varieties of grape, including Romeiko, Kotsifali and Liatiko.

CREUX

The French term for 'hollow'.

CRIADERA

Translates literally as nursery in Spanish and describes the first state of a sherry *solera*, where the youngest wine is beginning to age.

CRIANZA

Crianza means literally nursing in Spanish and refers to the ageing of Rioja. A Rioja labelled *con crianza* means that it has been matured for a minimum of twelve months in cask, and some months, usually six in bottle, and must not be sold before the third year after the vintage.

Sin crianza describes a young wine bottled during the year after the vintage.

BODEGAS CRILLON   ARGENTINA

A winery best known for sparkling Crillon. They do not own any vineyards.

CRIMEA   USSR

The vineyards of this part of the Soviet Union are in the hills around Simferopol and along the coast from Sebastopol to Feodosiya. The best-known wine is Massandra, the name used by the state cooperative to describe their dessert wines made from Muscatel.

CRIOLLA

The principal grape of Argentina, a red *Vitis Vinifera* probably related to the Pais of Chile and producing red wine in prolific quantity from irrigated vineyards around Mendoza. It derived from the early European vine cuttings brought by Spanish missionaries in the 16th century.

CRISP

Describes the acidity in white wine.

CRNO

Means red on a Yugoslav wine label.

CROATINA

A red grape grown in Piedmont and Lombardy, making notably Oltrepò Pavese and Gutturnio dei Colli Piacentini.

LUCIEN CROCHET   Loire: FRANCE

A reputable grower in Sancerre, with vineyards in the Clos du Chêne Marchand.

LE CROCK   Bordeaux: FRANCE

A Cru Grand Bourgeois of St-Estèphe.

CROFT

A name with a great reputation for port, but it has only been associated with sherry since 1970 when the owners of the firm, International Distillers and Vintners, set up Croft Jerez to supply their sherry needs. They were the first to launch a pale cream sherry, Croft Original. There is also Croft Particular Amontillado, Delicado fino and a good palo cortado.

The original port company, which is one of the oldest, was founded in 1678 by the Yorkshire Croft family. Quinta da Roêda at Pinhão forms the basis for their vintage port and Croft's Distinction Tawny is an important brand.

LA CROIX

Bordeaux: FRANCE

A second growth Pomerol *château* enjoying a good reputation and incorporating La Croix St-Georges and La Croix Toulifaut. There is also a La Croix in Fronsac.

LA CROIX DE GAY

Bordeaux: FRANCE

A small second growth Pomerol property making attractive wine.

CROIZET-BAGES

Bordeaux: FRANCE

A fifth growth Pauillac overshadowed by its more famous neighbour, Lynch-Bages, but nevertheless producing sound robust Pauillac. The second label is Enclos de Moncabon.

CROQUE-MICHOTTE

Bordeaux: FRANCE

A little-known Grand Cru Classé of the *graves* part of St-Émilion.

CROWN CORK

The closure commonly used on a champagne bottle during the *prise de mousse*. It looks like the ordinary metal top of a beer bottle, with a plastic pot inside to contain the sediment from the second fermentation.

CROWN OF CROWNS

An important Liebfraumilch brand produced by the company of Langenbach in Worms.

CROZES-HERMITAGE

Rhône: FRANCE

A wine from the northern Rhône. The vineyards encircle those of its more prestigious cousin, Hermitage. Eleven villages make up the appellation, including Crozes-Hermitage, but Tain l'Hermitage is the centre of the area.

Red Crozes Hermitage is made entirely from the Syrah grape and white Crozes Hermitage from Marsanne and Roussanne. Leading growers include Paul Jaboulet Aîné with his property Domaine de Thalabert and Max Chapoutier with les Meysonniers, Jean-Louis Pradelle, Domaine des Clairmonts, Desmeure Père et Fils.

CRU

Translates literally as 'growth', indicating a vineyard of particular quality and status and usually qualified by *Grand* or a numbered category such as *Premier* or *Deuxième Cru*.

CRU ARTISAN

A term that was used in Bordeaux to describe wine below the status of Cru Bourgeois. *Petit château* is now the more common description.

CRU BOURGEOIS

Cru Bourgeois is the category below the classed growths in the line-up of Médoc *châteaux*. There is a *Syndicat* of Crus Bourgeois to which a *château* owner must belong in order to have the position recognised. In addition, a dozen properties which are not members of the *Syndicat* have been semi-officially considered as exceptional since 1855. In 1978, the *Syndicat* had 68 Cru Bourgeois members with properties over seven hectares, where the owner makes his own wine and has met the quality requirements of the *Syndicat*. The classification of Cru Bourgeois also exists in Sauternes. Cru Grand Bourgeois, of which there are 41, has satisfied the same criteria as the Cru Bourgeois and the wine is aged in oak barrels.

CRU CLASSÉ

Translates literally as 'classed growth' and refers to the 1855 classification of the Haut-Medoc wines (with Sauternes and one Graves) of Bordeaux. These classed growths can command considerable premiums in price.

CRU GRAND BOURGEOIS EXCEPTIONNEL

Every ten years or so, the *Syndicat* of Médoc Crus Grands Bourgeois and Crus Bourgeois publishes a kind of *Syndicat* Honours List, denoting the best properties as Crus Grand Bourgeois Exceptionnels. At present in the 1978 list there are eighteen, which come from the communes of the classed growths of the Médoc. Their minimum vineyard size is seven hectares; the wine is aged in wood and always château-bottled.

CRU PAYSAN

A term that was used in Bordeaux to describe wine below the status of Cru Bourgeois. *Petit château* is now the more common description.

CRUCHEN BLANC

A rather dull white grape grown originally in the Landes district of south west France for *vin de table* and now planted quite extensively in South Africa and Australia where its name is wrongly associated with Riesling. It produces slightly aromatic white wine. See Cape Riesling.

CRUET   Savoie: FRANCE

One of the larger crus of Vin de Savoie. Production is dominated by the local cooperative, that makes white wine from Jacquère and Roussette grapes and red mainly from Gamay.

CRUSE

An important name in Bordeaux, one of the principal families of the Quai des Chartrons.

CRUSH

An American term used instead of press. Crush also refers to a vintage or harvest, in the sense of a winery's first crush.

CRUSHER

An American term for a *fouloir*.

CRUSHER-DESTALKER

The Anglophone equivalent of a *fouloir égrappoir*.

CRUSIUS   Nahe: GERMANY

Weingut Hans Crusius is a small family company which goes back to the 16th century and produces stylish oak-aged wines from Traiser Bastei and Rotenfels, Norheimer Klosterberg and Schlossböckelheimer Felsenberg grapes.

CRUSTED PORT

A term no longer recognised in Portugal, but is similar to vintage character port. Like vintage port, it throws a crust, but is a blend of wines of different vineyards and years, bottled after a longer period in wood, so that it is less long-lasting.

CRUZETA

Used for training the vines in the vineyards of Vinho Verde. A *cruzeta* is a wooden or concrete T-shaped support, with wires along which the vines are trained. This is the modern version of the traditional method of training vines on trees.

CUBZAC   Bordeaux: FRANCE

Also called Cubzaguais, a part of Bordeaux without its own appellation, around the town of St-André de Cubzac. The wines have the simple appellation Bordeaux but include three large properties: de Terrefort-Quancard, Timberlay and de Bouilh. There is also, confusingly, a Domaine de Beychevelle and a Cru Cantemerle.

CUCMONGA   California: USA

A disappearing wine region to the east of Los Angeles. It produces now unfashionable port and sherry style wines in hot sunshine and the vineyards are now more valuable as building land for the urban sprawl of L.A.

CUL DE BOUTEILLE
The French term for the *punt* of a wine bottle.

CULTURE BIOLOGIQUE See organic viticulture.

CULTURED YEAST See yeast.

CULTIVAR
A South African term for grape variety, used in the same way as the American term, varietal. For a South African label to mention a single cultivar, the percentage in the wine must not be less than 75%.

CUMIÈRES *Champagne:* FRANCE
A village on the Montagne de Reims with a reputation for red wine, as well as some of the best vineyards of the area.

CUPROUS CASSE See copper casse.

CURÉ-BON *Bordeaux:* FRANCE
Or Curé-Bon-le-Madeleine, as the label says, is a Grand Cru Classé of St-Émilion that was planted by a *curé* named Bon in the early 19th century.

DOMAINE DE CUREBOURSE *Bordeaux:* FRANCE
The second wine of the Durfort Vivens estate.

CUSSAC *Bordeaux:* FRANCE
A commune of the Médoc but it produces little wine.

CUVAISON
The period during which the juice is in contact with the grape skins. This really only applies to red wines. The length of the *cuvaison* will affect the quality and character of the wine; it is itself determined by the characteristics of the vintage.

CUVAISON *California:* USA
A Napa Valley winery founded in 1970 and after chequered beginnings now makes fine Cabernet Sauvignon, Chardonnay and Zinfandel from grapes bought from some of the best sites in the valley.

CUVE
The French term for 'vat'.

CUVE CLOSE
Also called *Charmat* or tank method, this is a process for making sparkling wine in bulk, developed by a French oenologist, Eugène Charmat, in 1910. Sugar and yeast are added to the still wine in the tank, where the second fermentation takes place; the wine is then clarified, filtered and bottled under pressure. The process could never replace the *méthode champenoise*, but it allows for the production of consistent and cheap, labour-saving sparkling wine.

CUVÉE
In French this literally means the contents of a vat or *cuve*, but has come to mean a quantity of wine made at the same time, under the same conditions or from the same vineyard. In Champagne, *vin de cuvée* is the first wine of the pressing. With expressions like *cuvée speciale* and *cuvée réserve* it describes a special lot of wine. *Cuvée du patron* is a common name for a restaurant house wine, chosen by the owner.

CUVÉE TRADITION
Cuvée Tradition is a description used by the Hugel company in Alsace, to describe a category of wine that is the quality above their basic wine. The definition has no legal backing.

CUVERIE
The collective term for a number of vats in a cellar.

CVNE SPAIN
CVNE or Compania Vinicola del Norte de España is an important Rioja *bodega* in Haro, founded just over 100 years ago, with vineyards supplying nearly half their needs. The range includes an oak aged white Monopole, 3 year old Cune and Imperial and Vina Real reservas.

CYPRUS
Cyprus has an important wine industry for table wines, sherry and Commandaria, her traditional dessert wine. Most of the vineyards are on the southern foothills of the Troodos mountains. The island is phylloxera-free and there are indigenous, ungrafted grape varieties, red Mavron and Ophthalmo, white Xynisteri, as well as Muscat d'Alexandrie. In addition, other European grape varieties are being introduced to the island, after a strict period of quarantine, such as Cabernet

Sauvignon, Shiraz, Chardonnay and Sauvignon. As yet, they are still very much at the experimental stage. The island's wine production is dominated by three wineries, Sodap, Keo and Etko-Haggipavlu, who produce a range of branded table wines and sherries.

CYPRUS SHERRY CYPRUS

Designed for the cheaper end of the British market with a full range of tastes from dry to very sweet; it has played an important part in the island's wine trade. Successful attempts have been made to encourage the growth of flor for *fino* sherries. Cream sherries are made from sun-dried grapes with *soleras* of barrels left in the sun to age. There are two important brands, Emva and Mosaic.

CZECHOSLOVAKIA

All the three provinces of Czechoslovakia, Bohemia, Moravia and Slovakia, produce wine, each with its own distinct traditions. The best Czech wines are white, from predominantly Rheinriesling and Welschriesling, called Vlassky Ryzling by the Czechs, as well as Müller-Thurgau, Sylvaner, Gewürztraminer, Ruländer and Grüner Veltliner. Limberger, also called Frankovka, makes the best red wine.

D

DO See Denominación de Origen.

DOC See Denominazione di Origine Controllata.

DOCG See Denominazione di Origine Controllata e Garantita.

DALLY PLONK NEW ZEALAND

The perjorative term used to describe the type of wine made in New Zealand before the revolution in her wine industry. It was usually a fortified wine, made from hybrid vines, mainly by the early Dalmatian immigrants, hence the name. Things have changed beyond all recognition now.

DALMATIA YUGOSLAVIA

Dalmatia produces Yugoslavia's most individual wines, a variety of heady reds such as Postup, Dingač and Faros, mainly from the Plavac Mali grape. Whites are less important in quantity, but more varied, with Čara Smokvica, Grk, Pošip and the island wines of Hvar Brač. A red and white dessert wine is called Prošek.

LA DAME BLANCHE Bordeaux: FRANCE

The white wine of Château du Taillan in the Médoc. No white wine may be called Médoc and so it only has the appellation of Bordeaux Blanc.

DAME-JEANNE

The French term for a large glass container, holding between one and ten gallons, usually covered in wicker like a Chianti *fiasco*. The English name is a demi-john.

In Bordeaux a *dame-jeanne* is the name of a bottle holding two and a half litres, a little over three standard bottles.

DAMES HOSPITALIÈRES

The name of a *cuvée* offered for sale at the Hospices de Beaune, namely Beaune les Bressandes, la Mignotte, les Teurons and Les Grèves.

DÃO PORTUGAL

One of the better known red wines of Portugal, produced in vineyards around the town of Viseu in the centre of the country. The delimited area covers about 1000 square miles, but only one twentieth is planted with vines, for the region is mountainous and divided by several rivers. The soil is mainly granite, and a considerable variety of grapes are permitted, Touriga Nacional, Alvarelhão, Tinta Amarela, Alfrocheiro Preto, Tinta Pinheira and Jaen for reds and Arinto do Dão, Borrado das Moscas, Cerceal, Barcelo, Encruzado and Verdhelo for whites. Cooperatives dominate the production and the Vinicola do Vale do Dão is important too. Red Dão needs considerable ageing in wood, at least three years followed by further time in bottle and reservas are aged for even longer. White Dão is also traditionally aged in wood, but there is a trend for a more youthful style of wine.

DAPHNES GREECE

A full-bodied sweet red wine from Crete, made from indigenous Cretan varieties of grape, notably Liatiko.

DASSAULT Bordeaux: FRANCE

A Grand Cru Classé of St-Émilion elevated in 1969. The property has recently been renovated and is making some charming wine.

DAUDET NAUDIN Burgundy: FRANCE

An old-fashioned Burgundy house based in Savigny les Beaune, making full-bodied soupy wines.

DAUZAC Bordeaux: FRANCE

A fifth growth Margaux; it has had a chequered history but, with a recent change of ownership, it may take on a new lease of life.

DE BORTOLI AUSTRALIA

Started by an Italian immigrant in the M.I.A. district of New South Wales in the 1920s and today demonstrates some of the potential of this part of the estate, producing, most notably, some astonishing botrytis Sémillons.

DEALCOHOLISED WINE

As the term implies, a wine which has had most of its natural alcohol removed, either by distillation or techniques involving centrifuge and filtration, in an attempt to make it acceptable to those wishing to reduce their alcohol consumption. More often, without alcohol, the taste is completely unbalanced but methods of production are improving with new technology. Dealcoholized wine must have less than .05% alcohol. However the introduction of more favourable duty rates for wines with less than 5.5° alcohol will have an impact.

DEALUL MARE ROMANIA

A wine region of southeastern Romania producing alcoholic, heavy red wines from Pinot Noir, Cabernet Sauvignon and Merlot grapes. Valea Călugărească, meaning Valley of the Monks, is the home of the country's experimental vineyards.

DÉBOURBAGE

The process of clearing the white wine must of *bourbes* or large lees, before fermentation begins. This can be done either by centrifuge, with bentonite or by cooling the must, adding a light dose of sulphur and allowing it to rest for twenty-four hours, during which time the lees fall naturally to the bottom of the vat.

DÉBOURREMENT

The French term for 'budbreak', describing the moment when the vine begins growing new shoots in the spring, usually in March when the average temperature has reached about 50°F or 10°C.

DEBRÓ HUNGARY

The town at the centre of the large vineyard area of Mátraalja in the north. The area is famous for Debröi Hárslevelü, an attractive, slightly sweet white wine.

DECANT

To pour wine from a bottle into another container, namely a decanter, in order to aerate the wine and allow it to breathe before it is drunk. Also to separate it from any sediment in the bottle.

DECANTER

A container into which a wine is decanted. At its simplest, it may be a plain glass carafe; at its finest, an elegant example of Georgian crystal.

DECANTER LABEL

Often a very decorative label hung round a decanter to indicate its contents. Often made in silver, they are valuable collectors' items dating back to the 18th century.

DÉGORGEMENT

The removal, after *remuage*, of the sediment created by the second fermentation in a bottle of champagne or *méthode champenoise* wine. There are two ways of doing this, *à la volée* and *à la glâce*. A la volée requires great skill and a sense of timing, to know when to bring the bottle upright after the cork is removed; too early and some sediment remains in the bottle; too late and some champagne is wasted. This method is rarely used today for *dégorgement à la glâce* is more reliable. The neck of the champagne bottle is dipped into chilled brine, so that the sediment freezes and adheres to the bottle's crown capsule, which can then be easily removed.

DEGREE DAY

The measurement for the heat summation of a vineyard. Degree Days are calculated by subtracting 50°F or 10°C from the average temperature for each day of the growing season. The remaining degrees are then totalled.

DÉGUSTATION

The French term for wine-tasting and the occasion at which it is tasted.

DEIDESHEIM *Rheinpfalz*: GERMANY

Rivals Forst in producing the finest wines of the Rheinpfalz. The wines of Deidesheim are perhaps a little more elegant than those of Forst. However, it is indisputably the wine centre of the Rheinpfalz where most of the important producers have their cellars, including Bassermann Jordan, von Bühl and Deinhard. The exception is Bürklin Wolf whose cellars are in Wachenheim. Deidesheim has villages in three *Grosslagen*: Schnepfenflug, Hofstück and Mariengarten. The only vineyard in Schnepfenflug is Letten, while Nonnengarten is in Hofstück, making Mariengarten the largest *Grosslage* with nine vineyards. The most important are Hohenmorgan, Kieselberg, Paradiesgarten, Leinhöhle, Herrgottsacker and Langenmorgen; Grainhübel, Kalkofen and Maushöhle are lesser-known.

DEINHARD & CO

Deinhard are an important family firm of German wine merchants, based in Koblenz with an office in London. They were founded in the 18th century, were one of the early makers of sparkling wine in Germany and they still are important producers of *Sekt* with Lila Imperial and Deinhard Cabinet. They own three estates; on the Rheingau with vineyards mainly in Oestrich, Winkel, Geisenheim and Rüdesheim; in the Palatinate at Deidesheim, with vineyards in Forst, Deidesheim and Ruppertsberg and on the Mosel with vineyards in Graach, Wehlen and Bernkastel, including part of the famous Doktor vineyards.

DELAFORCE

The port house of Delaforce was founded in 1868 by the Delaforce family who still run the company, although it is now part of International Vintners and Distillers. They own Quinta da Corte and their His Eminence's Choice, is a delicious old tawny.

DELAS Rhône: FRANCE

Important growers and *négociants* in the Rhône Valley, with vineyards in Hermitage, Cornas, Côte Rôtie, Crozes Hermitage, Condrieu and St-Joseph. Their best wines are their Hermitage, Cuvée Marquise de la Tourette, Cornas Chante Perdrix and Condrieu.

DELAWARE

A hybrid vine, grown in North America, Brazil and Japan. Unlike most hybrids, it is susceptible to *phylloxera* and the taste is more delicate than the average hybrid.

DELEGAT'S NEW ZEALAND

Founded in 1947 in the Henderson area. Today they have a reputation for Müller-Thurgau, especially Auslese quality, and oak aged Chardonnay. Cabernet Sauvignon is their only red wine.

DELORME Burgundy: FRANCE

An enterprising family company in Rully, they own an estate in Rully which has been built up since the early 1960s and now consists of Domaine de la Renarde for red Rully and white Rully Varot, as well as some Mercurey and Givry and vineyards for Crémant de Bourgogne.

DEMESTICA GREECE

The brand name for the basic red and white table wine made by the Greek company, Achaia Clauss. One of the most common Greek wines.

DEMI-JOHN   See Dame-Jeanne.

DEMI-QUEUE

A Burgundian barrel size, similar to a *pièce*.

DEMI-SEC

The French term for 'medium-dry'.

DENOMINACIÓN DE ORIGEN

The Spanish equivalent of the French system of appellation contrôlée, and was introduced with help from France. *Denominación de Origen* is only for wines with an established reputation, and with the climate, soil and viticultural practices to delimit a precise area of production. The first regulating body or Consejo Regulador was set up in Rioja in 1926 and others have gradually followed. Tighter controls are envisaged for D.O.s that achieve 'calificada' status. As yet there are none, although Rioja is an aspiring D.O.Ca.

DENOMINAZIONE DI ORIGINE CONTROLLATA

Since the introduction of the Italian wine law in 1963, some 230 wines are entitled to the category *Denominazione di Origine Controllata*, or DOC for short and the number increases every year. This represents 12% of Italian wine production. If a wine is DOC, it means that it comes from a delimited area, from specified grape varieties of limited yield and according to definite practices. A DOC may be large or small, a village or a province; there may be several wines within a DOC – the Alto Adige has 16 based on different grape varieties – or a single wine may be vinified in several ways – dry, medium sweet, sweet, sparkling and still. Although DOC establishes an element of authenticity, the final test of quality, as always, rests with the winemaker.

DENOMINAZIONE DI ORIGINE CONTROLLATA E GARANTITA

DOCG is the highest category of Italian wine. Only six wines merit this category so far: Barolo, Barbaresco, Brunello di Montalcino, Vino Nobile di Montepulciano and, more recently, Chianti and Albana di Romagna. The term implies that the area of origin and methods of production in vineyard and cellar are not only controlled but guaranteed and all wines are not only analysed but approved by a tasting panel.

DESMIRAIL   Bordeaux: FRANCE

A third growth Margaux. Although this wine features in the 1855 classification, the vineyard was sold to Château Palmer and incorporated in the property so that Desmirail in its own right has disappeared.

DESSERT WINE

Or pudding wine, a not uncommon description for a sweet wine, such as a Sauternes, or one of the Muscat wines of the south of France. These sweet wines have suffered a fall from favour; attempts to revive interest in them describe them as the ideal accompaniment to desserts or puddings. In fact, too sweet a pudding will overwhelm the wine and they are often best drunk on their own at the end of a meal.

DETZEM   Mosel-Saar-Ruwer: GERMANY

An unimportant wine village of the Mosel, just in the Mittelmosel, within the *Grosslage* of St. Michael.

DEUTSCHER SEKT   See *Sekt*.

DEUTSCHER TAFELWEIN

Deutscher Tafelwein, or German table wine, is the lowest category of wine made from grapes grown in Germany, produced in four broad Tafelwein regions; Rhein und Mosel, which subdivides into the sub-regions of Rhine and Moselle; Main, Neckar and Oberrhein, which splits into Romertor and Burgenau. Deutscher Tafelwein is made only from permitted grape varieties with a minimum amount of natural sugar and must come only from German grapes, unlike plain Tafelwein.

DEUTZ & GELDERMANN
                                    Champagne: FRANCE

A small, traditional champagne house.

DÉZELAY   SWITZERLAND

One of the best vineyards of Lauvaux, with its own appellation, producing some of Switzerland's best Fendant.

DEZIZES LES MARANGES   See les Maranges.

DHRON   Mosel-Saar-Ruwer: GERMANY

The neighbouring village of Neumagen on the Mosel and comes within the *Grosslage* of Michelsberg with two notable single sites, Hofberger and Roterd.

DIANA

A crossing of Silvaner and Müller Thurgau grape varieties which has now disappeared from use in Germany.

DIENHEIM   Rheinhessen: GERMANY

A village next to Oppenheim and with vineyards in the *Grosslage* of Oppenheim Krötenbrunnen and Güldenmorgen. The wines are not as good or as well-known as those of Oppenheim as most of the vineyards are on the plain.

DILLON   Bordeaux: FRANCE

A relatively unknown property in the Haut-Médoc belonging to the agricultural college at Blanquefort.

DIMIAT   BULGARIA

A white grape, very similar to the western European Chasselas and producing neutral white wine.

DINGAČ   YUGOSLAVIA

A red, full-bodied, heady wine, made from semi-dried Plavac Mali grapes, grown on the Pelješac peninsular in Dalmatia.

DIONYSIUS

The Greek god of wine. According to Greek mythology he was the son of Zeus and Semele, a god with prophetic gifts who spread the knowledge of vine cultivation over the known world and also developed his own cult with orgiastic Bacchic rites. He was also called Bacchos in Greek, which the Romans changed to Bacchus.

DIZY *Champagne*: FRANCE

An important champagne village on the Montagne de Reims.

DOISY-DAËNE *Bordeaux*: FRANCE

This second growth Sauternes is an example of successful experimental wine-making, under the ownership of Pierre Dubordieu. The dry wine, made from the unusual combination of 50% Sémillon grapes, 20% Sauvignon and 30% Muscadelle, Riesling and Chardonnay, is one of the best dry wines of the area. The Sauternes is pure Sémillon fermented in stainless steel vats, then aged briefly in new oak.

DOISY-DUBROCA *Bordeaux*: FRANCE

A second growth Sauternes in Barsac and the smallest portion of the original Doisy property. The vineyard is planted mostly with the Sémillon grape and the wines are well-made with Professor Peynaud's advice.

DOISY-VÉDRINES *Bordeaux*: FRANCE

A second growth Sauternes in Barsac, which has a good reputation for its barrel-fermented wines. A red wine is called Latour Védrines.

DOLCE

Dolce means sweet in Italian, sweeter than *abboccato* (medium dry) or *amabile* (medium sweet).

DOLCEACQUA   See Rossese di Dolceacqua.

DOLCETTO

A distinctively Piedmontese grape variety, making easy and early to drink red wines, under seven different DOCs.

DOLCETTO D'ACQUI *Piedmont*: ITALY

A DOC wine made from the red Dolcetto grape from vineyards around the town of Acqui Terme in Piedmont. To be *superiore*, it needs a year of ageing.

DOLCETTO D'ALBA *Piedmont*: ITALY

A DOC wine made from the red Dolcetto grape grown in vineyards around the town of Alba. If *superiore*, it has one year's ageing and is at its best between one and three years.

DOLCETTO D'ASTI *Piedmont*: ITALY

A DOC wine made from the red Dolcetto grape grown in the Monferrato hills in the province of Asti. This Dolcetto is easy to drink and needs one year's ageing to be *superiore*.

DOLCETTO DI DIANO D'ALBA *Piedmont*: ITALY

A DOC wine made from the red Dolcetto grape grown around the town of Diano and considered to be one of the best Dolcettos. One year's ageing makes it *superiore*.

DOLCETTO DI DOGLIANO *Piedmont*: ITALY

A DOC wine made from the red Dolcetto grape around the town of Dogliani, where the Dolcetto is reputed to originate. *Superiore* means one year's ageing.

DOLCETTO DELLE LANGHE MONREGALESI *Piedmont*: ITALY

A DOC wine made in minute quantities from the red Dolcetto grape in the Langhe hills between Dogliani and Mondori. One year's ageing makes it *superiore*.

DOLCETTO DI OVADA *Piedmont*: ITALY

A DOC wine made from the Dolcetto grape from the hills around Ovada in southeast Piedmont. *Superiore* means one year's ageing and the wine can be sturdy and long-lived.

DÔLE SWITZERLAND

A red wine produced all over the canton of Valais from Gamay and Pinot Noir grapes, in no precise proportions. Minimum alcohol is 12°, but chaptalisation is permitted and a tasting test is obligatory.

DOLUCA   See Kutman.

DOM PÉRIGNON

A legendary figure in Champagne. He was a Benedictine monk and the blind cellarmaster of the abbey of Hautvillers outside Épernay. In the late 1660s, he was the first person to appreciate the possibility of using cork as a stopper to retain the carbon dioxide resulting from a wine's second fermentation. He was also a talented blender and it is his work as a blender that laid foundations for champagne as it is today. His name is remembered in Moët et Chandon's prestige *cuvée*, Dom Pérignon.

DOMAINE

The French term for 'wine estate'.

DOMAINE BOTTLED

Indicates that the wine is bottled on the estate where it was produced, rather than by a *négociant*. or merchant.

PEDRO DOMECQ   SPAIN

The oldest, largest and one of the most important sherry houses, founded by Irish and French families in the 18th century, and now with 73 different *bodegas* in the Jerez area. Their range includes La Ina Fino; Rio Viejo, a dry *oloroso*; sweet Celebration Cream and Double Century. The present head of the company, Don José Ignacio Domecq, is known affectionately as 'the nose' of sherry, on account of his prominent feature. The firm has extended its interests to table wine in Mexico and Rioja, and like other sherry houses also produces a brandy.

LA DOMINIQUE   Bordeaux: FRANCE

A Grand Cru Classé of St-Émilion and a neighbour of Cheval Blanc on the *graves*.

DOMINUS   California: USA

The Californian creation of Christian Moueix; a red wine, made principally from Cabernet Sauvignon with some Cabernet Franc and Merlot. The grapes are grown at the Napanook vineyard and vinified in the Napa Valley in partnership with Robin Lail and Marcia Smith. Although 1983 was the first vintage, the 1984 vintage was the first release, in April 1988, after bottling in July 1986.

DONATIEN BAHAUD   Loire: FRANCE

Important Loire *négociants*, with a flagship property, Chateau de la Cassemichère in Muscadet. Le Chouan is the brand name for their pure Chardonnay *vin de pays*.

DONNAZ   Valle d'Aosta: ITALY

One of the two DOC Valle d'Aosta wines. It is virtually indistinguishable from neighbouring Carema in Piedmont. Made from the Piedmontese grape, Nebbiolo, it requires a minimum of four years' ageing, including at least two in wood, and has a minimum alcohol content of 12°. It rarely improves after five or six years and is not usually found outside the region.

DONNICI   Calabria: ITALY

A light red DOC wine, made from Gaglioppo and Greco Nero grapes near Cosenza. Best drunk young.

DOPFF & IRION   Alsace: FRANCE

An important Alsace house with their head office in the Château de Riquewihr, and distantly related to Dopff au Moulin. Their main wines, from single vineyards, are Riesling les Murailles, Gewürztraminer les Maquisards, Gewürztraminer les Sorcières and Muscat les Amandiers.

DOPFF AU MOULIN   Alsace: FRANCE

An important Alsace house, distantly related to Dopff & Irion, with cellars in Riquewihr. They are one of the larger producers of Crémant d'Alsace and also own vineyards on the Schoenenberg and Eichberg sites.

DORADILLO

A white grape which originated in Spain where it is no longer grown. Instead it is planted extensively

DORIN SWITZERLAND

The Vaudois name for Fendant. This is a white wine made from the Fendant grape, produced in the Vaud region, but without any village designation.

DORNFELDER

A new German red grape variety, a crossing of Helfensteiner (Frühburgunder x Trollinger) with Heroldrebe (Portugieser x Limberger). It is more successful than any of the constituent parts, producing some interesting wine.

DORSHEIM Nahe: GERMANY

One of the better villages of the Lower Nahe, near Bingen, coming within the *Grosslage* of Schlosskapelle. The best *Einzellage* is Goldloch.

DOSAGE

The sugar added to champagne in the *liqueur d'expédition* after *dégorgement*, determining the degree of sweetness of the wine, ranging from *Brut*, through *Extra Sec*, *Sec*, *Demi Sec* to *Doux*.

DOUBLE CURTAIN PRUNING

See Geneva Double Curtain.

DOUGLAS SOUTH AFRICA

Originally part of the Orange River area but given Wine of Origin status in 1981. The hot dry climate produces mainly dessert wines.

DOUKKLA See Casablanca.

DOURO

The river in Portugal along which the port vineyards are situated, in a demarcated area both for port and for table wine from the Spanish border to just below Regua and Lamego and including the valleys of its tributaries, Corgo, Torto, Pinhão and others. The Douro flows out into the Atlantic at Vila Nova de Gaia, where the port shippers have their lodges for the maturation of their wines. The Douro is dramatic; a single track railway follows the river, giving views of terraced vineyards, and slopes of rugged schist to which the vines cling tenaciously. The vineyards of the Douro are classified from A to F, according to yield, soil, gradient, altitude, climate, age of vines and quality of grapes; the classification of the vineyard determines the price of its grapes. Not all the wine of the Douro becomes port; much remains as table wine. The best are fruity red wines.

DOURO WINE SHIPPERS ASSOCIATION

Not, as its name might imply, a port trade organisation, but a subsidiary of the port house Barros & Almeida.

DOW

The port company of Dow merged in 1887 with Silva & Cosens so that Dow port is shipped by the Symington family who own Silva & Cosens. Dow's Boardroom Tawny and 30 year old Tawny are amongst their wines.

DOWNY MILDEW

A fungus which attacks the green parts of the vine especially in warm humid conditions. It manifests itself as an oily stain which later turns white on the undersides of leaves. Copper sulphate and Bordeaux mixture are the traditional treatments, now superseded by modern chemical products.

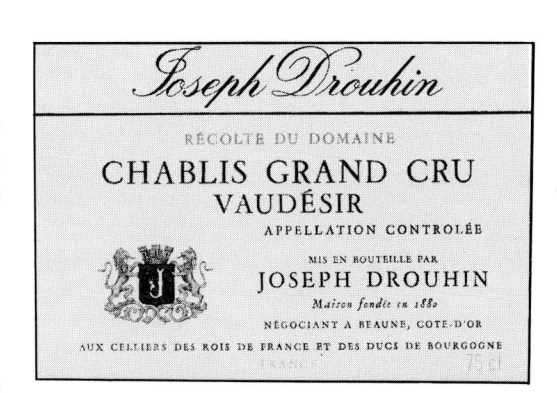

Joseph Drouhin
RÉCOLTE DU DOMAINE
CHABLIS GRAND CRU
VAUDÉSIR
APPELLATION CONTROLÉE
MIS EN BOUTEILLE PAR
JOSEPH DROUHIN
Maison fondée en 1880
NÉGOCIANT A BEAUNE, COTE-D'OR
AUX CELLIERS DES ROIS DE FRANCE ET DES DUCS DE BOURGOGNE
75 cl

DRĂGĂSANI ROMANIA

A wine region between the Danubian plain and the Transylvanian Alps. The best wines are aromatic whites from Sauvignon and Muscat Ottonel grapes.

DRAINAGE

It is essential for vines to grow in soil with good drainage. For instance, clay soil that is deficient in drainage, must be tempered with chalk or limestone. Vine roots must never become waterlogged.

DRATHEN Mosel-Saar-Ruwer: GERMANY

Ewald Theodor Drathen is a successful company dealing in inexpensive German wines and also owner of a small estate of vineyards on the lower Mosel at Alf, Neef and Bullay.

DREIMÄNNERWEIN

There are two stories attached to the name of this wine. One has it that the wine is so strong that three men must drink from a single glass of it, so that none of them risks getting drunk. The other has it that the wine is so bad that it takes three men to drink it; one to swallow it, one to hold the glass, and one to hold the unfortunate who is made to drink it!

DRIP IRRIGATION

A type of irrigation whereby each vine has its own water supply and is watered individually and sparingly, drip by drip.

JOSEPH DROUHIN Burgundy: FRANCE

Leading growers and *négociants* based in Beaune, with one of the largest estates, including vineyards in Chablis and on the Côte d'Or. Beaune Clos des Mouches is their best-known wine. New oak barrels feature in the vinification and the results are usually very successful.

DRUPEGGIO

A white grape, a small amount of which may be used in Orvieto.

DRY

Describes a wine without any residual sugar, that is fully fermented, with no trace of sweetness.

DRY CREEK California: USA

A small successful Sonoma winery in Dry Creek Valley, producing a good varietal range, and most notably Fumé Blanc.

DRY CREEK VALLEY California: USA

A part of Sonoma County, an AVA and a tributary of the Russian River, best known for Zinfandel, with some good Cabernet Sauvignon and Chardonnay too.

DRY FLY

An *amontillado* sherry, a brand name owned by the wine merchants, Findlater Mackie Todd & Co Ltd.

DRY SACK

An important sherry brand, owned by Williams & Humbert for their *amontillado*.

GEORGES DUBOEUF Burgundy: FRANCE

The best-known Beaujolais producer; some even call him the king of Beaujolais. He takes considerable responsibility for the success of Beaujolais Nouveau and markets the wines of many of the better small Beaujolais growers under his own label.

DUC DE MAGENTA Burgundy: FRANCE

An important estate based in Chassagne-Montrachet at the Abbaye de Morgeot, now under contract to Louis Jadot. It is known for Clos de la Chapelle, the vineyards belonging to the Abbey, and for Puligny-Montrachet, the Premier Cru from Clos de la Garenne in Puligny.

DUCRU BEAUCAILLOU Bordeaux: FRANCE

This second growth property, lying between Léoville Lascases and Beychevelle, makes wines typical of the best of St-Julien, with elegance and subtlety. Unusually for Bordeaux, the cellars are beneath the *château* which, also unusually, is the home of its owner, Jean-Eugène Borie. Beaucaillou means 'beautiful pebbles', in recognition of the contribution of the gravel soil to the quality of the wine. Lalande Borie is under the same ownership.

DUFF GORDON SPAIN

The company Duff Gordon was founded by the British consul in Cadiz, Sir James Duff. Gordon was another member of the family. In 1833 they went into partnership with Thomas Osborne who bought out the family in 1872. Since then the company of Osborne has continued to market Duff Gordon sherries which cover a wide range, including El Cid *amontillado* and Santa Maria Cream.

DUHART-MILON-ROTHSCHILD Bordeaux: FRANCE

A fourth growth Pauillac that was an important property in the mid-19th century and then went through a period of the doldrums until it was bought by the Rothschilds of Lafite in 1962. They have gradually renovated the property with considerable success.

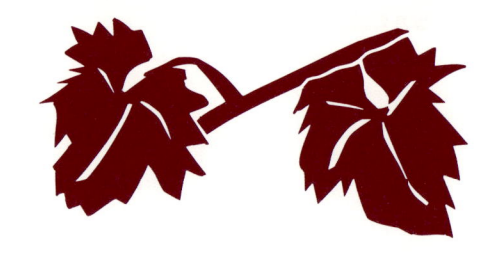

DOMAINE DUJAC
Burgundy: FRANCE

An outstanding estate in Morey St-Denis, producing long-lived wines, using new oak barrels and no filtration. The estate includes vineyards in Bonnes Mares, Echézeaux and Chambolle-Musigny.

DULCE DE ALMIBAR
SPAIN

Used in the making of pale cream sherry. It is produced by blending invert sugar with *fino* sherry which is then matured for a while until this unusually pale sweetener is added to the final sherry blend.

DULCE APAGADO
SPAIN

A type of sweet sherry, obtained by the addition of alcohol to unfermented must and used in the production of cream sherry.

DULCE PASA
SPAIN

A sweetening wine for sherry, made by leaving the grapes in the sun to dry so that the sugar concentrates. Their fermentation is then stopped with brandy.

DUMB

Describes a wine that is not yet showing its potential.

DURAS

The Duras grape has no connection with the Côtes de Duras, but is one of the lesser red grapes of south west France, one of the many permitted for red Gaillac, as well as for Estaing and for Vin de Pays des Côtes de Tarn.

DOMAINE DURBAN
Rhône: FRANCE

The leading estate in Beaumes de Venise, owned by the Leydier family with 22 acres of Muscat vines, as well as some vineyards for Côtes du Rhône Villages and in Gigondas.

DURBANVILLE
SOUTH AFRICA

A small Wine of Origin district, just outside Cape Town. Vineyards are being encroached upon by the expanding city and the only estate of any note is Meerendal where the climate is suitable for the production of fine red wines.

DURFORT-VIVENS
Bordeaux: FRANCE

A second growth Margaux *château* that belongs to the Lurton family, who are also proprietors of Brane-Cantenac. With a high percentage of Cabernet Sauvignon grapes, this wine can be hard and ungiving. The second wine is Domaine de Curebourse.

DURIF   see Petite Sirah

JEAN DURUP
Burgundy: FRANCE

Has a recently created estate in Chablis, including Fourchaume and Vaudevey. He believes in the extension of the vineyard area. His methods are modern, with no oak ageing. He is the owner of the Château de Maligny so his wines appear under that label, also Domaine de Paulière and Domaine de Valéry.

DUTCHESS

A white Labrusca grape grown in New York State.

DUTRUCH-GRAND POUJEAUX
Bordeaux: FRANCE

A Cru Grand Bourgeois Exceptionnel of the Moulis commune in the Haut-Médoc making consistent quality wine.

DUTY

The tax payable on alcoholic drinks. It is split into two parts, United Kingdom excise duty and a European duty on non-EEC wines. Duty is paid on the quantity rather than the value of the wine and according to alcoholic strength, varying for still, sparkling and fortified wine.

DYNASTY
CHINA

The brand name for a white Chinese wine made from local Chinese grapes and Muscat by Rémy Martin, in conjunction with the Chinese.

E

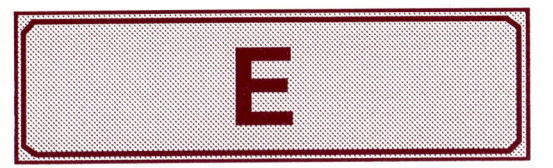

E.V.A. See English Vineyards Association.

EARLY BURGUNDY

A Californian synonym for the Abouriou grape, where it is grown for jug wine and is declining in importance.

EBURNEO   Tuscany: ITALY

A dry white *vino da tavola* made from Trebbiano and Chardonnay grapes at Podere di Cignano near Arezzo.

LES ECHÉZEAUX   Burgundy: FRANCE

An important Grand Cru vineyard in the village of Vosne-Romanée.

EDELFÄULE

The German term for 'noble rot'.

EDELKEUR   SOUTH AFRICA

The flagship white wine of the Nederburg estate, made from Steen which is occasionally blended, predominantly with Riesling, and always affected with noble rot, to produce a rich luscious dessert wine, South Africa's answer to Chateau d'Yquem, and similarly deserving bottle age.

EDELZWICKER

A blended wine from Alsace. Until recently a distinction was made between Zwicker and Edelzwicker, with the better grapes being used for the latter. The term Zwicker has now been abandoned and Edelzwicker is usually based on Pinot Blanc and/or Chasselas.

EDEN VALLEY   AUSTRALIA

A small wine area of South Australia, an offshoot of the Barossa Valley, producing wines similar to those of Barossa, but with slight climatic and soil variations.

EDNA VALLEY   California: USA

A new wine region and AVA of San Luis Obispo County, which is gaining a reputation for Chardonnay and Riesling.

ÉGALISSAGE

Another term for *assemblage*.

DOMAINE DE L'EGLISE   Bordeaux: FRANCE

A little-known *château* in Pomerol belonging to the Castéja family.

L'EGLISE-CLINET   Bordeaux: FRANCE

A second growth Pomerol property situated, not inappropriately, near the church of Pomerol. The wine enjoys a good reputation.

ÉGRAPPAGE

The French term for destalking grapes. Usually this is done by passing the bunches of grapes through a machine called an *égrappoir*. Opinions vary as to the necessity of *égrappage*; wines that are traditionally tough and tannic tend not to be *égrappé* and are fermented with the stalks, which can add more tannin, but also absorb some colour. The prevalent tendency is to *égrappe*, but with the increasing use of mechanical harvesters, this procedure has become less necessary.

ÉGRAPPOIR   See *égrappage*.

EGRI BIKAVER   HUNGARY

Better known as Bulls Blood, Hungary's most popular red wine. It comes from vineyards around the city of Eger and is made from Kadarka, Kékfrankos and Médoc Noir grapes. The wine is aged in large oak barrels, but has now lost some of its original strength. Eger also produces some good white wine from the Leányka grape.

EGUISHEIM   Alsace: FRANCE

One of the most important wine villages of Alsace; it has a Grand Cru site, Eichberg, and the village cooperative, with its modern equipment, is a large producer, especially of sparkling wine.

EGYPT

The story of modern winemaking in Egypt hinges upon one man, the pioneering Nestor Gianaclis, who planted a vineyard at Mariout, west of the Nile Delta near Alexandria in 1903. Today the main grape varieties are Chasselas, Pinot Blanc, Chardonnay, Pinot Noir, Gamay and Muscat Hamburg, plus local varieties, like Fayumi, Guizazi and Rumi. The Gianaclis wines are sold under picturesque brand names; the whites include Reine Cléopâtre and Cru des Ptolemées, and Omar Khayyam for the red. They are rarely found outside Egypt.

EHRENFELSER

A German grape variety, a crossing of Riesling and Silvaner developed in 1929. Generally tougher and more prolific than Riesling, but less able to age and with slightly less acidity. Plantings are increasing in the Rhine and Mosel.

EICHBERG   *Alsace*: FRANCE

A Grand Cru vineyard in the village of Eguisheim.

EINZELLAGE

Means in Germany an individual site, in other words a vineyard and the smallest unit which can be described on a label. In theory it must not be smaller than 5 hectares, but there are many exceptions, and applies only to quality wine.

EIS HEILIGEN   See Ice Saints.

EISACKTALER   *Trentino-Alto Adige*: ITALY

The German name for Valle Isarco.

EISENSTADT   AUSTRIA

One of the main wine towns of the vineyards of the Burgenland, with a reputation for fine dessert wines from the Esterhazy cellars.

EISWEIN   GERMANY

Literally means 'ice wine', a wine made from grapes that have been picked and pressed while frozen. As the water content of the grapes is thus removed in the form of ice, the sugar and acidity in the grapes become very concentrated. The sugar level must have reached *Beerenauslese* level. The risk of failure involved in making *Eiswein* is very great, as ripe grapes have to be left on the vines until December or January. More often it is a commercial gimmick, made in minute quantity and the wine does not have the elegance or balance of a *Beerenauslese*, although the quality has improved since 1982 when new regulations were introduced to raise the minimum level of sweetness.

EITELSBACH   *Mosel-Saar-Ruwer*: GERMANY

A wine village of the Ruwer and almost synonymous with one estate, the Karthäuserhofberg, an old Carthusian monastery. The *Grosslage* is Römerlay and single vineyards include Karthäuserhofberger Kronenberg, Karthäuserhofberger Sang, Karthäuserhofberger Burgberg and Marienholz.

EL BIERZO   SPAIN

A provisional D.O. of the province of Léon. Red Mencía and Alicante grapes produce fruity oak-aged reds, and white Palomino flowery fragrant whites.

EL DORADO   *California*: USA

An AVA of the Sierra Foothills in California, covering the gold rush county of El Dorado. Zinfandel is the main grape variety.

EL ROSAL   SPAIN

A small undemarcated wine region of Galicia where Vinho Verde look-alikes are produced from Albarino, Loureiro and Treixadura grapes.

ELBA   *Tuscany*: ITALY

The island where Napoleon was exiled briefly, which produces red and white DOC wine; the red from Chianti grapes and the white from Trebbiano. *Spumante* is also made.

ELBLING

A white grape, reputedly of antique origins, but today of little importance, except in Luxembourg where it is the second most widely planted grape variety, producing rather thin acidic wines that are best turned into sparkling wine. It is also grown in the Upper Mosel for Sekt.

ÉLÈVAGE

The general term for the rearing or upbringing of a wine, entailing ageing in cask or vat and maybe fining, filtering, blending and any other treatments from fermentation to bottling.

ELMHAM PARK — ENGLAND

Near Dereham in Norfolk, this is a small vineyard making a dry, flowery, white wine from Müller-Thurgau, Madeleine Angevine, Ortega, Reichensteiner and other grapes. Its owner, Robin Don, is the only Master of Wine to actually make wine commercially from his own vineyards.

ELTVILLE — Rheingau: GERMANY

One of the larger wine villages of the Rheingau and the home of the State Domain. It comes within the *Grosslage* of Steinmächer; the best *Einzellagen* are Taubenberg, Langenstück, Sonnenberg and Sandgrub. Several *Sekt* houses operate here, as well as Langwerth von Simmern.

ELVIRA

A white hybrid grape grown in small quantities in New York State.

EMERALD RIESLING

A Californian crossing of the Muscadelle and Riesling grape varieties, planted mainly in the San Joaquin valley where it produces quite full-bodied aromatic wines with some success.

EMILIA-ROMAGNA — ITALY

With Bologna as its capital, this is one of the largest wine-producing regions of Italy and best known for Lambrusco. There are three DOC grape varieties: Albano, Sangiovese and Trebbiano, and several other regional wines.

EMILIO LUSTAU — SPAIN

Emilio Lustau is an important family *bodega* making a fine range of sherries, not only under their own label, but also under customers' labels. Their Dry Lustau Oloroso and rare *almacenista* sherries are exceptional.

EMU WINE COMPANY — AUSTRALIA

Emu was the trademark of the Australian wine company, which was registered in London to sell wines from Australia in 1862. The company is now owned by Hardys. Emu Burgundy was a popular wine in pre-war Britain.

EMVA — CYPRUS

One of the leading brands of Cyprus sherry, owned by the company of Etko-Haggipavlu.

L'EN DE L'EL

Can also be called Len de L'Elh. One of the many grapes used for white Gaillac in south west France. In local patois it translates as loin de l'oeil or, far from the eye.

EN PRIMEUR

A term for the conditions of sale of French wine, usually claret, which is offered for sale before it has been bottled.

ENCÉPAGEMENT

The French term to describe the blend of different grape varieties in a wine and their proportion. As an example the traditional *encépagement* of the Médoc is two-thirds Cabernet Sauvignon to one third Merlot, with perhaps a little Petit Verdot.

L'ENCLOS — Bordeaux: FRANCE

A second growth Pomerol property with an excellent reputation.

ENCLOS DE MONCABON   See Croizet-Bages.

ENFER D'ARVIER — Valle d'Aosta: ITALY

One of the two DOC Valle d'Aosta wines. It is made from Petit Rouge grapes around the town of Arvier. Grape yields, and therefore production of this red wine, is tiny.

ENGLAND

The Romans brought vines to England and viticulture flourished throughout the Middle Ages. Henry II's marriage to Eleanor of Aquitaine and the dissolution of the monasteries both had a marked effect, causing a decline in English viticulture. The last few years have seen a definite revival in English and Welsh wines and there are now about 400 hectares of vines in southern England. Sussex, Kent, Surrey, Somerset, Norfolk and Suffolk are the most important counties. Nearly all the grapes are white; Müller-Thurgau and Seyval Blanc are the most popular, followed by Reichensteiner, Kerner and other new German varieties to make a Germanic style of wine, often with *Süssreserve*. Climatic conditions are often a handicap, but the new breed of English winemakers are acquiring confidence as they gain experience.

ENGLISH BOTTLING

Before it became increasingly common for wines to be bottled at source, fine English wine merchants prided themselves on their expertise at bottling. English bottled claret and port were highly rated, but disappeared when it became compulsory for classed growth claret and vintage port to be bottled at source.

ENGLISH VINEYARDS ASSOCIATION

Founded in 1967, this is the organisation that represents the winegrowers of the United Kingdom. It has set its own standards since 1978, issuing an EVA seal to wines of the required quality, as judged by tasting and analysis. There are about 400 members ranging in size of vineyard from half an acre to 48 acres.

ENGLISH WINE

On a label this describes a wine that is produced by grapes grown in England. Likewise, Welsh wine describes a wine made from grapes grown in Wales. The term should not be confused with British wine.

ENKIRCH Mosel-Saar-Ruwer: GERMANY

The last village of the Mittelmosel, before Koblenz, coming within the *Grosslage* of Schwarzlay.

ENOLOGY   See oenology.

ENOTECA

Literally means a wine library or wine shop in Italian. The most famous is the Enoteca Permanente Nazionale in Siena which has samples of every wine produced in Italy. There are other regional *enotecas*, e.g. the one for Chianti in Greve. One of the best wine shops is the Enoteca Trimani in Rome.

ENOTRIA

Enotria was the name given to Italy by the ancient Greeks and means 'the land of wine'.

ENTRAYGUES ET DU FELS
SOUTH WEST FRANCE

A lost wine of the upper reaches of the Lot valley, a tiny VDQS of red, white and rosé wines from a mixture of local and imported grapes. The red wine is made predominantly from Fer Servadou grapes, the rosé from Cabernet Franc and the white includes Chenin Blanc and Mauzac. Methods of production are primitive.

ENTRE-DEUX-MERS   Bordeaux: FRANCE

The region of Bordeaux situated between the two tidal rivers of the Garonne and the Dordogne. Although red wine is produced there, the appellation is only for white wine. The style of this wine has changed enormously in recent years; once, Entre-Deux-Mers was slightly sweet and bland, now it is crisp, dry and made purely from Sauvignon or a blend of Sémillon and Sauvignon grapes. The vineyards, on undulating hillsides, are some of the most attractive of Bordeaux.

ENZYME

Secreted by a yeast cell in order to convert the sugar in the grape into alcohol. Some twenty-two different enzymes are responsible for the chain reaction of fermentation.

ÉPERNAY   Champagne: FRANCE

One of the centres of the champagne trade and the town where many of the important houses have their cellars in the impressive Avenue de Champagne.

ÉPINEUIL Burgundy: FRANCE

A red wine-producing village near Chablis. It was reputed to have been one of Louis XIV's many favourite wines but then fell into severe decline but is now enjoying a small revival. The wine has its own appellation and is made by a handful of growers from the Pinot Noir grape.

LES ÉPINOTTES See Mélinots.

ÉPLUCHAGE

Practiced in Champagne, this entails the sorting of grapes after picking, and before pressing, to reject any imperfect grapes, which may be unripe or rotten.

ÉRAFLAGE

The removal of the stalks, the *rafle* of the grapes before fermentation. It is similar to *égrappage*.

ERBACH Rheingau: GERMANY

This village is the home of one of Germany's most famous vineyards, Marcobrunn, which means a boundary fountain, and which does indeed exist to mark the boundary between Erbach and Hattenheim. Ownership of the vineyard, but not the fountain, was in fact in dispute until the German wine law of 1971, as the following couplets relate:

To solve this thorny question
Of what is yours and what is mine,
Let Erbach keep the water,
Give Hattenheim the wine.

Erbach now shares the Grosslage Deutelsberg with Hattenheim but is in firm possession of the Marcobrunn vineyard, while other good sites include Honigberg, Siegelsberg, Rheinhell, Steinmorgen, Hohenrain, Michelmark and Schlossberg. Schloss Rheinhartshausen is the largest estate; Langwerth von Simmern, Schloss Schönborn and the State Domain are amongst other notable producers.

ERBALUCE DI CALUSO Piedmont: ITALY

A white DOC wine from around Caluso. It comes in three forms. The dry version is made from the Erbaluce grape and is light and acidic. Caluso Passito, made from semi-dried Erbaluce grapes and aged for five years, is a sweet, strong (13.5° minimum alcohol) dessert wine. Caluso Passito Liquoroso, aged for at least five years, is even sweeter and stronger as it is a fortified wine with up to 16° alcohol and is capable of great age.

ERDEN Mosel-Saar-Ruwer: GERMANY

A village on the Mosel, opposite Ürzig. However, the best vineyards of the village are next to those of Ürzig, specifically Treppchen, meaning 'little staircase', Prälat, and Herrenberg. Busslay on the village side of the river is planted with Müller-Thurgau grapes rather than Riesling. The best producers include the Bischöfliches Priesterseminar and Zach Bergweiler Prum. The *Grosslage* of the village is Schwarzlay.

ERZEUGERABFÜLLUNG

Means 'estate-bottled' in German and appears on a label to indicate that the wine has been bottled at source.

LOUIS ESCHENAUER

A Bordeaux *négociant* company originally from Alsace, that manages Châteaux Rausan Ségla, Olivier, Smith Haut Lafitte and La Garde.

ESCHOL see Trefethen.

ESKDALE NEW ZEALAND

The smallest winery of the Hawkes Bay area producing Chardonnay, Gewürztraminer, Cabernet Sauvignon and Pinot Noir. All the wines are aged in oak and Chardonnay is especially successful.

ESPALIER

A method of training vines, entailing one or two arms with several canes, supported by a trellis or wires.

ESPUMOSO

The Spanish term for sparkling wine.

ESSENCIA see Tokay.

EST! EST!! EST!!! di MONTEFIASCONE Latium: ITALY

A white DOC wine made from Trebbiano and Malvasia grapes from around Lake Bolsena. The story has it that, in 1111, Bishop Fugger was travelling to Rome for the coronation of the Emperor Henry V and he sent his servant on ahead to mark with Est! inns where the wine was especially good. At Montefiascone Est! Est!! Est!!! was marked on the door and, if the story is to be believed, the bishop never reached Rome, but stayed in Montefiascone. Today Est! Est!! Est!!! is not so exciting.

ESTAING — SOUTH WEST FRANCE

Prides itself on being the smallest VDQS of France, with a mere 6 hectares in production in 1985. It is a lost wine of the Lot Valley. Grape varieties are a mixture, Gamay, Cabernet Franc, Fer Servadou for reds and for white Chenin Blanc and Mauzac. Methods of production are primitive.

ESTATE WINE — SOUTH AFRICA

In South Africa this means that the wine comes from grapes grown and vinified on the estate. The wine may be bottled elsewhere.

ESTERHAZY — AUSTRIA

The company of the distinguished Austrian family, the Esterhazy'sche Schloss Kellerei, is the most important producer of the Burgenland, making some of the region's finest dessert wines.

ESTERS

Formed by the reaction between the acids in a wine and its alcohol. They contribute considerably to the bouquet of a wine.

ESTUFA

The *estufa* system describes an essential part of the process of making Madeira. Back in the 16th century Madeira wine was used as ballast by ships travelling to India, a journey which entailed two crossings of the Equator. The wine was found to improve enormously from the resulting heat treatment and today this is imitated for all qualities of Madeira by the use of an *estufa*, a special heated tank. The process is carefully controlled; the temperature must be 45°C with 5° tolerance each way. Three months is the minimum period; no maximum is fixed. Most producers prefer a lower temperature and a longer period up to six months. The *estufas* and their thermometers are sealed by the Madeira Wine Institute.

ESTUFAGEM

E*stufagem* is the Portuguese term to describe the process of heating Madeira in an *estufa*.

ÉTIENNE SAUZET — Burgundy: FRANCE

A fine estate in Puligny-Montrachet producing rich white wines that have been kept on their lees for a year. Their principal holdings are in the Premier Cru vineyards of Puligny, notably Puligny les Combettes.

ÉTIQUETTE

The French term for a wine label.

ETKO-HAGGIPAVLU — CYPRUS

One of the largest Cyprus wine producers, founded in 1844 and owner of the sherry brand Emva.

ETNA — Sicily: ITALY

As the name implies this is a DOC wine from the vineyards on the slopes of the volcano. Red, the most important, made from Nerello Mascalese grapes, is warm and fruity; *rosato* comes from the same grape and the dry white from Carricante and Catarratto. Bianco Superiore, with at least 80% Carricante, is more elegant.

L'ÉTOILE — Jura: FRANCE

One of the four appellations of the Jura, a hilltop village with its own microclimate, where only white wine and *vin jaune* is produced. The grape varieties are Chardonnay and Savagnin and a little Poulsard.

ETSCHTALER — Trentino-Alto Adige: ITALY

The German name for Valdadige.

EUCALYPTUS

Can describe the smell of New World Cabernet Sauvignon, notably that of Heitz Martha's Vineyard, which is surrounded by eucalyptus trees.

EUDEMIS

A grape berry moth, which feeds on grapes. It is treated with insecticides.

EUROBLEND

A table wine coming from more than one Common Market country. Often, it is mainly Italian wine, blended with some German *Süssreserve* (unfermented grape juice added to raise the level of sweetness) and, sold from Germany, with a German label and presentation so it can look misleadingly Germanic. Read the small print carefully, for the label must clearly state that it is a blend of wine from more than one country.

EVA SEAL

Awarded annually by the English Vineyard Association to English and Welsh wines which have reached a required standard on the basis of analysis and tasting. It is impossible for England to have a system of appellations with Common Market standards as the total production is less than that required to be considered an official wine-producing country. Also hybrid grape varieties are forbidden for quality wines in the EEC, but they are grown in English vineyards and are acceptable for English table wine.

L'ÉVANGILE   Bordeaux: FRANCE

One of the most important Pomerol *châteaux*, with an excellent reputation, situated on the Pomerol plateau, amongst all the best properties. The *encépagement* is classic for the area, ⅔ Merlot and ⅓ Cabernet Franc grapes.

LEN EVANS

One of the great personalities of the Australian wine industry. He is Chairman of both the Rothbury Estate in the Hunter Valley and Petaluma in South Australia. In addition he is a prolific wine writer and has done much to promote Australian wines.

ÉVENTAIL DES VIGNERONS PRODUCTEURS   Burgundy: FRANCE

A group of growers from all over Beaujolais and part of the Mâconnais who each make their own wine independently then join together to market it.

EXTRACT

Describes the soluble solids which contribute to a wine's body and substance.

EYRIE VINEYARDS   USA

One of the leading wineries of Oregon, where David Lett pioneered the planting of Pinot Noir in the state. His methods follow those of the Côte d'Or with oak aged wines; Chardonnay is fermented in wood too.

EZERJO

An indigeneous Hungarian white grape variety, widely planted on the Great Plain, but making its best wine in the district of Mor, as Móri Ezerjo, with unusually crisp acidity. The name means 'a thousand boons' or blessings.

F

FABER

A German white grape variety developed in 1929, a crossing of Weissburgunder and Pinot Noir. It is valued for its Riesling-like characteristics, with good sugar and acidity levels and is planted in the Rheinhessen and Nahe.

FACTORY HOUSE

The headquarters of the Association of British Port Shippers in Oporto, Portugal. At present there are twelve member firms. The imposing Factory House was built between 1790 and 1807. A traditional lunch is held every Wednesday for members and their guests; women are excluded.

FAIVELEY   Burgundy: FRANCE

One of the largest estates in Burgundy, with vineyards in the Côte d'Or and in Mercurey. They are based in Nuits St-Georges, Clos des Myglands in Mercurey is their best-known wine.

FALERIO DEI COLLI ASOLANI
The Marches: ITALY

A dry white DOC made mainly from Trebbiano Toscano grapes grown between Ascoli Piceno and the Adriatic coast.

FALERNUM   Latium: ITALY

Was a wine of ancient Rome, made to the south of the city in Latium and Campania and often flavoured with resin, salt water or honey. The tradition lives on; Falernum is produced in Latium, the red made from Aglianico and Barbera grapes, the white from Falanghina grown in vineyards near Gaeta. Further south in Campania, Falerno is made around Mondragone. It is a full-bodied red made from the Aglianico grape and the white is again made from Falanghina.

FALKENSTEIN-MATZEN   See Weinviertel.

FALLER FRÈRES   Alsace: FRANCE

One of the finest growers of Alsace. An alternative label is Théo Faller; the cellars are at Clos des Capucins outside Kayserberg and the estate is called Domaine Weinbach. They own part of the Schlossberg Grand Cru vineyard.

FALSET   see Tarragona.

FANLEAF   See *court noué*.

FARA   Piedmont: ITALY

A robust red wine made from Nebbiolo, Vespolina, and Bonarda grapes, grown around the village of Fara. It needs at least three years' ageing, including two in wood.

FARGUES   Bordeaux: FRANCE

One of the villages of the appellation of Sauternes.

DE FARGUES   Bordeaux: FRANCE

A Cru Bourgeois Sauternes in the commune of Fargues, owned by the Lur Saluces family who apply the same methods as for d'Yquem. The wine can be very good.

FARMYARD

Can refer to the rather earthy animal smell of some red Burgundies, made from Pinot Noir grapes.

FARO   Sicily: ITALY

A red DOC wine made in tiny quantities mainly from Nerello Mascalese grapes grown around Messina.

FAROS   YUGOSLAVIA

A Yugoslav red wine from the island of Hvar, made from the Plavac Mali grape, but a little lighter and drier than Postup or Dingač.

FASS

Means 'an oak barrel' in German. It does not indicate a specific size.

FATTORIA

Like *tenuta*, literally means a farm or estate in Italian. The word often precedes the name of an Italian wine estate, e.g. Fattoria delle Lodoline.

FAUGÈRES *The Midi:* FRANCE

First an appellation in its own right, but now part of the all-embracing Coteaux du Languedoc. It is a robust red made from Carignan, Cinsaut and Grenache grapes and an increasing amount of Mourvèdre and Syrah. The vineyards are centred on the village of Faugères in the first foothills of the Massif Central.

JEAN FAURÉ *Bordeaux:* FRANCE

A small little-known Grand Cru Classé of St-Émilion on the *graves*.

FAURIE-DE-SOUCHARD *Bordeaux:* FRANCE

A little-known Grand Cru Classé of St-Émilion, easily confused with its neighbour, Petit-Faurie-de-Soutard.

FAUSTINO MARTÍNEZ SPAIN

A Rioja firm run by the Martínez family since 1860, producing a third of their grapes from their own vineyards. Their range includes a non oak-aged white Faustino V, a red *reserva* Faustino V and a *gran reserva* Faustino I.

FAVONIO *Apulia:* ITALY

The brand name used by Attilio Simonini for the table wines produced on his estate in northern Apulia. All his wines are made from grapes not usually grown in Apulia, hence the low classification.

FAVORITA *Piedmont:* ITALY

A dry white wine, made from a little-known native vine, Favorita, grown in the Roeri and Langhe hills.

FAYE D'ANJOU *Loire:* FRANCE

One of the villages of the Coteaux du Layon whose name can feature on the label as Coteaux du Layon Villages – Faye d'Anjou.

FAZI-BATTAGLIA TITULUS *The Marches:* ITALY

One of the largest producers of Verdicchio, responsible for the introduction of the distinctive amphora bottle for Verdicchio.

FEHÉR

Describes white wine on a Hungarian wine label.

FEHER BURGUNDI

The Hungarian name for the Pinot Blanc grape.

LE FELS SOUTH WEST FRANCE

A tiny village included in the title and area of the VDQS of Entraygues.

FENDANT

The synonym, used in the Valais canton of Switzerland, for the Chasselas grape.

FÉRET   See Cocks et Féret.

FER / FER SERVADOU

A little-known red grape variety, grown in south west France, for Gaillac, Madiran, Béarn and the wines of the Aveyron. Fer is also the name for Malbec in Argentina.

FERMENTATION

In simple terms, this is the conversion of the grape juice into wine. The yeast in the bloom of the grapes feeds off the sugar in the grapes, transforming it into ethyl alcohol and carbon dioxide. The basic formula is $C_6H_{12}O_6$ (lexose sugar) $\rightarrow 2C_2H_6O$ (ethyl alcohol) $+ 2CO_2$ (carbon dioxide). The process entails a chain of chemical reactions and must be carefully controlled, with particular care paid to hygiene and temperature. The fermentation usually stops naturally when all the sugar has been used up by the yeast, or when the alcohol level becomes too high for the yeast to continue working, or alternatively, the fermentation may be stopped by mutage.

FERMOSELLE   SPAIN

An undemarcated wine region in the south east corner of the province of Zamora almost on the Spanish border. The wines claim a slight resemblance to those of the upper Douro but the region has lost the importance it had in the 18th century.

FERNÃO PIRES

A Portuguese white grape variety grown in small quantities throughout the country. It ripens early, and has also travelled to South Africa.

FERRARI   Trentino-Alto Adige: ITALY

A leading producer of *spumante* made by the *méthode champenoise* in the Italian province of Trento and made, predominantly from Chardonnay and Pinot Noir grapes. The range comprises Ferrari Brut, Brut di Brut Millesimato, Brut Rosé, Extra Dry and Riserva Giulio Ferrari.

PIERRE FERRAUD   Burgundy: FRANCE

A small Beaujolais producer with an excellent reputation.

FERREIRA

A. A. Ferreira is a family owned port house founded in 1751. Its most notable member was Dona Antonia Adelaide Ferreira who ran the company in the second half of the 19th century and built Quinta do Vesuvio and Quinta do Vale de Meão in the remotest part of the Douro. The company still owns extensive vineyards. Superiore Dona Antonio and Duque de Bragança are their fine tawnies. Hunt Roope is a subsidiary company, that in turn ships Tuke Holdsworth vintage ports and there is also a close link with MacKenzie & Co.

FERRIC CASSE   See iron casse.

FERRIÈRE   Bordeaux: FRANCE

A little-known third growth Margaux and the smallest surviving estate of the 1855 classification. The wine is made at Château Lascombes and is rarely seen abroad.

LA FÊTE DE LA FLEUR

A festival held at the end of June in Bordeaux to celebrate the flowering of the vines.

FETEASCA

The Roumanian synonym for the Léanyka grape of Hungary.

FETIASKA

The Bulgarian synonym for the Léanyka grape variety of Hungary.

FEUERHEERD

Founded in 1815 as a general trading company, and transformed into a port house in the 1880s. It is now owned by Barros Almeida.

FEUILLETTE

The traditional Chablis barrel size of 132 litres. Although the wine is no longer sold in a *feuillette*, prices are still reckoned in this unit.

FEUNIG

In German, describes a wine that is high in alcohol.

WILLIAM FÈVRE   Burgundy: FRANCE

An important grower in Chablis and the largest owner of Grand Cru vineyards. He is an exponent of Chablis aged in new oak barrels and strongly disagrees with the expansion of the Chablis vineyards. His wines are sold under the label Domaine de la Maladière.

FEYTIT-CLINET   Bordeaux: FRANCE

A little-known Pomerol *château* acquiring a good reputation under the management of J.-P. Moueix.

FEZ   See Meknès.

FIANO DI AVELLINO   Campania: ITALY

A dry white DOC wine, taking its name from the grape and made in the region of Campania. Fiano is a derivation of *Apianum*, the Latin name acknowledging the bee's (Apis) attraction to the grape. Fiano di Lapio, in the heart of the vineyards, is a subdenomination.

FIASCO

Literally means 'flask' in Italian and describes the wicker flask that used to be characteristic of the dumpy Chianti bottle, until modern technology rendered it impractical and unprofitable.

FIDDLETOWN *California:* USA

An AVA of the Sierra Foothills in Amador County. Zinfandel is the main grape variety.

FIEFS VENDEÉNS *Loire:* FRANCE

A recently promoted VDQS. A tricolour wine from the Vendée to the north of La Rochelle. The wines are light and fresh; whites come from the grape varieties Gros Plant, Chenin Blanc, Sauvignon and Chardonnay; rosés and reds from Gamay, Cabernet Franc, Cabernet Sauvignon, and Pineau d'Aunis.

FIELD CRUSHING

As the name implies, this is the crushing of grapes in the vineyard, a technique developed to prevent the oxidation of the grapes, when the vineyard is some distance from the winery.

FIELD GRAFTING

Describes the joining of a *vitis vinifera* scion to an American rootstock in the desired position in the vineyard. The roots have already developed before grafting takes place. This can only be done in a warm climate.

FIESTA DE LA VENDIMIA SPAIN

The famous festival held in Jerez every September to celebrate the beginning of the vintage. It is dedicated to a country or city that appreciates sherry and is a particularly flamboyant festival with flamingos, bull-fighting and a ceremony for the first pressing of the grapes.

DE FIEUZAL *Bordeaux:* FRANCE

A Graves from the commune of Léognan. A Cru Classé for red, but not for white wine, which is a more recent innovation for the property. The reds have the characteristic *goût de terroir* of the Graves.

FIGARI CORSICA

One of the separate zones within the overall appellation Vin de Corse. It covers the area around the town of Figari in the south of the island. Vineyards were planted extensively here by the wine growers returning from Algeria, but often on unsuitable land so that many vineyards have been converted into grazing land. The main producer is the local cooperative. Nielluccio and Malvoisie de Corse are the dominant grape varieties for red and white respectively, blended with those of the Midi.

FIGEAC *Bordeaux:* FRANCE

A Premier Grand Cru Classé, St-Émilion situated in the *graves* part of the vineyard. It is owned by the Manoncourt family who have put every effort into the quality of their wine. Unusually, Merlot grapes only account for a third of the vineyard, with another third each of Cabernet Franc and Cabernet Sauvignon. The wine aspires to rival the neighbouring Cheval Blanc.

FILHOT *Bordeaux:* FRANCE

A large, second growth Sauternes property with vineyards on sandy soil, producing lighter wines than traditional Sauternes. It used to belong to the Lur Saluces family.

FILLETTE

Means 'little girl' in French and is also a charming name for a half bottle of wine.

FILTRATION

The process of clarification of a wine, usually just before bottling, to remove any suspended particles in the wine. Filter sheets were once made of asbestos, but these are now forbidden; *kieselguhr* filters are common for large particles; *millipore* filters are very fine and remove yeasts and bacteria invisible to the naked eye.

FINDLING

A variation of the Müller-Thurgau grape, grown mainly in the Mosel.

FINESSE

Describes a wine with elegance and style.

FINGER LAKES   USA

The best known wine area of New York State, with vineyards around the elongated lakes of Seneca, Cayaga and others, that look like fingers on the map.

FINING

The clarification of the wine usually after the fermentation has finished. A substance is added which attracts the tiny particles suspended in the wine, causing them to coagulate and drop to the bottom of the vat. Fining materials vary from region to region and include real egg whites, powdered albumin, bentonite, gelatine, dried blood and isinglass. If a wine is aged in barrel or vat for several months, fining may be unnecessary as the wine deposits naturally.

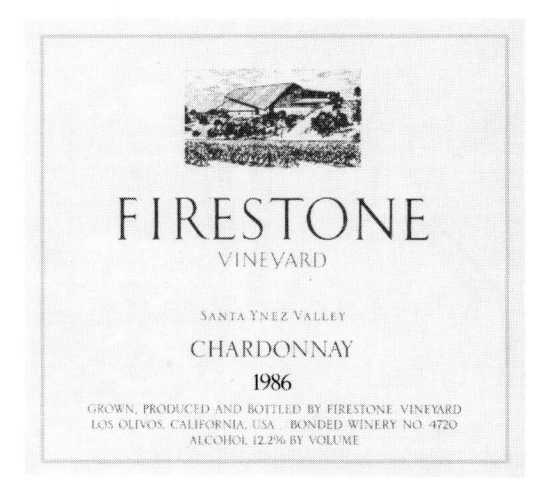

FINISH

Describes the final flavour a wine leaves in the mouth. This should be attractive, encouraging you to have another taste. Sometimes a wine has a short finish, or indeed no finish at all. A long finish is a sign of quality.

FINO   SPAIN

The driest and most delicate of sherries. Its distinctive taste depends upon the development of flor. It is a pale straw colour, only 15° to 18° and best drunk as soon after bottling as possible when it is at its freshest.

FIORANO   *Latium*: ITALY

The brand name used by the Principe de Venosa for the three table wines produced on his estate outside Rome. The red is a blend of Cabernet Sauvignon and Merlot grapes and the two whites are made from Malvasia di Candia and Sémillon.

FIRESTONE VINEYARD   *California*: USA

Run by the family better known for car tyres and in partnership with Suntory. This is the leading winery of the Santa Ynez Valley, with a reputation particularly for Pinot Noir, as well as Cabernet Sauvignon, Merlot, Johannisberg Riesling, Chardonnay and Gewürztraminer.

FIRM

Describes a wine with good structure; the opposite of flabby.

FIRN

The German term for 'maderised'.

DR. FISCHER   *Mosel-Saar-Ruwer*: GERMANY

Weingut Dr. Fischer is an important estate on the Saar with an 18th century house at the foot of the steep Wawerner Herrenberg vineyard and with other vineyards in Ockfen and Saarberg. The wines have the typical steeliness of the Saar.

FITOU   *The Midi*: FRANCE

The very first appellation of the Midi for table wine, created in 1946. It is a red wine and Carignan is still the dominant grape variety, with an increasing amount of Syrah or Mourvèdre, as well as Grenache or Lladoner. The vineyards are on the coastal plain below Narbonne, as well as

FIVE ROSES
Apulia: ITALY

A *rosato* made by Leone de Castris. Reputed to be the first Italian commercial *rosato* wine, it was first produced in the 1930s and acquired popularity during the war. Unusually, it improves after five or so years of cask ageing.

FIXED ACIDITY   See acidity.

FIXIN
Burgundy: FRANCE

One of the most northerly villages of the Côte d'Or and the only village appellation that can be declassified into Côte de Nuits Villages. Its Premiers Crus are most notably la Perrière (part), and Clos du Chapitre (part) as well as les Meix Bas (part), aux Chensots (part), les Arvelets (part), and les Hervelets (part). The most important estates in the village are Domaine Pierre Gelin and Domaine de la Perrière.

FLABBY

Describes a wine which lacks acidity, sometimes referring to wines from a hot country.

FLAGEY-ECHÉZEAUX
Burgundy: FRANCE

The village of Flagey-Echézeaux does not have its own appellation but does boast two Grands Crus: Grands Echézeaux and Echézeaux. The main grower of the village is Louis Gouroux.

FLASH PASTEURISATION

A means of sterilising ordinary sweet or semi-sweet table wines which may have some potential instability. It differs from basic pasteurisation in that the wine is heated to the higher temperature of about 90°C, as opposed to 65–70°, but only for one minute or less and then cooled very quickly. This may have a less detrimental effect on quality than more prolonged pasteurisation.

FLAT

Describes a sparkling wine which has lost its bubbles or a wine which is lacking in acidity so it tastes dull and one-dimensional.

FLEUR DU CAP
SOUTH AFRICA

The brand name for a range of table wines produced by the Oude Meester group on their Bergkelder estate. Cabernet Sauvignon is especially successful.

LA FLEUR-MILON
Bordeaux: FRANCE

A Cru Grand Bourgeois in Pauillac.

LA FLEUR PÉTRUS
Bordeaux: FRANCE

One of the top Pomerol properties. The 9 hectare vineyard is next to Pétrus. It comes third in the line-up of J.-P. Moueix *châteaux* after Pétrus and Trotanoy.

FLEURIE
Burgundy: FRANCE

One of the ten Beaujolais Crus with a right to a separate appellation. The wines are generally fruitier and with more finesse than other Beaujolais. The village cooperative makes good wine.

FLINTY

Describes a certain stoney characteristic apparent in some white wines, such as Pouilly Blanc Fumé.

FLOC DE GASCOGNE

An aperitif made in the Armagnac area from unfermented grape juice and Armagnac. Technically it is a ratafia.

FLOR

The film of saccharomyces yeast – it looks like a veil of cotton wool – that develops on the surface of *fino* and *manzanilla* sherry during ageing to give the wine its distinctive taste. It prevents the wine from oxidising or turning into vinegar. The phenomenon occurs particularly in Jerez. There are some natural *flor* sherries in South Africa and in Cyprus attempts have been made with varying success to induce the growth of *flor* as it is the *flor* character that above all gives *fino* sherry its individual taste and quality.

FLORA

A cross of the Semillon and Gewürztraminer grape varieties, developed in 1958 and grown with limited success in California.

LA FLORAISON

The French term for 'flowering'.

FLORIO   Sicily: ITALY

A large Marsala house, now incorporating Ingham, Whittaker and Woodhouse, as part of the Cinzano group.

FLOWERING

An important moment in the vine's annual cycle as it determines the potential quantity of the vintage. The vines flower for about two weeks, during which time warm dry weather is essential, otherwise pollination will not take place and the vines may subsequently suffer from *coulure* or *millerandage*.

FLOWERY

Describes a wine with a certain fragrance, reminiscent of flowers, for example young Mosel.

FLURBEREINIGUNG

Over recent years, many of the old German terraced vineyards have been abolished; vineyards have been reconstructed and reallocated amongst growers with the object of improving the quality of wine. Regional characteristics have been grouped together so that tiny parcels of vines are eliminated, yields are increased and the vineyards are easier to run and more accessible, with modern machinery and lower labour costs. This process is called F*lurbereinigung*.

FLUTE

The traditional tall thin green bottle from Alsace. It is also the name of the tall elegant glasses used for serving champagne.

FLÛTE D'ALSACE

The distinctive tall green bottle of Alsace. The shape and size were defined in 1959 and only certain other regions may use the bottle, namely Cassis, Château Grillet, red and rosé Côtes de Provence, Crépy, Jurançon, Rosé de Béarn and Tavel Rosé.

FLYER

Describes particles of sediment, detached from the main sediment, floating or flying around in the wine.

FOIANEGHE   Trentino-Alto Adige: ITALY

A distinctive red wine; a Cabernet Sauvignon and Franc blend, with some Merlot grapes, made from vineyards of the same name by Fedrigotti in Trentino. It is not DOC.

FOLLE BLANCHE

Once an important white grape variety used for distillation in the Charente and the Gers, but is now being replaced by Ugni Blanc. As a synonym of Gros Plant it is the grape for Gros Plant Nantais. A little is grown in California.

FONBADET   *Bordeaux*: FRANCE

The largest of the Cru Bourgeois estates of Pauillac.

FONDILLÓN   SPAIN

A rich alcoholic dessert wine made near Alicante, which acquires an almost Madeira-like flavour after ageing in cask for at least fifteen years, during which time the original quantity of wine halves.

FONPLÉGADE   *Bordeaux*: FRANCE

A Grand Cru Classé of St-Émilion, with a grand 19th century *château*, producing underrated wine of some finesse.

FONROQUE   *Bordeaux*: FRANCE

A Grand Cru Classé of St-Émilion and one of the J.-P. Moueix properties.

FONSECA

J. M. da Fonseca is one of the leading Portuguese wine companies, and has no connection with Fonseca port (see Guimaraens). The company was founded in 1834 in Azeitao and made a reputation first with Moscatel de Sétubal. After the war they created a fizzy rosé, Lancers, and they now produce a range of fine table wines, notably reds, Camarate, Pasmados, Periquita and Terras Altas Dão.

FONTANA CANDIDA   *Latium*: ITALY

The largest Frascati producer and now part of the Swiss Winefood group.

FONTANAFREDDA   *Piedmont*: ITALY

An important wine estate, founded by a son of King Victor Emmanuel II and now owned by the Monte dei Paschi di Siena bank. It is especially noted for its Barolo and Asti Spumante while making a range of other Piedmontese wines.

DOMAINE DE FONTARNEY   *Bordeaux*: FRANCE

The second wine of Château Brane-Cantenac.

FORÊTS   See Montmains.

CONTI FORMENTINI   *Friuli-Venezia Giulia*: ITALY

A family company which owns a 16th century castle where it produces a range of DOC Collio wines.

FORRESTER

Baron James Forrester was one of the great characters of the port trade, a member of the company then called Offley, Webber & Forrester. He explored the Portuguese Douro Valley more thoroughly than any of his English colleagues and wrote a pamphlet called 'A word or two on Port Wine' in which he criticised certain malpractices in the port trade, including the addition of brandy. He was drowned dramatically and tragically in the Douro.

FORST   *Rheinpfalz*: GERMANY

Rivals Deidesheim in producing the finest wines of the Rheinpfalz. The wines of Forst owe their individuality to the outcrops of black basalt in the heavy clay soil of the vineyards. The principal grape variety is Riesling. There are two *Grosslagen*: Schnepfenflug and Mariengarten. The most important vineyards within Schnepfenflug are Bischofsgarten, Süsskopf and Stift and, within Mariengarten, the best vineyards are Jesuitengarten, Freundstück, Kirchenstück and Ungeheuer. The less well-known are Elster, Pechstein and Musenhang. The main producers of the Rheinpfalz have property in Forst, such as von Bühl, Bassermann Jordan, Bürklin Wolf and Deinhard.

FORTA

A crossing of the Madeleine Angevine and Silvaner grape varieties, grown in Germany.

FORTIFIED WINE

A wine with an alcoholic strength higher than that of ordinary table wine, as some grape brandy has been added to it at some stage during its production. Snerry, Port, and Madeira are the most common; there are also Malaga, Montilla and Marsala and other lesser known wines.

LES FORTS DE LATOUR
Bordeaux: FRANCE

The second wine of the Château Latour estate.

FORWARD

Describes a wine that is advanced in maturity for its age and the quality of the vintage.

FQSANI
ROMANIA

The town of Fqsani in southern Moldavia gives its name to Romania's largest wine region, including the better-known name of Cotesti, for both red and white wine; Odobeşti which is best for whites and Nicoreşti for reds.

FOUDRE

A large oak or chestnut barrel holding several hectolitres and used in France, especially in The Aude and Provence, for maturing and storing wine. The effect of ageing wine in *foudres* is much less pronounced than with smaller *barriques*.

FOULAGE

For red wine vinification, this is the breaking of the grape skins to release the juice and bring the yeast into contact with the juice. Often the stalks are removed at the same time by a machine called a *fouloir égrappoir*. The grapes may not be pressed until after the alcoholic fermentation is finished.

FOULOIR ÉGRAPPOIR

The machine which gently crushes the grapes rather than pressing them hard, in order to break the skins and release the juice, while at the same time removing the stalks.

FOURCAS-DUPRÉ
Bordeaux: FRANCE

A Cru Grand Bourgeois Exceptionnel of Listrac in the Haut-Médoc, not as well-known as Fourcas-Hosten, but making good wine.

FOURCAS-HOSTEN
Bordeaux: FRANCE

A Cru Grand Bourgeois Exceptionnel of Listrac in the Haut-Médoc which has established an excellent reputation since a change of ownership in 1972. Professor Peynaud advises.

FOURCHAUME
Burgundy: FRANCE

A Chablis Premier Cru. It can be subdivided into Fourchaume, Vaupulent, Côte de Fontenay, Vaulorent and L'Homme Mort. A grower with vines in two or more sites may vinify all the wine together and call it Fourchaume or vinify each plot separately and call each wine by its individual name.

LES FOURNEAUX
Burgundy: FRANCE

A Premier Cru Chablis vineyard that can be subdivided into les Fourneaux, Morein and Côte des Près Girots. A grower with vines in two or more sites may vinify all the wine together and call it Les Fourneaux or vinify each plot separately and sell each wine by its individual name.

FOXY

The flavour associated with wines made from American vines, notably vitis labrusca. It is a peculiar wild earthy tang, relating not to the smell of the animal, but foxy in the sense of wild.

FRANC-MAYNE
Bordeaux: FRANCE

A little-known Grand Cru Classé of St-Émilion situated on the *côtes*.

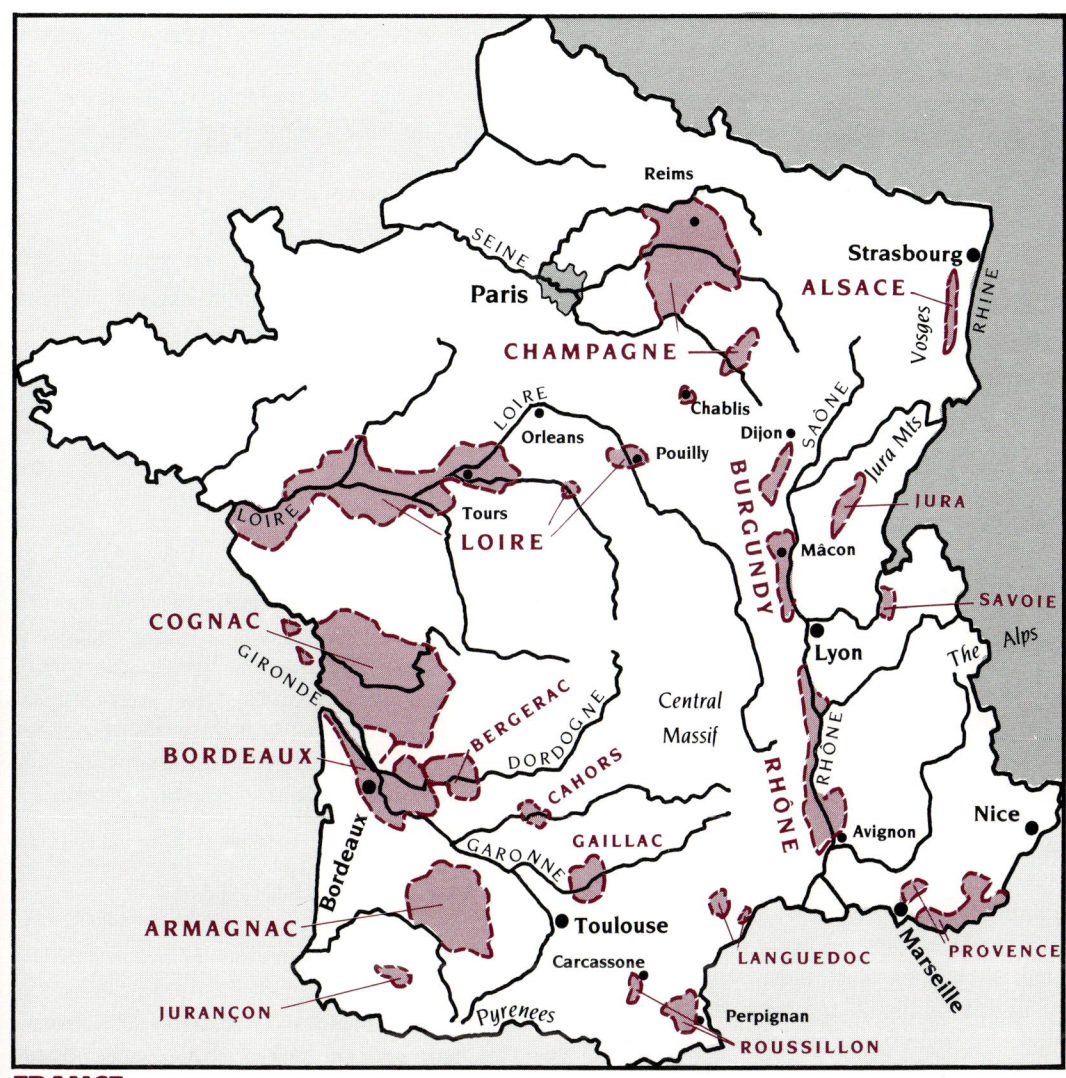

FRANCE

France is a myriad of wine delights. More than any other country in the world she sets the standards in her wines to which all others aspire. In Bordeaux she produces the epitome of Cabernet Sauvignon and luscious sweet Sauternes; in Burgundy the quintessence of Pinot Noir and Chardonnay; in Champagne the greatest sparkling wine; in the Rhône Valley the heights of Syrah and Viognier and in the Loire Valley some superb sweet Chenin Blanc and Sauvignon Blanc. Riesling and Gewurztraminer from Alsace have few rivals. In addition to these five main areas, there is a wealth of other individual wines, scattered all over the country, with the exception of northern France, but most notably in the south west, the Midi, Jura, Savoie, Provence and Corsica.

The French wine law of *Appellation Contrôlée* was instituted in 1936; since then the system has been developed to include Vin Délimité de Qualité Supérieure, *vins de pays* and finally anonymous *vin de table*. France is the world's largest wine producing country, with an average 70 million hectolitres per year, of which 20 million are AC or VDQS.

FRANCIACORTA Lombardy: ITALY

A DOC from vineyards around the town of Cortefranca. It comes in either white or red. The white is either still from Pinot Bianco or *spumante* with the *méthode champenoise*, or *cuve close* from Pinot Nero and Pinot Grigio. The *spumante* version can also be *rosato*. The red is made from an unusual blend of Cabernet Franc, Barbera, Nebbiolo and Merlot grapes, giving a rich mellow flavour.

FRANCO-FIORINO Piedmont: ITALY

A respected house, that does not own vineyards, but buys in grapes to make a full range of Piedmontese wines.

FRANCONIA

The English word for Franken.

FRANGY   see Roussette de Savoie.

FRANKEN GERMANY

A less well-known wine region of Germany, covering the northern part of Bavaria. The heart of the region is around Würzburg. The vineyards are on either side of the river Main, which carves a large W through the hills of Franken and meets the Rhine at Hochheim. Traditionally Frankenwein was sold in fat flagons called *bocksbeutel* and often called Steinwein after its most famous vineyard, Würzburger Stein. Unusually, the best wines are made with Silvaner rather than Riesling, for which the growing season is too short and the climate too harsh. Müller-Thurgau is now more important in quantity but less interesting in taste. New grape varieties, particularly Rieslaner, are also widely planted with some success. The region is divided into three *Bereichs*; Mainviereck, Maindreieck and Steigerwald, which are all frequently used on labels. Most of the wine is made by local cooperatives, apart from a few important wine estates, such as Bürgerspital, Juliusspital, Fürstlich Castell'sches Domänenamt, Weingut Hans Wirschling and the Staatlicher Hofkeller. The majority of the production is drunk locally so that the wines are little appreciated outside the area. *Trocken* wines are popular here and the term Frankisch trocken applies to wine with less than 4 g/l of sugar.

FRANKEN RIESLING

A Californian synonym for the Silvaner grape variety.

BADISCHES FRANKENLAND Baden: GERMANY

One of the seven Bereichs of Baden, but adjoins Franconia and has more affinities with that region. Müller Thurgau is the principal grape variety and much of the wine is bottled in the *Böcksbeutel*.

FRANKISCH TROCKEN   See Franconia.

FRANKLAND RIVER AUSTRALIA

The Frankland River region in Western Australia, is more commonly called Great Southern.

FRANSDRUIF

A South African name for the Palomino grape, meaning literally and illogically the French White. It is used for sherry in the Cape.

FRASCATI Latium: ITALY

The best-known Latium wine, made from Malvasia and Trebbiano grapes, almost in the suburbs of Rome around the towns of Monteporzio Catone and Frascati, up in the hills of the Castelli Romani. Usually full and dry, it is occasionally very sweet, made from semi-dried grapes, medium sweet, and even rarer, *spumante*. Frascati Superiore denotes 12° alcohol.

FRATELLI VALLUNGA
Emilia-Romagna: ITALY

A forward-looking family company, who are changing the image of the region's wines. In addition to Albana, Sangiovese and Trebbiano di Romagna, they make *spumante*, *vino novello* and, most notably, Rosso Armentano from Sangiovese, Cabernet and Pinot Noir grapes.

FRECCIAROSSA Lombardy: ITALY

One of the leading estates of the Oltrepò Pavese making fine table wines to enhance the reputation of the region.

FREE RUN JUICE

The English equivalent of *vin de goutte*.

FREE VINTNER see Vintner.

FREEMARK ABBEY California: USA

A Napa Valley winery which takes its name from its owners, not from any ecclesiastical associations. From the mid 1960s the winery has established a reputation for substantial Cabernet Sauvignon and honeyed Late Harvest Riesling.

FREISA D'ALBA Piedmont: ITALY

Although not a DOC wine, this is considered to be better than its neighbour, the DOC Freisa d'Asti. It is red and can be dry or medium sweet, still, *frizzante* or *spumante*.

FREISA D'ASTI Piedmont: ITALY

Freisa d'Asti is a little-known red DOC wine that can be dry or medium sweet, still, *frizzante* or *spumante*.

FREISA DI CHIERI Piedmont: ITALY

A red DOC wine of limited production made from the Freisa grape at Chieri, just outside the city of Turin. It can be dry or medium sweet, still, *frizzante* or *spumante*.

FREISAMER

A crossing of Silvaner and Pinot Gris grape varieties, grown mainly in Baden.

FREIXENET SPAIN

The second largest *cava* house and with Codorníu is responsible for 70% of the *cava* production. They have a modern winery at San Sadurni da Noya and were the first to introduce *girasols* for *remuage*. Their most popular wines are Brut Nature and Cordon Negro.

FRENCH COLOMBARD See Colombard

FRENCH OAK

French oak, as opposed to American oak is generally considered to be the best type of wood for ageing fine wine, with more subtle effects. It comes from a different species of oak, *quercus robor* and *quercus sessilis*, grown in the forests of Limousin, Nevers, Tronçais, Alliers and Vosges.

FRESCOBALDI Tuscany: ITALY

One of the most important and oldest makers of Chianti Rufina, with extensive vineyards in Tuscany, including Castello di Nipozzano. Montesodi is the name of the property's best wine. They are also leading producers of Pomino, white and red, and make Galestro, Vin Santo and other experimental wines on the family estates, as well as managing Castelgiocondo in Montalcino.

FRESH

Describes a young wine with youthful acidity and flavour.

FRESNO *California*: USA

The name of a town and a county in California's San Joaquin Valley, a fertile area for producing grapes prolifically for jug wine.

FRIEDRICH WILHELM GYMNASIUM *Mosel-Saar-Ruwer*: GERMANY

The Stiftung Staatliches Friedrich Wilhelm Gymnasium is one of the finest estates of the Mosel, founded in 1563 by the Jesuits, with cellars in Trier and vineyards along the Mosel and Saar, planted with a high proportion of Riesling. Ageing in oak is also practised and the results are Mosel wines at their best.

FRIULI-VENEZIA GIULIA ITALY

The province covering the northeast corner of Italy, bordering Yugoslavia and Austria. The region produces more red than white wine, but its white wines are making a much greater impact with modern production methods. The DOC zones are Aquilea, Collio Goriziano, Colli Orientali del Friuli, Grave del Friuli, Isonzo and Latisana, each qualified by several grape varieties, including Picolit, Italy's finest dessert wine.

FRIZZANTE

An Italian term for a lightly sparkling wine, that is not as fizzy as *spumante*.

FRONSAC *Bordeaux*: FRANCE

A Bordeaux village on the banks of the Dordogne near Libourne. The wines of the village are divided into two appellations: Fronsac, once called Côtes de Fronsac, and Côtes de Canon Fronsac. Both are red; the lower vineyards are Fronsac and the higher slopes Canon Fronsac. This is one of the areas that provides affordable, quick-maturing claret.

FRONTIGNAN

Frontignan or Muscat Frontignan or Frontignac can be New World synonyms for the Muscat Blanc à Petits Grains grape.

FROST

A climatic hazard in the northern vineyards of Europe. Winter frosts are less damaging unless the temperature drops to −25°C or below for a prolonged period of time. Much more serious are the spring frosts which can do considerable damage to a vineyard if they occur after the budbreak, in April or May. They may even destroy an entire crop by killing the young shoots. There are two methods of protection against frost damage, by aspersion (spraying the vines) and by lighting *chaufferettes* in the vineyards.

FRUCHTIG

The German term for 'fruity'.

FRUHROTER VELTLINER   See Veltliner

FRUITY

Describes the smell that comes from ripe grapes, not a smell of grapes themselves, but an attractive winey smell.

FRUŠKA GORA YUGOSLAVIA

The most important vineyard area of Vojvodina in northern Yugoslavia, concentrating on white wines from a variety of different grapes. Laski Rizling is the most important, but Gewürztraminer and Sauvignon are more exciting.

FRUTTATO

The Italian term for 'fruity'.

FUDER

The traditional Mosel cask with a capacity of approximately 1000 litres.

FUENMAYOR SPAIN

An important centre of production of Rioja.

FULL-BODIED

Describes a wine with lots of body, that is rich in alcohol and extract, like Châteauneuf-du-Pape, with 12.5° minimum alcohol.

FUMÉ BLANC

A synonym for the Sauvignon Blanc grape, in Australia and California.

FUNCHAL *Madeira*: PORTUGAL

The capital of Madeira, where the Madeira Wine Company and its members have their vinification plants and cellars.

FURMINT

The principal grape variety of Tokay, where it is blended with Hárslevelü and a little Muscat. As well as providing Hungary's legendary sweet wine, it is grown elsewhere in the country and eastern Europe for strong dry white wine, including possibly Yugoslavia's Pošip.

FÛT

A French term for a small oak barrel of indeterminate size.

G

mentation is stopped so that enough residual sugar remains to enable a second fermentation to take place after bottling the following spring. No dosage is necessary. Sometimes the remaining sediment is removed, by filtration or *remuage*, or it can be left in the bottle.

GAILLAC PERLÉ   see Gaillac.

GABIANO   Piedmont: ITALY
A red wine; a new DOC based on Barbera grapes from the village of Gabiano in the Monferrato Casalese hills. Production is tiny.

LA GAFFELIÈRE   Bordeaux: FRANCE
A Premier Grand Cru Classé St-Émilion known as la Gaffelière Naudes until Naudes was dropped from the label with the 1964 vintage. The property has belonged to the Counts of Malet-Roquefort for the last three centuries. The cellars have been modernised recently to enable better control of the fermentation.

GAGLIOPPO
A common red grape variety grown in Italy, in Abruzzi, Campania, Umbria and the Marches, producing full-bodied alcoholic wines, most notably Cirò.

GAILLAC   SOUTH WEST FRANCE
Can be red, rosé or white, dry or sweet, still or sparkling wine. The vineyards cover a large area around the town of the same name near the city of Albi.

The grape varieties of Gaillac are a mixture of those traditional to the area and those recently introduced. The most typical red grape of Gaillac is Duras but a variety of others such as Fer Servadou, Syrah, Gamay, Négrette, Cabernet Franc and Sauvignon and Merlot are also possible. With such a mixture the taste of Gaillac Rouge is very varied; it can be a *primeur* wine for immediate drinking or made to age.

Gaillac Rosé comes mainly from Syrah and Gamay. The white and sparkling wines are made mainly from Mauzac, plus l'En de l'El, Sauvignon and Sémillon. The dry white wines of Gaillac are usually called Gaillac Perlé. The real thing should have the faintest hint of a bubble of pearl, retaining a trace of CO_2 from the malolactic fermentation.

The *méthode gaillacoise* or *méthode rurale* for the production of sparkling wine in the area is claimed to be older than that of champagne. The first fer-

GAJA   Piedmont: ITALY
The star amongst Barbaresco producers, making Barbaresco and other Alba wines including Barolo since 1988 as well as Vinòt by *macération carbonique*. Also experimental Chardonnay and Cabernet.

GALESTRO   Tuscany: ITALY
A new white wine, created by the larger Chianti producers to use up their surplus white grapes. Trebbiano is the main grape, improved with Pinot Bianco, Grigio and Chardonnay, with a maximum alcohol of 10.5°, using modern vinification methods.

GALET
The large flat round pebbles characteristic of the vineyards of Châteauneuf-du-Pape. These originate from very old alpine glaciers. Generally the more stones there are, the riper the grapes will be as the stones absorb heat from the sun and reflect it back onto the vines.

GALICIA   SPAIN
The wines of the region of Galicia in north west Spain include three D.O.s, Rias Bajas, Valdeorras and Ribiero. There are close similarities to the adjoining Minho area of Portugal which makes fresh acidic Vinho Verde, both red and white.

GALLO
California: USA

The E. & J. Gallo winery, founded by Ernest and Julio Gallo at Modesto is California's and the world's largest winemaking plant, with a breathtaking capacity for storage and fermentation measured in millions of gallons in a space age winery in the San Joaquin Valley. Reliable jug wine such as Chablis Blanc and Hearty Burgundy are their main lines, but they also make varietals, port and sherry styles and sparkling wine.

GALLO NERO

Black Cockerel in Italian. The emblem of the Chianti Classico Consorzio. A black cockerel on the bottle distinguishes Chianti Classico from other Chiantis; however not all the producers within the zone are members of the Consorzio.

GAMAY

Gamay Noir à jus blanc to give it its full name and to distinguish the better version from various *teinturier* Gamays is above all the grape of Beaujolais. Outside Beaujolais it is an ingredient of Passe Tous-Grains and is grown in the Ardèche, in Savoie, in the Loire, in Touraine and Anjou for Anjou Gamay and Gamay de Touraine and as an ingredient of Coteaux d'Aubance and in the Haut Poitou and in Saint Pourçain, Côtes de Forez and Côtes Roannaises. Outside France a little is grown in Switzerland for Dôle.

In California a grape called Gamay Beaujolais has been identified as a clone of Pinot Noir, with nothing to do with Beaujolais or Gamay. Napa Gamay is the same as Valdiguié in the Midi. Contrary to popular misconception, Gamay is not the Kékfrankos of Hungary.

GAMBELLARA
Veneto: ITALY

A white DOC wine. Garganega is the principal grape variety and it comes in three versions: Gambellara Bianco, which is similar to Soave and is *superiore* at 11.5° alcohol; Recioto di Gambellara, from slightly dried grapes which can be still, *frizzante* or *spumante* and Vin Santo di Gambellara, a rare dessert wine.

GAMZA
BULGARIA

A traditional red wine grape grown extensively in Bulgaria and similar to the Hungarian Kadarka.

GANCIA
Piedmont: ITALY

A family firm who pioneered the *méthode champenoise* of *spumante* in Italy. Although known as a producer of vermouth, it is a leader in *spumante* with Gran Riserva Carlo Gancia Brut, Il Brut and Pinot di Pinot. They also have vineyards in Apulia.

LA GARDE
Bordeaux: FRANCE

A Graves property which produces red, and more recently, white wine. The vineyards have been extended by the owners, Eschenauer.

GARGANEGA

The principal grape of Soave. Elsewhere in the Veneto it is found in Gambellara, Colli Berici, Colli Euganei, Bianco di Custoza and Colli Morenici Mantovani del Garda Bianco.

GARIBALDI DOLCE
Sicily: ITALY

Was a popular brand name for Marsala Superiore (see Marsala).

GARRAFIERA

The Portuguese term for a selected vintage wine with some age. The minimum requirements are, for red wines, two years ageing before bottling, followed by one year in bottle before the wine is offered for sale, and for white wines, six months ageing before bottling, followed by six months ageing afterwards. The alcohol level must be half a degree higher than the usual minimum for the area. A *garrafiera* is considered to be a producer's best wine and is often much older than these regulations. It is only offered for sale when it is ready for drinking.

GARVEY
SPAIN

The sherry *bodega* Garvey was founded in 1780 by an Irishman, William Garvey. The company now own extensive vineyards and bodegas. Their *fino* sherry San Patricio is named after the patron saint of Ireland; Tio Guillermo is an exceptional *amontillado*. La Lidia *manzanilla*, Bicentenary Pale Cream, dry Ochavico and medium dry Long Life *olorosos* complete the range.

GATÃO
PORTUGAL

The brand name of a vinho verde produced by Borges & Irmão. It is slightly sweet.

GATTINARA
Piedmont: ITALY

A red DOC wine made around the town of the same name in the Vercelli hills, from Nebbiolo grapes which can be blended with 10% Bonarda. It needs four years' ageing, including two in barrel. Quality has improved recently and good Gattinara, such as that made by Luigi Dessiliani, is a serious wine.

GAVI   Piedmont: ITALY

An alternative name for the DOC, Cortese di Gavi.

GAVI DI GAVI   Piedmont: ITALY

A DOC Cortese di Gavi from the estate of La Scolca, it is generally considered to be the best wine from the Cortese grape, with considerable depth of flavour.

LE GAY   Bordeaux: FRANCE

A second growth Pomerol *château*, owned by the two elderly Robin sisters and marketed by J.-P. Moueix.

GAY LUSSAC

A French chemist who discovered the chemical formula for the fermentation process. He also worked on measuring alcohol and gives his name to the French measuring system which is based on a percentage of the total volume.

GAZIN   Bordeaux: FRANCE

One of the largest and best-known of the leading Pomerol properties. It is next to Pétrus. The wines have been criticised for inconsistency. There is a lesser property of the same name in the Graves and Château du Gazin in Canon Fronsac.

GEELONG   AUSTRALIA

A small wine region of Victoria, south west of Melbourne. The planting of Idyll Vineyard began the revival of the area's vineyards. The climate is cool, but low rainfall can be a problem. However the region shows great potential.

GEISENHEIM   Rheingau: GERMANY

Famous for its Wine Institute, this village has several fine vineyards, including Schlossgarten, Klaus, Mäuerchen and Rothenberg. The village comes within two *Grosslagen*: Burgweg and Erntebringer. Good producers include Deinhard, Schloss Schönborn and Balthasar Ress.

GEISENHEIM WINE INSTITUTE

The full title is Institut für Kellerwirtschaft der Forschungsanstalt Geisenheim and it is the leading German research station and oenology school. It experiments with new vine varieties and still uses traditional oak casks.

GEISWEILER   Burgundy: FRANCE

A house with large estates on the Hautes Côtes de Nuits at Domaine de Bévy and Domaine des Dames Hautes. They also deal in table wine and other appellations.

GENERIC

A term used to describe a type or style of wine rather than a specific vineyard, eg. generic Bordeaux or generic Chablis.

GENEROSO

An Italian term to describe a wine that is rich in alcohol, body and extract. In Spain it is used to mean an aperitif or dessert wine, like sherry or Malaga.

GENEVA   SWITZERLAND

The canton of Geneva divides into three areas, the largest being Mandement; the smaller areas are Arve-et-Rhône and Arve-et-Lac. The main grape variety is Chasselas, known as Perlant. Gamay and a little Müller-Thurgau are also grown.

GENEVA DOUBLE CURTAIN

A relatively new method of pruning vines and a variation of the Lenz Moser system. The vines are trained high so that the foliage and fruit form two curtains. The method is thought to assist ripening in cooler climates.

GENTIL AROMATIQUE

A synonym for the Rhine Riesling grape variety in Alsace.

GEORGIA   USSR

One of the most important wine regions of the Soviet Union with vineyards in the valley of the river Rion with its favourable microclimate. Georgia has a reputation for sparkling wine, usually called *champanski* and sometimes made from Chardonnay and Pinot Noir. Tsinandal and Napereuli are the best still white wines, and Saperavi and Mukuzani the best reds. Neutral white Rkatiseli is grown extensively around the Black Sea.

GERANIUMS

A smell of geraniums denotes a fault in winemaking, a breakdown of sorbic acid.

JEAN GERMAIN Burgundy: FRANCE

Maker of fine white wine, notably from Puligny-Montrachet and Meursault.

GERMAN WINE ACADEMY

Runs seminars on German wines at Kloster Eberbach for professionals and amateurs. A very good way of learning about German wine.

GERMANY

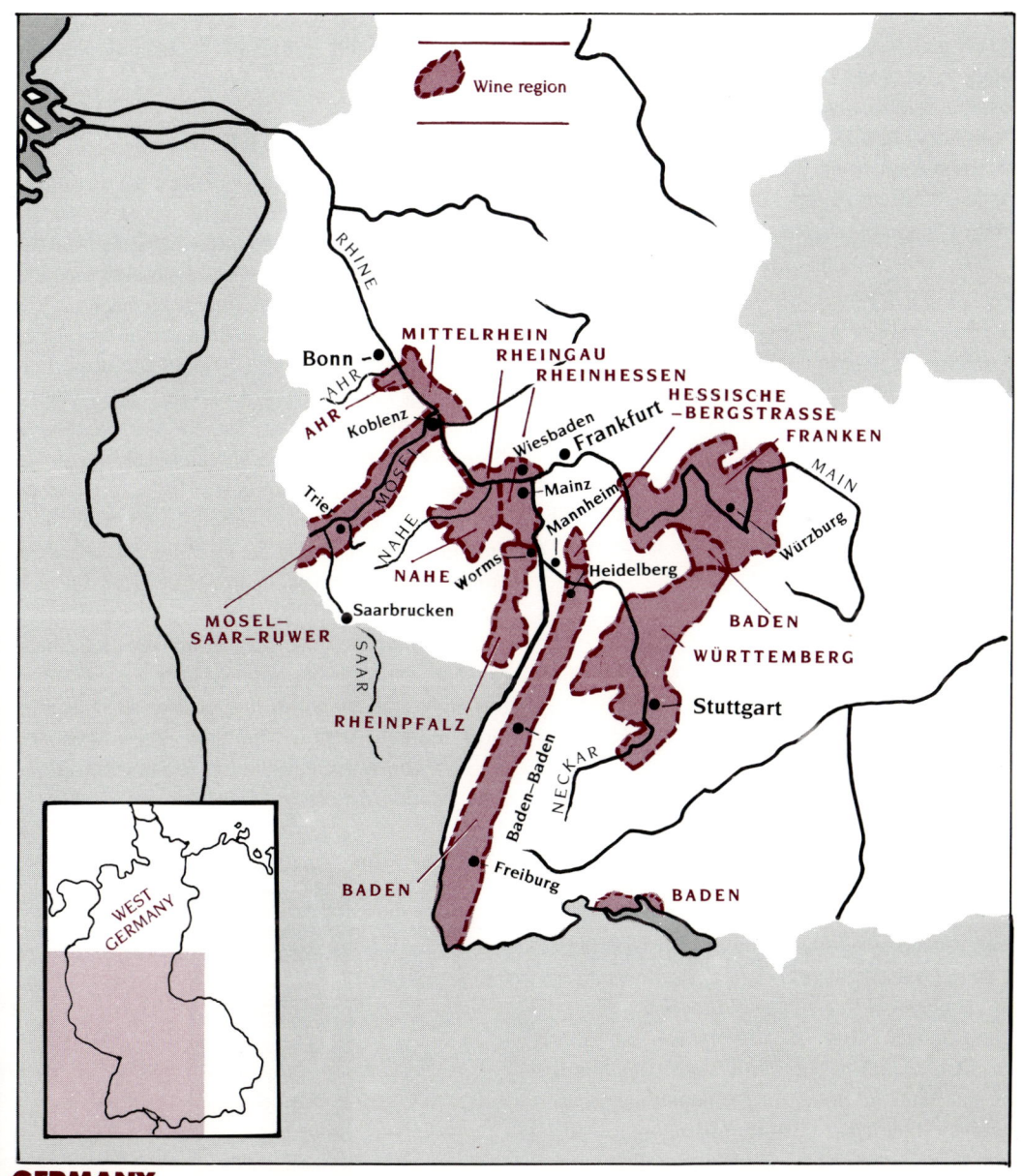

The home of some of the world's finest sweet white wine. In the main wine regions along the Rhine and the Mosel, the Riesling grape produces a wealth of deliciously honeyed wines, but always with the balancing acidity created by the northern climate. German wines are divided into four categories, in ascending order of quality: *Deutscher Tafelwein, Landwein, Qualitätswein* and *Qualitätswein mit Prädikat*. The *Prädikat* is determined by the amount of sugar in the must: again, in ascending order, they are: *Kabinett, Spätlese, Auslese, Beerenauslese* and lusciously sweet *Trockenbeerenauslese*. In addition there is an oddity, *Eiswein*, made from frozen grapes, which, since 1982, has had the same minimum sweetness level of *Beerenauslese*. The sweetest of these wines are made only in the best years when the grapes have been affected by noble rot.

There are eleven quality wine regions in Germany, mainly depending on the Rhine and Mosel, namely: Mosel-Saar-Ruwer, Nahe, Rheingau, Rheinhessen, Rheinpfalz or Palatinate, Mittelrhein, Ahr, Hessische Bergstrasse and then further south, Franconia or Franken, Württemberg and Baden.

It is indisputable that the Riesling grape produces the finest wines. Müller-Thurgau in recent years has been planted in favour of Silvaner, which used to be popular. In addition, there are a variety of experimental grape varieties, some more established than others, which have been introduced to combat the often difficult climatic conditions of a northern vineyard.

The majority of German wines are white; there is some red wine, notably in the Ahr region and also in Baden, for which the principal grape variety is the Spätburgunder.

GEROPIGA

Sweet grape must, or port, used occasionally in Oporto for blending.

GEVREY-CHAMBERTIN
Burgundy: FRANCE

With almost 500 hectares, has the largest area of vineyards of any Côte d'Or village, including some of the finest Grands Crus. In the Middle Ages, the Abbey of Cluny was an important vineyard owner. Gevrey added Chambertin to its name in 1847 by order of the king, Louis Philippe. Some of its vineyards go into the neighbouring village of Brochon.

The Grands Crus of the village are most important of all: Chambertin and Chambertin Clos de Bèze, followed by Chapelle-Chambertin, Charmes-Chambertin, Griotte-Chambertin, Latricières-Chambertin, Mazis-Chambertin, Ruchottes-Chambertin, and Mazoyères-Chambertin, which is occasionally found, though it can also be sold as Charmes-Chambertin.

The Premiers Crus vineyards are: Les Véroilles, le Clos St-Jacques, aux Combottes, Bel-Air, Cazetiers, Combe aux Moines, Estournelles, Lavaux, Pissenot, les Champeaux, les Goulots, Issarts, les Corbeaux, les Gemeaux, Cherbaudes, la Perrière, Clos Prieur, Clos du Fonteny, Champonets, au Closeau, Craipillot, Championnois (known as Petite Chapelle), Ergots and Clos du Chapitre (part).

The village of Gevrey is the home of many estates: Camus Père et Fils, Domaine Pierre Damay, Domaine Drouhin-Laroze, Domaine Joseph Roty, Domaine Armand Rousseau, Thomas Bassot and Louis Trapet.

GEWÜRZTRAMINER

Meaning spicy Traminer. One of the most distinctive of all grape varieties, easily recognisable for its pungent spicy aroma. The grape originates from the village of Tramin or Termeno in the Alto Adige in Italy. Gewürztraminer has a deep pink golden colour; it is a difficult grape to vinify well and is at its best in Alsace where it makes rich scented wines, notably as *Vendange Tardive* and *Sélection des Grains Nobles* in the best years. It is not grown anywhere else in France. In Germany it is found in the Palatinate and Baden; in Austria often as a *Beerenauslese* and in Eastern Europe too, where it is sometimes simply called Traminer or Traminac. A little is also grown in the Alto Adige as Traminer Aromatico. In Spain, Miguel Torres uses it for Vina Esmeralda.

California has some Gewürztraminer, but conditions are generally too hot so that the grapes ripen too early and the wines lack acidity. In Oregon it fares better. In Australia Traminer - Riesling blends are sometimes made, while the cooler vineyards of New Zealand achieve better results.

GHARB See Rabat.

GHEMME
Piedmont: ITALY

A red DOC wine, made around the town of the same name in the Novara Vercelli hills from 60–85% Nebbiolo grapes, with Vespolina and Bonarda. It needs four years' ageing including three in barrel and is a sturdy, robust wine.

GHIAIE DELLA FURBA
Tuscany: ITALY

A non-DOC wine made by Conte Contini Bonacossi at Tenuta Capezzana in Carmignano from equal parts of Cabernet Sauvignon, Cabernet Franc and Merlot grapes.

GIACOBAZZI
Emilia-Romagna: ITALY

One of Italy's largest producers of Lambrusco.

GIGONDAS
Rhône: FRANCE

A village in the southern Rhône which has had its own appellation for red wine since 1971. Grenache is the dominant grape, with Syrah, Cinsaut and Mourvèdre making a wine worthy of some bottle age. A little white and rosé wine is also made in the village but only with the appellation Côtes du Rhône. The largest grower is Gabriel Meffre; Pierre Amadieu and Hilarion Roux at Domaine les Pallières are also important.

GILBEY

One of the famous English wine trade names, also with associations in the spirit trade, for they began distilling gin in London in 1872. The company is now an important part of International Distillers and Vintners. It has associations with Château Loudenne in Bordeaux and several other foreign subsidiaries.

GILETTE
Bordeaux: FRANCE

A little-known Cru Bourgeois Sauternes in the commune of Preignac.

GIMMELDINGEN
Rheinpfalz: GERMANY

A village in the Rheinpfalz. Most of its wine is sold under the *Grosslage* name of Meerspinne.

GIPPSLAND
AUSTRALIA

A small vineyard area in Eastern Victoria which has experienced something of a revival since 1970 with the planting of the Lulgra Vineyard with Cabernet Sauvignon, Rhine Riesling and Sauvignon Blanc. The example has been followed by other wineries.

GIRASOL

Girasol, meaning sunflower in Spanish, is a special pallet used especially in Spain and increasingly in Champagne and elsewhere to replace the lengthy manual process of *remuage*. The bottles are placed neck down inside the metal frame, which can then be rotated daily, either manually or mechanically, or computer programmed for the more sophisticated cellars. The saving in labour and time is enormous, but for purists there is uncertainty as to whether the results are as satisfactory.

GIRO DI CAGLIARI
Sardinia: ITALY

A red, usually sweet DOC wine coming in four versions, made from the Giro grape grown north of Cagliari: dry and sweet with 14° alcohol, fortified dry and sweet. *Riserva* denotes two years' barrel age.

GIRONDE
Bordeaux: FRANCE

A *département*, an estuary and a village. The vineyard area of the *département* of the Gironde was delimited in 1911 so that only vineyards within this area are entitled to the name Bordeaux. Wines on the wrong side of the administrative boundary, such as Bergerac or Côtes de Duras, could no longer bask in the reflected glory of their better-known neighbour. The two great rivers of the Bordeaux vineyards, the Garonne and the Dordogne, flow into the estuary of the Gironde. Some of the best red wine vineyards of the Médoc are on the gravelly deposits of the Gironde where, as local tradition has it, the best wines are produced within sight of water. Finally there is a small village in the Entre-Deux-Mers, Gironde, which to avoid confusion, was renamed Gironde-sur-Dropt.

GIROPALETTE   See *girasol*.

GISBORNE   NEW ZEALAND
The Gisborne area of North Island has enjoyed a considerable expansion of vineyards in the past few years, to become New Zealand's largest wine region. The soil on the plains around the town of Gisborne on Poverty Bay is fertile and the climate provides ample rainfall and sunshine so that the vines are sometimes too productive. White grapes do best here, notably Müller-Thurgau, Gewürztraminer and Chardonnay; Cabernet Sauvignon is less successful.

GISCOURS   Bordeaux: FRANCE
A third growth Margaux; a large property now owned by the Tari family who used to make wine in Algeria. The vineyards have been enlarged and the property modernised so the wine is a candidate for promotion in the classification.

GISSELBRECHT   Alsace: FRANCE
Two Alsace wine houses answer to the name of Gisselbrecht, Maison Louis Gisselbrecht and the larger Willy Gisselbrecht et Fils. Both are at Dambach-la-Ville and have a sound reputation.

GITTON   Loire: FRANCE
An original producer in Sancerre. He makes several different wines according to soil and so produces at least eleven Sancerres, including les Montachins, les Belles Dames et les Romains, as well as two Pouilly Fumés.

GIVRY   Burgundy: FRANCE
A village on the Côte Chalonnaise that produces predominantly red wine from Pinot Noir grapes. It is said to have been one of the many favourite wines of Henri IV! The wine tends to be a little lighter than Mercurey and there are no Premier Cru vineyards. The principal growers are Domaine Thénard, du Gardin and Domaine Juillot.

A LA GLACE   see dégorgement.

DU GLANA   Bordeaux: FRANCE
A Cru Grand Bourgeois Exceptionnel St-Julien, one of the important unclassed growths of St-Julien, owned by Gabriel Meffre of the Rhône and making reputable wine.

GLEN ELGIN   see Tulloch.

GLENORA WINE CELLARS   USA
A small but successful winery of New York State, specialising in white wines, particularly Johannisberg Riesling and Chardonnay, as well as hybrids.

GLORIA   Bordeaux: FRANCE
A *chateau* in St-Julien, the creation of Henri Martin, a leading personality of the Médoc, mayor of St-Julien and Grand Maître of the Commanderie du Bontemps. He has assembled the vineyard from parcels of land from neighbouring Crus Classés, principally St-Pierre, and has established a good reputation for his wine

GLÜHWEIN
A German mulled wine made with red wine, sugar and spices.

GOBELET
A method of pruning the vine so it needs no support and the vine consists of a single trunk with several small branches, like a small bush. This is the most common method in Beaujolais.

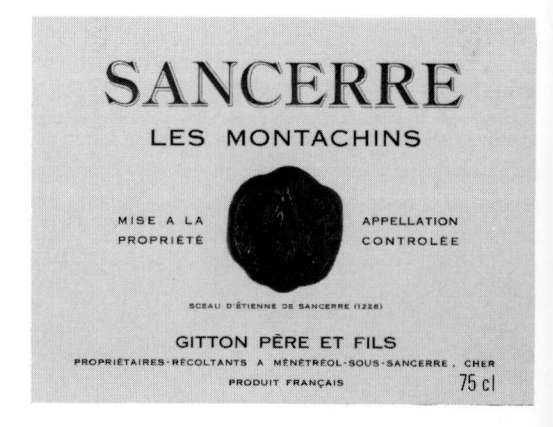

GOLD SEAL VINEYARDS — USA

One of the most successful and forward looking wineries of New York State, who pioneered the introduction of *vitis vinifera* vines into the State and have produced successful Chardonnay and Johannisberg Riesling. As yet others are slow to follow their example. They also make the standard *labrusca* wines.

GOLDENER OKTOBER

An important Liebfraumilch brand produced by the St. Ursula Weinkellerei in Bingen.

LA GOMBAUDE — Bordeaux: FRANCE

The second wine of the Lascombes estate.

GOMBAUDE-GUILLOT — Bordeaux: FRANCE

A little-known Pomerol *château* with a good reputation, situated almost in the village.

GÖNC   see Tokay.

GONZALEZ BYASS — SPAIN

An important sherry house, founded in 1835 by Don Antonio Gonzalez y Rodriguez whose London agent, Robert Blake Byass, joined him in partnership. The company is still family owned and has extensive vineyards. Tio Pepe is their leading *fino* sherry. In addition they have Elegante *fino*, la Concha medium *amontillado*, Alfonso dry *oloroso*, San Domingo pale cream, Nectar Cream and some wonderful old *olorosos* such as Apostoles Oloroso Muy Viejo and old dessert sherries, Matusalem and Solera 1847. Other interests include Rioja and Catalonia.

GOOSEBERRIES

Sometimes associated with wines made from Sauvignon Blanc grapes such as Sancerre.

GORDO

An Australian synonym for the grape variety Muscat d'Alexandrie.

GORE BROWNE TROPHY — ENGLAND

Awarded annually to the best English wine, in memory of Margaret Gore Browne who planted England's second new vineyard at Beaulieu Abbey in 1958.

GOTHIC WINDOWS   See tears.

HENRI GOUGES — Burgundy: FRANCE

A grower in Nuits St-Georges, mainly making Clos des Porrets, les St-Georges, les Pruliers and les Vaucrains. His wines no longer have their former depth and concentration.

GOULBURN VALLEY — AUSTRALIA

A small wine region in Victoria about 75 miles north of Melbourne. Microclimate and soil are varied, resulting in a diversity of wines. Chateau Tahbilk is the best producer.

GOULD, CAMPBELL

Gould, Campbell vintage port is shipped by the company of Smith Woodhouse.

GEORGES GOULET — Champagne: FRANCE

A small champagne house in Reims. Cuvée du Centenaire is their prestige *cuvée*.

GOÛT AMERICAIN

Describes, in Champagne, a sweeter blend made especially for the American market.

GOÛT ANGLAIS

Describes, in Champagne, a dry wine and, in Burgundy, a big smooth wine.

GOÛT FRANÇAIS
Describes a sweet wine in Champagne.

GOÛT DE TERROIR
A French term to describe an earthy smell or flavour coming from the soil. This is sometimes characteristic of Graves.

GOVERNO
A technique used in Italy for the production of Chianti. Its full name is *governo all'uso toscano* and it was refined by Barone Ricasoli in the mid-19th century. It is now less common since modern vinification techniques have advanced. The *governo* method consists of adding must from 5–10% of the grapes, which have been left to dry and concentrate, to vats of normally fermented wine, in order to cause a refermentation and give the wine more colour and alcohol. It makes the wine ready for earlier drinking but also makes it more susceptible to deterioration and is now only used by some producers to make a youthful style of Chianti and not for wines intended for maturation. The use of the *governo* method can be detected by a faint prickling in the mouth.

GOZO   See Malta.

GRAACH   *Mosel-Saar-Ruwer*: GERMANY
An important but tiny village in the Mittelmosel. The principal vineyards, with some of the best river sites, are Himmelreich, Domprobst and Josephshofer, which belongs to the Kesselstatt estate and is sold without using the village name. The *Grosslage* is Münzlay. Good producers are J.J. Prüm, von Schorlemer and the Friedrich Wilhelm Gymnasium.

GRACIANO
The Graciano grape is one of the ingredients of red Rioja, grown mainly in the Rioja Alta. Plantings have declined as yields are low, but the wine gives Rioja an attractive perfumed character.

GRACIOSA   see Azores.

GRAF VON NEIPPERG   *Württemberg*: GERMANY
Weingüter and Schlosskellerei Graf von Neipperg is an old 13th century estate, still run by the von Neipperg family. Red wine predominates, from Limberger, Müllerrebe and Spätburgunder grapes, with whites from Riesling and Traminer. The family also own property in Saint-Emilion.

GRAFTING
An essential procedure in most vineyards. Only American rootstocks are resistant to phylloxera, therefore *vitis vinifera* plants or scions have to be grafted onto other roots. This is usually done in a nursery and is called bench grafting, as opposed to field grafting, which is in the vineyard itself.

GRAHAM
A port house of Scottish origin. Their first recorded shipment was 27 pipes by John Graham in 1826. Quinta dos Malvedos near the Spanish border is made as a single *quinta* port, as well as being a base for fine vintage port. Graham is now part of the Symington family's empire of port houses.

GRANITE BELT   see Queensland.

GRAN RESERVA
The term Gran Reserva is used in Spain for a wine that has been aged for a minimum of two years in oak cask and three years in bottle and released in its sixth year. Gran Reservas are only made in exceptional years when the wine will benefit from such a lengthy maturation.

GRAND-BARRAIL-LAMARZELLE-FIGEAC   *Bordeaux*: FRANCE
The largest of the Grands Crus Classés vineyards of St-Émilion and therefore widely seen.

GRAND-CORBIN-DESPAGNE   *Bordeaux*: FRANCE
A Grand Cru Classé of St-Émilion on the *graves*, almost next to Pomerol.

GRAND CORBIN-PECRESSE   *Bordeaux*: FRANCE
Or Grand Corbin-Giraud, as its owner M. Giraud prefers to call it, is a Grand Cru Classé of St-Émilion.

GRAND-PUY-DUCASSE
Bordeaux: FRANCE

A fifth growth Pauillac. The *château* doubles as the *Maison du Vin* in Pauillac. The wine is not very well-known but is making something of a come-back after the vineyards were replanted in the 1970s.

GRAND PUY LACOSTE
Bordeaux: FRANCE

A fifth growth Pauillac. A property generally considered to be better than its classification which now belongs to the Borie family of Ducru Beaucaillou. They have modernised the estate and are making successful wine.

GRAND ROUSSILLON
The Midi: FRANCE

A *vin doux naturel* from Roussillon, rarely found now. The principal grape varieties are Grenache and Muscat.

LA GRANDE COTE D'AUXERRE
Burgundy: FRANCE

Outside the town of Auxerre in northern Burgundy, this was a famous red wine-producing vineyard in the Middle Ages. Migraine and La Chainette were the two finest sites, but the area fell into dramatic decline following the phylloxera crisis and Clos de la Chainette is all that remains today.

GRAND CRU

The best quality wine in several French appellations, notably in Alsace, Burgundy and parts of Bordeaux, where the best vineyards are described in this way.

GRAND CRU VINEYARDS
California: USA

A winery in the Sonoma Valley which concentrates on Gewürztraminer, including artificially botrytised wine, Sauvignon Blanc and Sémillon, as well as Chenin Blanc and Cabernet Sauvignon.

GRAND LISTRAC
Bordeaux: FRANCE

The brand name for the wine of the cooperative of Listrac.

GRAND MAYNE
Bordeaux: FRANCE

A little-known Grand Cru Classé of St-Émilion situated on the *côtes*.

GRAND NOIR DE LA CALMETTE

A *teinturier* grape variety at one time planted extensively in the Midi and also in the Charente for Cognac. High productivity is its only quality and plantings have declined dramatically.

GRAND PONTET
Bordeaux: FRANCE

A reputable Grand Cru Classé of St-Émilion situated on the *côtes*.

GRANDE MARQUE

Literally means 'a great brand' and, in Champagne specifically describes houses that belong to the Syndicat de Grandes Marques de Champagne. Their wines are therefore described as *grande marque champagne*.

LES GRANDES MAISONS D'ALSACE

A group of the nine most important Alsace shippers to Great Britain, designed to act as a promotional body for Alsace wines in general and their own houses in particular. They are Hugel, Trimbach, Dopff au Moulin, Dopff & Irion, Preiss Zimmer, Kuentz Bas, Leon Beyer, Schlumberger and Lorentz.

GRANDES-MURAILLES
Bordeaux: FRANCE

A tiny, relatively unknown Grand Cru Classé of St-Émilion.

GRANDS-ECHÉZEAUX
Burgundy: FRANCE

An important Grand Cru vineyard in the village of Vosne-Romanée.

GRANGE HERMITAGE
AUSTRALIA

One of the legendary wines of Australia. It is pure Shiraz, aged in small French barriques and produced by Penfolds. Hermitage is the Australian name for Shiraz and The Grange was where the Penfolds family first settled at Magill in South Australia when they arrived in the country in 1844. The wine was made for the first time in 1951 by Max Schubert; 1955 was a legendary vintage and a succession of usually fine wines have followed.

GRANITE

Often goes with schist and is found notably in Beaujolais and also in the northern Rhône area. The Gamay grape thrives on granite, enjoying the good drainage and high mineral content. Acidity is a dominant characteristic in the wines made from grapes grown on granite.

GRÃO VASCO

The brand name for the Dão wine produced by Sogrape in Portugal.

GRAPE VARIETY

The grape variety of a wine, a single variety or a blend of several, is one of the major factors in determining the taste of the wine. The grape variety gives a wine its essential character, but is influenced by the soil on which it is grown and the climatic conditions to which it is subjected and finally by the wine maker's methods of vinification. There are hundreds of different grapes used for wine making all over the world. Most of these come from the *Vitis Vinifera* family. Other vine families such as *Vitis Labrusca* or *Vitis Rupestris* and so on are found in some wine regions, notably North American, where they are native, and are used for grafting rootstock to combat *phylloxera*. These are loosely called American vines, while *hybrid* grape varieties are a cross between *Vitis Vinifera* and another member of the *Vitis* family.

GRAPEY

Describes the distinctive aroma of some grape varieties like Muscatel or Scheurebe.

GRAPPUT

A red grape variety grown in the Lot and Garonne and in the Gironde, but only of local and diminishing importance. It is a permitted variety of Côtes du Marmandais.

GRAŠA

A Roumanian white grape variety used mainly for the sweet wines of Cotnari.

GRAŠEVINA

The Yugoslav name for the Italian, Welsh or Laski Rizling grape variety.

ALFRED GRATIEN   Champagne: FRANCE

A small, traditional champagne house of fine quality.

GRATIEN MEYER   Loire: FRANCE

Good producers of sparkling Saumur and cousins of the champagne house, Alfred Gratien.

GRAUBÜNDEN   SWITZERLAND

Or Grisons, this is the source of the best-known wine from German-speaking Switzerland. The warm climate here ripens the Pinot Noir grapes with some good results.

GRAUVES   Champagne: FRANCE

The valley of Grauves is a less-favoured part of the vineyards of Champagne.

GRAVE DEL FRIULI
Friuli-Venezia Giulia: ITALY

The most important Friuli-Venezia Giulia DOC, accounting for half the region's wine production, based in the western part of the region. There are seven varieties in the DOC: Cabernet, mainly Franc; Merlot, amounting to half the DOC; Pinot Bianco, including some Chardonnay; Pinot Grigio; Refosco; Tocai and Verduzzo.

LA GRAVE TRIGANT DE BOISSET
Bordeaux: FRANCE

A second growth Pomerol *château* that has recently been acquired by J.-P. Moueix, which augurs well for the future.

GRAVEL

The dominant soil of the Haut-Médoc, notably in Margaux, but also in other areas. It produces wines with balance and delicacy, drains well and reflects the heat, but has less moisture retention than limestone. There is good aeration of the soil, too.

GRAVES   Bordeaux: FRANCE

The Graves is an important part of the vineyards of Bordeaux and unusual in that the appellation is for both red and white wine. More white wine used to be made, but the balance has now shifted and the better wines are generally considered to be the reds, which are not unlike those of the Médoc, but with a distinctive *goût de terroir*. The grape varieties are the same, predominantly Cabernet Sauvignon with Cabernet Franc and Merlot and, for the white wine, Sauvignon and Sémillon in varying proportions. The whites used to be rather sweet, but have changed with the demands of fashion to become increasingly drier. The name Graves comes from the gravelly soil; the area stretches from the suburbs of Bordeaux, south along the Garonne to Langon, with the enclave of Sauternes, Barsac and Cérons in the middle of the area. The best wines are produced in the six most northerly communes: Pessac, Talence, Leognan, Martillac, Villenave d'Ornon and Cadaujac. There are thirty-one other communes but few of real importance. The wines of the Graves were classified in 1953 and again in 1959 and include 13 reds and eight whites. All of these now come within the new, more limited appellation of Pessac-Léognan. Haut-Brion was the only estate included in the 1855 classification of the Médoc. The other four great red wine *châteaux* are La Mission Haut-Brion, Domaine de Chevalier, Pape Clement and Haut-Bailly. Laville Haut-Brion is indisputably the best of the whites.

GRAVES DE VAYRES
Bordeaux: FRANCE

A small enclave in the Entre-Deux-Mers region of Bordeaux, with more gravel in the soil than the neighbouring appellation, hence the name. There is no connection with the appellation of Graves. More white than red wine is made; the whites are sweeter than Entre-Deux-Mers and reds may bear a resemblance to lesser Pomerols.

GRAVES SUPÉRIEURES
Bordeaux: FRANCE

Identical to Graves, except that it has a higher degree of alcohol, 12° as opposed to 11°.

GRAVINA   Apulia: ITALY

A new DOC from near Bari. It is a dry white made from Greco di Tufo, Bianco d'Alessano, with Bombino Bianco, Trebbiano Toscano and Verdeca grapes. A *spumante* of the DOC is also permitted.

GRAY MONK — CANADA

A small British Columbian winery, growing five white European varieties: Pinot Auxerrois, Kerner, Pinot Gris, Johannisberg Riesling, Bacchus and Gewürztraminer. For reds, they prefer hybrids such as Maréchal Foch.

GRAY RIESLING

Gray Riesling in California or Grey Riesling in New Zealand is a synonym for the Trousseau Gris grape variety. In California it produces a rather neutral soft white wine, often bottled as a varietal. A little is grown in New Zealand, but of no importance.

GREAT SOUTHERN — AUSTRALIA

A wine region which covers a large area of Western Australia from Mount Barker to Albany, to Denmark, Rocky Gulley and Frankland River. It is also called Mount Barker. The climate is suitable for viticulture and there has been a gentle trend towards the creation of new vineyards prompted by an appellation system similar to that of the Margaret River. Fine red and white wines are being produced and Chateau Barker is one of the largest pioneering estates.

GREAT WESTERN — AUSTRALIA

Great Western is a wine region in Victoria, important above all for the production of sparkling wine. The region lies about 150 miles to the west of Melbourne. The climate is difficult, with low rainfall and occasionally severe frosts. Temperatures are cooler than usual in Australia, with a consequently longer ripening period. Seppelts are the biggest winery of the region, making various blends of Great Western 'Champagne'.

GREAT WESTERN CHAMPAGNE — USA

Great Western Champagne is a sparkling wine made by the Pleasant Valley Wine Company, New York State's oldest winery. Other hybrid wines are also produced.

GRECHETTO

A white Umbrian grape, used for Orvieto and other Umbrian DOCs, as well as for *Vin Santo*.

GRECO

A white southern Italian grape variety, at its best in Greco di Tufo and also found in Lacryma Christi del Vesuvio, Torre Quarto and Greco di Bianco.

GRECO DI BIANCO — *Calabria*: ITALY

A delicious white dessert DOC wine made around the town of Bianco from Greco grapes. It needs a minimum of one year's ageing, making it sweet and luscious with 17° alcohol. With further ageing it becomes drier.

GRECO DI TODI — *Umbria*: ITALY

A dry white *vino da tavola* made from the Grechetto grape grown around the small town of Todi in the Umbrian hills.

GRECO DI TUFO — *Campania*: ITALY

A dry white DOC wine made from Greco grapes grown around the village of Tufo. It is very occasionally *spumante* and can age quite well.

GREECE

The origins of Greek wine go back to mythology; in the Middle Ages it provided *malvasia* for malmsey sack, originating from the port of Monemvasia in the Peloponnese. Today, the country grows grapes for the table, for raisins and for wine all over the mainland and islands. Soil and climate vary enormously and methods are generally unsophisticated. The better wines are subject to an appellation system. Retsina is the most characteristic wine; sweet red dessert wines such as Mavrodaphne and dessert Muscat are most successful as well as some red table wines like Naoussa and Nemea. Achaia Clauss is the biggest producer while Château Carras is demonstrating the enormous potential for modernisation.

GREEN

Describes a wine with a high level of acidity, possibly made from unripe grapes.

GREEN SILVANER

Green Silvaner or Grüner Silvaner is the correct name for the grape variety commonly called Silvaner, as opposed to Blauer Silvaner, a pale red version grown around Württemberg.

GREEN GRAPE

A South African synonym for the Sémillon grape.

GREEN HUNGARIAN

A rather dull white grape variety of uncertain origins planted in limited quantities in California.

GRENOUILLES   Burgundy: FRANCE

The smallest of the seven Grand Cru vineyards of Chablis. It is nearest to the river Serein and doubtless the noise of the frogs was clearly audible in the vines – hence its name.

GRESSIER GRAND-POUJEAUX
Bordeaux: FRANCE

A traditional Haut-Médoc estate in the commune of Moulis which has been owned by the Saint Afrique family since 1724.

GREY RIESLING   See Gray Riesling.

GREY ROT   See *pourriture grise*.

GREYSAC   Bordeaux: FRANCE

A reputable property in the commune of Bégadan, Médoc.

GRGICH HILLS   California: USA

Austin Hills and Mike Grgich joined forces to found this Napa Valley winery in 1977. Chardonnay is their flagship; Johannisberg Riesling, Zinfandel and Cabernet Sauvignon also merit their reputation.

GRIGNOLINO D'ASTI   Piedmont: ITALY

A light red wine made from the Grignolino grape and up to 10% Freisa from vineyards around the town of Asti. It is Piedmont's largest DOC zone.

GRIGNOLINO DEL MONFERRATO CASALESE   Piedmont: ITALY

A light red DOC wine made from the Grignolino grape and up to 10% Freisa from vineyards in the hills around Casale Monferrato.

GRILLO

A white Sicilian grape variety used for Marsala.

GRINGET

The principal grape variety of sparkling Savoie wine from Ayze; it is a synonym for Savagnin from the Jura.

GREEN VALLEY-SOLANO
California: USA

An AVA in Solano County in northern California.

GREEN VALLEY-SONOMA
California: USA

One of the many AVAs of Sonoma County.

GREMIO

The Associaçao dos Exportadores do Vinho Porto was originally called the Gremio until the name was changed to Associaçao with the 1974 Revolution.

GRENACHE

A red grape of Spanish origin where it is called Garnacha and widely planted all over the country. It produces heavy alcholic wines which tend to age quickly and it needs blending with other varieties. It is found notably in Rioja, Navarra, Catalonia and Vega Sicilia.

In France it is planted in the Midi and is one of the thirteen varieties of Châteauneuf-du-Pape and is found in Côtes du Rhône and the other appellations of the southern Rhône, alongside Mourvèdre and Syrah, and also in Corsica and in Sardinia as Cannonau. It has also spread to the New World, Australia and South Africa and to California where it is grown for port type wines in the Central Valley.

Grenache Blanc is one of the white grapes of the Midi found notably in Châteauneuf du Pape, Coteaux d'Aix en Provence and Cassis. It is also grown in Spain as Garnacha Blanco in Rioja, and elsewhere. The wines are high in alcohol, low in acidity and oxidise easily.

GRINZING   AUSTRIA

One of Vienna's main wine villages, with *Heurigen* galore for the thirsty.

GRIOTTE-CHAMBERTIN
Burgundy: FRANCE

A little-known Grand Cru vineyard in the village of Gevrey- Chambertin.

GRIS DE BOULAOUANE
MOROCCO

A light, dry, refreshing rosé, coming from vineyards south of Casablanca.

GRISONS, SWITZERLAND   See Graubünden

GRK   YUGOSLAVIA

A sherry like wine from the island of Korčula off the Dalmatian coast.

GROLLEAU

A red grape variety grown mainly in the Loire valley for ordinary red and rosé wine, notably Rosé d'Anjou. It is now declining in favour of Gamay and Cabernet Franc.

GROOT CONSTANTIA   SOUTH AFRICA

The estate of Groot Constantia founded in 1685 represents the historic beginnings of the South African wine industry, producing the legendary Constantia, a rich dessert wine, which sadly is no longer made. The old Dutch house of Simon van der Stel is now a museum. The winery has recently been enlarged, the vineyards expanded and a wide range of table wines are produced, notably Pinotage, Cabernet Sauvignon, Sauvignon Blanc, Weisser Riesling and Heerenwood, a Cabernet Sauvignon, Shiraz blend.

GROPPELLO   *Lombardy*: ITALY

Comes from the southwest shores of Lake Garda, and is made mainly from the grape of the same name. A medium-bodied, fruity red *vino da tavola*.

GROS PLANT DU PAYS NANTAIS
Loire: FRANCE

A dry white wine from the same area as Muscadet, from vineyards around the city of Nantes. It is made only from Folle Blanche grapes, known locally as Gros Plant and is a crisp acidic wine. The better wines are bottled 'sur lie'.

GROSLOT   see Grolleau

GROSSLAGE

The German term for a combination of vineyards or *Einzellagen* (individual vineyards) within one *Bereich*. One name groups together several similar vineyards and is used only for *Qualitätswein* and wines with a *Prädikat*. The commercial advantage of a *Grosslage* name is that a larger amount of wine is available under one name rather than small amounts of several different wines.

GRUAUD-LAROSE   *Bordeaux*: FRANCE

A second growth St-Julien which has had a colourful history, belonging respectively to a M. Gruaud and a M. de Larose, and then the Cordier family whose showpiece it now is. The second wine is Sarget de Gruaud-Larose.

GRUMÉ   *Burgundy*: FRANCE

Describes a Beaujolais that has been selected at a blind tasting as one of the best wines of the area. It is therefore entitled to use a label saying *selectionné par les Grumeurs de l'Ordre des Compagnons du Beaujolais*.

GRUMELLO   *Lombardy*: ITALY

One of the four areas of Valtellina Superiore named after a 15th century castle.

GRUNER VELTLINER   see Veltliner

GUADET-ST-JULIEN
Bordeaux: FRANCE

A relatively unknown Grand Cru Classé of St-Émilion.

GUEDES

The most remarkable family in the Portuguese wine trade; the owners of the company Sogrape and the creators of Portugal's most successful wine, Mateus Rosé. Another branch of the family are responsible for Aveleda.

GUENOC VALLEY   California: USA

An AVA in Lake County. Cabernet Sauvignon is the main varietal.

GUERROUANE   MOROCCO

An *appellation d'origine garantie* in the region of Meknès Fez, producing wines from Cinsaut, Carignan, and Grenache grapes, found under the name of Chantebled. A *vin gris* from Cinsaut and Carignan is also included in the appellation.

GUIMARAENS

The port house of Guimaraens was first called Fonseca Monteiro & Co, but was established by the English Guimaraens family who took the name Fonseca for their wines. The company is now linked with Taylors, but the wine is kept quite separate. Their vineyards are the Quinta Santo Antonio and the Quinta do Cruzeiro. Bin 27 is a good young tawny.

GUIRAUD   Bordeaux: FRANCE

The only first growth Sauternes, apart from Yquem, in the village of Sauternes itself. After a period in the doldrums, it has recently changed ownership and the new proprietor is making his wine with meticulous care and great enthusiasm. At present there is a high proportion of Sauvignon grapes in the vineyard, so a dry wine is also made, G, as well as a red Pavillon Rouge de Château Guiraud from Cabernet Sauvignon and Merlot.

GUMPOLDSKIRCHEN   AUSTRIA

A pretty spa town in the Thermenland area of Niederösterreich, known for its rich heady white wine, made from Rotgipfler and Zierfändler grapes.

GUNFLINT

The characteristic smell of mature Chablis, a stoney flinty smell that the French call *pierre u fusil*.

GUNTERSBLUM   Rheinhessen: GERMANY

A large but relatively unknown wine town on the Rhein-front, coming within the *Grosslagen* of Krötenbrunnen and Vogelsgärtchen. The *Einzellagen* are Steinberg, Sonnenberg and Eiserne Hand, but are rarely seen outside Germany.

GUNTRUM

Louis Guntrum is a German family company with a thriving export business and owners of an estate in the Rheinhessen, with vineyards in Nierstein and Oppenheim. The company dates back to 1824, but earlier generations were brewers and coopers in the 14th century.

GUTEDEL

A German synonym for the Chasselas grape, where it was once widely grown in the Palatinate.

GUTENBORNER

A German crossing of the Müller Thurgau and Chasselas Napolean grape varieties, grown with some success on the Mosel and in England.

GUTTURNIO DEI COLLI PIACENTINI   Emilia-Romagna: ITALY

This was a red DOC in its own right from Emilia Romagna, made from 60% Barbera and Bonarda grapes. It used to be medium sweet and *frizzante*, is now dry and still, and has been incorporated as part of a larger DOC of Colli Piacentini, as Colli Piacentini Gutturnio.

GUYOT

A method of pruning vines, a variation of the *cordon* method, leaving in the case of a single *guyot*, a trunk and one arm, or for a double *guyot*, two arms. It is used in the fine wine regions of France and necessitates training the vines on wires.

GYPSUM

Gypsum, or yeso in Spanish, is calcium sulphate. The sherry grapes used to be lightly dusted with this before pressing, to improve the acidity level in the *must*. Nowadays it is added after crushing.

GYRASOL   See *girasol*.

GYROPALETTE   See *girasol*.

H

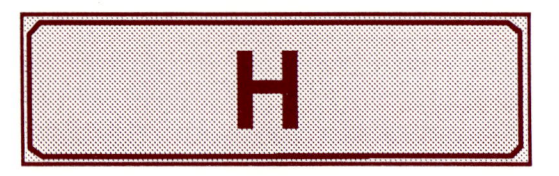

HABILLAGE
The overall term for the dressing of a wine bottle, including the label, capsule or foil and possibly *muselage*.

HAIL
A climatic hazard in many wine regions. The damage caused by hail is usually localised, but can be very severe, destroying an entire crop. It may also harm the following year's crop by damaging the potential new growth. Insurance against hail is possible, although expensive. Rockets are sometimes fired into the hail clouds in an attempt to disperse them, but are rarely very effective.

HALBFUDER
A traditional German Mosel cask size, holding about 500 litres of wine.

HALBSTÜCK
A traditional German cask size, containing 600 litres.

HALBTROCKEN
A description for medium dry wine in Germany and indicates that the sugar content is not more than 10 g/l greater than the total acid content with a maximum of 18 g/l. Landwein must not be sweeter than *halbtrocken*. These wines are generally more successful than *trockens*, but often still lack the real delicacy of German wine.

HALLGARTEN   Rheingau: GERMANY
A famous village on the river, with vineyards protected by the Taunus mountains. It comes within the *Grosslage* of Mehrhölzchen and the principal *Einzellagen* are Schonhell, Hendelberg, Jungfer and Würzgarten. Good producers include Deinhard and Schloss Schönborn, as well as the village cooperative.

Hallgarten or, in full, Arthur Hallgarten GmbH, is also the name of an important German wine company, based in Geisenheim and London, and specialising in estate wine.

HAMBLEDON VINEYARD   ENGLAND
Planted in 1951 by Sir Guy Salisbury-Jones, who was one of the pioneers of the new wave of English viticulture. Chardonnay, Pinot Noir and Seyval Blanc are grown on the chalky soil of the Hampshire downs.

HAMILTON RUSSELL VINEYARDS
SOUTH AFRICA

A new wine estate in the Overberg district of South Africa near the seaside town of Hermanus. Had its first vintage in 1981 and is rapidly creating a reputation for oak aged Cabernet Sauvignon, Pinot Noir, Chardonnay and Sauvignon Blanc. It is one of the most southerly of all the Cape wineries and benefits from a cooler climate.

HAMILTON'S EWELL VINEYARDS
AUSTRALIA

One of the oldest wineries of South Australia, with vineyards in the Eden Valley where they concentrate on white wines, of which Hamilton's Ewell Moselle and Vintage Sauternes are their best wines.

HANEPOOT
The South African name for Muscat d'Alexandrie which was possibly one of the first grapes introduced into the Cape and makes a successful dessert wine, sometimes sold as Hanepoot.

HANNS CHRISTOF
An important German branded wine, a *Kabinett* from the Palatinate, produced by the House of Deinhard. Hanns Christof Deinhard was probably the first member of the family involved in wine, back in the 1650s. The company was not founded until 1794 by Johann Friedrich Deinhard.

HANTEILLAN   Bordeaux: FRANCE
A Cru Grand Bourgeois of Cissac, Haut-Médoc. The property has been restored and is now making interesting wine.

HARASZTHY

The colourful 'Count' Agoston Haraszthy takes credit as the founder of the Californian wine industry. He travelled extensively in Europe between 1851 and 1862 and brought numerous vine cuttings back to California, possibly including the vine that became known as Zinfandel. He also wrote a book, 'Grape Culture, Wines and Wine Making'.

HARD

Describes a wine with an excess of tannin. Usually this fades with time.

THOMAS HARDY   AUSTRALIA

One of the most important wine companies of Australia. Its 19th century origins are in the McLaren Vale with the Tintara vineyard. The fifth generation run this family company which has expanded to include vineyards on the Murray River, and Siegersdorf in Barossa and at Keppoch. The company also bought the Emu Wine Company and Chateau Reynella. Eileen Hardy Dry Red is their best red wine; Cabernet Sauvignon is good too, and also Nottage Hill Claret and other Reserve Bin Reds, such as St. Thomas Burgundy, made from Shiraz, as well as good ports and sherries and a sweet Late Harvest Lexia.

HARO   SPAIN

Haro is in the centre of the Rioja Alta and the home of several *bodegas*.

HÁRSLEVELÛ

One of the principal grapes of Tokay in Hungary and not grown anywhere else in Europe. Its sweet spicy flavour gives attractive wines, notably around Debró. It has also been introduced into South Africa with some success. The name means 'lime leaf'.

HARSOVO   BULGARIA

A defined Controliran wine region of origin, making varietal wines from local red grapes.

HARVEYS OF BRISTOL

Harveys of Bristol have long been associated with sherry, but only established their own vineyards and *bodega* in Spain as recently as 1970. The company is now owned by Allied Breweries. They are responsible for the world's biggest selling sherry, Bristol Cream. Other wines in their range include Club Amontillado and Luncheon Dry Fino.

HATTENHEIM   *Rheingau*: GERMANY

One of the prettiest villages of the Rheingau, with a host of fine vineyards. It comes within the *Grosslage* of Deutelsberg; Steinberg, which requires no village name, is generally considered one of Germany's best vineyards, run by the State Domaine with its headquarters in neighbouring Kloster Eberbach. Nussbrunnen, Engelmannsberg, Hassel, Pfaffenberg, Wisselbrunnen, Schützenhaus and Mannberg are other important *Einzellagen*. Apart from the State Domain, notable producers include Schloss Schönborn, Langwerth von Simmern and Balthasar Ress.

HAUT-BAGES AVEROUS
Bordeaux: FRANCE

The second wine of the Lynch-Bages estate.

HAUT-BAGES-LIBÉRAL
Bordeaux: FRANCE

Fifth growth Pauillac. A little-known property which used to belong to the Cruse family. It was not *château* bottled until 1972 and has enjoyed an indifferent reputation that is now improving.

HAUT BAGES MONPÉLOU
Bordeaux: FRANCE

A Cru Bourgeois of Pauillac once part of the vineyards of Duhart Milon.

HAUT-BAILLY
Bordeaux: FRANCE

A Graves Cru Classé from the commune of Léognan. Produces only red wine and is considered one of the best properties of the Graves. A quarter of the vineyard consists of very old vines. The second wine is called La Parde de Haut-Bailly.

HAUT-BATAILLEY
Bordeaux: FRANCE

A fifth growth Pauillac. This property used to be part of Batailley, but was divided up by its owners, the Borie family. The vineyards have now been replanted, and the wines are lighter than the average Pauillac. The second wine is La Tour Aspic.

HAUT-BENAUGE
Bordeaux: FRANCE

A small, little-known appellation within the Entre-Deux-Mers, where the wine is considered to be of slightly better quality.

HAUT BOMMES
Bordeaux: FRANCE

A little-known but well-situated Cru Bourgeois in the commune of Bommes, making some excellent wine.

HAUT-BRION
Bordeaux: FRANCE

The only *château* of the Graves to be placed in the 1855 classification, it was mentioned by Pepys in the late 16th century. The property is now surrounded by the suburbs of Bordeaux and owned by the American banker, Clarence Dillon, who is also proprietor of the neighbouring property, La Mission Haut-Brion. The deep gravel soil gives rich-flavoured wines with the distinctive *goût de terroir* of the Graves. The second wine, unusually, is a non-vintage blend. Bahans-Haut-Brion. A small amount of white wine is also made.

HAUT COMTAT
Rhône: FRANCE

Until 1945 the two Côtes du Rhône Villages of St. Pantaléon-les-Vignes and Rousset-les-Vignes made a wine called Haut Comtat. In 1948 the name was abandoned in favour of Côtes du Rhône, which was in turn elevated to Côtes du Rhône Villages in 1969 and 1972 respectively.

HAUT-CORBIN
Bordeaux: FRANCE

A small little-known Grand Cru Classé of St-Émilion on the *graves*.

HAUT-MARBUZET
Bordeaux: FRANCE

A Cru Grand Bourgeois Exceptionnel of St-Estèphe with a high proportion of Merlot grapes, making it easier to drink than many of its neighbours.

HAUT-MÉDOC
Bordeaux: FRANCE

The southern half of the Médoc where the best *châteaux* are situated. It is an appellation in its own right and also includes the appellations of Margaux, St-Julien, Pauillac, St-Estèphe, Moulis and Listrac. The best wines of the appellation are Cantemerle and La Lagune.

HAUT MONTRAVEL
SOUTH WEST FRANCE

A slightly sweet wine produced in a small area within the zone of Bergerac. In comparison to Côtes de Montravel it is sweeter, but is more often sold as Côtes de Bergerac.

HEAT SUMMATION

Measured in degree days, this is a way of determining the overall temperature of a vineyard during the growing season, usually from the beginning of April to the end of October in the northern hemisphere. It is the total of the daily temperatures above 50°F or 10°C. Cool regions have a low heat summation, for example Chablis has 950 degree days, compared with Hermitage with 1,450 degree days.

HEAVY

Describes a wine that is too rich in alcohol and extract. Sometimes this is a question of context; a full-bodied red wine will be too heavy for a summer's day, but perfect for a winter's evening.

HEBEI   See China.

HECTARE

The land measure in Europe. 2.48 hectares equal one acre. Yields are given per hectare.

HECTOLITRE

One hectolitre equals one hundred litres. Yields in France are given as so many hectolitres per hectare. Hecto is a common abbreviation, especially when referring to barrel sizes.

HAUT POITOU   *Loire*: FRANCE

The vineyards of this aspiring AC are to the north of the city of Poitiers. The principal producer is the cooperative at Neuville de Poitiers. Unusually for France, most of the wines are named according to their grape variety, Sauvignon, Chardonnay, Gamay, Cabernet, as well as a sparkling wine made from pure Chardonnay.

HAUT-PRIEURÉ   *Bordeaux*: FRANCE

The third label of the Prieuré-Lichine estate.

HAUT-SARPE   *Bordeaux*: FRANCE

A Grand Cru Classé of the *graves* part of St-Émilion.

HAUTVILLERS   *Champagne*: FRANCE

The Benedictine abbey outside Épernay where Dom Pérignon worked as a cellarmaster and initiated the blending process of Champagne in the 1660s.

HAWKES BAY   NEW ZEALAND

One of the country's best wine regions and the biggest after Gisborne, with some of the oldest wineries. Situated on North Island, the climate is sunny and drier than Gisborne and the area has a wide variety of soil, encouraging the planting of several different grape varieties, notably Chenin Blanc, Chardonnay, Sauvignon Blanc, Cabernet Sauvignon and Müller-Thurgau. McWilliams, Te Mata and Eskdale are notable estates in the area.

HEALDSBURG   *California*: USA

An important town and wine centre in Sonoma County.

HEEMSKERK VINEYARDS   TASMANIA

One of the leading wineries of Tasmania, named after Abel Tasman's flagship on his voyage of discovery of Tasmania in 1642. The vineyard was established in 1975, with 20 hectares planted half in Cabernet Sauvignon. The balance is Chardonnay, plus a little Pinot Noir and Rhine Riesling. The oak aged Cabernet Sauvignon is showing great potential.

HEITZ WINE CELLARS   California: USA

Heitz is one of the great names of California with an outstanding reputation for Cabernet Sauvignon, most notably his flagship, Martha's Vineyard. Bella Oaks is good too. In addition this family run Napa Valley winery makes Chardonnay, and unexpectedly, Grignolino.

HELBON

Also called Chalybon, this was a Syrian sweet wine, appreciated by the Persian kings of antiquity.

HEGGIES   AUSTRALIA

One of the new vineyards of the Hill Smith family, in the hills above the Barossa Valley, with a cooler climate.

CHARLES HEIDSIECK   Champagne: FRANCE

A successful champagne house that is owned by Henriot and is therefore now part of the Moët Hennessy empire. The founder of the company was the 'Champagne Charlie' of the song.

HEIDSIECK MONOPOLE   Champagne: FRANCE

A popular *grande marque*. Piper Heidsieck and Charles Heidsieck are both part of the same family but are under quite separate ownership.

HEILIGENSTEINER KLEVNER : see Savagnin

HEILIGER DREIKÖNIGWEIN

The name given to an *Eiswein* made on 6th January.

HELFENSTEINER

A crossing of Frühburgunder and Trollinger, grown in small quantities in Württemberg.

HELICOPTER

Perhaps an unexpected piece of vineyard equipment. Helicopters have been used in some steeper vineyard areas, such as the Mosel, to spray the vines. More recently they have been used in California and at Château Pétrus to dry the grapes after a rainstorm during the harvest.

HENDERSON   NEW ZEALAND

A wine region on North Island to the west of Auckland, with some of the oldest vineyards of the country and a strong Dalmation influence. The area under vines, comprising mainly hybrids, has declined in recent years for the climate is unsuitable for viticulture having high rainfall with considerable risk of rot and soil too heavy for vines.

HENKEL & CO.

The largest *Sekt* producers in Germany, based in Wiesbaden since 1856. Henkel Trocken is their main brand.

HENRIOT   Champagne: FRANCE

A champagne house that owns Charles Heidsieck and is now part of the Moët-Hennessy group. It owns considerable vineyards of white grapes.

HENRIQUES & HENRIQUES

An independent Madeira company founded in 1850, with family vineyards that produce all their own grapes.

HENSCHKE   AUSTRALIA

An old established winery near the Barossa Valley in South Australia. Some of their vineyards have recently been replanted with Malbec, Chardonnay and Traminer; they make an interesting range of varietal wines. Hill of Grace and Mount Edelstone are two of their vineyards.

HERMITAGE   Rhône: FRANCE

One of the great wines of the northern Rhône. It can be white, but is more often red. The vineyards, which are tiny for a wine with a great reputation, are on the sunsoaked terraced hillsides above the town of Tain l'Hermitage. The red wine is made principally from the Syrah grape. Occasionally a little Marsanne may be included. Traditional growers age their wine in wood and it is a wine of considerable longevity. White Hermitage is made from a blend of Marsanne and Roussanne grapes. The best known Hermitage comes from the company of Paul Jaboulet Ainé under the label la Chapelle for the red wine and Chevalier de Stérimberg for the white. Other reputable producers include Max Chapoutier, Jean-Louis Chave, Henri Sorel, Jean-Louis Grippat, Delas Frères, Louis de Vallouit.

HERMITAGE

Sometimes called Red Hermitage or Hunter Hermitage, it is a synonym for the Syrah grape variety in Australia. Confusingly, in South Africa, Hermitage means Cinsaut.

HERMITAGE

The South African name for Cinsaut and one of the most widely grown cultivars of the Cape. It was first introduced to the country in the 1850s.

HERMITAGÉ

Refers to the 18th century practice of boosting weaker claret with more robust wine from the Rhône valley, especially from Hermitage. Often used in wine destined for a sea voyage. 1795 Lafite was a notable example.

HERMITAGE LA CHAPELLE
                                            Rhône: FRANCE

The brand name used by Jaboulet for their best *cuvée* of red Hermitage. The name refers to the tiny chapel of St-Christophe on the hill of the Hermitage vineyards.

HERMITAGING   See *hermitagé*.

HEROLDREBE

A German crossing of the Portugieser and Limberger grape varieties, grown mainly in the region of Württemberg.

HESSISCHE BERGSTRASSE GERMANY

Germany's smallest wine region, situated between the cities of Darmstadt to the north and Heidelberg to the south, with terraced vineyards overlooking the Rhine valley. It is split into two *Bereichs*, Umstadt, which is planted mainly with Müller-Thurgau grapes and, more importantly, Starkenberg, where Riesling is predominant. The best villages are Bensheim and Heppenheim, where the Eltville State Domain has vineyards. Otherwise production is in the hands of local cooperatives and the wines are rarely found outside the area.

HEURIGE   AUSTRIA

The traditional Viennese wine tavern in the outlying villages of the capital, such as Grinzing, where the young wines of the area are served with great jollity.

Heurige is also the name for the young wine, which takes this designation on 11th November until it is superseded by the next vintage.

HICKINBOTHAM WINEMAKERS
AUSTRALIA

The Hickinbotham family have played an important role in the Australian wine industry. Alan Hickinbotham was largely responsible for establishing Roseworthy College. They now own vineyards at Mount Anakie in Geelong, at Elgee Park south of Melbourne and at Meadowbank in Tasmania.

HILL SMITH   see Yalumba.

HILLCREST
USA

The first winery to be established in Umpqua Valley, Oregon after the repeal of Prohibition. White Riesling is the speciality; Cabernet Sauvignon is good too.

HIRONDELLE

A branded table wine owned by the brewery company, Bass Charrington. Its provenance has varied over the years, including Italy and Cyprus.

HOCHAR
LEBANON

The name of the family that created Château Musar in the Lebanon. Gaston Hochar founded the family business in 1930. His son, Serge, trained in Bordeaux and now makes the wine of Château Musar according to Bordelais tradition.

HOCHHEIM
Rheingau: GERMANY

The Rheingau village from which the English term 'Hock' originated. It stands apart from the rest of the Rheingau, separated by the urban sprawl of Wiesbaden, and forms something of a wine island, but with the distinctive characteristics of the Rheingau. The *Grosslage* is Daubhaus and the better *Einzellagen* include Domdechaney, Kirchstück, Hölle, Stein, Sommerheil and Königin Victoriaberg, which was named after Queen Victoria when she visited Hocheim in 1850. Good producers include the State Domain and Schloss Schönborn.

HOCK

Traditional English name for Rhine wine, possibly originating from the village of Hochheim.

HOFSTATTER
Alto Adige: ITALY

A family company which is one of the more important producers of the Alto Adige, making a comprehensive range of wines from their own vineyards as well as buying from other growers.

DR. HOGG MUSCAT

A peculiarly New Zealand grape variety grown in Poverty Bay, and once in the greenhouses of Victorian England for table grapes

HOGSHEAD

The term for a wooden cask, traditionally used for shipping wine in bulk. It can vary in size, but is usually about 250 litres.

HÖHE DOMKIRCHE
Mosel-Saar-Ruwer: GERMANY

One of the three main ecclesiastical estates of this region. It makes up the Bischöfliche Weingüter Trier, with vineyards on the Saar.

HOLLOW

Describes a wine with some initial flavour and finish, but which lacks a middle in its taste and is without any real substance.

L'HOMME MORT   See Fourchaume.

HONEYED

Describes some mature sweet wines, such as fine German wines.

HORTEVIE Bordeaux: FRANCE
A small property in St-Julien.

HOSBAG TURKEY
A red wine made from Gamay grapes in Trakya.

HOSPICES DE BEAUNE
Burgundy: FRANCE
The Hospices de Beaune are two charitable institutions, the Hôtel Dieu and the Hospice de Charité in the centre of Beaune, which have in the past been financed by legacies, particularly of fine vineyards. Now the estates of the Hospices de Beaune consist of some 131 acres of Grands and Premiers Crus vineyards in the Côtes de Beaune. The Hôtel Dieu was founded in 1445 by Nicolas Rolin, Chancellor to the Duke of Burgundy, Philippe le Hardi. Its brightly-coloured tiled roof is one of the landmarks of the town. The Hospices de Beaune wines are auctioned on the third Sunday in November. The first sale was held in 1853. This is the first appearance of the new vintage wines and used to be considered a guide to the general value and quality of the vintage. However, in recent years, some prices have reached artificially inflated levels. The purchaser takes delivery of the wine by the January following the sale and is responsible for its *élevage* and bottling.

HOSPICES DE NUITS
A charitable institution that was founded in 1692. Since 1961 it has held an annual auction on the Sunday before Palm Sunday. It owns nine hectares of *premier cru* vineyards in Nuits St. Georges as well as lesser *premiers crus*. The sale does not attract the same attention as the Hospices de Beaune sale.

HOT BOTTLING
A procedure to ensure the stability of a wine in bottles, probably a sweet or semi-sweet wine. The wine is pasteurised just before bottling and left to cool down in bottle.

HOTTE
The French term for a long basket, worn on the back, used for carrying grapes at the vintage. They are particularly used in Alsace and nowadays are more often made of lighter plastic.

HOUGHTON WINES AUSTRALIA
The leading estate of the Swan Valley and virtually synonymous with the wines of Western Australia. 1859 was their first vintage. The legendary Jack Mann, one of Australia's greatest winemakers, saw fifty vintages here and established a reputation for Houghton's White Burgundy. Hardys now own the estate.

HÖVEL Mosel-Saar-Ruwer: GERMANY
Weingut von Hövel is a fine 200 year old estate of the Saar with monastic cellars dating back to the 12th century. Vineyards include Scharzhofberg and sole ownership of Oberemmeler Hütte.

HOWELL MOUNTAIN California: USA
An AVA in Napa County in the eastern hills.

HUAPAI see Kumeu.

HUDSON VALLEY USA
One of the wine growing regions of New York State.

HUELVA SPAIN
A D.O. in south west Spain, between the Portuguese frontier and the Atlantic, making some white wine and some sherry-like wines, called *generosos*, which once used to be sent to Jerez for blending. The bulk of the region's production is basic table wine which is often distilled. The grape varieties include those of Jerez; Palomino and Pedro Ximénez, as well as Mantúa, Garrido fino and Pedro Luis.

HUET
Loire: FRANCE

A reputable grower in Vouvray with three vineyards, Le Haut Lieu, Le Mont and Le Clos du Bourg, which is reputed to have been a vineyard in the 5th century. He makes sparkling as well as still wines.

HUGEL
Alsace: FRANCE

One of the great names of Alsace. They are a family company of many generations, based in Riquewihr, with vineyards around the village including part of the Sporen and Schoenenberg sites. They were the instigators of *Sélection de Grains Nobles* and *Vendange Tardive* and also sell three other qualities of wine, Réserve Personnelle, Cuvée Tradition and then the standard quality.

HUGELLAND   See Neusiedlersee-Hugelland.

HUNGARY

Hungarian viticulture is full of variety. There are indigenous grapes with picturesque names like Szürkebarát, translating literally as Grey Friar, and more commonly called Pinot Gris, Hárslevelü (lime leaf), Ezerjó, (A thousand boons) and Kékfrankos, thought to be a relative of Gamay, as well as western European varieties such as Merlot, Pinot Noir, Silvaner and Gewürztraminer. The most common white grape is Olaszrizling, grown especially in the Pannonian Plain. There are several wine districts around Lake Balaton, namely Badacsony, Balatonfüred-Csopak, Somló, Mór and Balaton itself. Eger, in north eastern Hungary, is famous for its Bulls Blood, while Hungary's finest wine is the legendary Tokay Aszu, a dessert wine made from botrytis affected grapes. The sweetest of all, Tokay Essence, is credited with life-restoring powers.

CENTRAL EUROPE

HUNGERFORD HILL — AUSTRALIA

One of the largest wineries of the Hunter Valley region. The first vineyards were planted in 1967 and a modern winery built in 1972. Their red wines are aged in Nevers and Limousin oak; their white wines cool fermented and bottled young. They also own vineyards in Coonawarra and have a winery in the Riverland area of New South Wales. The 'Collection' series are their best wines.

HUNT ROOPE see Ferreira.

HUNTER RIVER RIESLING

An Australian synonym for the Sémillon grape, except in Western Australia.

HUNTER VALLEY — AUSTRALIA

One of the great wine regions of Australia. Traditionally the Hunter describes the Lower Hunter Valley around Pokolbin and Rothbury. There is a distinction between this and the upper Hunter which stretches from Denman to Scone. The fame of the Hunter rests upon its table wines. The Sémillon grape, also called Hunter Riesling, is particularly noted for white wines and Chardonnays are becoming important too. For red wines the traditional grape has been Hermitage, also called Shiraz. Some good Cabernet Sauvignon is made too. Climate varies from year to year, with varying amounts of rain, from flood to drought, so vintages are important. Hail can cause severe damage. The Upper Hunter has only really become established since the late 1960s. Investment by Penfolds has set the pattern for large scale development whereas boutique wineries abound in the Lower Hunter. The reputation of the area stands on its white wine, especially with Chardonnay and aromatic varieties.

HUNTER VALLEY RIESLING

The local name for the Sémillon grape in the Hunter Valley region of Australia, where it accounts for a large area of the vineyards.

HUNTINGDON ESTATE — AUSTRALIA

One of the leading properties of the Mudgee area in New South Wales, planted in 1969, mainly with Shiraz and Cabernet Sauvignon, and also some Chardonnay and Sémillon and a tiny amount of Pinot Noir, Merlot and Sauvignon. Chardonnay and Cabernet Sauvignon have done much to enhance the reputation of Mudgee.

HUXELREBE

A Germanic grape variety, a cross of Gutedel and Courtillier Musqué, developed in the 1920s and named after a Fritz Huxel. It is a very prolific variety, grown mainly in the Rheinhessen and Palatinate and usually provides Prädikat wines, even in poor years. It is also found in England.

HYBRID

A crossing between two vine species, usually *vitis vinifera* and an American variety such as *vitis labrusca*. The object of a hybrid is to produce a vine with the resistance to disease of the American species, and with the quality of fruit of *vitis vinifera*. The better known hybrids include Seibel and Seyve Villard. They are not permitted for the best quality wines, such as the QWPRD wines of the EEC.

HYDRAULIC PRESS   See press.

HYDROMETER

An instrument used to measure the sugar content of must and thereby indicate its potential alcohol. As sugar accounts for most of the increase in density of must above the density of water, the hydrometer can read a percentage of sugar at a specified temperature when floated in the grape must.

HYMETTUS   GREECE

A dry white unresinated wine made in Attica in vineyards near Mount Hymettus. It deserves a couple of years' ageing.

I

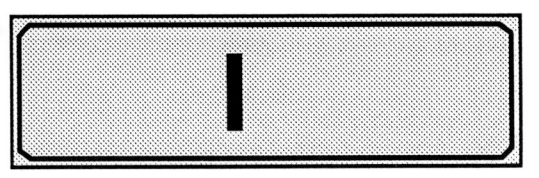

I.N.D.O. See Instituto Nacional de Denominación de Origen.

ICE SAINTS

Or E*is Heiligen*, as they are called in Germany, are the four saints on whose days in the middle of May there is the risk of a sharp frost which may damage the vines and thus reduce the potential harvest. They are St Pancratius on the 12th; St Servatius the 13th; St Bonifacius on the 14th and St Sophia on the 15th. Once these days are passed, the vines are free from danger of frost damage.

IDAHO USA

One of the three wine producing states of the Pacific North West. Grapes were grown here before Prohibition, but little interest was shown until Chateau Ste. Chapelle Vineyards were established in 1976. The growing season is long, with a cool climate. Chardonnay and Riesling both show considerable potential.

IDYLL VINEYARD AUSTRALIA

One of the leading properties of Geelong in Victoria. Cabernet Sauvignon and Shiraz form the bulk of the vineyard, with some Gewürztraminer and Chardonnay.

IGÉ See Mâcon Villages.

IGHTHAM ENGLAND

A tiny vineyard in Kent near Sevenoaks, established in the mid-1970s and planted with Müller-Thurgau, Reichensteiner, Huxelrebe and Schönburger. The grapes are vinified at Lamberhurst Priory.

DOMAINE DE L'ÎLE DE MARGAUX
Bordeaux: FRANCE

An individual property in Bordeaux, a vineyard on an island in the Gironde, but outside the appellation of Margaux.

ILLATS Bordeaux: FRANCE

One of the three communes of the Cérons appellation.

IMPÉRIALE

A Bordeaux bottle size, equalling eight ordinary bottles.

LA INA

La Ina is an important *fino* sherry brand, owned by the company of Pedro Domecq.

INDIA

Surprisingly, India is a wine producing country, most notably of *méthode champenoise* sparkling wine, made from Ugni Blanc, Pinot Blanc and Chardonnay, grown at high altitude in the Sahyadri mountains of the Western Maharashtra near Bombay and vinified by the former winemaker of Piper Heidsieck. It is sold under the name of Omar Khayyam.

INDICAZIONE GEOGRAFICA

A recently-introduced category of Italian wine, also called *vino tipico* and the equivalent to the French *vin de pays* and German *Landwein*. The term refers to a superior table wine, originating from a defined area and from specific grape varieties. Regulations are less stringent than for DOC and as yet not fully implemented but will include fine wines like Sassicaia, Tignanello and Fiorano.

INDIVIDUAL BERRY SELECTED

The New World equivalent of *Beerenauslese*, on a wine label, and the picking of individual berries which are probably affected by *botrytis*.

INDIVIDUAL BUNCH SELECTED

The New World equivalent of *Auslese* on a wine label, and the picking of individual bunches which are probably affected by *botrytis*.

INDIVIDUAL PADDOCK   see Rothbury.

INFERNO   Lombardy: ITALY

Meaning Hell, one of the four areas of Valtellina Superiore. A vineyard within the area is called Paradiso (Paradise)!

INGELHEIM   Rheinhessen: GERMANY

Now an industrial town rather than a wine village, it is within the *Grosslage* of Kaiserpfalz. It has a reputation for red wines made from Spätburgunder and Portugieser grapes which are unknown outside the region.

INGHAM

One of the Englishmen who followed the example of John Woodhouse and began making Marsala. The original company is now incorporated with Florio and is part of the Italian Cinzano group.

INGLENOOK VINEYARD   California: USA

Founded in 1881, survived Prohibition, and now owned by United Vintners, a subsidiary of Heublein. The winery produces a variety of wines from Napa and elsewhere; estate bottled wines from the Napa estate; a vintage line from the Northern coast counties and Navalle with a California appellation.

INNISKILLEN   CANADA

One of the most important wineries in Ontario, not for its size, but for the reputation it has created with its vitis vinifera wines since 1975. It concentrates on European varieties: Riesling, Gewürztraminer and oak-aged Chardonnay.

INSTITUT NATIONAL DES APPELLATIONS D'ORIGINE

Commonly known as the I.N.A.O., the body responsible for the implementation of the French laws of *Appellation Contrôlée*.
It lays down broad outlines which are enforced on a local basis, covering the areas of production, permitted grape varieties, minimal alcohol level, yields, viticultural and vinification practices, etc.

INSTITUTO NACIONAL DE DENOMINACIONES DE ORIGEN

The body designed to coordinate and control the activities of the Consejo Reguladores in each Spanish wine region. It was founded in 1972, has its headquarters in Madrid and in practice delegates much of its responsibility to the Consejo Reguladores.

INSTITUTO DO VINHO DO PORTO

The Portuguese body that directs and controls the production and sale of port. It has several functions; it determines how much of the wine produced in the Douro each year may be fortified to become port; it fixes the minimum and maximum prices for farmers and shippers; it controls annual shipping rights; it monitors movements of port and tastes and analyses all blends of port and issues shipments for export with a seal of guarantee and certificate of origin.

THE INTERNATIONAL WINE & FOOD SOCIETY

Founded in 1933 by André Simon, who was its first president. It is a non-profit making organisation with headquarters in London and regional branches in Britain and all over the world, aiming to increase the knowledge and appreciation of good wine and food amongst its members.

INZOLIA

One of the principal white grape varieties of Sicily, not found anywhere else in Italy and used for Marsala, Sicilian table wines and Bianco Alcamo.

IRANCY   Burgundy: FRANCE

A pretty village near Chablis in northern Burgundy that produces red wine from the Pinot Noir grape, to which some César is occasionally added to give the wine more body. Illogically, the best-known vineyard of the area is La Palotte which technically is outside the village and therefore only entitled to the appellation of Bourgogne Rouge, but the wine is made by the growers of Irancy. Irancy was given its own appellation in 1977 and in good years the wine will age as well as any from the Côte d'Or.

IRON

An important constituent in the soil of most fine vineyards, notably the Haut-Médoc, Châteauneuf-du-Pape and Pomerol, giving wines with good colour and bouquet. In some areas, its presence can be detected by the red colour of the earth.

IRON CASSE

Caused by a high iron content in the wine reacting in the presence of air to turn the wine cloudy. Two types of iron form precipitates in wine, white casse, which is due to ferric phosphate and blue casse, due to ferric tannate. These can both be prevented by not allowing the wine to come in contact with iron, but this is not always practicable. Otherwise the remedy is by fining, sometimes with blue finings.

IRON HORSE   California: USA

Iron Horse was founded in 1978, with vineyards in Sonoma County. It specialises in Cabernet Sauvignon, Chardonnay and Sauvignon Blanc and also makes sparkling wine. The winery is named after the miniature railway that was on the property.

IROULÉGUY   SOUTH WEST FRANCE

A small but growing appellation in the Pyrenees with a local reputation. The main producer is the cave cooperative of St Etienne de Baigorry, almost on the Spanish frontier. The tiny village of Irouléguy is one of the nine within the appellation. The wine is red or rosé, made from Tannat, Cabernet Franc and Cabernet Sauvignon grape varieties, by traditional methods of vinification.

IRRIGATION

Watering the vineyards is generally not acceptable in Europe for fine wine, except possibly for very young vines, which would otherwise suffer from drought. In Europe it is agreed that irrigated vines would produce uninteresting wine as the vines would make no attempt to search for water and nutrition from the soil. However there are other vineyards in the world which depend upon irrigation for their existence, notably parts of Australia, California and South America where the rainfall is insufficient and the quality of the wine is nonetheless acceptable.

ISABELLA

A red wine hybrid planted extensively in the Soviet Union for pink wine. It was one of the first crossings between Vitis Labrusca and Vitis Vinifera and has a strong foxy flavour.

ISCHIA   Campania: ITALY

The wines of the island are a red, made from Guarnaccia and Per'e Palummo grapes, and a white from Forastera and Biancolella. Both are light and best drunk young. A white *superiore* has a little more character.

ISINGLASS

A fining material, a proteinaceous substance obtained from the flotation bladder of a sturgeon.

ISKRA   BULGARIA

The brand name of Bulgaria's most popular sparkling wine, both red and white.

ISONZO
Friuli-Venezia Giulia: ITALY

A small DOC, near Gorizia and coming in ten variations: Cabernet, Sauvignon and Franc; Malvasia Istriana, a local Malvasia; Merlot, the most popular; Pinot Bianco; Pinot Grigio; Riesling Renano; Sauvignon; Tocai; Traminer Aromatico and Verduzzo Friuliano.

ISRAEL

Despite biblical traditions, modern winemaking in Israel is only a century old. Baron Edmond de Rothschild planted vineyards in the 1880s and built two new wineries, which were given to the country at the beginning of the century. Today, the principal grape varieties are Grenache and Carignan, with some Sémillon, Clairette and Muscat d'Alexandrie. Other varieties like Cabernet Sauvignon and Sauvignon Blanc are also beginning to appear. The main wine regions divide into three: in the north, on the slopes of Mount Carmel overlooking Haifa and around the northern shores of Lake Galilee; the central region, with the coastal plains inland from Jaffa and Tel Aviv where sweet dessert wines are produced and, in the south, there are vineyards around Beersheba and towards Ascalon. The Société Coopérative Vigneronne de Grandes Caves is the most important producer. Its brand name is Carmel.

D'ISSAN
Bordeaux: FRANCE

A third growth Margaux which has an attractive moated *château* that is owned by the Cruse family. The wines are considered untypical of Margaux.

ISTRIA
YUGOSLAVIA

A part of Yugoslavia, producing a variety of wines from the grape varieties Merlot, Cabernet, Pinot Noir and Teran (Refosco) for reds; Malvasia for dessert and normal still wines and Pinot Blanc for sparkling wine.

ITALIAN RIESLING see Welschriesling

ITALIAN SWISS COLONY
California: USA

One of California's largest wineries, producing jug and dessert wines and some standard varietals under the name of Colony.

ITALY

The world's largest wine-producing country with an average of 1,134,000 hectolitres per year. There is no province of Italy, from the Dolomites to the toe of Sicily, that does not make wine. Not for nothing was Italy called Enotria, the land of wine. The variety of Italian wines is infinite; there are about 230 wines classified as DOCG or DOC, a number which is growing all the time, in addition to those numerous *vini da tavola* which are often of considerable merit, but which do not conform to the DOC regulations of their area.

Best known of all Italian wines, with the possible exception of sparkling Lambrusco, must be Chianti from Tuscany. Central Italy produces similar wines based on the Sangiovese grape, and some good white wine, Verdicchio, Frascati and Orvieto. Piedmont in the north west is the home of Barolo, Barbaresco and other solid red wines from the Nebbiolo grape. The Veneto makes lighter reds, such as Valpolicella and Bardolino, and white Soave, and further north in the Alto Adige, Trentino and Fruili there are numerous red and white varietal wines. South of Rome, in the Mezzogiorno, vines proliferate; much of the production is destined for the Vermouth factories of Turin, but pockets of quality do exist, such as Taurasi, in Campania and Aglianico di Vulture. Sicily has made enormous progress in wine making with some individual wines, as well as Marsala. Sardinia, too, has potential. Sparkling wine, *spumante*, is a growing part of the Italian wine trade.

ITALY PARTICULAR
Sicily: ITALY

Was a popular brand name for Marsala Fine (see Marsala).

IZMIR
TURKEY

The Aegean coast around Izmir is one of the best Turkish wine regions. Cabernet Sauvignon and Merlot grapes are grown here for reds, and Sultanye (Sultana) for whites, as well as some Sémillon and Muscat for dessert wines.

ITALY

J

JABOULET
Rhône: FRANCE

Paul Jaboulet Aîné is one of the great names of Hermitage, an important *négociant* as well as a grower. The family own vineyards in Hermitage and Crozes Hermitage, but their range of wines covers the whole of the Rhône Valley, with Hermitage la Chapelle (red); Hermitage Chegalier de Stérimberg (white); Crozes Hermitage, Domaine de Thalabert (red); Crozes Hermitage Mule Blanche (white), St-Joseph la Grande Pompée; Côte Rôtie les Jumelles; Tavel l'Espiègle, Châteauneuf-du-Pape les Cèdres and Côtes du Rhône Parallèle 45.

JABOULET VERCHERRE
Burgundy: FRANCE

Négociants from Beaune, best known for their estate in Pommard, Clos de la Commaraine.

JACOB'S CREEK
AUSTRALIA

An important Australian red wine brand, owned by Orlando.

JACQUÈRE

The basic dry white wine grape of the Savoie, used as a base for light fresh acidic wines like Vin de Savoie and Vin du Bugey.

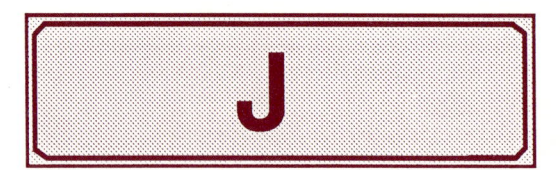

JACQUES BLANC
Bordeaux: FRANCE

A little-known Grand Cru Classé of St-Émilion, distinguished by its organic viticulture.

JACQUEZ

Jacquez or Jacquet is a synonym for the Black Spanish grape.

LOUIS JADOT
Burgundy: FRANCE

Important *négociants* and growers in Beaune and owners of the magnificent 15th century Couvent des Jacobins. Their vineyards include property in Beaune, Clos des Ursules and Boucherottes as well as Corton, Puligny-Montrachet and Chassagne-Montrachet.

JAHRGANG

The German word for 'vintage' or 'year'.

JAPAN

The origins of modern winemaking in Japan date back to the 1870s, with the end of Japan's isolationism. Today the main vineyard areas are on the island of Honshu, at Yamanashi and Yamagata, and also Nagano and Okayama. On Kyushu, grapes are grown around Fukuoka and, on Hokkaido, at Sapporo. The main grape varieties are Labrusca, Delaware, Campbell's Early and native Koshu, accounting for most of the production. There are some European varieties; Sémillon, Chardonnay, Riesling, Cabernet Sauvignon and Merlot. The overall climate of Japan does not lend itself to viticulture, with monsoons, typhoons and cold winds. Much depends upon individual microclimate. There are three main wine companies: Suntory, Mann's and Sanraku. The Japanese are anything but strict in their labelling regulations; nothing prevents them from blending their wine with imported wine and selling it as Japanese wine, and borrowing European classifications, eg Chateau X, *grand cru classé*.

JASMIN
Rhône: FRANCE

A small but excellent producer of long-lived Côte Rôtie.

JASNIÈRES
Loire: FRANCE

A white wine from the Loire valley made, confusingly, from vineyards in the valley of the Loir. It is made only from the Chenin Blanc grape and is usually very dry. Very occasionally, in the very best years, some semi-sweet wine is produced.

DOMAINE DE LA JAUBERTIE
SOUTH WEST FRANCE

One of the most forward looking estates of Bergerac, owned by an Englishman, Nick Ryman, and producing grapey Bergerac Sec and oak aged red Bergerac.

JEAN PERICO
SPAIN

A *cava* brand owned by Gonzalez Byass.

JEKEL VINEYARD
California: USA

A Monterey vineyard that had its first vintage in 1978 and established an instant reputation for Johannisberg Riesling. Cabernet Sauvignon and Chardonnay are good too.

JEREZ

The Spanish name for sherry, taking its name from the most important town of the area, at the centre of the sherry trade, Jerez de la Frontera.

JEROBOAM

A bottle size equal to four ordinary bottles in Champagne (300cl) and six ordinary bottles in Bordeaux (450cl).

JEROPIGA   See Geropiga.

JERUSALEM
YUGOSLAVIA

Yugoslavia's most famous vineyard, situated in the Ljutomer hills, with Crusader connections and today producing some of Ljutomer's best white wine.

JOHANNISBERG
Rheingau: GERMANY

One of the more famous names of Germany. It gives its name to the *Bereich* for the whole Rheingau. In California, the Rhine Riesling is often called the Johannisberger Riesling. The most reputed property of the village is Schloss Johannisberg. For many, the elegantly honeyed wines of Johannisberg are the epitome of the Rheingau. The village comes within the *Grosslage* of Erntebringer; vineyard sites, apart from the Schloss Johannisberg, include Hölle, Vogelsang, Klaus, Hasenberg, Mittelhölle, Goldatzel and Schwarzenstein. Amongst the good producers are Schloss Schönborn, Deinhard and Balthasar Ress.

JOHANNISBERG

A Swiss synonym for the Silvaner grape variety.

JOHANNISBERG RIESLING

The Californian synonym for the grape variety Rhine Riesling.

JOHANNISBERGER
SWITZERLAND

A white wine from the Valais made from vines reputedly introduced from Schloss Johannisberg, which have a predominantly Sylvaner flavour.

NATHANIEL JOHNSTON

An important family firm of *négociants* in Bordeaux who have been in business for over 250 years, specialising in fine wines.

JOLY (MADAME)
Loire: FRANCE

Owner of the superlative Loire vineyard, Coulée de Serrant in Savennières.

JONGIEUX
Savoie: FRANCE

A new cru of Vin de Savoie, for vineyards to the west of Lake Bourget. The wine can be red, white or rosé, mainly from Jacquère, Chardonnay, Mondeuse and Pinot Noir grapes.

JORDAN VINEYARD AND WINERY
California: USA

A Bordelais extravaganza built by William Jordan near Healdsburg. The winery imitates Bordeaux methods for Cabernet Sauvignon. The first vintage, 1976, was aged in barrels from Château Lafite and was an instant success on its release in 1980. Chardonnay and Merlot are made too.

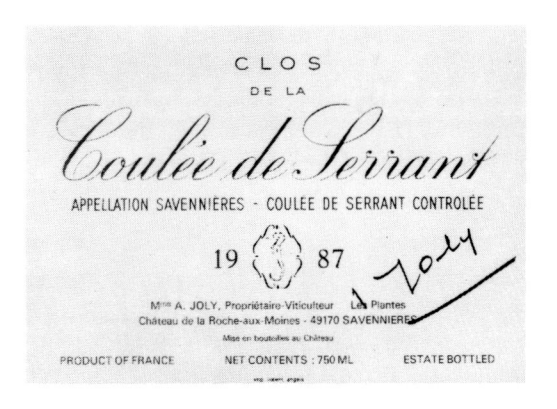

JUG WINE

An American term for basic table wine of no precise provenance or varietal though now less frequently used. Chablis or Burgundy were common descriptions. The wines are cheap, usually well made and technically sound and generally sold in larger containers than the standard 75cl. bottle.

JUHFARK

A white grape, grown in the Somló district of Hungary. The name translates poetically as Lamb's Tail.

JULIÉNAS   Burgundy: FRANCE

One of the ten Beaujolais Crus with a right to a separate appellation. Julius Caesar is reputed to have given his name to the village. Les Capitans and Château de Juliénas are two good properties.

JULIUSSPITAL   Franconia: GERMANY

Weingut Juliusspital is an important Wurzburg estate and a charitable institution founded in 1576 to support a hospital in Würzburg. Vineyards are in the most important sites of Franconia, Würzburger Stein, Iphofer Julius Echter Berg, Randersackerer Teufelskeller, Rödelseer Küchenmeister and others. Silvaner is the principal grape, with several other varieties. Wines are matured in wood in a magnificent 17th century cellar.

JUMILLA   SPAIN

A D.O. from near Valencia. Most of the production is heady, full-bodied 18° red wine, oak aged and made mainly from the Monastrell grape. The cooperative of San Isdro is the main producer. Unusually, owing to the high chalk content in the soil the region is phylloxera free and the vines ungrafted.

JUPONNE

The name given to a very new fat champagne cork, that has hardly spent any time in a bottle. The opposite is a *cheville*.

JURA   FRANCE

The wines of the Jura in eastern France come under four appellations and several colours and styles: Côtes du Jura (red, white, rosé and *Vin jaune*); Arbois (more red than white, as well as rosé and *vin jaune*); L'Etoile (white and *vin jaune*) and Château-Chalon (only *vin jaune*). Sparkling *méthode champenoise* wine is made too, with no precise appellation, as well as *vin de paille* and the Jura aperitif, Macvin. The vineyards are around the towns of Lons le Saunier and Arbois, where Louis Pasteur did much of his research on vinification, on attractive undulating hillsides with hilltop villages. The principal grape varieties are Chardonnay and Savagnin for white wine, and Poulsard and Trousseau, both peculiar to the Jura, for red and rosé, as well as Pinot Noir. *Vin Jaune* and Château-Chalon are made purely from Savagnin. Often it is hard to distinguish between red and rosé; the vinification process is the same for both, with a long maceration on the skins to extract the maximum amount of colour from the Poulsard and Trousseau, which are generally lacking in colour. Most wines spend a minimum of twelve months in large or small oak barrels.

JURADE DE ST-ÉMILION

The wine brotherhood of St-Émilion in Bordeaux, established in its modern form in 1948. The original Jurade dates back to the time of Henry II when it was a body of men responsible for administering the commune of St-Émilion, including its commercial interests, which were almost entirely based on wine. They proclaimed the *ban des vendanges* and checked on the quality of wine. They were disbanded during the French Revolution.

JURANÇON

The grape variety Jurançon comes in three colours, blanc, noir and rouge. Jurançon Blanc is an indifferent grape, still used in small quantities for Armagnac. Jurançon Noir and Jurançon Rouge are two very similar grape varieties, found in south west France. Jurançon Noir can feature up to 10% in Cahors and also in the red wines of the Aveyron, Entraygues, Estaing and Marcillac. Both Noir and Rouge are allowed for red Gaillac.

JURANÇON   SOUTH WEST FRANCE

A white wine produced in the foothills of the Pyrenees around the town of Pau. It can be dry or sweet. The grape varieties are predominantly Gros and Petit Manseng and Courbu. The grapes destined for Jurançon Moelleux are left on the vines until well into November so that they become overripe, dried by the southern winds from the Pyrenees, in a process called *passerillage*. The sweet wines are usually aged in wood for several months; the dry wines are bottled early and drunk young.

K

KMW AUSTRIA

The abbreviation of Klosterneuburger Mostwaage which, describes the Austrian system of measuring mustweight for *Prädikat* wines, based on the percentage of sugar in the juice.

K.W.V. SOUTH AFRICA

The Ko-operatiewe Wjnbouwers Vereniging van Zuid-Afrika Beperkt, or more comprehensibly the Cape Wine Farmers' Association. The K.W.V. was founded in 1918 by the South African government to protect the country's grape growers from low prices by fixing a minimum price for wine and distilling any surplus. In practice it has more far reaching powers. It is not allowed to sell wine within South Africa except to other wineries and has dominated the export market from South Africa.

The K.W.V. has five wineries; its headquarters are at Paarl on the Laborie estate, as well as vineyards in Stellenbosch, Worcester, Robertson and Montagu. Brandy, sherry and port style wines account for the greater part of its production. Cape Cavendish sherry is a worthy imitation of a Spanish sherry. Table wines include a good Chenin Blanc, a red wine, Roodeberg made from a blend of Pinotage, Shiraz, Cinsaut and Tinta Barocca.

KABINETT

The lowest category of German *Prädikat* wine, made from grapes which are normally ripe and will not need any additional sugar to increase the alcohol level. The statutory sugar content, measured as the oechsle degree for a *Kabinett* wine varies according to grape variety and area. For a Riesling in the Rheingau it is 73° and 70° in the cooler Mosel. The term *Kabinett* was first used at Kloster Eberbach by the Duke of Nassau, originally for particularly fine wines which were kept in a grower's private cellar or *Cabinet*.

KADARKA

The principal red grape variety of Hungary and grown all over the country. It is an ingredient of Bulls Blood, giving tannin and spicyness. On the Great Plain the wines are lighter. It is also grown in Roumania and in Bulgaria where it is called Gamza.

KAEFFERKOPF Alsace: FRANCE

One of the best vineyard sites of Ammerschwir, but not classified as a Grand Cru as it is too large an area with a very varied soil composition that gives wines with too broad a range of quality.

KAISER STUHL AUSTRALIA

The label under which the Barossa Cooperative Winery of South Australia sold its wine, notably rosé and also sparkling wine. However, the cooperative was taken over by Penfolds in 1982 and the label has become a Penfolds brand.

KAISERSTUHL – TUNIBERG
Baden: GERMANY

One of the seven *Bereichs* of Baden, northwest of Freiburg. The Kaiserstuhl is an extinct volcano and the Tuniberg a modest hill on whose slopes a substantial amount of wine is produced after much reconstruction of the vineyards. The most popular wine here comes from Müller-Thurgau, closely followed by Spätburgunder for *Weissherbst*, while Ruländer makes a more distinguished white wine. The region is divided into two *Grosslagen*: Vulkanfelsen and Attilafelsen.

KALLSTADT Rheinpfalz: GERMANY

A village in the Mittelhaardt area of the Rheinpfalz. There are two *Grosslagen* in the village: Kobnert, with the *Einzellage* Steinacker, and Saumagen, which is made up of the three best vineyards of the village: Nill, Kirchenstuck and Horn. However, in practice, wine from these vineyards is usually sold under the better-known *Grosslage* name.

KALTE ERNTE

A popular drink in Germany translating as Cold Duck, made by mixing still and sparkling wine, flavoured with lemon rind and sugar.

KALTERERSEE See Lago di Caldaro.

KANZA See Attica.

KANZEM Mosel-Saar-Ruwer: GERMANY
A small wine village of the Saar, producing fine steely Riesling in good years, especially from the Vereinigte Hospitien and Bischöfliches Priesterseminar. The *Grosslage* is Scharzberg and the main vineyards are Altenberg, Schlossberg Horecker and Sonnenberg.

KANZLER
A crossing of the Müller-Thurgau and Silvaner grape varieties, grown mainly in the Rheinhessen.

KASEL Mosel-Saar-Ruwer: GERMANY
The largest and best wine village of the Ruwer, coming within the *Grosslage* of Römerlay. The vineyards are Herrenberg, Dominikanerberg, Kehrnagel, Hitzlay, Nies'chen, Paulinsberg and Timpet. The main producers are the Bischöfliche Weingüter and von Kesselstatt.

KEKFRANKOS see Blaufrankisch

KÊKNYELÛ
An indigenous Hungarian white grape variety, grown mainly in Badacsony. The name means 'blue stalked'.

KELLER
Means 'cellar' in German. A *Kellerei* is larger, a winery.

KELLERMEISTER
Means 'cellarmaster' in German, the person responsible for making the wine and running the cellar.

KENDERMANN
Hermann Kendermann GmbH is a successful German export company based in Bingen, with a successful Liebfraumilch brand, Black Tower.

KEO CYPRUS
One of Cyprus' main wine producers founded in 1920 and making a successful range of wines, notably red Othello, dry white Aphrodite, sweet white St. Pantaleimon and slightly *pétillant* Bellapais. Domain d'Ahéra is their best red wine, Mosaic is the brand name of their sherry.

KEPPOCH-PADTHAWAY AUSTRALIA
A little known wine region of South Australia, about 40 miles north of Coonawarra. Keppoch takes its name from a proposed town that was never built; Padthaway is the name of a village. Some of the bigger companies, Wynns, Thomas Hardy, and Seppelt and Lindemans have vineyards here and the area is developing a reputation for white wines.

KERNER
One of the new German grape varieties, developed in 1969, and now planted mainly in the Rheinpfalz and Rheinhessen. It is a crossing of red Trollinger and white Riesling, and has some Riesling characteristics with a high yield and good resistance to frost. It is also grown in south Africa.

KESSELSTATT Mosel-Saar-Ruwer: GERMANY
Weingut Reichsgraf von Kesselstatt is the largest private estate of the Mosel, made up of four separate estates, as well as having very close ties with other vineyards. The four estates are Der Josephshof at Graach, and Kasel and Oberemmel in Piesport. It is planted almost entirely in Riesling and includes some of the best sites on the Mosel. It is owned by Günther Reh who operates from the baroque Kesselstatt Palace in Trier.

KESTEN   *Mosel-Saar-Ruwer*: GERMANY

A small village within the *Grosslage* of Kurfürstlay, with only one significant vineyard, Paulinshofberg.

KEYNESTON   AUSTRALIA

A small wine area of South Australia, an offshoot of the Barossa Valley, producing wines similar to those of Barossa, but with slight climatic and soil variations.

KHALOKHORIO   CYPRUS

A village in Cyprus where they make Commandaria purely from Xynisteri grapes so that it is light and can be drunk younger than usual.

KHAN KRUM   BULGARIA

A defined Controliran wine region concentrating on the production of Gewürztraminer as a varietal wine.

KHINDOGNY

A red grape widely planted in the Soviet Union, especially in Azerbaijan, giving colourful tannic wines.

KIANGSU   See China.

KIEDRICH   *Rheingau*: GERMANY

An attractive town with the ruined castle of the Electors of Mainz, the Scharfenstein, crowning its sweep of vineyards. It comes within the *Grosslage* of Heiligenstock and the best E*inzellagen* are Gräfenberg and Wasseros. Sandgrub and Klosterberg produce spicey, honeyed wines too. Good producers include Schloss Groenesteyn and the State Domain at Eltville.

KIESELGUHR

A type of diatomaceous earth used to filter wine.

KIMMERIDGE

The clay soil is found in the Chablis area, which is one of the factors giving Chablis its individual taste. The Dorset village of Kimmeridge, on the other side of the Parisian Basin gave the soil its name. It dates back to the Upper Jurassic age, 180 million years ago.

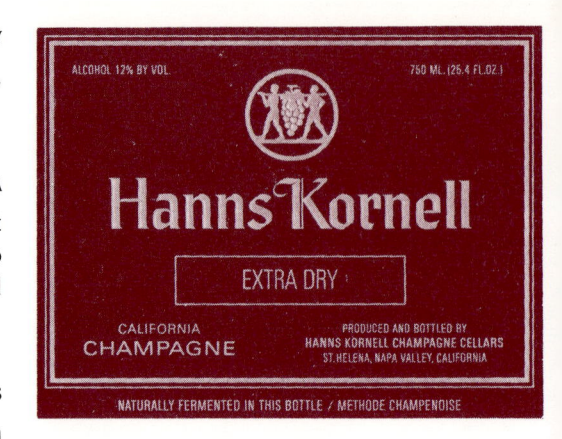

KINHEIM   *Mosel-Saar-Ruwer*: GERMANY

A village on the Mosel within the *Grosslage* of Schwarzlay, with wines of no special distinction.

KIR

An aperitif which is especially popular in Burgundy. It is made from a dry, white wine, like Aligoté, to which is added a touch of blackcurrant liqueur, *cassis*. It is named after a leader of the French resistance and former mayor of Dijon, Canon Félix Kir. A Kir Royale is made with sparkling wine.

KIRMISI

The Turkish word for 'red'.

KIRWAN   *Bordeaux*: FRANCE

A third growth Margaux, from the commune of Cantenac, which owes its name to an Irishman who came to an untimely end during the French Revolution. The property is now owned by Schröder & Schyler, who have been replanting the vineyard and modernising the cellars, resulting in a happy improvement in the wine.

KITTERLÉ   *Alsace*: FRANCE

A Grand Cru vineyard in the town of Guebwiller.

KLEIN KAROO   SOUTH AFRICA

The Klein Karoo or Little Karoo is the most easterly of the vineyards of South Africa, an arid region running north of the Landeberg mountain region from Montague, east through Barrydale, Ladismith to de Hoop. Irrigation is essential here and the wine either becomes dessert wine or is destined for the distillery.

KLEINBERGER

A synonym of Elbling.

KLEVNER

A Swiss synonym for the Pinot Noir grape. See also Clevner.

KLOSTER EBERBACH
Rheingau: GERMANY

A 12th century Cistercian monastery which is the headquarters of the Verwaltung der Staatsweingüter Eltville. Annual wine auctions are held in the monastery as well as the German Wine Academy courses.

KLOSTERNEUBURG
AUSTRIA

An important wine centre in the Donau-Carnuntum region, to the north of Vienna, with a magnificent baroque abbey and the wine estate, the Chorherrenstift.

KLÜSSERATH
Mosel-Saar-Ruwer: GERMANY

A Mosel wine village just in the Mittelmosel and included in the *Grosslage* of St. Michael. There are two vineyards, Bruderschaft and Königsberg. The main grower is the Friedrich Wilhelm Gymnasium.

KNIGHTS VALLEY
California: USA

An AVA of Sonoma County, first planted in the 1960s, and now with a reputation for Johannisberg Riesling.

KNIPPERLÉ

A white grape variety that was planted extensively in Alsace at the beginning of the century, but it is very susceptible to rot and has consequently now almost disappeared from the area.

KNUDSEN ERATH
USA

One of the pioneer wineries of Oregon, founded in 1972, and now the state's largest winery, making good Pinot Noir, Riesling and sparkling wine.

KOBNERT
Rheinpfalz: GERMANY

A *Grosslage* in the Mittelhaardt area of the Rheinpfalz covering vineyards from the villages of Herxheim, Leistadt, Freinsheim and part of Kallstadt.

KOCHER-JAGST-TAUBER
Württemberg: GERMANY

The smallest of the three *Bereichs* of Württemberg and the tiniest in Germany, covering the valleys of the three rivers, tributaries of the Neckar and the Main, from which it takes its name.

KOKKINELI
GREECE

The Greek term for a rosé wine, often nearer red in colour.

KOMETENWEIN See comet wine.

KÖNIGSBACH
Rheinpfalz: GERMANY

A village with four vineyards in the *Grosslage* of Meerspinne, namely Oelberg, Jesuitengarten, Idig and Reiterpfad.

KOPKE

C. N. Kopke is reputed to be the oldest port shipper of all, founded in 1638 by Christopher Kopke and now owned by Barros Almeida.

KORBEL
California: USA

F. Korbel & Bros is the pioneer winery for sparkling wine in California. The Korbels had their first vintage in 1881. The Sonoma winery is now owned by the Heck family who have renovated the cellars to expand production and make a streamlined 'champagne'.

HANNS KORNELL CHAMPAGNE CELLARS
California: USA

Follows its German origins in producing sparkling wine, mainly from Johannisberg Riesling grapes, by the Champagne method.

KOSHU   JAPAN

A thick-skinned white grape variety, planted in Japan, that is suitable for the country's humid climate and produces palatable white wine.

KOSMET   YUGOSLAVIA

Also known as Kosovo, is a mountainous province in northern Yugoslavia adjacent to Albania and noted for its red wines from Cabernet Sauvignon grapes and for a wine from Pinot Noir grapes, which is sold under the name of Amselfelder.

KOSOVO   see Kosmet.

KOWERICH   see Leiwen.

KRAJINA   YUGOSLAVIA

A Serbian vineyard area, planted mainly with Gamay, Pinot Noir, Merlot, Cabernet, Laski Rizling and Muscat Ottonel grapes.

KRALEVO   BULGARIA

A defined Controliran wine region of origin, concentrating on the production of Riesling wines.

KRASKI TERAN   YUGOSLAVIA

The best red wine of the Slovenian part of the Istrian peninsular. Teran is the local name for Italian Refosco and Kraski refers to the particular limestone formation of Krass on which the vineyards are planted.

KRETZER

Describes a rosé wine in the Alto Adige, an alternative description to *rosato* in this German-speaking part of Italy.

KREUZNACH

Nahe: GERMANY

One of the two *Bereichs* of the Nahe, covering the northern part of the area with the *Grosslagen* of Kronenberg, Schlosskapelle, Sonnenborn and Pfarrgarten.

KRONDORF   AUSTRALIA

A company in the Barossa Valley which had a chequered history until it came under new ownership in 1978. All the major grape varieties of Australia are grown, and blended with grapes from Coonawarra and McLaren Vale as well as Barossa. Rhine Riesling, oak-aged Cabernet Sauvignon and selected wines under a Burge & Wilson (new owners) label are the best wines.

KRÖV   *Mosel-Saar-Ruwer*: GERMANY

A village best known for its *Grosslage* Nacktarsch, which means 'bare bottom'. Labels are usually in bad taste, showing a little boy being spanked with his pants down. The wine tends to be better than the label.

KRUG   *Champagne*: FRANCE

One of the great Champagne names and one of the most traditional producers, with fermentation in oak barrels. Two wines are made: N.V. Grande Cuvée and a vintage wine in limited quantities.

CHARLES KRUG WINERY

California: USA

Now run by Peter Mondavi, brother of Robert, and one of the Napa Valley's most historic wineries. Charles Krug was making wine in the Napa Valley as early as 1858. Today their reputation is mainly for white wine.

KUENTZ BAS
Alsace: FRANCE

An important family company in Alsace with cellars at Husserein-les-Châteaux. Their range of wines includes Cuvée Réservée and the better Réserve Personnelle.

KUMEU/HUAPAI/WAIMAUKU
NEW ZEALAND

A wine region of North Island, in the province of Auckland, with vineyards around the towns of the same name. The vineyard area has increased over the past decade with established companies planting new vineyards here, attracted by the favourable microclimate with its low rainfall. Red wines do well here. Reputable estates include Delegat's, Nobilo, Matua Valley, Selaks and Cooks.

KUTMAN
TURKEY

One of the better Turkish wine producers who sell their wines under the Villa Doluca label. The company was founded in 1920 and is based at Mürefte on the Sea of Marmara. They make two types of red: Doluca from Cinsaut and Papazkarasi and Villa Doluca from Gamay, Papazkarasi and Cabernet Sauvignon, as well as some oak-aged Sémillon.

L

L.B.V.   see Late Bottled Vintage.

LABARDE   Bordeaux: FRANCE
One of the villages near the village of Margaux and included in the appellation. Giscours is the best property.

LABÉGORCE   Bordeaux: FRANCE
There are three properties, l'Abbégorce de Gorsse, Labégorce Zédé and Labégorce that were once a single estate in Margaux belonging to the La Bégorce family in the early 14th century. Labégorce is considered to be the best of the three.

LACRIMA
A red grape variety found in limited quantities in central Italy.

LACRIMA DI MORRO   The Marches: ITALY
Also called Lacrima di Morro d'Alba, a new red DOC from the Marches near Ancona. A soft red wine from Lacrima grapes, it is sometimes made with the Chianti *governo* method.

LACRIMA DI TERRA D'OTRANTO   See Alezio.

LACRYMA CHRISTI DEL VESUVIO   Campania: ITALY
A tricolour wine. Legend has it that Christ shed tears on Vesuvius and vines grew where the tears fell. The story is better than the wine: red and *rosato* come from Olivella, Piedirosso and Aglianico grapes grown on the lower slopes of the volcano. White, which can be dry, medium sweet, fortified or *spumante*, is made from Greco del Vesuvio, Coda di Volpe and Falanghina.

LACTIC ACID
As found in milk, one of the constitutents of wine. It is present in young wine and increases after the malo-lactic fermentation.

LADOIX SERRIGNY   Burgundy: FRANCE
Much of the wine from this village has the right to the Grands and Premiers Crus appellations of Aloxe-Corton, so little is left to be sold as Ladoix Serrigny and, in practice, most of that is declassified into Côte de Beaune Villages. The principal growers of the village are Capitaine Gagnerot and Prince Florent de Mérode.

PATRICK DE LADOUCETTE   Loire: FRANCE
An excellent producer and promoter from the central vineyards of the Loire, with three labels, Pouilly Fumé de Ladoucette from Château du Nozet, a prestige cuvée Pouilly Blanc Fumé Baron de L, and Sancerre Comte Lafond. His interests also extend to Vouvray, in the company of Marc Brédif, and to Chablis.

LAFAURIE-PEYRAGUEY   Bordeaux: FRANCE
A first growth Sauternes in the commune of Bommes with a *château* of 13th century origins. The property belongs to Cordier, but the wines are not generally considered to merit their classification. A more successful dry wine is also produced.

LAFITE   Bordeaux: FRANCE
One of the great wines of Bordeaux, a first growth from the commune of Pauillac that has been owned by the Rothschild family since 1868. It is the largest of the first growth *châteaux* and makes wines of proverbial longevity. The second wine of the property is called Moulin des Carruades. It was originally called Carruades de Lafite after a particular part of the vineyard, but the name was changed to avoid confusion. Quality is of paramount importance. The soil is gravel on limestone, the vines an average of fifty years old and the *encépagement* Cabernet Sauvignon 70%, Merlot 20% and Cabernet Franc 10% with a tiny amount of Petit Verdot. The fermentation takes one to three weeks depending on the conditions of the vintage. The wine is aged after the *assemblage* in new *limousin barriques*. Its development is carefully followed until bottling in the third spring after the vintage. This is wine-making at its best.

LAFLEUR   Bordeaux: FRANCE
A tiny Pomerol *château* owned by the two elderly Robin sisters and marketed by J.-P. Moueix. The wine has an excellent reputation.

LAFLEUR GAZIN Bordeaux: FRANCE

A tiny Pomerol *château* lying on the best part of the plateau of Pomerol. The wine is marketed by J.-P. Moueix and enjoys a good reputation.

LAFLEUR DU ROY Bordeaux: FRANCE

A minor Pomerol *château* on the outskirts of Libourne.

LAFÕES PORTUGAL

A little known wine coming from a determinate, but not yet demarcated area, between Vinho Verde and Dão. The most typical red grapes are Amaral and Touriga, making wines that are light and fruity.

RAYMOND LAFON Bordeaux: FRANCE

A Cru Bourgeois Sauternes, owned by the *régisseur* of d'Yquem, who applies the same principles to his own cellar as in the great *château*.

LAFON ROCHET Bordeaux: FRANCE

After an undistinguished history, this fourth growth St-Estèphe *château* was bought by Guy Tesseron, who has rebuilt and modernised the property. His efforts are now bearing fruit and the wine is acquiring a good reputation.

LAGAR

Lagar in Portuguese, or *lago* in Spanish is an old-fashioned stone trough used for treading grapes. They are still used in some of the more traditional port houses.

LAGO   see Lagar.

LAGO DI CALDARO
Trentino-Alto Adige: ITALY

Also called Kalterersee, a soft red DOC wine made from Schiava Grossa, Gentile and Grigia grapes, grown along the Adige valley and taking its name from the lake near Bolzano. It is best drunk young. *Classico* means that it comes from near the lake; *auslese* or *scelto* that the grapes are selected with 11° alcohol as opposed to 10.5°.

LAGRANGE Bordeaux: FRANCE

Two important properties have the same name, a third growth St-Julien and a Pomerol estate. The first has gone through a period in the doldrums and is now enjoying something of a renaissance under the ownership of the Japanese company Suntory and the guidance of Professor Peynaud. The second is a second growth Pomerol *château* producing wines of excellent quality in small quantity. J.-P. Moueix make and distribute it. There is also a little-known property of the same name in Lussac-St-Émilion.

LAGREIN

A red grape peculiar to the Trentino-Alto Adige, where it makes light red and rosé wines. Lagrein Dunkel is soft and deep red; Lagrein Kretzer an elegant rosé.

LÁGRIMA SPAIN

The term used to describe the best Málaga, made without any mechanical pressing of the grapes, only from the free run juice. Lágrima literally means tear and an even sweeter version is Lágrima Cristi.

LAGUARDIA SPAIN

An important centre in the Rioja Alavesa.

LA LAGUNE Bordeaux: FRANCE

A third growth Ludon, the first *château* you reach, driving to the Médoc from Bordeaux. The property was modernised in the late 1950s. New oak barrels are used every year and the wine is consistently good.

LAKE COUNTY   California: USA

A growing wine area of northern California. It was first planted with vines in the 1880s, declined with Prohibition and is now undergoing a revival, with two AVAs, Clear Lake and Guenoc Valley. Cabernet Sauvignon is the most important grape variety.

LAKE'S FOLLY   AUSTRALIA

A winery in the Hunter Valley district of New South Wales, created by one of the personalities of the Australian wine trade, Dr. Max Lake. He broke with Hunter Valley tradition by planting Cabernet Sauvignon rather than Shiraz and by using new oak for maturation. Chardonnay is another enthusiasm.

LALANDE BORIE   Bordeaux: FRANCE

Owned by the Borie family of Ducru Beaucaillou, where the wine is made. It is a separate wine, rather than a second label for the greater *château*.

LALANDE DE POMEROL   Bordeaux: FRANCE

A commune next to the Pomerol vineyards with its own appellation, which also covers the wines of the adjacent commune of Néac. The wines are like lesser Pomerols, but with a higher percentage of Cabernet Franc grapes.

JACQUES LALANNE   Loire: FRANCE

A fine producer of Quarts de Chaume in the Anjou-Saumur region, using traditional methods with meticulous care.

LAMARQUE   Bordeaux: FRANCE

A commune of the Médoc, but it produces little wine.

DE LAMARQUE   Bordeaux: FRANCE

A Haut-Médoc Cru Grand Bourgeois in the village of Lamarque and a fine example of a medieval fortress, now making some good wine after a period of neglect.

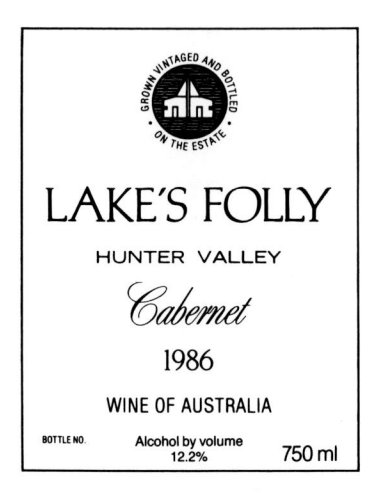

LAMBERHURST PRIORY   ENGLAND

One of England's largest vineyards with 48 acres of vines near Tunbridge Wells in Kent. It was established in 1972, is planted mainly with Müller-Thurgau and Seyval Blanc grapes, also some Schönburger and Reichensteiner. It is owned by Kenneth McAlpine.

LAMBLIN ET FILS   Burgundy: FRANCE

A *négociant* company with modern cellars in Maligny near Chablis. Their methods are modern, with stainless steel vats and no oak. Their main vineyards are Les Clos, Valmur, Fourchaume, and Mont de Milieu.

LAMBRUSCO   Emilia-Romagna: ITALY

Italy's most popular wine abroad. It is usually red, though now can be white and *rosato*, always *frizzante*, often sweet, but sometimes dry. Unclassified Lambrusco is made in the Po valley around the towns of Reggio and Emilia; in addition there are four DOCs: Lambrusco di Sorbara, Lambrusco Grasparossa di Castelvetro, Lambrusco Reggiano and Lambrusco Salamino di Santa Croce.

LAMBRUSCO GRASPAROSSA DI CASTELVETRO   Emilia-Romagna: ITALY

A DOC from south of Modena, from Lambrusco Grasparossa grapes. It is usually dry, sometimes medium sweet and always *frizzante*.

LAMBRUSCO REGGIANO
   Emilia-Romagna: ITALY

A light DOC wine made from a blend of different Lambrusco grapes in large quantities for export. It is best drunk young and fresh, dry or medium sweet and always frizzante.

LAMBRUSCO SALAMINO DI SANTA CROCE   Emilia-Romagna: ITALY

A DOC made from Lambrusco Salamino grapes from around Modena, including the village of Santa Croce. It is dry or medium sweet and always *frizzante*.

LAMBRUSCO DI SORBARA
   Emilia-Romagna: ITALY

A DOC which comes mainly from Lambrusco di Sorbara grapes grown to the north of Modena. It is *frizzante* made by the *Charmat* method. The dry version is considered one of the best Lambruscos.

LAMEZIA   Calabria: ITALY

A light red DOC wine, made from a mixture of grapes, Nerello Mascalese, Nerello Cappuccio, Gaglioppo and Greco Nero, grown around Lamezia Terme near Catanzaro. It is best drunk young.

LAMOTHE   Bordeaux: FRANCE

A little-known second growth Sauternes, made for early drinking.

LA LANDONNE   Rhône: FRANCE

The brand name under which Guigal sell their pure Côte Brune wine from the Côte Rôtie.

LANDWEIN

A new category of German wines, designed to equate to *Vin de Pays* in France and also meaning 'country wine'. It is different from *Tafelwein* as it has a higher natural alcohol content and cannot be sweeter than medium-dry. There are fifteen different regions for *Landwein*: Ahrtaler Landwein, Starkenburger Landwein, Rheinburgen Landwein, Landwein der Mosel, Landwein der Saar, Nahegauer Landwein, Altrheingauer Landwein, Rheinischer Landwein, Pfälzer Landwein, Fränkischer Landwein, Regensburger Landwein, Bayerischer Bodensee-Landwein, Schwäbischer Landwein, Unterbadischer Landwein and Sudbadischer Landwein.

LANCERS

A slightly sweet carbonated rosé wine produced with some success by the Portuguese company of J. M. da Fonseca. Some white and a little red is also made under the same label.

LANESSAN   Bordeaux: FRANCE

A Cru Grand Bourgeois Exceptionnel, Haut-Médoc in the village of Cussac, which has a long-established reputation. There is also a fine museum of carriages.

LANGENBACH

Langenbach are an important German export house based in Worms and part owners of the Liebfrauenstift Kirchenstuck vineyard which gave its name to Liebfraumilch. Crown of Crowns is their Liebfraumilch brand.

LANGENLONSHEIM   Nahe: GERMANY

A little-known town within the *Grosslage* of Sonnenborn. Its wine rarely travels outside Germany.

LANGHORNE CREEK   AUSTRALIA

A small area of vineyards in South Australia, 25 miles south east of Adelaide on the Bremer River. The soil is rich and fertile; the rainfall low and the combination gives distinctive wines. Bleasdale Vineyards are the pioneer winery of the area, now changing from fortified to table wines.

LANOLIN

A soft, sweet, possibly slightly oily smell, like lanolin, associated with Chenin blanc and Sémillon grapes in good years.

LANSON *Champagne*: FRANCE

A champagne house known for its N.V. Black Label, made with modern techniques.

LARCIS-DUCASSE *Bordeaux*: FRANCE

A Grand Cru Classé of St-Emilion lying in the commune of St-Laurent-des-Combes. It has a good reputation.

LARMANDE *Bordeaux*: FRANCE

A little-known St-Emilion Grand Cru Classé on the *côtes*.

LARMES

The French term for 'tears'

HENRI LAROCHE *Burgundy*: FRANCE

An important *négociant* company in Chablis with large estates. Methods combine the modern and the traditional with stainless steel fermentation vats and experimental use of new oak barrels. Their principal vineyards are Blanchots, Les Clos, Bougros, Fourchaume, Montmains, Vaillons and Beauroy.

LANGLOIS CHÂTEAU *Loire*: FRANCE

Important producers of sparkling Saumur and now owned by Bollinger.

LANGOA-BARTON *Bordeaux*: FRANCE

A third growth St-Julien owned by the Irish Barton Family since 1821. Curiously, the wine was not *château* bottled until 1969, but bottled by Barton & Guestier. Léoville-Barton is made here too.

LANGWERTH VON SIMMERN *Rheingau*: GERMANY

To give the estate its full title, Freiherrlich Langworth von Simmern'sches Rentamt, is an important estate owned by the von Simmern family since 1464. Vineyards include parcels in Erbacher Marcobrunn, Rauenthaler Baiken and Hattenheimer Nussbrunnen, planted extensively with Riesling vines which give fine results.

LANIOTE *Bordeaux*: FRANCE

A little-known St-Émilion Grand Cru Classé situated on the *côtes*.

LATE HARVEST

The New World term for *Spätlese* or *Vendange Tardive* on a wine label, meaning quite simply that the grapes were picked later than the rest of the harvest and so have a higher concentration of sugar.

LATISANA   *Friuli-Venezia Giulia:* ITALY

A little-known DOC with seven varieties. Most important are Merlot, Cabernet Franc, Sauvignon and Tocai, as well as Pinot Bianco, Pinot Grigio Refosco and Verduzzo.

LATIUM   ITALY

This region, with Rome at its centre, is best known for its white wines, especially Frascati, but also Est! Est!! Est!!! and Marino. Lesser-known reds such as Fiorano and Torre Ercolana may well offer more exciting drinking. Grape varieties for whites are Malvasia and Trebbiano; reds are a mixture including Cesanese, Montepulciano, Sangiovese, and Cabernet and Merlot.

LATOUR   *Bordeaux:* FRANCE

One of the three first growth properties of Pauillac, lying on the village's southern boundary. The *château* takes its name from a medieval fortress. Today there is a squat domed tower in the vineyard. From 1963 to 1989 Lord Cowdray was the principal shareholder and responsible for modernising the *chais* with stainless steel fermentation vats. Latour has set such high standards that it has, rather unfairly, acquired a reputation for its 'off' vintages, rather than for the great years. Les Forts de Latour is made from young vines, and from two smaller vineyards that are next to the main vineyard. Although sometimes described as the second wine of Latour, technically it is not.

LOUIS LATOUR   *Burgundy:* FRANCE

A famous Beaune house, which has a reputation for its white wines, especially Corton-Charlemagne and for its red Corton, sold as Château Corton-Grancey. They have other vineyards on the Côte de Beaune; Montagny and Mâcon Lugny are other specialities.

LAROSE TRINTAUDON   *Bordeaux:* FRANCE

Both vineyards and *château* of this Haut-Médoc Cru Grand Bourgeois property have been renovated by the Forner family from Rioja with notable success.

LAROZE   *Bordeaux:* FRANCE

A little-known but well-run St-Émilion Grand Cru Classé situated on the *côtes*.

LARRIVET HAUT-BRION   *Bordeaux:* FRANCE

A small Graves property producing some red and a small amount of white wine.

LASCOMBES   *Bordeaux:* FRANCE

A second growth Margaux *château*, that was restored and enlarged by Alexis Lichine in the 1950s. Bass Charrington are now the owners. The second wine is Château La Gombaude.

LASERRE   *Bordeaux:* FRANCE

Called La Serre on the label, this is a Grand Cru Classé of St- Emilion. It has a high proportion of Merlot grapes and makes a sound wine.

LASKI RIZLING   see Welschriesling

LATE BOTTLED VINTAGE   PORTUGAL

Late Bottled Vintage, or LBV for short, is aged longer in wood and bottled later than vintage port, between four and a half and six years after the vintage. It comes from a year that is not a declared vintage. It provides an affordable way of drinking a vintage style wine.

LATOUR DE FRANCE *The Midi*: FRANCE

A village within the area of Côtes du Roussillon with its own appellation. The wine is similar.

LATOUR À POMEROL Bordeaux: FRANCE

The village name is attached to the name of the *château* in order to avoid confusion with another property in the Médoc. This comes fourth in the hierarchy of J.-P. Moueix *châteaux* and is situated across the road from Pétrus.

LATOUR-VEDRINES See Doisy-Védrines.

LATTE

The French term for the thin strip of wood which separates one layer of bottles from another in a wine bin in a traditional cellar, when the wine is not stored in pallets.

LAUDUN Rhône: FRANCE

One of the villages of the appellation Côtes du Rhône Villages in the southern Rhône. Amphorae dating back to 300BC have been found there. In the 18th century the reputation of its white wine travelled to Paris and beyond. Today the village produces red, white and rosé wines. The red is most important, but the white is better than average quality.

LAUERBURG Mosel-Saar-Ruwer: GERMANY

A small but important family estate on the Mosel with vineyards in Graach and Bernkastel, including part of the Bernkastel Doktor vineyard.

MICHEL LAUGEL Alsace: FRANCE

A large family company from Alsace, based in Marlenheim, a village with a reputation for Pinot Noir, so that Pinot Noir, Cuvée du Mariage de l'Ami Fritz is one of their best wines. They are also important producers of Crémant d'Alsace.

LAUJAC Bordeaux: FRANCE

One of the leading properties of Bégadan, Médoc.

LAURENT PERRIER Champagne: FRANCE

An important champagne house. Their *cuvée de prestige* is Cuvée Grand Siècle and they produce a non-dosaged wine, Ultra Brut.

LAUZET

A little-known white grape occasionally used for Jurançon.

LAVAUX SWITZERLAND

One of the three main wine regions in the canton of the Vaud, with vineyards on the steep shores of Lake Geneva, between Lausanne and Montreux. Fendant, also called Dorin locally, is the main grape variety. Dézelay and Marsens are reputed vineyards with their own appellation.

LAVILLE-HAUT-BRION Bordeaux: FRANCE

Cru Classé Graves from the commune of Talence. The white wine made from the vineyards next to those of La Mission-Haut-Brion. The blend is Sauvignon and Sémillon grapes fermented in oak barrels, making a wine that benefits from ageing in the bottle.

LAVILLEDIEU SOUTH WEST FRANCE

An expanding VDQS from vineyards around the village of the same name near the town of Montauban. The sole producer is the local cooperative, making red and rosé wine from Negrette, Gamay, Cabernet Franc, Syrah and Tannat grapes.

LAZIO See Latium.

LEACOCK

An important Madeira house, founded in 1754 and now part of the Madeira Wine Company.

LÉANYKA

Léanyka, translating literally as 'little girl' is a widely planted grape variety in Hungary, especially on the Great Plain and produces the better wine of the Eger area, with a spicy aromatic taste. It is also grown in Roumania as Feteasca and in Bulgaria as Fetiaska.

LEASINGHAM   see Stanley.

LEBANON

The Lebanon, as a Muslim country, is not a serious wine producer. However, the pioneering Château Musar in the Bekáa Valley demonstrates that conditions there are favourable to viticulture. The Jesuits first built a winery at Ksara in the Bekáa Valley in 1857. It was reputed to be the largest wine cellar in the Middle East but is now secularised and better known for the quality of its arrack. There are a few other aspiring wine estates, notably Domaine des Tournelles, who follow French methods, while the Lebanese concerns still favour the unsophisticated use of *amphorae*.

LECONFIELD   AUSTRALIA

A new winery in Coonawarra, established in 1974 by Sydney Hamilton at the age of 76, on his retirement from the family wine business. The winery concentrates on Bordeaux style Cabernet Sauvignon as well as some Rhine Riesling. Both are oak-aged and grapes are harvested exclusively by hand.

LEES

The deposits or sediment that fall out of a wine when it is left to rest in vat or barrel after fermentation. They consist of particles of colouring matter, dead yeast and so on, left from the fermentation. These are left to settle and then the clear wine is racked and run off into another recipient.

LEEUWIN ESTATE   AUSTRALIA

One of the most important vineyards of the Margaret River region in Western Australia, with the most sophisticated winery. Robert Mondavi advises; French barrels are changed each vintage and the Chardonnay and Pinot Noir have attracted particular attention.

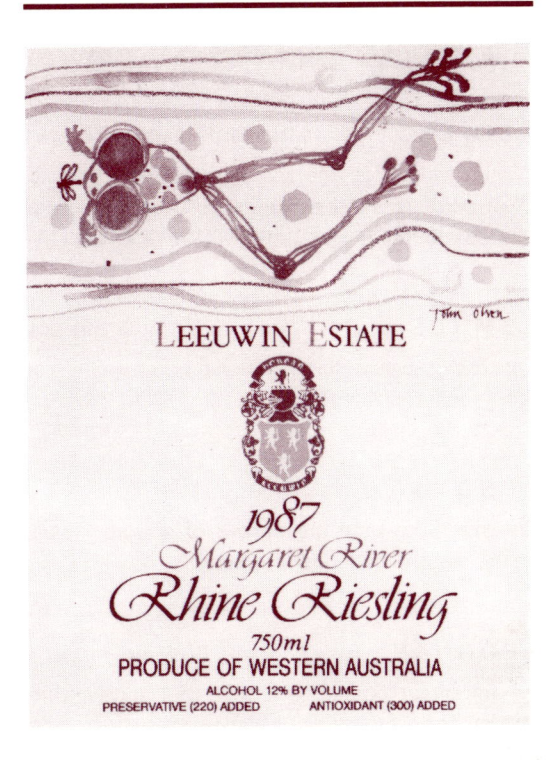

LEFLAIVE   Burgundy: FRANCE

Domaine Vincent Leflaive is a notable white wine estate of the Côte d'Or, including Bâtard- and Chevalier-Montrachet, Puligny Premiers Crus, les Pucelles, Clavoillons and Combettes. Methods are traditional. Oliver Leflaive, nephew of Vincent, runs a successful négociant company, also with an excellent reputation.

CHARLES LEFRANC

One of the early pioneers of the Californian wine industry and the founder of the Almadén Winery in 1852. His name lives on, as it is used by Almadén for their best quality wines.

LEGA DEL CHIANTI

In its present form it is an Italian voluntary association designed to protect and promote the quality of Chianti Classico. The original organisation goes back to the 13th century when the feudal barons of Radda, Gaiole and Castellina, towns in the heart of Chianti, formed a league to protect their various interests, including their vineyards.

LEGS   See tears.

LEIWEN Mosel-Saar-Ruwer: GERMANY
A wine village on the Mosel within the *Grosslage* of St. Michael. The best vineyard, Laurentiuslay, is shared with the neighbouring village of Köwerich.

LEMNOS GREECE
One of the Aegean islands which produces a Muscat wine similar to that of Samos.

LENGTH
Describes the time the flavour of a wine lingers in the mouth; the longer the better.

LEOGNAN Bordeaux: FRANCE
An important commune within the Graves, with several fine estates. See Pessac Leognan.

LEÓN SPAIN
A region of northern Spain with a long tradition of wine-making. As yet it has no D.O.s, but several undemarcated areas are recognised, namely El Bierzo which is a provisional D.O., as well as Comarca de León, Valdevimbre, Dos Oteros, La Bañeza, Valderas and Ribera Alta del Cea. The long-winded name of the main producer of León wines has been reduced to the unfortunate initials of VILE.

JEAN LEÓN SPAIN
One of the most innovative winemakers of Penedès, who has planted Cabernet Sauvignon and Chardonnay with successful results.

CHATEAU LEONAY   See Leo Buring.

LÉOVILLE-BARTON Bordeaux: FRANCE
A second growth St-Julien which was once part of Léoville-Lascases until it was purchased by the Irish Barton family in 1826. The wine is made at Langoa-Barton.

LÉOVILLE-LASCASES Bordeaux: FRANCE
A second growth which is indisputably one of the finest wines of St-Julien. Léoville-Barton and Léoville-Poyferré were originally part of the same estate. The wine is now made by Michel Delon whose family have run the property for three generations. The second wine is Clos de Marquis and the Delon family also own Château Potensac, a Grand Cru Bourgeois.

LÉOVILLE-POYFERRÉ Bordeaux: FRANCE
A second growth St-Julien, once part of Léoville-Lascases and recently overshadowed by its more famous cousin, whereas in the 19th century it was considered an exceptional second growth. Its second wine is Château Moulin-Riche.

LEROY Burgundy: FRANCE
Leroy are not only growers and *négociants*, but co-proprietors of the famous Domaine de la Romanée-Conti. Their wines, including Chambertin, Musigny, Clos de Vougeot, Pommard and Auxey-Duresses are made to last, with long maceration and no filtration.

LESBIAN

One of the wines of ancient Greece, a sweet wine presumably coming from the island of Lesbos.

LESSONA   Piedmont: ITALY

A little-known red DOC wine made from Nebbiolo grapes with up to 25% Vespolina and Bonarda, grown in vineyards around the town of the same name in the Vercelli hills. It requires two years' ageing.

LEVANTE   SPAIN

A general term to cover the demarcated areas of Valencia, Utiel-Requena, Alicante, Jumilla and Yecla in south east Spain. Some wines of individual character are made, but primarily it is a region for bulk table wines.

LEVERANO   Apulia: ITALY

A new DOC from Apulia. Red, which is capable of ageing, and *rosato* come from Negroamaro grapes, and white is made to drink young from Malvasia grapes.

LEXIA

An occasional synonym for the grape variety Muscat d'Alexandrie in Australia.

LIAOMING   See China.

LIATIKO

A red grape variety planted in Crete. It takes its name from Greek for July, Louliatiko, which is when it ripens.

LICENCE

Authorises the sale of wines, spirits and beers. These come in various forms, an off-licence, on-licence, retail licence and wholesale licence. Wines and spirits are considered separately.

ALEXIS LICHINE

One of the more colourful figures in Bordeaux and owner of Prieuré Lichine. Alexis Lichine's company is now owned by Bass Charrington, along with Lascombes.

LIE

The French term for 'lees'.

LIEBFRAUMILCH   GERMANY

Ironically, Liebfraumilch is the most popular German wine outside Germany, while it is little known in the country itself. The term means literally 'milk of Our Lady' and the name originates from the vineyard of the Liebfrauen Kirche in Worms. Liebfraumilch is made principally from Müller-Thurgau, Silvaner, Kerner and Riesling grapes and is produced mainly in the Rheinpfalz and Rheinhessen. It can also come from the Nahe. It is a Q*b*A wine and therefore must have the prerequisite amount of sugar in the must. Its prime quality is to be soft, fruity and pleasant without any distinctive characteristics. The Liebfraumilch market is dominated by brands like Blue Nun, Black Tower and Crown of Crowns.

LIESER   Mosel-Saar-Ruwer: GERMANY

A small village with a castle owned by the von Schorlemer family. It comes partly within the *Grosslage* of Kurfürstlay with the Schlossberg vineyard. It also includes the *Grosslage* of Beerenlay, with the vineyard of Niederberg-Herden.

LIGHT

Describes a wine of low alcohol, lacking in body. Light is also the official term for unfortified table wine.

LIGHT WINE

Colloquially called soft or lite wine, and also low calorie wine, is the result of a current trend in California towards wines that are low in alcohol, around 7° to 8°. When California first introduced wine laws, a wine had legally to have a minimum of 10° alcohol, and most wines were often much higher. Greater awareness of alcohol and calories has encouraged this trend towards light wines. See also dealcoholized wine.

LIMBERGER   see Blaufrankisch

LIMEKILN   California: USA
An AVA within San Benito County.

LIMESTONE
Features in many of the vineyards of France, notably in parts of Bordeaux and on the Côte d'Or. It is absorbant with good drainage, while retaining moisture. It also retains heat and gives wines with a good varietal character, alcohol and a flavour with balanced acidity and finesse.

LIMOUSIN OAK
One of the principal types of French oak used for making wine barrels. In contrast to Nevers oak, it comes from a warm mild climate and the wood is looser grained, from quicker growing trees, so that the wine picks up more character than from Nevers oak.

LINDEMAN   AUSTRALIA
One of the most important names of the Australian wine industry. The early origins of the company go back to the planting of a vineyard in the Hunter Valley in 1843. Ben Ean is now their base in the Hunter Valley and the name of their 'Moselle'. As well as other vineyards in the Hunter Valley, they own Leo Buring, Rouge Homme in Coonawarra, vineyards on Corowa, a modern winery and vineyards at Keradoc in north east Victoria and vineyards at Padthaway in Southern Australia. In the past the company has done much to introduce new techniques; today they have a reputation for sound brands, and good varietals, blending wines consistently over several regions.

LINDOS   See Rhodes.

LIOT   Bordeaux: FRANCE
A little-known Cru Bourgeois Sauternes in the commune of Barsac. The vineyards have an unusually high proportion of Muscadelle.

LIQUEUR D'EXPÉDITION
The mixture of wine, cane sugar and occasionally, grape spirit which is added to a bottle of champagne after *dégorgement*. The wine in the mixture should be the same as that already in the bottle. The cane sugar determines the ultimate sweetness of the champagne.

LIQUEUR MUSCAT   AUSTRALIA
A fortified liqueur wine made from the Brown Muscat grape, grown in the Rutherglen district of northeast Victoria. The grapes are picked when they are very ripe and sweet and the wine is aged in old oak barrels, often in a kind of *solera* system, in very hot conditions. The resulting wine is rich and treacly, not unlike liquid marmalade. It makes a delicious dessert wine.

LIQUEUR DE TIRAGE
The solution of wine, yeast and sugar that is added to still champagne to induce the second fermentation.

LIQUOROSO
In Italy, describes a dessert wine, such as Marsala, which has been fortified with alcohol.

LIRAC   Rhône: FRANCE
A wine village of the southern Rhône producing red, white and rosé wines under the village name. The rosé competes with Tavel; the reds are generally light and fruity and best drunk young, as are the rosé and white. The grape varieties are mainly Grenache, Cinsaut, Syrah and Clairette.

LISTAN
A synonym for the Palomino grape in the Midi.

LISTEL
The brand name used by Les Salins du Midi the biggest vineyard owner of France. It is a play on words of the name of one of their main vineyard areas, the Ile de Stel.

LISTRAC
Bordeaux: FRANCE

One of the two lesser appellations of the Médoc in that it lies away from the Gironde. There are no classed growths among the wines of Listrac. Fourcas Hosten, Fourcas Dupré and Clarke are the most notable properties.

LITE WINES
see light wines.

LITTLE KAROO
see Klein Karoo.

LIVERMORE VALLEY
California: USA

The most important wine region and the only AVA of Alameda County to the east of San Francisco. Wente Bros. and Concannon are the best names, with a reputation for white wine.

LIVERSAN
Bordeaux: FRANCE

A Cru Grand Bourgeois from Saint Saveur, Haut-Médoc, with a good reputation.

LJASKOVETZ
BULGARIA

A defined Controliran wine region concentrating on white wine made from Aligoté.

LJUTOMER
YUGOSLAVIA

Yugoslavia's most famous vineyard district, situated in the Drav region of Slovenia. It is planted mainly with Laski Rizling, for Lutomer Laski Rizling, but there is also Rhine or Renski Riesling, Sauvignon, Gewürztraminer and Pinot Blanc and Gris, all of which make very acceptable white wine.

LOAM

A loose-grained porous soil that is quite fertile and therefore not responsible for any particularly fine wines.

LOCOROTONDO
Apulia: ITALY

A dry white DOC wine from Apulia, made from Verdeca and Bianco d'Alessano grapes, grown around the town of Locorotondo. *Spumante* is also permitted.

LODGE

The traditional name for a port shipper's establishment in Vila Nova da Gaia the suburb of Oporto in Portugal, with offices, tasting room and cellars for ageing and blending the port.

LODI
California: USA

A town and important wine region of the San Joaquin Valley, known for its jug wines.

LES LOGES
Loire: FRANCE

An important village in the appellation of Pouilly Fumé.

LOGRONO
SPAIN

The capital of Rioja, a bustling city with some *bodegas* as well as the offices of the official bodies of the region.

LOIRE   FRANCE

The Loire Valley is one of the most varied wine regions of France. The river rises in the Ardèche and on its 635 mile journey to the Atlantic flows by numerous different vineyards, as well as orchards, fertile pastures and Renaissance châteaux. Not for nothing is the Loire valley known as the Garden of France. Travelling downstream, the first important vineyards you reach are those of Sancerre and Pouilly Fumé, with neighbouring Reuilly, Quincy and Ménétou Salon making similar wines from Sauvignon Blanc and some Pinot Noir. The vineyards of Touraine include Vouvray, a versatile appellation of sweet, dry and sparkling wines, and similar Montlouis and the red wines of Bourgueil and Chinon. Anjou is known for its pink wines and for the sweet wines of Coteaux du Layon, Quarts de Chaume and Bonnezeaux, as well as the individual wines of Sancerre. The lower reaches of the Loire around Nantes are the home of Muscadet.

LONG

Length of taste is an element of quality for a wine.

LONG ISLAND   USA

Long Island in New York State produces a small but growing amount of wine around Cutchogue on the north eastern tip of the island, where the maritime climate is more favourable to vines than in the rest of the state. Chardonnay is especially successful.

LONTUÉ   See Chile.

LOONG YAN   CHINA

A white Chinese grape variety translating literally as 'Dragon's Eye'.

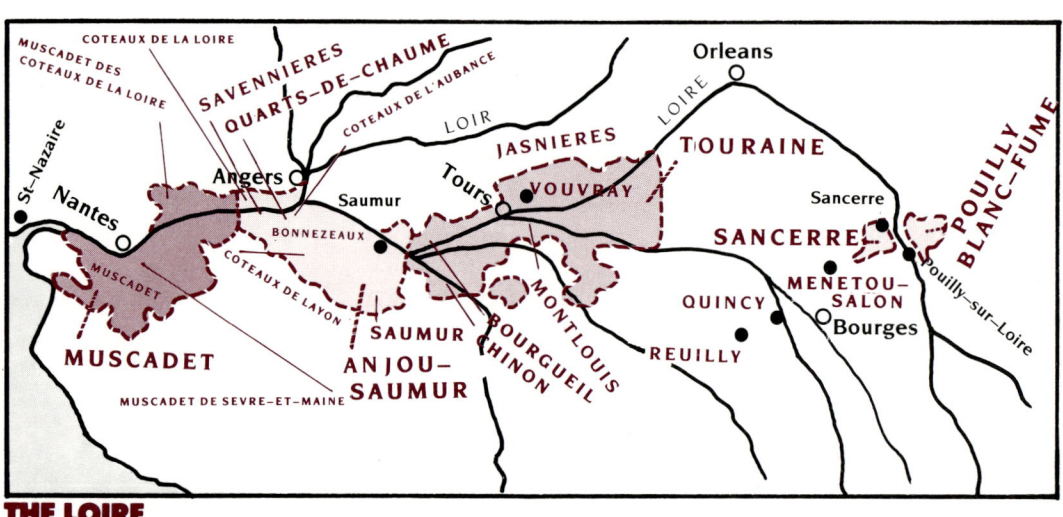

THE LOIRE

LONDON PARTICULAR   Sicily: ITALY

Was a popular brand name for Marsala Superiore (see Marsala).

LONDON WINERY   CANADA

In London Ontario, this is one of the more traditional Canadian wineries, making sherry-style wines like London Cream sherry, and hybrid table wines from Maréchal Foch and Baco grapes. London Chablis also features on its list.

LÓPEZ DE HEREDIA VINA TONDONIA   SPAIN

One of the most traditional Rioja companies, a family *bodega* founded in 1877. Their own vineyards give them half their requirements and all their wines are fermented in wood and aged in oak for a minimum of three years. Their range includes red and white Tondonia and Bosconia and younger Cubillo.

LORCH
Rheingau: GERMANY

With Lorchhausen, the last two villages of Rheingau coming within the *Grosslage* of Burgweg and producing some sound Riesling.

LORCHHAUSEN
Rheingau: GERMANY

With Lorch, the last two villages of the Rheingau, coming within the *Grosslage* of Burgweg and producing some satisfactory Riesling.

GUSTAV LORENTZ
Alsace: FRANCE

An Alsace house based in Bergheim. They have vineyards on the Kanzlerberg and Altenberg sites.

LORON
Burgundy: FRANCE

An important family firm of *négociants* in Beaujolais, dealing in table wine as well as Cru and estate Beaujolais.

LOS OTEROS
SPAIN

An undemarcated region within the Comarca de Leon. Wine production is primitive and the most typical wine is a light *clarete* made from the Prieto Picudo grape.

LOTA

The Portuguese term for a parcel of wine from an individual port vineyard. Similar *lotas* are blended together.

LOUDENNE
Bordeaux: FRANCE

A Cru Grand Bourgeois in the commune of St-Yzans, Médoc, that has belonged to the Gilbeys since 1875. Unusually, nearly a quarter of the vineyard is devoted to white wine but the reputation of the property really stands on its red wine.

LOUPIAC
Bordeaux: FRANCE

A sweet white wine appellation. The vineyards are separated from those of Sauternes by the Garonne. The autumnal climate sometimes allows for the development of noble rot; methods are similar to Sauternes and a higher yield is permitted. Usually the wines are lighter. Ricaud is one of the best properties.

LOUREIRO

One of the principal grape varieties for the white Vinho Verde of Portugal, producing attractive fragrant wines.

LA LOUVIÈRE
Bordeaux: FRANCE

The largest property of the Graves, making good red and white wine in the modern style after the replanting of the vineyards in the 1960s by the Lurton family.

LOW CALORIE WINE see light wine.

LOZITZA
BULGARIA

A defined Controliran wine region of origin, concentrating on the production of Cabernet Sauvignon wines.

LUDON
Bordeaux: FRANCE

One of the communes within the Haut-Médoc with La Lagune as its best wine.

LUGANA
Lombardy: ITALY

An elegant dry white DOC wine from Trebbiano di Lugana, grown south of Lake Garda. A *spumante* version is also made.

LUGNY See Mâcon Villages.

LUNGAROTTI — Umbria: ITALY

The enterprising and pioneering family who dominate the production of Torgiano. As well as making red and white Torgiano, called respectively Rubesco and Torre di Giano, and a *rosato* Castel Grifone from the same grapes as Rubesco, they are experimenting successfully with Cabernet Sauvignon and Chardonnay grapes and even make a sherry-style wine called Soleone, and also a *Spumante*.

LUPÉ CHOLET — Burgundy: FRANCE

A house from Nuits St-Georges, known for their *monopole* of Nuits St-Georges Château Gris.

LUR SALUCES

The family have owned d'Yquem since 1785, when Josephine Sauvage d'Yquem married the Comte de Lur Saluces. The present Comte Alexandre is also the proprietor of a Sauternes Cru Bourgeois, de Fargues.

LUSSAC — Bordeaux: FRANCE

One of the so-called 'St-Émilion satellites'. These six surrounding parishes used to sell their wine as St-Emilion until the appellation was delimited in 1936. The name of the parish is now hyphenated onto the St-Émilion name.

LUXEMBOURG

The vineyards of Luxembourg stretch along the Mosel some 40 miles from Remich to Wasserbillig near the French border. The main grape varieties are Rivaner, with Elbling, Auxerrois and Riesling, and a little Gewürztraminer, Pinot Gris and Pinot Blanc. There are no red wines and the whites are not unlike their German counterparts: low in alcohol, light, flowery and acidic. About 1,200 growers cultivate some 1,300 hectares of vines, so most of the production is in the hands of cooperatives. Caves Bernard Massard are important producers of sparkling wines. Luxembourg wines are labelled according to their grape variety and graded into four categories: *marque nationale*, *vin classé*, *premier cru* and *grand premier cru*, the best of all.

LYNCH-BAGES — Bordeaux: FRANCE

Although only a fifth growth Pauillac, it has a well-deserved reputation, producing rich plummy wines. It has Irish origins in the Lynch family. The second label is Haut-Bages Averous and a small amount of white wine is also made from Sémillon grapes.

LYNCH-MOUSSAS — Bordeaux: FRANCE

A fifth growth Pauillac. The family's name was Lynch, and Moussas is the name of the tiny hamlet where the vineyard is situated. It is a tiny, little-known property making consistent wine.

LES LYS   See Vaillons.

M

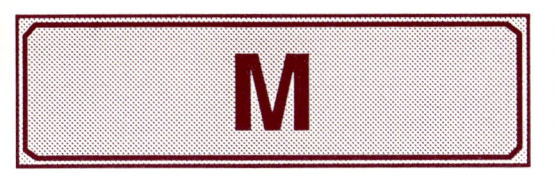

M.A.
On a champagne label, this indicates a *marque auxiliaire* or subsidiary brand, rather than the company's principal name.

M.I.A.   AUSTRALIA
M.I.A. is the common abbreviation of the Murrumbidgee Irrigation Area, the wine region in New South Wales.

M.O.G.
Stands for 'Material other than Grapes' and is the term used in assessing the quality of grapes picked by a mechanical harvester, to check whether other foreign matter like leaves and stones have also been picked up by the machine.

MACABEO   See Maccabeo

MACAU   Bordeaux: FRANCE
One of the communes within the Haut-Médoc, with Cantemerle as its best wine.

MACCABEO
Maccabeo or Macabeo is a Spanish white grape variety, planted widely for white Rioja and called Viura in the region. It is grown elsewhere in northern Spain, particularly in Penedès for sparkling wine, blended with Xarel-lo and Parellada. It is an uninteresting grape and requires blending with other more enlivening varieties. It is also grown in the Midi, notably in the Pyrénées Orientales for local vin de pays and Côtes de Roussillon Blanc.

MACERATION
The period during which the juice is in contact with the grape skins. In the case of white wines this may not occur at all, or only last a few hours, and in the case of red wines, several days. The difference between maceration and *cuvaison* is that the *cuvaison* and fermentation may last longer than the period of maceration. The length of maceration depends on the quality of the grapes and the required depth of colour of wine, in the case of red wine.

MACÉRATION CARBONIQUE
A relatively new technique of vinification used to produce fresh fruity red wines that are low in tannin and high in colour. Whole bunches of grapes are put into the vat, which is already filled with carbon dioxide. A fermentation begins inside the grapes, while the juice of some of the grapes at the bottom of the vat, which have been crushed by the weight of the grapes on top, also begins fermenting in the normal way. Colour and fruit is extracted in this way, but not tannin, so early-to-drink red wine is the result. This method of vinification is particularly used in Beaujolais and in the Midi, with attractive results. Unlike a normal fermentation, the pressed juice is better than the free-run juice.

MACHARD DE GRAMONT   Burgundy: FRANCE
An estate in Nuits St-Georges, known especially for its Nuits St-Georges Premiers Crus, Pommard, and Savigny les Beaune. They only bottle the best wines of each vintage.

MACHARNUDO   SPAIN
The best of all the *albariza* areas of Jerez, to the north of the town. The name sometimes appears on a sherry label.

MACHURAZ   Savoie: FRANCE
One of the villages with the status of cru in the VDQS of Vin du Bugey. In practice the name is never used.

MacKENZIE & CO   see Ferreira.

MÂCON Burgundy: FRANCE

The wine, which can be red, white or *rosé*, is named after the town in southern Burgundy; the area is called the Mâconnais. The white wines are made from Pinot Blanc grapes and Chardonnay and the reds are made from Gamay. White is generally more successful. The cooperatives are the most important producers of the region.

MÂCON PINOT CHARDONNAY
Burgundy: FRANCE

This appellation is sometimes found for white Mâcon. Pinot Chardonnay does not exist as a grape variety; this is a reference to the fact that white Mâcon can be made from Pinot Blanc as well as Chardonnay.

MÂCON SUPÉRIEUR
Burgundy: FRANCE

Differs from simple Mâcon only in alcoholic content as it must be one degree higher; 10° of alcohol for red and 11° for white wine.

MÂCON VILLAGES Burgundy: FRANCE

Can be a red or white wine from the Mâcon area and may also include the name of the village on the label. The red appellation is quite rare; in contrast, 43 villages may produce the white wine. The better-known villages include Chardonnay, which may have given its name to the grape variety, Lugny, Viré, Azé, Clessé, Igé, Vergé, Prissé and La Roche Vineuse. Louis Latour specialises in Mâcon Lugny.

MÂCONNAIS Burgundy: FRANCE

The overall name for the area of southern Burgundy, around the town of Mâcon, which produces a variety of wines ranging from red, rosé and white Mâcon, Mâcon Villages, Mâcon Supérieur, Saint Véran, Pouilly Vinzelles, Pouilly Loché and Pouilly Fuissé. The area also produces a substantial amount of Bourgogne, Bourgogne Grand Ordinaire, Bourgogne Passe Tout Grains and Crémant de Bourgogne. The predominant grape varieties are Chardonnay for white wine and Gamay for red wine.

MACULAN Veneto: ITALY

A small family company making oak-aged Breganze Rosso and Bianco, as well as Torcolato, a rich dessert wine from dried Vespaiolo grapes, which created their reputation.

MACVIN Jura: FRANCE

The typical aperitif of the Jura made, like ratafia, from grape must and *marc*.

MADARGUES FRANCE

A cru of the V.D.Q.S. Côtes d'Auvergne.

MADEIRA Madeira: PORTUGAL

A Portuguese fortified wine that takes its name from the island of Madeira, where it is produced. There are four main types of Madeira, based on four respective grape varieties; these are Sercial; Verdelho, said to be the same as Pedro Ximénez; Bual and Malmsey. Negramole, Moscatel and Terrantez are also grown on the island's volcanic soil. The method of production is unique and involves, as well as fortification, a process of heating called *estufagem*. Vinification takes place in Funchal, the capital of the island. The dry Sercial and Verdelho are fermented fully and fortified later; the sweet Bual and Malmsey have their fermentation checked by the addition of brandy. The wine is then baked in *estufas* for a minimum of three months at an average temperature of 45–50°C. This is an imitation of the heating of the wine that took place when it was used as ballast by the Portuguese ships travelling to India. It was discovered that the wine proved better after the long hot voyage. The wine is then blended and occasionally aged in a *solera* system like sherry.

Madeira is the most long lived of wines and improves considerably with age. Vintage Madeiras are made in particularly fine years.

Madeira suffered considerably from phylloxera and oidium. The island's heyday was in the Victorian era; this was the wine that gave its name to the cake. Sadly, today, Madeira has declined in popularity but there are hopes of a revival in its fortunes.

THE MADEIRA WINE COMPANY

Changed its name from The Madeira Wine Association in 1981. It comprises a group of seven leading Madeira shippers who sell to Britain, including Blandy, Cossart Gordon, Leacock, Lomelino, Rutherford & Miles. It accounts for about half the island's production.

LA MADELEINE Bordeaux: FRANCE

A tiny Grand Cru Classé of St-Émilion situated on the *côtes*.

MADELEINE ANGEVINE

A white grape grown to a limited extent in England. It is a crossing between Précoce de Malingre and Madeleine Royale.

MADERA California: USA

The name of a city, a county and an AVA in the fertile San Joaquin valley, with vineyards producing grapes prolifically for jug wine.

MADERISÉ

The French term for 'maderised'.

MADERISED

Describes an overmature wine; that is oxidised, flat and browning in colour.

MADIRAN SOUTH WEST FRANCE

A tough red wine from the foothills of the Pyrenees from around the village of the same name. The grape varieties are principally Tannat, softened by Cabernet Sauvignon and Cabernet Franc. The wine requires a minimum of one year's ageing in wood or vat. There are several individual growers, but the most important producers are the two cave cooperatives at Saint Mont and Crouseilles.

MADURO

Vinho maduro means in Portuguese a mature table wine, as opposed to a young *vinho verde*.

MAGARATCH RUBY

A Russian crossing of the Cabernet Sauvignon and Saperavi grape varieties, now grown in the Crimea, where it produces some successful red wines.

MAGDELEINE Bordeaux: FRANCE

A Premier Grand Cru Classé St-Émilion. A tiny property next to Belair owned by J.-P. Moueix and making very successful wine. The vineyard consists of 80% Merlot and 20% Cabernet Franc grapes.

MAGENCE Bordeaux: FRANCE

An excellent Graves property in the commune of St-Pierre-de-Mons. It makes a crisp white wine of pure Sauvignon grapes and a fruity red wine.

MAGNESIUM

An important constituent in the soil of a vineyard and essential in the process of photosynthesis, converting starch into sugar. It must be in balance with potassium for both to be assimilated properly by the vine.

MAGNUM

A double bottle size (150cl).

MAGON TUNISIA

A full-bodied red wine made from Cinsaut and Mourvèdre grapes grown at Tébourba in the valley of Oeud Medjerdah, west of Tunis.

MAGRO

The Italian term for 'thin'.

MAILBERG   See Weinviertel.

MAILLY *Champagne:* FRANCE

A champagne village on the Montagne de Reims; there is a successful village cooperative.

MAINDREIECK *Franconia:* GERMANY

The most important of the three *Bereichs* of Franconia, including the vineyards of Wurzburg, Randersacker, Volkach, Nordheim and Escherndorf and fine sites, where the soil is limestone. Wines are often sold under the *Bereich* name as the several *Grosslagen* names are relatively unknown.

MAINVIERECK *Franconia:* GERMANY

One of the three *Bereichs* of Franconia, divided into two *Grosslagen*, Reuschberg and Heiligenthal.

MAINZ *Rheinhessen:* GERMANY

The city of Mainz is the capital of the federal state of Rheinland-Pfalz. As such it is the wine capital of Germany and the home of many of the industry's institutions. The Mainzer Weinbörse is an important annual trade fair. There are vineyards in the suburbs of Mainz, sold under the *Grosslage* name of St. Alban.

MAIPO CHILE

Near Santiago, this is one of the main wine-producing areas of Chile. The low rainfall necessitates irrigation but, with the oceanic climate, conditions are particularly suitable for Bordeaux grape varieties.

HENRI MAIRE *Jura:* FRANCE

As the owner of four estates around Arbois and also as a *négociant*, Henri Maire is the most important producer of the wines of the Jura. He also deals in wines from Burgundy and Bordeaux as well as marketing branded table wine. The family goes back to the 16th century, but it is the present head of the house that has, for many people, made his name synonymous with the wines of the Jura, combining modern techniques and traditional practices in his wine-making.

MAITRE DE CHAI

A Bordelais term for a cellar master, responsible for the vinification and ageing of the wine, a man of considerable experience and expertise.

MAJORCA

There are two main wine areas on the island of Majorca, Binisalem and Felanito, planted with local grape varieties, making red and rosé wines at the local cooperatives for everyday drinking.

MÁLAGA SPAIN

A currently neglected fortified wine which was at the height of its popularity in the last century. Today the name Málaga is more often associated with seaside holidays. The vineyards are on the hills behind the town of Málaga in the three main áreas, Antequerra, Borge and Mollina, but to qualify for the D.O. the wine must be matured in Málaga itself, in *soleras* similar to those of Jerez. The principal grape varieties are Pedro Ximénez and Moscatel and a variety of styles are made, ranging from the very sweet to the fairly dry. They are:
— Blanco Seco – usually dry and nutty, made from Pedro Ximénez

- Semi Dulce – a drier Málaga
- Pajarete – a dry or semi dry Málaga
- Pedro Ximénez, made from that grape alone, with a full-bodied soft, flavour
- Moscatel, made purely from the Moscatel grape; of varying age and colour
- Dulce Color – the most popular Málaga, sweetened with *arrope* and very rich, almost cloying
- Lágrima, made purely from free run juice, sweet and aromatic
- Lágrima Cristi, an even sweeter version of Lágrima
- Tintillo, an unusual red Málaga.

MALARTIC-LAGRAVIÈRE
Bordeaux: FRANCE

A Cru Classé Graves from the commune of Léognan. Produces both red and white wine. There is very little production of white but it is an unusually pure Sauvignon. The red is a fine wine for ageing, made from modern methods.

MALBEC

Also called Cot, Pressac, and Auxerrois, is one of the grapes of Bordeaux. It is less widely grown in the Médoc, but is still popular in Blaye and Bourg. It is really in its element in Cahors, where it accounts for at least 70% of the blend, with Merlot and Tannat. It is also grown a little in the Loire valley, where it is blended with Gamay and Cabernet Franc.

In Argentina it is surprisingly popular and successful; some is grown in Chile too and there is a little in Australia, for blending with Cabernet Sauvignon, while in California it is of little significance.

MALESCOT ST-EXUPÉRY
Bordeaux: FRANCE

A third growth Margaux which was, for a long time, the property of the Counts of St-Exupéry. It has an attractive house in the centre of Margaux and vineyards to the north of the town. It is now owned by the Zuger family who also own Marquis d'Alesme-Becker and are making good wine.

MALIC ACID

As found in apples and other fruits, one of the constituents of wine. It accounts for the greenness of a wine made from unripe grapes, and diminishes considerably after the malo-lactic fermentation.

MALIGNY
Burgundy: FRANCE

One of the larger villages within the vineyards of Chablis.

DE MALLE
Bordeaux: FRANCE

A second growth Sauternes in the commune of Preignac, with a beautiful house and garden. Vinification entails the use of stainless steel vats and oak barrels. The dry wine is called Chevalier de Malle and the red wine Château de Cardaillon.

MALMSEY
Madeira: PORTUGAL

The sweetest of the four types of the fortified wine, Madeira, a rich full-bodied dessert wine made from the Malvasia or Malmsey grape. Brandy is added to stop the fermentation and retain sufficient sugar in the wine. The Duke of Clarence drowned in a butt of Malmsey in Shakespeare's play, Richard III.

MALO-LACTIC FERMENTATION

The secondary fermentation that takes place after the main alcoholic fermentation, when the malic acid in the wine is converted into lactic acid, thereby reducing the total acidity in the wine. All red wines undergo a malo-lactic fermentation, but not all white wines do, as it may be desirable to retain a higher level of acidity. In some areas of southwest France and in Alsace, for example, they believe that the malo-lactic fermentation adversely affects the taste of the wine.

MALTA

Malta produces a small amount of wine from vineyards scattered along the western and southern sides of the island and also on Gozo. The vines are mainly local varieties, but there has also been some experimentation with French and Italian varieties, particularly Muscat for dessert wines. The wine producer is the Marsovin company which makes branded table wines for local consumption.

MALVASIA

An antique white grape variety grown in diminishing amounts, mainly in Spain and Italy, but also a little in Portugal, Yugoslavia, France, Austria and Germany. To add to the confusion, Malvoisie is often a synonym for grapes that have nothing to do with Malvasia, namely for Pinot Gris in Switzerland and in the Loire valley; in Limoux for Maccabeo; in the Languedoc for Bourboulenc and in Corsica for Vermentino.

Malvasia is at its best in central-southern Italy. It is used as Malvasia di Candida and Malvasia di Lazio for Frascati, Marino and Est! Est!! Est!!! In Chianti it is disappearing as the proportion of white grapes has been reduced but is still found in Galestro and used for *Vin Santo*. Some is also grown in Friuli and Emilia Romagna, while Malvasia delle Lipari and Malvasia di Sardegna are heady, sweet or dry wines.

Malvasia gives its name to Malmsey in Madeira and it is grown in Portugal for table wines.

MALVASIA DI BOSA *Sardinia*: ITALY

A DOC dessert wine or aperitif made from the white Malvasia di Sardegna grapes grown around Bosa. *Secco* and *dolce* have 15° minimum alcohol; *liquoroso secco* and *liquoroso dolce* 17.5°.

MALVASIA DI CAGLIARI
Sardinia: ITALY

Made from the white Malvasia grapes grown on the Campidano plains, north of Cagliari. There are four versions in the DOC *secco* and *dolce* at 14° minimum alcohol, *liquoroso secco* and *liquoroso dolce* at 17.5°. The dry is best drunk young, the others may be kept.

MALVASIA DI CASORZO D'ASTI
Piedmont: ITALY

A cherry-coloured sweet *spumante* DOC wine made from the Malvasia Rosso grape, grown in the hills around Casorzo between Turin and Asti.

MALVASIA DI CASTELNUOVO DON BOSCO *Piedmont*: ITALY

A cherry-coloured sweet *spumante* DOC wine made from the Malvasia Rosso grape grown in tiny quantities in the hills around Castelnuovo Don Bosco.

MALVASIA DELLE LIPARI
Sicily: ITALY

A DOC dessert wine made on the Lipari or Aeolian islands north of Messina from Malvasia di Lipari grapes. The basic wine has minimum alcohol of 11.5°, and is quite sweet and fragrant. *Passito* at 18° and fortified at 20° are more long-lived and substantial. The best producer is Carlo Hauner on the island of Salina.

MALVOISIE SWITZERLAND

A dessert wine from the Valais, made from Pinot Gris grapes. See also Malvasia.

MAMERTINE

Was a wine of ancient Rome, made in Calabria. Julius Caesar drank it to celebrate his 3rd consulship in 46 BC. Modern Mamertino is made in Sicily from semi-dried Cataratto, Inzolio and Grillo grapes and is slightly sweet and raisiny.

MAMERTINO *Sicily*: ITALY

The modern version of a wine which was once enjoyed by Julius Caesar. It is made from Cataratto, Inzolia and Grillo grapes and is the colour of old gold and smells of raisins. As medium sweet it is a dessert wine, as dry an aperitif.

MAMMOLO

A local Tuscan grape variety which can be used in small proportions for Chianti and other Tuscan reds.

LA MANCHA SPAIN

One of the D.O.s of central Spain, in the heart of the plain of La Mancha, which is the largest wine producing region of Spain. The main grape variety is Airén, for light neutral white wines; much of them are destined for distillation.

MANCHUELA SPAIN

One of the D.O.s of central Spain, producing bulk table wines; whites from the Airén grape and red, clarets and *vinos de doble pasto* from Bobal.

MANDEMENT SWITZERLAND

The main vineyard area in the canton of Geneva, with vineyards of Chasselas on the right bank of the Rhône and the town of Satigny at its centre. The cellars of the Coopérative Vin Union are in Geneva.

MANDILARIA

A red grape variety planted extensively on the Greek islands.

MANDROLISAI Sardinia: ITALY

A DOC wine, made from Bovale Sardo, Cannonau and Monica grapes grown around Sorgono in central Sardinia. The dry red takes a couple of years' ageing, the *rosato* is best young.

MANICLE Savoie: FRANCE

One of the crus of the Vin du Bugey. In reality only one grower makes the wine, from Chardonnay and Pinot Noir grapes, grown on what is reputed to have been the vineyard of Brillat Savarin. Methods are primitive and the wine surprisingly good.

MANNEQUIN

Was the traditional large wicker basket used for the vintage in Champagne. It was oval in shape with tall sides slanting inwards towards the base and held about 176 lbs of grapes. These have been replaced by more functional rectangular containers.

MANSENG

Manseng, the grape for Jurançon, is grown in south west France and comes in two forms, Gros and Petit. Petit is better, especially when left to dry on the vines until November for Jurançon moelleux. Sometimes it even develops *botrytis*. Gros Manseng, with larger berries, is the basis of Jurançon sec, when blended with Courbu, and occasionally Lauzet. Gros and Petit Manseng area also used for Pacherenc du Vic Bilh and Blanc de Béarn. Manseng Noir is a little known red grape variety occasionally found in Béarn and the Pyrenees.

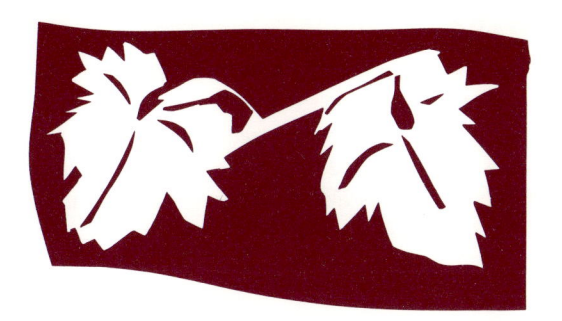

MANTINIA GREECE

A dry, slightly aromatic, white wine produced in the heart of the Peloponnese, from the Moschofilero grape.

MANTONICO DI BIANCO Calabria: ITALY

A dry or slightly sweet white wine made from semi-dried Mantonico grapes grown around the town of Bianco. When aged in barrel, this develops a sherry-like taste with 15° alcohol.

MANZANILLA SPAIN

A distinctive sherry made only in Sanlúcar de Barrameda. It is a dry *fino*, but with a particular salty tang resulting from its maturation by the sea. If it is moved to Jerez de la Frontera the saltiness fades and never returns. When *manzanilla* ages, it becomes *manzanilla pasada*. The name *manzanilla* in Spain also means camomile tea and may have derived from a similarity of flavour.

LES MARANGES Burgundy: FRANCE

A new appellation grouping three villages of the Côte d'Or: Sampigny, Cheilly and Dezize, whose wines were previously sold as Côte de Beaune Villages.

MARAŠTINA

The most widely grown white grape variety of the Dalmatian coast; labelled as Maraština, it comes from vineyards around Čara Smokvica.

DE MARBUZET Bordeaux: FRANCE

A Cru Grand Bourgeois Exceptionnel of St-Estèphe. It belongs to Bruno Prats of Cos d'Estournel and enjoys a good reputation.

MARC

The residue of stalks, pips and skins left after pressing. Called pomace in English. In Champagne, it is also the capacity of a traditional press of 4000 kilos, which yields 2266 litres of juice, or 13 *pièces*. Confusingly, it is also the term for a spirit made from the distilled residue or pomace, such as Marc de Bourgogne.

MARCHES   ITALY

The Marche or Marches in English, so called because they were once a border region of castles like the Welsh Marches, are best known for white Verdicchio. Two red DOCs also merit note: Rosso Piceno and Rosso Cònero.

MARCILLAC   SOUTH WEST FRANCE

A VDQS from the upper reaches of the Lot valley in the Aveyron. The wine is red with a little rosé, made predominantly from the Fer Servadou grape plus a little Gamay and Jurançon Noir. The production is dominated by the cave cooperative of Valady, with a few independent producers.

MARCOBRUNN See Erbach.

MARCOTTAGE

Was the traditional way of propagating vines before the phylloxera crisis. It works in the same way as for strawberries. A vine shoot, still attached to the vine, is pushed into the ground, so that it grows roots, while the exposed end grows leaves. It is then cut from the parent vine.

MARÉCHAL FOCH

A French red hybrid grape variety, a *riparia rupestric* crossing with Goldriesling and grown in Canada as it is resistant to hard winters.

MAREMMA   Tuscany: ITALY

The coastal region of Tuscany near Grosseto makes non-DOC red and *rosato* mainly from Sangiovese grapes and white from Trebbiano, Vermentino and, unusually, Ansonica.

MARESTEL   see Roussette de Savoie.

MARGARET RIVER   AUSTRALIA

One of the new wine districts of Western Australia, a coastal area around the town of Margaret River 200 miles south of Perth. Vines were first grown here in the 19th century but it is only in the last 20 years that there has been a viticultural revival with the realisation of the suitability of the climate, with its high winter rainfall and warm summers. The Margaret River is the first Australian wine region to have a Certificate of Origin, setting standards of authenticity. The most important estates are Leeuwin, Cape Mentelle, Moss Wood and Vasse Felix.

MARGAUX   Bordeaux: FRANCE

Both a village and an appellation in the Médoc and one of the best *châteaux* of this appellation. The appellation of Margaux includes not only *châteaux* in the village but also from the neighbouring villages of Labarde, Arsac, Cantenac and Soussans. The wines of Margaux are elegant, have finesse and develop with age into delicate bottles. They are produced on pebbly gravel soil. The quintessence of Margaux is undoubtedly Château Margaux, one of the four Premiers Crus of the 1855 classification. It went through a period of the doldrums in the early 1970s until it was bought by André Mentzenopoulos in 1976. He, then his widow and daughter, have invested time and money in restoring the vineyards, cellars and house to their former glory and the wine is now once again worthy of its classification. A white wine is produced, called Pavillon Blanc de Château Margaux, and the second red wine is called Pavillon Rouge.

MARIE JEANNE

A name for a magnum in the Coteaux du Layon.

MARIENSTEINER

A crossing of the Silvaner and Rieslaner grape varieties grown in the Rheinhessen, Palatinate and Franconia.

MARIGNAN   *Savoie*: FRANCE

One of the crus of Vin de Savoie, a small vineyard near Lake Léman, planted with Chasselas for still white wine.

MARIN   *Savoie*: FRANCE

A village in Haute Savoie, and an aspiring cru of the appellation Vin de Savoie, mainly for white wine from the Chasselas grape.

MARIN   *California*: USA

An unimportant wine county, across the Golden Gate from San Francisco, that is more important for its proximity to Napa and Sonoma than for its own wine industry.

MARINO   *Latium*: ITALY

A dry white DOC wine which is very similar to Frascati, though perhaps a little fuller. It is also made from Malvasia and Trebbiano grapes. *Superiore* denotes 12.5° alcohol. *Spumante* is rare.

MARKGRÄFLERLAND   Baden: GERMANY

One of the seven Baden *Bereichs*, covering a fertile flat stretch of land from Freiburg to Baden, where Gutedel is the main grape variety and makes light neutral *spritzig* wine. A cross between Gutedel and Silvaner, called Nobling, shows some character and Müller-Thurgau and Spätburgunder grapes are important too. There are three *Grosslagen*: Lorettoberg, Burg Neuenfels and Vogtei Rötteln.

MARL

A mixture of clay and lime, found notably in Chablis, where there are limestone-rich muds, packed with fossilised oyster shell.

MARLBOROUGH   NEW ZEALAND

The most important wine region of South Island, which has been developed over the last fifteen years. There is a long ripening season, with warm dry summers and cool autumns, so that Müller-Thurgau, Sauvignon Blanc, Rhine Riesling and Cabernet Sauvignon do well here. Montana is the most important winery of the region.

MARONEAN

One of the wines of ancient Greece, described by Pliny as being dark in colour and generally mixed with eight parts water to one of wine.

MARQUIS-D'ALESME-BECKER
Bordeaux: FRANCE

A third growth Margaux. Once belonged to the Marquis d'Alesme and, after a chequered history, is now owned by the Zuger family of Malescot St-Exupéry. The wine is sound Margaux from modern methods.

MARQUIS DE ST-ESTÈPHE
Bordeaux: FRANCE

The brand name for the wine of the cooperative of St-Estèphe.

MARQUIS-DE-TERME
Bordeaux: FRANCE

A fourth growth Margaux; a little-known but respected wine, seen more often in France than abroad.

MARSALA
Sicily: ITALY

A port which gave its name to a fortified wine. The grape varieties are Grillo, Catarratto and Inzolia, grown in the province of Trapani in western Sicily. The method of production and development of the wine owes much to a Liverpool merchant, John Woodhouse who, finding the western Sicilian wine to his liking, added brandy to it to preserve it on the voyage home. Its success was such that Woodhouse founded a company in Sicily and his example was followed by other Englishmen. The basic character of Marsala depends upon the oxidation of the grapes, which gives the wine its distinctive taste. The base wine must have a minimum of 12° natural alcohol. To this base wine can be added concentrated must for extra sweetness, grape spirit for extra strength and *cotto* (a grape must that has been reduced to a syrupy mixture of caramelised sugar by cooking for twenty-four hours) which gives colour. It also used to be possible to add a *mistella* called *sifone*, which was a blend of sweet wine from semi-dried grapes. A mixture of *sifone* and *cotto* was called *concia*, but this is now an out-of-date process.

The following types of Marsala are permitted under the reforming regulations of 1984: in colour: *oro* (golden), *ambra* (amber), *rubino* (ruby), which can be made from red grapes, and in flavour: *secco* (dry), *semi secco* (medium dry) and *dolce* (sweet). The different qualities are as follows: The most common is Marsala Fine, with a minimum of one year's ageing and 17° alcohol. Marsala Superiore has two years' ageing and 18° alcohol, while Marsala Superiore Riserva has four years' ageing. These can be sweet or dry, depending on the producer's preference; Marsala Vergine must have a minimum of five years' ageing and 18° alcohol. It is always aged in a *solera* system and must contain no *cotto*, concentrate or *sifone*. Marsala Stravecchia or Riserva (either name is used) is aged for a minimum of ten years. This is the best of all, with the *solera* ageing allowing the true flavour of the Marsala to develop. The wine that was originally called Marsala Speciale and flavoured with egg, coffee, etc and used for cooking, is no longer called Marsala at all, but Cremoso Zabaione Vino Aromatizzato, if 80% of the mixture is Marsala. If there is only 60%, the concoction is labelled *preparato con l'Impiego di vino Marsala* and if there is less than 60%, no mention of Marsala may appear on the label.

MARSANNAY
Burgundy: FRANCE

The village of Marsannay or Marsannay-la-Côte, as it is also called, situated in the suburbs of Dijon, used to be distinguished with its own appellation Bourgogne Rosé Marsannay for rosé made from Pinot Noir. However, from 1987, the appellation has been altered to allow red, white and rosé wines under the name of Marsannay. The village is the home of the famous estate, Domaine Clair Daü.

MARSANNE

The principal white grape variety of the northern Rhône, used for white Hermitage, Crozes Hermitage, St-Péray and St-Joseph, with Roussanne. It can also be founded in the Swiss canton of the Valais as Ermitage and in the state of Victoria in Australia.

MARSENS
SWITZERLAND

Next to Dezelay in the region of Lavaux, this has its own appellation and a comparable reputation for Fendant wines.

MARTHA'S VINEYARD

An important Californian vineyard owned by Joseph Heitz, producing Cabernet Sauvignon, which has a distinctive flavour coming from the eucalyptus trees surrounding the vineyard. The price matches the reputation.

MARTILLAC
Bordeaux: FRANCE

An important commune within the Graves, with several fine estates.

MARTINA FRANCA
Apulia: ITALY

A dry white DOC wine from Apulia, very similar to neighbouring Locorotondo. A *spumante* is allowed.

MARTINBOROUGH — NEW ZEALAND

A small and as yet unknown wine area of North Island, just north of Wellington, with conditions well suited to the production of Gewürztraminer and Sauvignon Blanc.

MARTINENS — *Bordeaux*: FRANCE

A Cru Grand Bourgeois of Margaux.

MARTINEZ GASSIOT

A port house founded in 1797 by Sebastian Gonzalez Martinez who was joined by Peter Gassiot in 1822. In 1901 they were bought by John Harvey of Bristol and are now part of Allied Breweries.

LOUIS MARTINI — *California*: USA

A family run winery, founded in the Napa Valley in 1922. They own vineyards over the Napa and Sonoma Valleys. Cabernet Sauvignon and Zinfandel are their best varietals, and Barbera, in accordance with their Italian origins.

MARTINI & ROSSI — *Piedmont*: ITALY

The name Martini instantly means vermouth, but the company is also an important producer of Asti Spumante and a Riserva Montelera Brut Champenoise.

MARTINSTHAL — *Rheingau*: GERMANY

A little-known village that comes within the *Grosslage* of Steinmächer. The best *Einzellagen* are Langenberg and Wildsau.

MARYLAND — USA

The first French-American hybrids were planted in America in Maryland in the 1940s, by Philip Wagner at Boordy Vineyards. Others have followed his example and gone further to plant *vitis vinifera* vines too.

LA MARZELLE — *Bordeaux*: FRANCE

A small Grand Cru Classé of St-Émilion on the *graves*.

MARZEMINO

A local red grape variety of the Trentino district of north east Italy, one of the types of DOC of Trentino and also grown for the non DOC wine of Marzemino di Isera.

MASI — *Veneto*: ITALY

A large family company with a fine reputation for Bardolino, Soave, Valpolicella and other wines.

MASIA BACH   SPAIN

A Penedès wine estate, now owned by Codorníu, but originally set up by the Bach brothers in 1920, with a flamboyant Florentine villa as its centre. They make good red wines and a sweet Extrísimo Bach.

MASIANCO   Veneto: ITALY

A dry, white non-DOC wine from the Veneto, made by Masi from Garganega, Trebbiano and Durello grapes, grown in Valpolicella.

MASSACHUSETTS   USA

The island of Martha's Vineyard off the Massachusetts coast boasts one winery, Chichama Vineyards, which produces *vitis vinifera* grapes: Chardonnay, Riesling, Cabernet Sauvignon, Pinot Noir and Rkatiseli.

MASSANDRA   See Crimea.

PAUL MASSON VINEYARDS
            California: USA

One of California's largest and oldest wineries. Paul Masson was a Frenchman from Beaune who came to California in 1878. Today they produce an enormous range of wines, with varietals, jug wine, sparkling and dessert wines, even vermouth and brandy. They own vineyards in the Central Valley and Monterey County and buy grapes from all over California; the main winery is at Gonzalez.

MASTER OF WINE

A member of the British wine trade who has passed vigorous tasting and theory examinations, thus obtaining the trade's highest professional qualification and membership of the Institute of Masters of Wine. The Institute was founded in 1953; membership 35 years later still only numbers about 120 people who work in the British wine trade and abroad. Since 1988 the examinations have been open to candidates from abroad.

MASTROBERARDINI   Campania: ITALY

A 100 year old family company with a reputation based upon their production of the individual wines of Campania. The DOC wines are Greco di Tufo, Fiano di Avellino and Taurasi.

MATANZAS CREEK   California: USA

A small winery in Sonoma, in operation since 1977, with a reputation for pure varietals, Cabernet Sauvignon, Merlot and Chardonnay.

MATARO

An Australian synonym for the Mourvèdre grape.

MATAWHERO   NEW ZEALAND

A winery in the Poverty Bay area of the North Island with an excellent reputation for Gewürztraminer. Müller-Thurgau and Chardonnay are good too. Some reds, Cabernet Sauvignon and Pinot Noir, are made but are of less importance.

MATEUS ROSE

One of the world's leading wine brands, a lightly carbonated rosé wine in a dumpy bottle, produced by Sogrape in Portugal. It was created by the Guedes family in the 1930s.

MATINO   Apulia: ITALY

A red and *rosato* DOC wine from the southern part of Apulia, made from Negroamaro grapes.

MATRAS   Bordeaux: FRANCE

A little-known Grand Cru Classé of St-Émilion with a large proportion of old vines. M*atras* means crossbow in French, so perhaps there was an association with an archer from the Hundred Years' War.

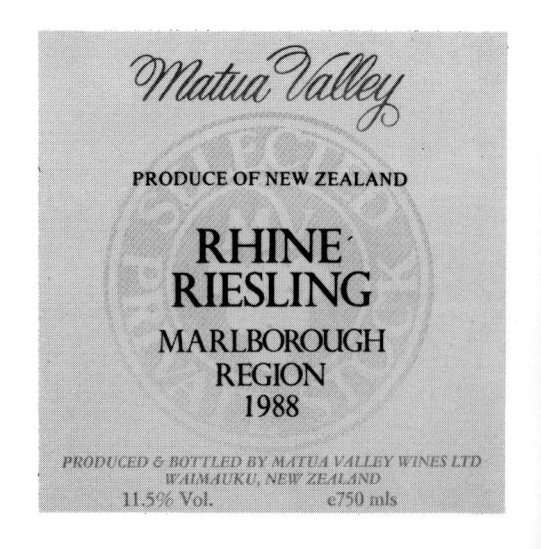

Matua Valley

PRODUCE OF NEW ZEALAND

RHINE
RIESLING

MARLBOROUGH
REGION
1988

PRODUCED & BOTTLED BY MATUA VALLEY WINES LTD
WAIMAUKU, NEW ZEALAND

11.5% Vol.   e750 mls

MATUA VALLEY　　　NEW ZEALAND
One of the most innovative estates of New Zealand, set up in the Huapai area in 1974. Whites are better than reds, notably Sauvignon Blanc. The estate has also pioneered Sémillon in New Zealand.

MATURATION
The ageing of a wine is an important part of the vinification process of fine red and, to a lesser extent, white wine. Ageing in barrel allows for the tannins to mellow and the wine to oxidise slightly; new barrels may contribute tannin and flavour to the wine; old barrels only allow for an exchange of air with the wine. The process continues once the wine is bottled; a fine wine will develop further complexities of flavour with bottle age.

MATURE
Describes a wine that is at the peak of its development before it begins to fade. Wines vary enormously in the amount of time they take to reach full maturity, from a few months to several years, depending on their structure, tannin, acid and alcohol content. An immature wine tastes unharmonious.

MAUCAILLOU　　　*Bordeaux*: FRANCE
An important Haut-Médoc property in Moulis, owned by the *négociant* company of Dourthe.

PROSPER MAUFOUX
Burgundy: FRANCE
A reputable *négociant* based in Santenay, known especially for his share in Domaine St-Michel in Santenay.

MAULE　See Chile.

MAUREZIN　　　*Bordeaux*: FRANCE
A little-known Grand Cru Classé of St-Émilion, and also a *château* in Moulis.

MAURY　　　*The Midi*: FRANCE
A sweet dessert wine, *a vin doux naturel* from around the town of Maury in the *département* of the Pyrénées Orientales. The principal grape varieties are Grenache and Muscat.

MAUZAC BLANC
A white grape grown in Gaillac for still and sparkling wine and in the Aude for sparkling wines, notably for Blanquette de Limoux, where it accounts for 80% of the blend, with its high acidity.

MAVRODAPHNE
An indigeneous red Greek grape variety, producing full-bodied wines that are sometimes slightly fortified. It accounts for one of the four appellations of the Patras area of Greece, where it makes a rich, dark dessert wine, sweet and high in alcohol at about 15° and needing several years ageing. It is also grown on the island of Cephalonia.

MAVRON
The principal native black grape of Cyprus, making many of the island's robust table wines as well as some Commandaria. Mavro means black in Greek.

MAVRUD　　　BULGARIA
An indigenous black grape, producing the country's more distinctive red wines, especially in the Maritsa basin to the south of the Balkan mountains, in the Controliran region of Asenovgrad.

MAXIMIN-GRÜNHAUS　see von Schubert.

MAY WINE
A traditional German drink, made from a light Rhine wine, in which the aromatic leaves of woodruff have been infused, served as a cold punch and decorated with fruit.

MAYACAMAS VINEYARDS
California: USA
Named after the mountain range dividing the Napa and Sonoma Valleys. The grapes for Chardonnay and Cabernet Sauvignon are grown on the estate, while those for the chewey Late Harvest Zinfandel are bought in from the best vineyards.

MAZIS-CHAMBERTIN
Burgundy: FRANCE
A Grand Cru vineyard in the village of Gevrey-Chambertin.

MAZOUNA — ALGERIA

Part of the combined quality zone of Tanghrite, Aîn Merane and Mazouna. Originally called Renault under the French VDQS system and situated on the hills near Dahra. Known for full-bodied red wines.

MCDOWELL VALLEY — California: USA

An AVA in Mendocino County, inland near the Russian River.

MCLAREN VALE — AUSTRALIA

An important part of a larger area of South Australia, called the Southern Vales, just south of Adelaide. The town of McLaren Vale is at its centre. The climate is temperate and conditions ideal for viticulture. Reynella and Tinfara are the best estates of this expanding area.

MCWILLIAMS — AUSTRALIA

The leading winery of the Murrumbidgee Irrigation Area. The family planted the first vines of the Murray River in 1877. Today they have wineries at Yenda, Hanwood and Beelbungera as well as at Robinvale in Victoria. The Hunter Valley is important for them too, where they make wines under the Mount Pleasant label; Sémillon and Hermitage are the main varietals. They have remained a family firm and produce an enormous range of reliable wines from New South Wales.

McWilliams also have an interest in New Zealand with extensive vineyards in Hawkes Bay. Fortified wines are important and of their table wines, Chardonnay and Cabernet Sauvignon are the best.

MECHANICAL HARVESTER

A machine used for picking grapes. The grapes are shaken off the vines and sucked up on a conveyor belt. These machines have become increasingly widespread over the last few years, even in some of France's most traditional vineyards, as employing extra labour for the vintage has become so much more expensive. Mechanical harvesters have other advantages: they are faster; the grapes can be picked at the optimum moment, in hotter countries even at night. They pick only the grapes and not the stalks, which removes the need for *égrappage* in some areas and can change the character of a wine, where the grapes have been traditionally fermented with their stalks. The use of mechanical harvesters is forbidden in Champagne and Beaujolais as the appellation regulations require the picking of whole grapes, while with mechanical harvesters the grapes are inevitably slightly damaged.

MEDEA — ALGERIA

One of the seven quality zones in the province of Alger, a hilly region and cooler than the rest of the country's vineyards, where some better grape varieties such as Cabernet and Pinot Noir are grown as well as Carignan and Grenache. The wines have balance and bouquet.

MEDIUM-DRY

Describes a wine with a little residual sugar, but dry enough to drink during a meal.

MEDIUM-SWEET

Describes a wine with a considerable amount of sugar, but not sweet enough to be a dessert wine. Many German wines come into this category.

MÉDOC — Bordeaux: FRANCE

One of the largest red wine regions of Bordeaux. It divides into eight appellations, the Haut-Médoc in the south which includes the separate villages of Margaux, St-Julien, Pauillac, St-Estèphe, Moulis and Listrac, and the north, which is traditionally known as the Bas-Médoc, has the appellation of Médoc. It is an enormous area, stretching 50 miles from Blanquefort in the south to Soulac in the north. The best 63 wines of the Médoc were classified into five categories in 1855 and most of these still rank amongst the greatest wines of the region, if not of the world. The blend of grape varieties is predominantly Cabernet Sauvignon, with Cabernet Franc and Merlot and some Petit Verdot and Malbec.

MÉDOC NOIR

This is, illogically, the Hungarian name for the Merlot grape.

MEERENDAL   SOUTH AFRICA

The only estate of the Durbanville district of South Africa, making full-bodied Shiraz and Pinotage.

MEERLUST   SOUTH AFRICA

One of the oldest estates of the South African Stellenbosch region. An excellent reputation has been created by the present owner for its red wines made from Cabernet Sauvignon, Pinot Noir, Cabernet Franc, and Merlot. Rubicon is their brand name for a Bordeaux blend.

GABRIEL MEFFRE   Rhône: FRANCE

This company is the largest owner of appellation vineyards in France, with properties all over the southern Rhône. Most important are Châteauneuf-du-Pape Château du Vaudieu; in Gigondas Domaine des Bosquets and Château Raspail and for Côtes du Rhône Domaine du Bois des Dames and Château de Ruth. Methods are modern and the results sound.

MEHANA   BULGARIA

Means 'bistro' in Bulgarian and is the popular brand name for the basic range of Bulgarian wines, red and three flavours of white: dry, medium and sweet.

MEHRING   Mosel-Saar-Ruwer: GERMANY

A village on the Mosel, just on the edge of the Mittelmosel. The wines do not attain the same heights as the principal villages. The *Grosslagen* are St Michael for the better south-facing sites and Probstberg for the others.

MEKNÈS-FEZ   MOROCCO

The biggest wine region of Morocco, with five designated areas, or *appellations d'origine garantie*, namely, Sais, Beni Sadden, Zerkhoun, Beni M'Tir and Guerrouane. The vineyards are on the most northerly slopes of the Atlas mountains and the wine is mainly red.

MELINI   Tuscany: ITALY

Now part of the Swiss Winefood group, the company owns large vineyards in the Chianti area, as well as dealing in most other Tuscan wines. They also market Serristori Chianti under the name of Macchiavelli, as he once lived in the estate house in exile from Florence.

MÉLINOTS   Burgundy: FRANCE

A Premier Cru Chablis vineyard that can be subdivided into Mélinots, Roncières and Les Épinottes. A grower with vines in two or more sites may vinify all the wine together and call it Mélinots or vinify each parcel separately and sell it by its individual name.

MELISSA   Calabria: ITALY

A DOC wine produced around the town of the same name and resembling its neighbour, Cirò. The red, made mainly from Gaglioppo grapes, improves with bottle age and is *superiore* after two years. The dry white comes from Greco Bianco.

ALPHONSE MELLOT   Loire: FRANCE

Important in Sancerre, both as a grower and as a *négociant*. His most famous wine is Domaine la Moussière.

MELNIK   BULGARIA

A concentrated powerful red wine made in the southwest of the country near the Yugoslav frontier. It is also the name of the town around which the vineyards are situated.

MELON DE BOURGOGNE

More commonly called Muscadet, which is the only wine of any note made by this grape. It originated in Burgundy, and can still be planted there in theory, but very rarely in practice. It is especially resistant to cold weather, rarely shows any ageing potential and produces light wine with a steely acidity.

MENDOCINO
California: USA

The most northern wine area of California, with five AVAs, Mendocino County, covering the whole county, Anderson Valley near the Pacific, Cole Ranch, Potter Valley and McDowell Valley inland. The main varietals are Zinfandel, French Colombard, Cabernet Sauvignon and Carignan.

MENDOZA
ARGENTINA

The province of Mendoza is the most important wine region of Argentina. Irrigated vineyards produce grapes in prolific quantity. Red wines are best, made from Malbec, Cabernet Sauvignon and other more recent introductions such as Syrah, Tempranillo, Lambrusca and Barbera. Local Criolla is still important, while the small proportion of white wine comes from Pedro Ximenez, Chenin Blanc, Moscatel, Palomino, and, more recently, from Chardonnay, Riesling and Sémillon.

MÉNÉTOU SALON
Loire: FRANCE

An appellation of the central vineyards of the Loire valley. Sauvignon is grown for the white wine and Pinot Noir for the red and rosé. The whites are crisp and pungent; the rosés pale and pretty and the reds light and fruity. They are not unlike Sancerre, but much less well-known.

MENISCUS

The term for the rim of the wine in the glass. The density of colour indicates the richness and age of the wine.

MENJUCQ

Based outside Pau, an important *négociant* house specialising in the wines of south-west France.

MÉNTRIDA
SPAIN

A little known area of central Spain, south west of Madrid. Most of the production is full-bodied red from Garnacha Tinta and sold in bulk, often for blending or for distillation.

MENTZENOPOULOS

The late André Mentzenopoulos came to the fore in Bordeaux when he bought the run-down Château Margaux in 1977. Since then he, his wife and daughter have transformed the *château* into one of the showpieces of the Médoc and restored the wine to its rightful place in the 1855 classification.

MERANER HUGEL   See Meranese di Collina.

MERANESE DI COLLINA
Trentino-Alto Adige: ITALY

Also called Meraner Hugel, this DOC is the local red Merano wine. It is made from Schiava grapes and is for early drinking.

MERCAPTAN

A very unpleasant smell, indicating a fault in the wine, coming from hydrogen sulphide produced by yeast which has combined with other elements in the wine.

MERCED
California: USA

A wine growing county of the fertile San Joaquin Valley, producing mainly jug wines.

MERCIER
Champagne: FRANCE

A large champagne house that is part of the Moët Hennessy group.

MERCUREY
Burgundy: FRANCE

The most important village of the Côte Chalonnaise, producing the best red wines of the region from Pinot Noir grapes. Its name comes from the Roman god to whom a temple above the village was dedicated. There are five Premier Cru vineyards: Clos du Roi, Clos-Voyen, Clos Marcilly, Clos des Fourneaux, Clos des Montaigus.

The principal growers include Domaine Jeannin-Naltret, Michel and Louis Juillot, François Protheau and the Château de Chamirey.

MERLOT

The grape variety most commonly associated with Bordeaux where it is often overshadowed by Cabernet Sauvignon for in the Médoc and Graves Cabernet Sauvignon accounts for two thirds of the *encépagement*. However in Pomerol and St-Émilion, Merlot comes into its own as the larger part of the blend, with delicious results. Merlot buds and ripens early, but is susceptible to spring frost and notably to *coulure* at the flowering. It is liable to rot in wet vintage. It is also grown in the other vineyards of Bordeaux and the south west and has spread to the Midi as an *améliorateur* variety with some success.

Merlot is popular in Italy, notably in the north east where it produces soft cheap wine of little distinction in large quantities, notably in Veneto and Friuli. In Spain there is a tiny amount at Vega Sicilia.

It is also found in eastern Europe, in Yugoslavia and in Hungary as Médoc Noir, where it is a constituent of Bulls Blood. Roumania and Bulgaria also have extensive vineyards of Merlot.

In California there are a few examples of pure Merlot; usually it is blended with Cabernet Sauvignon, notably in Opus One. It also grows well in Washington State, but not in Oregon. In the southern hemisphere it has met with little enthusiasm. There is a little in South Africa at Meerlust for Rubicon, while in Australia Shiraz is preferred for blending with Cabernet Sauvignon. There is a tiny amount in Argentina and Chile.

MERRITT ISLAND   *California*: USA

An AVA on the banks of the Sacramento River in Yolo County in the Central Valley.

MERZEGUERA

Merzeguera or Meseguera is a white grape variety grown around Alicante and Valencia for ordinary table wine.

LOUIS MÉTAIREAU   *Loire*: FRANCE

One of the top names in Muscadet. He works with eight other growers; they select their best wines in an objective 'blind' tasting; each grower bottles his own wine which is then sold under the Louis Métaireau label. Seven of the nine have bought the Grand Mouton estate which they run together.

METALLIC

A metallic flavour in wine results from some contamination during its making, storing or bottling.

METATARTARIC ACID

Can be added to wine in small quantities to prevent precipitation of tartrate crystals.

MÉTHODE ANCIENNE

A term that is sometimes used in connection with red burgundy to describe the method of making heavy, soupy, deep-coloured wines, with a longer fermentation or maceration period than is usual today, and the inclusion of a higher percentage of the stalks. In fact, burgundy had traditionally been a light elegant wine, made with a relatively short fermentation. The heavier style of the *méthode ancienne* came into fashion at the end of the last century at a time when burgundy was difficult to sell and had to last longer before consumption. It has now almost completely disappeared.

MÉTHODE CHAMPENOISE

The term for the method of making champagne that was developed in the Champagne region and has been imitated not only in other parts of France, but also elsewhere in Europe and the New World. The essence of *méthode champenoise* is that the second fermentation takes place in the bottle in which the wine is subsequently sold, entailing the application of a *liqueur de tirage*, maturation on the lees for a minimum of twelve months, *remuage* and *dégorgement* and the addition of a *liqueur d'expédition*. The term *méthode champenoise* could be used to describe any sparkling wine made in this way until 1985, when the EEC decided to restrict it to champagne only, with an eight year derogation period. This is a retrograde step which will only result in confusion over the quality of lesser sparkling wines.

MÉTHODE GAILLACOIS   see Gaillac.

MÉTHODE RURALE   see Gaillac.

METHUEN TREATY

The Methuen Treaty of 1703 gave Portuguese wines a duty advantage over French wines: the duty was one third less than on French wines. In return, English woollen cloth was exported to Portugal free of duty. This measure gave an enormous boost to the wine trade of the Douro and inspired Swift's poem:

Be sometimes to your country true.
Have once the public good in mind.
Bravely despise champagne at court,
And choose to dine at home with port.

METHUSELAH

A champagne bottle size equal to eight ordinary bottles (600cl).

METODO CLASSICO

The Italian term for champagne method or *méthode champenoise*.

METODO FRIULIANO

Describes a method of vinification in Italy, which aims to achieve very fresh white wine by slowly fermenting only the free-run juice at a low temperature and then keeping it in an environment as free from oxygen as possible, until bottling. This is now common practice amongst modern winemakers all over Italy. Friuli takes credit for being the first region to use the method in Italy. The resulting wine is fresh and fruity, with a crisp acidity and clean finish.

METSOVO   GREECE

A red wine made in Epirus from Cabernet Sauvignon grapes which were planted after the phylloxera crisis.

MEUNIER

One of the three grapes used for champagne along with Pinot Noir and Chardonnay. Although it is not rated as highly as the other two, it is the most widely planted of the three. The vine is called Pinot Meunier as it is an off-shoot of the Pinot family; the leaves look as though they have been sprayed with flour (Meunier means miller in French). It produces grapes with a high amount of acidity and is particularly resistant to frost. Elsewhere in France it can also be found in the Loire valley around Orléans. A little is grown in Australia, also for sparkling wine where it can be known as Miller's Burgundy.

MEURSAULT   Burgundy: FRANCE

The village of Meursault is one of the largest villages of the Côte de Beaune. Its vineyards spread for two and a half miles and fall into three distinct parts. To the north of the village are the vineyards that border Volnay, producing red wine that is generally sold as Volnay Santenots. In the south are the great white vineyards of the village and above them are the white vineyards that are next to the hamlet of Blagny. They can be sold under the appellation Meursault Blagny.

The Premiers Crus vineyards are: les Perrières, les Perrières Dessus, les Perrières Dessous, les Charmes Dessus, les Charmes Dessous (part), le Poruzot Dessus, le Poruzot (part), les Bouchères, les Santenots Blancs, les Santenots du Milieu, les Caillerets, les Pêtures, les Cras, les Gouttes d'Or, and at Blagny la Jennelotte, la Pièce sous le Bois, sous le Dos de l'Ane (part), les Genevrières Dessus (part) and les Genevrières Dessous (part).

There are numerous growers and estates offering Meursault: Robert and Michel Ampeau, François Gaunoux, Jean Germain, Comtes Lafon, Domaine Joseph Matrot, Michelot, René Monnier, the Château de Meursault which is owned by Patriache Père et Fils of Beaune, Ropiteau Frères, Guy Roulot and Domaine de Blagny.

La Paulée de Meursault is one of the gastronomic highlights of the area; it is the lunch that takes place the day after the Hospices de Beaune sale, making it the third event of Les Trois Glorieuses.

MEXICO

Winemaking in Mexico began with the Spanish conquest at the beginning of the 16th century. Today, wine is produced mainly for brandy, but there has been some international investment and some encouragement to plant European grape varieties. The main wine areas are Baja California, the Guadalupe Valley, San Juan del Rio, in Querétaro at Aguascalientes in the south, and Saltillo, Parras and Torreon to the west of Monterrey.

JOS MEYER   Alsace: FRANCE

A family company from Alsace based in Wintzenheim and specialising in wines from Wintzenheim and the adjoining village of Turckheim. Labels include les Lutins made from Pinot Auxerrois, Riesling les Pierrets and Gewürztraminer les Archenets.

MEYNEY   Bordeaux: FRANCE

A Cru Bourgeois Exceptionnel. A large St-Estèphe property that belongs to the Cordier family who are making sound reliable wine. The second wine is Prieur de Meyney.

MÉZESFÉHER

An indigeneous white Hungarian grape variety, grown on the Great Plain around Lake Balaton and Eger for sweet dessert wines. The name means white honey.

LOUIS MICHEL   Burgundy: FRANCE

One of the best wine-makers in Chablis; he owns Premier and Grand Cru vineyards and his wines are found under the label Domaine de la Tour Vaubourg as well as under his own name. He makes a wine to last, but without any ageing in oak barrels.

MICHIGAN   USA

Michigan is important in terms of wine production, but the wine industry has had a chequered history and is now undergoing something of a revival, mostly near Lake Michigan and Chicago. The Brone Champagne & Wines Company works with American hybrids, the St. Julian Wine Company with a range of *labrusca* and hybrid vines. At Château Grand Travers there is Riesling and Chardonnay grown in a mild micro-climate and also at Tabor Hill.

MICROCLIMATE

One of the factors that explain why one vineyard may produce superlative wine and the neighbouring vineyard only ordinary wine. The changes from one hillside to another come from a difference of microclimate, with varying temperature, wind and susceptibility to frost or hail.

MIDDELVLEI   SOUTH AFRICA

An important red wine estate in Stellenbosch, concentrating on Pinotage, and more recently Cabernet Sauvignon. The Momberg family have owned it since the 1930s.

MIDI   FRANCE

The Midi is France's oldest and largest vineyard. It stretches from the Pyrenees to the estuary of the Rhône, including the *départements* of the Pyrenees Orientales, Aude Hérault and Gard. This is a region in transition; the climate is good for wine making, but the original criterion for wine production was quantity irrespective of quality which encouraged the growers to produce enormous quantities of undrinkable characterless wine, *le gros rouge*, which formed the basis of the wine lake. There was no economic advantage in making the better wines of which the area is capable. Things are now changing gradually; grape varieties like Cabernet Sauvignon and Merlot are being introduced into the region. Vinification methods are improving enormously; *macération carbonique* in particular has revitalised some dull wines. The principal appellations of the Midi are Costières du Gard, Côtes du Roussillon, Minervois, Corbières and Coteaux du Languedoc. It is also the region for *vin doux naturel* and numerous *vin de pays*, whose producers, unbound by the legislation of the *appellation contrôllée* system, are able to experiment with improving grape varieties.

MIGRAINE   Burgundy: FRANCE

Was one of the best vineyards of the once famous Grande Côte d'Auxerre.

MILDARA WINES
AUSTRALIA

An important Australian company based, confusingly, in Mildura in north west Victoria. Their reputation was founded on sherry and brandy. They have also expanded into Coonawarra, especially for red wines. Once a family firm, they are now a public company.

MILDEW   See downy mildew and oidium.

MILLER'S BURGUNDY

An Australian synonym for the Pinot Meunier grape.

MILLERANDAGE

Or 'shot berries' in English, is a disorder of the vine which occurs when the flowering takes place in unsatisfactory climatic conditions. This results in imperfect fertilisation so the grapes develop unevenly or not at all and the resulting crop is very small.

MILLÉSIME

The French term for 'vintage' or 'year'.

MILLIPORE FILTER

A very fine sterile filter, designed to remove the minutest yeasts and bacteria from a wine.

MINERVOIS   *The Midi:* FRANCE

Minervois is one of the most important wines of the Midi; it is mainly red, but can be rosé and white, coming from vineyards to the east of Carcassonne. The main grape varieties are Carignan, Grenache, and Cinsaut with an increasing amount of Mourvèdre and Syrah. The area is divided into the plain along the banks of the river Aude and the arid plateau 600 feet higher where the village of Minerve is situated in dramatic scenery. Local cooperatives are important producers, as well as the large company of Chantovent and some small independent growers. The best Minervois is aged in small oak barrels.

MINHO   PORTUGAL

A province of northern Portugal where vinho verde is produced. The northern boundary of the demarcated area is the River Minho.

MIRALDUOLO   *Umbria:* ITALY

The vineyard from which Lungarotti, the main producers of Torgiano, makes their Cabernet Sauvignon and Chardonnay wines.

MIRAMAR WINES   AUSTRALIA

A successful new property in the Mudgee district of New South Wales. Its first vintage was in 1977, concentrating on Cabernet and Shiraz, with some Rhine Riesling, Chardonnay, Sémillon and others. A Sémillon Chardonnay blend has proved particularly successful.

MIRASSOU VINEYARDS   *California:* USA

Five generations of Mirassous have been making wine in California since the 1860s. They were the pioneers of field crushing and have produced some fine white wines from their Monterey estate.

LA MISE

The French term for bottling.

MISE EN BOUTEILLE

On a French wine label this literally means 'bottled'. Further information is then given: *au domaine*, at the property; *au château*, at the château; *dans nos caves*, in our cellars.

MISKET — BULGARIA

Bulgaria's most popular white wine, produced from the indigenous red Misket grape, vinified off the skins.

MISSION

The original grape of California, first planted there by a Jesuit priest in 1697 and spread with the missionaries to become, by the mid 19th century, California's most important grape. It is still planted today, mainly in southern California, for simple red wine. It may have some affinity with Chile's Pais.

MISSION — NEW ZEALAND

New Zealand's oldest winery, founded by the Brothers of the Society of Mary in 1851 and still in their hands. They own vineyards in Hawkes Bay, including Taradale for Sémillon and Sauvignon Blanc and Meanee for Cabernet Sauvignon and Merlot.

LA MISSION-HAUT-BRION
Bordeaux: FRANCE

A classed growth Graves at Pessac in the suburbs of Bordeaux which was, until the 17th century, part of the Haut-Brion estate and which is, once again, under the same ownership after its recent sale by the Woltner family. The wine is different in style from Haut-Brion, but as well considered. La Tour Haut-Brion is the second wine and the property also produces one of the best white Graves, Laville Haut-Brion.

MISSION HILL VINEYARDS — CANADA

In British Columbia, this winery had a chequered career from 1966 until its new ownership in 1981, since when it has been turned into a model winery, making three categories of wines: Mission Ridge for table wines; Mission Hill vineyards for varietals and Mission Hill Private Reserve for *vitis vinifera* varietals such as Gewürztraminer, Johannisberg Riesling, Chenin Blanc, Pinot Noir and Cabernet Sauvignon.

MISSOURI — USA

Wine was made in Missouri in the 19th century, but only two monastically owned wineries survived Prohibition. The first American appellation was given to Augusta, a designated area to the west of St. Louis in 1980. The climate is too cold for *vitis vinifera*; the best wines come from hybrids.

MISTELLE

Grape must which has been prevented from fermenting by the addition of alcohol. All the sugar remains in the must and it is often used as a base for vermouth and other wine aperitifs. Ratafia and similar drinks such as Floc de Gascogne and Pineau de Charente are technically mistelles.

MITTELBURGENLAND — AUSTRIA

One of the subregions of the Burgenland, where red wine is particularly important, made from Blaufrankischer and Blauer Zweigelt. There is also some Müller-Thurgau and Welschriesling. Deutchkreuz is best for white wine, while the villages of Lehmden, Horitschon and Neckenmarket make red wine.

MITTELHAARDT DEUTSCHE WEINSTRASSE
Rheinpfalz: GERMANY

One of the two Rheinpfalz *Bereichs*, created in 1971. It covers the northern part of the region between Kleinbockenheim on the edge of the Rheinhessen and Neustadt and therefore includes some of the finest villages of the Rheinpfalz, as well as, in the north, some of the least exciting wines of the region. Logically, this area should have been split in two, to retain the former distinction between the Unterhaardt and Mittelhaardt.

MITTELHEIM
Rheingau: GERMANY

One of the lesser known villages of the Rheingau, coming within the *Grosslagen* of Erntebringer and Honigberg, with wines similar to neighbouring Oestrich.

MITTELMOSEL
Mosel-Saar-Ruwer: GERMANY

Refers to the middle reaches of the Mosel, an area synonymous with Bereich Bernkastel.

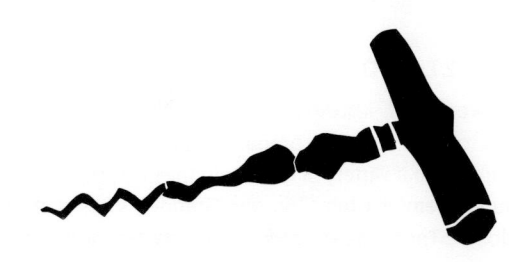

MITTELRHEIN   GERMANY

One of the lesser wine regions of Germany, covering 100 kilometres from Oberdiebach opposite Lorch as far as Königswinter just south of Bonn. The river flows through the dramatic scenery of the Rhine gorges and past the famous Lorelei rock. Riesling is the main grape variety and the area is divided into three *Bereichs*: Siebengebirge, Rheinburgengau and Bacharach, which in turn are split into eleven *Grosslagen*. The best vineyards are around Bacharach, Oberwesel and Boppard.

MOBILE BOTTLING MACHINE

A travelling bottling plant. It is increasingly prestigious for a wine to be bottled *au château* or *au domaine*, but not all small winemakers are able to afford the investment in bottling equipment. Consequently, in order to be able to bottle their own wines, they hire the services of a mobile bottling machine.

MODESTO   *California*: USA

Modesto in the San Joaquin Valley is the home of California's largest winery, E. & J. Gallo.

MOËLLEUX

The French term for a soft rich wine, but not necessarily very sweet.

MOËT ET CHANDON *Champagne*: FRANCE

One of the most famous names of Champagne and one of the largest producers. Dom Pérignon is their prestige *cuvée* and they own Château de Saran, where they produce a white Côteaux Champenois. Their interests extend far beyond champagne. They make sparkling wine in California at Domaine Chandon and they are developing vineyards in Spain, in Penedès and in Australia near Melbourne. They are also important producers of sparkling wine in Argentina and have interests in Brazil, West Germany and Austria. Back in Champagne they are leading the research into 'billes' to assist the second fermentation and remuage.

MOILLARD   *Burgundy*: FRANCE

Growers and *négociants* in Nuits St-Georges and one of the largest companies on the Côtes de Nuits, with a variety of different vineyards including Nuits Premier Crus Clos des Grandes Vignes and Clos de Thorey as *monopoles*. Methods are modern.

MOIMENTA DA BEIRA   see Beiras.

MOLDAVIA   USSR

The part of the Soviet Union on the Romanian border which produces wines not unlike those of her neighbour. Feteascá is the principal grape variety for medium-dry white wine. Aligoté, Sauvignon, Gewürztraminer, Rhine and Welschriesling and Rkatiseli are also to be found, as well as Cabernet Sauvignon, Merlot and Malbec for red wines, which, together with Saperavi and Rara Neagra, make a good red wine called Negru de Purkar.

MOLETTE

A white grape grown in the Savoie around Seyssel, mainly as a base for sparkling wine.

MOLINARA

One of the grapes used for Valpolicella and Bardolino.

MOLISE   ITALY

One of the smallest Italian regions in southern Italy and, until recently, without any DOC wines. It now has two: Biferno and Pentro di Isernia. The principal grape varieties of the region are Trebbiano and Montepulciano.

MOMMESSIN   *Burgundy*: FRANCE

Beaujolais growers whose claim to fame is ownership of Clos de Tart, a Grand Cru of Morey St-Denis.

MONASTRELL

One of the mostly widely planted red grapes of Spain. It is grown all over the Levante, especially in Alicante and is the main grape of Yecla and Jumilla. It also appears in Catalonia. The wines are sturdy and robust and capable of ageing.

MONBAZILLAC   SOUTH WEST FRANCE

An appellation for sweet white wine within the area of Bergerac. It is made mainly from Sémillon, with some Muscadelle and Sauvignon. The centre of the vineyards is the village of Monbazillac with its imposing château. The vineyards are close to the Dordogne so that in the best years they have the necessary microclimate of damp misty mornings followed by warm autumnal sunshine to induce the development of noble rot. The grapes for Monbazillac must always reach a natural degree of 14°, otherwise they are declassified into Côtes de Bergerac. The fermentation is stopped when the right balance of sugar and alcohol is obtained, ideally 14° alcohol + 4° sugar. Like Sauternes, Monbazillac benefits from some bottle age and has suffered from the lack of popularity of sweet wines.

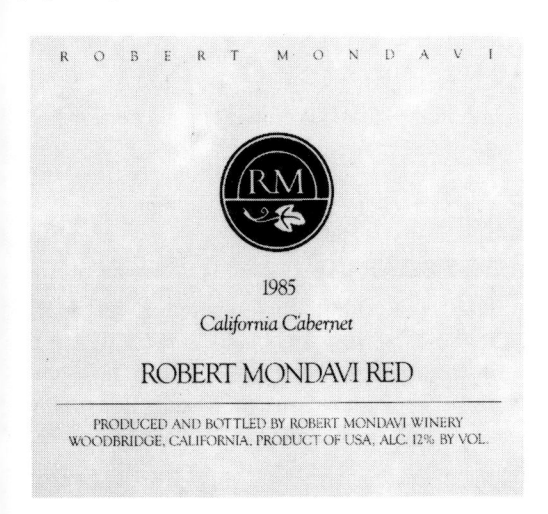

MONDAVI   California: USA

Robert Mondavi is one of the great names of the Californian wine industry. In 1966 he founded the first new winery to be built in California since Prohibition. The winery, inspired by the architecture of a Spanish mission building, boasts modern equipment, a forest of French oak barrels and is run with superb technical expertise. There is meticulous care and attention to detail but on a large scale. Cabernet Sauvignon Reserve is Mondavi's best wine; Chardonnay and Fumé Blanc are good too and there are other varietals. Oakville Vineyards is a second label. Opus I, a Cabernet Sauvignon/Merlot blend is the fruit of a joint venture between Robert Mondavi and Baron Philippe de Rothschild.

MONDEUSE

A distinctive red grape of the Savoie and the Bugey regions of France, where it is either blended with Gamay or Pinot Noir or made into a varietal wine with an earthy fruitiness. Mondeuse Blanche is occasionally to be found.

In Italy, Mondeuse Noire is called Refosco and grown in Friuli for a varietal wine in the DOCs of Grave del Friuli, Colli Orientali del Friuli and Latisana. The best clone is Refosco del Peduncolo Rosso, so called because the stalks are slightly red when the grapes are ripe. A little is also grown as Mondeuse in north east Victoria for table wine and in the Argentine as Refosco.

MONICA DI CAGLIARI   Sardinia: ITALY

A red DOC wine made from the Monica grape grown north of Cagliari. The wines are more often sweet than dry, coming in four versions: *secco* with 14° alcohol; *dolce* with 14.5°; *liquoroso secco* and *liquoroso dolce* with 17.5°.

MONICA DI SARDEGNA   Sardinia: ITALY

A dry red DOC wine, made from the Monica grape, grown all over the island. *Superiore* denotes one year's ageing in barrel and it develops well after three years.

MONIMPEX

The organisation responsible for most of Hungary's wine exports.

MARQUÉS DE MONISTROL   SPAIN

An important producer of both sparkling and still wine in Penedès, since 1882 and 1974 respectively. They are now owned by Martini & Rossi and make a good range of *cavas* as well as oak-aged red *reservas*.

MONSECCO   Piedmont: ITALY

A red wine made by Conte Ravizza; a particularly fine Gattinara known for its longevity.

MONT DE MILIEU   *Burgundy*: FRANCE
A Chablis Premier Cru.

DOMAINE DU MONT D'OR
                                            SWITZERLAND
One of the best Swiss wine producers at Sion in the Valais, making Johannisberg, Arvine, Dôle and Fendant.

DOMAINE DE MONT REDON
                                          Rhône: FRANCE
The largest estate of Châteauneuf-du-Pape, with particularly stoney vineyards that traditionally produce some of the toughest wine of the area.

MOUNT LA SALLE   see Christian Brothers.

MONTAGNE   *Bordeaux*: FRANCE
One of the so-called satellites of St-Émilion. These six surrounding parishes used to sell their wine as St-Émilion until the appellation was delimited in 1936. The name is hyphenated onto St-Émilion.

MONTAGNE DE REIMS
                                         Champagne: FRANCE
An important part of the Champagne vineyards especially for red grapes, which is split into two zones, to produce *vins de la montagne* and *vins de la rivière*.

MONTAGNIEU   *Savoie*: FRANCE
One of the crus of the Vin de Bugey, notably for sparkling wine, made by the *méthode champenoise* from the grape varieties Chardonnay, Pinot Noir and Jacquére, and also Roussette, depending on the grower's preference. A little still red and white is also produced and there was a tradition for naturally sparkling Montagnieu, which is now rarely found.

MONTAGNY   *Burgundy*: FRANCE
One of the four appellations of the Côte Chalonnaise. It produces purely white wine from the Chardonnay grape. If the wine reaches 11.5° of alcohol as opposed to 11°, it is entitled to the appellation Premier Cru. The principal grower is Domaine Martial de Laboulaye at Château de Buxy and the Cave Cooperative at Buxy is important too.

MONTALBANO   *Tuscany*: ITALY
One of the Chianti Putto zones, to the west of Florence, next to Carmignano.

MONTANA   NEW ZEALAND
One of New Zealand's leading wineries, with vineyards and cellars in Gisborne, Marlborough and Blenheim, and a bottling plant in Auckland. The first wine was made in 1944 by Ivan Yukich; production boomed in the 1970s, with a move to Marlborough in 1973. Their range is extensive and sound; Marlborough Sauvignon Blanc and Marlborough Rhine Riesling are especially good. Ormond is their second label.

MONTANCHEZ   SPAIN
A small village in the Extremadura that is famous for its red wine which has a sherry-like *flor*. It is aged in earthenware *tinajas* and is drunk locally as an aperitif.

MONTE ANTICO   *Tuscany*: ITALY
Made between Siena and Grosseto. The red is made from mainly Sangiovese and Canaiolo grapes and the white from Trebbiano and Malvasia.

MONTE CRISTO   SPAIN
An important Montilla company with a large export business to Britain.

MONTE SAN PIETRO   See Colli Bolognesi.

MONTECARLO   *Tuscany*: ITALY
A DOC wine with a fine reputation for white, made from 60–70% Trebbiano, and other more distinctive grapes, Sémillon, Pinot Bianco and Grigio, Vermentino, Sauvignon and Roussanne. Less exciting red comes from Sangiovese and Canaiolo.

MONTECOMPATRI COLONNA
                                            Latium: ITALY
A little-known white DOC produced from vineyards between the two towns with the same names. The grape varieties are Malvasia and Trebbiano.

MONTÉE DE TONNERRE
Burgundy: FRANCE

A Premier Cru Chablis vineyard that can be subdivided into Montée de Tonnerre, Chapelot and Pied d'Aloup. A grower with vines in two or more sites may vinify all the wine together and call it Montée de Tonnerre, or vinify each parcel separately and call each wine by its individual name.

MONTEFALCO
Umbria: ITALY

A DOC from around the town of the same name. The DOC comes in two versions: Montefalco Rosso and Sagrantino di Montefalco. The former is a full-flavoured red wine made from Sangiovese grapes with some Trebbiano and Sagrantino. Sagrantino di Montefalco comes purely from the indigenous Sagrantino grape. It can be dry, or better if made from dried raisin like grapes to give a rich full-bodied, medium-dry dessert wine with at least 14° alcohol.

MONTELLO E COLLI ASOLANI
Veneto: ITALY

One of the newest Veneto DOCs, made from three grape varieties: Cabernet Sauvignon and/or Franc, becoming *superiore* after two years' ageing; Merlot, again *superiore* after two years' ageing and, the most important, Prosecco, usually *frizzante* or *spumante*. Venegazzù comes within the area of the DOC, but does not usually conform to its regulations.

MONTEPULCIANO

A red grape variety grown in central and southern Italy, notably for Montepulciano d'Abruzzo, but also in the Marches for Rosso Cònero. There is no connection with Vino Nobile di Montepulciano.

MONTEPULCIANO D'ABRUZZO
Abruzzi: ITALY

A DOC wine which bears no relationship to Vino Nobile di Montepulciano, being named after a grape and not a town. The wine comes in two versions, red, and *rosato*, (called Cerasuolo). Both are made from Montepulciano with up to 15% Sangiovese grapes, grown around L'Aquilia. Red is aged for two years and has a rich fruitiness. Cerasuolo is vinified lightly on the skins to be a pretty *rosato*.

MONTEREY
California: USA

An important wine growing county of California that has expanded enormously during the 1970s. There are now four AVAs, Monterey for the whole county, Carmel near the Pacific Ocean, Arroyo Seco and Chalone in the Salinas Valley where vineyards are densest. The main varietals are Cabernet Sauvignon, Chenin Blanc, Pinot Noir, Riesling, Chardonnay, Zinfandel, Petite Sirah and Sauvignon Blanc.

MONTEREY VINEYARD
California: USA

A large operation in Monterey, dealing mainly in varietal wines, most notably Thanksgiving Riesling and December Zinfandel, as well as light Rieslings. They also make white Zinfandel and blended red and white wines, known in the United States as Classic Red and Classic White.

MONTERMINOD — see Roussette de Savoie.

MONTEROSSO VAL D'ARDA
Emilia-Romagna: ITALY

Was a dry white DOC made from Malvasia di Candia, Moscato Bianco, Trebbiano and Ortruga grapes. It has now been incorporated into the larger DOC of Colli Piacentini, as Colli Piacentini Monterosso Val d'Arda.

## MONTERREY	SPAIN

Sometimes called Valle de Monterrey; a recently demarcated area of Galicia, along the valley of the river Taméga, and subdivided into Verín, Monterrey, Castielo and Oimbra. 70% of the wine is red and usually stronger than other Galician wines. The main producer is the local cooperative.

## MONTESCUDAIO	Tuscany: ITALY

A DOC wine in three versions: red, mainly from Sangiovese grapes; white from Trebbiano and rare Vin Santo made in the traditional way.

MONTESODI   See Frescobaldi.

## MONTHÉLIE	Burgundy: FRANCE

A predominantly red wine village on the Côte de Beaune somewhat overshadowed by its neighbours, Volnay and Pommard. The best-known Premier Cru is Champs Fulliot; others include sur Lavelle, les Vignes Rondes, le Meix Bataille, les Riottes, la Taupine, le Clos Gauthey, le Château Gaillard, le Cas Rougeot and les Duresses (part). The most notable growers are the Suremain family who own the Château de Monthélie. Domaine Monthélie-Douhairet and Charles Boussey also have vineyards in the village.

MONTHOUX   see Roussette de Savoie.

## MONTILLA	SPAIN

Montilla Moriles, to give the D.O. its full name, is a Spanish wine not unlike sherry so that until the area was demarcated in 1945, large quantities of wine were sent to Jerez for blending. The vineyards are on the chalky soil around the town of Montilla in southern Spain and the nearby village of Moriles. The main grape variety is Pedro Ximénez. The wines are fermented in earthenware *tinajas* and then matured in a *solera* system, but rarely require fortification as they are usually already high enough in alcohol. Similar categories to sherry apply to Montilla, but as the sherry shippers have contested their use, Montilla is more often labelled fine dry, medium and cream. Ironically the term *amontillado* originates from Montilla.

## MONTLOUIS	Loire: FRANCE

A white wine from the Loire valley, coming in various degrees of dry, semi-dry and moelleux; still, pétillant and mousseux. It is almost identical to Vouvray; only the river separates Montlouis on the south bank from Vouvray on the north bank. Chenin Blanc is the only grape variety.

## MONTMAINS	Burgundy: FRANCE

A Premier Cru Chablis vineyard that can be subdivided into Montmains, Forêts and Butteaux. A grower with vines in two or more sites may vinify all the wine together and call it Montmains or vinify each plot separately and sell each wine under its individual name.

## MONTMÉLIAN	Savoie: FRANCE

One of the crus of Vin de Savoie, producing white wine from the Jacquère grape.

MONTPELLIER

The home of one of the best university oenology departments of France, important not only for its teaching, but also for its experimental research work.

## MONTPEYROUX	The Midi: FRANCE

Formerly a VDQS, Montpeyroux is now part of the new all-embracing appellation of the Coteaux du Languedoc. Red and rosé wines from vineyards to the north of Béziers, made from 50% Carignan with Grenache, Cinsaut, Syrah and Mourvèdre to produce solid fruity wines.

## LE MONTRACHET	Burgundy: FRANCE

Indisputably the finest of all white burgundies. It is a 7.49 hectare plot of land, split between the villages of Puligny and Chassagne which is owned principally by the Marquis de Laguiche, Baron Thénard, Bouchard Père & Fils, Fleurot-Larose, Roland Thévenin and the Domaine de la Romanée-Conti.

MONTRAVEL — SOUTH WEST FRANCE

A white appellation within the zone of Bergerac, adjoining the vineyards of Bordeaux. Montravel Sec, Côtes de Montravel and Haut Montravel are all possible labels, but many growers prefer to call their wines Bergerac or Côtes de Bergerac.

MONTRAVEL SEC — SOUTH WEST FRANCE

A white wine produced in a small area within the zone of Bergerac. It is identical to Bergerac Sec and is rarely found as the growers who make it prefer to sell their wine as Bergerac.

MONTRE

Another term for *la sortie*.

LE MONTRE CUL — Burgundy: FRANCE

Dijon's last vineyard, tenaciously cultivated in a suburb of apartments and office blocks. The vineyard is steep and terraced, imagination explains the origin of the name *cul*, French slang for 'behind'.

MONTROSE — Bordeaux: FRANCE

Always considered the most traditional of the Médoc *châteaux*, isolated to the north of St-Estèphe. With a high proportion of Cabernet Sauvignon grapes, it used to make tough, uncompromising wines, but more recently has adopted a much lighter style of wine for earlier maturity.

MONTS DU TESSALAH — ALGERIA

One of the seven quality zones in the northeast part of the country, near Sidi-bel-abbès, producing fairly undistinguished red wines.

MOORE'S DIAMOND

A white hybrid grape variety occasionally found in New York State.

MÓR — HUNGARY

A village to the west of Budapest which enjoys a reputation for its white Mori Ezerjó. It is usually dry, but in exceptional years, botrytis develops to make a sweet wine.

ALOIS MORANDELL — AUSTRIA

One of Austria's better wine merchants, selling the wines of small growers from all over the country.

MORAVIA — CZECHOSLOVAKIA

The vineyards of Moravia south of Brno adjoin the Weinviertel of Austria and there are similarities in the wine. Grüner Veltliner is the main grape variety with some Sauvignon and Gewürztraminer.

MORBIDO

The Italian term for 'soft'.

J. MOREAU ET FILS — Burgundy: FRANCE

The best-known name on the Chablis market, the most important *négociant*, no longer family owned, in the town of Chablis and the largest vineyard owning family including Chablis, Domaine de Biéville and a part of the vineyard of Les Clos, called Clos des Hospices. The Moreau style of Chablis favours vinification in stainless steel and no oak ageing. Moreau Blanc, a white *vin de table*, bearing no relation at all to Chablis, is a successful brand.

MOREIN   See Les Fourneaux.

MORELLINO DI SCANSANO — Tuscany: ITALY

A red DOC wine from near Grosseto, made purely from Sangiovese grapes. Two years' ageing gives a *riserva*.

ALBERT MOREY   Burgundy: FRANCE

An old family *domaine* in Chassagne-Montrachet, making both red and white wines with considerable talent.

MOREY ST-DENIS   Burgundy: FRANCE

The village of Morey is an important village of the Côte de Nuits. It acquired its epithet St-Denis as recently as 1927. It is a small village and the wines were unknown before the introduction of *appellation contrôlée* as they tended to be sold as Gevrey-Chambertin or Chambolle-Musigny. The villages contain four Grands Crus: Bonnes Mares, which it shares with the neighbouring village of Chambolle-Musigny; Clos St-Denis; Clos de Tart and Clos de la Roche.

The Premiers Crus vineyards of the village are: les Larrets, which is more commonly known as Clos des Lambrays; les Ruchots; les Sorbés; Clos Sorbés; les Millandes; Clos des Ormes (part); Meix Rentiers; Monts-Luisants; les Bouchots; Clos de la Bussière; aux Charmes; les Charrières; Côte Rôtie; Calonères; Maison Brûlée; les Chabiots; les Mochamps; les Froichots; les Fremières; les Genevrières; les Chaffots; les Chénevery (part); la Riotte; Clos Baulet; les Gruenchers, les Façonnières.

The principal estates are Heretiers Cosson, Domaine Dujac and Domaine Ponsot.

MORGON   Burgundy: FRANCE

One of the ten Beaujolais Crus with a right to a separate appellation. The village of Morgon is in the middle of the vineyards. Morgon is amongst the most long-lived Beaujolais wines and Château de Bellevue has a good reputation.

MORILES see Montilla.

MORILLON BLANC

A little-used synonym for the Chardonnay grape. 19th century authorities describe it as the grape responsible for Chablis. Morillon Noir is a possible synonym for Pinot Noir.

MORIO-MUSCAT

Named after Peter Morio, this is a cross of Silvaner and Pinot Blanc, two fairly neutral grape varieties that together have produced an overpoweringly aromatic grape, which is planted mainly in the Rheinhessen and Rheinpfalz. This variety is now declining in popularity but is still used to boost the flavour of Liebfraumilch.

MOROCCO

Viticulture in Morocco arrived with the French settlers in the 1920s. There is a quality system similar to that of France and the best wines are designated *appellation d'origine garantie*. Four main areas produce wine: around Meknès-Fez in the foothills of the Atlas mountains; near Rabat, around Casablanca and, of lesser importance, in the Berkane-Oujda area near the Algerian border. The grape varieties are French, mainly Carignan, Cinsaut and Grenache with Alicante Bouschet for quantity and Syrah and Mourvèdre for interest. The production of white wine is negligible, but there are acceptable reds and rosés. Cooperatives dominate the industry.

J. W. MORRIS WINERY   California: USA

Previously known as J. W. Morris Port Works. Concentrates on Californian port style wines made from overripe Zinfandel, Carignan, Ruby Cabernet and Petite Sirah.

MORRIS WINES   AUSTRALIA

A winery in north east Victoria with a reputation based on the quality of their Liqueur Muscat. Their Mia Mia vineyard at Rutherglen is also planted with other varieties to produce some good red and white table wines, including, unusually, Durif.

MORTON ESTATE — NEW ZEALAND

The principal property of the Bay of Plenty, a new estate with its first vintage in 1983. Gewürztraminer, Chardonnay and Sauvignon Blanc are early successes. They also make a sparkling wine by the champagne method, with champagne grape varieties and champagne yeasts.

MOSAIC — CYPRUS

One of the leading brands of Cyprus sherry, owned by the company of Keo.

MOSCADELLO DI MONTALCINO
Tuscany: ITALY

A new DOC, reviving an old tradition of sweet *spumante* produced around Montalcino from a clone of the Moscato grape called Moscadello. The newcomers to the area, Banfi, were the prime movers of the DOC with their space-age winery. There is also a passito version.

MOSCATEL

A common synonym for the grape variety Muscat d'Alexandrie in Spain and Portugal.

MOSCATO D'ASTI NATURALE
Piedmont: ITALY

The base wine from which Asti Spumante is made, produced in large quantities in vineyards south of Asti from Moscato Bianco or Moscato di Canelli grapes. It is usually *frizzante* from refermentation in the bottle and the best has the rich fresh flavour of the Muscat grape.

MOSCATO BIANCO

The Italian synonym for the grape variety Muscat Blanc à Petits Grains.

MOSCATO DI CAGLIARI
Sardinia: ITALY

A DOC dessert wine made from the Moscato grape grown north of Cagliari. Sweet has 15° minimum alcohol, fortified sweet has 17.5° and a good muscat flavour.

MOSCATO GIALLO

One of grape varieties of the sixteen wine types of the DOCs of the Alto Adige and the Trentino. It is also called Goldenmuskateller and is a variation of Muscat Blanc à Petits Grains.

MOSCATO DI NOTO — *Sicily*: ITALY

A rare DOC dessert wine. Made from the Moscato Bianco grape grown around Noto in southeast Sicily, it comes in three versions, a semi-sweet table wine best drunk young, a *spumante* and a fortified at 22° minimum alcohol.

MOSCATO DI PANTELLERIA
Sicily: ITALY

Technically a DOC dessert wine produced on the remote island of Pantelleria, which is closer to Tunisia than to Italy. It is made in several versions from Zibibbo, (a type of muscat grape). The basic wine, from normally ripe grapes, can be *naturale*, fragrant with 12.5° alcohol; *naturalemente dolce*, sweeter and richer at 17.5°; *spumante naturale*, a sparkling wine, and fortified as *liquoroso*. Alternatively, it can be made from semi-dried *passito* grapes as *naturalemente dolce* at 14°, *liquoroso*, fortified at 21.5° and *extra* at 23.5°. The local cooperative calls it *passito extra Tanit*.

MOSCATO ROSA

One of the grape varieties of the sixteen wine types of the DOCs of the Alto Adige and the Trentino. It is also called Rosenmuskateller and is a variation of Muscat Blanc à Petits Grains.

MOSCATO DI SARDEGNA
Sardinia: ITALY

A *spumante* DOC wine, made from Moscato grapes, grown in vineyards all over the island. It is grapey and fairly sweet, not unlike Asti Spumante.

MOSCATO DI SIRACUSA
Sicily: ITALY

A DOC dessert wine made in very limited quantities, if at all, from the Moscato Bianco grape grown around Siracusa.

MOSCATO DI SORSO SENNORI
Sardinia: ITALY

A DOC dessert wine made from the Moscato grape, grown around the towns of Sorso and Sennori. As well as a table wine, it is fortified as *liquoroso dolce*.

MOSCATO DI STREVI   *Piedmont*: ITALY

Strevi has a good reputation for its Moscato which is usually *spumante* or *frizzante*.

MOSCATO DI TRANI   *Apulia*: ITALY

A sweet white DOC wine from Apulia made from the Moscato Reale grape, grown around Trani. As *dolce naturale* it has 15° alcohol and, as *liquoroso*, 18°.

MOSCOPHILERO

A white or pink grape variety grown mainly in the Peloponnese; it ripens late and makes light fruity wines.

MOSEL

One of the world's great wine rivers and an important part of the vineyards of Germany. The river rises in the Vosges mountains and joins the Rhine at Koblenz. The main vineyard area is between Trier and Koblenz and on the two tributaries, the Saar and the Ruwer, however there are also vineyards in northern France (*vins de la Moselle*) and Luxembourg.

MOSEL-SAAR-RUWER   GERMANY

The all-embracing regional name given to the wines of these three rivers. The area is divided into four *Bereichs* and twenty *Grosslagen*, with 525 individual vineyards in nearly 200 wine-producing villages. The best vineyards, apart from those on the tributaries of the Saar and the Ruwer, are on the Mittelmosel, which covers the area around Bernkastel. The Saar and the Ruwer are grouped together in one *Bereich*. Riesling grown on the attractive steep hillsides.

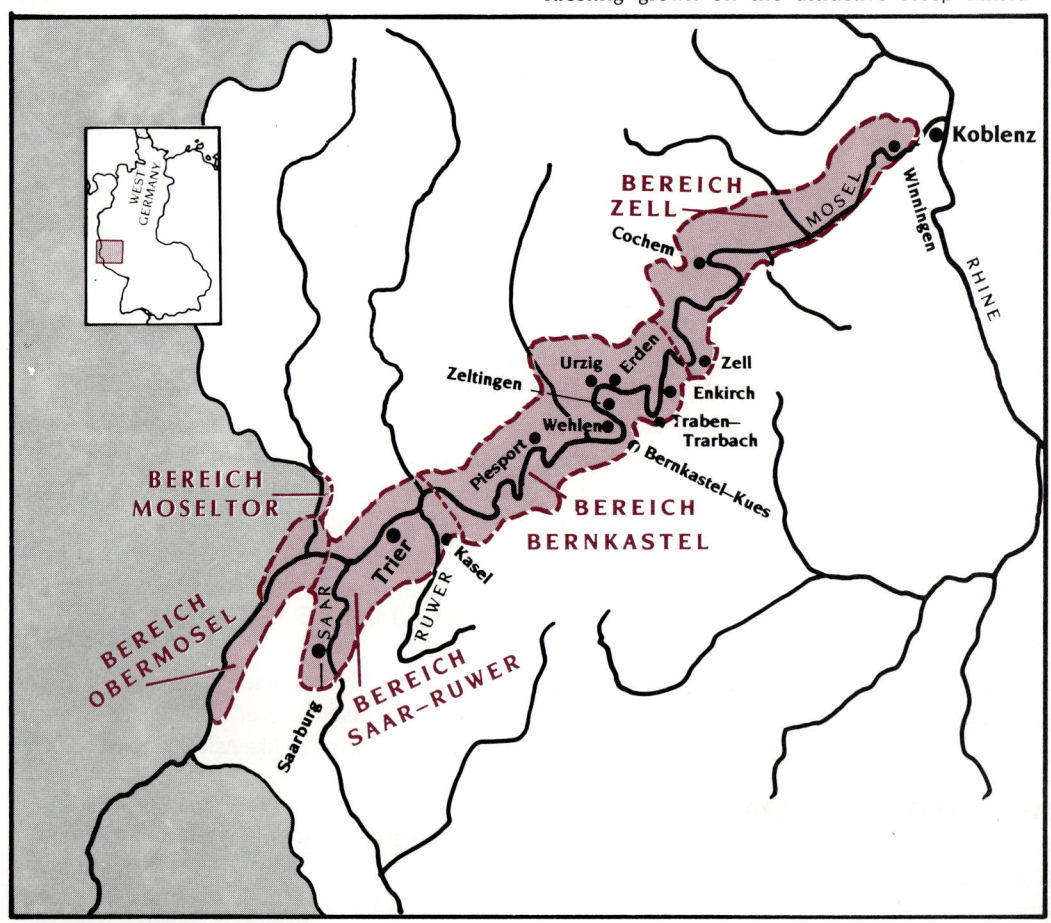

MOSEL-SAAR-RUWER

makes the best wine where the slatey soil gives it a unique steely flavour, while the Müller-Thurgau grape thrives on the flatter vineyards with richer soil, to give generous quantities of sound everyday drinking wine. In the ripest years, elegantly honeyed *Auslese* from the Mosel is hard to better.

MOSELBLÜMCHEN

Meaning 'little flower of the Mosel', describes a blend of Mosel wines, usually of *Tafelwein*, but possibly of *Qualitätswein* standard, which is generally sold under a brand name.

MOSELTALER Mosel-Saar-Ruwer: GERMANY

A new category of Mosel wine authorised as a kind of Liebfraumilch.

MOSELTOR Mosel-Saar-Ruwer: GERMANY

Bereich Moseltor, meaning 'the gate of the Mosel', is a small district adjoining the Obermosel. Elbling, for *Sekt*, is the principal grape variety.

LENZ MOSER AUSTRIA

The wines of Austria are almost synonymous with the company of Lenz Moser. Doktor Moser was one of the leading viticulturalists of the country earlier this century and he developed a system of training vines on high trellises which has been adopted in Austria and in other parts of the world. Schluck is the company's white wine brand, while their reputation rests upon fine estate wines.

MOSS WOOD AUSTRALIA

The second vineyard of the Margaret River was planted in 1969 and now rivals Cape Mentelle as the finest winery of the area. The ten hectares are planted with Sémillon, Chardonnay, Cabernet Sauvignon and Pinot Noir. All four wines are aged in oak.

MOU

The French equivalent of 'flabby'.

MOUEIX

There are two Moueix companies dealing with the wines of St-Emilion and Pomerol. Armand Moueix, who are based at Château Taillefer in Pomerol and, more importantly, Jean-Pierre Moueix, who include the best *châteaux* of Pomerol in their portfolio, notably Pétrus and Trotanoy.

MOULDY

A smell stemming from rotten grapes or dirty casks.

MOULIN-DU-CADET Bordeaux: FRANCE

A Grand Cru Classé of St-Émilion from the house of J.-P. Moueix.

MOULIN DES CARRUADES Bordeaux: FRANCE

The second wine of Lafite, made from young vines.

MOULIN-RICHE Bordeaux: FRANCE

The second wine of The Léoville-Poyferré estate.

MOULIN TOUCHAIS Loire: FRANCE

This wine has acquired a reputation as the best Anjou Blanc, partly because the Chenin Blanc grapes come in fact from vineyards within the Coteaux du Layon. There is a windmill on the site and the wine is made by the Touchais family who have kept enormous stocks of old vintages. The wines, with their delicious honeyed character, have aged perfectly.

MOULIN À VENT Burgundy: FRANCE

One of the ten Beaujolais Crus with a right to a separate appellation. The vineyards are in the villages of Chénas and Romanèche Thorins; the name, given in 1936, comes from the last remaining Beaujolais windmill. The wines of Moulin à Vent are longer-lasting than any other Beaujolais. Château de Jacques is a particularly fine estate.

LA MOULINE Rhône: FRANCE

The brand name under which Guigal sell their pure Côte Blonde wine from the Côte Rôtie.

MOULINET Bordeaux: FRANCE

A second growth Pomerol *château* isolated on the edge of Pomerol and owned by A. Moueix.

MOULIS Bordeaux: FRANCE

One of the lesser appellations of the Médoc in that it lies away from the river on a plateau, further inland, north west of Margaux. The best wines of Moulis are around the village of Grand Poujeaux and often hyphenate their names to Grand-Poujeaux, such as Dutruch-Grand-Poujeaux. Although no wines of Moulis feature in the 1855 classification, Chasse Spleen is recognised today as Cru Classé quality.

MOUNT ARARAT   See Turkey and Armenia.

MOUNT BARKER AUSTRALIA

Another name for the Great Southern area of Western Australia.

MOUNT EDEN VINEYARDS
California: USA

A winery in Santa Clara with an early chequered history. The vineyards were first owned by Martin Ray, one of the colourful figures of the Californian wine industry. Today they continue to produce fine Chardonnay, Cabernet Sauvignon and Pinot Noir.

MOUNTAIN SPAIN

An old name for the wine of Málaga, which is produced on the mountainous slopes inland from the city.

MOUNTAIN OF RHEIMS   See Montagne de Reims.

MOURISCO

A grape variety that is authorised, but not recommended for white port. Mourisco Tinto is well considered for red port, while Mourisco de Semente is less favoured.

MOURVÈDRE

The red grape variety that accounts for a minimum of half the blend for Bandol. Here it is at its best for it is a difficult grape to ripen, needing long hours of warm sunshine. It also features in Châteauneuf-du-Pape, Côtes de Provence, Côtes du Rhone and other appellations of the Rhône and the Midi.

In Australia where it is called Mataro, it is usually blended with Shiraz, often for a port style wine. Some is grown in California too.

MOUSSE

The French term to describe the bubbles in a sparkling wine. See *prise de mousse*.

MOUSSEUX

Literally means 'sparkling' so *vin mousseux* describes any sparkling wine without a precise appellation. When it is permitted to mention *méthode champenoise* on the label, *vin mousseux* usually implies the *cuve close* method of production.

MOÛT

The French term for 'must'.

MOUTON D'ARMAILHACQ   See Mouton-Baronne-Philippe.

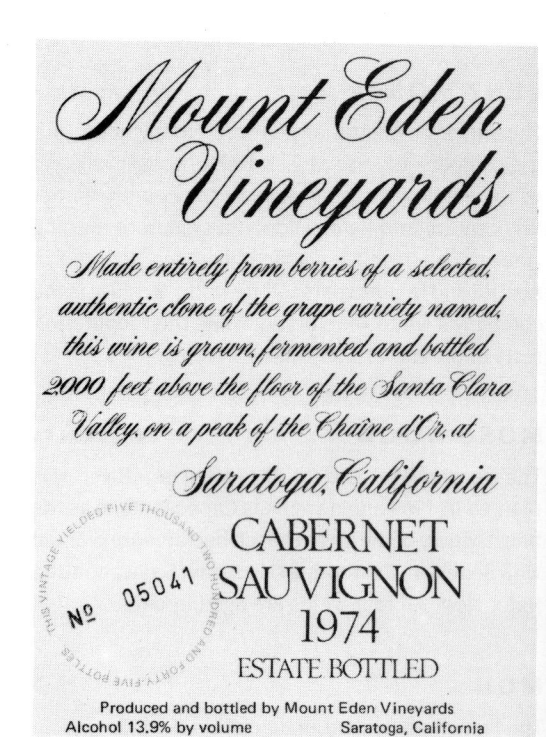

MOUTON-BARONNE-PHILIPPE
Bordeaux: FRANCE

A fifth growth Pauillac. This property was classified in 1855 as Mouton d'Armailhacq, bought by Baron Philippe de Rothschild in 1933 and renamed Mouton Baron Philippe in 1956. Then, with the 1976 vintage, the name was changed again to Mouton Baronne Philippe in memory of the Baron's wife Pauline who died in 1974. The wines are made with the usual Mouton care.

MOUTON CADET

An important claret brand that was developed by Baron Philippe de Rothschild during a run of bad vintages during the early 1930s. It was once appellation Pauillac, but now is simple Bordeaux Rouge.

MOUTON-ROTHSCHILD
Bordeaux: FRANCE

One of the three first growths of Pauillac. It only acquired that status with the 1973 vintage, thanks to the energies of its former owner, Baron Philippe de Rothschild. He took over the neglected property in the early 1920s and devoted himself to it for the next sixty years. Mouton is known for its series of labels; one is commissioned each year from a famous artist such as Picasso or Chagall. The Baron's American wife was responsible for the collection of works of art relating to wine that is displayed in a museum in their house. It is open to the public by appointment. Mouton is made predominantly from Cabernet Sauvignon grapes with a tiny amount of Merlot and Cabernet Franc. Blackcurrant is the quintessential flavour, with enormous staying power.

LA MOUTONNE
Burgundy: FRANCE

A vineyard on the slopes of the Grand Cru vineyards of Chablis which, for various bureaucratic anomalies, does not have the official status of a Grand Cru. It lies within Preuses and Vaudésir and is a parcel of land that once belonged to the monks of the nearby Cistercian abbey of Pontigny who were reputed to have danced *comme de petites moutonnes* after they had liberally imbibed their wine!

MTSVANE

One of the best white grape varieties of the Soviet Union, grown in Georgia and the Crimea for aromatic fruity wines.

MUDGEE
AUSTRALIA

A wine region of New South Wales, close to the Hunter Valley, but very different in climate, with a longer ripening period and later harvest resulting from the high altitude. Wine was made here in the 1850s, then the industry died out until the late 1960s, since when something of a renaissance has taken place. Several grape varieties are grown. Chardonnay is very successful amongst the whites and Cabernet Sauvignon produces some good reds, along with Shiraz and Pinot Noir. Mudgee has had its own appellation since 1979. Huntingdon and Craigmoor are good estates.

MUFFA NOBILE

The Italian term for *pourriture noble*. Picolit is the most notable example of an Italian wine with it.

MUGA
SPAIN

A small family Rioja *bodega* making traditional Rioja, 40% from their own vineyards and the rest from grapes bought from local farmers. The wine is fermented and aged in wood with meticulous care. The name Muga is reserved for wine from their own vineyards. Their reserva is called Prado Enea. They also produce a little dry white wine and some *cava*.

MUID

An old French barrel size.

MÜLHEIM
Mosel-Saar-Ruwer: GERMANY

A Mittelmosel village of lesser importance within the *Grosslage* of Kurfürstlay. It is overshadowed by its neighbours, Bernkastel and Brauneberg, but does produce some good wine, notably from the estate of Max Ferdinand Richter and their Helenenkloster vineyard.

MULLED WINE
The English equivalent of Glühwein, a heated wine, flavoured with spices. Traditionally, it should not be heated over a stove, but warmed by placing a red hot poker in the pan.

RUDOLPH MÜLLER
Mosel-Saar-Ruwer: GERMANY

An important German export house, and owner of vineyards on the Mosel, as well as a producer of sparkling wine.

MÜLLER-SCHARZHOF
Mosel-Saar-Ruwer: GERMANY

Weingut Egon Müller-Scharzhof is one of the finest Saar estates, with origins going back to the 13th century. It is owned by Egon Müller, with cellars in Wiltingen. The vineyards include part of the Scharzhofberg and Braunsfels, which are planted almost entirely with Riesling. The estate also administers Weingut Le Gallais at Wiltingen.

MÜLLER-THURGAU
A white grape, and the most long-established crossing of two varieties. It was created by a Doctor Müller who was born in the Swiss canton of Thurgau, who crossed Riesling with Silvaner in the 1880s. There is some discussion as to whether it was not a crossing of two different Rieslings which will never be finally determined. Today it is Germany's most popular grape variety, producing light flowery wine in prolific quantities, and a vital constituent of Liebfraumilch. It fares well in England and Luxembourg too and in the high vineyards of Trentino-Alto Adige. Switzerland, Austria, Yugoslavia and Hungary all maintain its popularity, but in the New World it is little favoured, except in New Zealand, where it has been extensively planted.

MUMM
Champagne: FRANCE

A large champagne house, owned by Seagrams. Their dry wine is sold under the brand name Cordon Rouge and the medium-dry is Cordon Vert.

MÜNSTER-SARMSHEIM
Nahe: GERMANY

The last Nahe village before Bingen, coming within the Grosslage of Schlosskapelle. The best E*inzellage* is Dautenpflänzer, where the State Domain makes full-bodied Riesling.

MURÉ
Alsace: FRANCE

A family company in Rouffach whose estate is called Clos Saint Landelin, which is now part of Grand Cru Vorbourg.

MURFATLAR
ROMANIA

A wine region in the far southeast of the country, taking its name from the town at its centre and producing heavy dessert Muscat wines as well as some dry Chardonnay. Vines have been grown here for centuries.

MURRAY RIVER
AUSTRALIA

The Murray River in north west Victoria provides the essential water for the vineyards of the region. Here the Murray Valley vineyards produce mainly Shiraz and Sémillon grapes from phylloxera free irrigated vineyards, including Swan Hill, Mildura, Marbein, Red Cliffs and Robinvale.

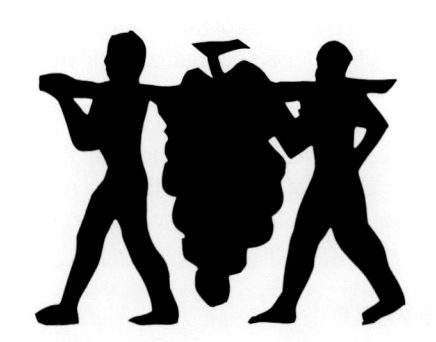

MARQUÉS DE MURRIETA SPAIN

One of the oldest *bodegas* of Rioja, founded in 1870 and still run by the same Murrieta family. Traditional methods are retained and their reputation is excellent, especially for their most notable and long-lived *reserva*, Castillo de Ygay.

MURRUMBIDGEE IRRIGATION AREA AUSTRALIA

Often referred to as M.I.A. or Riverina, provides as much as one tenth of Australia's wine in the fertile land around Griffith in the south west of New South Wales. Grapes flourish here and most varieties are cultivated. McWilliams are the leading winemakers who are introducing new techniques and changing the area's wines from fortified to light table wines. Murrumbidgee means 'big water' in Aborigine.

MUSCADELLE

A grape variety grown in Bordeaux, as a very unimportant part, 5% at the most, of the blend for Sauternes, with Sémillon and Sauvignon. It is also found in the Premières Côtes de Bordeaux, the other sweet appellations of the Gironde and in Monbazillac. In Australia it has transpired that what the Australians call Tokay and use for making so called Liqueur Tokay is in fact Muscadelle. It is planted in South Australia and around Rutherglen in Victoria. A little Muscadelle is grown in California where it is called Sauvignon Vert.

MUSCADET *Loire*: FRANCE

One of the most popular white wines of the Loire Valley and of France. It comes from vineyards around the city of Nantes, almost on the Atlantic coast. There are three appellations: Muscadet, Muscadet de Sèvre et Maine and Muscadet des Coteaux de la Loire. The simple Muscadet appellation is the lowest of the three, coming from an area to the south and south west of Nantes. It is permitted a higher yield of 50 hectolitres, as opposed to 40 hectolitres per hectare for the other two. Muscadet is also the name of the grape that makes the wine. It came originally from Burgundy, where it is called the Melon de Bourgogne. Muscadet is unique in having a maximum, rather than a minimum alcoholic content in its appellation regulations, namely 12.3°. Good Muscadet should be light and dry and is delicious with seafood; the best wines are bottled 'sur lie'.

MUSCADET DES COTEAUX DE LA LOIRE *Loire*: FRANCE

One of the three appellations of Muscadet. As the name implies, it comes from vineyards on the banks of the Loire, to the east of Nantes. The production is tiny compared with the principal appellation of the area. Muscadet de Sèvre et Maine.

MUSCADET DE SÈVRE ET MAINE *Loire*: FRANCE

One of the three and the most important appellation of Muscadet. It covers the vineyards of Muscadet in the Sèvre et Maine district south east of Nantes, and because of its size there is considerable variation in the quality of the wine. The best comes from the two villages of Vallet and Saint Fiacre.

MUSCADINE

A more familiar name for the *vitis rotundifolia* family of vines, which are widely grown in the southeastern United States. Scuppernong is the most common grape variety.

MUSCARDIN

One of the permitted red grape varieties of Châteauneuf-du-Pape. It is possibly unique to Châteauneuf, but in reality is hardly ever found there.

MUSCAT D'ALEXANDRIE

One of the Muscat family, a very old grape variety which now produces much better table grapes than wine grapes, for it does not have the character and flavour of Muscat Blanc à Petits Grains. However it is still grown in several countries for wine. In the south of France it is used for *vins doux naturel*, especially Rivesaltes; in Spain around Alicante and Valencia and in Malaga where it is called Moscatel; in Portugal it makes Moscatel de Setúbal and in Italy Moscato di Pantelleria. It is planted extensively in Australia, where it is called Gordo Blanco, for cream sherry. Lexia is a better example of a sweet Australian wine and in South Africa it is called Hanepoot and is at its best for sweet fortified wines.

MUSCAT BLANC À PETITS GRAINS

The best grape variety of the large Muscat family, making much more interesting wine than Muscat d'Alexandrie or Muscat Ottonel. In France it is a vital part of the better *vins doux naturels* of the Midi and for Muscat de Beaumes de Venise. It also grows in the Rhône valley at Die for Clairette de Die Tradition. In Italy it is widely grown as Moscato for Asti Spumante. The Goldenmuskateller and Rosenmuskateller of the Alto Adige are variations of the grape variety. Muscat Blanc à Petits Grains accounts for the better muscat wines of Greece, notably of Samos. A little is grown in Hungary for Tokay.

In the New World some is grown in California as Muscat Canelli; in Australia it produces the famous Liqueur Muscats of Victoria. Some is produced in South Africa and South America too. Unexpectedly it is Muscat Ottonel that accounts for a large part of Muscat d'Alsace.

MUSCAT CANELLI

A synonym used in California for the grape variety Muscat Blanc à Petits Grains.

MUSCAT DE FRONTIGNAN
The Midi: FRANCE

A *vin doux naturel* made, as the name implies, from the grape variety Muscat Blanc à Petits Grains, grown around the town of Frontignan, south west of Montpellier. The wines are deep golden, sweet, aromatic dessert wines with a distinctive rich muscat flavour. It is also a synonym for the grape variety Muscat Blanc à Petits Grains.

MUSCAT GORDO BLANCO

Muscat Gordo Blanco, or simply Gordo is an Australian synonym for the grape variety Muscat d'Alexandrie.

MUSCAT DE KELIBIA   TUNISIA

A dry white Muscat wine, made from vineyards on Cap Bon, an area particularly famous for its Muscat.

MUSCAT DE LUNEL   *The Midi*: FRANCE

A *vin doux naturel* made, as the name implies, from the grape variety Muscat à petits grains ronds, grown around the town of Lunel to the east of Montpellier. The wines are golden, sweet, aromatic dessert wines with a distinctive rich muscat flavour.

MUSCAT DE MIREVAL
The Midi: FRANCE

A *vin doux naturel* made, as the name implies, from the Muscat Blanc à Petits Grains grown around the town of Mireval to the south west of Montpellier. The wines are golden, sweet, aromatic dessert wines, with a distinctive rich muscat flavour. Production is very small.

MUSCAT OTTONEL

A newer Muscat variety developed in the last century and now widely grown in Alsace, where it has to some extent replaced the Muscat d'Alsace. However, although its perfume is finer, it has the disadvantage of being sensitive to *coulure*. It is also grown in Austria, in the Rust and Neusiederlersee regions, for dessert wines and also in Hungary and Roumania. Some is grown in South Africa too.

MUSCAT OF RION   GREECE

One of the four appellations of the Patras area, a sweet white dessert wine from the Muscat grape.

MUSCAT DE RIVESALTES
The Midi: FRANCE

Muscat de Rivesaltes is a *vin doux naturel* from Rivesaltes in the *département* of the Pyrenées Orientales, made half from Muscat d'Alexandrie and half from Muscat Blanc à Petits Grains.

MUSCAT DE SAINT-JEAN-DE-MINERVOIS   *The Midi:* FRANCE

A *vin doux naturel* made from the Muscat Blanc à Petits Grains grape grown around the village of St. Jean de Minervois within the appellation of Minervois.

MUSCAT DE TERRACINA   See Muscat de Tunisie.

MUSCAT DE TUNISIE   TUNISIA

A Tunisian designation for a dessert Muscat wine that is fortified to at least 17° of alcohol and made from any of three types of Muscat: Alexandrie, Frontignan or Terracina, which is a peculiarly Tunisian grape variety.

MUSELAGE

The wire muzzle around a champagne or sparkling wine cork, designed to keep the cork very firmly in place.

LE MUSIGNY   Burgundy: FRANCE

A Grand Cru vineyard in the village of Chambolle-Musigny, with a reputation for fine red wine. A very small amount of white is also made.

MUST

Freshly-crushed grape juice, which has not yet begun to ferment.

MUST WEIGHT

Determined by the amount of sugar the grapes contain, which in turn indicates how ripe they are. The must weight is measured regularly before the vintage to decide the picking date. There are several systems for measuring must weight, namely Brix, Baumé, Oechsle and Balling.

MUSTIMETER

Also called a hydrometer, this is an instrument used to measure the density of must, and thereby calculate the potential alcohol of the wine.

MUSTY

A stale smell, originating from a faulty cork or cask. It may disappear once the wine is allowed to breathe.

MUTAGE

The French term for stopping an alcoholic fermentation, either by the addition of grape spirit, to make a *vin doux naturel*, or by the use of sulphur dioxide and filtration to leave some residual sugar in the wine.

MYCODERMI ACETI
Another name for acetobacter.

MYCODERMI VINI
Mycodermi vini, as they were called by Pasteur, or *candida mycodermi*, the more usual name today, are the yeasts which support other yeasts, like *saccharomyces oviformis* in the development of the *flor* on the *fino* sherry and *vin jaune*. They were originally thought to cause the *flor*.

MYRAT   Bordeaux: FRANCE
Classified as a second growth Sauternes but, unfortunately, the vines were pulled up in 1976.

N

N.M.

On a champagne label, this means that the wine has been produced by a *négociant manipulant*.

NACKENHEIM   Rheinhessen: GERMANY

One of the lesser-known towns on the Rheinfront within the *Grosslagen* of Spiegelberg and Gutes Domtal. The best vineyard is the Rothenberg, called after the sandy red soil.

NAGYBURGUNDI

The Hungarian name for the Pinot Noir grape.

NAHE   GERMANY

One of the smaller wine regions of Germany and a tributary of the Rhine, joining the river at Bingen, opposite Rüdesheim. Its vineyards are surrounded by those of the Mosel, the Rheinhessen and the Rheingau and share some of the characteristics of each, tempered with their own individuality. The region is divided into two *Bereichs*, Schlossböckelheim for the northern part and Kreuznach for the southern half, with a total of seven *Grosslagen*. The best vineyards are between Schlossböckelheim and Bad Kreuznach. Riesling vines are grown on the best sites, but other varieties make up over half the production.

NAIRAC   Bordeaux: FRANCE

A second growth Sauternes in Barsac, its reputation has enjoyed a renaissance under the ownership of an American enthusiast Tom Heeter. It now belongs to Nicole Tari of Château Giscours. Professor Peynaud advises, methods are traditional and meticulous, with oak barrels for fermentation and ageing.

NAOUSSA   GREECE

One of the better red wines from Thessalonika in northern Greece. It comes from the Xynomavro grape grown on the slopes of Mount Velia and is a robust red of some character. Many Greeks consider it to be their best wine.

NAPA   *California*: USA

The name of a county, a town and a valley, in northern California, close to San Francisco. The name means Valley of Plenty. This is California's most well known wine region with many of the State's great producers. The AVA of the Napa Valley covers the whole valley and there are two smaller AVAs within the valley. Carneros near San Pablo Bay and Howell Mountain in the eastern hills. The Napa Valley itself runs from the bay of San Francisco to the slopes of Mount St. Helena, entailing considerable climatic changes and consequently a variety of grapes. Chardonnay and Cabernet Sauvignon are the best varietals, but others produce fine wines too.

NAPA GAMAY   See Valdiguié.

NARBAG   TURKEY

A sweet white Turkish wine made from Narince grapes grown at Tokat in central Anatolia.

NARDO   *Apulia*: ITALY

A sturdy red non-DOC wine, made from Negroamaro and Malvasia Nera grapes near Lecci.

NASCO DI CAGLIARI   *Sardinia*: ITALY

A rare DOC made from dried Nasco grapes. It may be dry or sweet, or fortified as *liquoroso secco* and *liquoroso dolce naturale*. Riserva denotes two years' ageing in barrel, when it acquires a sherry-like flavour.

NATURAL YEAST   See yeast.

NATURWEIN

A term still used in Austria, also found in Germany before the introduction of the 1971 wine law. It described a wine without any added sugar, i.e. completely natural.

NAVARRA SPAIN

A province of northern Spain, with a D.O. covering vineyards south of Pamplona. The area is further subdivided into Baja Montaña, Valdizarbe, Tierra de Estella, Ribera Alta and Ribera Baja. The main grape varieties are red Garnacha Tinta, Tempranillo, Graciano and Mazuelo and white Viura, Malvasia and Garnacha Blanca. The best wines, oak aged reds, compare with Rioja.

NÉAC Bordeaux: FRANCE

A commune next to the Pomerol vineyards. It has its own appellation but the growers prefer to use the more attractive name of the adjacent commune Lalande de Pomerol. The wines are like lesser Pomerols but with a higher proportion of Cabernet Franc grapes.

NEBBIOLO

A peculiarly Italian grape variety, not found outside the vineyards of northern Italy where, in Piedmont, it makes some of Italy's best red wines, notably Barolo and Barbaresco, as well as forming most or all of the blend for Gattinara, Ghemme, Lessona, Sizzano and others. As Spanna, Nebbiolo is made into a *vino da tavola*; on the Swiss border in the Valtelline, it makes Sassella, Grumello, Valgella and Inferno and is also found in the Valle d'Aosta and near Brescia, where it is part of Franciacorta Rosso. Tannin is the grape's main characteristic, producing tough solid wines that need years of ageing in bottle after a lengthy maturation in large Slavonian oak barrels. The name Nebbiolo is said to originate from the nebbia or fog that often covers the vineyards of Piedmont.

NEBBIOLO D'ALBA Piedmont: ITALY

A red DOC wine made from the Nebbiolo grape produced around the town of Alba. In some places it overlaps with Barolo and Barbaresco vineyards and is made when the grapes are not good enough for the DOCG wines. Nebbiolo must have a minimum of 12° alcohol and be aged in wood for at least a year. Medium sweet and *spumante* versions can be found locally.

NEBBIOLO DELLE LANGHE Piedmont: ITALY

A red wine which, as the name implies, is made from the Nebbiolo grape in the Langhe hills of Piedmont, the area of Barolo and Barbaresco. Sometimes it is made from wines rejected for these denominations, or is just a less aged, simpler wine.

NEBBIOLO DEL PIEMONTE Piedmont: ITALY

Describes wine from the Nebbiolo grape which does not come from any of the DOC zones of Piedmont.

NEBUCHADNEZZAR

A champagne bottle size equal to twenty ordinary bottles (1500cl).

NEDERBURG SOUTH AFRICA

Known for the quality of its wines for it is one of the finest estates of Paarl in South Africa and also for its annual wine auction, which since 1975 has attracted international attention. Gunter Brozel is the estate's talented winemaker who, in keeping with his German traditions, makes a rich botrytis wine, Edelkeur, as well as a Cabernet Sauvignon based wine, Baronne, Paarl Riesling and other table wines. Brozel took over from Johann Graue, a German immigrant who developed the Nederburg estate during the 1940s and 1950s.

NÉGOCE

The collective word to describe the activity of the *négociants* in a region.

NÉGOCIANT

A wine merchant whose original role was that of salesman for the wines of the area in France and abroad, but that is now only one aspect of the work. Through a *courtier*, the *négociant* buys wine, and sometimes grapes or must, which may be blended, bottled and sold under this name. The *négociant éleveur* matures wines in his/her own cellars and is responsible for the *élevage*, or upbringing, of the wine. *Négociants* are tending to lose their importance in some parts of France as small growers tend increasingly to bottle and sell their own wine.

NEGRAMOLE

Negramole, or tinta negra mole, is the most prolific grape of Madeira, accounting for between 50% and 60% of the island's total production. Most Madeira has Negramole as its base; it has developed from crosses involving Pinot Noir and Grenache and has been grown on the island since the beginning of the 19th century.

NEGRARA

A red grape occasionally used for Valpolicella and Bardolino.

NÉGRETTE

A red grape variety peculiar to south west France. It can be used in Gaillac and Lavilledieu, but is at its best in the Côtes du Fronton, where it accounts for 50–70% of the blend. It is also grown in California where it is called Pinot St. George.

NEGRU DE PURKAR   See Moldavia.

NEGUS

An old-fashioned hot drink, made with red wine or port and spices which was popularised under Queen Anne, by Colonel Francis Negus.

NELSON   NEW ZEALAND

One of the wine regions of New Zealand's South Island. The climate is one of frosty winters, long warm summers and cool wet autumns. Interest in the area is new. A wide range of grape varieties, including Müller-Thurgau, Riesling, Gewürztraminer, Pinot Noir and Cabernet Sauvignon have been planted on the varied soils. Vineyard holdings tend to be small, attracting the *boutique* style of winery.

NEMATODE

A pest that, in its larva form, can do considerable damage in a vineyard, attacking vine roots and eventually destroying the vine. They were first identified in California in 1930 and, to combat them, the soil needs to be fumigated after being left fallow for a couple of years. Nematode-resistant rootstock can also be used.

NEMEA   GREECE

A full-bodied red wine, generally considered to be one of Greece's best, made in the northeastern Peloponnese near Corinth from Agiorgitiko grapes grown in hilly vineyards.

NENIN   Bordeaux: FRANCE

One of the largest and best-known properties of Pomerol, coming in the second rather than the top rank, with consistent quality.

NERELLO

One of the main grape varieties of Sicily and comes in two versions, Nerello Mascalese, which is good for alcohol and colour and at its best in Etna Rosso, and the better Nerello Cappucci, which contributes to Corvo Rosso.

NEUBURGER

A crossing of Weissburgunder and Silvaner grape varieties, grown extensively in Austria, but little elsewhere. It produces some full-bodied, rather neutral white wine.

NEUCHÂTEL   SWITZERLAND

The canton of Neuchâtel, to the north of Geneva, is planted mainly with white Chasselas, while Pinot Noir is considered the best wine. No Gamay is grown in the canton so any red wine can be assumed to be Pinot Noir and to have some character. Sometimes it comes as pale *œil de perdrix* or even lighter *blanc de noir*. Chasselas is light and often bottled *sur lie*.

NEUMAGEN   Mosel-Saar-Ruwer: GERMANY

A wine village of the Mittelmosel, said to be the oldest wine producing village of Germany, going back to the Romans. It comes within the *Grosslage* of Michelsberg and the best single sites are Rosengärtchen, Engelgrube and Laudamusberg.

NEUSIEDLERSEE AUSTRIA

One of the subregions of Burgenland and also Europe's largest inland lake. The climate is warm and sunny and the Welschriesling grows well on the sandy soil. Grüner Veltliner, Müller-Thurgau, Weissburgunder, Muscat Ottonel and Neuberger are also grown. The Seewinkel is included in this region.

NEUSIEDLERSEE-HUGELLAND
AUSTRIA

One of the sub-regions of the Burgenland with vineyards on the south east slopes of the Leitha mountains. As well as Grüner Veltliner there is Welschriesling, Müller-Thurgau, Weissburgunder and Neuberger. Blaufrankischer grows well in the vineyards of Pottelsdorf. The town of Rust is at the centre of the area and Eisenstadt is the home of the Esterhazy estate.

NEUSTADT Rheinpfalz: GERMANY

An important town with wine villages in its suburbs. It is the home of the viticultural and oenological school of the Rheinpfalz as well as an experimental station.

NEVERS OAK

One of the principal types of French oak, used for making wine barrels. In contrast to Limousin oak, it comes from slow growing forests in a cooler climate so that the wood is dense and tightly grained and therefore the wine absorbs less oak character than with Limousin oak.

NEW HAMPSHIRE USA

New Hampshire boasts one winery, White Mountain Vineyards, which produces a range of generically labelled hybrid wines.

NEW SOUTH WALES AUSTRALIA

One of the most important wine producing states of Australia, with several important vineyard areas: Corowa, Cowra, Hunter Valley, Mudgee, the Murrumbidgee Irrigation Area, also called Riverina, and Rooty Hill, as well as scattered vineyards over the state at Young, Camden, Orange and elsewhere. See individual entries.

NEW YORK STATE USA

The second most important American wine producing state after California. Only a small part of the production comes from *vitis vinifera* vines. Most of the vineyards are planted with *vitis labrusca*, with its peculiar foxy characteristics, there are some French-American hybrids too. Gold Seal, Taylors and Great Western are the largest wineries, with a recent increase in smaller wineries too. There are five vineyard areas. Most important is the Fingers Lakes, with the Chatauqua district on the eastern side of Lake Erie, Niagara county to the west of the Niagara Falls, the Hudson Valley, and finally a small but growing district on the north eastern tip of Long Island.

NEW ZEALAND

New Zealand is a rising star in the wine firmament. Her wine industry took off in the 1960s when a considerable number of vineyards were planted in the North Island with European grape varieties, especially white varieties, and in the 1970s vines moved to the South Island. The principal wine areas are now Auckland, Hawkes Bay, Poverty Bay and Gisborne on the North Island and Marlborough on the South Island. The climatic conditions of each area vary quite considerably, but New Zealand has the advantage of a long growing and ripening season, resulting in wines with a good acidity balance. At present Müller-Thurgau is the most important variety with Chardonnay, Gewürztraminer, Sauvignon Blanc and Cabernet Sauvignon all gaining some success.

The major producers are Cooks and Montana; other reputable estates include Babich, Nobilo and Morton Estate. New Zealand wines are beginning to make an impact on the export market.

NIAGARA

A crossing of the Concord and Cassady vines grown in the eastern United States to make a foxy white wine.

NIAGARA COUNTY USA

One of the wine regions of New York State, with vineyards to the west of the Niagara Falls.

NORTHLAND

HUAPAI/KUMEU/AUCKLAND

Auckland

WAIKATO

BAY OF PLENTY

Gisborne

POVERTY BAY

HAWKES BAY

MANAWATU/WELLINGTON

NELSON

Wellington

MARLBOROUGH

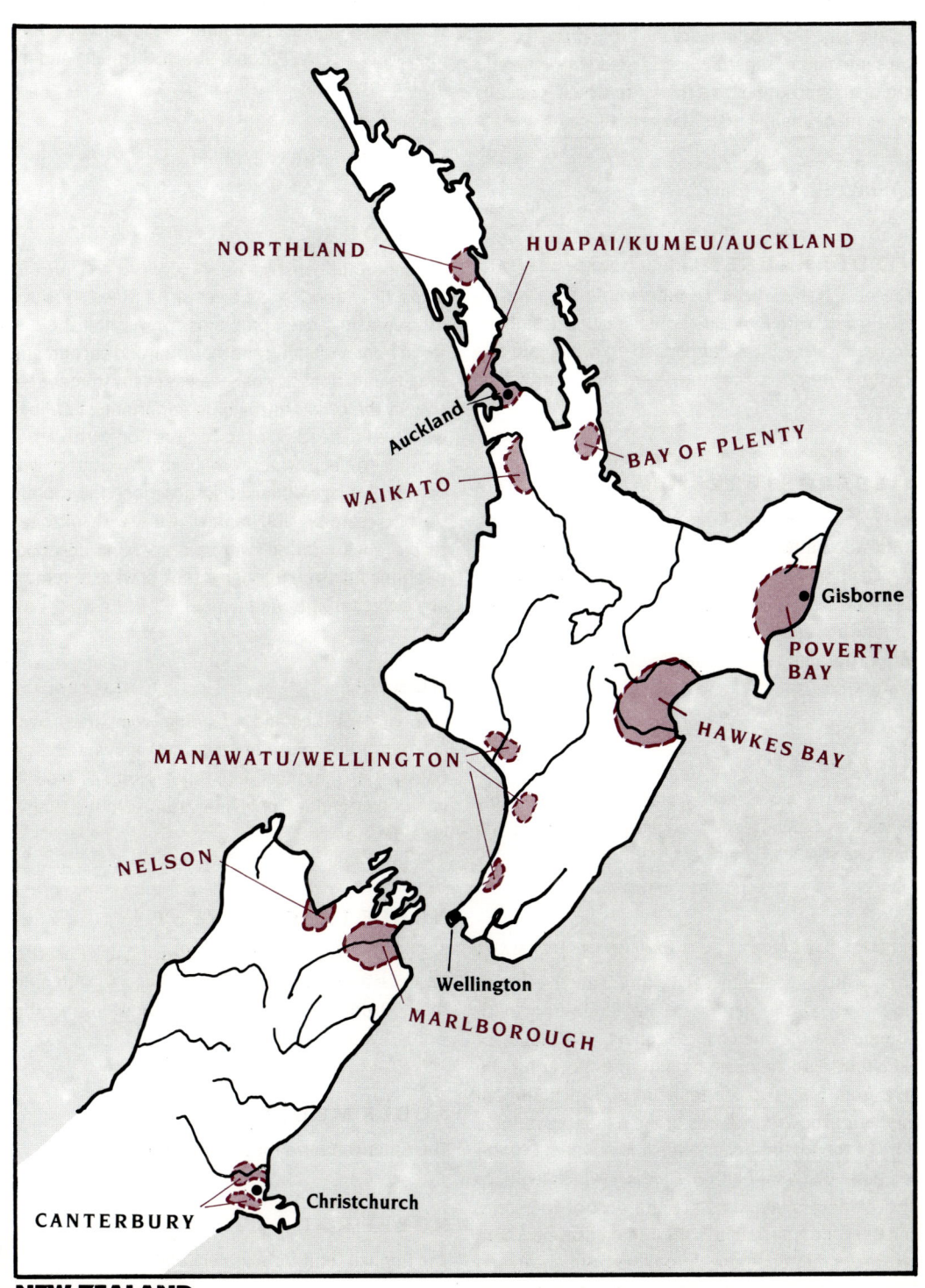

CANTERBURY

Christchurch

NEW ZEALAND

NICASTRO
Calabria: ITALY

A table wine from Calabria made around the town of the same name. The fruity red is made from Nerello and Gaglioppo grapes and the white, which is usually dry, is made mainly from Malvasia Bianca.

NICORESTI   See Foșani.

NIEDERHAUSEN
Nahe: GERMANY

The best Nahe village, coming within the *Grosslage* of Burgweg, with E*inzellagen* which include Steinberg, Hermannshöhle and Hermannsberg, which are fine Riesling vineyards. The State Domaine has its cellars here.

NIEDERÖSTERREICH
AUSTRIA

Or Lower Austria, the largest wine region of Austria subdivided into five smaller areas, mostly between the Danube and Czechoslovakia, namely Wachau, the Weinviertel, Kamptal-Donauland, Donauland-Carnuntum and Thermenland. The principal grape variety throughout is Grüner Veltliner for dry, spicey, white wine.

NIELLUCCIO

A distinctive red Corsican grape variety, possibly related to Sangiovese, producing substantial red and rosé wines, at their best in Patrimonio.

NIERSTEIN
Rheinhessen: GERMANY

The heart of Rheinhessen, an attractive riverside town at the centre of the Rhein-front with numerous wine merchants' cellars. The name of Nierstein also belongs to a *Bereich*, covering the area from Mainz to Mettenheim and including all the better known vineyards of the region, covering a third of the Rheinhessen. Niersteiner Gutes Domtal is a particularly well-known *Grosslage*, which includes fifteen villages inland and to the west of Nierstein, and only one Nierstein E*inzellage*, Pfaffenkappe. There are three other *Grosslagen*: Spiegelberg, Auflangen and Rehbach. The *Grosslagen* names are much more often used than those of the *Einzellagen*, the better ones including Paterberg, Rüchkchen, Hölle, Rosenberg, Pettenthal, Hipping, Ölberg and Zehnmorgen. The best Niersteins are beautiful ripe wines made from Riesling. Müller-Thurgau and other grapes produce the more mundane Liebfraumilch type of wine. Good producers include Anton Balbach, Sittmann and the local cooperative.

NIPOZZANO   See Frescobaldi.

NITROGEN

An important constituent of balanced soil, encouraging new wood and flowering of vines. However in excess it causes problems, preventing the new wood from hardening and maturing and encouraging fungus infections. It washes away easily from the top soil. In the cellar, nitrogen is important as an inert gas, used instead of, or in conjunction with, carbon dioxide to keep wine away from any contact with oxygen. Nitrogen-blanketing describes the topping up of a partially full tank of wine with nitrogen, to prevent oxidation. Nitrogen sparging describes bubbling nitrogen through a tank of wine to remove any oxygen in the wine.

NOBILO
NEW ZEALAND

One of New Zealand's leading companies, with a reputation especially for its red wines, Cabernet Sauvignon, Pinotage and Pinot Noir, as well as good Chardonnay. Their vineyards are in the Huapai area.

NOBLE LATE HARVEST

A South African white wine classification used to describe a wine picked at 28° Balling and with more than 50 gms of sugar after fermentation, in other words, a wine with *botrytis*.

NOBLE MOULD

The American term for *pourriture noble*.

NOBLE ROT

The English term for *pourriture noble*.

NOBLESSA

A crossing of the Madeleine Angevine and Silvaner grape varieties, grown mainly in Baden.

NOBLING

A German crossing of the Silvaner and Gutedel grape varieties, grown mainly in Baden.

NOËL-BOUTON   Burgundy: FRANCE

Important growers in Rully at Domaine de la Folie, making white Rully, Clos St-Jacques and red Rully, Clos de Bellecroix, as well as some Bourgogne Aligoté. New barrels are an important aspect of the vinification process.

NON-VINTAGE

A term used to describe wine sold without any mention of the year of harvest. For an ordinary wine drunk within the year, this information may be superfluous; in better quality wines it implies a blend of vintages. Champagne and port which are only sold as vintage wines in exceptional circumstances are usually non-vintage wines from a blend of years. Sherry too is another example.

NORHEIM   Nahe: GERMANY

A small village on the Nahe coming within the *Grosslage* of Burgweg and producing wine from Müller-Thurgau, Silvaner and Riesling grapes. The best vineyards are Dellchen and Kafels.

NORTH COAST   California: USA

An ill-defined term for the counties north of San Francisco, covering all the grape growing areas within the counties of Lake, Mendocino, Napa, Sonoma and Solano.

NORTH EAST VICTORIA
AUSTRALIA

An important wine region of Victoria, making the best fortified and dessert wines of Australia, as well as some excellent red wines. Rutherglen is the centre of the area, which is bounded by the Murray River and part of the Australian Alps. Summers are hot and dry; winters in the Alps are very cold. Most of the vineyards are centred on the King, Ovens and Murray Rivers and are planted with a range of grapes for table wines, as well as for the traditional fortified wines.

NORTHLAND   NEW ZEALAND

As the name implies, New Zealand's most northern wine region, where James Busby made the country's first wine in the 1830s. Today viticulture is unimportant in the area. Hybrids such as Albany Surprise, Baco 22A and Seibel 5455 are the main grape varieties and the wines are generally unexciting, sweet fortified wines, typical of New Zealand's wines two decades ago.

NOSE

A term used for the smell of the wine. It can also be used as a verb, 'to nose' the wine.

NOSTRANO   AUSTRIA

An everyday red table wine produced in the Italian-speaking canton of Ticino, from a miscellany of grapes.

NOUAISON

The French term to describe the setting of the grapes which occurs after the flowering.

NOUVEAU

The French term for a new wine, used most commonly in connection with Beaujolais, but also other wines, when they are first released towards the end of November. The description is generally valid until Christmas.

NOVI PAZAR   BULGARIA

A defined Controliran wine region concentrating on the production of Chardonnay as a varietal wine.

NOVO SELO
BULGARIA

A defined Controliran wine region of origin, concentrating on the production of wines from the Gamza grape.

NUITS ST-GEORGES Burgundy: FRANCE

The town of Nuits St-Georges is the commercial centre of the Côte de Nuits. Many producers and *négociants* have their cellars there; makers of fruit liqueurs and sparkling Burgundy are important too.

This must be one of the most popular wine names in the English- speaking world, perhaps because of its association with our patron saint. The vineyards of Nuits St-Georges fall into three sections: to the north those next to the village of Vosne; to the south, with the vineyard of les St-Georges, and thirdly, the vineyards of the neighbouring village of Prémaux, which are sold under the appellation of Nuits St-Georges.

The Premiers Crus vineyards are numerous: les St-Georges, les Vaucrains, les Cailles, les Porets, les Pruliers, les Hauts Pruliers (part), aux Murgers, la Richemone, les Chabœufs, la Perrière, la Roncière, les Procès, Rue de Chaux, aux Boudots, aux Cras, Aux Chargnots, aux Thorey (part), aux Vignes-Rondes, aux Bousselots, les Poulettes, aux Crots (part), les Vallerots (part), aux Champs Perdrix (part), Perrière Noblet (part), aux Damodes (part), les Argillats (part) Chaînes Carteaux (part) and aux Argillats (part).

For Premier Cru vineyards in the commune of Prémeaux, see under Prémeaux.

There are numerous growers and shippers with their headquarters in Nuits St-Georges. Amongst them are Jean Claude Boisset, J. H. Faiveley, Geisweiler et Fils, Domaine Henri Gouges, Labouré Roi, Lupé Cholet et Cie, Domaine Machard de Gramont, Tim Marshall, Moillard-Grivot and Morin Père et Fils.

As in Beaune, there is an Hospices de Nuits which was founded in 1692 and which, since 1961, has held an annual auction of the wine from nine hectares of the town's Premiers Crus vineyards. The sale does not attract the same attention as its counterpart in Beaune.

NURAGUS DI CAGLIARI
Sardinia: ITALY

The most important DOC wine of Sardinia, a dry white made from the Nuragus grape, grown north of Cagliari.

NUS
Valle d'Aosta: ITALY

A village in the Valle d'Aosta which is noted for Malvoisie de Nus, a wine made from semi-dried grapes and fermented for 40–50 days in a sealed vat, then aged in oak barrels for two to three years. Crème du Vien de Nus is a red wine from a native grape Vien de Nus, with Petit Rouge and Merlot.

NUTTY

Describes full-bodied mature white wines, such as fine white Burgundies or medium-dry sherries.

NYCTERI   See Santorini.

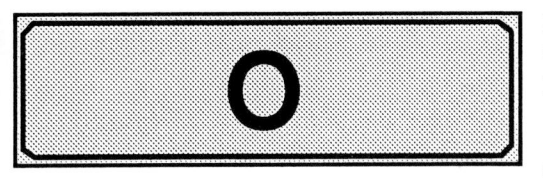

OAK

The best wood for making wine barrels, though sometimes chestnut is used. The most famous oaks are from Nevers and Limousin in France; Alliers, Tronçais and Vosges also produce good oak. In Italy, Slavonic oak from Yugoslavia is the most common while in California they have American oak, such as Tennessee or Kentucky, or imported French oak. Oak barrels are made either by steaming or charring the wood. Specialists can detect the difference of flavour stemming from the type of wood and the method of manufacture.

OAKVILLE California: USA

An important village in the Napa Valley, noted especially for the Robert Mondavi winery.

OBEREMMEL Mosel-Saar-Ruwer: GERMANY

A village on the Saar with some fine vineyard sites, Karlsberg, Hütte, Artenberg, Raul, Agritiusberg and Rosenberg. Notable producers include von Hövel, Kesselstatt, Friedrich Wilhelm Gymnasium. The *Grosslage* is Scharzberg.

OBERMOSEL Mosel-Saar-Ruwer: GERMANY

Bereich Obermosel covers the vineyards on the Mosel above Trier from Igel to the Luxembourg border. The main grape variety is Elbling, mostly used for *Sekt*.

OBIDOS PORTUGAL

One of the undemarcated wine regions of western Portugal producing mainly white wine.

OCKFEN Mosel-Saar-Ruwer: GERMANY

An important village on the Saar coming within the *Grosslage* of Scharzberg. The best vineyards are Bockstein and Geisberg. There is also Kupp, Herrenberg, Hippenstein, Zickelgarten and Neuwies. Good producers include the Staatsweingut and Dr. Fischer and Freidrich Wilhelm Gymnasium.

ODOBESTI   See Fosani.

OECHSLE

The German system for estimating the potential alcohol and quality in the grape juice. The specific gravity of the must indicates the number of grams by which one litre of must is heavier than one litre of water. The sugar content represents 25% of this calibration, so with a reading of 100° oechsle, 100 litres will contain about 25 kilos of sugar. The oechsle weight shows the specific gravity in an abridged form. If the oechsle degree is 72°, the specific gravity of the must is 1072. The reading of must weight determines the quality of the wine from *Tafelwein* to *Trockenbeerenauslese*. Oechsle was the name of the inventor, a German physicist.

ŒIL DE PERDRIX

Translates literally as 'partridge eye' and describes the tawny gold colour of some wines, for example some of the wines of the Jura.

OEILLADE

An obscure dull white grape of south eastern France which is hardly grown today.

OENOLOGY

The science of winemaking, covering all aspects of vinification from fermentation to maturation and including more general aspects of wine. An oenologist is a trained winemaker, often with a degree in the subject.

OENOPHILE

A connoisseur of wine, a well-informed, enthusiastic wine-lover.

OESTE PORTUGAL

The overall name given to western Portugal, covering the area north of the Tagus to Obidos and from the Atlantic to the Ribatejo. It is important for the production of bulk table wines.

OESTRICH
Rheingau: GERMANY

One of the largest villages of the Rheingau, with vineyards forming a wide semi-circle round the village. It is within the *Grosslage* of Gottesthal, apart from parts of the Klosterberg vineyard which are in the *Grosslage* of Mehrhölzchen. Lenchen is generally considered the best *Einzellage*; in addition there is Doosberg, Klosterberg and Schloss Reichartshausen, originally a monastic vineyard which does not need the village name.

OFF-LICENCE

Allows the sale of wines and maybe spirits for consumption away from the premises where they are purchased.

OFFICE DU VIN

The official French organisation which controls all matters pertaining to the production of *vins de pays* and *vins de table*.

OFFLEY FORRESTER

This port house dates back to 1751. It included Baron James Forrester amongst its members and is now owned jointly by Sandeman and St. Raphael. Quinta Boa Vista provides the basis of their vintage wines.

OHIO
USA

Ohio is the third largest wine producing state of the United States. The vineyards on the islands or shores of Lake Erie are planted mainly with hybrid vines, notably Catawba. However, experimental vineyards of *vitis vinifera* are making inroads into a flourishing industry.

OIDIUM

Also known as 'powdery mildew', a vine disease which first appeared in Europe in the 1850s. It attacks the leaves and berries, eventually killing the vine, and affects the taste of the wine. Sulphur is an efficient remedy.

OJO DE LIEBRE

A Catalonian synonym for the Tempranillo grape.

OKANAGAN RIESLING

A white grape grown in the Okanagan Valley in British Colombia which was brought to Canada from Hungary and developed for its resistance to low winter temperatures.

OLARRA
SPAIN

One of the larger and more modern *bodegas* of Rioja, with the traditional ageing in American oak *barricas*. The winery is in the shape of a three pointed star to symbolise the three subregions of Rioja. The bodega has no vineyards; the range includes Cerron Añón *reservas* and some sound white wine.

OLASZRIZLING   See Welschriesling

OLFACTORY

The adjective pertaining to a person's sense of smell and perception of the bouquet of a wine.

OLIFANTSRIVIER
SOUTH AFRICA

A northern wine region of South Africa, including the wards of Spruitdrift and Cedarberg. The vineyards are mainly along the river between Trawal and Koekenaap. They are heavily irrigated and provide wine for distillation, an industry now reduced in importance.

OLIVE FARM WINES
AUSTRALIA

Olive Farm Wines dates back to the settlement of Western Australia in the 1830s when both vines and olives were planted by Thomas Waters. Today after a recent revival, they make an excellent range of varietal and generic wines.

OLIVIER
Bordeaux: FRANCE

A Cru Classé Graves from the commune of Léognan. Produces both red and white wine though the white is better-known. The moated *château* dates back to the 11th century and was once the Black Prince's hunting lodge.

OLOROSO
SPAIN

The darkest, richest and most full-bodied sherry. It has very little *flor* and really develops its flavour with ageing in wood. An unblended *oloroso* is completely dry, but it is often used as a base for cream sherry with sweet Pedro Ximénez wines and *vino de color*.

OLTREPÒ PAVESE   Lombardy: ITALY

A large but relatively unknown DOC from vineyards in the Po Valley near Pavia. The DOC covers ten wines: Oltrepò Pavese Rosso, a mixture of grape varieties and styles, the best are full-bodied and slightly tannic; three more individual reds, Barbacarlo, Buttafuoco and Sangue de Giuda and six varietal names: Barbera, Bonarda, Cortese, Moscato, Pinot Grigio and Pinot Nero, which can be still, red, white, *rosato* and, more commonly, *spumante* when it is white or *rosato*, and often not DOC if blended with other grape varieties, and Riesling, both Renano and Italico. Barbera and Bonarda both age well; Cortese is light and dry and the Moscato is usually *spumante* dessert wine. Barbacarlo, which is named after the estate of the best producer, can be medium sweet and is always *frizzante*; Buttafuoco comes from Uva Rara, Croatina and Barbera grapes, is sometimes *frizzante* and means 'sparking like fire'. Sangue di Guida, or 'Judas's blood' is often *frizzante* and predominantly made from Croatina.

OMAR KHAYYAM

See India and Egypt. The names given to wines in these two countries were obviously inspired by the Indo-Persian poet, who wrote the Rubaiyat, a wonderful celebration of wine.

ON-LICENCE

Allows the sale of wines for consumption on the premises where they are purchased, in other words, a public house, restaurant or wine bar.

ONDENC

A little known white grape variety of south west France, occasionally found in Gaillac, Côtes de Duras and the white appellations of Bergerac. It was also taken to Australia by James Busby where it is used for sparkling wine in Victoria.

ONTARIO   CANADA

One of the two main wine-producing states in Canada. The vineyards are on the Niagara peninsular, next to New York State's Niagara county, and are planted with similar grape varieties, originally Labrusca. Increasingly, hybrids and *vitis vinifera* are grown. The climate is generally milder than neighbouring British Columbia but still with seasonal extremes of temperature. The main wineries are Andres, Brights and Château Gai. Inniskillen is establishing a good reputation with Chardonnay and other *vitis vinifera*.

OPIMIAN

Was a wine of ancient Rome, similar to Falernian.

OPOL   YUGOSLAVIA

A dry rosé wine made from a blend of grapes grown on the Dalmatian coast.

OPORTO   PORTUGAL

The city that gave port its name. The first recorded shipment of Vinho do Porto was registered by the Oporto customs in 1678. An English colony began to settle there during the reign of Charles II and, as port became increasingly popular, those families established a thriving trade. Today textiles are the dominant industry, but wine is still of considerable importance.

OPPENHEIM   Rheinhessen: GERMANY

A small but important wine village of the Rheinhessen, it has several important cellars and a viticultural institute. The wines are comparable to its neighbour Nierstein, coming in two *Grosslagen*, Guldenmorgen for the better sites and Krötenbrunnen. The *Grosslagen* are better known than any *Einzellagen*, of which there are several, including Herrenberg, Sackträger and Schlossberg. The better wines are made from Riesling grapes and can have considerable character. Good producers include Louis Guntrum, Sittmann and the State Domain Research and Training Institute of Rheinland-Pfalz.

OPTHALMO

An ancient red grape variety indigenous to Cyprus and used for Commandaria and the island's table wines.

OPTIMA

The Optima grape is a new German crossing of Silvaner x Riesling with Müller Thurgau, giving a wine with low acidity and high must weight, best blended with other grapes. It is grown in the Mosel and Rheinhessen, mainly to achieve wines of Prädikat quality. It is also grown in England.

OPUS I

The result of the joint venture between Robert Mondavi in California and Baron Phillippe de Rothschild in Bordeaux. It combines Californian technology and Bordelais expertise exercised on Cabernet Sauvignon grapes with a small percentage of Merlot and occasionally Cabernet Franc grown in the Napa Valley.

ORBELLO   Piedmont: ITALY

A red wine made from Nebbiolo grapes with some Vespolina and Croatina, grown at Bramaterra in the Vercelli hills by Fabrizio Sella.

OREGON   USA

Oregon is one of the three wine producing states of the Pacific North West. Vines were planted there in the 19th century, but failed to survive Prohibition. It was not until the 1960s that interest was revived, especially in the Willamette Valley where the Oregon wine industry is concentrated. The mountain ranges of the Coast Range in the west and the Cascades in the east moderate any temperature extremes but allow sufficient rainfall. The best wineries of the state are Eyrie Vineyards, Hillcrest Vineyard, Tualatin Vineyards, Sokal Blosser Winery and Knudsen Erath. Pinot Noir, grown in a considerably cooler climate than California, is making interesting wine. Chardonnay is good too. A grape variety on the label indicates a minimum of 90%, except for Cabernet Sauvignon which is 75% to allow for blending with Merlot and Malbec. Three regional designations are permitted, Willamette Valley, Umpque Valley and Rogue Valley. Grapes from Washington State are often blended with those from Oregon.

ORGANIC VITICULTURE

The cultivation of vines without the use of chemical weedkillers, fertilisers or treatments. A winemaker who practices organic viticulture, of which there are a growing number, fertilises the vineyard with natural manure, uses the traditional treatment of *bouille bordelaise* and tills the vineyard, rather than using weedkillers.

ORIAHOVITZA   BULGARIA

A defined Controliran wine region of origin, concentrating on the production of varietal Cabernet Sauvignon and Merlot wines.

ORLANDO   AUSTRALIA

The more familiar name of the company of G. Gramp, and the label under which their wines are sold. Their winery is at Jacob's Creek in the Barossa Valley part of Southern Australia, which provides the name for their leading brand, a red 'claret'. Whites are their best wines, notably Rhine Riesling, including Spätleses and an experimental vineyard producing steely Steingarten. Cabernet Sauvignon is good too.

L'ORMARINS   SOUTH AFRICA

An estate in Paarl, in the Franschhoek Valley, which was producing wine as early as 1825, since when it has had a chequered history. The vineyards have recently been replanted and the cellars modernised for the production of fine white table wine, notably Sauvignon Blanc and Rhine Riesling.

LES ORMES-SORBET
                              Bordeaux: FRANCE

A Cru Grand Bourgeois in the commune of Conquèques, Médoc.

LES-ORMES-DE-PEZ
                              Bordeaux: FRANCE

A Cru Grand Bourgeois of St-Estèphe with a good reputation and under the same ownership as Lynch-Bages.

ORTA NOVA   Apulia: ITALY

Red and *rosato* DOC from Apulia, in the province of Foggia, made principally from Sangiovese, but other grapes such as Uva di Troia, Montepulciano and Trebbiano Toscano are also allowed.

ORTEGA

The Ortega grape is a recent German crossing of Müller Thurgau and Siegerkebe grown mainly in the Mosel and in England but of limited interest for although it is useful to boost must readings for Prädikat wines, it is very susceptible to rot and other diseases.

ORTENAU Baden: GERMANY

One of the seven Baden *Bereichs*, covering the area to the south of Baden Baden. It is split into two *Grosslagen*: Fürsteneck and Schloss Rodeck. Here, Spätburgunder is the dominant grape variety for a popular wine called Affentaler which sports a monkey on the bottle, as well as lighter *Weissherbst* and *Rotgold*.

ORVIETO Umbria: ITALY

A white DOC wine taking its name from the hilltop town. Made from a mixture of Trebbiano, Verdello, Grechetto, Malvasia and other grapes, traditionally it was abboccato and slightly honeyed, but now tends more often to be dry. Both are best drunk young. The *classico* zone covers vineyards around the town.

OSBORNE

A sherry firm associated with Duff Gordon, but also with sister companies in Mexico, Portugal and Rioja. They have a modern winery in Puerta de Santa Maria in the Jerez district of Spain, and their range includes Quinta *fino*, Coquinero *amontillado*, Bailen *oloroso*, and Osborne Cream. They are also very important brandy producers.

OSTUNI Apulia: ITALY

A DOC wine in two forms: a dry white made from Impigno and Francavilla grapes, and Ottavianello, from the grape of the same name, which makes a light red wine for early drinking.

OTHELLO CYPRUS

Keo's brand name for their standard red wine.

DOMAINES OTT Provence: FRANCE

Ott is one of the most important names of Provence. The family have three properties, Château de Selle and Clos Mireille in the Côtes de Provence and Château Romassan in Bandol. Clos Mireille on the coast near St. Tropez produces white wine from Ugni Blanc and Semillon, while Château de Selle makes red and rosé as well. This old Provençal family have done much for the wines of their region; they experiment with different grape varieties and practise organic viticulture on all their estates. Their head office is in Antibes.

OTTAVIANELLO See Ostuni.

OUDE MEESTER SOUTH AFRICA

The Oude Meester Group is an important force in the South African wine industry, for table wines as well as fortified wine and brandy. The Bergkelder at Stellenbosch, which is a member of the group, with its own ageing and bottling plant, markets the wines of eighteen top estates, as well as making wine from grapes bought in Stellenbosch and Paarl. The Fleur du Cap range and Grunberger Stein are typical of their quality.

OUILLAGE

The procedure of topping up barrels which have ullaged. During the course of ageing in barrel, a certain amount of wine is absorbed by the barrel and also evaporates, especially if the bung of the barrel is on top of the barrel and exposed to air, rather than on the side and kept more airtight by the wine. Humidity, the cellar temperature and the thickness of the barrel also affect the rate at which the wine evaporates, from half a glass to a bottle per week. In theory, the topping up or *ouillage* should be done with the same wine; in practice, some winemakers are less conscientious.

OUVRÉE

An old Burgundian measure of land, equalling about one twenty-fourth of a hectare.

OVENS VALLEY AUSTRALIA

A small wine area of Northeast Victoria. Wynns sell Ovens Valley Shiraz.

OVERBERG — SOUTH AFRICA

The southernmost Wine of Origin district of South Africa, including the ward of Walker Bay and previously known as the Caledon district. The region is mountainous with vines in the Villiersdorp and Bot river areas, with a cool climate and high rainfall. Hamilton Russell vineyards is the best estate.

OVERCROPPING

The encouragement of a vine to produce an excessive yield, either by pruning to leave too many buds, or by irrigating excessively in an irrigated vineyard to the detriment of the quality of the wine and the vigour of the vine.

OVERGAAUW — SOUTH AFRICA

A wine estate in the Stellenbosch area. The estate concentrates on red wines, most notably Cabernet Sauvignon. It is the only South African estate to make Sylvaner as a cultivar. Its Chenin Blanc has a good reputation too.

OXIDASIC CASSE

Can occur in a wine made from overripe or rotten grapes. The wine goes cloudy when exposed to air and changes colour; red wines turn brown and white wine yellow. Treatment includes the use of sulphur and ascorbic acid.

OXIDATION

The changes in wine, resulting from exposure to air; in a small quantity this can be beneficial, in excess it harms the wine because it causes the wine to oxidise, lose its fruit and age prematurely.

OXIDISED

Describes a wine that has been adversely affected by exposure to air and oxygen, losing its fruit and freshness.

P

p.H.

The measure of hydrogen ions or acidity in a wine, coming mainly from malic and tartaric acid. The lower the pH in a wine, the higher the acidity so, as the pH reading rises from 3 to 4, the number of hydrogen ions goes down and the acidity reduces. Free hydrogen ions can have an important effect on wine, affecting its colour, flavour, stability and resistance to bacteria growth. The malo-lactic fermentation increases the pH, while the addition of acidity decreases it. Acidity is also relevant in judging the ripeness of grapes; white grapes would be picked with a pH of between 3.1 and 3.4, and red grapes between 3.4 and 3.6.

P.L.C. See Plafonde Limite de Classement.

P.X.

An abbreviation for the Pedro Ximénez grape, which is used principally for making sweet wine in Jerez. There is a story that the grape was brought to Jerez in the 16th century by a member of the army of the Emperor Charles V, Pieter Siemens.

PAARL   SOUTH AFRICA

One of the best wine of origin districts, coming within the Coastal Region and including the ward of Franschhoek. It lies some fifty miles north of Cape Town and is the home of two important organisations, the K.W.V. and Nederburg. The countryside is breathtaking and the climate ideally suited to the production of grapes, especially for white wine and for sherry.

PAARL RIESLING

A South African synonym for the Cruchen Blanc grape. See Cape Riesling.

PACHERENC DE VIC BIHL   SOUTH WEST FRANCE

A white wine originally from the identical area of its red counterpart, Madiran. It can be dry, or sweet if it is made from overripe grapes, with a distinctive perfumed flavour, coming from a combination of four grape varieties, Gros and Petit Manseng, Petit Courbu and Arruffiac. The appellation nearly disappeared earlier this century but is now enjoying something of a revival.

PACIFIC NORTH WEST   USA

A general term to describe the vineyards of the three north American states of Oregon, Washington and Idaho. There are two distinct viticultural areas; the cool foggy coastal area of Oregon and the dry and sunsoaked land of Washington. Wine-making began in the Pacific North West in the 19th century, but until the mid 1960s the wines were mostly fruit wines, and nothing to do with grapes.

PADOUEN   Bordeaux: FRANCE

A little-known Cru Bourgeois Sauternes on the northern edge of Barsac where very good dry and sweet wines are made with great care.

PADTHAWAY See Keppoch.

PAGADEBIT   Emilia-Romagna: ITALY

An unusual off-dry white wine made by Mario Pezzi at Bertinoro from the almost obsolete Pagadebit Gentile grape. It is best drunk as an aperitif.

PAICINES   California: USA

An AVA within San Benito County.

PAIS

The main grape variety of Chile, possibly brought to the country by the Jesuit missionaries in the 16th century. Today it is producing *vin ordinaire* in large quantities from irrigated vineyards and is being replaced by better varieties.

PALATE

In wine terminology, this is the sense of taste. A person who has a fine palate has a perceptive sense of taste. A palate can be trained and educated. 'On the palate' in tasting notes means the taste of the wine, as registered by the taste buds which are situated on the tongue. Sweetness is registered at the tip of the tongue; sourness on the upper edges; bitterness at the back and saltiness at the sides. The palate usually confirms what the taster has already noted about the appearance and smell of a wine.

PALATINATE   GERMANY

This is the English name for the Rheinpfalz region of Germany.

PALE CREAM

Tastes like a cream sherry while looking the pale yellow colour of a *fino*. It is made by blending fino with pale *dulce apagado*. Croft were the first shippers to develop this style of sherry; it is designed to appeal to the snobbery of a preference for sweet wine while wishing to be seen to be drinking a dry wine!

PALETTE   Provence: FRANCE

The tiny appellation of Palette outside Aix-en-Provence is virtually synonymous with one property, Château Simone, which has been owned by the same family for two centuries. The appellation, created in 1948, covers red (50%), white (30%) and rosé (20%). The 20 hectare property of Château Simone is planted mainly with Mourvèdre, Grenache and Syrah for the red and rosé plus tiny quantities of other obscure Provençal grape varieties, as well as Ugni Blanc, Grenache Blanc, Picpoul and various types of Muscat for the white wine. Methods are meticulous and traditional; white wines are fermented and aged in wood; reds are fermented in cement and spend at least two years in wood and are fined with real egg whites. Château Simone prides itself on its tradition.

PALETTE

A wooden or metal cage used in cellars and warehouses for stacking cases of wine.

PALMA

Palma describes a *fino* sherry of the highest quality. As the wine ages, it becomes *dos palmas*, *tres palmas* and even *cuatro palmas*. The classification depends on the shippers' taste and one man's *palma* may be another's *tres palmas*. The term *palma cortado* describes, in the classification of musts, a fuller *fino* tending towards *amontillado*.

PALMELA   PORTUGAL

A wine region in the Arrábida Peninsular just south of Lisbon, a determinate, as opposed to a designated area, and therefore a likely candidate for promotion. The region is particularly suitable for the production of rosé wines.

PALMER   Bordeaux: FRANCE

A third growth Margaux from the commune of Cantenac which is generally thought to rank after Château Margaux in quality and which commands a price accordingly. The property is named after General Palmer, its owner in the early 19th century. It is now divided between the English Sichels, the Dutch Mahler-Besses and the French Miaihles. There is an unusually high proportion of Merlot grapes, 40%, which gives the wine richness and finesse. 1961 was a legendary vintage.

PALO CORTADO   SPAIN

A maverick sherry; it is neither quite an *amontillado*, nor an *oloroso*. It does not develop a *flor*; is quite alcoholic at 17.5° to 23° and according to age can be classified as *dos*, *tres* or *cuatro cortados*. Genuine *palo cortado* is rare and expensive as a *palo cortado solera* is very difficult to operate.

PALOMINO

The grape variety of Jerez, responsible for the best wines of the region. It has travelled to South Africa, California and Australia, where it is also used for sherry style wines and also makes rather flat table wines. In the Midi it is called Listan and produces dull *vin ordinaire* and is tending to disappear from the area.

LA PALOTTE   See Irancy.

PAMID   BULGARIA

A light red, almost rosé wine, made in northern Bulgaria, as well as in the Plovdiv area of the upper Maritsa valley, from the grape of the same name.

PANNONIAN PLAIN HUNGARY

The Pannonian or Great Plain provides half of Hungary's wine. The land is flat and the soil very sandy and therefore phylloxera free. Light white wines are made from Ezerjó, Olaszrizling, Müller-Thurgau and Leányka grapes, while Kadarka and Kekfrancos dominate the black grapes for everyday red wine.

LE PAPE Bordeaux: FRANCE

A little-known, unclassified Graves property in the commune of Léognan, making both red and white wine.

PAPE-CLÉMENT Bordeaux: FRANCE

A Cru Classé Graves from the commune of Pessac and one of the most important vineyards in the region. It was planted, in 1300, by the Archbishop of Bordeaux who, in 1306, became Pope Clément V, the first of the Avignon popes and also the pope of Châteauneuf-du-Pape. Only red wine is produced, using a high proportion of Merlot grapes and no Cabernet Sauvignon. It enjoys a fine reputation.

LA PARDE DE HAUT-BAILLY
Bordeaux: FRANCE

The second wine of Haut-Bailly.

PARDUCCI WINE CELLARS
California: USA

The best known winery of Mendocino is family run by the fourth generation and is especially successful for French Colombard and Petite Sirah, with other varietals in the range.

PARELLADA

One of the white grapes used for sparkling wine in Catalonia, Spain, along with Macebeo and Xarel-lo. As a table wine it is at its best in Torres' Vina Sol, when grown in the cooler vineyards of the upper Penedés.

PAREMPUYRE Bordeaux: FRANCE

One of the riverside communes of the Médoc. It produces very little wine today in its rich alluvial soil.

PARFUM

The French term for 'aroma'.

PARRINA Tuscany: ITALY

A tiny DOC from southern Tuscany. The red is based on Sangiovese grapes and the white on Trebbiano.

PARSAC Bordeaux: FRANCE

One of the so-called 'satellites' of St-Émilion. These surrounding six parishes used to sell their wine as St-Émilion until the appellation was delimited in 1936. The name of the parish was hyphenated onto St-Émilion. In 1973, the growers were given the choice of declaring their wines as Puisseguin and by 1975 the appellation of Parsac had disappeared.

PASADO

A Spanish term used to describe old fino and amontillado of fine quality.

PASCAL Rhône: FRANCE

A leading wine house of the southern Rhône, with vineyards in Vacqueyras and Domaine du Grand Montmirail in Gigondas. In addition they produce good quality Côtes du Rhône and Côtes du Rhône Villages.

PASMADOS PORTUGAL

One of the fine red wines in the portfolio of J. M. da Fonseca, produced from a blend of red grapes of the Alentejo and aged in wood.

PASO ROBLES California: USA

An important town in the county of San Luis Obispo and AVA of the county, that is especially noted for Zinfandel.

PASQUIER DESVIGNES
Burgundy: FRANCE

A *négociant* company based in the Beaujolais region who have diversified into other wines from Burgundy and elsewhere.

PASSAGE AU FROID   See cold stabilisation treatment.

PASSERILLAGE

A process practised in Jurançon in south west France in order to obtain overripe grapes for the sweet wines. The grapes are left hanging on the vines until late in the year so that the juice concentrates as the grapes are dried by the warm autumnal winds from the Pyrenees.

PASSITO

An Italian wine made from grapes which have been semi-dried before pressing so that the juice is more concentrated than usual and the wine is therefore stronger and sweeter than normal.

PASSITO DI CHAMBAVE   See Chambave.

LOUIS PASTEUR

The famous French chemist from Arbois in the Jura who based his researches on the wines of his region. He isolated the microorganisms that cause grape juice to ferment and gave his name to the process of pasteurization.

PASTEURISATION

The practice named after Louis Pasteur of heating wine to about 65-70°C for a few minutes in order to stabilise it and kill any bacteria or remaining yeast. Usually this is done just before bottling and only for cheap bulk wines, not for fine wine. Sometimes a wine, such as Asti Spumante, is heated to a cooler temperature of about 50°C for a longer period, an hour or so, after bottling.

PATA DE GALINA
SPAIN

Means literally hen's foot and describes an *oloroso* sherry with a hint of natural sweetness derived from traces of glycerine.

PATACHE D'AUX
Bordeaux: FRANCE

One of the most important wines of the commune of Bégadan in the Médoc with a good reputation justified by consistent wine-making.

PATERNINA
SPAIN

One of the largest *bodegas* of Rioja, with a modern winery, including a cellar of 53,000 *barricas* for the maturation of 12 million litres of wine. Banda Azul is their popular red; Viña Vial a more mature wine. The white Banda Dorada has been changed from an oak aged to a dry fresh style.

PATRAS
GREECE

The main wine region of the Peloponnese at the north of the gulf of Corinth with four appellations; Muscat of Rion, Mavrodaphne, a liqueur wine named after the grape, Patras and Muscat of Patras. Patras is a simple red wine made from the Rhoditis grape while Muscat of Patras is a rich dessert wine.

PATRIACHE PÈRE & FILS
Burgundy: FRANCE

Patriache are important merchants in Beaune with a dual image. They own the Château de Meursault and several Beaune Premiers Crus and buy regularly at the Hospices de Beaune sales. On the other hand, their bestseller is Kriter, a branded sparkling wine, without any appellation. They have other branded table wines, too.

PATRIMONIO CORSICA

A separate appellation, covering vineyards from around the village of Patrimonio and the town of St. Florent in north west Corsica. The wines are red, dry white and rosé and some vin doux naturel is also made from the Muscat grape but is not as yet entitled to the appellation. The local Nielluccio grape grows especially well on the chalk soil and many red wines are made from that alone. The minimum alcohol is 12.5° with a maximum yield of 45 hectolitres per hectare.

PAUL BOUCHARD   See Bichot.

PAUL MASSON VINEYARDS
California: USA

One of California's largest and oldest wineries. Paul Masson was a Frenchman from Beaune who came to California in 1878. Today they produce an enormous range of wines, with varietals, jug wine, sparkling and dessert wines, even vermouth and brandy. They own vineyards in the Central Valley and Monterey County and buy grapes from all over California; the main winery is at Gonzalez.

PAUILLAC *Bordeaux*: FRANCE

The most important commune in the Médoc for the quantity of fine wine. Three of the five first growths are here: Latour, Lafite and a latecomer, Mouton Rothschild. If the Cabernet Sauvignon grape is characterised by cigar boxes in St-Julien, in Pauillac it is rich blackcurrants. At the other end of the classification there are numerous fifth growths, including Grand Puy Lacoste and Lynch Bages.

PAVEIL DE LUZE *Bordeaux*: FRANCE

A Cru Grand Bourgeois in Margeaux that has belonged to the de Luze family since 1862.

PAVIE *Bordeaux*: FRANCE

The largest of the Premiers Grands Crus Classés of St-Émilion, situated partly on the *côtes* and partly on a sandy plain.

PAVIE-DECESSE *Bordeaux*: FRANCE

A Grand Cru Classé of St-Émilion, adjoining Pavie on the *côtes*.

PAVIE-MACQUIN *Bordeaux*: FRANCE

A Grand Cru Classé of St-Émilion, adjoining Pavie on the *côtes*. Albert Macquin was a pioneer in grafting European vines on to American rootstock.

PAVILLON BLANC *Bordeaux*: FRANCE

The white wine of Château Margaux.

PAVILLON-CADET *Bordeaux*: FRANCE

A little-known Grand Cru Classé of St-Émilion.

PAVILLON ROUGE *Bordeaux*: FRANCE

The second wine of Château Margaux.

PAVLIKENI BULGARIA

A defined Controliran wine region of origin, producing Cabernet Sauvignon, Merlot and Gamza.

PAXARETE SPAIN

A very sweet wine made from the Pedro Ximénez grape, used in the production of cream sherries to add sugar and colour.

PÉCHARMANT SOUTH WEST FRANCE

A small appellation within the zone of Bergerac. The wines are made from the same grape varieties as Bergerac Rouge and include a little Malbec, but are distinguished from Bergerac Rouge by having more tannin and weight and are therefore longer lived. The two best properties are Château Tiregand and Domaine de Haut Pécharmant.

PÉCS HUNGARY

A Hungarian wine district in the south between Lake Balaton and the Yugoslav border. The wines are mainly white from Olaszrizling.

PÉDESCLAUX *Bordeaux*: FRANCE

A fifth growth Pauillac which is one of the more obscure *châteaux* of the 1855 classification, making solid but unexciting wines from vineyards scattered over the commune of Pauillac.

PEDRO XIMENEZ

A white grape grown all over southern Spain. Although it is an ingredient of sherry, it is more important in Montilla, accounting for 95% of the vineyards, as well as for the sweetest Málaga. Elsewhere in southern Spain it makes neutral alcoholic table wine. In Australia it is grown for sherry style wines and is blended with Palomino.

PELURE D'OIGNON

The 'colour of onion skin' describes the colour of *vin gris* or very pale *rosé*.

PEÑAFLOR ARGENTINA

Argentina's largest wine company, based in Mendoza with four modern wineries and a huge range of wines, including the Trapiche and Andean brands.

PENEDÈS SPAIN

One of the most important D.O.s of Spain, covering an area south west of Barcelona. The area is divided by climate and altitude into three sub-regions, Lower Penedès, the hottest region nearest the coast, which is best for red grapes; Middle Penedès at an altitude of 200 metres where white Xarel-lo and Macabeo are grown for sparkling wine, and finally the higher and cooler Upper Penedès where Parellada and other white grapes are successful. Penedès is particularly known for its *cava* wines, but also has some good producers of table wine, notably Torres, Masía Bach and Jean Léon.

PENFOLDS AUSTRALIA

Penfolds is one of the largest wine companies of Australia with a reputation based upon their Grange Hermitage. Dr. Penfold settled in Magill in 1844 and began making wine for his anaemic patients. Today the company's wineries are extensive: Auldana, Modbury and Kalimna are individual vineyards in South Australia. They have interest in the Barossa Valley with their ownership of the Barossa Cooperative Winery and in the Hunter Valley, McLaren Vale, the M.I.A., Coonawarra, and Clare Valley. They are an enormous sparkling wine producer. They, in turn, are now owned by the brewers, Tooth & Co. Their red wines are particularly good, with Cabernets and Cabernet Shiraz blends; St. Henri Claret is a great red; Minchinbury Champagne a good sparkling wine and Grandfather's Port was legend amongst Australian port. Magill remains the company's headquarters, while Nuriootpa in Barossa is their main production centre. Penfolds also have a small interest in New Zealand, relying on contract growers for their grapes. Autumn Riesling-Silvaner is their best white wine and there are other sound white varietals.

PENNSYLVANIA USA

The south eastern part of the state of Pennsylvania has just a few wineries with pockets of *vitis vinifera* vines, such as Allegro Vineyards, as well as the easier hybrids.

PENSHURST ENGLAND

Near Tunbridge Wells in Kent, this is a small vineyard planted mainly with Müller-Thurgau and Reichensteiner grapes. There is a wallaby on the label, to maintain the owner's Australian connections.

PENTRO Molise: ITALY

Also called Pentro di Isernia, one of the two DOC Molise wines from the province of Isernia. The red and *rosato* are made from Montepulciano and Sangiovese grapes and the white is made from Trebbiano Toscano and Bombino Bianco grapes.

PEPPERY

Describes a characteristic in raw young red wine which will mellow in time. Some red Rhône wines are described as peppery.

PERGOLE TRENTINE

Used, particularly in the Trentino region of Italy, to train the vines. They are L-shaped supports, extending the vine away from the hillside, allowing the foliage the maximum exposure to sunlight.

PERIQUITA

A red grape variety grown all over southern Portugal; it ages well and is at its best as a constituent of J. M. da Fonseca's branded wine, Periquita. There are plans for the area of production to be demarcated as Arrabida.

PERLAN
SWITZERLAND

The name used in the canton of Geneva for the grape variety, Chasselas.

PERLANT
Another term for pétillant.

PERLÉ
Another term for pétillant or perlant.

PERLE
The Perle grape is a German Gewürztraminer x Müller-Thurgau crossing, giving flowery wine and planted mainly in Franconia. It is usefully resistant to spring frost.

PERLWEIN
German semi-sparkling *Tafelwein*, produced by artificially carbonating the wine, or possibly by the *charmat* method. It is a way of livening up dull table wine.

PERNAND VERGELESSES
Burgundy: FRANCE

A predominantly red wine village, although it has a reputation for its Aligoté. However, part of the vineyards of Corton Charlemagne, as well as Corton, fall within its boundaries. Its Premier Cru vineyards are Île de Vergelesses, les Basses Vergelesses, Creux de la Net (part), les Fichots and en Caradeux (part).

The main growers are Domaine Bonneau de Martray, P. Dubreuil. Fontaine Père et Fils and Robert Rapet et Fils.

PERONOSPERA
A synonym for 'downy mildew'.

PERPETUELLE
This is a Cahors tradition, now carried on only by one grower, Jean Jouffreau. Some wine from the greatest years is kept in oak barrels that are regularly topped up, but never bottled. The results are amazing.

PERRIER-JOUËT
Champagne: FRANCE

A fine champagne house, whose prestige *cuvée*, Belle Époque, is distinctive due to its Art Nouveau bottle.

PERSISTENCE
The French term for 'length'.

PERU
Has just one winery, Tacama Vineyards in the Ica province. The country would normally be too hot for successful viticulture, but these vineyards benefit from the influence of the cool Pacific Ocean. Cabernet Sauvignon, Sauvignon Blanc and a *méthode champenoise* wine are their successes.

PESQUERA
SPAIN

A rising star amongst Spanish wines, in the D.O. of Ribera del Duero. Alejandro Fernandez has planted Tempranillo on the banks of the Duero and makes two wines, one that is aged in American oak for one year, and a riserva which is aged in American oak for two years.

PESSAC-LÉOGNAN
Bordeaux: FRANCE

A new appellation since 1987 that covers the most important part of the Graves, that is closest to the city of Bordeaux and contains fifty-five estates including all the classed growths of the Graves.

PETALUMA
AUSTRALIA

One of the most important wineries of South Australia, establishing with Brian Croser, one of Australia's leading winemakers, and with the participation of Bollinger, a reputation for champagne method sparkling wine made from Pinot Noir and Chardonnay. Still wines are produced too, notably Rhine Riesling from the Clare Valley and a predominantly Cabernet with Shiraz blend.

PÉTILLANT

A French term for 'slightly sparkling', which usually describes wines which owe their sparkle to the unfermented sugar in the wine when it was bottled, which has subsequently fermented and produced a small amount of carbon dioxide. The maximum pressure for a *pétillant* wine in France is two atmospheres.

PÉTILLANT DE RAISIN
SOUTH WEST FRANCE

A refreshing, very slightly alcoholic drink that has been made in the Gaillac region since the 1950s and is often more advertised by small growers than their wines. The grape juice, from the Mauzac grape only is flash pasteurised and bottled under sterile conditions at a communal plant.

PETIT CHABLIS Burgundy: FRANCE

The lowest category of Chablis. It is intended to describe the wine produced from the lesser vineyards of the area. The name sounds deprecating, almost petty rather than *petit*, and its commercial success is doubtful. Consequently, many of the better sites have been ungraded into Chablis and the area of Petit Chablis is declining.

PETIT CHÂTEAU

A general term used by Bordeaux merchants to describe a property from one of the outlying appellations such as Côtes de Bourg, Côtes de Franc and so on, which have no official status in the hierarchy of Bordeaux, but make good honest claret. Any good wine merchant should offer a list of *petits châteaux*, clarets which are ready to drink earlier and are much less expensive than the great names, but none the less enjoyable for that.

PETIT-FAURIE-DE-SOUTARD
Bordeaux: FRANCE

A Grand Cru Classé of St-Émilion, once part of Château Soutard.

PETIT MESLIER

A white grape variety, grown in limited quantities in the Aube district of Champagne, but it is gradually being replaced by other varieties as it is sensitive to rot and *coulure* and susceptible to frost.

PETIT VERDOT

A grape variety which forms a small part of the Bordelais blend of the Médoc. Some châteaux have abandoned it completely, while others retain about 5% in their blend. It gives colour, tannin and alcohol, but is a late ripener and unsatisfactory in poorer years. Some attempts are also being made to grow it in California.

PETIT VILLAGE Bordeaux: FRANCE

Generally considered to be one of the top Pomerol properties, owned by the Prats family of Cos d'Estournel. The vineyards include a high proportion of Cabernet Sauvignon grapes.

PETITE ARVINE See Arvine.

LA PETITE MONTAGNE
Champagne: FRANCE

A less-favoured part of the vineyards of Champagne.

PETITE SIRAH

The more common synonym for the Durif grape variety of the southern Rhône. In fact, in France, it is hardly ever found, while in California it is widely grown, mainly in Monterey and San Joaquin where it makes fairly tannic fruity wines.

PÉTRUS Bordeaux: FRANCE

The star of the Pomerol *châteaux*, never officially classified, but recognised as equal to the first growths of the Médoc. The vineyard is only 11 hectares, planted 95% with Merlot grapes which thrive on the clay soil of the property. The *château* is owned partly by the Loubat family and partly by the company of J.-P. Moueix of Libourne. It is their oenologist who makes the wine, with meticulous care and great talent. The resulting wine commands a price higher than the first growths of the Médoc.

PEWSEY VALE AUSTRALIA

One of the new vineyards of the Hill Smith family in the hills above the Barossa Valley, with a cooler climate.

PROFESSOR ÉMILE PEYNAUD

Past head of the oenology department of Bordeaux University who, in retirement, advises numerous wine makers, not only in Bordeaux, but as far afield as Greece and Spain.

PEYRABON *Bordeaux*: FRANCE

A Cru Grand Bourgeois and the largest property in St-Saveur, Haut-Médoc.

DE PEZ *Bordeaux*: FRANCE

A Cru Bourgeois and one of the leading properties of St-Estèphe. The high proportion of Cabernet Sauvignon grapes gives the wine considerable richness and concentration.

PEZA GREECE

A full-bodied sweet red wine from Crete, made from indigenous grape varieties, which are generally called Mavro Romeiko, as well as Kotsifali for bouquet and body and Mandilari for colour.

PHÉLAN-SÉGUR *Bordeaux*: FRANCE

A Cru Bourgeois Exceptionnel and one of the most important properties of St-Estèphe. The estate was created by M. Phélan, partly from land belonging to the Marquis de Ségur.

JOSEPH PHELPS VINEYARDS *California*: USA

Joseph Phelps Vineyards have been in operation since 1972. Their first winemaker, Walter Schug, created the winery's reputation for Johannisberg Riesling, as is fitting for a graduate of Geisenheim. They have achieved great things with the Syrah grape; Cabernet Sauvignon is good too.

PHENOLIC COMPOUNDS

Phenolic compounds are the aromatic substances found in the stalks, pips and skins of grapes. There are two types, anthocyans and tannins.

PHOSPHORUS

A necessary soil constituent for a healthy vine, helping in the conversion of starch to sugar, strengthening the roots and encouraging the production of flowers and then fruit.

PHYLLOXERA

A disease of the vine, caused and spread by an aphid, the *phylloxera vastatrix*, which attacks the roots of vines. It was brought to Europe from the United States and did enormous damage to the vineyards of France in the 1870s. It has now spread all over Europe and to many of the vineyards of the New World. The only cure is to graft *vitis vinifera* on to American rootstocks which are resistant to phylloxera.

LE PIAN MÉDOC *Bordeaux*: FRANCE

One of the communes within the Haut-Médoc appellation, but it produces very little wine.

PIAT *Burgundy*: FRANCE

An important *négociant* company dealing in the wines of Beaujolais and the Mâconnais. They use a special bottle based on the Beaujolais *pot* and have an important red and white brand, Piat d'Or.

PIAT D'OR

A leading French table wine brand, both red and white, produced by the company of Piat in the Beaujolais.

PIAVE *Veneto*: ITALY

A large DOC zone in the eastern Veneto, covering vineyards on either side of the river Piave. There are four varieties: Cabernet del Piave, from Cabernet Sauvignon and/or Franc grapes, which becomes *riserva* after three years; Merlot del Piave, the most important, aged for two years; Tocai del Piave, a light wine, and Verduzzo del Piave with more acidity and character.

ALBERT PIC *Burgundy*: FRANCE

Was a famous Chablis company, bought in 1957 by A. Régnard et Fils when the last member of the Pic family died. The name is now used as a *sous marque* for Régnard.

PIC ST-LOUP

The Midi: FRANCE

Formerly a VDQS, Pic St-Loup is now part of the new appellation of Coteaux du Languedoc, taking its name from a 2000 foot peak to the north of Montpelier. It is predominantly a red wine, made from Carignan, Grenache and Cinsaut grapes with some Syrah and Mourvèdre.

PICARDIN

A white grape permitted in Châteauneuf-du-Pape and not found anywhere else. Picardin Noir can be a synonym for Cinsaut.

PICCONE

Piedmont: ITALY

A robust red wine made from Nebbiolo, Vespolina and Bonarda grapes grown in the Vercelli hills by Fabrizio Sella.

PICHET

A small receptacle, usually in the form of a pottery jug, used for serving unbottled wine in a French restaurant. In England, the equivalent is a carafe.

PICHON-LONGUEVILLE BARON

Bordeaux: FRANCE

A second growth Pauillac which shared the same history as its neighbour, Pichon Longueville Comtesse de Lalande, until part of the estate was inherited by the Comtesse de Lalande. Pichon Baron, as it is generally called, makes tougher wines than its neighbour.

PICHON-LONGUEVILLE COMTESSE DE LALANDE

Bordeaux: FRANCE

A second growth Pauillac which shared the same history as its neighbour, Pichon-Longueville Baron, until part of the estate was inherited by the Comtesse de Lalande. Pichon Lalande or Pichon Comtesse, as it is generally called, is a smooth, perfumed wine, with a high proportion of Merlot grapes. The second wine is called Réserve de la Comtesse.

PICO   see Azores.

PICOLIT

Friuli-Venezia Giulia: ITALY

One of Italy's best dessert wines. It is one of the wines of the Colli Orientali del Friuli DOC. Production is tiny as the Picolit vine suffers from pollination deficiencies. Alcohol is a minimum of 15° and the taste is sweet or medium sweet with a gentle honeyed flavour. Two years' ageing is necessary for a *riserva*.

PICPOUL

A dull white grape, at its best in Picpoul de Pinet. It is also allowed in Châteauneuf-du-Pape. Picpoul Noir is also grown in the Midi, but is not of any importance.

PICPOUL DE PINET

The Midi: FRANCE

Formerly a VDQS, Picpoul de Pinet is now part of the new appellation of the Coteaux du Languedoc. It is a dry white wine, made predominantly from the Picpoul grape grown in the vineyards around the town of Pinet, just outside Béziers. The cave cooperative is the main producer.

PIÈCE

The traditional barrels from several regions of France. In Burgundy it holds from 212 to 228 litres; in Champagne 205 litres; in the Loire Valley about 220 litres and in Châteauneuf du Pape 225 litres.

PIED D'ALOUP   See Montée de Tonnerre.

PIED DE CUVE

If a vat is slow to start fermenting of its own accord, it may be helped by the addition of a *pied de cuve*, which is prepared by picking the grapes of a few vines, just before the main harvest, warming the must until the fermentation starts and a large quantity of yeast develops. This is then added to the first vats to start the fermentation.

PIEDMONT

ITALY

Piedmont is one of Italy's most important wine-producing regions, with 26 DOCs and 2 DOCGs though, in volume terms, it is only sixth in the regional line-up. Red wine is more important than white. The Nebbiolo grape produces the finest red wines, such as Barolo and Barbaresco. Barbera and Dolcetto make more every day wines. In white wine there is Cortese, at its best made from Gavi, and Asti Spumante from the Moscato grape. The main vineyard areas are in the Langhe and Monferrato hills around Alba, Asti and Alessandria and in the foothills south of the Valle d'Aosta producing Gattinara, Ghemme and Lessona.

PIERCE'S DISEASE

A vine disease found in California. The leaves turn yellow, the fruit wilts and the vine ultimately dies. The disease is spread by insects which can be eliminated with insecticides.

PIEROPAN   Veneto: ITALY

A family company generally considered to produce one of the best Soave. The family's Riesling Italico is good, too.

PIERRE À FUSIL   See gunflint.

PIESPORT   Mosel-Saar-Ruwer: GERMANY

One of the best-known villages of the Mosel. Its most famous vineyard is Goldtröpfchen, 'a little drop of gold', in this case sunshine. The *Grosslage* (large vineyard area) is Michelsberg and other important *Einzellagen* (individual registered and numbered vineyards within the *Grosslagen*) are Guntersly, Treppchen and Falkenberg. Good producers include Vereinigten Hospitien, Bischöfliches Konvikt and von Kesselstatt.

PIGATO

The Pigato grape is used to produce dry white wine on the Italian Ligurian coast.

PIGEAGE

The traditional way of mixing the grape skins with the fermenting must, by gently squashing the grapes with human feet, possibly clad in gumboots.

PIGNOLETTO   See Colli Bolognesi.

PIKETBERG   SOUTH AFRICA

Piketberg, or Piquetberg, is a small Wine of Origin district, north of Tulbagh, towards the Olifantsrivier. Irrigation is needed in the vineyards and the high temperatures produce dessert wines or wine for distillation.

LES PILIERS CHABLISIENS
Burgundy: FRANCE

The Chablis wine brotherhood whose main object is to promote Chablis with various ceremonies throughout the year and an annual *Fête du Vin* on the fourth Sunday in November.

PILTON MANOR   ENGLAND

A vineyard with a good reputation near Shepton Mallet in Somerset, planted in 1966, mainly with Müller-Thurgau and Seyval Blanc vines.

PINARD

The French slang word to describe a coarse rough red wine.

PINEAU D'AUNIS

A lesser red grape variety of the Loire Valley, no relation to Pinot and grown mainly in Anjou and Touraine, usually for rosé wine.

PINEAU DES CHARENTES

An aperitif produced in the Cognac area from unfermented grape juice, which is prevented from fermenting by the addition of Cognac. Technically it is a ratafia.

PINEAU DE LA LOIRE   see Chenin Blanc

PINENC

A synonym used in Madiran and Béarn for the Fer or Fer Servadou grape.

PINHEL   PORTUGAL

Pinhel is a proposed demarcated wine region of Portugal. It is in the Beiras province, adjacent to Dão and has long been known for its white wines, although reds dominate the production in quantity.

PINOT AUXERROIS   See Auxerrois

PINOT BEUROT

A name used in the Côte d'Or, France, for the small amount of the Pinot Gris grape that is grown in the area.

PINOT BIANCO   see Pinot Blanc

PINOT BLANC

This grape is the white version of Pinot Noir, but nowhere does it produce wines of such interest. That role is taken by Chardonnay. Pinot Blanc is an established variety in Alsace for simple table wine, possibly part of an Edelzwicker blend, or as a base for Crémant d'Alsace. Pinot Blanc can also be found in the Côte d'Or in tiny quantity.

In Germany and Austria Pinot Blanc is called Weissburgunder. Some is produced in Baden and in the Palatinate, sometimes as *trocken* or *halbtrocken* wines. In Austria it is found near the Yugoslav border and is popular across the frontier, notably in Slovenia and Slavonia, as Belic Pinot. There is a little in Hungary too.

In Italy there has been some confusion between Pinot Bianco and Chardonnay and often an indistinguishable mixture of the two has been planted. Most Pinot Blanc is found in Friuli, the Veneto, Trentino and Alto Adige, but it has spread further south. It is used for sparkling wines, notably in the Oltrepò Pavese.

There is confusion in the New World too. Most Australian Pinot Blanc is really Chardonnay, while most South African Chardonnay is probably Pinot Blanc. In California there is a little serious oak-aged Pinot Blanc, from Chalone vineyards.

PINOT DROIT

This grape variety is one of the many types of Pinot Noir found in Burgundy, so called because the vines grow up straight, rather than trailing along the ground. Yields are large and regular but the resulting wine is dull and insipid.

PINOT GRIGIO

The Italian term for the Pinot Gris grape.

PINOT GRIS

A grape, whose synonyms include Ruländer, Tokay d'Alsace, Pinot Beurot, Pinot Grigio and Szürkebarat and is at its best in Alsace, France, where it produces a lightly spicey wine, which in the best years will have *noble rot*, be vinified as *Vendange Tardive or Sélection des Grains Nobles* and have considerable ageing potential. An insignificant amount is grown in Burgundy and there are scattered amounts elsewhere in eastern France. In Germany, as the Ruländer, it produces aromatic wines, fuller and heavier than Riesling. In Italy it enjoys a certain favour as Pinot Grigio, especially in Friuli-Venezia Giulia and also in the Alto Adige, the Oltrepò Pavese and in the Colli Piacentini of Emilia Romagna.

Switzerland has some Pinot Gris, under the name of Malvoisie in the Valais; there is some too in Luxembourg, Austria, Yugoslavia and Roumania. In Hungary it goes under the name of Szürkebarat and is successfully grown near Lake Balaton. In the New World it has had little impact, with a few plantings in California, Australia and New Zealand.

The grape itself is neither red nor white; it makes its best wines in a cooler climate where the fruit and flavour is allowed to develop.

PINOT MEUNIER   See Meunier

PINOT NERO

The Italian term for the Pinot Noir grape.

PINOT NOIR

The grape variety of fine red Burgundy and also plays an important part in champagne. It is an elusive grape variety; its characteristics are hard to define and it does not have the adaptability of Cabernet Sauvignon. It is difficult to grow and especially susceptible to rot. It enjoys a long growing season in a cool climate and is not so successful in hotter countries, hence its better results in Oregon than in California.

Pinot Noir is at its best in the hands of the top producers of the Côte d'Or, where it will have a sweetness of flavour reminiscent of raspberries, with undertones of vegetables and chocolate. The colour is never very deep. It will mature well with oak ageing and can attain great heights, but less reliably than Cabernet Sauvignon and can often disappoint.

As well as on the Côte d'Or and Côte Chalonnaise and in the Mâconnais, it is grown in the Yonne in Irancy and Coulanges-la-Vineuse. It forms an important part of the champagne blend, at its best in the villages of the Montagne de Reims and also for still *coteaux champenois* like Bouzy. Elsewhere in France, it features in the rosé and red wines of Sancerre, occasionally in Côtes de Toul gris; it is accepted as one of the grapes of Alsace, more often as a rosé than a red wine and is also grown in the Jura and in Savoie.

Across the Rhine in Germany it makes some of the red wines of the Rhine, notably at Assmannshausen and in the Ahr, as Spätburgunder, and also in Baden and Wurttemberg. The same Prädikat categories apply as for the white wines, giving a curiously sweet flavour. Pinot Noir has also crossed the English channel; one grower in the Thames Valley makes it and it is also found south of the Alps, growing in the cool Alto Adige and over north eastern Italy as Pinot Nero. The Oltrepò Pavese uses it for sparkling wine and there is some grown in the Aosta valley.

In Switzerland it is a constituent of Dôle and also features as a single varietal.

Pinot Noir is planted in eastern Europe; Austria has a little; it is grown in Yugoslavia as Burgundac Crni and in Hungary as Nagyburgundi at Villany. It has crossed the Atlantic to California, where it enjoys some success in the cooler regions of the state, notably in Los Carneros. Cooler Oregon produces much better results, more elegant wines than the heavy Californian versions. Success has been limited in Australia too, with Tyrell's Hunter Pinot Noir and in the Margaret River. Some is grown in New Zealand and in South Africa as well as a little in Chile.

PINOT ST. GEORGE

A synonym for the Négrette grape in California, where it makes rather uninteresting wine.

PINOTAGE

A peculiarly South African grape variety, a cross of Pinot Noir and Cinsaut developed in 1925. If it is not allowed to overproduce it makes warm earthy red wine.

PIPE

A large cask used as the traditional measure for buying, storing and selling port. The exact size of the pipe varies according to purpose. A Douro pipe holds 550 litres, for the traditional formula is 440 parts must to 110 parts brandy. Lodge pipes vary between 580 and 620 litres and a shipping pipe is 534 litres.

PIPER HEIDSIECK   *Champagne*: FRANCE

A popular champagne and one of the *grandes marques*. Florens Louis is the luxury *cuvée*; a dry wine with no dosage is called Brut Sauvage. The family is related to Charles Heidsieck and Heidsieck Monopole.

PIPETTE

An instrument for obtaining wine from a barrel or vat. The wine is sucked up the thin glass tube from the vat like a straw and a thumb is held over the top while the wine is transferred to the glass.

PIQUÉ

The French term for 'pricked'.

PIQUEPOUL   see Picpoul

PIQUETTE

A general term for any mediocre wine, and more precisely, it is a wine made by adding water to pressed grape skins. It is very low in alcohol, thin and tart.

PIQÛRE

A wine ailment; a grey film appears on the surface of the wine, turning the alcohol into vinegar.

JOÃO PIRES
PORTUGAL

A wine company that produces a pure dry Muscat wine from the Portuguese Setúbal peninsular under that name. It is also known for two other wines, Tinta da Anfora, from the Alentejo, which is a blend of Periquita, Trincadeira, Aragonez and Moreto, aged in oak and chestnut barrels for a few months, and Quinta da Bacalhao in the Azeitao. The vineyard is planted with 90% Cabernet and 10% Merlot and the wine is aged in new oak for between 9 and 14 months.

PLAFONDE LIMITE DE CLASSEMENT

Translates literally as 'classification ceiling' and allows an extra percentage, usually 20% on top of the annual yield, provided that the wine is of satisfactory quality. If not, the production of the vineyard is declassified into table wine.

PLANTS NOBLES

Describes true *vitis vinifera* plants for wines of quality, as opposed to any hybrid vines for *vin ordinaire*.

PLAVAC MALI

The principal red grape variety of Dalmatia in Yugoslavia, making most notably Postup, Dingač and Faros wine. The basic red wine of the Dalmatian coast is also simply called Plavac.

PLETTENBERG
Nahe: GERMANY

Or Reichsgräflich von Plettenberg'sche Verwaltung is an important family estate going back to the 18th century. Their main vineyards are at Bad Kreuznach and Schlossböckelheim. They are planted with 65% Riesling grapes and the balance is Müller-Thurgau and other new varieties. They are vinified in modern cellars.

PLEURS

The tears which come from a vine after it has been pruned, when the sap rises.

PLINCE
Bordeaux: FRANCE

A second growth Pomerol *château*, which was once well-known in England.

PLONK

A slang word used for any cheap, but not necessarily cheerful red or white wine. The origin of the word is uncertain, possibly from World War I army slang for *vin blanc*, in cockney rhyming style as 'plink plonk'. It has also been associated with Australian soldiers in France.

PNEUMATIC PRESS   See press.

PODENSAC
Bordeaux: FRANCE

One of the three communes of the Cérons appellation.

LA POINTE
Bordeaux: FRANCE

A large Pomerol *château*, coming in the second growth and producing some excellent wine from gravel and sand vineyards close to Libourne.

POL ROGER
Champagne: FRANCE

A small champagne house associated with Winston Churchill. On his death, the label was given a black border.

POLLINO
Calabria: ITALY

A red DOC wine, made from Gaglioppo and Greco Nero grapes grown around Monte Pollino. It is *superiore* after two years' ageing and develops well after some bottle age.

POLYPHENOLS

Another term for phenolic compounds, the colouring matter in red wine. They are composed of anthocyanins and tannins.

POMACE   See *marc*.

MARQUÉS DE POMBAL

The Marqués de Pombal, as well as being Prime Minister to the Portuguese king Joseph I, had a long-lasting effect on the development of port, by establishing the demarcated area of the Douro and by founding the Royal Oporto Wine Company, which had the sole right to distil grape brandy and controlled all grape prices. These measures considerably improved the quality of port.

POMEROL Bordeaux: FRANCE

The smallest of the main Bordeaux wine regions. It adjoins St-Émilion, taking its name from the village at the centre of the vineyards. Until about a hundred years ago, the wines were hardly known outside their own locality and it was only during the 1960s that they really acquired any international reputation. Unlike the other important appellations of Bordeaux, the principal *châteaux* have never been classified. It is, however, accepted that Pétrus equals the first growths of the Médoc in quality and nowadays far outstrips them in price. The soil of the best *châteaux* is a mixture of gravel and clay. The *encépagement* is similar to St-Émilion, with a high percentage of Merlot and Cabernet Franc grapes, rather than Cabernet Sauvignon. The wines of Pomerol are often described as a cross between the Médoc and St-Émilion; they have the richness of St-Émilion, but less alcohol and tannin than Médoc and, in reality, an individuality of their own.

POMINO Tuscany: ITALY

A small red and white DOC, whose production is dominated by Frescobaldi. Grape varieties are unusual: Pinot Bianco and Grigio, Chardonnay and Sauvignon for white; Sangiovese, Canaiolo, Cabernet Franc and Cabernet Sauvignon, Merlot and other French varieties for the red. Both can be very good, especially when barrel-aged.

POMMARD Burgundy: FRANCE

An important village on the Côte de Beaune. It has suffered from the popularity and pronounceability of its name to the extent that wines of doubtful origin used to be sold as Pommard because demand far outstripped supply.

The vineyards are split in two, on hillsides which are on either side of the village. To the south with east-facing slopes are the Premiers Crus vineyards of les Rugiens, les Rugiens Haut (part), les Croix Noires, les Chaponières, les Fremiers, le Clos Micot, Derrière Saint-Jean, les Chanlins Bas (part) and les Combes Dessus (part).

To the north of the village, where the wines are a little lighter, are the Premiers Crus of les Petits Epenots (part), Clos de la Commaraine, les Epenots, Clos Blanc, les Arvelets, les Charmots, les Argillières, les Pézerolles, les Boucherottes, les Saucilles, la Refène, Clos de Verger, la Platière (part) and la Chanière (part). The most impressive building in the village is the Château de Commaraine which dates back to 1180 and is now owned by the shippers Jaboulet Vercherre. There is a more modern Château de Pommard.

POMMÉRY & GRENO Champagne: FRANCE

A champagne house based in Reims with large vineyard holdings and nine miles of chalk cellars that were excavated by the Romans.

PRINCE PONIATOWSKY Loire: FRANCE

One of the great names of Vouvray, making wines of considerable ageing potential from two vineyards, Clos Baudoin and Aigle Blanc.

PIERRE PONNELLE Burgundy: FRANCE

A small Burgundian house based outside Beaune with vineyards in Musigny, Bonnes Mares, Charmes-Chambertin, Clos Vougeot, Corton Clos du Roi and Beaune Grèves.

PONTAC

A red grape variety found in South Africa. It was introduced to the country early in its history and may have been named after the Pontac family who were important landowners in the Médoc. It has contributed to Constantia and South African port but is now disappearing as its yields are low and the vines have little resistance to disease.

PONTAC-MONPLAISIR
Bordeaux: FRANCE

A Graves from the commune of Villenave d'Ornon, a little-known property making good red and white wine.

PONTET-CANET
Bordeaux: FRANCE

A fifth growth Pauillac. This is a large, well-known estate with a somewhat tarnished reputation. 1929 was a great wine, but the wine was not *château*-bottled until 1972. It is now owned by the Tesseron family of Lafon Rochet in St-Estèphe.

POP WINE

An American term for a beverage that is not strictly wine. It may include some wine, but is more often made from other fruits and flavourings and may also be carbonated.

POPE VALLEY
California: USA

Part of the county of Napa, in the hills to the east of Calistoga. As it is technically outside the geographical delimitation of the Napa Valley, it is seeking its own appellation.

PORT
PORTUGAL

The most famous Portuguese wine and known as the Englishman's wine for the English played an important part in its development. Even today the port trade is dominated by British names, Graham, Cockburn, Warre, Sandeman, Taylor and so on. Port is a fortified wine. It is produced in a demarcated area of the Douro valley and made from a mixture of grape varieties. The most important are Bastardo, Mourisco, Touriga Francesca, Donzelinho Tinto, Tinta Roriz, Tinta Cão, Touriga Nacional and Tinta Francisca for red port. The fermentation is stopped by the addition of brandy to retain some sweetness in the wine. It is then aged for a varying length of time, depending on the desired style of port. A variety of alternatives are possible, according to the quality of the young wine. A vintage may be declared, or it may be a Late Bottled Vintage, Vintage Character or Crusted, Ruby or Tawny, which may be young, or aged in wood for several years. A small amount of white port is made too. The French drink port as an aperitif; in England it is very much an after dinner drink, to sip on its own, or maybe with stilton and walnuts.

PORT FUNNEL

A funnel used for decanting port, usually with a piece of muslin inserted to catch the sediment. Traditional port funnels were made of silver or silver-plated and could be very elaborate and ornate, or elegant and plain.

PORT WINE INSTITUTE
see Instituto do Vinho do Porto.

PORTE GREFFE

The French term for 'rootstock'.

PORTETS
Bordeaux: FRANCE

An important commune within the Graves, with several good estates.

PORTLANDIAN

A calcareous clay and one of the soil constituents of the vineyards of Chablis. Purists maintain that it does not produce wine as good as that from the similar kimmeridge soil, so vineyards of Petit Chablis tend to be on portlandian soil.

PORTO VECCHIO
CORSICA

Porto Vecchio is one of the separate areas within the overall appellation Vin de Corse. The area around the town of Porto Vecchio was extensively planted by the wine growers returning from Algeria, but most of the vineyards have since been pulled up, leaving just one successful estate, Domaine de Torraccia. The dry white wine is made mainly from Malvoisie de Corse and the rosé and red principally from Nielluccio and Grenache.

PORTUGAIS BLEU

The French synonym for Blauer Portugieser. In France it is one of the many grape varieties allowed in red Gaillac from south west France.

PORTUGAL

The vineyards of Portugal cover a large part of the country and are full of hidden potential. First and foremost there is Port, the fortified wine from the Douro which includes a range of styles from basic ruby to fine vintage Port. Madeira is the other significant fortified wine.

In 1988 there were ten demarcated areas: Madeira, Port, Bairrada, Douro – for table wine, Vinho Verde,

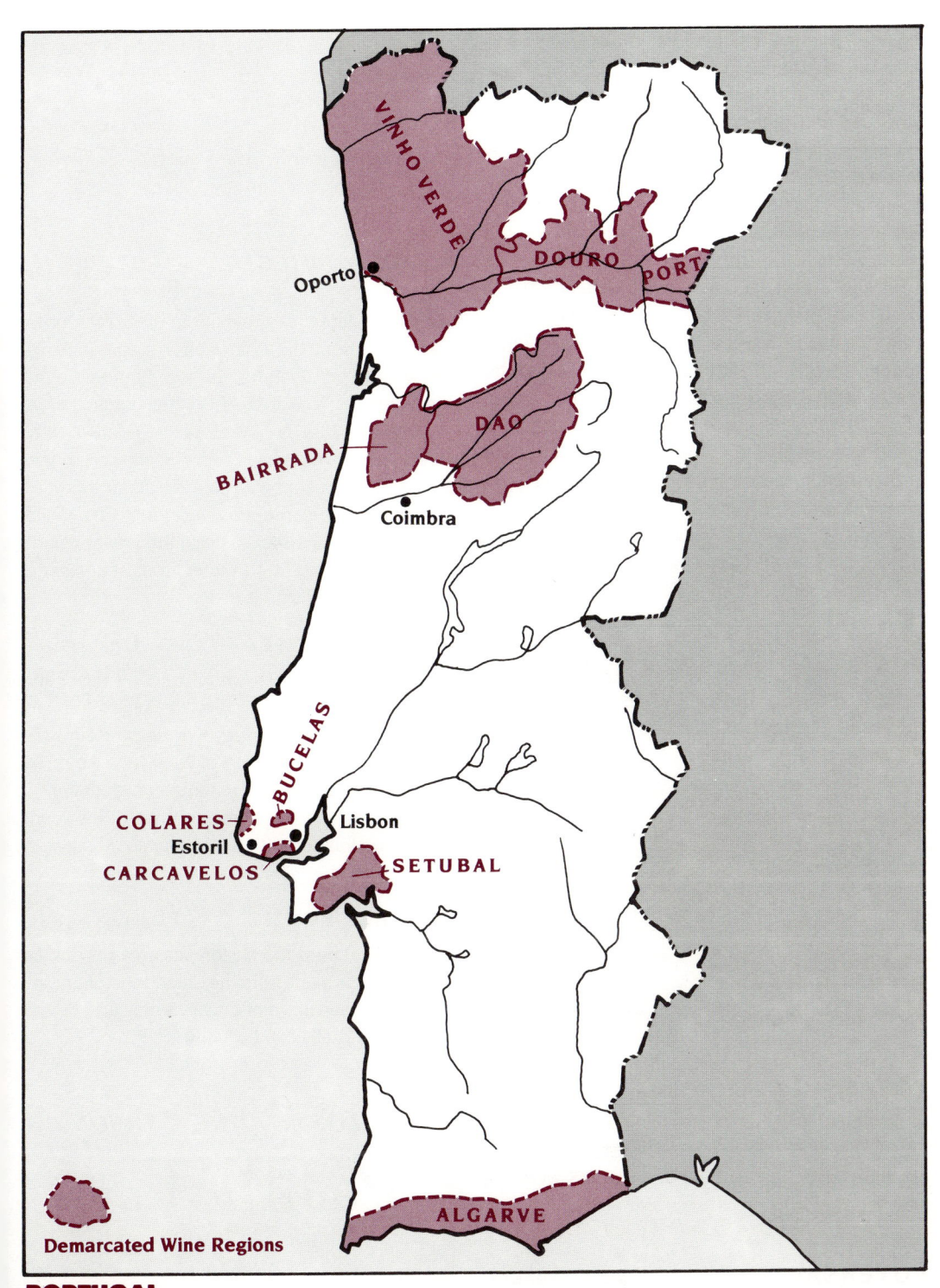

PORTUGAL

VINHO VERDE
DOURO
PORT
Oporto
BAIRRADA
DÃO
Coimbra
BUCELAS
COLARES
Lisbon
Estoril
CARCAVELOS
SETÚBAL
ALGARVE

Demarcated Wine Regions

PORTUGAL

267

Dão, Bucelas, Colares, Setúbal and Carcavelos. The region of Alentejo has five determinate areas and there are a further 20 in the pipeline.

Vinho Verde is Portugal's most popular white wine. Dão and increasingly Bairrada are important red wines. In addition there are other *denominacão de origem*, little known wines from around Lisbon, Colares, Carcavelos and Bucelas, and a sweet dessert wine, Setúbal, as well as the table wines of the Douro.

Portugal's best known wine is Mateus Rosé, a pretty fizzy pink wine that has been imitated by others, notably Lancers. The best reds are often from no specific area; a reputable producer and the word *garrafeira* denote a stylish mature wine. A mass of basic table wine is also produced in Portugal for the climate is kind to grapes, with the influence of the Atlantic ocean bringing warm summers and sufficient rain.

Portuguese wines are making a growing impact abroad, and their future is rosy, especially as vinification methods improve.

POŠIP   YUGOSLAVIA

A dry, full-bodied alcoholic white wine made on the island of Korčula off the Dalmatian coast from the grape of the same name.

POSTUP   YUGOSLAVIA

A full-bodied sweet red wine made from the Plavac Mali grape grown north of Dubrovnik with about 15° alcohol and aged in oak barrels for years.

POT

The 50 centilitre bottle size peculiar to Beaujolais.

POTASSIUM

In the soil of a vineyard this affects cell growth and enzyme activity in the vine. It is essential for ripening the wood of the vine and for developing shoots for next year's crop.

POTENSAC   Bordeaux: FRANCE

A Médoc Cru Bourgeois. One of the best wines of the commune of Ordonnac and enjoys a fine reputation under the ownership of the Delon family of Léoville-Lascases.

POTTER VALLEY   California: USA

An AVA in Mendocino County, inland near the Russian River.

POUGET   Bordeaux: FRANCE

A little-known fourth growth Margaux in the commune of Cantenac run by the owners of Boyd Cantenac.

POUILLY FUISSÉ   Burgundy: FRANCE

One of the white wine appellations of the Mâconnais. It is made from the Chardonnay grape, grown in the villages of Chaintré, Fuissé, Pouilly, Solutré and Vergisson. The rock of Solutré dominates the countryside. This is where primitive man drove thousands of wild horses over the cliff top to their deaths 75,000 years ago. There are single vineyards worthy of note in the area, including Château de Fuissé. Pouilly Fuissé has acquired a popularity which has caused it to suffer from the vagaries of extreme price fluctuations.

POUILLY FUMÉ   Loire: FRANCE

One of the best known white wines of the central vineyards of the Loire valley. It comes from the Sauvignon Blanc grape, grown in vineyards in seven communes around the town of Pouilly-sur-Loire. The taste is crisp and steely, reminiscent of gunflint or gooseberries and the wines are best drunk young. There is no relation with the similar sounding name Pouilly Fuissé.

POUILLY LOCHÉ   Burgundy: FRANCE

A white wine from the Mâconnais area of southern Burgundy. It is made from the Chardonnay grape and is grown in the village of Loché. It may also be sold as Pouilly Vinzelles and usually is.

CLOS JOANNE D'ORION

Pouilly-Fumé

Appellation Pouilly-Fumé Contrôlée

Gitton Père & Fils

Propriétaires-Récoltants à Pouilly-sur-Loire, France

12°9 GL   MIS EN BOUTEILLE A LA PROPRIÉTÉ   750 ml

PRODUIT FRANÇAIS

POUILLY SUR LOIRE Loire: FRANCE

Not only the town at the centre of the appellation of Pouilly Fumé, but also the name of the second wine of the area. It is made from the Chasselas grape, better known as a table grape and is merely a pleasant quaffable white wine whose production is gradually disappearing.

POUILLY VINZELLES
Burgundy: FRANCE

A white wine from the Mâconnais area of southern Burgundy. It is made from the Chardonnay grape grown in the village of Vinzelles and may include wine from Loché too. It is a cheaper alternative to Pouilly Fuissé.

POUJEAUX Bordeaux: FRANCE

A well-run Cru Grand Bourgeois Exceptionnel and one of the leading wines of the Moulis commune of Haut-Médoc.

POULSARD

A red grape peculiar to the Jura, and one of the grape varieties for Arbois and Côtes du Jura, making distinctive pale red wines.

POURRITURE GRISE

Caused by the same fungus responsible for *pourriture noble*. *Pourriture grise* develops in prolonged humid conditions when there is none of the necessary warmth to dry off the grapes. It attacks the leaves and fruit and spoils the taste of the wine. Its development can be prevented with spray treatments.

POURRITURE NOBLE

The condition caused by the very special fungus, *botrytis cinerea*, that is responsible for the world's finest dessert wines, notably Sauternes in France, *Auslese* and better in Germany and Tokay in Hungary. It requires special climatic conditions: damp misty autumnal mornings followed by warm sunny afternoons allowing the grapes to dry and their juice to concentrate. The process is unpredictable and hazardous. In bad weather, *pourriture noble* becomes *pourriture grise* instead.

DOMAINE DE LA POUSSE D'OR
Burgundy: FRANCE

An estate in Volnay with a high reputation. It has three *monopoles* in Volnay: Clos de la Bousse d'Or, Clos des Soixante Ouvrées and Clos d'Audignac, as well as other vineyards. The wines are designed to combine finesse with longevity.

POVERTY BAY   see Gisborne.

POWDERY MILDEW   See oidium.

PRÄDIKAT   See Qualitätswein mit Prädikat.

PRAMAGGIORE Veneto: ITALY

The town of Pramaggiore gives its name to two DOC wines: Cabernet di Pramaggiore and Merlot di Pramaggiore. Cabernet is *riserva* after three years' ageing with 12° alcohol and Merlot after two years, also with 12°.

PRAMIAN

One of the great wines of ancient Greece, said by Homer to have been Nestor's favourite and the base of Circe's magic potion. It was described as being 'strong and nutritious'.

PRÉCOCE

The French term for 'forward'.

PREDICATO

A new classification for wines from the hills of central Tuscany in Italy, pioneered by a few leading producers, Antinori, Frescobaldi and Ruffino. Although they are only *vino da tavola*, they have their own self-imposed set of regulations, and so far there are four categories: Predicato di Cardisco, red wine based on Sangiovese with up to 10% other grapes, but not Merlot or Cabernet; Predicato di Biturica, red wine from a minimum of 30% Cabernet with Sangiovese and up to 10% other grapes; Predicato del Muschio, white wine from Chardonnay or Pinot Bianco, in which case up to 20% Rhine or Italico Riesling, Pinot Grigio or Müller Thurgau can be included; Predicato del Selvante, white wine from Sauvignon, allowing up to 20% of other grapes.

PREIGNAC
Bordeaux: FRANCE

One of the villages of the Sauternes appellation.

PREISS HENNY
Alsace: FRANCE

An Alsace company based in Mittelwihr.

PREISS ZIMMER
Alsace: FRANCE

A producer of Alsace wines from vineyards around Riquewihr.

PRÉMEAUX
Burgundy: FRANCE

The village next to Nuits St-Georges. Its village wines are sold under the name of Nuits St-Georges. It also boasts some Premiers Crus vineyards: Clos de la Maréchale, Clos Arlots, Clos des Argillières, Clos des Grandes Vignes, Clos des Corvées, Clos des Forêts, les Didiers, aux Perdrix, les Corvées Paget, le Clos St-Marc. The principal growers of the village are the Domaine Daniel Rion and Charles Viénot.

PREMIÈRES CÔTES DE BLAYE
Bordeaux: FRANCE

One of the three appellations of the Blaye vineyard, which is next to those of Bourg on the right bank of the Gironde. It covers mainly red wines made from Merlot and Cabernet Franc grapes. Better properties include Peyredoulle, Segonzac, Haut-Sociondo, Grand Barrail, Bourdieu. Very little white wine is made under this appellation.

PREMIÈRES CÔTES DE BORDEAUX
Bordeaux: FRANCE

One of the peripheral Bordelais appellations. The area extends along the right bank of the Garonne facing the Graves. The wines are red and white, with a distinct shift towards red in recent years. Whites are tending to become drier and are better in the southern part of the area, while reds are best in the north. Château names are not important here; these are the petits châteaux at the beginning of a good wine merchant's claret list.

PRESS

The piece of equipment used to press the grapes for white and rosé wine, and to extract juice from the grape skins and pulp in the case of red wine. The most common form of press is a horizontal hydraulic press which is the modern adaptation of the old wooden vertical press. The modern press can be programmed, rather like a dishwasher. The metal plates squeeze the grapes according to the required amount of pressure. A pneumatic press, sometimes called a bladder press, is a gentler version. A rubber bag inside the press is inflated so that it squeezes the grapes against the sides of the press. It is not as harsh as the hydraulic press.

PRESSAC

A synonym for the Malbec grape in Saint-Emilion.

PRESSOIR

The French word for 'press'.

PREUSES
Burgundy: FRANCE

One of the seven Grand Cru vineyards of Chablis.

PRICKED

An unpleasant sharp taste, coming from an excess of volatile acidity, indicating the wine has almost turned to vinegar.

DOMAINE JACQUES PRIEUR
Burgundy: FRANCE

A remarkable wine house, based in Meursault, with vineyards in great sites, notably Chambertin and Montrachet. Methods are modern and the results successful.

PRIEUR DE MEYNEY Bordeaux: FRANCE
The second wine of Château Meyney.

LE PRIEURÉ Bordeaux: FRANCE
A small little-known Grand Cru Classé of St-Émilion.

PRIEURÉ-LICHINE
Bordeaux: FRANCE

A fourth growth Margaux. Once the *prieuré* for the monks of Cantenac and now owned by Alexis Lichine who was responsible for restoring the vineyard and *château*. The second label is Château Clairefort and the third, Haut-Prieuré.

PRIMEUR
Vin de primeur describes a very young wine; in Beaujolais, the term is almost synonymous with *Nouveau*. See *en primeur*.

PRIMITIVO
A grape variety generally thought to be the European parent of Zinfandel. It is grown mainly in Apulia, Italy, for full-bodied wines like Primitivo di Manduria and Primitivo di Gioia.

PRIMITIVO DI MANDURIA
Apulia: ITALY

A heady red DOC wine made around the town of Manduria from the Primitivo grape. It comes in several versions, dry or slightly sweet, and then the sweeter types, *dolce naturale* with 16° minimum alcohol, *liquoroso dolce naturale* at 17.5° and *liquoroso secco* at 18°. All will age well, the *liquoroso* almost indefinitely.

PRIORATO SPAIN
An enclave within the larger D.O. of Tarragona. The name means Priory and comes from the ruined monastery of Scala dei Dei. The vineyards are in terraces on steep hillsides, with volcanic soil, and produce rich full-bodied red wines from Garnacha Tinta, Garnacha Peluda and Cariñena, and whites from Garnacha Blanca, Macabeo and Pedro Ximénez. Rancio is also made.

PRISE DE MOUSSE
The term used in Champagne for the process of second fermentation, entailing the conversion in the bottle of the *liqueur de tirage* into alcohol and carbon dioxide, to create the essential sparkle in champagne.

PRISSÉ   See Mâcon Villages.

PROCANICO
A synonym for the Trebbiano grape.

PROHIBITION
Prohibition, which forbade the sale and distribution of alcoholic beverages lasted in the United States from 1920 to 1933. It had a disastrous effect on the Californian wine industry; those wineries that managed to survive, did so by growing grapes for home winemakers, for there was no ban on making your own wine, provided you did not sell it; and by making sacramental and tonic wines. Tonic wines, supposedly for medicinal purposes, flourished, as did all manner of illegal drinks.

PROKUPAC
An important Yugoslav grape variety for red wine, grown all over Serbia and also used for rosé wine which the Yugoslavs call Ružica.

PRONTA BEVA
The Italian term for a wine that will be quick to mature and ready to drink soon.

PROSECCO
A white grape grown in north east Italy, mainly for sparkling wine, notably in Prosecco di Conegliano-Valdobbiadene.

PROSECCO DI CONEGLIANO – VALDOBBIADENE Veneto: ITALY
A white DOC wine, the name covers a variety of styles, which are made mainly from the Prosecco grape and can be still, *frizzante* and *spumante*. The *spumante* may be dry, medium dry or medium sweet. Most common is

a light *spumante* made by the *méthode champenoise*. Superiore di Cartizze, or simply Cartizze, describes a wine from the heart of the area, around the town of Cartizze.

PROŠEK — YUGOSLAVIA

Yugoslavia's best dessert wine, produced on the Dalmatian coast from a blend of red and white grapes, sweet and luscious with 15° natural alcohol.

PROTEIN CASSE

Occurs if there is too much protein in a wine, so it reacts with the tannins and coagulates to form a haze and then a deposit. Bentonite fining to remove the excess protein is the remedy.

PROVENCE — FRANCE

The wines of Provence cover a variety of appellations. The largest is Côtes de Provence, typified by pale pink wine in an amphora shaped bottle. More serious is red Coteaux d'Aix-en-Provence, with its subsection of Coteaux des Baux-en-Provence. These two are separated by the recently elevated VDQS of the Coteaux Varois. To the north there are the growing Côtes du Lubéron on the foothills of the Montagne de Lubéron, and to the east the little known Coteaux de Pierrevert. Within these larger appellations there are four smaller enclaves, Bellet, Palette, Cassis and Bandol, and also the regional Vin de Pays des Maures, du Mont Caume, d'Argens and du Var.

PROVIAR — ARGENTINA

The Argentinian subsidiary of Moët & Chandon, producing sparkling wine by the *méthode champenoise*. Baron B is their top brand. They make still wine, too.

LA PROVIDENCE — Bordeaux: FRANCE

A little-known but recommended Pomerol *château*.

PROVIGNAGE

An old method of propagating a vine. The old vine was buried, leaving a single shoot coming out of the ground, which then developed roots and took nourishment from the old vine. Phylloxera has ended this method of propagation.

PRUGNOLO

A clone of the Sangiovese grape variety grown in Montepulciano for Vino Nobile.

PRUINA

The waxy substance on the skin of a grape to which the yeast and bacteria adhere to form a bloom, a coating which is especially noticeable on black grapes.

PRÜM — Mosel-Saar-Ruwer: GERMANY

Weingut J.J. Prüm is one of the finest estates of the region, with cellars in Wehlen and vineyards in Wehlener Sonnenuhr – the famous sundial which the vineyard was named after was built by an earlier member of the family – as well as at Graach, Zeltingen and Bernkastel, all planted with a very high proportion of Riesling vines. This estate should not be confused with Weingut S.A. Prüm Erben, an estate which was created when the original Prüm family property was divided amongst the heirs or *Erben*.

PRUNING

Carried out each year to remove the excess parts of the vine, so that it can be trained in the desired way to be easy to cultivate and treat. Pruning achieves an optimum balance between the growth of the vine and the size of the crop. The amount of pruning depends upon the vigour of the vine, its age, climatic conditions and the fertility of the soil. Methods of pruning vary from region to region: *cordon*, *gobelet* and *espalier* are the most common.

PTG   See Bourgogne Passe-Tout-Grains.

PUCKERING
Or mouth-puckering, a sensation caused by a high tannin content in young wine.

PUDDING WINE   See dessert wine.

PUISSEGUIN   Bordeaux: FRANCE
One of the so-called 'satellites' of St-Émilion. These surrounding six parishes used to sell their wine as St-Émilion until the appellation was delimited in 1936. The name of the parish is hyphenated onto St-Émilion. Puisseguin now includes the wines of Parsac.

PUJOLS SUR CIRON
                     Bordeaux: FRANCE
An important commune within the Graves, producing good white wine.

PULCIANELLO
Was the typical Orvieto bottle in Italy, a squat straw-based flask which has now suffered the same fate as the Chianti flask and fallen victim to modern technology.

PULIGNY-MONTRACHET
                       Burgundy: FRANCE
The reputation of the village of Puligny was founded on its red wine, but today it produces considerably more white wine and owes its reputation to the white vineyards of Le Montrachet, which it shares with the village of Chassagne, also Chevalier-Montrachet and Bienvenues-Bâtard-Montrachet.

The Premiers Crus vineyards are Clos du Cailleret, les Combettes, les Pucelles, les Folatières (part), Clavoillons, Champ Canet, les Chalumeaux, les Referts, Sous le Puits, la Garenne, Hameau de Blagny.

Several reputable merchants and growers are based in the village, including Domaine Carillon, Domaine Leflaive, Domaine Etienne Sauzet and Domaine Roland Thévenin, who occupy the Château de Puligny Montrachet.

PUNT
The indentation in the bottom of some wine bottles, notably champagne bottles. It is more common in older bottles, and was originally designed to reinforce the bottle and to hold any sediment at the bottom of the bottle.

PUPILLIN   Jura: FRANCE
A village within the appellation of Arbois. It is allowed to attach the village name to the appellation as Arbois — Pupillin. The wines are very similar to those of Arbois.

PUPITRE
The wooden boards used for *remuage*, made up of two heavy hinged boards, each with sixty holes, cut at 45°, which hold a bottle at any angle from vertical to horizontal.

PUTT   see Tokay.

PUTTO   See Chianti Putto.

PUTTONY   see Tokay.

PYRALIS
A meal moth, producing larvae which feed on the leaves and fruit of the vines. It is best treated with insecticides.

PYRENEES   AUSTRALIA
As yet a relatively unknown area on the Australian wine map, situated north west of Ballarat in Victoria and including the towns of Avoca, Moonambel and Redbank. The first winery of the recent revival was Château Remy and others have followed. The climate is mild. Distinctive minty red wines are characteristic of the potential of the area.

Q

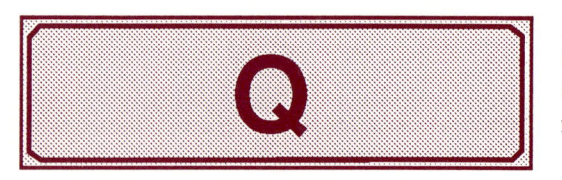

Q

The quality seal for Sicilian wine. The system is controlled by the regional government which is responsible for selecting the wine eligible for this seal of approval, with the aim of encouraging improvement in Sicilian wines. Wines of appropriate quality carry a Q on the label.

QbA   See *Qualitätswein*.

QmP

A common abbreviation for *Qualitätswein mit Prädikat*.

QUAI DES CHARTRONS

The address in Bordeaux of many of the principal *négociants*, for whom it was convenient to have offices and cellars on the quayside. These important Bordelais families were often referred to collectively as the 'Chartronnais'.

QUALITÄTSWEIN

The full title is *Qualitätswein bestimmter Anbaugebiet*, often abbreviated to Q*b*A, and it is the most important category by German wine law. It means, literally, 'quality wine from designated areas of origin'. There are eleven such areas: Mosel-Saar-Ruwer, Nahe, Rheingau, Rheinhessen, Rheinpfalz, Ahr, Mittelrhein, Hessische Bergstrasse, Franconia, Württemberg and Baden. A *Qualitätswein* comes from one of these areas, from permitted grape varieties, with enough natural sugar to raise the wine above *Tafelwein* level. It is subject to chemical analysis and a tasting test to ensure its authenticity.

QUALITÄTSWEIN MIT PRÄDIKAT

These are the finest of German wines. There are five categories of *Prädikat*, or predicate in English, determined according to the *Oechsle* reading, in other words the amount of natural sugar in the grapes. In ascending order they are Kabinett, Spätlese, Auslese, Beerenauslese and Trockenbeerenauslese as well as Eiswein. The sweetest of these are made only in the best years when the grapes have been affected by noble rot. Austria uses these terms too.

QUARLES HARRIS

One of the port houses that is owned by the Symington family. The company owns no vineyards but has good contacts with the Douro farmers. Harris is the brand name for their wood ports.

QUARTO VECCHIO   Veneto: ITALY

A non-DOC wine made from Cabernet and Merlot grapes grown in the Po valley, by the company of the same name. *Riserva* is aged in wood for five years.

QUARTS DE CHAUME   Loire: FRANCE

One of the most important sweet white wines of the Loire Valley, situated within the Coteaux du Layon, south of the hamlet of Chaume. The name derives from the fact that the local lord, Seigneur de la Guerche, used to demand payments in the form of a quarter of the vintage. In the best years the grapes are affected by *pourriture noble*; they are picked in several "tries" and the yield is the lowest of the Loire valley, 22 hectolitres per hectare. The results can be delicious, elegantly honeyed wines capable of considerable maturity.

QUATOURZE   The Midi: FRANCE

Formerly a VDQS, Quatourze is now part of the all-embracing appellation of the Coteaux du Languedoc. The most interesting wine is red, made from Carignan, Grenache, Syrah and Mourvèdre, grown on a plateau just outside Narbonne. White wine is made from Maccabeo.

QUINTA

The Portuguese word for a country property. It may be small or large, rustic or palatial, but must include agricultural land. Wine and port estates are often called *quintas*.

QUINTA DE BACALHÔA   PORTUGAL

One of the most exciting and innovative wine estates of Portugal, producing *barrique* aged Cabernet Sauvignon that is marketed by João Pires.

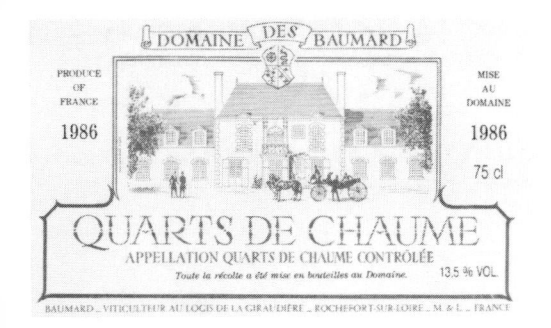

QUATTRO VICARIATI
Trentino-Alto Adige: ITALY

A distinctive red wine made from Cabernet and Merlot grapes aged in the barrel for two years by the area's largest cooperative, Cavit.

QUINTA BOA VISTA   PORTUGAL

Though no longer owned by the port shippers Offley Forrester, this vineyard still forms the basis of Offley vintage port. Baron Forrester, who died in 1862, is reputed to have planted the vineyards.

QUEENSLAND   AUSTRALIA

There are two small wine regions in Queensland, in the Granite Belt, 125 miles south west of Brisbane and at Roma, 320 miles west of Brisbane, where there is just one enthusiastic winemaker. Normally the climate is too hot for successful viticulture.

QUINTA DO BOMFIM   PORTUGAL

Owned by the Symington family who ship Dow's port through their company Silva & Cosens. Quinta do Bomfim forms the basis of Dow vintage port with its fine position on the Douro.

QUELLTALER   AUSTRALIA

Meaning Springvale, an old winery in the Watervale area of South Australia, now owned by Remy Martin. It is especially noted for its dry white hock, Rhine Riesling and a Riesling Traminer. Cabernet Sauvignon and a Granfiesta sherry are good too.

QUINTA DA EIRA VELHA   PORTUGAL

A port estate owned by the Newman family who sell their production to Cockburns. In 1978 a single *quinta* vintage port was declared.

QUINTA DA FOZ   PORTUGAL

Quinta da Foz is the estate that forms the backbone of Cálem's ports.

QUEUE

An old-fashioned Burgundian measure for two *pièces*. Sales at the Hospices de Beaune were traditionally by the *queue*.

QUINTA DOS MALVEDOS   PORTUGAL

An estate near the Spanish border in the Douro Valley that is owned by the house of Graham. They sell it in non-vintage years as a single *quinta* wine, that is, released for sale only when the wine is ready for drinking; otherwise it forms the basis of their vintage port.

QUEYSSAC-LES-VIGNES
SOUTH WEST FRANCE

A village in the Lot valley with a dying tradition for Vin de Paille.

QUINCY   *Loire:* FRANCE

One of the wines of the Central Vineyards of the Loire. Like Pouilly Fumé it is only white, made from the Sauvignon grape, grown almost exclusively in the village of Quincy.

QUINTA DO NOVAL   PORTUGAL

The port estate of Quinta do Noval is owned by the van Zeller family whose company was originally called A. J. da Silva, until the name was changed to Quinta do Noval – Vinhos Sarl. Some ungrafted 'nacional' vines are grown here (national as opposed to foreign); they only produce a tiny amount of wine, which is sometimes sold as a pure 'Nacional' vintage, such as the legendary 1931. In addition to ordinary vintage port, the company produces fine tawnies and late bottled vintage wines.

QUINTA DA ROÊDA   PORTUGAL

Belongs to the port shippers Croft. In vintage years the wine is included in the vintage; in some non-vintage years it is sold as a single *quinta*. The estate is the centre of Croft's vinification plant.

QUINTA DA VARGELLAS   PORTUGAL

Quinta da Vargellas is an estate owned by the port shippers, Taylor, Fladgate & Yeatman and is sold as a single *quinta* wine in non-vintage years.

QUINTAL

The Italian measure for a hundred kilograms; yields in Italy are given in quintals per hectolitre. In theory, a quintal will give you a hundred hectolitres of juice, but in practice DOC regulations restrict the amount of juice obtainable, usually to 70%.

R

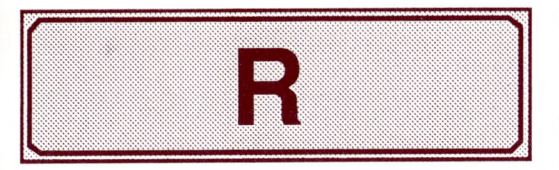

RACE
The French term for 'breed'.

RACKING
The running or pumping of clear wine off its lees from one barrel or vat to another. This is done after fermentation and at intervals during the maturation of a wine, if it is aged in barrel before bottling.

R.D.
Stands for *récemment dégorgé* and is used as a trademark by the champagne house of Bollinger. Literally, it means 'recently disgorged', but indicates a wine that has been kept under ideal conditions in the producer's cellars for a few years until it is disgorged in readiness for sale.

R.M.
On a champagne label, this means that the wine has been produced by a *récoltant manipulant*, in other words an individual grower.

RAFFAULT   Loire: FRANCE
An important name in Chinon, with various members of the family owning different estates. Jean Maurice Raffault makes separate wines from different soils, Clos des Lutinières, Les Galluches, Les Picasses Isore and Clos de Galon. Raymond Raffault's estate is called Domaine de Raifault. Olga is perhaps the best known Raffault, making excellent Chinon.

RAFFIAT DE MONCADE
A white grape, grown in south west France, which gives Pacherenc de Vic Bilh its distinctive character.

RABAT   MOROCCO
A sizeable wine-producing region of Morocco, with vineyards at Gharb, Chellah, Zemmour and Zaer, all producing soft red wines for early drinking.

RAHOUL   Bordeaux: FRANCE
One of the better estates of Portets in Graves, with, until recently, a talented Danish winemaker, Peter Vinding Diers. He also makes the wine at neighbouring Domaine la Grave.

RABAUD-PROMIS   Bordeaux: FRANCE
A first growth Sauternes in the commune of Bommes. Relatively unknown, it is no longer considered to merit its classification.

RAIMAT   SPAIN
Raimat is the leading estate of the new D.O. of Costa del Segre in Catalonia. It is owned by Codorníu, who have planted classic French grape varieties, Chardonnay for a Cava and Cabernet Sauvignon and Merlot, as well as some Tempranillo for a red wine sold under the name of Raimat Abadia.

RABELAIS   See Aïn Merane.

RABIGATO
A Portuguese white grape variety, grown in the Douro for port and elsewhere for table wine, notably Vinho Verde.

RAINWATER   Madeira: PORTUGAL
The name used to describe a blend of light Madeira which became popular in America in the 18th century. There are various stories as to the origin of the name, which entailed the diluting of the contents of some casks of Madeira with rain. The recipient of the wine failed to realise this, enjoyed it, asked for more and Rainwater was born. It appeared frequently on lists of Madeira from the late 18th century. Today it is used to describe a light wine made from a blend of grapes and varies from shipper to shipper.

RABLAY SUR LAYON   Loire: FRANCE
One of the villages of the Coteaux du Layon whose name can feature on the label as Coteaux du Layon Villages – Rablay sur Layon.

RABOSO DEL PIAVE   Veneto: ITALY
The red grape variety Raboso, from the Piave valley in the Veneto, makes some distinctive wines which are sometimes blended with Cabernet. It is a recent DOC.

DIEGO RALLO & FIGLI   Sicily: ITALY

An important wine producer, a family company making table wines, DOC and others, as well as some of the best Marsala.

RAMANDOLO   Friuli-Venezia Giulia: ITALY

A sub-denomination within the DOC of the Colli Orientali del Friuli, a wine made from the Verduzzo grape, which can be dry, or medium sweet if made from slightly dried grapes.

RAMISCO

The red Portuguese grape responsible for Colares, with small thick-skinned berries, producing sturdy wine in small quantities.

RAMITELLO   Abruzzi: ITALY

Ramitello is the name of a vineyard, a red wine made from Montepulciano and Sangiovese grapes and a white wine made from Trebbiano and Malvasia. Both wines can also be *frizzante*.

RAMONET-PRUDHON   Burgundy: FRANCE

From Chassagne-Montrachet, one of the great producers of white Burgundy, including Bâtard-Montrachet and Bienvenues-Bâtard-Montrachet. Their red wine is good, too.

RAMOS PINTO

A port house, founded by Adriano Ramos Pinto in 1880, with the *quinta* of Bom Retiro forming the basis for their vintage wines.

RANCIO

Describes the oxidised taste of fortified wine.

RANINA

The Yugoslav and Hungarian synonym of the Bouvier grape.

RAPITALÀ   Sicily: ITALY

One of the better Sicilian estates, making Bianco Alcamo and full-flavoured red table wine.

RAPOSEIRA

A Portuguese company producing sparkling wine in Lamega to the south of the Douro.

RAPSANI   GREECE

A deep red wine from the slopes of Mount Olympus in Thessaly. It benefits from some bottle age.

RASPBERRIES

Raspberries are associated with some young red wines, such as Valpolicella and young Pinot Noir.

RASTEAU   Rhône: FRANCE

A *vin doux naturel* from the southern Rhône for which the village has its own appellation. Table wines are also made in the area and Rasteau is also one of the seventeeen Côtes du Rhône Villages. The *vin doux naturel* is made from the Grenache grape, vinified as if for white wine. The Côtes du Rhône Villages, red, white and rosé, is made from the hotchpotch of grapes generally grown in the southern Rhône, mainly Grenache, Cinsaut, Mourvèdre and Syrah.

RATAFIA

The typical aperitif from Champagne, made from grape must which is prevented from fermenting by the addition of *marc de champagne*, the local brandy, and then aged for a few months in barrel. Ratafia can be red, white or rosé. The origin of the name comes from the Latin, *rata fiat*, which became *ratafié* in French, meaning 'the drink taken to celebrate the conclusion of a legal or commercial agreement.' Ratafia is also made in Burgundy for local consumption, and a similar drink is found in other parts of France as Pineau de Charente, Floc de Gascogne and Macvin in the Jura.

RENATO RATTI   Piedmont: ITALY

Based at Abbazia dell'Annunziata, a relatively new estate in Piedmont, making a small amount of exceptional Barolo, Barbaresco and other Alba wines in a 15th century abbey.

RAUENTHAL   Rheingau: GERMANY

A village in the foothills of the Taunus mountains which comes within the *Grosslage* of Steinmächer. It also has some exceptionally fine E*inzellagen*, especially Baiken and Gehrn. Rothenberg, Langenstuck and Nonnenberg are good too, with a distinctive spiciness and flavour. Respected producers include Langwerth von Simmern, Schloss Reinhartshausen and Schloss Schönborn.

RAUSAN SÉGLA Bordeaux: FRANCE

A second growth property in Margaux, part of the 18th century estate of the Marquis de Rauzan. It now belongs to Eschenauer who have been replanting the vineyard. After a period in the doldrums the wines merit their classification again.

RAUZAN-GASSIES Bordeaux: FRANCE

A second growth Margaux *château* which, after a faded reputation for the last decade or two, is now enjoying a revival in its fortunes.

RAVAT

A hybrid grape variety, both red and white, with several variations, grown in the north American continent.

RAVELLO Campania: ITALY

Though not DOC, this is one of the better wines of the Amalfi coast, produced around the town of Ravello. Red and *rosato* are made from Per'e Palummo, Aglianico and Merlot grapes; white is made from Coda di Volpe, San Nicola and Greco. The best reds age well.

FRANÇOIS RAVENEAU
Burgundy: FRANCE

One of the finest growers of Chablis. His wines are the essence of tradition, matured in oak barrels for at least 12 months and matured in bottle for several years. His main vineyards are Valmur, Les Clos, Blanchots, Vaillons and Montée de Tonnerre.

RAY

Martin Ray was once one of the controversial figures of the Californian wine industry. He owned the Paul Masson winery for a short spell at the' end of the 1930s. His original winery has been divided and part is now Mount Eden Vineyards, while part is run by his son, who follows his father in making expensive and sometimes memorable bottles, notably of Chardonnay.

RAYA

While the wine for sherry is still on its lees, it is classified as to whether it is developing a *flor* and will become a *fino* or *amontillado*, or whether it has little or no flor and will become an *oloroso*. Finos and amontillados are marked with one *raya* or line; *olorosos* with two *rayas*. The term *raya* can also be used to describe the coarser styles of *oloroso*, which can be called *raya olorosa*.

RAYNE-VIGNEAU Bordeaux: FRANCE

A first growth Sauternes in the commune of Bommes, originally known as Château Vigneau. It is a large estate and famous for the semi-precious stones which have been found in the vineyard. Modern methods produce sound but unexciting wines. A little dry wine is made as Rayne Vigneau Sec.

REBÊCHE

Or *vin de rebêche*. This is the third part of juice in the pressing of champagne grapes, coming after the *cuvée* and the *vins de tailles*. In practice it is never used for champagne but is sent to the distillery, if indeed it is made at all.

REBELLO VALENTE

Once an old port house but now the name of a vintage port shipped by Robertson Bros. who are a subsidiary of Sandeman. The grapes are still trodden by foot and the wines are tannic and robust.

REBULA see Ribolla

REBULA OF BRDA YUGOSLAVIA

An individual white wine from the coastal region of Slovenia, golden, pungent and very dry. Rebula is similar to the Ribolla of Friuli.

RÉCEMMENT DÉGORGÉ See R.D.

RECIOTO

A Valpolicella or Soave which has been made from dried grapes; the resulting wine may be sweet or dry; if a Valpolicella is dry it is also described as *amarone*. *Recioto* is so called because the grapes come from the upper edge of the bunches, called the ears or *recie*, that receive most sun.

RECIOTO DI SOAVE Veneto: ITALY

A dessert wine from the same grapes as ordinary Soave, but semi-dried before pressing to give sweetness and alcohol. Recioto may also be *spumante* and, if fortified, *liquoroso*.

RECIOTO DELLA VALPOLICELLA
Veneto: ITALY

Made from the same grape varieties as Valpolicella, pressed after they have been dried for two or three months so that they make a sweet dessert wine. *Spumante* is also popular and a fortified version is made too.

RECIOTO DELLA VALPOLICELLA AMARONE
Veneto: ITALY

Made from the same grape varieties as Valpolicella, pressed after they have been dried for two or three months and fermented dry to give a rich warm wine with a slightly bitter or *amarone* finish, capable of long life and highly rated amongst the wines of the Veneto.

RÉCOLTE
The French term for 'harvest'.

RED BIDDY
A mixture of rough brandy and sweet red wine, which was served in Victorian pubs as a cheap substitute for port.

RED MISKET
This is, contradictorily, a white grape variety grown in Bulgaria for grapey table wines.

RED TRAMINER
Red Traminer, Traminer Rosso or Roter Traminer can be a synonym for the Gewürztraminer grape as the grape skins tend to be pinkish red rather than green in colour.

REDMAN
AUSTRALIA

The name Redman is synonymous with the pioneers of the vineyards of Coonawarra. Bill Redman came to Coonawarra in 1901; the family created the Rouge Homme label, which is now owned by Lindeman. A small family Redman winery was opened in 1969 which produces fine Cabernet Sauvignon.

REDWOOD VALLEY
California: USA

A small wine area in Mendocino County, a tributary of the Ukiah Valley and as yet not an AVA.

REFRACTOMETER
An instrument used for measuring the maturity of grapes in the vineyard. Light passing through a drop of juice held between two prisms bends at a different angle according to its sugar content. A scale read through the eyepiece gives the percentage of sugar in the juice.

REGALEALI
Sicily: ITALY

The brand name of a range of wines that feature amongst the best Sicilian table wines, made by the Conte Tasca d'Almerita. A fresh dry white comes from Catarratto, Inzolia and Sauvignon grapes; a superior quality white called Nozze d'Oro, and a crisp *rosato* come from Nerello Mascalese and Perricone grapes. Red is from the same grapes, as well as a richer, more long-lived *riserva* Rosso del Conte.

RÉGION DE MERCUREY   See Côte Chalonnaise.

RÉGISSEUR
The Bordelais term for the employee who runs a *château* for its owners and has overall charge of the vineyard and cellars, entailing considerable responsibility.

A. RÉGNARD ET FILS
Burgundy: FRANCE

A *négociant* company in Chablis. Although they do not own any vineyards of their own, their list includes the whole range of Chablis wines. The company incorporates the famous Chablis name of Albert Pic. Their methods are traditional and the wines sound.

REGNER
A crossing of Luglienca Bianca, a table grape, and Gamay, grown mainly in the Rheinhessen.

RÉGNIÉ
Burgundy: FRANCE

Was one of the more distinctive of the many villages of the appellation Beaujolais Villages and has been elevated with the 1988 vintage to the status of a Beaujolais Cru.

REGUA
PORTUGAL

The unprepossessing Portuguese town at the centre of the port district. The Casa do Douro is based there, but otherwise there is little of interest.

FRANZ REH
Mosel-Saar-Ruwer: GERMANY

Franz Reh und Söhne GmbH, a family company, a successful export house and an estate owner with vineyards in Leiwen and Trittenheim. They also own the Marienhof estate in Piesport.

REHOBOAM

A champagne bottle size equal to six ordinary bottles (450cl).

REICHENSTEINER

A German grape variety, developed in 1978 from a crossing of Müller Thurgau with Madeleine Angevine from France x Early Calabrese from Italy. It is named after a castle in Mittelrhein, resembles Müller Thurgau and produces neutral wine in generous quantities in Germany and wines of some character in England.

REIL
Mosel-Saar-Ruwer: GERMANY

A little known village on the Mosel. The *Grosslage* is Vom Heissen Stein and the best vineyards Goldlay and Sorentberg.

REIMS
Champagne: FRANCE

Reims or Rheims is not only the city where the kings of France are crowned, in the cathedral of St. Rémy, but also the capital of Champagne. Many of the important champagne houses have their cellars here, with magnificent chalk cellars quarried by the Romans.

REMOISSENET PÈRE ET FILS

Important *négociants* in Beaune, with a small estate. Grèves and Toussaints are their best wines.

REMONTAGE

An essential part of red wine vinification describing the process of pumping the fermenting juice over the cap of skins in order to extract colour and tannin. This is usually done twice a day during the fermentation. Most cellars are equipped with mechanical pumps and *remontage* has, to some extent, replaced the traditional *pigeage*.

REMSTAL-STUTTGART
Württemburg: GERMANY

One of the three *Bereichs* of Württemberg, around the city of Stuttgart and the valley of Rems. Grape varieties include Riesling and Müller-Thurgau for whites, Trollinger and Müllerrebe for reds.

REMUAGE

The technique evolved by the champagne house of Clicquot in the early 1800s to rid a bottle of champagne of the sediment resulting from the second fermentation. The operation of remuage is carried out by a *remueur*. The bottles are placed almost horizontally in *pupitres* then twisted and tilted a little each day so that, at the end of the process, the sediment rests on the cork or capsule of the now vertical bottle, and is ready for *dégorgement*. It is *remuage* that distinguishes champagne from the less sophisticated wines made with the *méthode rurale*.

REMY PANNIER
Loire: FRANCE

Important *négociants* dealing in the whole range of wines from the Loire. They own vineyards for Anjou Blanc and Cabernet d'Anjou.

RENAULT   See Mazouna.

RENDEMENT

The French term for the yield or amount of wine that can be produced from a vineyard.

RENDEMENT ANNUEL

Takes into account the climatic conditions of the year and adjusts the *rendement de base* accordingly, as proposed by the growers.

RENDEMENT DE BASE

The basic yield allowed for an appellation, measured in hectolitres per hectare.

RENISHAW — ENGLAND

England's most northerly vineyard with two acres in Derbyshire, planted in 1972 with Seyval Blanc, Reichensteiner and other vines.

RENMANO See Berri.

RESERVA

Reserva in Spain indicates that the wine has been aged for a minimum of one year in oak cask and released in its fourth year. Reservas are only made in good years when the grapes are of sufficient quality giving wine that will sustain maturation. See also gran reserva.

In Portugal the term describes a wine of outstanding quality, with a vintage year. The alcohol level must be half a degree higher than is normal for the wine, but otherwise there are no ageing regulations. All depends upon the individual producer.

RÉSERVE DE L'AMIRAL See Beychevelle.

RÉSERVE DE LA COMTESSE — Bordeaux: FRANCE

The second wine of the Pichon-Longueville Comtesse de Lalande estate.

RÉSERVE PERSONNELLE

A description used by the Hugel company in Alsace to denote a better quality wine. The term has no legal backing and there are several other similar terms used by other Alsace houses such as Réserve Spéciale, Réserve Exceptionnelle and so on, again depending purely upon the opinion of the producer.

RESIDUAL SUGAR

The natural grape sugar left in a wine after the fermentation has finished; the grapes may be very rich in sugar in the case of Late Harvest wines, so the yeast die naturally before they have consumed all the sugar, or the fermentation may be stopped by the use of sulphur dioxide, chilling and a very fine filtration to leave some residual sugar.

BALTHASAR RESS — Rheingau: GERMANY

A 100 year old family firm of wine merchants, with vineyards in the finer sites of the Rheingau, including Rüdesheim, Geisenheim, Winkel, Oestrich. They also lease the previously neglected Schloss Reichartshausen.

RETAIL LICENCE

Allows for the sale of wine in quantities of less than one dozen bottles. It is essential for a wine merchant to hold a retail licence, obtained by application to the local magistrates.

RETSINA — GREECE

That most characteristic of Greek wines, usually white, occasionally rosé, flavoured with the resin of the Alep pine, which is added to the must during fermentation. The grape varieties are Savatiano and Rhoditis, grown in Attica, Euboea and the Peloponnese. The taste goes back to antiquity when pine resin was used to seal *amphorae* of wine. Today it complements rich oily, Greek food.

RETZ See Weinviertel.

REUILLY — Loire: FRANCE

One of the wines of the Central Vineyards of the Loire, made from vines around the village of Reuilly. The white wine comes from the Sauvignon grape and is similar to Sancerre, and there is a rosé, usually made from Pinot Gris, or occasionally Pinot Noir. A tiny amount of red wine is also made from Pinot Noir.

RÈZE — SWITZERLAND

A little-known white grape of the Valais, giving acidic white wine, it is aged in a type of *solera* system, using small casks, in the cold glacial atmosphere of the Val d'Anniviers in the Valais, and so it is known as *vin du glacier*.

RHEINGAU — GERMANY

For many, the wines of the Rheingau are the epitome of fine German wines, slightly honeyed, with balance and elegance. The heart of the Rheingau runs from Rüdesheim to Rauenthal,

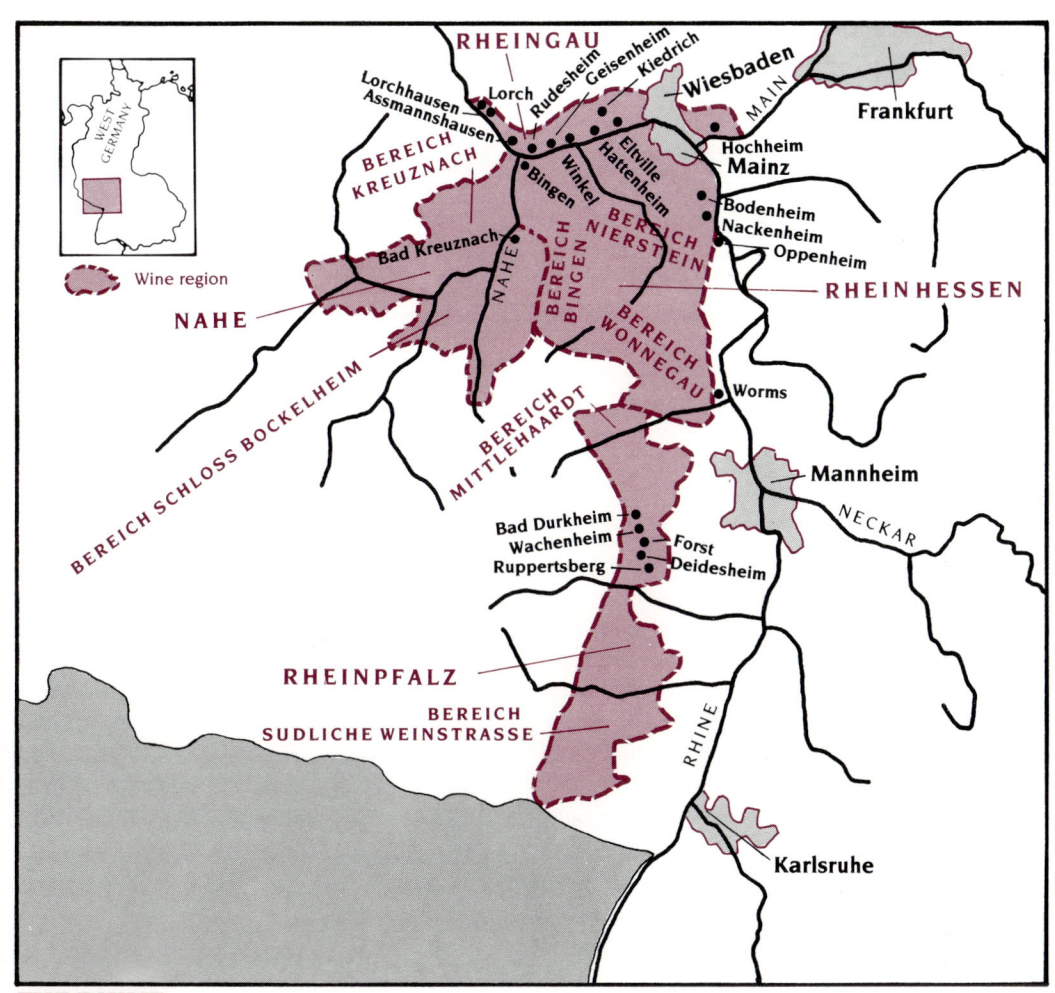

THE RHINE

a small stretch of southeast-facing vineyards on the banks of the Rhine, sheltered by the Taunus mountains. After Rüdesheim, the Rhine turns north and the region includes Assmannshausen, better known for its red wines. Beyond Wiesbaden and Mainz, there is Hochheim, almost a wine island on its own. One *Bereich*, Johannisberg, covers the Rheingau, and that in turn is split into ten *Grosslagen*: Burgweg, Erntebringer, Deutelsberg, Steinmächer, Steil, Honigberg, Gottesthal, Mehrhölzchen, Heiligenstock and Daubhaus. This small area, and especially the better sites, are planted with a high proportion of Riesling vines and contain some of the best estates of Germany, such as Schloss Vollrads, Schloss Johannisberg, Schloss Schönborn, Deinhard, Groensteyn, the State Domain at Eltville and Schloss Rheinhartshausen, with a myriad of fine vineyards.

RHEINHESSEN GERMANY

The largest wine region of Germany, bordered by the Rhine in the north and east and the Nahe in the west. It is divided into three Bereichs; Nierstein, Bingen and Wonnegau. The best wines come from the villages of the Rheinfront between Dienheim and Nackenheim, with Nierstein at their centre, where there is a high proportion of Riesling, grown on red slate in south facing terraced vineyards. In other parts a variety of other grapes, both red and white, such as Kerner and Bacchus, are grown, including a considerable amount of Müller Thurgau much of which is destined for Liebfraumilch. The wines of the Rheinhessen are generally fuller and fatter than those of the Rheingau.

RHEINPFALZ GERMANY

Germany's largest wine-producing region; in area it is slightly smaller than the Rheinhessen, but its yields are nearly always greater. The vineyards are almost a logical continuation of those of Alsace. The Rheinpfalz vineyards cover 80 kilometres along the slopes of the Haardt mountains from Kleinbockenheim, on the edge of the Rheinhessen, to Schweigen on the French frontier. Logically they can be divided into three distinct areas: an area formerly called the Unterhaardt that runs from the Rheinhessen to Herxheim, where average undistinguished wines are produced; the heart of the Rheinpfalz, which is the Mittelhaardt, between Herxheim and Neustadt where great wines are made, particularly in villages like Forst, Deidesheim, Ruppertsberg and Wachenheim. These two areas are now grouped together under the Bereich name of Mittelhaardt Deutscher Weinstrasse. The third area, formerly the Oberhaardt and now called Bereich Südliche Weinstrasse, runs from Neustadt to the French border and produces sound everyday drinking wines.

The principal Rheinpfalz grape variety is the Müller-Thurgau. Riesling is much less important than in the more northerly vineyards, although it is the main variety on the best sites. Scheurebe also makes some very successful wines. Other varieties include red Portugieser, making the region an important producer of red wine, Silvaner, Morio-Muskat, Kerner, Ruländer and Gewürztraminer. The region has the warmest and driest climate of Germany's vineyards.

RHINE RIESLING see Riesling

RHODE ISLAND USA

Vitis vinefera grapes have been grown on Rhode Island since the early 1970s, with a few small wineries, notably Prudence Island Vineyards.

RHODES GREECE

Produces a variety of wines all over the island, but only the northern slopes are entitled to an appellation. A dry white wine from the Athiri grape is called Lindos; there is red wine from the Amorgiano grape and some Muscat similar to that of Samos.

RHODITIS

A white Greek grape variety grown mainly for retsina and at its best around Patras and in the Peloponnese.

RHÔNE FRANCE

The Rhône is the all embracing term for the vineyards that depend upon the River Rhône, going from Côte Rôtie in the north below Vienne through Hermitage and Cornas and down to the south to Châteauneuf-du-Pape and similar surrounding wines, including Côtes du Rhône. The wines of the northern Rhône are quite distinct from those of the south. In the north the grape varieties are Syrah for red wines and Viognier or Marsanne and Roussanne for whites. In contrast Châteauneuf-du-Pape can be made from any combination of thirteen grape varieties of which red Grenache is the most usual, while Côtes du Rhône includes even more.

THE RHÔNE VALLEY

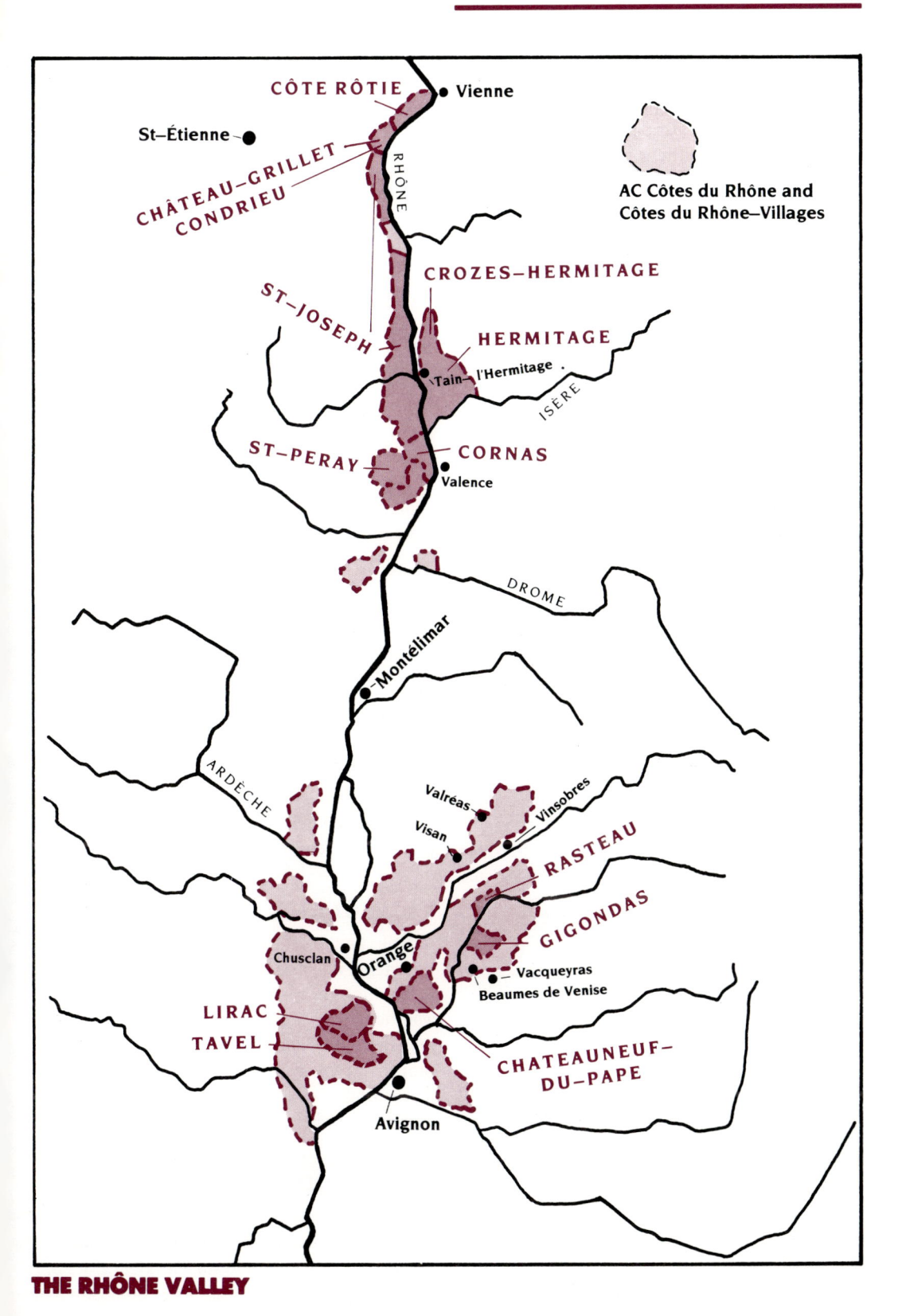

- CÔTE RÔTIE
- CHÂTEAU-GRILLET
- CONDRIEU
- ST-JOSEPH
- CROZES-HERMITAGE
- HERMITAGE
- ST-PERAY
- CORNAS
- RASTEAU
- GIGONDAS
- LIRAC
- TAVEL
- CHATEAUNEUF-DU-PAPE

AC Côtes du Rhône and Côtes du Rhône–Villages

Vienne, St-Étienne, Tain-l'Hermitage, Valence, Montélimar, Valréas, Vinsobres, Visan, Chusclan, Orange, Vacqueyras, Beaumes de Venise, Avignon

ISÈRE, DROME, ARDÈCHE, RHÔNE

RIAS BAJAS — SPAIN

Rias Bajas is a new Spanish D.O. in the region of Galicia. The vineyards are planted with the Albarino grape, grown in the fiords between the Portuguese border and Santiago. The wine is white and light, with a hint of sparkle, like Vinho Verde.

RIBATEJO — PORTUGAL

This province of Portugal to the north of Lisbon is an important wine producing area. Most of the vineyards, which are to the north of the River Tagus, are planted with a mixture of grape varieties; Trincadeira, Mortágua and João de Santarém for reds and Fernão Pires, Terrantez, Rabo da Ovelha, Boais and Jampal for whites. Carvalho, Ribeiro & Ferreira are the largest private company in the region and cooperatives are important too. The best reds are full-bodied and robust; the whites tend to be rather earthy. Carvelho, Ribeiro & Ferreira produce some fine red *garrafeiras* and their Serradayres, meaning mountain air, is their best wine.

RIBEAUVILLÉ — Alsace: FRANCE

An important Alsace wine town and its vineyards include the Grand Cru sites of Geisberg, Kirschberg and Osterberg.

RIBEIRO — SPAIN

The most important D.O. of Galicia in isolated north west Spain, with similarities to the adjoining Minho area of Portugal. The region is subdivided into three; Ribeiro de Avia, Ribeiro del Mino and Ribeiro de Arnola. A mixture of grapes produce a crisp, fragrant white wine similar to Vinho Verde. The best varieties are Treixadura, Torrentés, Godello, Macabeo, Albilla and Loureiro. The best red wine is made from Sousón.

RIBERA DEL DUERO — SPAIN

A newly demarcated area and D.O. of northern Spain, mainly in the province of Burgos, with vineyards on the river Duero, which is the Douro of Portugal. However the best wines are made around the towns of Peñnafiel and Valbuena in the province of Valladolid. The principal grapes are the Tinto Fino and Tinto Aragonés, which is similar to the Tempranillo, and makes wonderful oak aged wines, especially the famous Vega Sicilia, but more accessibly at the Cooperative de Ribera del Duero.

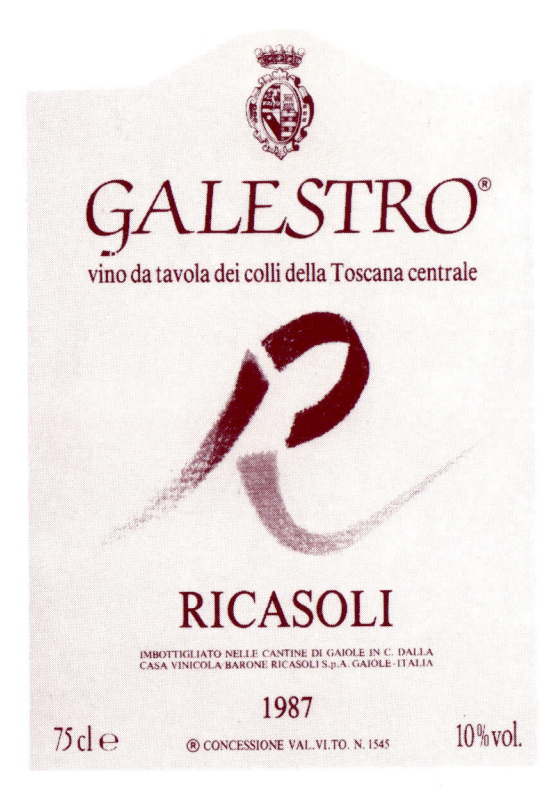

RIBERA D'EBRE   see Tarragona.

RIBOLLA — Friuli-Venezia Giulia: ITALY

A dry white wine included in the DOCs of Collio and Colli Orientali del Friuli, made from the indigenous grape of the same name.

RICASOLI — Tuscany: ITALY

Barone Bettino Ricasoli was the second prime minister of a united Italy in the 1850s and can also be described as the father of modern Chianti, for it was he who refined the *governo* system and laid down the guidelines for vinification at the family property of Castello di Brolio. Today the company makes Chianti and a large range of Tuscan wines, as well as Orvieto.

RICCADONNA — Piedmont: ITALY

A family company with a reputation for Asti Spumante, as well as Vermouth and Marsala. President Brut Riserva Privata, President Extra Brut and President Riserva Crystal Extra Secco are their top brands.

RICHEBOURG Burgundy: FRANCE

An important Grand Cru vineyard in the village of Vosne-Romanée.

RIDDLING

The American term for *remuage*.

RIDGE VINEYARDS California: USA

An isolated winery on a ridge in Santa Clara County which has established a fine reputation for Zinfandel. They are one of the few Californian wineries to use natural yeast; vinification methods are traditional. The wines are labelled according to their provenance, such as the adjoining Montebello Vineyard, as well as Paso Robles, York Creek and others.

RIED AUSTRIA

The Austrian term for a vineyard which has about the same status as an *Einzellage* in Germany.

RIESLANER

A crossing between the Riesling and Silvaner grape varieties, grown mainly in Franconia, but susceptible to rot and *coulure* and not really planted elsewhere.

RIESLING

Several different grape varieties include Riesling in their name. The best is the Rhine Riesling of Alsace and Germany, usually simply called Riesling, which is also termed Johannisberg Riesling and White Riesling. This Riesling should not be confused with the others, Welsch, Gray and Emerald Riesling, which bear no comparison with this elegant grape variety.

Rhine Riesling produces Alsace's best wines, usually fermented dry, but in the best years as *Vendange Tardive* and *Sélection de Grains Nobles*, they are richer and sweeter. In Germany this is the grape responsible for the finest *Prädikat* wines, epitomised by elegantly honeyed Moselle Auslese. Riesling tends to ripen late and benefits from the long warm autumns which brings *noble rot* for *Beerenauslesen* and *Trockenbeerenauslesen* in the best years.

In North East Italy, some Riesling Renano is produced; it is grown in Eastern Europe too, but Welschriesling is more common there.

Riesling has spread to the New World; in California there are Late Harvest Rieslings with *botrytis*, though the wines tend to be a little heavier than their German counterparts. In Oregon too some good wines are made. Riesling in Australia is at its best in the Barossa valley, where it was introduced by Silesian immigrants and is now grown all over the continent. New Zealand has a little Riesling too. In South Africa it is called Weisser Riesling to distinguish it from the inferior South African or Cape Riesling; the wines tend to be off dry.

RIESLING ITALICO see Welschriesling

RIESLING RENANO

The Italian name for the grape variety Rhine Riesling.

RIESLING-SYLVANER

A synonym for the Müller-Thurgau grape variety in New Zealand and Switzerland.

RIEUSSEC Bordeaux: FRANCE

The only first growth Sauternes in the commune of Fargues. It is an important *domaine* that has recently come under the control of Baron Éric de Rothschild. The wine is fermented in stainless steel and aged in new oak barrels. The dry wine is called R.

RIGAL SOUTH WEST FRANCE

Important *négociants* and producers of Cahors, with Chateau St-Didier and Prieuré de Cénac as their flagship properties.

RINCE COCHON

Literally means 'pigswill' and is the Beaujolais equivalent of Kir or *vin blanc cassis* made with red instead of white wine.

RIO NEGRO
ARGENTINA

A province of southern Argentina, with important vineyards in the valley of the river bearing the same name. Temperatures are cooler than elsewhere in the country, and the wines are therefore less alcoholic. Pinot Noir, Malbec, Cabernet Sauvignon and Barbera grapes are grown for red wines and Sauvignon, Pedro Ximenez, Sémillon and Chenin Blanc make crisp whites. Bodegas Canale is the best producer.

RIOJA

The best known of all Spanish table wines. It comes from northern Spain, from vineyards around the town of Logroño and along the river Ebro. The area is split into three; Rioja Baja, Rioja Alta and Rioja Alavesa. This was the first Spanish wine region to be demarcated, with the formation of a *Consejo Regulador* in 1926. The wines have a characteristic vanilla taste coming from their ageing in *barricas* of American oak, resulting in four categories of quality, *sin crianza*, *con crianza*, *reserva* and *gran reserva*. The principal grape varieties are Tempranillo, Graciano, Mazuelo and Garnacha for reds and rosés; Viura, Malvasia and Garnacha Blanca for whites. White Rioja is traditionally aged in oak too, but increasingly less so with producers favouring a fresher style of wine. There are numerous reputable *bodegas* producing good Rioja.

RIOJA ALAVESA
SPAIN

The smallest of the three subregions of Rioja and generally considered to produce the best wines, from a high proportion of the Tempranillo grape, grown on a mixture of chalk and clay. The wines tend to mature more quickly and be less long lasting than those of the Rioja Alta.

RIOJA ALTA
SPAIN

One of the three subregions of Rioja, with the main production centres of Haro and Logroño. The soil is a mixture of chalky and iron rich clay and alluvial silt and Tempranillo is the most important grape. The wines tend to be long lasting.

LA RIOJA ALTA
SPAIN

A well established traditional Rioja *bodega* based in Haro with vineyards in the Rioja Alta and Rioja Baja. Their range includes a young Viña Alberdi, a light Viña Arana, soft velvety Viña Ardanza and a stylish 904 *reserva*. Metropol Extra is a traditional oak-aged white, while Leonora has just a hint of oak.

RIOJA BAJA
SPAIN

The largest of the three subregions of Rioja, covering the south east part of the area. The soil is different from elsewhere in the region, with alluvial silt and clay rich in iron, and the climate is semi-arid. The main grape variety is Garnacha Tinta which gives wines that are high in alcohol, but quick to oxidise. The wines are coarser than those of the Rioja Alavesa and Alta and are often used for blending.

BODEGAS RIOJANES
SPAIN

An old fashioned Rioja *bodega* and some of their wine is still fermented in open stone *lagos*. Their range of wines consists of a traditional white Medieval, a semi sweet Albina, young Canchales, a *clarete* Vina Albina and a red Monte Real.

RIPAILLE
Savoie: **FRANCE**

One of the better crus of vin de Savoie, made only from the eighteen hectare vineyard of the Chateau Ripaille on the shores of Lake Léman. It is a still white wine made from the Chasselas grape.

RIPASSO

Describes a technique used in the making of Valpolicella. In the spring the young wine is passed over the lees of Reccioto, which has just finished fermentation. This is possible as Reccioto is not vinified until January or February, when the grapes have dried sufficiently.

RIPEAU   Bordeaux: FRANCE

A well-known Grand Cru Classé of St-Émilion on the *graves* with a sound reputation.

RIQUEWIHR   Alsace: FRANCE

One of the most picturesque of the wine villages of Alsace. It is the home of several important wine houses and also includes the Sporen and Schoenenberg sites among its vineyards.

MARQUÉS DE RISCAL   SPAIN

The oldest Rioja *bodega*, founded in 1860 by the Marqués de Riscal who was the first to introduce Bordelais methods to Rioja. They have a small parcel of vineyards, some of which are planted with Cabernet Sauvignon. Methods are traditional and meticulous; all the wines are aged in wood for at least four years, followed by further ageing in bottle. White Marqués de Riscal comes from Rueda.

RISERVA

An Italian term for a wine that has been aged for a longer time than usual in barrel, and possibly also in bottle, and is therefore of a better vintage and quality than the basic DOC wine.

RISERVA SPECIALE

An Italian term for a wine that has been aged for a longer time in barrel, and maybe bottle, than either the basic DOC or a *riserva* wine and is therefore of even better quality. In the case of Barbaresco, the ageing period is four years as opposed to three for a *riserva* and two for the basic DOC.

RIUNITE   Emilia-Romagna: ITALY

One of the largest wine producers in the world, grouping 21 cooperatives, making Lambrusco Reggiano as well as white and *rosato spumante* for export to the United States through the American house of Villa Banfi.

LA RIVA   SPAIN

A small sherry *bodega*, with an excellent reputation, especially for old *olorosos* and *palo cortados*.

RIVANER

A synonym for Müller-Thurgau in Luxembourg, Yugoslavia and sometimes England.

RIVERINA   AUSTRALIA

Riverina is another name for the Murrumbidgee Irrigation Area, a wine region in New South Wales.

RIVERLAND   AUSTRALIA

Covers the Murray Valley area of South Australia. The vineyards depend upon irrigation, are generally fertile and originally only produced wine for distillation. Today production is destined for every-day table wines, drinkable but undistinguished. Berri and Renmano are two of the most important producers.

RIVERSIDE   California: USA

A relatively new wine producing county of California, to the south of Los Angeles. The principal grape varieties are Riesling, Cabernet Sauvignon, Chardonnay and Sauvignon Blanc. There is one AVA, Temecula.

RIVESALTES   The Midi: FRANCE

A *vin doux naturel* from the *département* of the Pyrénées Orientales which can be red, white or rosé, made from Grenache, Muscat, Malvoisie or Maccabéo. Muscat de Rivesaltes is a separate appellation.

RIVIERA DEL GARDA DI BRESCIANO   Lombardy: ITALY

A large DOC from southwest of Lake Garda in the province of Brescia. Red and claret are made from Groppello, Sangiovese, Barbera and Marzemino grapes; *superiore* denotes one year's ageing. Comparisons can be made with Valpolicella and Bardolino across the lake.

RIZLING SZILVANI

A Hungarian synonym for the Müller-Thurgau grape variety.

RKATSITELI

A white grape variety of Russian origin, widely planted in the Soviet Union, for dessert wines as well as table wines in Georgia. It is also grown in Eastern Europe. A small amount is grown in California; Concannon Winery bottles it as a light varietal wine, with acidity and delicate spiciness.

ROAIX   Rhône: FRANCE

One of the villages of the appellation Côtes du Rhône Villages from the southern Rhône. It shares a cooperative with Séguret that produces mainly red wine of average quality.

ROBE

The French term to describe colour and appearance. An attractive-looking wine will have *une belle robe*.

ROBERT   See Tanghrite.

ROBERTSON   SOUTH AFRICA

A Wine of Origin district, coming within the larger Breede River Valley district and including the wards of McGregor, Vinkrivier, Goree, Riverside, Ellandia, Boesmansrivier, Agterkliphoogte, Le Chasseur, Hoopsrivier and part of Bonnievale. This is a hot, dry region, requiring irrigation to make good table and fortified wines. Important estates include De Wetshof, Zandvliet and Mont Blois.

ROBOLO   see Ribolla

ROBUST

Describes a tough, full-bodied wine.

ROCCA DELLE MACIE   Tuscany: ITALY

A new modern estate in the heart of Chianti Classico, making streamlined Chianti and Galestro.

LA ROCHE AUX MOINES   Loire: FRANCE

A vineyard and an appellation within the appellation of Savennières. The growers make not only Savennières la Roche aux Moines, but also dry white, rosé and red Anjou. Important estates are Domaine de la Bizolière, Chateau d'Epiré and Château de Chamboureau.

LA ROCHE VINEUSE   See Mâcon Villages.

ROCHEFORT-SUR-LOIRE   Loire: FRANCE

One of the villages of the Coteaux du Layon whose name can feature on the label as Coteaux du Layon – Rochefort-sur-Loire.

ROCHEGUDE   Rhône: FRANCE

One of the villages of the appellation Côtes du Rhône Villages in the southern Rhône. The main producer is the village cooperative.

ANTONIN RODET   Burgundy: FRANCE

An important *négociant* company based in Mercurey, whose principal vineyards are Clos du Roi and Chateau du Chamirey.

LOUIS ROEDERER   Champagne: FRANCE

A champagne house with a justifiably fine reputation, especially for their prestige *cuvée*, Cristal Brut, which comes, unusually, in a clear bottle.

They are the only champagne house to keep their reserve wines in large oak barrels, which give their wines a particular richness. They also have an estate in California's Anderson Valley as well as vineyards in Tasmania.

ROERO   Piedmont: ITALY

A recent DOC for red wine made almost entirely from Nebbiolo grapes with a touch of Arneis. Produced in the province of Cuneo, from the vineyards of several villages. If 12° of alcohol, as opposed to the minimum 11.5°, it may be *superiore*, and cannot be sold until the June following the vintage.

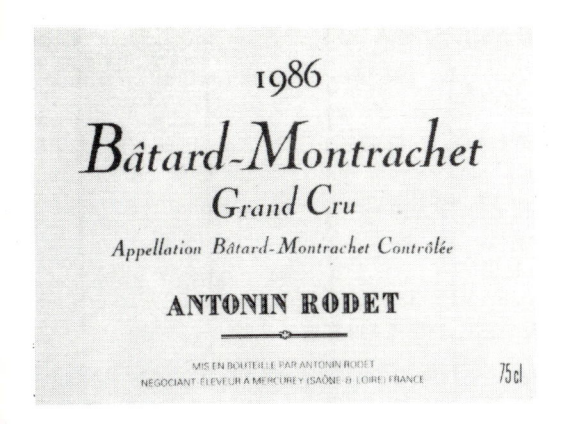

1986 Bâtard-Montrachet Grand Cru — Appellation Bâtard-Montrachet Contrôlée — ANTONIN RODET — 75cl

ROGUE VALLEY — USA
One of the three designated wine areas of Oregon, covering the counties of Jackson and Josephine, centred on Grant's Pass.

NICOLAS ROLIN
Chancellor to the Duchy of Burgundy under Philip the Good. He amassed a fortune while serving the duke and, in 1443 endowed an almshouse and hospital, the Hôtel-Dieu in Beaune. Three of the *cuvées* offered at the sale of the Hospices de Beaune are named after him, in accordance with the custom of using the names of the Hospices' major benefactors, namely Beaune les Cents Vignes, Beaune les Grèves and Beaune en Genet.

ROLLAND — Bordeaux: FRANCE
A Pauillac Cru Grand Bourgeois.

ROLLE
Similar to white Vermentino and found in Provence, notably for Bellet.

ROMA   see Queensland.

ROMAIN   see César

LA ROMANÉE — Burgundy: FRANCE
The tiniest Burgundy Grand Cru vineyard, in the village of Vosne-Romanée.

ROMANÉE-CONTI — Burgundy: FRANCE
A very small Grand Cru vineyard in the village of Vosne-Romanée, owned by the Domaine de la Romanée-Conti which is in turn owned by the de Vilaine and Leroy families. The *domaine* includes vineyards in Richebourg, Romanée-St-Vivant, Grands-Echézeaux, Echézeaux and Montrachet, as well as the whole of La Tâche. These are amongst the most famous wines of Burgundy.

ROMANÉE-ST-VIVANT — Burgundy: FRANCE
A Grand Cru vineyard in the village of Vosne-Romanée.

ROMANIA
One of the world's largest wine producers with vineyards all over the country. Grape varieties are both international and indigenous, including Cabernet Sauvignon, Chardonnay, Ruländer, Muscat, white Fetească, Grasă and Tămîioasa, red Băbească and Fetească Negra. Tirnave is considered to produce the country's best wines, while Cotnari is an individual dessert wine. Most is drunk in Romania or exported to the Soviet Union, and caters for the Soviet taste for heavy, sweet alcoholic wines.

ROMARANTIN
A little known white grape variety of the Loire valley, used mainly in *vins de pays*.

RÖMER
A German wine glass or rummer. The stem is usually amber or green and the glass has a fat clear or engraved bowl.

ROMER (DU HAYOT) — Bordeaux: FRANCE
A second growth Sauternes in Barsac, producing a light modern-style wine, aged in tank.

RONCIÈRES   See Mélinots.

RONDINELLA
One of the grapes used for Valpolicella and Bardolino.

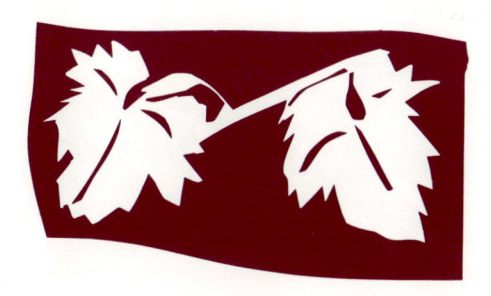

ROODEBERG — SOUTH AFRICA

One of the better red wines of the K.M.V., a full-bodied blend of Pinotage, Shiraz and Tinta Barocca, aged in wood for two years.

ROOTSTOCK

Refers to the roots onto which the scions of *vitis vinifera* are grafted. These are phylloxera-resistant vines, such as *vitis labrusca* and never *vitis vinifera*, which is susceptible to phylloxera.

ROOTY HILL — AUSTRALIA

A vineyard area that is now disappearing under the encroaching suburbs of Sydney.

ROPITEAU FRÈRES

Burgundy: FRANCE

Négociants in Meursault who belong to Chantovent; who handle two family estates, Domaine A, Ropiteau Mignon and Domaine Maurice Ropiteau, concentrating mainly on white wines.

ROSADO

Means pink in Portuguese and Spanish.

ROSATELLO — *Tuscany*: ITALY

A light *rosato* wine from Sangiovese grapes produced all over Tuscany.

ROSATO

Rosé or pink in Italian, referring to wine.

RÖSCHITZ   See Weinviertel.

ROSÉ

The French term for 'pink'

ROSÉ D'ANJOU — *Loire*: FRANCE

A cheerful, slightly sweet, pink wine from Anjou, made mainly from the Groslot grape. Cabernet Franc and Sauvignon, Gamay, Pinot d'Aunis and Malbec are also permitted grape varieties but only account for 10% of the production. It is also possible, but unusual to find Rosé d'Anjou Pétillant.

ROSÉ DE LOIRE — *Loire*: FRANCE

An appellation that covers both Anjou and Touraine, which was created in 1974 to describe a dry rosé. It is made from at least 30% Cabernet, as well as the Groslot, Pineau d'Aunis, Gamay and Pinot Noir grape varieties.

LA ROSE PAUILLAC

Bordeaux: FRANCE

The label for the wines of the Pauillac *cave coopérative*.

ROSÉ DES RICEYS — *Champagne*: FRANCE

An appellation within the boundary of the Champagne area for a *rosé* made from Pinot Noir grapes.

ROSEMOUNT — AUSTRALIA

A relatively new but important estate in the Upper Hunter part of New South Wales, with vineyards in Coonawarra too. Chardonnay and Cabernet Sauvignon are their best wines, with Show Reserves and even better, from the single vineyard of Roxburgh.

ROSETTE — SOUTH WEST FRANCE

A tiny appellation for slightly sweet white wine within the zone of Bergerac, but in fact it is virtually no longer made and any wine sold instead as Côtes de Bergerac.

ROSEWORTHY

Roseworthy Agricultural College in South Australia is the leading oenological centre of Australia, founded in 1883. It has trained many of Australia's finest winemakers and also conducts a considerable amount of research work.

ROSSESE DI DOLCEACQUA
Liguria: ITALY

One of the two Liguria DOCs, made from the Rossese grape around the town of Dolceacqua. It is a fruity red wine and becomes *superiore* after one year's ageing.

ROSSO

Red in Spanish, Portuguese and Italian, referring to wine.

ROSSO BARLETTA
Apulia: ITALY

A dry red DOC wine made from the Uva di Troia grape grown around the town of Barletta. If designated *invecchiato*, it has been aged for two years.

ROSSO CANOSA
Apulia: ITALY

A robust red DOC wine, made mainly from Uva di Troia grapes grown around Canosa. *Riserva* denotes two years' ageing.

ROSSO DI CERIGNOLA
Apulia: ITALY

A red DOC wine from Apulia, made mainly from Uva di Troia and Negroamaro grapes, grown around Cerignola. *Riserva* denotes three years' ageing and it matures well.

ROSSO DELLE COLLINE LUCCHESI
Tuscany: ITALY

A red DOC from the hills around Lucca. Grape varieties are the same as for Chianti, but the wine is lighter.

ROSSO CÒNERO
The Marches: ITALY

A full-flavoured red DOC wine made principally from Montepulciano grapes and possibly some Sangiovese, grown in the hills of Monte Conero, south of Ancona. It develops well with bottle age.

ROSSO DI MONTALCINO
Tuscany: ITALY

A recent red DOC, coming from the same grape and vineyards as Brunello di Montalcino, but with one year's minimum ageing before release.

ROSSO PICENO
The Marches: ITALY

A red DOC made from 60% Sangiovese and 40% Montepulciano grapes grown over a large area. *Superiore* indicates a restricted area between Ascoli Piceno and San Benedetto del Tronto. Ageing in cask and then bottle improves the wine further.

ROTBERGER

Rotberger is a crossing of the Trollinger and Riesling grape varieties, grown in tiny quantities in Germany, mainly in Baden and also a little in Lamberhurst, in England for light red and rosé wines.

ROTGIPFLER

A white Austrian grape variety, grown with Zierfandler to make Gumpoldskirchner, giving the wine weight. Once it was grown in Baden and Alsace but has disappeared from those areas.

ROTGOLD
Baden: GERMANY

Also called Badisch Rotgold, a *Qba* rosé made in Baden by mixing Ruländer and Spätburgunder grapes.

ROTHBURY
AUSTRALIA

One of the leading estates of the Hunter Valley in New South Wales, with a spectacular winery and notable cask- cum banqueting- hall, holding 62 45 hectolitre casks. Shiraz, Cabernet Sauvignon, Pinot Noir and Sémillon are the most important grape varieties. The best wines go under the black 'Individual Paddock' label; next are the individual vineyards and then the ordinary varietals. Rothbury also own the Lachlan Valley vineyard in central New South Wales.

BARON PHILIPPE DE ROTHSCHILD

The owner of Château Mouton Rothschild in Bordeaux until 1988. He devoted his life to the success of this Médoc property, achieving the only alteration in the 1855 classification with the elevation of Mouton from second to first growth. Bordeaux's most successful brand, Mouton Cadet, was also his creation.

ROTLING

A German *rosé* wine made by blending red and white grapes, or their pulp, but not their must or wine.

ROUCHET   Piedmont: ITALY

A rare red wine made from the Rouchet grape, grown in the hills around Castagnoli Monferrato by Antica Casa Vinicola Scarpa. The production is minute.

ROUGE

The French term for 'red'.

ROUGE HOMME   AUSTRALIA

An estate created by the Redman family in Coonawarra, with vineyards on the area's famous terra rossa soil. The property now belongs to Lindeman. The main grape variety was Shiraz, but the range has now been diversified to include a particularly good Cabernet Sauvignon.

ROUGEON

Rougeon or Seibal 5898 is a red wine hybrid vine grown in north America, notably in Canada.

ROUGET   Bordeaux: FRANCE

A second growth Pomerol *château*. New ownership since 1974 is changing this old-fashioned, solid property.

DOMAINE G. ROUMIER
Burgundy: FRANCE

A small family estate in Chambolle-Musigny, with vineyards in Bonnes Mares, le Musigny and les Amoureuses.

ROUSSANNE

One of the white grape varieties of the northern Rhône, and can be used with Marsanne for white Hermitage and the other white appellations of the area. Its flavour is more delicate than Marsanne and it is better able to age. It can also feature in Châteauneuf-du-Pape and in Côtes du Rhône and can even be found in Montecarlo in Tuscany and as Bergeron in Savoie.

DOMAINE ARMAND ROUSSEAU
Burgundy: FRANCE

A reputable estate in Gevrey-Chambertin, making rich long-lived wines, notably from Clos de Bèze, Mazis and Charmes-Chambertin and Gevrey Clos St-Jacques.

ROUSSET-LES-VIGNES Rhône: FRANCE

One of the villages of the appellation Côtes du Rhône Villages in the southern Rhône. It shares a cooperative with St. Pantaléon les Vignes and produces predominantly red wine.

ROUSSETTE DE BUGEY Savoie: FRANCE

Now describes a style of wine, rather than a wine from a specific grape variety. Roussette is the same grape as Altesse, but nowadays the wine is usually made mainly from Chardonnay, with perhaps some Roussette. It is a still wine.

ROUSSETTE DE SAVOIE
Savoie: FRANCE

A dry white wine, that once was made purely from Roussette, but now includes as much as 50% Chardonnay. Four village crus are allowed for Roussette de Savoie, namely Marestel, Monthoux, Monterminod and Frangy. These wines are made purely from Roussette. Roussette de Seyssel is a separate appellation.

ROXBURGH   see Rosemount.

THE ROYAL OPORTO WINE COMPANY

Or to give its full Portuguese name, Real Companhia Vinicola do Norte de Portugal was founded in 1754 by the Marques de Pombal, Prime Minister of King Joseph I, and took on the sole rights to distill grape brandy for the fortification of port and also controlled all grape prices. Today the company's interests are half in port and half in other wines, including sparkling wine.

ROZOVA DOLINA   BULGARIA

Means Valley of Roses, a defined Controliran wine region of origin, for the production of mainly white Misket as a varietal wine.

RUBESCO   See Torgiano and Lungarotti.

RUBICON   SOUTH AFRICA

Rubicon is the brand name for one of the red wines of the Meerlust estate, a Bordeaux blend of 65% Cabernet Sauvignon, 10% Cabernet Franc and 25% Merlot, so called because the owner of the estate thought he figuratively crossed the Rubicon in making such a style of wine.

RUBINO DI CANTAVENNA
Piedmont: ITALY

A little-known DOC wine made from 75–90% Barbera grapes with some Freisa and Grignolino, grown around Cantavenna in the province of Alessandria. It is similar to Barbera di Monferrato.

RUBIRED

A hybrid grape variety grown in California, used to give colour to jug red and port wines, with its *teinturier* character.

RUBY CABERNET

A red grape; a Californian crossing of Carignan and Cabernet Sauvignon, designed to improve jug wines of the San Joaquin valley, as it does well in hot irrigated areas. For this reason it has also been planted in parts of Australia.

RUBY PORT   PORTUGAL

A basic young port with a deep colour, aged in wood for only two or three years and therefore relatively inexpensive. It is not a wine of sufficient character to withstand longer maturation and is ready for early drinking.

RUCHOTTES-CHAMBERTIN
Burgundy: FRANCE

A Grand Cru vineyard in the village of Gevrey-Chambertin.

RÜDESHEIM   Rheingau: GERMANY

This village, opposite Bingen, where the Nahe joins the Rhine, is one of the most important of the Rheingau, known to tourists for its wine bar-lined Drösselgasse. The steep vineyards are on the foothills of the Taunus mountains and several carry the name Berg as well as a site name, of which Rottland, Roseneck and Schlossberg are the best. The *Grosslage* of the village is Burgweg, and other good vineyards include Klosterberg, Rosengarten, Bischofsberg and Klosterlay. The best producers are Schloss Groenesteyn, the State Domain at Eltville and Schloss Schönborn.

Rüdesheim, confusingly, is also the name of a small village of the Nahe, coming within the *Grosslage* of Rosengarten, with wines made mainly from Müller-Thurgau and Silvaner. There is no comparison with the Rüdesheim of the Rheingau.

RUEDA   SPAIN

An important white wine region and D.O. to the south west of Valladolid. The main grape varieties are the indigenous Verdejo and the more recently introduced Palomino. Traditional Rueda is allowed to develop a *flor* and tastes like coarse sherry. The modern wine is fresh and clean, typified in the wine of Marqués de Riscal.

RUEDO   SPAIN

A white table wine from Montilla with 14° alcohol, and unlike most Montilla, not aged in a *solera*.

RUFFINO   Tuscany: ITALY

The largest Chianti house, with not only 954 acres of vineyards but an enormous production from purchased grapes and wine. Their best-known wine is Chianti Classico Riserva Ducale.

RUFINA   Tuscany: ITALY

The smallest of the Chianti Putto zones to the east of Florence producing wines comparable to Chianti Classico. The permitted yield for this zone and for Colli Fiorentini is smaller than for the other Chianti Putto. Frescobaldi at Castello di Nipozzano are notable producers.

RUINART   Champagne: FRANCE

A very stylish champagne house founded in 1729 and part of the Moët Hennessy group. Don Ruinart, a *blanc de blancs* is their prestige *cuvée*.

ZOILO RUIZ-MATEOS   SPAIN

The sherry company of Zoilo Ruiz-Mateos was founded by the man of the same name in 1857. They have vineyards in the best *albariza* areas and make a range of very fine sherries under the Don Zoilo label.

RULANDAC SIVI

A Yugoslav synonym for the Pinot Gris grape.

RULÄNDER

The German name for Pinot Gris, as the grape variety was identified by a German wine merchant, Johann Seger Ruländ in the Palatinate in 1711.

RULLY   Burgundy: FRANCE

A village on the Côte Chalonnaise that has an appellation for both its red and white wine. Sparkling wine is also an important part of the village economy. The Premier Cru vineyards of Rully are Margoté, Gresigny, Vauvry, Mont-Palais, Meix-Caillet, les Pierres, la Bressande, Champ-Clou, la Renarde, Pillot, Cloux, Raclot, Rabourcé, Écloseaux, Marisson, la Fosse, Chapitre, Préau, Moulesne.

Emile Chandesais is an important *négociant* here. Amongst the growers, those with the best reputation are Noël Bouton at Domaine de la Folie and Jean-François Delorme at Domaine de la Renarde. The latter includes red and white Rully les Varots.

RUMASA   SPAIN

Rumasa was an important Spanish holding company run by Don José Maria Ruiz-Mateos with considerable interests in the Spanish wine trade in Jerez, Rioja and Penedès. The company has been expropriated by the Spanish government and most of its associate companies are continuing to function under new ownership.

RUPESTRIS   See *vitis rupestris*.

RUPPERTSBERG   Rheinpfalz: GERMANY
One of the four great names of the Rheinpfalz. All the vineyards of the village are within the *Grosslage* Hofstück. They are Reiterpfad, Hoheburg, Linsenbusch, Gaisböhl, Spiess and Nussbien.

RUSSE RIVERSIDE   BULGARIA
A defined Controliran wine region for white wine from Muscat and Rkatziteli.

RUSSIA   USSR
As a republic of the Soviet Union, Russia contains three wine-producing regions; around Rostov for red, white and sparkling wines from indigenous grape varieties; around Anapa and Novorossiysk on the Black Sea, again for red, white and sparkling wines from grapes that include Riesling and Cabernet and, thirdly, a region next to Azerbaijan for dessert wines. For the rest of the country, see under Soviet Union.

RUSSIAN RIVER VALLEY
California: USA
An important wine region and AVA of Sonoma County, running from the county boundary to Healdsburg. It is a very versatile area, with considerable soil and climatic variations, resulting in a successful mixture of grapes.

RUST   AUSTRIA
One of the most famous Austrian wines, taking its name from an old town of the Burgenland in the Neusiedlersee-Hügelland district. Ruster *Ausbruch* is an especially luscious nobly-rotten wine.

RUTHERFORD HILL WINERY
California: USA
A winery in the Napa Valley which is associated in ownership with Freemark Abbey, but with entirely separate facilities and an individual style of winemaking. Gewürztraminer, Zinfandel and Chardonnay are their best wines.

RUTHERFORD & MILES
An important Madeira house, founded in 1814 and now part of the Madeira Wine Company. Old Trinity House is a brand name.

RUTHERGLEN   AUSTRALIA
The centre of the wine growing district of Northeast Victoria. It boomed with the gold rush and again with the grape rush, declined under phylloxera and is now enjoying a renaissance. The vineyards are on the King, Oven and Murray Rivers, with cold winters and dry summers. Liqueur Muscats are the speciality of the region.

RUSTENBERG   SOUTH AFRICA
The South African estates of Rustenberg and Schoongezicht, under single ownership since 1945, are two adjacent Stellenbosch wine estates with separate histories, which operate as a single wine-making unit, using the cellars at Schoongezicht. The Schoongezicht vineyards concentrate on Cabernet Sauvignon and Pinot Noir. In the Rustenberg vineyards Cabernet Sauvignon is important too. All red wines are labelled Rustenberg and all the whites Schoongezicht.

RUSTICO   Abruzzi: ITALY
A rough red mountain wine made from Montepulciano and Sangiovese grapes.

RUWER *Mosel-Saar-Ruwer*: GERMANY

One of the tributaries of the River Mosel, rising in the Hansrück hills and flowing into the Mosel at the village of Ruwer close to Trier. The main wine villages of the Ruwer valley are Waldrach, Kasel and Eitelsbach. In ripe years the region produces deliciously elegant wines with a firm acidity similar to those of the Saar, which shares the Bereich.

RUŽICA

The Yugoslav term for rosé wine.

S

S.I.C.A.V.A.   Burgundy: FRANCE
The Société d'Intérêt Collectif Agricole du Vignoble Auxerrois is a kind of cooperative that has members amongst the growers of the villages of St-Bris-le-Vineux, Chitry-le-Fort, Coulanges-la-Vineuse and Irancy. The cellars are in the hamlet of Bailly and its sole purpose is to make Crémant de Bourgogne. The grape varieties are principally Aligoté with Sacy and Chardonnay for white, Pinot Noir for white and rosé and Gamay for rosé alone.

SAAR   Mosel-Saar-Ruwer: GERMANY
One of the tributaries of the River Mosel, rising in the Vosges mountains. In ripe years the Saar valley produces deliciously elegant wines with a firm steely acidity coming from the hard slatey soil. It shares a *Bereich* with the Ruwer. The main villages are Serrig, Wiltingen, Ayl and Ockfen.

SAARBURG   Mosel-Saar-Ruwer: GERMANY
Saarburg on the Saar has become the centre of the Saar wine trade. The *Grosslage* is Scharzberg and the vineyard sites include Antoniusberg, Klosterburg, Fuchs, Schlossberg and Rausen.

SABLANT
Was an 18th century name for a *crémant* champagne.

SABLES   Bordeaux: FRANCE
One of the so-called satellites of St–Émilion. These six surrounding communes used to sell their wine as St-Émilion until the appellation was defined in 1936. The name of the parish is hyphenated onto the St-Émilion name. In fact the appellation for Sables, the least important of the six, ended with the 1973 vintage.

SABLET   Rhône: FRANCE
One of the villages of the appellation Côtes du Rhône Villages in the southern Rhône. As the name implies, most of the vineyards are planted on sandy soil. The Villages wines are red and rosé; there is a cooperative and several private domaines, notably Château du Trignon and Domaine du Parandou.

SACCHAROMYCES ELLIPSOIDEUS
The most important variety of natural yeast.

SACCHAROMYCES OVIFORMIS
The yeast responsible for the development of *flor* on *fino* sherry. This thick layer of yeast regulates the access of air to the must and eliminates the harmful vinegar-producing bacteria.

SACCHOROMETER
Another name for a 'mustimeter'.

SACK
The old name for sherry and was also used in the 16th century to describe the wine exported from Málaga and Canary. The term originates from the Spanish word 'sacar' meaning to export. Sack often featured in the works of Elizabethan playwrights.

SACRAMENTO   California: USA
An enormous valley that forms part of the fertile Central Valley of California, as an extension of the San Joaquin Valley. Viticulture here, as elsewhere, suffered considerably with Prohibition, but has undergone a considerable revival in the past decade with grapes destined mainly for jug wines. The most important varietals are French Colombard, Chenin Blanc, Barbera, Carignan, Grenache, Ruby Cabernet and Zinfandel.

SACY
A rather thin, acid white grape variety which was widely planted in the Yonne, in France, until Chardonnay was established as the one and only variety for Chablis. Today Sacy is used for Crémant de Bourgogne and white Bourgogne Grand Ordinaire. It is also found in white Saint-Pourcain along with Sauvignon and Chardonnay, where it is called Tresalier.

SAGRANTINO   See Montefalco.

SAHEL   See Casablanca.

SAINT-AMOUR Burgundy: FRANCE

One of the ten Beaujolais Crus with a right to a separate appellation. Apocryphal stories attribute its name to its aphrodisiac powers. The wines are best drunk young and the Château de Saint-Amour has a good reputation.

SAINT-AUBIN Burgundy: FRANCE

The original St-Aubin was a medieval bishop of Angers. The village is a little apart from the main slope of the Côte d'Or. The vineyards of the neighbouring village of Gamay, that gave its name to the grape, share the appellation. The production, in round terms, is one third white and two thirds red, often sold as Côte de Beaune-Villages. The Premier Cru vineyards are: la Châtenière, les Murgers-des-Dents de Chien, en Remilly, les Frionnes, sur le Sentier du Clou, sur Gamay, les Combes, Champlots. The most important grower in the village is Jean Lamy. Raoul Clerget also specialises in the appellation.

SAINT-AUBIN DE LUIGNÉ Loire: FRANCE

One of the villages of the Coteaux du Layon whose name can feature on the label as Coteaux du Layon Villages – Saint Aubin de Luigné.

SAINT BONIFACIUS See Ice saints.

SAINT-BRIS-LE-VINEUX Burgundy: FRANCE

A village near Chablis that has a reputation for its Sauvignon sold under the label Sauvignon de St-Bris. Growers there grow a mixture of grape varieties: Aligoté is well considered and there is some Chardonnay, Gamay, Sacy and Pinot Noir too. Sometimes the name Côteaux de St-Bris appears on a label.

SAINTE CHAPELLE USA

The leading winery of Idaho, and until 1982 the state's only winery. Its own grapes are supplemented from Oregon and Washington State. Riesling, Gewürztraminer and Chardonnay are showing potential in the cooler climate of Idaho.

SAINT-CHINIAN The Midi: FRANCE

First an appellation in its own right, but now part of the all-embracing Coteaux du Languedoc. It is a predominantly red wine, made from Carignan, Cinsaut and Grenache, with an increasing amount of Syrah and Mourvèdre, grown on vineyards around the town of St-Chinian. The Cave Cooperative de Berlou is the most important producer.

SAINTE-CROIX-DU-MONT Bordeaux: FRANCE

A sweet white wine appellation; the vineyards are separated from those of Sauternes by the river Garonne. The autumnal climate sometimes allows for the development of noble rot, methods are similar to Sauternes and higher yields are allowed, with 40hl/ha, but in a good year the wines can be comparable but lighter.

SAINT-DRÉZERY The Midi: FRANCE

Formerly a VDQS, St-Drezery is now part of the new all-embracing appellation of the Coteaux du Languedoc, a red wine from the village of the same name near Montpellier. Carignan is the main grape variety, making a typical Midi wine.

SAINT-ÉMILION Bordeaux: FRANCE

Situated on the right bank of the Gironde. After the Médoc, it is the most important part of the Bordeaux vineyards. In contrast to the Médoc, Merlot is the dominant grape variety and the usual blend of St-Émilion is about 60% Merlot with 30% Cabernet Franc and maybe a little Cabernet Sauvignon. The wines of St-Émilion tend to be richer and softer than those of the Médoc. The soil and geography of St-Émilion divides the vineyards into two distinctive areas: the rocky hillside vineyards around the town of the *côtes* and the sandy gravelly plain of the *graves* which is next to the vineyards of Pomerol.

The appellation of St-Émilion was defined in 1936 and consists of eight communes: St-Émilion, St-Christophe des Gardes, St-Étienne de Lisse, St-Hippolyte, St-Laurent des Combes, St-Pey d'Armens, St-Sulpice de Faleyrens and Vignoiret. In addition there are the surrounding communes or satellites, as they are called, of Sables, Lussac, Montagne, St-Georges, Puisseguin and Parsac, which hyphenate their name onto that of St-Émilion.

St-Émilion has long been considered something of the country cousin of the Médoc. Consequently it was not classified until 1954 and the classification is designed for regular revision. There are two *châteaux*, Ausone and Cheval Blanc, in the Premier Grand Cru Classé A category and nine in the B category, followed by 72 Grands Crus Classés, last defined in 1985 and, finally, well over 150 Grands Crus, which are reassessed annually.

St-Émilion itself is an attractive hilltop town with a 9th century monolithic church, a medieval keep with ruined ramparts and narrow cobbled streets. The vineyards come right up to the walls of the town, and as well as wine, it is also famous for macaroons.

SAINT-ÉMILION

A synonym for the Trebbiano grape, commonly used in Cognac and also California.

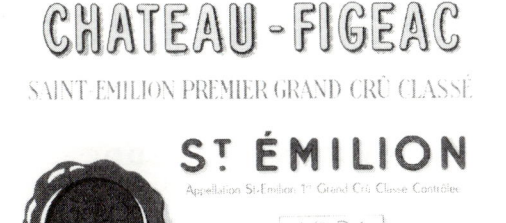

SAINT-ESTÈPHE   Bordeaux: FRANCE

The most northern of the four main communes of the Haut-Médoc. Although it produces more wine than the others, it has fewer classed growths; *Crus Bourgeois* are more significant. The quality range is broader and the taste typified by a certain dry austerity. Cos d'Estournel and Montrose are second growths; Calon Ségur a third growth, Cos Labory a fifth; Meyney, Phélan Ségur and Les Ormes-de-Pez rank among the *Crus Bourgeois*.

SAINT-FIACRE   Loire: FRANCE

An important village within the appellation of Muscadet de Sèvre et Maine.

SAINTE-FOY-BORDEAUX
Bordeaux: FRANCE

A little-known Bordeaux appellation. Only the Dordogne river separates it from Bergerac, with which it has much more affinity. More white wine is made than red.

SAINT-GEORGES   Bordeaux: FRANCE

One of the so-called St-Émilion satellites. These surrounding six parishes used to sell their wine as St-Émilion until the appellation was delimited in 1936. The name of the parish is hyphenated onto St-Émilion.

SAINT-GEORGES-CÔTE-PAVIE
Bordeaux: FRANCE

A little-known Grand Cru Classé of St-Émilion next to Pavie.

SAINT-GEORGES D'ORQUES
The Midi: FRANCE

Formerly a VDQS, St-Georges d'Orques is now part of the new all-embracing appellation of the Coteaux du Languedoc, a red wine from vineyards to the west of Montpellier. Carignan (maximum 50%), Cinsaut (minimum 15%) and Grenache (10–40%) are the main grape varieties, making a wine with good colour and body.

SAINT-GERVAIS
Rhône: FRANCE

One of the villages of the appellation Côtes du Rhône Villages in the southern Rhône, having been elevated to that status in 1974. The vines are mainly Grenache and Cinsaut and the production of the village is dominated by the cave cooperative that makes red and some rosé wines.

SAINT HUBERTUSWEIN

The name given, in Germany, to an *Eiswein* made on 3rd November.

SAINT-JEAN DE LA PORTE
Savoie: FRANCE

One of the crus of Savoie; in practice it never appears on a label and the wine is sold as Vin de Savoie.

SAINT-JEOIRE PRIEURÉ
Savoie: FRANCE

One of the crus of Savoie; in practice it rarely appears on a label and is sold as Vin de Savoie.

SAINT-JOSEPH
Rhône: FRANCE

A wine of the northern Rhône; it is usually red, but can also be white and is made from either Syrah or a blend of Marsanne and Roussanne grapes. The appellation was only created in 1956. The wine is produced from a large area around the village of Mauves; St-Joseph is the name of a nearby hill. The wines tend to be lighter than those of Hermitage across the river. The best growers are Pierre and Gustave Coursodon, Jean-Louis Grippat, Jean-Louis Chave, Jean Marsanne and Raymond Trollat.

SAINT-JULIEN
Bordeaux: FRANCE

One of the principal and the smallest communes of the Médoc. The soil is a mixture of gravel and clay which gives wines the breed of Margaux and the body of Pauillac. A very large proportion of the properties of St-Julien are of Cru Classé quality or, if not, Cru Bourgeois. There are no first growths in the commune, but a rich variety of second growths including Léoville Lascases, Léoville Poyferré, Léoville Barton, Ducru Beaucaillou and Gruaud Larose, as well as wines of lesser status.

SAINT KATHARINEWEIN

The name given, in Germany, to an *Eiswein* made on 25th November.

SAINT-LAMBERT DU LATTAY
Loire: FRANCE

One of the villages of the Coteaux du Layon whose name can feature on the label as Coteaux du Layon Villages – Saint-Lambert du Lattay.

SAINT LAURENT

A red grape variety found almost exclusively in Austria, producing soft fruity wines. It buds and ripens early and gives good yields.

SAINT-LAURENT DE MEDOC
Bordeaux: FRANCE

One of the Médoc communes, but without its own appellation. It has three classed growths: Belgrave, La Tour Carnet and Camensac.

SAINT MAGDALENER See Santa Maddalena.

SAINTE-MARIE D'ALLOIX
Savoie: FRANCE

One of the crus of Savoie; in practice it never appears on a label and the wine is sold as Vin de Savoie.

SAINT-MARTIN

The patron saint of drunkards. He was also an early bishop of Tours in the 4th century who is attributed with the discovery of the beneficial effects of pruning vines, when his donkey ate some young vine shoots. It was subsequently realised that those vines grew more vigorously the following year.

SAINT MARTINSWEIN

The name given, in Germany, to an *Eiswein* made on 11th November.

SAINT MAURICE-SUR-EYGUES
Rhône: FRANCE

One of the villages of the appellation Côtes du Rhône Villages in the southern Rhône. The village cooperative produces mainly red wine, primarily from the Grenache grape.

SAINT-NICHOLAS DE BOURGUEIL
Loire: FRANCE

A red wine from the Loire valley and the only commune within the vineyards of Bourgueil with its own appellation. The grape variety is Cabernet Franc, with a little Cabernet Sauvignon. The only difference is one of yield, 35 hectolitres per hectare for St-Nicholas de Bourgueil and 40 hectolitres per hectare for Bourgueil; otherwise the taste of the wine is similar, with St-Nicholas de Bourgueil possibly a little lighter than Bourgueil.

SAINT NIKOLAUSWEIN

The name given, in Germany, to an *Eiswein* made on 6th December.

SAINT PANCRATIUS   See Ice Saints.

SAINT PANTALEIMON
CYPRUS

Keo's brand name for their sweet white wine.

SAINT-PANTALÉON LES VIGNES
Rhône: FRANCE

One of the villages of the appellation Côtes du Rhône Villages from the southern Rhône. It shares a cooperative with Rousset-les-Vignes and produces predominantly red wine.

SAINT-PÉRAY
Rhône: FRANCE

The most southern vineyards and village of the northern Rhône. It is a pocket of sparkling wine in a predominantly red wine area. Wagner is purported to have consumed large quantities of it while he was composing Parsifal. St. Péray is made by the *méthode champenoise* predominantly from the Marsanne grape. Some Roussanne and Roussette can also be included. Leading growers include Jean-François Chaboud, Alain Voge, Auguste Clape.

SAINT-PIERRE
Bordeaux: FRANCE

A fourth growth St-Julien. In the 1855 classification, this property was divided in two, St-Pierre Sevaistre and St-Pierre Bontemps-Dubarry. It is now under one owner and making something of a comeback.

SAINT-PIERRE DE MONS
Bordeaux: FRANCE

An important commune within the Graves, producing particularly good white wine.

SAINT-POURÇAIN SUR SIOULE
Loire: FRANCE

A tricolour VDQS wine from the vineyards around the town of Saint-Pourçain on the banks of the Allier and its tributary the Sioule. The white wines are dry and crisp, made predominantly from the Tressalier (or Sacy) grape as well as some Chardonnay and Sauvignon. Gamay and Pinot Noir are the grapes for the red and rosé wines, which may resemble lighter versions of Beaujolais.

SAINT-ROMAIN
Burgundy: FRANCE

The village of St-Romain, like St-Aubin, is more part of the *arrière côte* than the main Côte de Beaune and it was only recognised as an appellation in its own right in 1967. Twice as much white as red wine is produced from its steep vineyards. There are no Premiers Crus and the principal growers are Henri Buisson. Fernand Bazenent, René and Alain Cras, and Roland Thévenin.

SAINT-SATURNIN — The Midi: FRANCE

The former VDQS of St-Saturnin is part of the new appellation of the Coteaux du Languedoc, with red and rosé wines made from the grape varieties Carignan, Grenache, Cinsaut and a little Syrah and Mourvèdre. The only producer is the modernised cooperative in the village of St-Saturnin.

SAINT-SAUVEUR — Bordeaux: FRANCE

One of the communes within the Haut-Médoc appellation. Its better wines are similar to lesser Pauillacs.

SAINT SERVATIUS See Ice Saints.

SAINT-SEURNIN DE CADOURNE — Bordeaux: FRANCE

One of the communes within the Haut-Médoc appellation making wines that resemble St-Estèphe.

SAINT SOPHIA See Ice Saints.

SAINT-VÉRAN — Burgundy: FRANCE

One of the Mâconnais white wine appellations. It only came into existence in 1971 and was created to offer an alternative to the extortionately-priced Pouilly Fuissé, instead of Beaujolais Blanc. The wine is made from the Chardonnay grape grown in the villages of Chanes, Leynes, Pruzilly, St-Vérand and Saint-Amour.

SAINT-VINCENT

The patron saint of French wine growers; his feast is commemorated, particularly in Burgundy, on 22nd January. The story has it that he became thirsty in heaven and asked to return to earth so that he might taste the great wines of France again. Every intention to return to heaven was undone by the wines of the Graves. He was in the cellar of La Mission Haut-Brion in a drunken stupor and turned into stone. There is a statue to St Vincent in the cellars of La Mission Haut-Brion, and in other French wine cellars too.

SAINT-YZANS — Bordeaux: FRANCE

An important commune within the Médoc appellation. Its principal property is Loudenne.

SAINTSBURY — California USA

The first Saintsbury wines were made in 1981. Named after George Saintsbury, this winery concentrates on Chardonnay and Pinot Noir, notably from the cool region of Carneros, with considerable success.

SAINTSBURY CLUB

A dining club founded in memory of Dr. George Saintsbury who wrote 'Notes on a Cellarbook', published in 1920. He was known for his particularly fine cellar.

SAIS — MOROCCO

An *appellation d'origine garantie*, in the region of Meknès Fez.

SAKAK — BULGARIA

A defined Controliran wine region of origin, for the production of Merlot and Cabernet Sauvignon as varietal wines.

DE SALES — Bordeaux: FRANCE

The largest Pomerol property, of second growth rather than top class. The *château* is 18th century and the vineyards have been owned by the de Laage family for 400 years. The second label is Chantalouette.

SALICE SALENTINO — Apulia: ITALY

A red and *rosato* DOC wine made mainly from Negroamaro grapes grown around the town of Salice Salentino. The *rosato* can be aged for a year and designated *prodotto invecchiato*. The red is a *riserva* after two years' ageing and can be long-lived.

SALINAS
California: USA

The broad Salinas Valley is the main wine area of the central coast of California, with most of the vineyards of Monterey County and two AVAs, Arroyo Seco and Chalone. Climate varies, with an appropriate variety of grapes.

LES SALINS DU MIDI
The Midi: FRANCE

The principal producer of Vin de Pays du Golfe du Lion and the biggest vineyard owner of France with land on the phylloxera-free sand dunes of the Gulf of Lions. The company's principal estates are Domaines du Villeroy, de Jarras and du Bosquet as well as Château la Gordonne, a Côtes de Provence and the Abbaye de Ste-Hilaire in the Coteaux Varois. Many of its wines are sold under the brand name Listel.

SALMANAZAR

A champagne bottle size equal to twelve ordinary bottles (900cl).

SALON LE MESNIL
Champagne: FRANCE

A champagne house and one of the finest producers of *blanc de blancs* champagne.

SALTA
ARGENTINA

The province of Salta is mountainous and arid, but there is one small oasis of vineyards where the particular microclimate of the valley of Cafayate allows for the cultivation of 1500 hectares of vines. The main grape variety is the white Torrontes for spicey, aromatic wines. Bodega La Rosa is the best producer.

SALTRAM
AUSTRALIA

An old Barossa Valley winery established in the 1860s. Since then its ownership has been varied and it now belongs to Seagrams, with a range of good varietals, also using grapes from Coonawarra, Hunter Valley, Clare Valley, and McLaren Vale. Memare Brook Cabernet Sauvignon (75%) Shiraz (25%) and Bin 88 Selected Vintage Claret are the best wines.

SALVAGNIN
SWITZERLAND

A red wine from the Vaud, a blend of Gamay and Pinot Noir grapes, or just Gamay, making a lighter version of Dôle.

SAMOS
GREECE

The island of Samos has a reputation for its sweet unfortified Muscat produced from steep, terraced vineyards all over this mountainous island.

SAMPIGNY LES MARANGES   See Les Maranges.

SAN BENITO
California: USA

The vineyards of San Benito form part of the Central Coast area of California, with three AVAs, La Cienega, Paicines and Limekiln. Chardonnay, Pinot Noir and Cabernet Sauvignon are the main varietals.

SAN BERNARDINO COUNTY
California: USA

A relatively unimportant wine producing county of the South Coast area of California, planted mainly with Mission and Zinfandel grape varieties.

SAN COLOMBANO AL LAMBRO
Lombardy: ITALY

One of the more distinctive and recent DOC wines from the outskirts of Milan. Red, from a mixture of Barbera, Bonarda, Merlot, Cabernet and Malbec grapes, is dry, sometimes *frizzante* and benefits from some ageing. White is best drunk young and comes from Verdea, Riesling Tocai and Pinot Grigio grapes.

SAN DIEGO
California: USA

An unimportant wine-growing county of Southern California, almost adjoining the Mexican border, with one small AVA, San Pasqual.

SAN GIOCONDO
Tuscany: ITALY

A *novello* wine made from Chianti grapes by Antinori.

SAN GIORGIO
Umbria: ITALY

The name given to the Lungarotti blend of Torgiano Rosso to which 20% Cabernet Sauvignon grapes have been added. This is a superlative *vino da tavola*.

SAN JOAQUIN *California:* USA

The name of a valley and a county, forming part of the enormous Central Valley of California, where grapes grow prolifically to produce huge quantities of jug wines. California's largest wineries are here. The most important varietals are French Colombard, Chenin Blanc, Barbera, Carignan, Grenache, Ruby Cabernet and Zinfandel, which flourish in the hot climate.

SAN JUAN ARGENTINA

An important wine region to the north of Mendoza. The climate is hotter and dryer, so the vines are irrigated. White grapes dominate the production for sherry styles that are then aged in wooden casks in the sun.

SAN LUIS OBISPO *California:* USA

A county of the Central Coast area of California, that is growing in importance, with a range of grape varieties, Zinfandel, Cabernet Sauvignon, Chardonnay and others. It has four AVAs, Paso Robles, Templeton, and York Mountain in the north and Edna Valley in the south.

SAN PASQUAL *California:* USA

An AVA in San Diego County.

SAN PATRICIO

A sherry brand named after the patron saint of Ireland, owned by Garvey for their *fino* sherry.

SAN SADURNIU DE NOYA SPAIN

A small town in Pendès that is the centre of the Spanish *cava* trade.

SAN SEVERO *Apulia:* ITALY

A tricoloured DOC wine from northern Apulia. The red and *rosato* are made from Montepulciano d'Abruzzo grapes with some Sangiovese. The dry white comes from Trebbiano Toscano and Bombino Bianco.

SANCERRE *Loire:* FRANCE

White Sancerre is one of the most popular wines of the Loire Valley. It is made from the Sauvignon grape, grown in Sancerre and thirteen other surrounding villages and has a distinctive steely taste. There is also Sancerre Rosé and Rouge, made from Pinot Noir and less successful than the white wine. The small town of Sancerre perches on a hill overlooking the vineyards, with narrow windy streets and medieval houses.

SANDEMAN

One of the largest port and sherry shippers, with a worldwide reputation based on their early advertising with their trademark of the Don. The company was founded in 1790 by George Sandeman and is now owned by Seagrams, but still with close family involvement. They only began buying vineyards in Portugal in the Douro in the 1970s and now have extensive estates. They are associated with Robertson, Offley Forrester, Diez Hermanos and Rodriguez Pinho. In Jerez they make fine sherry by traditional methods, including Dry Don Amontillado, Apitiv fino and Armada Cream.

SANFORD & BENEDICT VINEYARDS *California:* USA

A small winery at the western end of the Santa Ynez Valley, that specialises successfully in Pinot Noir and Chardonnay.

SANGIOVESE

The Sangiovese grape is grown all over central Italy. There are numerous different clones and variations, dividing broadly into Sangiovese Grosso and Sangiovese Piccolo, with a considerable range in quality. Sangiovese is at its best for Brunello di Montalcino, made purely from the Brunello clone of Sangiovese Grosso, which was isolated by the Biondi Santi family in the last century. Sangiovese is the principal grape variety of Chianti where it is blended with other grapes. It does particularly well with Cabernet Sauvignon, in wines like Carmignano and Tignanello, as it can lack colour and tannin and is often rather astringent so that it benefits from the extra flavour of the Cabernet. For Vino Nobile di Montepulciano the blend is similar to Chianti and the Sangiovese clone is Prugnolo.

Sangiovese Piccolo is commonly planted in Emilia-Romagna, where its yields are prolific and the wine rather dull. Sadly it is also present in some Chianti vineyards, as well as in the Marches, Latium and Umbria.

SANGIOVESE DEI COLLI PESARESI
The Marches: ITALY

A little-known red DOC made from Sangiovese grapes grown around Pesaro and Urbino.

SANGIOVESE DI ROMAGNA
Emilia-Romagna: ITALY

A DOC wine made from a different strain of Sangiovese grape to that found in Tuscany. If aged for two years, it qualifies for *riserva* but is best drunk as a youthful red wine.

SANGIOVETO

A Tuscan name for the Sangiovese grape variety.

SANGRIA

A typical Spanish drink, a cold punch made from red wine, lemon juice and soda water, ideal for quenching the thirst on a hot summer's day.

SANGUE DI GIUDA   See Oltrepò Pavese.

SANLUCAR DE BARRAMEDA   SPAIN

A seaside town close to Jerez de la Frontera that is famous for *manzanilla* sherry.

SANSONNET
Bordeaux: FRANCE

A little-known Grand Cru Classé of St-Émilion next to Trottevielle.

SANT'ANNA DI ISOLA CAPO RIZZUTO
Calabria: ITALY

A light, youthful red DOC wine made from Gaglioppo and other grapes grown on the Ionian coast around the town of the same name.

SANTA BARBARA
California: USA

A wine producing county of the Central Coast, but only since the 1960s. It has two AVAs, the adjoining Santa Ynez and Santa Maria Valleys. Chardonnay, Gewürztraminer, Chenin Blanc and Riesling are the main grape varieties.

SANTA CLARA
California: USA

The wine producing county immediately south of the Bay of San Francisco. Its vineyards come within the AVA of Santa Cruz Mountain which extends into Santa Cruz and San Mateo Counties. Cabernet Sauvignon is the most important varietal.

SANTA CRUZ
California: USA

A Central Coast county, but a relatively unimportant wine region.

SANTA CRUZ MOUNTAIN
California: USA

An AVA in Santa Clara County, extending into Santa Cruz and San Mateo counties, producing good Chardonnay and Cabernet Sauvignon, in a cool climate.

SANTA MADDALENA
Trentino-Alto Adige: ITALY

Also called St Magdalener, a small village outside the town of Bolzano which gave its name to what was once considered the best Alto Adige wine and is now a soft red wine made from the Schiava grape. It is best drunk young.

SANTA MARIA VALLEY
California: USA

One of the two AVAs of Santa Barbera County, and very similar to the adjoining Santa Ynez Valley.

SANTA YNEZ VALLEY
California: USA

An AVA in Santa Barbara County in southern California, with a good reputation for Pinot Noir grapes in its cooler areas. Riesling, Chardonnay, Gewürztraminer and Chenin Blanc are good too.

SANTENAY   Burgundy: FRANCE

The southernmost village of the Côte de Beaune. It produces predominantly red wine but also a little white. The full name of the village is Santenay-les-Bains, thanks to two springs that are reputed to cure gout and rheumatism. The following vineyards are classified as Premier Cru: les Gravières (part), le Clos des Tavannes (part), la Comme (part), Beauregard (part), le Passe Temps, Beaurepaire, la Maladière. The most important grower of the village is the Prosper Maufoux *négociant* company. Other estates include Domaine Lequin-Rossot, Domaine Fleurot-Larose, Domaine de l'Abbaye de Santenay and the Château de Santenay.

SANTORINI   GREECE

This volcanic island of the Cyclades has a particular microclimate with strong winds and hot sunshine so the wines are high in both alcohol and acidity. The best are white and may be sweet or dry, made from Assyrtiko grapes and called Nycteri locally. There is also a wine not unlike a French *vin de paille*.

SAPERAVI

A red grape grown extensively in the Soviet Union and also in Bulgaria. The name means 'dyer' and the juice is bright pink, giving rich wines with an ability to age.

SARAP

The Turkish word for 'wine'.

SARDINIA   ITALY

The second largest Mediterranean island produces an enormous variety of wines. The industry is dominated by cooperatives, with the exception of one company, Sella & Mosca. There are 14 DOC wines, as well as non-DOC versions of the main grapes, Vermentino, Torbato and Cannonau, demonstrating modernisation of methods. Traditional strong dessert wines are still produced, such as Vernaccia di Oristano and aromatic Muscatels.

SARGET DE GRUAUD-LAROSE
                              Bordeaux: FRANCE

The second wine of the Gruaud-Larose estate.

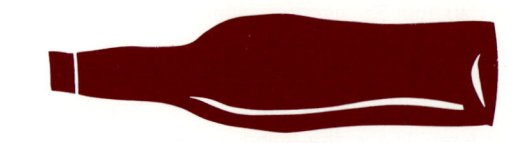

SARMENT

The French word for the cuttings taken from the vines at pruning. They will often be gathered up and used for barbecues. A *grillade aux sarments* is a gastronomic delight in most wine regions.

SARMENTO   Tuscany: ITALY

Not a novello, but a light red wine to be drunk the summer following the vintage, introduced for the first time in 1988, by the big four Tuscan producers, namely Frescobaldi, Antinori, Ruffino and Melini. The grapes are Sangiovese and Canaiolo, grown in the central hills of Tuscany. The vinification allows for some *maceration carbonique* and the wine is not released for sale until May. The recommendation is to drink it slightly chilled, like white wine.

SARRAU   Burgundy: FRANCE

An important Beaujolais house whose principal estate is Château des Capitans in Juliénas, with other estates in the region and a *négociant* activity extending from Chablis to Châteauneuf-du-Pape.

SARTÈNE   CORSICA

One of the separate areas within the overall appellation Vin de Corse and covers the vineyards to the north and south of the historic town of Sartène on the west coast. The white wine is made from Malvoisie de Corse and the local Sciacarello grapes give particularly good results on the granite soil, when blended with other Corsican and Midi grape varieties for red and rosé. The maximum yield is 45 hectolitres per hectare and the minimum alcohol level 11.5°.

SASSELLA   Lombardy: ITALY

One of the four areas of Valtellina Superiore, generally considered the best.

SASSICAIA   Tuscany: ITALY

A red wine made from barrel-aged Cabernet Sauvignon grapes, with some Cabernet Franc, on the estate of the Marchese Incisa della Rochetta near Bolghieri on the coast. Production is small and the wine merits its fine reputation.

SAUMUR Loire: FRANCE

An attractive town on the Loire, with an imposing château and a famous riding school, as well as vineyards that produce red, white, rosé and sparkling wines. The sparkling wine, Saumur Mousseux, is more important than the still wine and many of the producers have their cellars in Saumur. Saumur Blanc is made mainly from the Chenin Blanc grape, with a little Chardonnay and Sauvignon. It is usually rather dry and acidic. There are two types of red Saumur, Saumur Rouge and Saumur Champigny. Saumur Rouge is the lesser of the two but both are light fruity wines made from Cabernet Franc and occasionally Cabernet Sauvignon and Pinot d'Aunis. Pink Saumur is known as Cabernet de Saumur.

SAUMUR CHAMPIGNY Loire: FRANCE

The better of the two red wines of Saumur. The vineyard area has increased in recent years, thanks to the main producer, the cave cooperative of Saint Cyr en Bourg. The predominant grape variety is Cabernet Franc and the wine has a little more substance than Saumur Rouge.

SAUMUR D'ORIGINE   see Saumur Mousseux.

SAUMUR MOUSSEUX Loire: FRANCE

Saumur is the home of the sparkling wine industry of the Loire. Many of the best producers have had their cellars there, since the first sparkling Saumur was produced by Jean Ackerman in 1811. Saumur Mousseux, which can be red, white or pink, is made from several possible grapes: Chenin Blanc, Chardonnay, Sauvignon, Cabernet Franc, Cabernet Sauvignon, Malbec, Gamay, Groslot, Pineau d'Aunis and Pinot Noir, grown in a large area around the town. The method is identical to that of Champagne, as introduced by Jean Ackerman and the limestone or tufa of Saumur provides an ideal atmosphere for maturing the wine in miles of underground cellars. The name Saumur Mousseux has a slightly pejorative note, and so Saumur d'Origine sometimes appears on a label.

SAUSSIGNAC SOUTH WEST FRANCE

A small appellation around the village of Saussignac within the zone of Bergerac. It was originally called Côtes de Saussignac, but the name was recently shortened. The wine is identical to Côtes de Bergerac and in reality many growers prefer to sell their wine under that label rather than as unknown Saussignac.

SAUTERNES Bordeaux: FRANCE

One of the great sweet wines of the world. It comes from part of the vineyards of Bordeaux, from a small area within the Graves, limited by the Garonne and consisting of five communes: Sauternes itself, Bommes, Fargues, Preignac and Barsac, which is also a separate appellation. Wine from Barsac may call itself Sauternes, but wine from outside Barsac may not be labelled Barsac.

The particular honeyed character of Sauternes comes from the special climatic conditions that, in good years, encourage the development of noble rot so the grape juice is rich and concentrated. The little River Ciron, that crosses the vineyards of Sauternes, is especially responsible for the necessary microclimate of autumnal misty mornings. The desired conditions do not occur every year and in a decade there are at least two or three years when little Sauternes is made.

The best Sauternes is made with painstaking care. The grape varieties are Sémillon, Sauvignon and maybe a little Muscadelle and the maximum yield is 25 hl/ha. There are several pickings, or *tries*, which means only overripe, or, in the very best years, nobly rotten grapes are picked, grape by grape. The juice is fermented, in new oak barrels at the best properties, and the fermentation can last two to six weeks. When about 14° alcohol is reached the yeast stops working, leaving a rich sweet wine which is then aged in oak barrels for up to three and a half years.

The Sauternes *châteaux* were classified in 1855; the best is indisputably d'Yquem and there are eleven first growths, fifteen second growths and a number of Crus Bourgeois.

Sauternes is drunk with puddings, and is also a delicious accompaniment to *foie gras* and blue cheese. However the difficult economics of production mean that some *châteaux* also make drier wines with the

Château d'Yquem
Lur-Saluces
— 1983 —

Bordeaux Blanc appellation, to use the cachet of the *château* name.

Unfortunately the name Sauternes has been borrowed in other parts of the world, to describe any sweet white wine.

SAUVIGNON BLANC

This grape produces crisp dry white wine with a strong varietal character and an aromatic flavour, variously described as gooseberry leaves or attributed with feline associations. Sauvignon Blanc is at its best in the Loire Valley in France; the appellations of Sancerre and Pouilly Fumé, as well as lesser Ménétou Salon, Reuilly and Quincy depend upon it. It is also grown for Sauvignon de Touraine and for some of the *vins de pays* of the Loire Valley. Further west in northern Burgundy at St-Bris le Vineux, there is an enclave of Sauvignon, a VDQS wine, Sauvignon de St-Bris. Further south it is one of the grapes of white Bordeaux and of the peripheral appellations. Bordeaux Blanc and Entre Deux Mers are becoming drier thanks to Sauvignon. Here it can benefit from the rounding influence of Semillon, notably in fine Graves and it is an essential ingredient of Sauternes. The white wines of Bergerac, Côtes de Duras, Côtes de Marmandais are based on Sauvignon. Some is planted by adventurous growers in the Midi and in Provence it is one of the permitted grape varieties of Coteaux d'Aix en Provence.

A little Sauvignon is grown by Miguel Torres in Penedès; otherwise it is not found in Spain. It has crossed the Alps to northern Italy and appears in the Alto Adige and Friuli. There is some in Eastern Europe too.

More exciting are the Sauvignons of the New World, typified by the Fumé Blanc, a common American synonym, particularly of Robert Mondavi. Pure Sauvignon is rarely oak aged in Europe, whereas in California it is more common practice. Sauvignon has spread to Argentina and now also to Chile. In South Africa it has had a little success, as typified by that of L'Ormarins. In Australia, it is planted mainly in South Australia, but not in any quantity, and is attaining some success in New Zealand, such as Montana's Marlborough Sauvignon.

Sauvignon is enjoying a fashion as a distinctive, easy-to-identify, easy-to-drink grape variety. It rarely ages well and lacks the nuance and subtlety of grapes like Rhine Riesling and Chardonnay.

SAUVIGNON DE ST-BRIS
Burgundy: FRANCE

A wine made from the Sauvignon grape grown in vineyards around the village of St-Bris-le-Vineux in northern Burgundy. As the Sauvignon is not considered a Burgundian grape, the wine only has the status of VDQS.

SAUVIGNON VERT

A Californian synonym for the Muscadelle grape.

SAUVION
Loire: FRANCE

An important family of growers and *négociants* in Muscadet. They own Chateau de Cléray, apparently the first Muscadet to be shipped to the Peoples' Republic of China and deal in many other properties.

SAVAGNIN

A grape variety peculiar to the Jura where it is the only grape allowed for *vin jaune* and Château Chalon. For the ordinary white wines of the Jura it is usually blended with Chardonnay. There may be a relationship between Savagnin and Gewürztraminer.

Savagnin Noir is a synonym for Pinot Noir. Savagnin Rosé is a little-grown grape variety of Alsace, sometimes called Clevner d'Heiligenstein or Heiligensteiner Klevner.

SAVATIANO

Greece's most popular white grape variety, grown extensively for retsina.

SAVENNIERES
Loire: FRANCE

Savennières is one of the smallest appellations of Anjou, a unique dry white wine, made purely from Chenin Blanc, with a quite individual flavour, neither sweet nor really dry and capable of considerable longevity. There are two particularly fine vineyards with their own appellation, Coulée de Serrant and La Roche aux Moines. The maximum yield is only 30 hectolites per hectare and the minimum alcohol is unusually high at 12°. Jean Baumard, with Clos du Papillon is an important grower.

SAVIGNY-LES-BEAUNE
Burgundy: FRANCE

This village is the third largest producer of wine on the Côte de Beaune after Beaune and Pommard, but its reputation is not at the same level. The Premier Cru vineyards are: les Vergelesses, aux Vergelesses known as Bataillière, les Marconnets, la Dominode, les Jarrons, Basses-Vergelesses, les Lavières, aux Gravains, les Peuillets (part), aux Guettes (part), les Talmettes, les Charnières, aux Fourneaux (part), aux Clous (part), aux Serpentières (part), les Narbantons, Haut Marconnets, Haut Jarrons, Redrescuts (part), les Rouvrettes (part), aux Grands Liards (part), aux Petits Liards (part) and Petits Godeaux (part).

Growers in Savigny include Simon Bize, Domaine Chandon de Briailles, Doudet Naudin, Laurent Gauthier, Albert Lacroix, Pierre Petitjean, Girard-Vallot and Henri de Villamont.

SAVOIE
FRANCE

Vin de Savoie has been an appellation since 1973 for dry white, red and rosé wines, as well as a little rosé and some white sparkling wine, called Vin de Savoie Mousseux. The vineyards are in the *départements* of Savoie and Haute Savoie, around Chambéry and Lake Bourget and further north towards Lake Léman. Reds and rosés made from Gamay and Pinot Noir are generally light and fruity, while red made from Mondeuse is more substantial. Jacquère is the characteristic white grape of the vineyards south of Chambéry, while Chasselas is the dominant white variety towards Lake Léman. Roussette, also called Altesse, is also grown, as well as Chardonnay and a little Aligoté for crisp dry whites. There are sixteen crus of varying importance, which are allowed to add their name to the appellation, or label their wine under that name alone, namely Abymes, Apremont, Arbin, Ayze, Charpignat, Chautagne, Chignin, Chignin-Bergeron, Cruet, Jongieux, Marignan, Montmélian, Ripaille, St. Jean de la Port, St. Jeoire-Prieuré and Ste. Marie d'Alloix. The new addition of Marin is foreseen.

SAVUTO
Calabria: ITALY

A red DOC wine made from Gaglioppo and Greco Nero grapes grown on the hills along the Savuto river. With two years' ageing it becomes *superiore* and develops well into a fragrant red.

SCALE see solera.

SCHARZHOFBERG see Wiltingen.

SCHAUMWEIN

The German term for sparkling wine, without any specific qualifications. The better *Schaumwein* or *Qualitätsschaumwein* is called *Sekt*.

SCHENK
SWITZERLAND

The largest vineyard owner and wholesaler of Swiss wines, with subsidiaries in France, Spain and northern Italy. Their property includes a host of wine estates with a good reputation.

SCHEUREBE

A German grape variety, a cross between Silvaner and Riesling, developed by Georg Scheu in 1916. It is one of the more successful new German crossings, with good yields and distinctive character, ripening well and susceptible to botrytis. The perfume is characterised by grapefruit pith.

SCHIAVA

Known as Trollinger in Wurttemberg, as Vernatsch in the Südtirol, and as Black Hamburg in England, where it is a table grape. It is the most prolific red grape of the Trentino-Alto Adige area of northern Italy, where its most distinctive wine is often the soft, easy to drink St-Magdalener. Variations of the grape include Grossvernatsch or Schiava Grossa, Kleinvernatch or Schiava Piccola or Gentile and Grauvernatsch or Schiava Grigia.

SCHILLERWEIN

German rosé wine made from red and white grapes which were once planted and harvested together unlike Weissherbst which comes only from red grapes. It is very popular in Württemberg. *Schillern* means 'to change colour' and the name originates from the wine's varying shades of red.

SCHIOPPETTINO
Friuli-Venezia Giulia: ITALY

A non-DOC wine from Friuli-Venezia Giulia, this is a curiosity made from the indigenous red Ribolla Nera or Schioppettino grape at Albano di Prepotto in the Colli Orientali del Friuli.

SCHIST

A decomposed granite and the principal soil of the port vineyards in the Douro, resulting in heavy full-bodied wines. Generally, it is more suited to red than white wines and is particularly hard to work.

SCHLEGELFLASCHE

The German term for the traditional long-necked bottle used for Rhein and Mosel wines. Before the standardisation of bottle sizes, German bottles were particularly long and elegant, but have now tended to become fatter.

SCHLORLEMER
Mosel-Saar-Ruwer: GERMANY

Hermann Freiherr von Schlorlemer GmbH, one of the largest estates of the region made up of five properties, namely: Weingut Meyerhof, Weingut Schloss Lieser, Weingut Schlangengraben, Weingut Franz Duhr Nachf and Weingut Clemens Freiherr von Schlorlemer and now owned by Peter Meyer Horne KG in Bernkastel. Their vineyards are in Graach, Bernkastel, Wehlen, Zeltinger, Ockfen and Wiltingen. They also make *Sekt*. The estate of Stephanus Freiherr von Schlorlemer at Lieser is an independent producer of fine Mosel wines.

SCHLOSS

The German equivalent of a French *château*, but usually less common.

SCHLOSS GROENSTEYN
Rheingau: GERMANY

An estate originating in 1400, owned by the Barons von Ritter zu Groensteyn since 1640 and run from their baroque mansion, or schloss, in Kiedrich, with cellars in Rüdesheim. Most of the vineyards are planted with Riesling vines, and the sites are principally in Rüdesheim and Kiedrich. The wines are aged in wood and attain great quality.

SCHLOSS JOHANNISBERG
Rheingau: GERMANY

One of the great estates of the Rheingau and owned by descendants of Prince Metternich, who was given the property by the Austrian Emperor after the Treaty of Vienna in 1816. It was at Schloss Johannisberg that the messenger carrying permission to begin the vintage failed to arrive, leading to the discovery of the quality of noble rot in Germany. The estate was also the first to plant Riesling unmixed with other varieties in 1716 and the vineyards are still pure Riesling. Wines are matured in oak. Different coloured capsules are used to indicate different qualities and the wine is sold without any vineyard names.

SCHLOSS REINHARTSHAUSEN
Rheingau: GERMANY

An important estate with origins reputedly dating back to Charlemagne, now owned by the Prince of Prussia. Vineyards include sites in Erbach, Hattenheim, Kiedrich, Rauenthal and Rüdesheim, with sole ownership of Erbacher Siegelsberg and Erbacher Rheinhell. Traditional casks are used and the vineyards are planted mainly with Riesling vines.

SCHLOSS SCHÖNBORN
Rheingau: GERMANY

The first vineyards were acquired by the von Schönborn family in 1349 and they still own this large estate. Riesling is the main grape in their vineyards, which include parcels in Oestrich, Rüdesheim, Geisenheim, Winkel Johannisberg, Erbach, Hockheim and Hattenheim. Their cellars are at Hattenheim and the wines are aged in oak.

SCHLOSS VOLLRADS
Rheingau: GERMANY

Built by the Greiffenclau family in the 14th century. The family had been making wine since the 12th century. Their original Grey House in Winkel is now a restaurant. The large estate is planted almost exclusively with Riesling vines. Different-coloured capsules on the labels indicate the various styles and qualities: green for *QbA*, blue for *Kabinett*, pink for *Spätlese*, white for *Auslese*, gold for *Beerenauslese* and *Trockenbeerenauslese*, with silver bands for dry wine and gold for sweeter wine. No extra vineyard name is needed after Schloss Vollrads. The present owner of the estate favours the trend towards drier wines. Graf Matuschka Greiffenclau has also bought the neighbouring Furst Löwenstein estate in Hallgarten.

SCHLOSSBERG
Alsace: FRANCE

A Grand Cru vineyard in the village of Kientzheim.

SCHLOSSBÖCKELHEIM
Nahe: GERMANY

An important village, coming within the Grosslage of Burgweg. Kupfergrube, named after a copper mine, is the best site; Felsenberg and Konigsfel are good too. Good growers include August Anheuser, von Plettenberg and the State Domain. It is also the name of one of the two Nahe *Bereichs*, covering the southern part of the area, with the *Grosslagen* of Burgweg, Paradiesgarten and Rosengarten.

SCHLÜCK
AUSTRIA

The brand name of a white wine made from Grüner Veltliner grapes by Lenz Moser.

SCHLUMBERGER
Alsace: FRANCE

One of the great names of Alsace. A company based in Guebwiller with a large domaine, including vineyards on the Kitterlé, Kessler, Spiegel and Saering sites, making them the largest owners of Grand Cru vineyards. They make excellent *Vendange Tardive* wines under the names of Cuvée Christine, Cuvée Anne and Cuvée Ernest.

SCHODEN
Mosel-Saar-Ruwer: GERMANY

An undistinguished wine village of the Saar, coming within the *Grosslage* of Scharzberg.

SCHOENENBERG
Alsace: FRANCE

One of the best vineyard sites of Riquewihr, which was classified as a Grand Cru in 1987. Part of it is owned by Hugel and is one of the sources of their *Sélection de Grains Nobles* wines.

SCHOLTZ HERMANOS
SPAIN

One of the best Málaga producers. The company was once owned by the German Scholtz family but is now under Spanish control. Its most famous wine is Solera Scholtz 1885, a nutty dessert wine. Others include a 10 years old Seco Añejo, a 10 year old Lágrima and a Málaga Dulce Negro.

SCHÖNBÜRGER

The Schönburger grape is a new crossing developed in 1971 and grown in Germany and England. It is a crossing of Pinot Noir crossed with IPI or Pirovano 1, which is itself a crossing of Chasselas Rosé and Muscat of Hamburg. The grapes are pink, the wine white.

SCHOONGEZICHT see Rustenberg.

SCHOPE

An Alsace word to describe a large drinking vessel, originating from chope, the French word for a tankard.

SCHOPPENWEIN

Describes wine sold by the glass or carafe in German cafés and wine bars rather than by the bottle.

SCHRAMSBERG VINEYARD

RESERVE

PRODUCED AND BOTTLED BY
SCHRAMSBERG VINEYARDS
CALISTOGA, CALIFORNIA

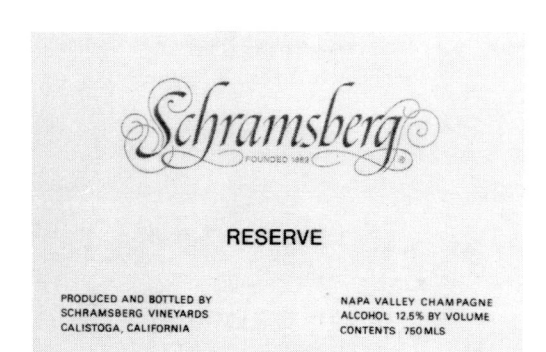

NAPA VALLEY CHAMPAGNE
ALCOHOL 12.5% BY VOLUME
CONTENTS 750 MLS

California: USA

Founded by Jacob Schram in the Napa Valley in 1862. Robert Louis Stevenson came here on his honeymoon and described the visit in the *Silverado Squatters*. After Jacob Schram's death, the estate had a chequered history until it was bought by Jack and Jamie Davies, whose aim to produce champagne method wines has been successfully achieved. Their main wines are a Blanc de Blancs, mainly from Chardonnay and Pinot Blanc and a fuller Blanc de Noirs, with some Pinot Noir.

SCHUG CELLARS *California*: USA

Walter Schug, the former winemaker at Joseph Phellps has set up his own winery to specialise in Pinot Noir and Chardonnay. His first vintage was in 1983.

SCHWARZRIESLING

A synonym for the Pinot Meunier grape in Germany.

SCIACARELLO

A Corsican red grape variety, usually blended with Nielluccio, Grenache and Cinsaut and at its best around Sartène where it gives the wines a distinctive perfumed character.

SCIACCHETRA   See Cinqueterre

SCION

The fruit-bearing part of a *vitis vinifera* wine that is grafted onto an American rootstock as a precaution against phylloxera.

LA SCOLCA *Piedmont*: ITALY

A small estate which is establishing an international reputation for Gavi dei Gavi.

SCREWPULL

The newest version of a corkscrew, looking rather like an outsize clothes peg with a coil. The cork is extracted from the bottle by continuing to turn the screw in the same way that it was inserted, so the cork is levered out of the bottle with minimum effort.

SCUPPERNONG

The most widely planted vine of the Muscadine family, a white grape grown extensively in the eastern United States, especially in Carolina and Florida where it can withstand the humid conditions.

SEAVIEW CHAMPAGNE CELLARS
AUSTRALIA

Old champagne cellars in South Australia with a new name, founded as Australian Wines in 1919. and now owned by Penfolds.

SEBASTIANI VINEYARDS
California: USA

The first Sebastiani, Samuele, was a Tuscan farmer who came to California in 1892. The present generation make a full range of table, dessert, aperitif and sparkling wines. Most notable are Barbera and Zinfandel.

EYE OF THE SWAN
1987 NORTH COAST
PINOT NOIR BLANC

Sebastiani
A SEBASTIANI FAMILY SELECTION
ALCOHOL 12.4% BY VOLUME

SECCO
The Italian term for 'dry'.

SÉCHET   See Vaillons.

SECONDARY FERMENTATION
Another term for malo-lactic fermentation, as it occurs after the main alcoholic fermentation. Second fermentation describes the fermentation in bottle or tank for sparkling wines.

SECOND WINE
The term used in Bordeaux to describe the lesser wine now made by many of the important *châteaux*. The wine should be produced from the same vineyard as the *grand vin* and made in the same cellars. It is a way for the *château* to use wine from young vines or lesser *cuvées*, without detracting from the *grand vin*. Réserve de la Comtesse from Pichon Lalande is a notable example.

SEEWINKEL   AUSTRIA
Within the area of Neusiedlersee, comprising the three villages of Illnitz, Podersdorf and Apetlon, squeezed between the Neusiedlersee and Hungary.

SEGURA VIUDAS   SPAIN
An important *cava* house at San Sadurniu da Noya. Their best wine is Reserva Heredad and they also make sparkling wine for their associate companies René Barbier and Condé de Caralt.

SEGURET   Rhône: FRANCE
Séguret is one of the villages of the appellation Côtes du Rhône Villages from the southern Rhône. It shares a cooperative with Roaix that produces mainly red wine of average quality.

SEIBEL
The Frenchman who gave his name to numerous different hybrids, both red and white, called Seibel plus a number, each one also going under a different name, such as Aurora, which are planted extensively in the United States and disappearing from France.

SEKT
A short term for *Qualitätsschaumwein*, or 'quality sparkling wine'. Deutcher Sekt must now be made in Germany from grapes grown in Germany. The largest producer is Henkel; others include Sohnlein, Deinhard, Kupferberg and Burgeff, usually using the *charmat* method. The *méthode champenoise* is rarely used in Germany and sometimes the transfer method of bottle fermentation is to be found. Where Sekt specifies a region of origin, grape variety and vintage, it must be made with at least 75% of grapes from the region, with 75% of the mentioned grape variety and with 75% of wine from the vintage.

SELAKS   NEW ZEALAND
An old established family winery at Kumeu on North Island. Their first vintage was in 1934. A champagne method Champelle, an oak aged Sauvignon Blanc Sémillon blend and Rhine Riesling are amongst their better wines.

SELECTION DE GRAINS NOBLES
A term used in Alsace to denote wine made from grapes that are particularly rich in sugar and even affected by noble rot. The concept was first established by the house of Hugel and now applies to Riesling, Muscat, Pinot Gris and Gewürztraminer. It has been part of the *appellation contrôlée* law since 1984 and is very strictly controlled. A grower must declare his intention to make *Sélection de Grains Nobles* before picking; the *oechsle* degree must be a minimum of 110° for Riesling and Muscat and 120° for Gewürztraminer and Pinot Gris. The wines can be sweetish with some residual sugar, or fermented completely dry. Chaptalization is forbidden; there is a compulsory analysis and tasting test in March, eighteen months after the vintage, before the wine can be sold. It must be from a single vintage which is stated on the label.

SELLA & MOSCA — Sardinia: ITALY

The most enterprising wine producer of Sardinia. A private company, founded 80 years ago and applying modern methods to Sardinian grapes to produce a range of successful wines, both traditional and innovative, from Vernaccia and Cannonau grapes to Vermentino and Torbato. I Piani is an important red table wine in their range.

SÉMILLON

The principal grape for Sauternes and the other sweet wines of Bordeaux and south west France. The classic blend for Sauternes is 80% Sémillon, 20% Sauvignon, with perhaps a drop of Muscadelle. The thin skinned Sémillon is particularly susceptible to *pourriture noble*. In the Graves and Entre-Deux-Mers it is the base of many dry white wines and is particularly amenable to oak ageing, in the finest properties like Château Laville-Haut-Brion.

Elsewhere in Europe, Sémillon is insignificant. In the New World it is widely planted in Chile; there is some in Argentina, a little in South Africa, where it is called Green Grape, but it is in Australia where it really comes into its own. Hunter Valley Sémillon ranks amongst the best white wine of Australia, a full-bodied wine, developing considerable character with barrel and bottle age. Some Sémillon is grown in New Zealand and blended with Sauvignon, while in California it is of little importance.

SEÑORIO DE SARRÍA — SPAIN

One of the best wine estates of Navarra. The abandoned property was bought and restored by a Señor Huarte in 1952. Traditional Spanish grapes are grown, as well as a small amount of Cabernet Sauvignon; the wines are made and aged like Rioja. The range includes a dry white and rosé, a three year old Viña Ecoyen, a more mature Viña del Perdon and best of all a *reserva* Gran Viña del Señorio de Sarría.

SEPPELT & SONS — AUSTRALIA

One of the largest Australian wine companies with vineyards at Great Western, at Keppoch, at Seppeltsfield in the Barossa Valley, at Drumberg and Rutherglen in Victoria, at Barooga in New South Wales, at Qualco in South Australia and at Partalunga near Adelaide. Their main winery is at Seppeltsfield. Château Tanunda is another winery in the Barossa Valley. They are one of the leading producers of sparkling wine, with Great Western 'champagne' and have an impressive range of table and fortified wines, Bin Range for generic wines, Reserve Bin Range for varietals and Black Label range for better quality varietals as well as district varietal wines. Moyston Claret and Arawatta Riesling are good standard lines.

SEPTIMER

A crossing of the Gewürztraminer and Müller-Thurgau grape varieties grown mainly in Rheinhessen.

SERBIA — YUGOSLAVIA

Serbia covers most of eastern Yugoslavia and accounts for a large part of the country's wine production. The main grape varieties are Prokupac for red wine and Smederevka for white; there is also Cabernet Sauvignon, Merlot and Gamay. The best vineyard is Župa, south of Belgrade and the Royal Serbian Cellars are important producers. The provinces of Vojvodina and Kosmet are significant too.

SERCIAL — Madeira: PORTUGAL

The driest of the four styles of the fortified wine, Madeira. It is thought to originate from the Riesling grape, though it bears little relationship to any other Riesling wines. It is best drunk as an aperitif. The must is fermented so that virtually no sugar is retained in the wine before fortification.

SERRIG
Mosel-Saar-Ruwer: GERMANY

The uppermost village of the Saar, where an unfavourable climate produces steely Rieslings in the best years. It comes within the *Grosslage* of Scharzberg. The main vineyards are Antoniusberg, Schloss Saarfelser, Schlossberg, Kupp, Heiligenborn, Schloss Saarsteiner, Herrenberg, Vogelsang and Würtzberg. Good producers include the State Domain, Bert Simon and the Vereinigte Hospitien.

SETINE

Was an ancient Roman wine said to be the favourite of Augustus Caesar and rated highly by Pliny. It was made at Setia on the Appian Way.

SETTESOLI
Sicily: ITALY

A wine company which sells its wines under the same name, a warm Bonero Rosso di Menfi and a dry Bianco di Menfi.

SÉTUBAL
PORTUGAL

Sétubal, across the Tagus from Lisbon, is famous for its Moscatel and also produces a large quantity of red wine. The area was demarcated in 1907 but is now under review with a possible further delimitation for Periquita and a reduction in the area of Sétubal around Azeitão. Moscatel de Sétubal is made from two grape varieties, Moscatel de Sétubal, a local name for Muscat d'Alexandrie, and Moscatel de Málaga. As it is a fortified wine, fermentation is stopped by the addition of grape brandy. It is then left in large containers for several years until bottling so that the sugar and alcohol increase as the liquid evaporates. The most common wines are a grapey six year old and a darker honeyed 25 year old.

SEVENHILL CELLARS
AUSTRALIA

The Sevenhill winery in Clare is known particularly for its production of sacramental wine as it is run by the Jesuits. They first settled in the area in 1845 and planted the first vines a few years later.

SEYSSEL
Savoie: FRANCE

An AC wine of Savoie, with vineyards around the town of the same name, on either side of the Rhône. The still wine is made from the Roussette grape, also called Altesse, and labelled Roussette de Seyssel. Seyssel Mousseux is a *méthode champenoise* wine, made mainly from Molette. Varichon et Clerc are the best known producers.

SEYVAL BLANC

A French hybrid vine which is grown with considerable success in England. It is a cross between two other hybrids, Seibal 5056 and Seibel 4986.

SEYVE-VILLARD 5276

A synonym for the Seyval Blanc grape variety. There is also Seyve-Villard 12,375, a synonym for Villard Blanc which is grown widely in southern France for indifferent white wine, while Seyve Villard 18,315 is a synonym for Villard Noir, another French hybrid.

SFURZAT
Lombardy: ITALY

Sfurzat or Sfursat or Sforzato is a DOC wine that comes from the DOC area of Valtellina and is made from semi-dried Nebbiolo grapes to give a full-bodied rich alcoholic wine.

SHANTUNG   See China.

SHARIS   See China.

SHENANDOAH VALLEY
California: USA

An AVA of the Sierra Foothills in Amador County. Zinfandel is the main grape variety.

SHERIS   See China.

SHERRY
SPAIN

Sherry is the classic Spanish aperitif. It is produced around the towns of Jerez de la Frontera, Sanlucar de Barrameda and the port of Cadiz. The best sherry grape is the Palomino, which grows best on the chalky *albariza* soil. Next in importance is the Pedro Ximénez which is used mainly for sweet dessert wine. A small amount of Moscatel is grown too.

Sherry is a fortified wine so that brandy is added to it at some stage during the production to raise the alcohol level. Unlike table wines, sherry depends upon an element of oxidation to obtain its distinctive character, resulting from the *flor* which develops, particularly on *fino* and *manzanilla* sherry. The *solera* system also distinguishes sherry from most other wines. Older wine is refreshed with similar younger wine and the method depends upon the fact that the more mature wine passes on its characteristics to the younger wine.

Sherry ranges from the very dry to the very sweet, from aperitif to dessert wine, from crisp *fino* and salty *manzanilla*, through fuller *amontillado* and *olorosos*, to cream and brown sherries, with *palo cortado* and *amoroso* sherries as well. Sherry is never a vintage wine; a date on the label refers to the year a *solera* was started.

True sherry comes from Spain; however its success has been imitated in other parts of the world, namely South Africa, Australia and Cyprus (see separate entries). Although these wines may be called sherry, the regulations covering the labelling are very strict and the word sherry must be immediately preceded by the country of origin.

Finally there is British sherry, which bears no resemblance to the real thing. It is a concoction from dehydrated must, reconstituted under factory conditions in this country.

SHIRAZ

An Australian and South African synonym for the Syrah grape, while white Shiraz describes Trebbiano in Australia.

SHIROKA MELNISHKA LOSA

The full name for Melnik, meaning 'broad vine of Melnik', which produces red wines in Bulgaria around Melnik in the southwest of the country. They are often aged in oak and have good fruit.

SHORT

Describes a wine which has no length or finish; the taste ends abruptly, denoting a lack of quality.

SHOT BERRIES   See Millerandage.

SHOT BOTTLE

A shot bottle was an old port bottle that would be filled with shot and shaken so that the inside of the bottle was scratched and rough, enabling the deposit of sediment from a vintage port to cling firmly to the side of the bottle.

SHUMEN   BULGARIA

Shumen, in northern Bulgaria, has a reputation for some good Chardonnay, as well as Italian Riesling, Rhine Riesling, Gewürztraminer, Sauvignon Blanc and Dimiat wines.

SIAURAC   Bordeaux: FRANCE

The most important Lalande de Pomerol *château*.

SICAREX MEDITERRANNÉE

Sicarex Mediterrannée, or to give its full name, the Societe d'Intérêt Collectif Agricole de Recherches Expérimentales pour l'Amélioration des Produits de la Vigne was a French government funded organisation based at Domaine de l'Espiguette in the Midi. Sadly it has been disbanded, as it was performing useful work as an experimental research station demonstrating how better grape varieties, such as Merlot and Cabernet, could improve the wines of the Midi.

SICHEL

An important wine name in four countries: Germany, France, England and the United States. In Germany, the company produce a leading Liebfraumilch, Blue Nun, which is distributed by members of the family in London and New York. In Bordeaux, another branch of the family owns d'Angludet, a share in Palmer and operates a successful *négociant* company dealing in Bordeaux and the wines of the Midi and south-west France.

SICILY   ITALY

Legend has it that the first vine was brought to Sicily by Bacchus who made wine at the foot of Mount Etna. Today, Sicily is the largest wine-producing region of Italy, with ten DOCs, including fortified Marsala, several dessert wines and a host of unclassified table wines. Production is dominated by cooperatives. The best wines carry a Q on the label for quality.

SIDI RAIS   TUNISIA

A dry rosé, with a hint of Muscat, made by the U.C.C.V.T.

SIDI SALEM TUNISIA

A red wine made by the Tunisian Office des Terres Domainiales at Kanguet in the Mornag hills.

SIEGERREBE

A German grape variety, a crossing of Madeleine Angevine and Gewürztraminer, grown mainly in the Rheinhessen and Palatinate. Its flavour can be rather overwhelming and so it is often used as part of a blend to add weight and sugar.

SIERRA FOOTHILLS *California*: USA

A general term to cover California's most easterly wine region, with the three counties of El Dorado, Amador and Calaveras. Zinfandel and Chenin Blanc are the most important varietals and the area includes three AVAs, El Dorado, Shenandoah Valley and Fiddletown.

SIFONE See Marsala.

SIGALAS RABAUD *Bordeaux*: FRANCE

A first growth Sauternes in the commune of Bommes which was once part of the large Rabaud estate. Methods are modern with ageing in tank, not barrels.

SIGOGNAC *Bordeaux*: FRANCE

A Médoc Cru Bourgeois from the commune of St-Yzans which is making good wine after recent modernisation.

SIGOULÈS SOUTH WEST FRANCE

The village with an important cave cooperative for the production of Bergerac.

SIKLÓS HUNGARY

A wine region in northern Hungary, with a reputation for red wine from the Kadarka and Blau Portugieser grape varieties.

SILLERY *Champagne*: FRANCE

Sillery is one of the famous Champagne villages on the Montagne de Reims. In the 17th century, the wine was sold as Sillery.

SILVA & COSENS

The port house, which owns the brand Dow, which is named after a Victorian partner of the company. It is now part of the Symington empire.

SILVANER

The grape variety at one time widely planted in Germany, but in recent years has mostly been replaced by Müller Thurgau. It does still make some interesting wine in Franconia, but elsewhere usually produces relatively unexciting, slightly grassy white wine. In Alsace it is one of the basic grape varieties used in Edelzwicker and is often replaced by Pinot Blanc. In Switzerland where it is sometimes called Johannisberg, it compares favourably with Chasselas. In the New World it has enjoyed little favour. In France it is called Sylvaner.

SILVERADO TRAIL *California*: USA

Silverado Trail is on the western side of the Napa Valley, with many wineries situated on the valley slopes, such as Stag's Leap, Heitz and Joseph Phelps.

SIMI *California*: USA

A large winery at Healdsburg in Sonoma that was founded by Italian emigrants in 1876. It survived the Prohibition by selling sacramental wine. After a succession of owners, it now belongs to Moet Hennessy and is producing some fine varietal wines under a talented winemaker, Zelma Long.

SIMMONET-FEBVRE Burgundy: FRANCE

One of the *négociant* companies of Chablis. They own a few vineyards in Mont de Milieu and Preuses, as well as dealing in the full range of Chablis. They are also the only people in Chablis to make sparkling wine, Bourgogne Mousseux.

ANDRÉ SIMON

André Simon 1877 to 1970 was one of the great characters of the British wine trade, a wine merchant and author of numerous wine books. He founded the International Wine & Food Society and was its first president for many years.

BERT SIMON Mosel-Saar-Ruwer: GERMANY

Weingut Herrenberg Bert Simon is an important estate in Serrig, founded in 1968 by Bert Simon from part of the von Schorlemer estate. Riesling is the main grape variety with, unusually, some Weissburgunder.

SIMONSIG SOUTH AFRICA

Simonsig in Stellenbosch is one of South Africa's largest wine estates, producing a wide range, with particular emphasis on white wine, including one of the few champagne method wines of the Cape, called Kaapse Vonkel.

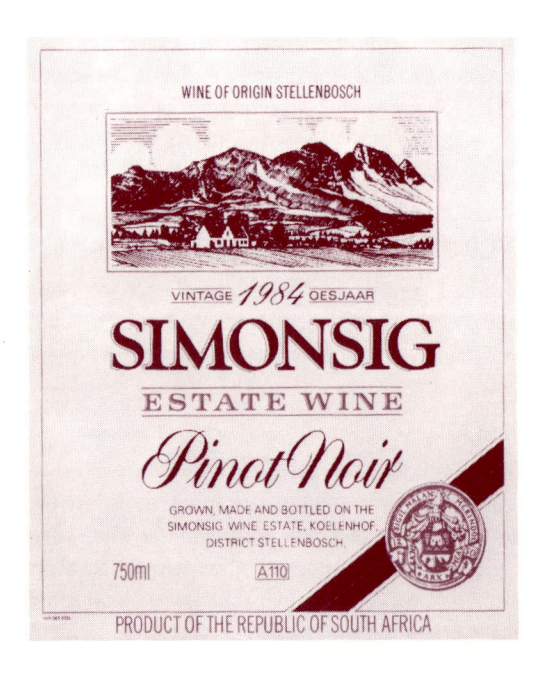

SIMONSVLEI SOUTH AFRICA

An important wine cooperative at Paarl with a range of award winning wines.

SIN CRIANZA see crianza.

SINKIANG See China.

SION SWITZERLAND

The town of Sion in the Valais gives its names to an appellation for wine made from Fendant grapes grown in the surrounding villages. Domaine du Mont d'Or is the best producer.

SIPON YUGOSLAVIA

A dry white wine, made in the Drava region of Slovenia from the grape of the same name.

SIRAN Bordeaux: FRANCE

A property in Margaux that is classified as a Cru Bourgeois Supérieur, but is generally considered to be better than some classed growths. It is now owned by the Miaihle family who have done much to enhance the reputation of the wine.

SITIA GREECE

A full-bodied sweet red wine from Crete, made from indigenous Cretan varieties of grape, notably Liatiko.

SITTMANN Rheinhessen: GERMANY

Weingut Carl Sittmann is the largest private estate of the Rheinhessen with vineyards in Oppenheim, Alsheim and Nierstein and cellars in Oppenheim. In addition they are a merchant house. Riesling represents a small proportion of their wines, with a variety of other grapes, and a good regional spread.

SIZZANO Piedmont: ITALY

A small DOC made from 40–60% Nebbiolo grapes with Vespolina and Bonarda, grown around Sizzano in the Novara hills. It must be aged for at least three years, including two in the barrel. It is a robust red wine and can age well in good vintages.

SKIN CONTACT see Macération.

SLATE

The principal soil constituent of the Rheingau and part of the Mosel, particularly suitable for the Riesling grape. It is permeable with a good mineral content and retains the heat well which is significant in helping to ripen grapes in a cool northern climate. Slate gives the Riesling grape some of its finesse and complexity.

SLAVONIA   YUGOSLAVIA

Once part of Austria and on the borders of Austria and Hungary Slavonia has three main vineyard areas, namely, the Drava, including Ljutomer and Ormož; the Sava region in the south where Laski Rizling is grown and the coastal region where Cabernet Sauvignon and Merlot are grown, as well as Teran for Kraski Teran, the region's best red wine. There is also an individual white wine, Rebula of Brda.

SLAVONIC OAK

Slavonic or Yugoslav oak is used, particularly in Italy, for the very large barrels traditional particularly in the wine cellars of Piedmont for ageing Barolo and Barbaresco. The wood gives a 'burnt oak' flavour to the wine.

SLOVAKIA   CZECHOSLOVAKIA

The largest wine-producing province of Czechoslovakia. The main vineyard area is near Bratislava, around the towns of Modra and Pezinok towards the Little Carpathians, while in the south corner around Malá Trna, a Czech version of Tokay is made from Furmint, Hārslevelü and Muscat grapes. Elsewhere the principal grape varieties are Welschriesling and Müller-Thurgau for whites, with an Austrian influence, and a little Limberger for reds.

SLOVIN   YUGOSLAVIA

The main wine producer of Slovenia, with cellars in Ljubljana and all over Yugoslavia, a large exporter and responsible for the popular Lutomer Laski Rizling.

SMEDEREVKA

A Yugoslav grape variety grown extensively in Serbia for dry white wine.

SMITH-HAUT-LAFITTE
Bordeaux: FRANCE

An important Cru Classé, Martillac property in the Graves. White wine of pure Sauvignon grapes and, reliable classified red wine are made.

SMITH WOODHOUSE

The port house of Smith Woodhouse was founded by Christopher Smith in 1784, who was joined by William Woodhouse in 1810. The company is now owned by the Symington family and also ships Gould, Campbell port.

SOAVE   Veneto: ITALY

Italy's most popular dry white wine. It is made principally from Garganega grapes, with some Trebbiano Toscano and Trebbiano di Soave in a large area with the town of Soave at the centre. Vineyards near the town are described as *classico*. *Superiore* has 11.5° minimum of alcohol and is aged for nine months. *Spumante* is also made and a Recioto di Soave. Bolla and Pieropan are amongst the best producers.

SODAP   CYPRUS

One of Cyprus' main wine producers, a group of cooperatives making red Afames, white Arsinoe, Salamis and Kolossi table wines and Lysander sherry.

SOFT WINES   see light wines.

SOGRAPE

Sogrape – Vinhos de Portugal, to give the company its full name, is Portugal's largest wine company and the makers of Mateus Rosé. It was founded in 1942 by the Guedes family and is still controlled by them. They also produce Vinho Verde and their subsidiary company, Vinicola do Vale do Dao makes a fine Dão Grão Vasco. They have two highly modernised vinification centres in the Douro and in Bairrada for Mateus Rosé.

SOIL

One of the elements that determines the character of a wine. Generally, vines perform better on poor soil, where nothing much else will grow, so the vine roots have to go deep for water and nourishment. Soil in the world's vineyards may vary enormously from slate, limestone, clay, schist and granite. It is the slight variations in soil that account for the differences between one vineyard and another, explaining, for instance, why, in the Médoc, one *château* is a second growth, while a neighbouring property is only a fifth growth. The French *appellation contrôlée* system uses soil to delimit vineyard areas and to determine quality. Californians, on the other hand, tend to attribute greater importance to climate and vinification techniques.

SOKOL BLOSSER

One of the largest wineries in Oregon in the USA, with a wide range of varietal wines.

SOLAIA   Tuscany: ITALY

A red wine made by Antinori purely from Cabernet grapes and aged in new wood for two years.

SOLANO COUNTY   California: USA

Solano County comes within the large AVA of the North Coast, with two smaller AVAs in the county, Green Valley-Solano and Suisun Valley.

SOLAR DAS BOUÇAS   PORTUGAL

One of the best *vinho verde* estates, making wine from Loureiro and Trajadura grapes by modern methods.

SOLERA

The term for the ageing system for sherry and also madeira. The sherry butts are arranged in a series of scales or tiers, containing the same style of wine, with each scale younger than the last. As wine is drawn off from the oldest butts, they are refreshed with a slightly younger wine, and so on down the scale, so that the youngest scale is replenished from the *criadera*, and that in turn with *añada* wine. The solera system depends upon the fact that the younger wine immediately takes on the characteristics of the older wine. Soleras for *fino* and *manzanilla* require more scales than for *oloroso*, perhaps as many as seven with up to fourteen for *manzanilla*.

DOMAINE DE LA SOLITUDE
Rhône: FRANCE

Domaine de la Solitude is a Châteauneuf-du-Pape property whose owner is the leading exponent of vinification by *macération carbonique* for the appellation. The resulting wine is easier to drink than many of its neighbours.

SOLLEONE   Umbria: ITALY

The sherry-like aperitif made by Lungarotti in Torgiano from Trebbiano and Grechetto grapes with a modified *solera* system.

SOLOPACA   Campania: ITALY

A little-known red and white DOC wine from Campania. The red is made from Sangiovese grapes, with some Aglianico and Piedirosso and is soft and fruity. The white is from Trebbiano Toscano and Malvasia grapes and is undistinguished.

SOMLÓ   HUNGARY

Wine from this region in the hills north of Lake Balaton once enjoyed a reputation, like Tokay, for its restorative powers. Today its importance and its vineyards are much reduced, with some Furmint, Juhfark and Olaszrizling.

SOMMELIER

The French term for 'wine waiter'. In good restaurants, this is someone with considerable knowledge of the subject. The Guild of Sommeliers is an organisation including people from other parts of the wine trade as well as wine waiters.

SOMONTANO — SPAIN

A recent D.O. of Aragón in the foothills of the Pyrenees. The wines are light, red and fruity, made from a mixture of grapes including Alcañón, Macabeo, Garnacha Tinta, Mazuelo and Parraleta.

SONNENGLANZ — Alsace: FRANCE

A Grand Cru vineyard in the village of Béblenheim.

SONOMA — California: USA

The name of a town, a valley, an AVA and a county. The valley is an important AVA within the county, running parallel to the Napa Valley, with the attractive town of Sonoma at its centre. The main grape varieties are Chardonnay, Cabernet Sauvignon, Zinfandel, Pinot Noir, Sauvignon Blanc, French Colombard and Riesling. The county has more AVAs than any other, demonstrating the area's importance as a wine region, namely, in the north, Alexander Valley, Chalk Hill, Dry Creek Valley, Green Valley-Sonoma, Knights Valley and Russian River Valley, and in the south Sonoma Carneros, Sonoma Mountain and the Sonoma Valley.

SONOMA CARNEROS — California: USA

One of the many AVAs of Sonoma County.

SONOMA MOUNTAIN — California: USA

One of the many AVAs of Sonoma County.

SONOMA VALLEY — California: USA

One of the many AVAs of Sonoma County.

SONOMA VINEYARDS — California: USA

Created by Rodney Strong, building upon the success of his mail order business, Tiburon Vintners. The present winery, with a building designed like a Maltese cross, was opened in 1971. The best wines are from the Russian River Valley. There is a joint venture with Piper Heidsieck known as Piper-Sonoma.

SOPRON — HUNGARY

A wine region almost on the Austrian border, close to the Neusiedlersee and, enjoying a cool microclimate, produces a light red wine from the Kékfrankos grape.

SORBIC ACID

A permitted additive in wine, used as an antiseptic for sweet wines, preventing the development of yeasts. Used in excess it may break down and then smells of geraniums.

SORNI — Trentino-Alto Adige: ITALY

A small Trentino DOC. The red is made from Schiava, Teroldego and Lagrein grapes; the white mainly from Nosiola and, if it has 11° alcohol, it can be designated *scelto*.

SORRENTINE

Was a wine of ancient Rome. Some said it was good for the health; others described it as 'generous vinegar'.

SORTIE

The emergence of the very tiny grapes before the flowering, which gives the very first indication of the potential size of the harvest.

SOTHEBY'S

The oldest of the two principal London auction houses, founded in 1744, with an important department for wine auctions, covering all types from *vin ordinaire* to the very oldest and rarest. Some reach record-breaking prices, such as an imperial of Château Mouton Rothschild 1924 sold for £9350 in September 1984. They also hold regular wine auctions in Geneva, Tokyo and Johannesberg.

SOUCHE

The French term for 'vine shoot'. At times when there has been great pressure and demand upon the Bordeaux market, wines have been sold *sur souche*, that is before the grapes have even been picked and the wine made.

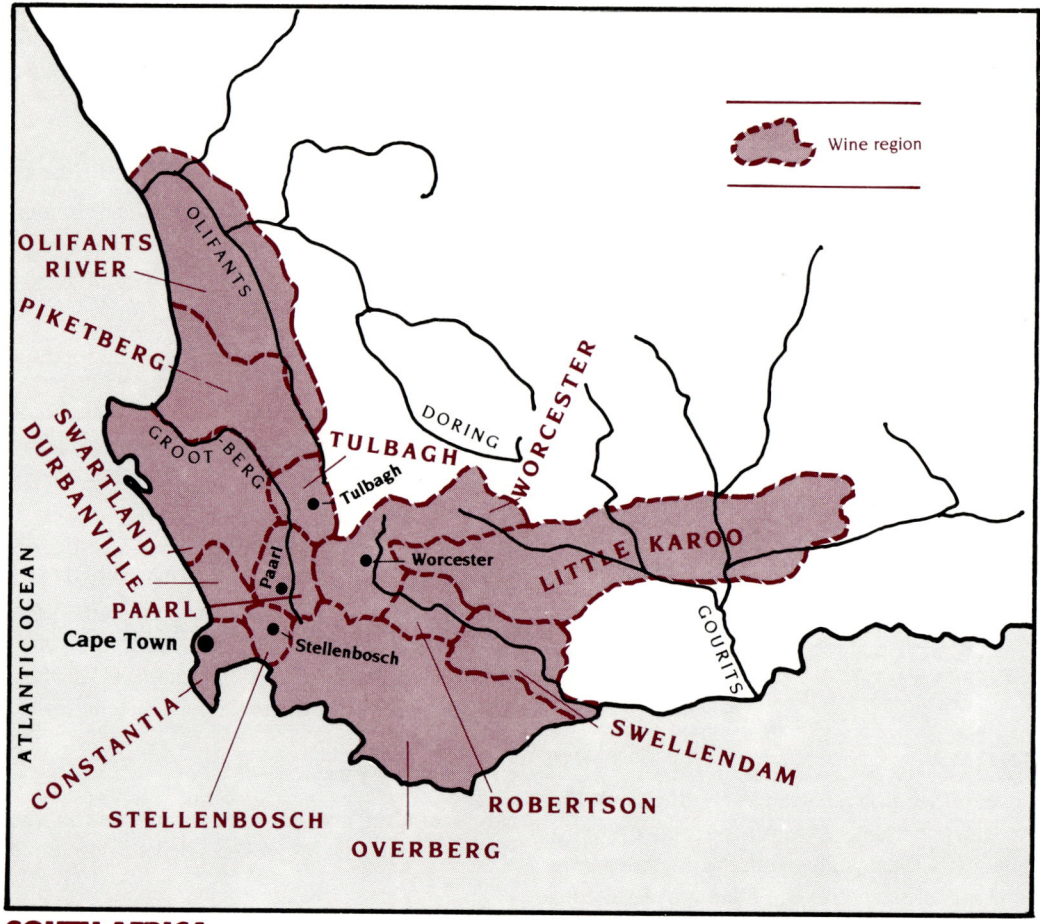

SOUTH AFRICA

YVES SOULEZ — Loire: FRANCE

An important producer of Anjou wines, with two estates in Savennières, Château de Chamboureau and Château de la Bizolière.

SOUS-MARQUE

A sub-brand. Wine producers who have given an importer the exclusivity of their own name may, in order to increase their sales in the importer's country, use another name, a *sous-marque*, for a second importer. This is a popular device amongst Bordeaux and Burgundian *négociants*.

SOUSÃO

A red grape authorised for port.

SOUSSANS — Bordeaux: FRANCE

One of the villages near to the village of Margaux and included in the appellation.

SOUTARD — Bordeaux: FRANCE

One of the better Grands Crus Classés of St-Émilion, making elegant wine in a beautiful 18th century *château*.

SOUTH AFRICAN RIESLING   see Cape Riesling.

SOUTH AFRICA

Jan van Riebeck planted vines in South Africa in 1652. A dessert wine, Constantia, was greatly prized in the 18th and 19th centuries, and more recently South Africa's wine production was concentrated on port and sherry styles, until about twenty years ago, when table wines began to come into their own. The appellation system of Wines of Origin was instituted in 1973 and there are now 17 areas of origin. In the Coastal Region there are Constantia, Durbanville, Stellenbosch, Paarl, Tulbagh and Swartland. In the Breed River Valley there are Worcester, Robertson and Swellendam and there are also Boberg, Overberg, Olifantsrivier, Piketberg, Klein Karoo, Benede-Orange, Douglas and Andalusia. Some of these areas are in turn divided into wards. Climate varies enormously. In the more northern areas rainfall is lacking and the vineyards are irrigated. In cooler Paarl and Stellenbosch the climate is very favourable to the cultivation of vines and some excellent wine is made.

Grape varieties, or to use a South African term, cultivars, are in the main those of Europe, with certain differences. Chenin Blanc, called Steen in the Cape, is the most important white grape. Cape Riesling and Colombard are widely planted too, while Rhine Riesling, Sauvignon and Chardonnay are becoming increasingly popular for better quality whites. For red wines, Cinsaut is the most popular grape for everyday wines; Pinotage is declining in importance, while Cabernet Sauvignon, with or without Merlot, produces the best red wines. There is also Shiraz and a little Pinot Noir.

The K.W.V., the wine farmers' cooperative, is an important force in the South African wine industry, controlling the supply and demand of grapes. Its regulations on the type of vines that can be planted and the land on which they can be grown have had an inhibitive effect and it is only in the last ten years that individual wine estates have begun to break away from their restrictions and plant more exciting grape varieties in their vineyards.

A large proportion of South Africa's wine production is destined for fortification, as either port or sherry style wines. For sherry the Palomino grape of Jerez, with Steen and Sémillon, is widely grown in the hotter wine regions of the Cape, notably in Boberg and Klein Karoo. The best wines are produced by the KWV under the brand name of Cape Cavendish, as dry, medium or cream sherry (Spanish names are not permitted). The production process follows that of Spain with a *solera* system and some *flor* does develop naturally for the dry wine.

SOUTH AMERICA

The two principal wine countries of South America are Chile and Argentina, which also ranks as one of the world's largest wine-producing countries. Mendoza is the principal vineyard area and Criolla the main indigenous grape, but European grapes have also been successfully adopted. Chile is one the few remaining phylloxera-free countries in the world. Her vineyards are surrounded by the Andes to the east and the Pacific to the west. The best wines come from the Maipo Valley where Cabernet Sauvignon is particularly successful. Brazil, with its enormous domestic consumption of wine has a growing industry that is attracting some foreign investment. Uruguay, too, has a large domestic market for wine, but has an unsophisticated industry. Elsewhere, there are pockets of vines, with Bolivia, Ecuador, Colombia, and Paraguay making wine for home consumption. Peru has one small vineyard of interest.

SOUTH COAST   *California*: USA

A general term to describe the vineyards of southern California, in the states of San Luis Obispo and Santa Barbara, extending to the Mexican border.

SOUTH COAST ROSÉ   BULGARIA

A defined Controliran wine region concentrating on the production of rosé wine from Cabernet Sauvignon.

SOUTH WEST COASTAL PLAIN
AUSTRALIA

An area of Western Australia, around Perth, which has the unifying feature for its wineries that they are all situated on particularly sandy, fertile soil, where the climate is good for viticulture. Most of the wineries are small newcomers.

SOUTHERN VALES   AUSTRALIA

A small wine growing district of South Australia just south of Adelaide, almost in a suburban sprawl. The climate is favourable to viticulture and Château Reynella is an important estate. See also McLaren Vale.

SOUTIRAGE

The French term for 'racking'.

SOUVERAIN CELLARS   California: USA

Souverain Cellars in Sonoma are owned by a cooperative with vineyards in Sonoma, Mendocino and Napa, and make a sound range of varietal table wines.

SOVIET UNION

The Soviet Union is a large wine producer, coming third after Italy and France. The republics with vineyards for wine, rather than table grapes, are Moldavia, the Ukraine, Russia, Georgia, Armenia and Azerbaijan, with most vineyards being around the north and eastern shores of the Black Sea. Sparkling wine, *champanski* and sweet port, madeira and sherry styles dominate production. There are indigenous varieties of grape as well as some western introductions.

SPAIN

Spain has the largest area under vines of any European country, but only comes third in production after Italy and France. Her yields in some areas

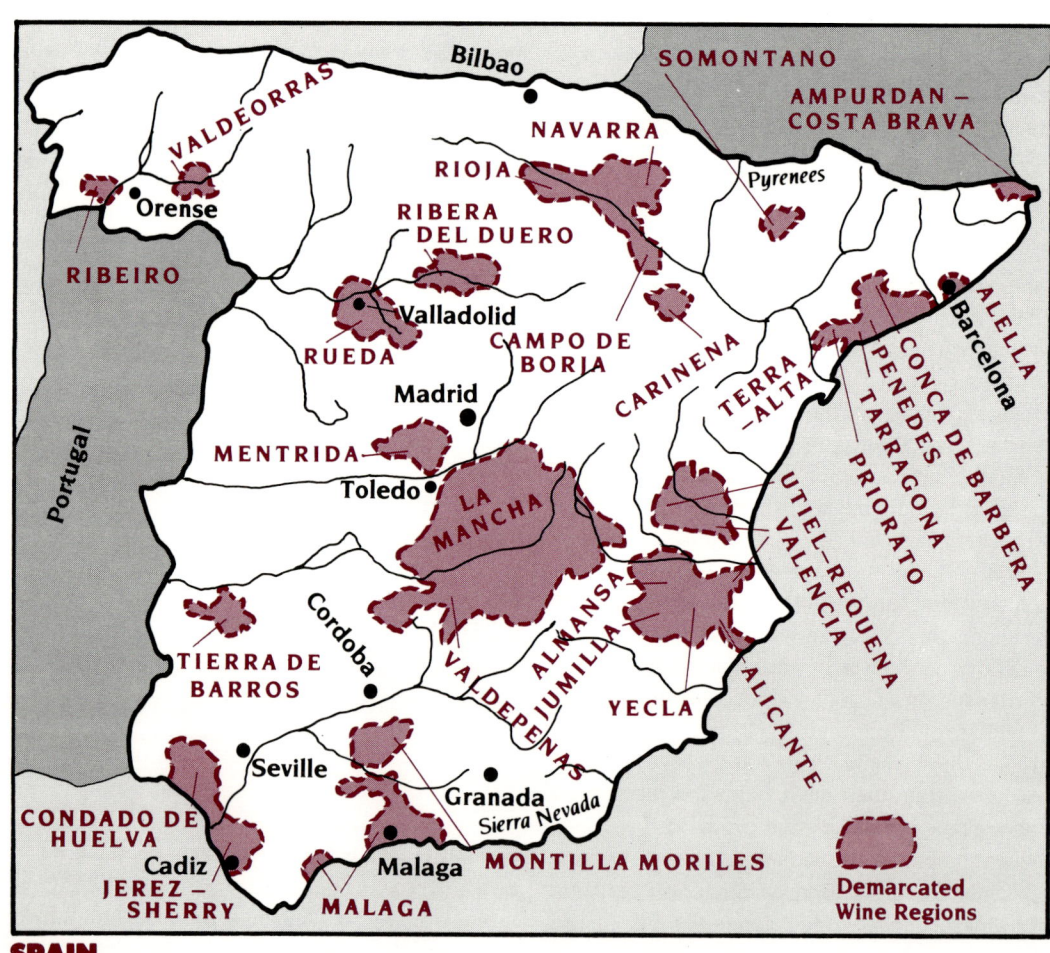

SPAIN

are tiny, where the land is arid, the vines old and the viticulture unsophisticated.

Above all, Spain is known for sherry, one of the finest and most versatile of fortified wines. In addition there are Montilla and Malaga in southern Andalusia.

Among her table wines, Rioja is the most important, mainly for fine oak aged red wines. Penedès is noted for red and white table wines and for sparkling *cava* too. In the north there are other smaller areas of interest, Léon, Navarra, Ribero for legendary Vega Sicilia and Galicia for fragrant dry white wines.

The central plateau of La Mancha produces a third of all Spanish wine; most of it is for sale in bulk rather than bottle, and the majority of the grapes are white.

The coastal region of the Levante, with DOs like Jumilla and Utiel Requena produces full-bodied earthy red wines.

Rioja was the first area to be delimited with a *Denominación de Origen* and several others have followed with a total now of 32 areas, each controlled by a Consejo Regulador.

SPALLIERA

The Italian term for the *cordon* system of pruning.

SPANNA Piedmont: ITALY

The local name for the Nebbiolo grape in the Novara Vercelli hills, and is also applied to non-DOC wines. At its best, it is greater than Gattinara and at its worst, best forgotten. Antonio Vallana & Figlio have a justifiably excellent reputation for their long-lived Spanna.

SPARKLING WINE

A general term to describe a wine containing bubbles of carbon dioxide, originating usually from a second fermentation which has taken place in the bottle, as in *méthode champenoise*, or in a tank, as for *cuve close*, or by the transfer method which is a mixture of both. It is also possible for carbon dioxide to be injected into a wine, but then the pressure is not great enough for it to be truly sparkling.

SPÄTBURGUNDER

The German name for the Pinot Noir grape variety.

SPÄTLESE

The second category of German Prädikat wines, meaning 'late picked'. The grapes cannot be picked earlier than seven days after the start of the harvest for the particular variety in the specific area. The delay in picking means that the grapes develop more sugar, so the resulting wines are lightly honeyed. The statutory sugar content, measured as the oechsle degree for *Spätlese* varies according to grape variety and area. For a Riesling in the Rheingau it is 85° and in the Mosel 76°. In Austria it is the first category.

SPÄTROT AUSTRIA

A synonym for Zierfändler grapes, used to make Gumpoldskirchen wine.

SPECIAL LATE HARVEST

A South African category, describing a wine with 20–30 gms of sugar per litre, without the addition of any sweetening. It comes between Late Harvest and Noble Late Harvest.

SPECIFIC GRAVITY OF MUST

Measured with a hydrometer to determine the sugar content and therefore the potential alcohol. There are various systems for this, Oechsle in Germany, Baumé in France, and Balling and Brix in the United States.

SPICEY

A smell particularly associated with Gewürztraminer grapes. Indeed Gewürz means 'spice' in German.

SPIGOT

A plug or peg on a wine barrel, inserted into the vent hole and used for drawing off a sample of wine.

SPITOON

A receptacle used for spitting at a tasting. It may be as simple as a wooden wine box filled with sawdust, or in a tasting room, a basin with a constant flow of water.

SPITZENWEIN AUSTRIA

An Austrian term for *Prädikatwein*.

SPOREN   Alsace: FRANCE

One of the best vineyard sites of Riquewihr, which was recognised as a Grand Cru in 1987. It is partly owned by Hugel and is one of the sources of their *Sélection de Grains Nobles* wines.

SPOTS FARM   ENGLAND

An award-winning vineyard near Tenterden in Kent, planted in 1977 with Müller-Thurgau, Güttenborner and Reichensteiner grapes.

SPRING MOUNTAIN   California: USA

Part of the Napa Valley to the west of St. Helena. The only winery is Spring Mountain Vineyards.

SPRING MOUNTAIN VINEYARDS   California: USA

Named after the mountain on whose slopes the vineyards are planted. The estate was created by Mike Robbins in the mid 1970s and has acquired a reputation for Cabernet Sauvignon and Chardonnay.

SPRINGETON   AUSTRALIA

A small wine area of South Australia, an offshoot of the Barossa Valley, producing wines similar to those of Barossa, but with slight soil and climatic differences.

SPRITZIG

Means 'lightly sparkling' in German, and is a term used to describe a wine with a faint hint of carbon dioxide. The wines from the Mosel often have this effect, which is experienced as a slight prickle on the tongue and which keeps them fresh.

SPUMANTE

Sparkling wine in Italy, made either by the *méthode champenoise* or *cuve close* method.

SQUILLACE   Calabria: ITALY

A dry white youthful wine, made mainly from Greco Bianco and Malvasia grapes grown around the town of Squillace.

SQUINZANO   Apulia: ITALY

A red and *rosato* DOC wine made from Negroamaro grapes grown around the town of Squinzano. The sturdy red is *riserva* after two years' ageing, the *rosato* is best drunk young.

STAG'S LEAP WINE CELLARS   California: USA

A Napa Valley winery created by Warren Winiaski, an academic turned wine grower, at the beginning of the 1970s. Cabernet Sauvignon quickly established a reputation; Chardonnay and Merlot are highly prized.

This is not to be confused with the neighbouring Stag's Leap Winery.

STAMBOLOVO   BULGARIA

A defined Controliran wine region of origin, concentrating on the production of Merlot as a varietal wine.

STANLEY WINE COMPANY   AUSTRALIA

An important winery in the Clare-Watervale district of South Australia, dating back to 1893. Their principal grape varieties were initially Rhine and Clare Riesling, Cabernet Sauvignon and Shiraz, but now they concentrate on white wines. Bin 49 Cabernet is good too. Leasingham is their brand name, once a small village near Watervale.

STATE DOMAIN   GERMANY

Known also by its German title, Verwaltung der Staatlichen Weinbaudomane, this consists of three large estates at Eltville on the Rheingau, Niederhausen in the Nahe and Trier on the Mosel as well as a small and less well-known estate in Baden at Meersburg on Lake Constance. They were all founded by the Prussian royal family; the larger estates carry the distinctive German eagle on the label. Each is run as a separate estate, with an excellent reputation.

STEELY

Describes a dry white wine, with a fair measure of acidity, such as Chablis or Sancerre.

STEEN

The South African name for the Chenin Blanc grape variety.

STEIERMARK AUSTRIA

Neighbouring Yugoslavia in the southeast, this is one of Austria's main wine regions. It is split into three subregions with considerable variation in soil and climate: Weststeiermark, Süd-oststeiermark and Südsteiermark. The production of white wines from Welschriesling and Müller-Thurgau, Gewürztraminer and Pinot Blanc grapes is mainly for local consumption.

STEIGERWALD Franconia: GERMANY

The smallest of the three *Bereichs* of Franconia, situated to the east of the Main. The best-known villages are Iphofen, Rödelsee and Castell where full-bodied wines are produced from heavy clay soil in fine summers.

STEINBERG See Hattenheim.

STEINWEIN Franken: GERMANY

Used to describe wine sold in the distinctive *bocksbeutel* from Würzburg but since the reform of the German wine laws in 1971, only wine from the *Einzellage* of Stein should be called Steinwein.

STELLENBOSCH SOUTH AFRICA

One of the best Wine of Origin districts of South Africa and, after Constantia, the oldest wine area, named after Simon van der Stel who arrived here in 1679. The area, 30 odd miles to the east of Cape Town, includes the ward of Simonsberg-Stellenbosch and has some of the best slightly mountainous terrain and moderate climate for viticulture in the Cape, and accordingly some of its finest wine estates. The attractive Cape Dutch town of Stellenbosch forms the centre of the area. Meerlust, Koopmanskloof, Rustenberg, Kanonkop and Simonsig are amongst the best estates and Stellenbosch Farmers' Winery is another important producer.

STELLENBOSCH FARMERS WINERY SOUTH AFRICA

Stellenbosch Farmers' Winery is the largest winery and wholesaler of South Africa. It produces a small part of its own grapes, but buys from private producers and cooperatives to make a very comprehensive range of wines, table, sparkling and fortified. Zonnebloem and Oude Libertas are their two prestige brands. The Nederburg estate is part of the organisation.

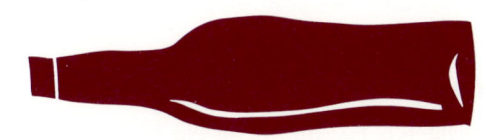

STERLING VINEYARDS California: USA

A showpiece winery in the Napa Valley, that was founded in 1964. The first wines were made in 1969 and in 1977 it was bought by Coca Cola. It is now owned by Seagrams. This is the only winery you approach by cable car. The cellars are immaculate and the wines, just four varieties, Cabernet Sauvignon, Chardonnay, Merlot and Sauvignon Blanc, are made with precision. Their White Cabernet has met with great acclaim in California.

STILL WINE

A table wine without any carbon dioxide to make it bubbly.

STONY HILL VINEYARDS California: USA

A small Napa Valley winery created in the 1960s and producing excellent Chardonnays, as well as Riesling, Gewürztraminer and Sémillon.

STRAVECCHIO

An Italian term for 'very old'. It occasionally appears on wine labels, for example, Stravecchio di Sicilia, a sherry-like wine made by Corvo in Sicily.

STRAVECCHIO SICILIANO
Sicily: ITALY

An individual wine made by Giuseppe Coria from Calabrese and Frappato grapes, (as Cerasuolo di Vittoria is, too) and aged in barrel for 20 or 30 years in a kind of *solera* system, where a little wine is drawn off each year and replaced with young wine.

STRESSED VINES

A Californian term describing vines which have to struggle to survive. Quite simply they are under stress, but the poor soil in which they grow encourages them to send down roots deep in search of nourishment and water, resulting ultimately in wines of greater complexity than if they had an easy life with freely-available water.

STROHWEIN

The German equivalent of the French *vin de paille*. Its production has been illegal in Germany since 1971.

STRUB
Rheinhessen: GERMANY

Weingut J. & H. Strub is an old family estate in Nierstein with a fine reputation, making wines from Riesling, Silvaner, Müller-Thurgau and Ruländer grapes.

STÜCK

The standard cask size of the Rhine region of Germany, it holds 1200 litres.

STYRIA   See Steiermark.

SUAU
Bordeaux: FRANCE

Suau is a lesser-known second growth Sauternes in Barsac.

SUBOTIČA
YUGOSLAVIA

A flat, sandy region of Yugoslavia just south of the Hungarian border, growing mainly white Ezerjó Laski Rizling and red Kadarka grapes.

SUD-OSTSTEIERMARK
AUSTRIA

Kloch is the centre of this region that forms the transition between the dry climate of the Danube and the warm climate of the Mediterranean. Gewürztraminer is particularly successful here, as well as Welschriesling, Müller-Thurgau and Weissburgunder.

SÜDLICHE WEINSTRASSE
Rheinpfalz: GERMANY

One of the two Rheinpfalz *Bereichs* created in 1971 and covering the southern part of the region, formerly called the Oberhaardt, from Neustadt down to the French border. The area produces sound everyday wines, which the Germans call *Schoppenwein*. The principal *Grosslagen* are Königsgarten and Ordensgut and most of the wine is made by cooperatives.

SUDSTEIERMARK
AUSTRIA

The town of Leibnitz is the centre of the most southern part of the wine region of Steiermark; Gamlitz is another important wine village.

SÜDTIROL   See Alto Adige.

SUDUIRAUT
Bordeaux: FRANCE

A first growth Sauternes, near to Yquem and the largest property of the area. The *château* and gardens were designed by Le Nôtre. After a chequered history in the first half of this century, Suduiraut now enjoys a reputation second only to Yquem.

SUHINDOL
BULGARIA

A defined Controliran wine region of origin, producing some of the country's best Cabernet Sauvignon and Gamza wines.

SUISUN VALLEY
California: USA

An AVA in Solano County in northern California.

SULPHUR DIOXIDE

SO_2, is the form of sulphur used in winemaking and in the vineyard. In the cellar, it is an important antiseptic that eliminates wild yeasts, destroys harmful bacteria and protects the must from oxidation. It can be used to stop a fermentation if it is necessary to retain some sweetness in the wine. Attempts are being made to produce wine with minimal or no sulphur dioxide at all. This is very difficult and virtually all wine does contain some. Maximum levels are strictly controlled and measured in analysis as combined and free sulphur. The combined sulphur has joined up with the other constituents of the wine, while the free sulphur continues to act as a general preservative and antioxidant. Sulphur tablets are used in traditional cellars to sterilise wooden barrels before use; they are burnt inside the barrel.

In the vineyard, sulphur sometimes forms part of a treatment against disease, such as oidium, but has tended to be superseded by modern products.

SULTANA

A white grape grown extensively in California and, as the name might suggest, it is more often turned into raisins than wine. However it does thrive in the Central Valley as a constituent of quaffable neutral jug wine. It originated in Asia Minor and is still grown there as a table grape and on some of the Mediterranean islands for wine. Some is grown too in Australia in the irrigated Murray Basin of Victoria and a little in South Africa, mainly for distillation. Also a synonym for Thompson Seedless.

SUMAC RIDGE   CANADA

A small British Columbian winery, created in 1979 and making half hybrid and half *vitis vinifera* wines, notably Chardonnay, Johannisberg Riesling and Chenin Blanc.

SUNGURLARE   BULGARIA

A defined Controliran wine region in eastern Bulgaria concentrating on white wine from the red Misket grape, vinified off the skins.

SUNTORY   JAPAN

Japan's largest grape grower and wine producer. They make Saki, whisky and other spirits as well. They also have a share in the Californian winery, Firestone and own the classed growth Médoc chateau, Lagrange.

SUPÉRIEUR

In France this usually denotes an extra degree of alcohol than the basic wine, and sometimes a smaller yield, eg Bordeaux Supérieur, with a minimum alcoholic degree of 10.5, against 10 for Bordeaux, and a maximum basic yield of 40 hl/ha against 50 hl/ha.

SUPERIOR OLD MARSALA
Sicily: ITALY

Was a popular brand name for Marsala Superiore (see Marsala).

SUPERIORE

Refers to an Italian wine which has a higher level of alcohol e.g. Frascati Superiore, or a longer ageing as in Valpolicella. The one exception is Rosso Conero where *superiore* also implies different grape varieties.

SUPERIORE DI CARTIZZE   See Prosecco di Conegliano.

SUR LATTES

A term used in Champagne to describe the purchase (by a champagne house) of wine that has undergone its second fermentation. So, the only way in which the purchaser can influence the quality of the wine is in the final dosage. Nevertheless, the wine is sold under the purchaser's label, which is contentious from the point of view of quality and reputation. However, it only represents a very small percentage of the market.

SUR LIE

Sur lie literally means 'on the lees'. Traditionally the best Muscadet was left in contact with the sediment or lees resulting from fermentation until the spring. When the wine was drawn off, it was found to contain a minute amount of carbon dioxide which kept the wine fresh. This idea has developed so that the better growers bottle their wines straight from the vat without filtering them to produce wines with some depth of flavour and freshness. Less reputable producers can inject a hint of CO_2 into their wines. Gros Plant du Pays Nantais can also be bottled *sur lie*.

SÜSSRESERVE

Süssreserve is a vital part of German wine making and means literally, sweet reserve. It is the unfermented grape juice added to a wine before bottling to bring it up to the required level of sweetness. It is widely used for wines up to and including Auslese level. Its use is strictly controlled and it should be of the same origin and quality as the wine to which it is added. Certainly its judicious use enhances the quality of the lower categories of German wine.

SUTTER HOME WINERY   *California*: USA

The Sutter Home Winery was founded in 1874; the Sutter family continued to operate during Prohibition and today the winery specialises in full-bodied Zinfandel which accounts for 85% of its production.

SUZE-LA-ROUSSE   Rhône: FRANCE

A village in the southern Rhône Valley, the home of a cooperative, individual estates producing Côtes du Rhône and a Université du Vin that is housed in an ancient château that dominates the village.

SVICHTOV   BULGARIA

A defined Controliran wine region of origin, concentrating on the production of Cabernet Sauvignon as a varietal wine.

SWAN VALLEY   AUSTRALIA

An important wine region of Western Australia on a fertile plain just north east of Perth. The climate is hot with rainfall in winter and spring. The wines tend to be alcoholic and heavy but recently there has been a trend towards lighter varietals, notably by Houghton Wines.

SWARTLAND   SOUTH AFRICA

A comparatively new South African Wine of Origin district, with an expansion of vineyards around the southern areas of Malmesbury, Darling and Riebeek, including the Wards of Riebeekberg and Groenekloof. The Atlantic Ocean modifies the climate, but rainfall is minimal necessitating irrigation and the principal grape varieties such as Palomino and Steen produce dessert wines. Allesverloren is a reputable estate. Red wine from this area is used by the K.W.V. for Roodeberg.

SWEATY SADDLE

An evocative tasting term describing some Australian red wines, notably from the Hunter Valley. Imagination conjures up the smell.

SWEETWATER

An Australian synonym for Palomino.

SWELLENDAM   SOUTH AFRICA

A Wine of Origin district, the most easterly region of the Breede River Valley. It includes part of the Ward of Bonnievale. Most of the production is sweet dessert wines.

SWITZERLAND

The wines, like the country, divide into three nationalities. Those of the French-speaking cantons, notably the Vaud and the Valais, are the best. The principal grape variety is the Chasselas, also called Fendant, Dorin and Perlan. Pinot Noir makes the best red wines; some Gamay is grown too, as well as less well-known Swiss grape varieties. Schenk is the largest wine company. The best-known red wine is Dôle, a blend of Gamay and Pinot Noir grapes, from the Valais.

SYLVANER

French synonym for the Silvaner grape variety.

SYMINGTON

One of the great port families, but of fairly recent standing. The first, A. J. Symington, moved from Graham to Warre in 1905 and the family developed the Oporto end of Warre's business. Now, as well as owning Graham and Warre, the family also own Silva & Cosens with Dow's port and Smith Woodhouse with Gould, Campbell.

SYRAH

The red grape variety of the northern Rhône, producing the area's great red wines, Côte Rôtie, Hermitage, Cornas, Crozes-Hermitage and St-Joseph, where the taste is typified by the distinctive flavour of peppery blackcurrant gums. It is also one of the thirteen varieties of Châteauneuf-du-Pape, is found in the Côtes du Rhône and planted throughout the Midi, including Provence, as a *cépage améliorateur*, where it is increasing in importance in the region's numerous *vins de pays*. As a varietal wine it is found in Syrah de l'Ardèche.

It is widely planted in Australia, where it is better known as Shiraz or, occasionally, Hermitage. A little is grown in California, where it has no relation to Petite Sirah. There is also some in Argentina and South Africa.

SZAMORODNI   see Tokay.

SZÜRKEBARAT

The Hungarian name for the Pinot Gris grape, translating literally as Grey Monk. It is grown in the hills of Badascony near Lake Balaton.

T

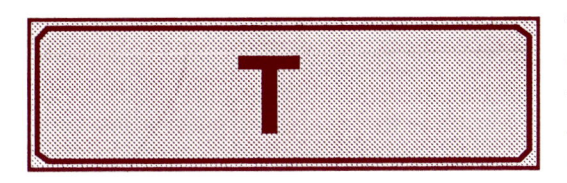

T-BUDDING

T-budding is a technique developed in California and also Australia (where it is called green grafting), to enable a quick conversion from one grape variety to another. The fruit bearing part of the vine is sawn away and a bud of the new variety grafted into the trunk. Thus only one year's fruit is lost in the vineyard. Many vineyards have been converted from red to white wine in this way.

LA TÂCHE Burgundy: FRANCE

An excellent Grand Cru vineyard in the village of Vosne-Romanée, owned by the Domaine de la Romanée-Conti.

TAFELWEIN

Table wine, the very lowest category of wine produced in Germany. More often than not, simple *Tafelwein* is a Euroblend, a mixture of wine from Italy with German *Süssreserve*. Wine that comes from Germany alone is called *Deutscher Tafelwein*.

DU TAILLAN Bordeaux: FRANCE

A Cru Grand Bourgeois of the Haut-Médoc from the village of Le Taillan and the first Médoc *château* just north of Bordeaux. There is also a white wine called La Dame Blanche.

LE TAILLAN Bordeaux: FRANCE

One of the communes within the Haut-Médoc appellation, but it produces very little wine.

TAILLE

The French term for 'pruning'. *Vin de taille* is part of the pressing of a Champagne *marc*.

TAILLEFER Bordeaux: FRANCE

A second growth Pomerol property belonging to A. Moueix's company.

TAIN L'HERMITAGE Rhône: FRANCE

The town that gave its name to one of the finest wines of the northern Rhône, namely Hermitage, and where many of the producers have their cellars, notably Jaboulet and Chapoutier.

TAITTINGER Champagne: FRANCE

An important champagne house in Reims with magnificent medieval cellars. Comtes de Champagne Blanc de Blancs is their prestige *cuvée*.

TALBOT Bordeaux: FRANCE

A fourth growth St-Julien. This property commemorates John Talbot, Earl of Shrewsbury, who lost the battle of Castillon, and hence Gascony, to the French in 1453. It is now owned by the Cordier family. The second label is Connétable Talbot and a small amount of white wine, called Caillou Blanc, is made.

TALENCE Bordeaux: FRANCE

Although now part of the suburbs of Bordeaux, this is an important commune in the Graves.

TALTARNI AUSTRALIA

Meaning red earth in Aborigine. One of the leading wineries of the Pyrenees area of Victoria in Australia, with a mixture of Australian, French and Californian influence. The owner is Dominique Portet, brother of Bernard Portet at Clos du Val in the Napa Valley. Their father was the *régisseur* of Chateau Lafite. Wine making here is a combination of French tradition and Australian technology - oak ageing and strict temperature control. The principal varietals are Cabernet Sauvignon, Malbec, Shiraz and Sauvignon Blanc.

TAMIANKA BULGARIA

An indigenous white grape variety producing a heavy dessert wine.

TĂMIÎOASĂ ROMANEASCA

An old Roumanian grape variety making aromatic sweet wines.

TANGHRITE — ALGERIA

Part of the combined quality zone of Tanghrite, Aîn Merane and Mazouna. Originally called Robert under the French VDQS system, it is situated on the hills near Dahra and known for full-bodied reds.

TANIT   See Moscato di Pantelleria.

TANK METHOD   See *Cuve close*.

TANNAT

A red grape variety of south west France, at its best in Madiran where it forms between 40% - 60% of the blend, making wines deep in colour, and as the name suggests, high in tannin and worth ageing. It also features in Tursan, Côtes du St. Mont, Irouléguy, Latour and Béarn.

TANNIC

The adjective from tannin, used to describe its presence in a wine.

TANNIN

A vital contitutent of fine red wines, playing an important part in the maturation, conservation and colour intensity of a *vin de garde*. Tannins comes from the skins, pips and stalks of the grapes and are absorbed by the must during fermentation. They give the wine its colour after the anthocyans have faded when the wine is about two or three years old. Tannin can be detected on the taste buds by a puckering sensation, similar to strong tea. As the wine ages, the tannin diminishes and the wine softens. It is therefore essential for a *vin de garde* to have sufficient tannin in early youth for it to age, but also enough fruit to balance the reduction of tannin.

TAPPIT HEN

A rare bottle size of port, equalling three standard bottles.

TARRAGONA — SPAIN

The largest demarcated region and D.O. of Catalonia, which is divided into three subregions, Camp de Tarragona, Falset and Ribera d'Ebre. Tarragona Clásico is a sweet dessert wine, fortified and sweetened by the addition of *mistela*. This was the wine described as Poor Man's Port in the last century. Today Tarragona is often used for blending with other lighter wines and the region produces Sangria and altar wines too.

TARRANGO

The Tarrango grape, a crossing of Touriga and Sultana, was developed in Australia for the hotter irrigated vineyards to produce soft early maturing wine in generous quantities.

TART

Describes a wine with too much acidity, caused by unripe grapes.

TARTARIC ACID

One of the principal acids found in wine, and rarely in any fruit other than the grape. When a wine is chilled below freezing point, the tartaric acid will precipitate into tartrate crystals, or tartrates. Tartaric acid may be added to wines or must lacking in acidity.

TARTRATES

Develop in a wine if it is subjected to an extremely cold temperature for any length of time; they come from a precipitation of the tartaric acid in the wine. This can happen inadvertently in the bottle and does not in any way denote a defect in the wine, only that the winemaker did not subject the wine to cold stabilisation treatment in the cellar. Many less well-equipped winemakers hope this will happen naturally during a cold winter.

TASMANIA

The potential of this southernmost part of Australia as a wine region is just being discovered. Vineyards have been planted around Hobart and Launceston, mainly with French and German varieties which are thriving in the favourable climate. Aromatic whites, Riesling and Gewürztraminer. are particularly successful, and also oak-aged Chardonnay and Cabernet Sauvignon. Heemskirk, Lorraine, Pipers Brook and Moorilla are the main estates.

TASTEVIN

A small shallow silver cup, used for tasting wines

in a cellar, especially in Burgundy. The raised indentations reflect the colour of the wine and show its depth.

TASTING

The moment and the occasion when you sample a wine and appreciate its qualities. This may be a single bottle before dinner in your own home, or several bottles at a meeting of a wine society or at a professional gathering or tasting. The senses of sight and smell as well as the palate are used in the art of tasting a wine.

TAURASI   Campania: ITALY

One of the best wines of Campania; a full-bodied red DOC made from the Aglianico grape grown around the village of Taurasi. It requires three years' ageing and four if it is *riserva*.

TAVEL   Rhône: FRANCE

Possibly the best rosé wine of France, coming from the southern Rhône. It is made primarily from the grape varieties Grenache and Cinsaut, with some Clairette, Bourboulenc, Syrah, Mourvèdre, Picpoul and Carignan, grown in vineyards around the village, and is a dry fruity wine best drunk when it is young and fresh. The leading estates are Domaine de la Genestière, Domaine de la Forcadière, Le Vieux Moulin de Tavel, Château d'Aquéria and the Cave Cooperative des Grands Crus de Tavel.

TAWNY PORT   PORTUGAL

A blend of wines from different years that have been matured in wood until they are ready for drinking. The colour turns tawny with age and they are lighter and more elegant than vintage port. Twenty year old tawny means that the wine is a blend of wines with an average age of twenty years. Cheap tawny is often a blend of red and white port.

TAYLOR, FLADGATE & YEATMAN

The company that produces Taylor's port and one of the great British port shippers. The house was founded by Job Bearsley in 1692; Joseph Taylor arrived in 1816; John Fladgate in 1837 and Morgan Yeatman in 1844, whose descendants still run the company. They own Quinta da Vargellas which is sold as a single *quinta* port in non-vintage years. Fonseca is an associate company.

TAYLOR WINE COMPANY   USA

One of the largest wineries of New York State, making a range of sparkling wines, which they call champagne, dessert wines and jug wines. They introduced the French-American hybrids to the state in the 1880s.

ANDRÉ TCHELISTCHEFF

The Russian born, French trained wine-maker of Beaulieu Vineyards in California. He created his reputation with Georges de Latour Private Reserve and his career from 1936 has covered the revival of the California wine industry since Prohibition.

TE KAUWHATA   NEW ZEALAND

The home of New Zealand's Government Viticultural Research Station and also of one of the country's most important wineries, Cooks.

TE MATA   NEW ZEALAND

A historic winery of the Hawkes Bay area. Vines were first planted here in 1892 and after a chequered history the property was revived in 1974. Cabernet Sauvignon, Sauvignon Blanc and Chardonnay are the main varietals. Coleraine is a vineyard planted with the Bordeaux grape varieties, Cabernet Sauvignon and Franc and Merlot. Castle Hill is an estate of the winery making Sauvignon Blanc.

TEARS

The streaks of wine visible on the side of the glass when you swill a wine round. 'Legs' and 'gothic windows' are other poetic associations for the same image. A lot of tears is an indication of a high level of alcohol.

TEINTURIER

Teinturier describes a black grape that has red rather than white pulp and juice. The term translates literally as a dyer and its principal use is to supplement the colour of less substantial grape varieties. Alicante Bouschet is widely planted in the south of France for this very purpose. Gamay Noir à jus blanc is given this rather long-winded name to distinguish it from the various Teinturier Gamay varieties.

TEKAL   TURKEY

The biggest Turkish wine producer, a state monopoly controlling 21 wineries from all regions.

TEMECULA   *California*: USA

An AVA of southern California, in Riverside County, planted mainly with Sauvignon Blanc, White Riesling and Chardonnay.

TEMPERATURE SUMMATION

Another term for heat summation.

DOMAINE TEMPIER   *Provence*: FRANCE

One of the finest estates of Bandol. The owner did much to establish the reputation of the appellation and has encouraged the planting of Mourvèdre. The estate is based on three vineyards, making two thirds red and one third rosé. Methods are traditional and unsophisticated and the results are long-lived wines of immense complexity.

TEMPLETON   *California*: USA

An AVA in the northern part of San Luis Obispo County.

TEMPRANILLO

The best red grape variety of Rioja, Spain, accounting for about 40% of the area and planted mainly in the Rioja Alta and Rioja Alavesa. It has thick skins, giving deep coloured wine, without too much alcohol and blends well with Garnacha, Mazuelo and Graciano. It is also grown to a limited extent in Penedès and Navarre, more so in Valdepeñas, as well as in the Alentejo and Douro districts of Portugal. The Californian grape Valdepenas, may also be Tempranillo.

TENDONE

An Italian term for a method of pruning and training vines similar to the *cordon* system. The vines may be higher or lower, depending on the preferences of the region, but always on wires, with the advantage of providing shade. Many Italian vineyards are adapting to this from the *alberello* system, especially as it tends to be more productive.

TENT   *Madeira*: PORTUGAL

A strong red wine that used to be made on the island of Madeira. It was made from the Negramole grape and was much enjoyed by the Victorians.

TENUTA

Like *fattoria*, means farm or estate in Italian. The word often precedes the name of an Italian wine estate, e.g. Tenuta Santa Margherita.

TERBASH

A white grape variety grown in Tadzhikistan, Uzbekistan and the Crimea for dessert wines.

TERLANO   *Trentino-Alto Adige*: ITALY

Also called Terlaner, a DOC from the Alto Adige, coming in six versions, all white: Pinot Bianco, Riesling Italico, Riesling Renano, Sauvignon, Sylvaner and simple Terlano, which denotes at least 50% Pinot Bianco grapes. The vineyards are around the town.

TEROLDEGO

An Italian red grape grown in the Trentino for the DOC of Teroldego Rotaliano. It is not unlike Gamay in character.

TEROLDEGO ROTALIANO
Trentino-Alto Adige: ITALY

One of the best DOC red wines of northern Italy, made on the Rotaliano plain from the grape of the same name. It needs at least two years' ageing and is *superiore* with 12° alcohol. A *rosato* is also made.

TERRA ALTA   SPAIN

A new and little-known D.O. of south west Catalonia, making full-bodied red and white wines from vineyards on mountainous terrain.

TERRA ROSSA

Describes the distinctive red soil of Coonawarra in South Australia, a narrow strip of red loam some 15 kilometres long and less than 1.5 kilometres wide, sometimes much less, with a limestone and clay subsoil. Cabernet Sauvignon and Shiraz are the main grape varieties grown on this soil.

TERRANO DEL CARSO
Friuli-Venezia Giulia: ITALY

A curiosity from the Istrian peninsula. A red non-DOC wine made from Terrano grapes, it is the traditional table wine of Trieste.

TERRANTEZ

An old Madeira grape variety, usually white, though a black version does exist, that almost disappeared after the *phylloxera* crisis as it is prone to disease and produces low yields. Today it is considered a rarity and old vintages of the 19th century and earlier are highly rated.

TERRAS ALTAS

The brand name for the Dão wines produced by the Portuguese company of J. M. da Fonseca.

TERRET

One of the permitted but insignificant grape varieties of Châteauneuf-du-Pape. Terret Gris and Terret Blanc are also grown in southern France for *vin de pays*.

DU TERTRE
Bordeaux: FRANCE

A fifth growth Margaux. The only classified growth of the Arsac commune. It belongs to the Gasqueton family who also have a share in Calon Ségur. They have restored the vineyard and *château* and have improved the wines considerably.

TERTRE-DAUGAY
Bordeaux: FRANCE

A Grand Cru Classé of St-Émilion. The property has been renovated since a change of ownership in 1978.

TÊTE DE CUVÉE

A similar term to *vin de tête* and used in Champagne to describe the first juice of a pressing, with the best balance of acidity, sugar and extracts.

TEXAS
USA

The state university of Texas has planted vineyards in the western part of the state, where conditions are similar to the Central Valley of California. There are now three AVAs: Bell Mountain, Mesilla Valley and Fredericksberg. Llano Estacado is the best winery.

THANISCH
Mosel-Saar-Ruwer: GERMANY

An old family estate going back to the mid-17th century. Its reputation is based on ownership of part of the Bernkasteler Doktor vineyards, with other vineyards in Bernkastel and Graach.

THASIAN

One of the wines of ancient Greece, described as a 'rich and rosy' wine and said to have been a noble growth when mellowed with age.

DOMAINE THÉNARD
Burgundy: FRANCE

The largest estate in Givry, making Premier Cru Givry Boischevaux, Cellier aux Moines and Clos St-Pierre. However, they are better known as owners of one of the largest plots of Le Montrachet.

THERMOVINIFICATION

A technique developed in France for making red wine. The grapes are crushed and the must heated to 69–71°C (156–160°F) to extract colour from the skins. It is maintained at that temperature for thirty minutes, cooled and pressed to separate the juice from the skins so that the fermentation takes place away from the skins, as for a white wine vinification. The aim is to produce a softer, less tannic, red wine.

THEUNISKRAAL
SOUTH AFRICA

A consistently popular estate in the Tulbagh district of South Africa, which concentrates on white wine, making successful Cape Riesling, Late Harvest Steen, Sémillon and Gewürztraminer.

ROLAND THÉVENIN
Burgundy: FRANCE

A grower and *négociant*, also the owner of Domaine du Moulin aux Moines at Auxey-Duresses. As the former owner of the Château de Puligny-Montrachet, he made his name in Puligny-Montrachet, especially les Folatières.

THIN

Describes a wine which lacks body and fruit.

THOMPSON SEEDLESS

Another name for the Sultana grape variety, named after William Thompson, who first grew it commercially in California.

THORIN
Burgundy: FRANCE

An important family company in Beaujolais whose reputation stands on two properties, Château des Jacques in Moulin-a-Vent and Château de Loyse in Beaujolais Blanc.

THÖRNISCH
Mosel-Saar-Ruwer: GERMANY

A Mosel wine village of little importance within the *Grosslage* of St. Michael.

THREE CHOIRS
ENGLAND

Takes its name from the Three Choirs Festival, a Gloucestershire vineyard planted with Müller-Thurgau and Reichensteiner.

TIBOUREN

A red grape grown mainly in Provence and is at its best as part of a well made Côtes de Provence rosé.

TICINO
SWITZERLAND

The vineyard of Italian-speaking Switzerland, producing red wine from a mixture of Italian varieties and increasingly from the Merlot grape, which thrives in this area. The term VITI guarantees quality with a tasting test.

TICKLER

An old cellar instrument for extracting a bung from a cask.

TIEFENBRUNNER
Alto Adige: ITALY

A family company which is one of the most talented wine makers of the Alto Adige, producing a wide range of wines from nearly 40 acres of vines. Most notable are Riesling, Chardonnay and Goldenmuskatel. They own the highest vineyard of the region, Feunberg, at 1,000 metres.

TIERRA DE BARROS
SPAIN

A newly demarcated region in south west Spain in the Extremadura, producing quantities of cheap neutral white wine, used for blending. Some distinctive red wine is made in the village of Salvatierra de Barros.

TIERRA DE MADRID
SPAIN

An undemarcated wine area near Madrid, producing robust red wines. It is subdivided into three districts, San Martin de Valdeiglesias, Navalcarnero and Arganda-Colmenar de Oreja.

TIGNANELLO
Tuscany: ITALY

A red *vino da tavola* made by Antinori on their Chianti estate of Santa Cristina, with about 10% Cabernet Sauvignon added to Chianti grapes and aged in *barriques*. This wine is characteristic of the new wave of Tuscan experimentation.

TIMOK
YUGOSLAVIA

A Serbian vineyard area, producing mainly Gamay, Pinot Noir, Merlot and Cabernet grapes.

TINAJA

A large earthenware vat, rather similar to the original Ali Baba jars, used for storing wine all over Spain and for the fermentation and maturation of wine in Montilla and also La Mancha.

TINO

A large oak vat which is used in Spain for the secondary fermentation and racking of wine.

TINTA BARROCA

One of the red grapes grown in the Douro for port, giving a high yield of robust wine. It is also planted extensively in South Africa for port style wines.

TINTA CÃO

One of the red grapes grown in the Douro for port. It gives very good wine, but in small quantity. It is also used for Dao.

TINTA CARVALHA

One of the red grape varieties authorised in the Douro for port.

TINTA FRANCESCA

One of the grape varieties grown in the Douro for red port. It has for a long time been erroneously linked with Pinot Noir, but there is no ampelographical link.

TINTA MADEIRA

A white grape variety grown to a limited extent on Madeira, and also in California, for port type wines.

TINTA RORIZ

A Portuguese synonym for Tempranillo where it is grown in the Douro and Alentejo.

TINTILLO   see Málaga.

TINTO

Tinto describes a deep red wine in Spanish, as opposed to a lighter *clarete*. Tinto is also used in Portuguese to describe a red wine.

TINTO AMARELLO

One of the red grapes grown in the Douro for port and also to a lesser extent for Dão and also for Bairrada where it is called Trincadeiro. It is colourful and prolific.

TIO PEPE

One of the biggest selling *fino* sherries; the brand is owned by Gonzalez Byass.

TIRNAVE   ROMANIA

One of the main production centres for Romanian wine, on the Transylvanian plateau in the north of the country. White wines are best here, notably Welschriesling, Gewürztraminer, Muscat Ottonel, and a white blend called Perla de Tirnave made from the indigenous Alba and Regala grapes, variations of Fereascá.

TISDALL WINES   AUSTRALIA

A new enterprise in the Goulburn Valley district of Victoria, with two vineyards, Mount Helen and Rosbercon, planted with Cabernet Sauvignon, Merlot, Pinot Noir, Chardonnay, Rhine Riesling, Sauvignon Blanc and Gewürztraminer, as well as more unusual varieties suited to the climatic conditions of the area, such as Emerald Riesling, Colombard, Ruby Cabernet and Barbera. Oak ageing is a distinctive characteristic of the Tisdall wines.

TOCAI FRIULIANO

As the name implies, is widely grown in the Friuli region of Italy. It has no relationship with Tokay d'Alsace, nor with Tokay in Hungary. In Friuli it produces fairly neutral dry white wine all over the province, and in the Veneto in the DOCs of Colli Berici, Piave and Tocai di Lison and is the base of Breganze Bianco and other non DOCs of the area.

TOCAI DI LISON
Veneto: ITALY

A dry white DOC wine made from Tocai grapes in the east of the region. The vineyards around the town of Lison are *classico*.

TOCAI DI SAN MARTINO DELLA BATTAGLIA
Lombardy: ITALY

A dry white DOC produced from Tocai Friuliano and Tocai Italiano grapes grown south of Lake Garda around the town of the same name. It is best drunk young.

TOCAI ROSSO

A red grape of the Veneto used for one of the DOCs of Colli Berici and occasionally found elsewhere.

TOKAY
HUNGARY

One of Hungary's finest wines and Tokay Aszú is one of the world's great dessert wines. The wine takes its name from the small town of Tokay in the foothills of the Carpathians. The River Bodrog, a tributary of the Danube, provides the necessary climatic conditions for botrytis to develop on the grapes. Three grape varieties are used, Furmint, Hárslevelü and to a lesser extent Muscat. There are several types of Tokay, namely Tokay Szamorodni, meaning 'as it comes', in other words nothing is added to the wine, which can be either dry or sweet, depending on the proportion of grapes affected with botrytis. Next is Tokay Aszú. Aszú is the term for the handpicked overripe grapes, affected by botrytis and fermented in small 140 litre casks called *gönc*. So many *puttonyos* of this pulp are added to the base wine to make Tokay Aszú. A *puttony* or *putt* consists of 25 kilos of grapes and Tokay Aszú is classified according to the number of *puttonyos* added. Three, four or five is usual; six is exceptional. After fermentation the wine is aged for not less than two years more than the number of *puttonyos* that were added and it can last for many years. Next comes Tokay Aszú Essencia made from selected botrytised grapes, and even sweeter than six *putts*, with a slow fermentation and long ageing in oak. Greatest of all is pure Tokay Essence from hand-picked botrytised grapes, pressed by their own weight and fermented very slowly and matured for many years. This is the drink – it rarely reaches more than 2° alcohol – that is attributed with life restoring powers. It is very rare indeed.

TOKAY

An Australian synonym for the Muscadelle grape.

TOKAY D'ALSACE

A synonym, used in Alsace for the Pinot Gris grape. The confusion of names has something to do with a Baron Schwendi who is supposed to have fought the Turks at Tokay and brought vines back from the area to his estate in Alsace. The EEC authorities want to abolish the name.

TOLLANA WINES
AUSTRALIA

Tollana is the brand name of a company called Tolley, Scott & Tolley Ltd, in the Barossa Valley. Their vineyards are in Eden Valley, particularly at Woodbury and Roeslers Vineyard and at Waikerie in Riverland. They were the first to use a mechanical harvester in Australia and their wines are generally reliable.

TOLLOT-BEAUT
Burgundy: FRANCE

A family estate with an excellent reputation based on vineyards in Chorey-les-Beaune and Beaune as well as some Corton and Corton-Charlemagne.

TOMBALADERO

The Portuguese equivalent of a *tastevin*.

TONDONIA   see López de Heredia.

TONEL

The term used in Spain to describe a large storage cask holding several butts, and in Portugal several pipes.

TONNEAU

A Bordeaux barrel size of 900 litres, equaling four *barriques*.

TONNELIER

The French term for a 'cooper'.

TORBATO DI ALGHERO Sardinia: ITALY

A fine dry non-DOC white wine made from the Torbato grape grown around Alghero. It is best drunk young.

TORCOLATO Veneto: ITALY

A curiosity from the Veneto made near Breganze by the Maculan company, from semi-dried white Vespaiolo, Tocai and Garganega grapes as a rich dessert wine.

TORGIANO Umbria: ITALY

A small DOC made around the town of the same name. The production is dominated by one enterprising family, Lungarotti. The red wine, called Rubesco, is made from Sangiovese, Canaiolo, Montepulciano and Ciliegiolo grapes; the *riserva* is aged in wood for three years, resulting in a richly elegant wine. The white, called Torre di Giano, is made from Trebbiano and Grechetto and is best drunk young.

TORO SPAIN

Toro, or Comarca de Toro is a newly demarcated area, or D.O. to the east of Zamora in one of the most arid parts of Spain. The wines are mainly full-bodied reds, some of which undergo considerable oak ageing.

TORRE DI GIANO See Torgiano and Lungarotti.

TORRE ERCOLANA Latium: ITALY

A little-known red wine made from Cesanese, Merlot and Cabernet grapes in almost equal proportions and produced in minute quantities by the Cantina Colacicchi.

TORRE QUATRO Apulia: ITALY

The name under which some of the best, though non-DOC Apulian wines are made by the Cirillo Farrusi family. The red, made from Malbec, Uva di Troia and Negroamaro grapes, is aged in wood and develops with bottle age. *Rosato*, based on Malbec and white from Trebbiano and Bombino Bianco grapes, are best drunk young.

TORRES SPAIN

One of the great names of the Spanish wine trade, a family company based at Vilafranca del Penedès in Catalonia. The family have been producing wine since the 17th century, but the present winemaker, Miguel Torres, has been responsible for a considerable programme of innovation, while retaining the best of Spanish tradition. In addition to the usual Spanish varieties, they have planted several foreign grapes, Cabernet Sauvignon, Chardonnay, Gewürztraminer, Riesling, Pinot Noir and others. The winemaking is carefully controlled; whites with cool fermentation; reds aged in *barricas* for less time than is usual in Spain. They produce a considerable variety of wines; in white, dry fruity Vina Sol, Gran Viña Sol and Gran Viña Sol Green Label with a hint of Chardonnay; grapey Viña Esmeralda from Muscat and Gewürztraminer; a Riesling based Waltraud and in red, Tres Torres, Gran Sangre de Toro, Coronas, Gran Coronas and best of all with some Cabernet Sauvignon, Gran Coronas Black Label. Miguel Torres is one of the few winemakers with vineyards in both hemispheres as the family have recently expanded into Chile with considerable success and has also planted vineyards in Sonoma in California.

TORRES VEDRAS PORTUGAL

An undemarcated wine region of western Portugal, important for its bulk table wines, produced by the regional cooperative. The reds are full-bodied and very alcoholic.

TORRETTE

Valle d'Aosta: ITALY

A red wine from the Valle d'Aosta, made from Petit Rouge grapes grown around the village of St Pierre.

TORRONTES

A white grape grown in Argentina.

TOSCANELLO

The name given to a two litre wicker-covered flask in Orvieto.

PASCUAL TOSO

ARGENTINA

A small family company, producing some reliable Cabernet Sauvignon in Mendoza.

TOTAL ACIDITY   See acidity.

TOUGH

Describes a wine with an excess of tannin, which will probably mellow with age.

LA TOUR ASPIC

Bordeaux: FRANCE

The second wine of The Haut-Batailley estate.

LA TOUR-BLANCHE

Bordeaux: FRANCE

A first growth Sauternes in the commune of Bommes. In 1910, the proprietor gave the property to the French State to be run as an agricultural school. Students participate in the winemaking and it is a centre for experimental work in viticulture and vinification. Unfortunately the quality of the wine generally does not merit its place in the classification.

LA TOUR DE BY

Bordeaux: FRANCE

A Médoc Cru Grand Bourgeois and the most important property of Bégadan, with a reputation for enjoyable wine. There is a tower in the vineyard.

LA TOUR-CARNET

Bordeaux: FRANCE

A fourth growth St-Laurent estate which has a moated medieval castle. The property was restored in the 1960s and is now producing sound wine.

LA TOUR-FIGEAC

Bordeaux: FRANCE

A Grand Cru Classé of St-Émilion in the *graves* and once part of Figeac.

LA TOUR-HAUT-BRION

Bordeaux: FRANCE

A Cru Classé Graves. This is a tiny property next to La Mission-Haut-Brion, and under the same ownership, is making red wine. The two wines are made identically, so this is really the second wine of The La Mission-Haut-Brion estate.

LA TOUR-MARTILLAC

Bordeaux: FRANCE

A Cru Classé Graves Martillac property producing both red and white wine. The estate is noted for its old vines, as some of the vineyard was planted in 1884. Both red and white are classified.

LA TOUR-DE-MONS

Bordeaux: FRANCE

One of the leading properties in the commune of Soussans, Margaux, with an excellent reputation meriting classed growth status.

LA TOUR-DU-PIN-FIGEAC

Bordeaux: FRANCE

A well-known Grand Cru Classé of the *graves* of St-Émilion. The property is split in two: half belongs to the Belivier family and half to A. Moueix et Fils, with the latter making markedly better wine.

TOURAINE

Loire: FRANCE

An important province of the Loire vineyards, with the town of Tours as its capital. Legend has it that it was the donkey of the patron saint of Tours, St. Martin, that ate some vine shoots so that it was subsequently realised that the remaining shoots bore even better fruit. Thus the practice of pruning the vine was begun. The wines of Touraine comprise an enormous diversity, with the red wines of Chinon, Bourgueil and St. Nicholas de Bourgeuil, as well as Vouvray, Montlouis, Touraine Azay le Rideau, Touraine Amboise and Touraine Mesland.

TOURAINE AMBOISE Loire: FRANCE

A mainly red and rosé Loire appellation with vineyards around the attractive town of Amboise. The black grapes are Gamay for a light, fruity red and for rosé; Malbec for a tougher red wine and Cabernet Franc and Cabernet Sauvignon for dry rosés. A very small amount of white wine is made from Chenin Blanc.

TOURAINE AZAY-LE-RIDEAU
Loire: FRANCE

The village of Azay-le-Rideau with its beautiful Renaissance château gave its name to this white and rosé wine. The white, made from Chenin Blanc, is dry or semi sweet, the rosé, from mainly Groslot, is dry and refreshing.

TOURAINE MESLAND Loire: FRANCE

The vineyards of Touraine Mesland are on the north bank of the Loire around the village of Mesland. The white is made from Chenin Blanc; the red is more important and comes mainly from Gamay and also Cabernet Franc, Cabernet Sauvignon and Malbec. This could be a region of considerable potential.

TOURIGA FRANCESCA

One of the best red grape varieties for port, with good flavour and sound yields.

TOURIGA NACIONAL

The best grape for making port; production is tiny; the wine is very dark and perfumed with high extract and tannin to form the base of vintage port. It is also grown for Dão and in Australia.

TOURNE

A bacterial spoilage of a wine. Bacteria attacks the tartaric acid which results in a loss of tartrates, an increase of volatile acidity and a decrease of fixed acidity, with gassiness, haze and loss of colour.

TRABEN-TRARBACH
Mosel-Saar-Ruwer: GERMANY

Really two villages, Traben on the left bank of the Mosel and Trarbach on the right bank, with several wine growers' cellars. The vineyards come within the *Grosslage* of Schwarzlay.

TRAISEN Nahe: GERMANY

A small village on the Nahe, coming within the *Grosslage* of Burgweg, with wines ranging from ordinary Müller-Thurgau to wonderful Riesling, grown in the Bastei and Rotenfels vineyards. Crusius is the best producer.

TRAKYA TURKEY

Or Thrace in English, one of the main wine-producing regions of Turkey, with vineyards on the European side of the Bosphorus. Some European grape varieties are grown, mainly Cinsaut, Gamay and Sémillon, as well as local Turkish varieties.

TRAMINER   see Gewürztraminer

TRAMINER AROMATICO   see Gewürztraminer

TRAMINER MUSQUE

Another name for the Gewürztraminer grape.

TRANSFER METHOD

The transfer method is a method of making sparkling wine that is a cross between the *méthode champenoise* and the *charmat* or *cuve close* process, to avoid the labour-intensive processes of *remuage* and *dégorgement*. The second fermentation takes place in the bottle, after the required period of maturation time on the lees. Then the wine is transferred into the vat, filtered and bottled, all under pressure.

TRANSVASAGE

Another name for the transfer method of making sparkling wine. In Champagne however, it describes the decanting under pressure of the contents of one bottle to another, which is necessary for either very small or very large bottles which are impractical for a *remueur* to manipulate.

LOUIS TRAPET
Burgundy: FRANCE

A small family estate with vineyards in Gevrey-Chambertin, notably Le Chambertin. The winemaking is traditional.

TRÀS-OS-MONTES
PORTUGAL

A large mountainous province of Portugal to the north of the Douro, with Vila Real as the main wine region. The wines are mainly red and rosé with a little white. Most of the vineyards are in the valleys of tributaries of the Douro river. Sogrape have a winery here for Mateus Rosé.

TREBBIANINO VAL TREBBIA
Emilia-Romagna: ITALY

Was a white DOC wine from Emilia-Romagna, made from Ortruga, Malvasia, Moscato Trebbiano and Sauvignon grapes, grown in the Trebbia Valley. It was usually dry, but sometimes medium sweet and *frizzante*, and has now been incorporated as part of the larger DOC of Colli Piacentini Trebbianino Val Trebbia.

TREBBIANO

The world's most prolific grape variety, producing rather dull white wine, either as table wine or for distillation. In France, where it is called Ugni Blanc, it is grown in the Charente and Gers for Cognac and Armagnac; it also features in several of the white wines of the Midi, usually blended with something more exciting. It accounts for several Italian wines, and if not the dominant variety, forms part of the blend of so many wines, particularly in central Italy. It is a vital ingredient of Soave, Verdicchio, Frascati, Orvieto and so on. The precise version of Trebbiano varies according to region. It is also one of the grapes used for Chianti but increasingly less so, but still provides the backbone of white Tuscan wines like Galestro, and also Vin Santo. It has been introduced to the New World, notably Australia and California, mainly for distillation.

TREBBIANO DI ABRUZZO
Abruzzi: ITALY

A dry white DOC wine made from local Trebbiano, Trebbiano Toscano or Bombino Bianco grapes. It is usually dry and bland and can be *frizzante*.

TREBBIANO DI ROMAGNA
Emilia-Romagna: ITALY

A white DOC wine from Emilia-Romagna. It is usually dry and still and rather bland, though the Trebbiano vines grown in Romagna are considered more distinctive than other Trebbianos. *Spumante* can occasionally be found.

TREFETHEN VINEYARDS
California: USA

Although grapes have been grown on the site in the Napa Valley since the 1880s, Trefethen Vineyards did not make its first wines until 1973, which were Chardonnay and Riesling. Cabernet Sauvignon and Pinot Noir followed, as well as Eschol Red and White which recalls the former name of the property.

TRENTINO
ITALY

Although politically linked with the neighbouring Germanic Alto Adige region, Trentino is purely Italian. Within the region there are three individual DOCs: Teroldego Rotaliano, Casteller and Sorni. All other DOC wine comes under one heading, Trentino, and is defined according to grape variety. Reds are *riserva* after two years. The list is: Cabernet; Lagrein, red and *rosato*; Marzemino; Merlot; Moscato, sometimes dry and sometimes a dessert wine produced in small quantity, a rich fortified wine can also be found; Pinot Bianco, which often includes Chardonnay and Pinot Grigio and can be *spumante*; Pinot Nero; Riesling, both Renano and Italico; Müller Thurgau and Traminer Aromatico. There is also a tradition for Vin Santo, DOC, made from Nosiola and Pinot Bianco, with three years' ageing.

TRESALIER   see Sacy.

TRESSEAU   see Tressot

TRESSOT

A red grape that is permitted in the red appellations of the Yonne, in France, notably Irancy, but in reality it has virtually disappeared.

TRIAGE

Describes the picking of the grapes for Sauternes and other sweet wines dependent on botrytis affected grapes. Several pickings or 'tries' are necessary, so that the grapes are picked only as they become affected by noble rot. The vintage at a Sauternes château can last for several weeks, with as many as ten 'tries'.

TRIE   See Triage.

TRIER   Mosel-Saar-Ruwer: GERMANY

Trier is the oldest city of Germany with early Roman origins and involved in viticulture for almost as long with vineyards today within the city boundaries. The *Grosslage* is Römerlay; the *Einzellagen* names are unknown outside Germany and the city is the home of several important wine estates such as the Bischöfliche Weingüter, Friedrich Wilhelm Gymnasium and Vereinigte Hospitien.

TRIMBACH   Alsace: FRANCE

One of the great producers of Alsace wine with cellars at Ribeauvillé. They own the vineyard of Clos Sainte Hune at Hunawihr and other labels include Cuvée Frédéric Emile for Riesling and Cuvée des Seigneurs de Ribeauvillé for Gewürztraminer.

TRIMOULET   Bordeaux: FRANCE

A little-known Grand Cru Classé of St-Émilion situated on the *côtes*.

TRINCADEIRO   see Tinto Amarello

TRITTENHEIM Mosel-Saar-Ruwer: GERMANY

A small wine village on the Mosel that was already known for its wine in the 9th century and said to be the site of the first planting of Riesling on the Mosel in the 16th century. The *Grosslage* is Michelsberg and the best vineyards are Apotheke and Altärchen. The Bischöfliches Priesterseminar and Friedrich Wilhelm Gymnasium are good growers.

TROCKEN

Trocken is a new description for German wine and means quite simply dry. The use of the term is defined: the residual sugar content must not be greater than 4 g/l, or 9 g/l if the total acidity is less than the residual sugar content by no more than 2 g/l, (e.g. residual sugar 9 g/l, total acidity not less than 7 g/l). *Trocken* wines have become something of a fashion in Germany, with the desire to produce wines to accompany food. The Rheinpfalz, Rheinhessen and Baden are the most important areas for *trocken*, but the export market is less enthusiastic, for without sugar and with low alcohol, German wines seem skeletal rather than elegant.

TROCKENBEERENAUSLESE

The sweetest category of German Prädikat wine, meaning literally, 'a selection of dried berries'; in other words, grapes so affected by noble rot that they have become shrivelled and raisin-like. The resulting wines are rich and luscious and will age well. *Trockenbeerenauslese* wines, or TBA for short, are made only in the very best years with fine autumn weather. The quantities are minute and the price inevitably high. The necessary sugar content, measured as oechsle level, is 150° for all grapes in all regions, giving a potential alcohol of 21.5°. In fact, with so much sugar in the must, the fermentation is very difficult and slow and the alcohol level is usually a mere 5.5°, which leaves a very sweet wine.

TROESMES   See Beauroy.

LES TROIS GLORIEUSES
                              Burgundy: FRANCE

These are the annual festivities held in the Côte de Beaune on the third weekend in November. The first event is a dinner at Clos Vougeot, held on the eve of the second event, the Hospices de Beaune sale of their wine, and the third is the Paulée de Meursault, a Monday lunch where all the growers bring bottles from their cellars.

TROIS MOULINS   Bordeaux: FRANCE

A little-known, tiny Grand Cru Classé of St-Émilion.

TROLLINGER   see Schiava

TRONÇAIS OAK

One of the types of French oak widely used for wine barrels. It comes from forests near those of Nevers and has similar characteristics with dense, tightly grained wood so that the wine absorbs less oak character.

TRONQUOY-LALANDE
Bordeaux: FRANCE

A Cru Grand Bourgeois of St-Estèphe that was once more important than it is today. The wine has some character.

TROPLONG MONDOT
Bordeaux: FRANCE

One of the leading Grands Crus Classés of St-Émilion, it has an excellent reputation and a beautiful position with views over the Dordogne. Monsieur Troplong was president of the senate during the Second Empire.

TROTANOY
Bordeaux: FRANCE

Despite the lack of official classification of Pomerol, Trotanoy is generally accepted as coming second to Pomerol. The tiny 9 hectare vineyard is the property of J.-P. Moueix and the wine is made in their usual meticulous way.

TROTTEVIELLE
Bordeaux: FRANCE

A Premier Grand Cru Classé St-Émilion owned by the Castéja family, who also own Batailley in the Médoc. The wine is full-flavoured but not designed for a long life.

TROUSSEAU

The French synonym for the red Bastardo grape, found in France in the Jura, while Trousseau Gris is another name for the Californian Gray Riesling.

TSINGTAO
CHINA

A district in the province of Shantung, which had vineyards and cellars at the beginning of the century. The white wine was often oxidised, not unlike sherry. Today, there are modernising projects for the future.

TUALATIN VINEYARDS
USA

Tualatin Vineyards of Oregon were created in the early 1970s and produced their first wine in 1976. White wines, Riesling, Muscat and Gewürztraminer are successful, as well as oak-aged Pinot Noir. 'Estate bottled' on the label differentiates between wines produced from their own grapes and wines from grapes from Washington and Idaho as well.

TUKE, HOLDSWORTH   see Ferreira.

TULBAGH
SOUTH AFRICA

A Wine of Origin district within the Central Region of South Africa, to the north of Paarl. With Paarl it comes within the Boberg region for fortified wines. Rainfall and temperature can vary enormously depending on microclimate. A variety of grapes are grown – whites are best of all – notably on three important estates, Montpellier, Twee Jonge Gezellen and Theuniskraal.

TULLOCH
AUSTRALIA

This company in the Hunter Valley was started when John Tulloch accepted a 20 hectare vineyard at Glen Elgin in payment of an overdue debt in 1893. Hunter River Riesling and Private Bin Dry Red Hermitage are amongst their best wines, characteristic of the Hunter. They also produce wines from other parts of Australia.

TUMULTUOUS FERMENTATION
Describes the first stage of the alcoholic fermentation, when the yeasts are very active and the fermentation bubbling energetically. This is the moment when the greatest attention must be paid to the control of the fermentation temperature.

TUNISIA
The wine industry of Tunisia has had a strong French influence. The vineyards are all in the north of the country, stretching from Cap Bon, past Carthage and Tunis to Bizerta. There is a vague classification of *vin supérieur de Tunisie*, but no precise appellation system. Grape varieties are French in origin, mainly Alicante Bouchet, Carignan and Grenache, with some Mourvèdre, Cabernet Sauvignon and Pinot Noir for reds and rosés, while white wines are mainly made from Clairette and Ugni Blanc. More important is Muscat for dessert wines. The Union des Caves Coopératives Vinicoles de Tunisie is the best producer of this largely state-controlled industry.

TURKEY
Noah may have planted vines on Mount Ararat, so Turkey has some claim to be one of the very first producers of wine. Today the potential of the country is enormous, but undeveloped. Trakya or Thrace, Izmir on the Aegean and Anatolia are the main wine regions. The vines are native or imported, with Papazkarasi, Adakarasi, Karasakiz, Gamay, Cinsaut, Pinot Noir and Cabernet Sauvignon for reds and Apincak, Beylerce, Riesling, Sémillon, Chardonnay and Silvaner for whites. Tastes range from very dry to very sweet and through every shade of colour from white, to red and tawny. The industry is dominated by Tekal, a state monopoly, but there are also several private wineries, notably Kutman with Villa Doluca.

TURSAN   SOUTH WEST FRANCE
A tricolour VDQS wine from the foothills of the Pyrenees, which made its reputation for its white wine. The main grape varieties for red and rosé are Cabernet Franc and Tannat. The now undistinguished white is made solely from a local grape, Barroque. The only producer of any significance is the cave cooperative at Geaune.

TUSCANY   ITALY
Above all, known for Chianti, but boasts a galaxy of fine red and white wines, with three DOCGs, Chianti, Vino Nobile di Montepulciano and Brunello di Montalcino, several DOCs and outstanding *vini da tavola*. The Sangiovese grape dominates the region's red wines, but other non-Italian varieties are being introduced, notably Cabernet Sauvignon. White wines and vinification methods are improving, especially with new wines such as Galestro coming from the surplus of white grapes no longer needed for Chianti. The principal DOCs are Bianco della Valdienievole, Bianco di Pitigliano, Bianco Pisano di San Torpé, Bianco Vergine della Valdichiana, Carmignano, Elba, Montecarlo Bolgheri, Montescudaio, Parrina, Morellino di Scansano, Parrina, Rosso delle Colline Lucchesi, Vernaccia di San Gimignano and Pomino.

TWEE JONGE GEZELLEN   SOUTH AFRICA
Translating as Two Young Batchelors, this is one of the important wine estates of the Tulbagh district. Its reputation stands upon its white wine; this was one of the first estates to experiment with cool fermentation in the 1950s. More recent work covers cultured yeasts and night harvesting.

TYPÉ
Means, in French, 'of its type' and implies that a wine is typical and characteristic of what one would expect from the area or grape variety.

TYRELL VINEYARDS   AUSTRALIA
The oldest company of the Hunter Valley, with a reputation today for tradition and excellence, especially for Pinot Noir and Chardonnay, and also for Shiraz and Sémillon, often denoted by bin numbers. Long Flat Red is their most popular wine. Ashmans is the name of the company's original vineyard.

U

U.C. DAVIS
Or alternatively the University of California at Davis is the famous viticulture and oenology school responsible for training the new generation of California winemakers. It also conducts extensive research in all aspects of wine.

U.C.C.V.T.   TUNISIA
Or Union des Caves Coopératives Vinicoles de Tunisie, this is the biggest wine producer in Tunisia, linking fourteen local cooperatives. Their wines are generally sound.

UGNI BLANC
The French synonym for the Trebbiano grape.

UITKYK   SOUTH AFRICA
An important wine estate in Stellenbosch. Its origins date back to the early 18th century, but the estate has been recently renovated and expanded by the current owners. Its reputation stands upon two special labels, Carlonet for red and Carlsheim for white wine, as well as Cape Riesling.

UKIAH VALLEY   *California*: USA
Part of the vineyard area of Mendocino County, but not an AVA. It has a short, but warm growing season so that the grape varieties French Colombard, Petite Sirah and Zinfandel have established a reputation. Sauvignon Blanc and Johannisberg Riesling are also gaining in importance.

UKRAINE   USSR
There are three wine regions within the Ukraine: the coastal region south of the Dnieper; the foothills of the Carpathians, both of which are important for quantity production, while the central and southern Crimea, one of the oldest wine regions of the Soviet Union, has a reputation for dessert wines.

ULL DE LLEBRE
A Spanish synonym for the Tempranillo grape.

ULLAGE
The space between the cork and the level of the wine in the bottle. Very old wine bottles will often be ullaged as some wine has inevitably evaporated. If this has occurred with a young wine, it is an indication of a faulty cork.

ULTRA BRUT
The name of Laurent Perrier's Champagne, without any dosage.

UMANI RONCHI   *The Marches*: ITALY
One of the most important producers of Verdicchio, and other wines from the Marches.

UMBRIA   ITALY
This region owes its wine-making origins to the Etruscans. Orvieto is its best-known wine; Torgiano, dominated by the Lungarotti family, has a fine reputation and lesser-known DOCs are Colli del Trasimeno, Colli Perugini, Colli Altotiberini and Montefalco. Grape varieties are a mixture of traditional Italian and foreign introductions: Sangiovesi, Trebbiano, Grechetto, with Cabernet Sauvignon and Chardonnay.

UMPQUA VALLEY   USA
One of the three designated wine areas of Oregon, covering the county of Douglas, around Roseburg.

UNBALANCED
Describes a wine that is lacking in balance, with one or more components in excessive or insufficient quantity.

UNGSTEIN   *Rheinpfalz*: GERMANY
A village in the Mittelhaardt area of the Rheinpfalz. It is situated in two *Grosslagen*, Hochmess and Honigsäckel, which cover the three *Einzellagen* of Weilberg, Herrenberg and Nussriegel.

UNIACKE ESTATE WINES   CANADA
A small British Columbian winery, experimenting with Johannisberg Riesling Late Harvest grapes.

UNTERMOSEL *Mosel-Saar-Ruwer*: GERMANY

Synonymous with Bereich Zell, which is on the Mosel before Koblenz.

URGÜP TURKEY

A dry white Turkish wine made in central Anatolia from Emir grapes.

URUGUAY SOUTH AMERICA

The wines of Uruguay are made very much for the domestic market. The wine industry is unsophisticated, relying mainly on American hybrid vines. Some European varieties are grown, notably those of Bordeaux.

ÜRZIG *Mosel-Saar-Ruwer*: GERMANY

A village on the Mosel, with red clay soil on slate giving its wines a distinctive taste. Würzgarten is the best site. The *Grosslage* of the village is Schwarzlay and notable producers include Rudolf Müller.

UTIEL REQUENA SPAIN

One of the D.O.s of the Levante, covering an area inland from Valencia, planted mainly with the Bobal grape, for delicate rosé, full-bodied reds and *vino de doble pasto*.

UVA RARA

A little known red grape grown in Lombardy for inclusion in the blend of Oltrepò Pavese Rosso.

V

v.c.c.   See vin de consommation courante.

v.d.n.   See Vin doux naturel.

v.d.q.s.   See Vin Délimité de Qualité Supérieure.

V.Q.P.R.D.

Vin de Qualité Produit dans une Région Déterminée, a Common Market term to describe a quality wine, be it A.O.C., V.D.Q.S., Qualitätswein, D.O.C.G. or D.O.C. or the equivalent. The English translation is Q.W.P.S.R. in other words, Quality wine produced in a specified region.

V.S.R.

Vin Sans Récolte, sometimes found on French wine labels to indicate a non-vintage wine.

VACCARESE

One of the thirteen grape varieties allowed in Châteauneuf-du-Pape, and not found anywhere else, in or outside France.

VACHERON   Loire: FRANCE

The great name of Sancerre, making both excellent white and red wine, as well as rosé. His white wine vineyards are Les Romains, Le Clos des Roches and Le Paradis; the red Les Cailleries and the rosé Les Guignes Chèvres.

VACQUEYRAS   Rhône: FRANCE

Rivals Cairanne as the best of the villages of the appellation Côtes du Rhône Villages in the southern Rhône. Vines were grown here in the 15th century and Raimbaud, the Provençal troubadour was born here so that the village cave cooperative is called Le Troubador in his memory. Good Vacqueyras is red, rich and full-bodied; white and rosé are best avoided.

VADUZER   LIECHTENSTEIN

The red wine of Liechtenstein, named after the capital, Vaduz. It is made from the Blauburgunder grape and is more rosé than red in colour.

VAILLONS   Burgundy: FRANCE

A Premier Cru Chablis vineyard which can be subdivided into Vaillons, Châtains, Séchet (or Séché), Beugnon and Les Lys. A grower with vines in two or more sites may vinify all the wine together and call it Vaillons or vinify each plot separately and sell each wine by its individual name.

VAL DE SALNÉS   SPAIN

An area of Galicia where the Albarino grape produces light, fragrant, somewhat acidic white wines. It is not a D.O. but is subject to some supervisory regulations.

VALAIS   SWITZERLAND

One of the main wine-making cantons of Switzerland, producing predominantly white wine from the Fendant grape, as the Chasselas is called locally. There is also Switzerland's best red wine, Dôle, made from Pinot Noir and Gamay. Other wines include Sion, Johannisberger, Malvoisie, Amigne and Arvine. The climate is generally dry and sunny and the vineyards are on arid mountain slopes.

valbuena   see Vega Sicilia.

VALCALEPIO   Lombardy: ITALY

A bi-coloured DOC produced between Bergamo and Lake Iseo. The red, made from Merlot and Cabernet Sauvignon grapes, needs at least two years' ageing; the white from Pinot Bianco and Grigio is dry, light and best drunk young.

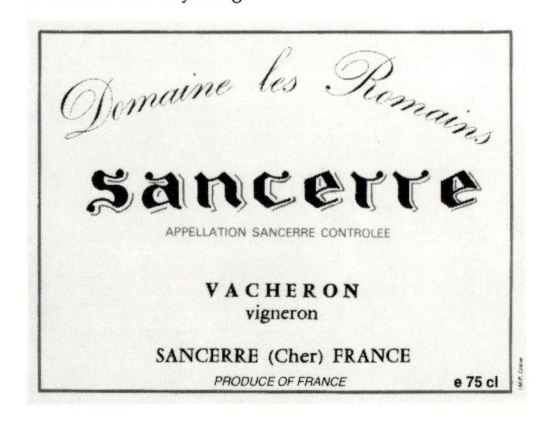

Domaine les Romains
Sancerre
APPELLATION SANCERRE CONTROLEE
VACHERON
vigneron
SANCERRE (Cher) FRANCE
PRODUCE OF FRANCE   e 75 cl

VALDADIGE *Trentino-Alto Adige:* ITALY

Called Etschtaler in German, this is a DOC covering vineyards in both regions of the Alto Adige and Trentino along the Adige river. It is red and white and grape varieties are sometimes mentioned on the label.

VALDEORRAS SPAIN

One of the D.O.s of Galicia in north west Spain, covering the mountainous valley of the river Sil and divided into three subregions, Rúa-Petín, Larouca and El Barco de Valdeorras. The dry light white wine is made mainly from Xerez, a type of Palomino grape, and the red comes from the Garnacha de Alicante grape.

VALDEPEÑAS SPAIN

One of the D.O.s of central Spain, covering the arid plains to the south of Ciudad Real. Airén is the most important grape in the vineyards and produces neutral white wines. However the most typical wines are red, made from Cencibel and Garnacha, traditionally vinified in earthenware *tinajas* and sold within a couple of years. Most Valdepeñas is drunk in the cafés of Madrid.

VALDEVIMBRE SPAIN

One of the subdistricts of the Comarca de Léon. The best wines are fruity *claretes*, traditionally with a refreshing prickle originating from a second fermentation.

VALDIGUIÉ

A red grape of southwest France, grown for its high yields and resistance to *oidium*, but otherwise deficient in any other character and tending to disappear. In California, it is confusingly called Napa Gamay where it makes a light red wine.

VALENÇAY *Loire:* FRANCE

A small VDQS of Touraine. The wine is mainly red from the grape varieties Gamay, Cabernet Sauvignon and Franc, Malbec and Pinot Noir; these are also permitted for the rosé. The white comes from a minimum of 60% Pineau Menu, Chardonnay or Sauvignon and a maximum of 40% Chenin Blanc or Romorantin.

VALENCIA SPAIN

A large area behind the city of Valencia, producing basic table wine in vast quantities. It includes the former D.O. of Cheste and the subregions of Alto-Turia, Clariana and Valentino. White wines are more important than red, from the Merseguera, Pedro Ximénez and Moscatel grape varieties.

VALENTINO SPAIN

The most important subregion of Valencia. The best white wines are dry, from Merseguera and Pedro Ximénez grape varieties and the sweet wines come from Moscatel grapes.

VALGELLA *Lombardy:* ITALY

One of the four areas of the Valtellina Superiore, and the most prolific.

VALLE D'AOSTA ITALY

Italy's tiniest province at the end of the Mont Blanc tunnel with some of the highest vineyards in Europe. At present there are only two DOC wines, Donnaz and Enfer d'Arvier, but a variety of notable *vini da tavola*. As well as French grape varieties like Gamay and Pinot Noir, and also Müller Thurgau, there are local grapes such as Petit Rouge and Gros Vien.

VALLE ISARCO *Trentino-Alto Adige:* ITALY

Also called Eisacktaler in German, this is the DOC covering the vineyards along the Isarco valley, south of the Brenner pass. Five white grape varieties are permitted: Müller Thurgau, Pinot Grigio (Ruländer), Sylvaner (at its best here), Traminer Aromatico (Gewürztraminer) and Veltliner, which is DOC only in this area. Production is dominated by the local cooperative.

VALLE DE MONTERREY see Monterrey.

VALLÉE DE LA MARNE *Champagne:* FRANCE

A less-favoured part of the vineyards of Champagne.

VALLET Loire: FRANCE
An important village within the appellation of Muscadet de Sèvre et Maine.

VALMUR Burgundy: FRANCE
One of the seven Grand Cru vineyards of Chablis.

VALPOLICELLA Veneto: ITALY
The most important Veneto red wine, made from Corvina Veronese, Rondinella and Molinara grapes. It compares with Bardolino but has more substance, especially as Recioto della Valpolicella and Recioto della Valpolicella Amarone. The *classico* zone has the towns of Negrar, Sant'Ambrogio and Fumane at its centre. *Superiore* denotes one year's ageing. Good producers include Allegrini, Tedeschi, Masi and Le Ragose.

VALPOLICELLA VALPANTENA Veneto: ITALY
A special denomination coming from the area of the Valpantena and made in the same way as other Valpolicelli.

VALRÉAS Rhône: FRANCE
One of the villages of the appellation Côtes du Rhône Villages of the southern Rhône. There is a long tradition of wine making in the village and today it has a flourishing cooperative and several estates, most notably Le Val des Rois.

VALTELLINA Lombardy: ITALY
A DOC area around Sondrio on the Swiss border where Nebbiolo grapes, locally called Chiavennasca, flourish. Simple red from a minimum of 70% Nebbiolo is produced throughout the area; Valtellina Superiore covers four smaller DOCs: Grumello, Inferno, Sassella and Valgella. Sfurzat comes from semi-dried grapes.

VALTELLINA SUPERIORE Lombardy: ITALY
The name applied to four smaller areas of the DOC Valtellina, namely Grumello, Inferno, Sassella and Valgella. It is made from 95% Nebbiolo grapes, with a minimum of two years' ageing and it benefits from further ageing in bottle.

VAN RIEBEECK
Jan van Riebeeck was the first winemaker in South Africa. As the first commander of the Cape in the employ of the Dutch East India company, he planted a vineyard and recorded the very first pressing of the grapes on 2nd February 1659. With the words 'Praise be to God', wine was pressed for the first time from Cape grapes.

VANILLA
A characteristic smell of many Riojas, notably *reservas* and *gran reservas*, that have been aged for some years in American oak barrels.

VARICHON ET CLERC Savoie: FRANCE
Varichon et Clerc, founded in 1901, are the principal producers of sparkling Seyssel, a *méthode champenoise* wine of Savoie. The principal grape varieties are Molette and Roussette and their best wine is Royal Seyssel. They also make a still Roussette de Seyssel and a Pétillant de Savoie as well as *méthode champenoise* wine without an appellation.

VARIETAL
An American term for grape variety. A 'varietal wine' implies that the wine is made predominantly or solely from one grape variety. For a wine label in the United States to mention a single variety, the percentage in the wine must not be less than 75%.

VARNA BULGARIA
A defined Controliran wine region of origin, concentrating on the production of Chardonnay as a varietal wine.

DOMAINE DES VAROILLES Burgundy: FRANCE
An estate in Gevrey-Chambertin with a reputation for long lasting Burgundy. Their wines include four *monopoles*: Clos des Varoilles, la Romanée, Clos du Meix des Ouches and Clos du Couvent.

VASLIN
Important manufacturers of wine presses, whose equipment is commonly found in France.

VASSE FELIX   AUSTRALIA

A pioneering vineyard of the Margaret River in Western Australia, the first to be planted this century, with its first vintage in 1971. Cabernet Sauvignon and Rhine Riesling are the main grape varieties, with a little Hermitage, Malbec and Gewürztraminer.

VAT

A container, of varying size, used for the fermentation, storage or ageing of wine. It may be made of wood; cement, in which case it may be lined with enamel paint, glass or epoxy resin; fibre glass; steel, again lined with a neutral material; or stainless steel. Cement vats are the most traditional, having superseded wood, and stainless steel, now taking over from cement, are the most modern, expensive and efficient to use.

VAUCOUPAIN   Burgundy: FRANCE

An alternative spelling for Vaucoupin the Premier Cru Chablis.

VAUD   SWITZERLAND

The biggest wine-producing canton of Switzerland, with vineyards on the northern shore of Lake Geneva. It divides into three main areas, La Côte, Chablais and Lavaux. Fendant is the main grape variety, making dry white wine.

VAUDÉSIR   Burgundy: FRANCE

One of the seven Grand Cru vineyards of Chablis.

VAUDEVEY   Burgundy: FRANCE

A Chablis Premier Cru vineyard. Its vines only came into production with the 1983 vintage, but the site was a flourishing vineyard before the phylloxera crisis.

VAUGIRAUT   See Vosgros.

VAULORENT   See Fourchaume.

VAUPULENT   See Fourchaume.

VECCHIO

Or *vecchia*, an Italian term for 'old' which can refer to a specific ageing period for some wines.

VECCHIO SANPERI   Sicily: ITALY

An unfortified Marsala, made mainly from Grillo grapes, aged in a *solera* system for ten years. Has a taste like dry old Amontillado.

VEGA SICILIA   SPAIN

A legendary name amongst Spanish wines, coming within the D.O. of Ribero del Duero. The estate has been planted for over a hundred years with the Bordeaux grapes, Cabernet Sauvignon, Merlot and Malbec which are blended with native grapes, Tinto Aragonés, Garnacha and white Albillo. Vega Sicilia, aged in oak for not less than ten years and for a further period in bottle, is an amazingly deep, complex wine. Three and five year old Valbuena are also produced by the *bodega*.

VELENCHE

Another term for a *pipette*.

VELLETRI   Latium: ITALY

A bi-coloured DOC coming from vineyards around Velletri. The red is made from Cesanese, Montepulciano and Sangiovese grapes; the white, from Malvasia and Trebbiano, can be dry or medium sweet.

VELTLINER

Comes in two versions, Grüner and Frühroter. Grüner Veltliner is the white grape of Austria and is grown only in central Europe; a little in Yugoslavia, Hungary, Czechoslovakia and Roumania. In Austria it produces lightly spicey wines with quite high acidity. Frühroter Veltliner is a separate variety, part of the DOC of the Valle Isarco, where it is called simply Veltliner and it also grows elsewhere in the Alto Adige, but mainly in Austria.

VELVETY

Describes a soft, smooth wine with an element of richness.

VENDANGE

The French term for 'grape harvest'.

VENDANGE TARDIVE

A term used in Alsace for wine made, as the name implies, from late picked grapes. The concept was established by the house of Hugel and since 1984 has been part of the *appellation contrôlée* law for Riesling, Muscat, Pinot Gris and Gewürztraminer. Growers must declare their intention to make *Vendange Tardive* wines before picking; the minimum sugar levels are 95° *oechsle* for Riesling and Muscat and 105° *oechsle* for Gewürztraminer and Pinot Gris. The wines can be sweetish, with some residual sugar, or fermented completely dry. Chaptalization is forbidden; there is a compulsory analysis and tasting test in March, eighteen months after the vintage, before the wine can be sold. They must be from a single vintage which is stated on the label.

VENDANGEUR

The French term for a grape-picker. As mechanical harvesters become more prevalent, *vendangeurs* are no longer needed, which takes some of the colour out of the vintage. However, in some regions such as Champagne and Beaujolais, where whole grapes must be picked, they will never be replaced, nor in Sauternes where great experience is required to pick the right grapes.

VENDEMMIA

An Italian term referring to the grape harvest, or a year's vintage.

VENDITA DIRETTA   See *vente directe*.

VENEGAZZÙ   Veneto: ITALY

Comes within the DOC of Montello e Colli Asolani, but the DOC regulations are not observed and Conte Loredan makes a stylish red wine from Cabernet Sauvignon, Cabernet Franc, Malbec and Merlot grapes. There is also a pure Venegazzù Cabernet and a Venegazzù Bianco from Pinot Bianco, as well as a *spumante*.

VENENCIA

In Spain, especially in Jerez de la Frontera, a small silver cup, traditionally on a long whalebone handle, used for sampling sherry from the butt.

VENENCIADOR

The man, often colourfully dressed, who in Spain uses a *venencia*, the long handled sherry sampling cup, with some flamboyance and considerable expertise.

VENETO   ITALY

One of the largest wine-producing regions of Italy. It rivals Emilia-Romagna and Sicily in quantity and is top in quantity of DOC wine. The principal DOCs are Valpolicella, Bardolino and Soave, but the variety of the Veneto is enormous and, with Italy's most important oenology school at Congeliano, its production methods are amongst the country's most modern.

VENTE DIRECTE

The French term describing the sale of wine by the producer directly to the consumer. In many French wine regions a considerable amount of wine is sold in this way without going through a merchant. The Italian equivalent is *vendita diretta*.

VÉRAISON

The moment at which the grapes change colour from youthful green to reddish purple or yellowish green. This usually occurs in August and is the beginning of the final stage in the ripening of the grapes.

VERBESCO Piedmont: ITALY

A light, dry, *frizzante* white wine made by a group of Piedmont producers, mainly from Barbera grapes. Modern technology is used.

VERDEJO

A white grape variety indigenous to the Rueda district of Spain, where it produces some crisp nutty wines.

VERDELHO Madeira: PORTUGAL

A type of the fortified wine, Madeira, sweeter than Sercial but not as sweet as Bual. It is a medium brown, dry nutty flavoured wine made from the Verdelho grape.

VERDENZ Mosel-Saar-Ruwer: GERMANY

A village on a tributary to the Mosel and within the *Grosslage* of Kurfürstlay. Verdenzer Kirchberg can be good in a fine vintage.

VERDICCHIO DEI CASTELLI DI JESI The Marches: ITALY

The best-known of the various Verdicchio wines, coming from the hills around the town of Jesi. The castles are an illusion. *Classico* covers most of the area. As well as the Verdicchio grape, 20% Trebbiano and Malvasia is also allowed and the resulting wine is light and dry and best drunk young. Good *spumante* wine is also made by the *méthode champenoise*.

VERDICCHIO DI MATELICA The Marches: ITALY

A white DOC similar to Verdicchio dei Castelli di Jesi.

VERDICCHIO DI MONTANELLO The Marches: ITALY

A good *vino da tavola* from the Marches that compares favourably with other DOC Verdicchio.

VERDICCHIO PIAN DELLE MURA The Marches: ITALY

A still and a *spumante* wine from the Marches, made from the Verdicchio grape.

VERDIGNY Loire: FRANCE

One of the most important villages of the vineyards of Sancerre. Les Mont Damnés is one of the better sites.

VERDUZZO FRIULIANO

A white grape producing dry wines in the Veneto such as Verduzzo del Piave.

VEREINIGTEN HOSPITIEN Mosel-Saar-Ruwer: GERMANY

The Güterverwaltung Vereinigten Hospitien is an old charitable institution in Trier. It has ancient cellars built when it was a Roman warehouse. Napoleon united the various Trier charities in the Benedictine abbey of St. Irminen. This continues nowadays as a hospice, like its counterpart in Beaune, financed by its vineyards. These include sole ownership of Schloss Saarfelser, Serriger Schlossberg, Wiltinger Hölle, Piesporter Schubertslay and Trierer Augenscheiner, as well as other sites in Serrig, Wiltingen, Kanzem, Piesport and the Scharzhofberg. On the labels, there is a figure, in gold, of St. James of Compostella, Sanctus Jacobus.

VERGÉ See Mâcon Villages.

VERMENTINO

A white grape found chiefly on Corsica and Sardinia and in Liguria.

VERMENTINO DI GALLURA
Sardinia: ITALY

A dry white DOC wine made from the Vermentino grape, grown on the Gallura Peninsula. *Superiore* denotes at least 13.5° alcohol, though the trend today is towards a lighter wine. Some of Sardinia's better dry white wines come from the Vermentino grape, with its delicate flavour.

VERNACCIA

The name of two different white Italian grapes, as well as one red. Vernaccia di San Gimignano makes a dry white wine; Vernaccia di Oristano in Sardinia is a sherry-like wine and quite different, while Vernaccia Nera is grown in the Marches for Vernaccia di Serrapetrona.

VERNACCIA DI ORISTANO
Sardinia: ITALY

A DOC which is Sardinia's answer to sherry, made from over-ripe Vernaccia grapes grown near Oristano. It is quite different from the other Vernaccias of Italy. At least two years' ageing in barrel is required in a *solera* type system. *Superiore* denotes three years' and *risesrva* four years' barrel age. The wine is usually unfortified at 15° alcohol or can be fortified, dry or sweet, at 16.5°–18°.

VERNACCIA DI SAN GIMIGNANO
Tuscany: ITALY

This was Italy's first DOC wine, a dry white made from the Vernaccia grape grown around San Gimignano. It is quite different from the other Vernaccias of Italy. *Riserva* denotes one year's ageing though usually it is a wine for early drinking.

VERNACCIA DI SERRAPETRONA
The Marches: ITALY

A curious *spumante* red DOC made around the town of Serrapetrona from red Vernaccia grapes. It can be dry, medium sweet or sweet and is usually made by the *charmat* method.

VERNATSCH   see Schiava

GEORGES VERNAY
Rhône: FRANCE

The leading grower of Condrieu, with a special *cuvée*, Coteaux de Vernon, which is aged for an extra year in cask. He also has small vineyards in Côte Rôtie, St-Joseph, and Côtes du Rhône.

VÉRONIQUE

A bottle shape almost identical to the flûte d'Alsace, except that it has rings or ridges round the neck.

VERTHEUIL
Bordeaux: FRANCE

One of the communes within the Haut-Médoc appellation next to St-Estèphe.

VERTZAMI

A red grape grown on the Ionian islands of Greece and noted for its very deep colour and high alcohol.

VERWALTUNG

A term which can appear on a German wine label in the title of some German estates and means administration, eg. Reichgräflich von Plettenberg'sche Verwaltung.

VERWALTUNG DER STAATLICHEN WEINBAUDOMÄNEN NIEDERHAUSEN – SCHLOSSBOCKELHEIM
Nahe: GERMANY

The Nahe State Domain was founded in 1902 by the King of Prussia and is now owned by the State of Rheinland-Pfalz. Today it is considered to be one of the finest estates in Germany producing wines, mainly from Riesling grapes, with meticulous vinification and careful maturation in wood. The principal vineyard sites are at Schlossböckelheim and Niederhausen and it also has sole ownership of Niederhausen Hermannsberg, Traisen and others. Labels carry the black eagle of Prussia.

VERWALTUNG DER STAATLICHEN WEINBAUDOMÄNEN
Mosel-Saar-Ruwer: GERMANY

A large Mosel estate owned by the State of Rheinland-Pfalz and created by the King of Prussia in 1896. Labels still carry the black Prussian eagle. The vineyards include parcels of Ockfener Bockstein and Herrenberg, Serriger Vogelsang, Avelsbacher Hammerstein and Trierer St. Maximiner Kreuzberg. There is also a testing station for new vine varieties and viticultural methods and some *Sekt* is made too.

VERWALTUNG DER STAATSWEINGÜTER ELTVILLE *Rheingau*: GERMANY

The largest estate in the Rheingau, with some vineyards in the Hessische Bergstrasse. The estate was based on the monastic vineyards which were ceded to the Duke of Nassau under Napoleon and then to the Kingdom of Prussia and now belong to the State of Hessen. Kloster Eberbach is the headquarters of the estate. Vineyards include parcels in Assmannshausen for red wine, as well as sole ownership of the famous Steinberg vineyard and parts of other famous sites, such as Rüdesheimer Berg Roseneck, Erbacher Marcobrunn, Rauenthaler Baiken, Hocheheimer Kirchenstück. Dr. Hans Ambrosi, the leading German wine authority, runs the estate.

VERZENAY *Champagne*: FRANCE

An important champagne village on the Montagne de Reims.

VESPAIOLO

A white grape grown in the Veneto. It features in the DOC of Breganze.

VESUVIO   See Lacryma Christi del Vesuvio.

VEUVE CLICQUOT *Champagne*: FRANCE

The lady who gave her name to this champagne house was widowed at the age of 27 in 1805 and, left to run her husband's business, made its fortune by selling wine to the Russian court after the Napoleonic wars. She invented the process of *remuage*. The company today is highly respected and its prestige *cuvée* is called La Grande Dame. The firm has recently been acquired by the Moët Hennessy group.

VEUVE DU VERNAY *Bordeaux*: FRANCE

A popular brand of sparkling wine, produced in Bordeaux from grapes of indeterminate provenance, by the *cuve close* method.

VICTORIA   AUSTRALIA

One of the main wine producing states of Australia, with several important vineyard areas: Central Victoria, including Ballarat and Bendigo, Geelong, Goulburn Valley, Great Western and Avoca; the Murray River; North Eastern Victoria around Milawa and Rutherglen and the Yarra Valley. See separate entries.

VIDAL FLEURY   Rhône: FRANCE

An important grower and *négociant* for Côte Rôtie and Hermitage, with vineyards on both slopes of the Côte Rotie. The company is now owned by another *négociant*, Guigal.

VIDE

A voluntary organisation of (currently) some 30 producers from all over Italy. The initials stand for Vitivinicoltori Italiani di Eccellenza (Italian wine growers and makers of excellence). The official title of the organisation is Associazione Vitivinicoltori Italiani and members produce wine from their own grapes and then submit their wine to rigorous chemical and organoleptic analysis. Bottles of wine which pass this test display the VIDE neck label.

VIEILLES VIGNES

Literally means 'old vines' in French. Sometimes, an estate which has parcels of much older vines will vinify the grapes separately as a special *cuvée* of wine. It is thought that older vines produce better wine, but usually a smaller quantity. Their root systems have developed sufficiently to enable them to reach distant sources of nourishment. Bollinger have a champagne *cuvée* Vieilles Vignes, made from ungrafted vines which never succumbed to phylloxera.

VIENNA   AUSTRIA

The vineyards of Vienna mingle with the suburbs to the north and south of the capital and the Vienna woods, and the wines rarely travel further than the nearest *heurige*.

VIETTI   Piedmont: ITALY

A small producer with a fine reputation for Barolo, Barbaresco and other Alba wines.

VIEUX CHÂTEAU CERTAN   Bordeaux: FRANCE

Despite the lack of official classification, this is regarded as one of the best Pomerol wines. There is a 17th century *château* and the property belongs to the Belgian Thienpont family.

DOMAINE DU VIEUX TÉLÉGRAPHE
                                           Rhône: FRANCE

An important estate in Châteauneuf-du-Pape, making traditional wine with modern equipment. Clappe, the inventor of the optical telegraph system, built a tower on the vineyard in 1793 to help with his experiments, hence the name of the property.

VIGNE

The French word for vine.

VIGNERON

The French term for a winemaker; it usually implies someone who has their own vineyards and makes their own wine. They then bottle and sell it themselves, under their own label, or sell the wine to a *négociant*.

VIGNERONS DE SAUMUR À ST-CYR EN BOURG   Loire: FRANCE

An important growers' cooperative dealing in the sparkling and still wines of Anjou and Saumur.

JEAN LOUIS VIGNES

The first commercial wine-grower of note in California. He brought European vine cuttings to California in the 1830s and is remembered with Vignes Street in L.A.

VIGNES MÈRES

The vines which provide the phylloxera-resistant rootstock for the grafting of *vitis vinifera*. They are usually hybrid varieties, grown in nurseries for the purpose.

VIGNETO

The Italian term for 'vineyard'.

VIGNOBLE

The French term for a 'vineyard'.

VIGOUROUX SOUTH WEST FRANCE

An important *négociant* for Cahors who has made his reputation by replanting the arid vineyards of Château Haute Serre.

VILA NOVA DE GAIA PORTUGAL

The main suburb of Oporto across the mouth of the Douro where by law all the port shippers have to have their offices and lodges where they mature their wine. Vila Nova de Gaia provides a much more humid atmosphere with less temperature fluctuations than the hot dry Douro valley.

VILAFRANCA DEL PENEDÈS SPAIN

The town at the centre of the most important part of the Catalonian vineyards, those of Penedès, with an important wine museum.

A. & P. DE VILAINE Burgundy: FRANCE

The co-owners of the great Burgundy estate, Domaine de la Romanée-Conti, and also the owners of a large vineyard on the Côte Chalonnaise at Bouzeron, where they have contributed much to the success of Aligoté de Bouzeron. They also make good Bourgogne Blanc and Rouge.

VILLA MARIA NEW ZEALAND

A large winery in South Auckland with a reputation for white wines, notably Late Harvest Müller-Thurgau and a Private Bin Sauternes. Gewürztraminer and Sauvignon Blanc are good too; Cabernet Sauvignon is their best red.

VILLA MOUNT EDEN California: USA

Founded in 1970 in the Napa Valley near Oakville and has established a fine reputation, notably for white wines, Gewurztraminer and Chardonnay, and also for Cabernet Sauvignon.

HENRI DE VILLAMONT Burgundy: FRANCE

This estate was founded by the Swiss company Schenk and owns vineyards in Savigny, Chambolle-Musigny and Grands-Echézeaux. They found and sold the famous Barolet collection of fine old Burgundies in 1968.

VILLÁNY HUNGARY

A Hungarian wine region in the south western part of the country known for its red wine, especially from the Pinot Noir grape which is called Villányi Burgundi in Hungary.

VILLARD

A French hybrid grape, grown widely in southern France for indifferent white wine, while Villard Noir, another French hybrid is also planted in southern France, especially in the Tarn. Much of its production goes to the distillery.

VILLEGEORGE Bordeaux: FRANCE

The leading property of Avensan. Although part of the vineyard is entitled to the appellation of Margaux, the appellation of the *château* is Haut-Médoc. Unusually, the vineyard is planted with 50% Merlot grapes.

VILLENAVE-D'ORNON Bordeaux: FRANCE

An important commune within the Graves, producing more white wine than red

VIN

The French word for wine.

VIN DE CONSOMMATION COURANTE

Another term for *vin de table*.

VIN DE CORSE CORSICA

The appellation that covers the whole of the island of Corsica. Within the appellation there are five smaller areas, namely Calvi, Coteaux du Cap Corse, Figari, Porto Vecchio and Sartène. The permitted grape varieties are both traditionally Corsican, namely Vermentino, which is also called Malvoisie de Corse, for white wine and Sciacarello, Nielluccio and other more obscure varieties for red and rosé wine, as well as the grape varieties found commonly in the Midi, such as Grenache, Cinsaut and Carignan. There is however a definite trend in favour of the traditional varieties so that a Vin de Corse from Nielluccio and Sciacarello can have its own very distinctive flavour.

VIN COTTO

Literally meaning 'cooked wine' in Italian, is a peculiarity of the Abruzzi. It is not unlike one of the production processes for Marsala: the must is cooked so that it concentrates into a syrupy consistency, fresh must is then added and the mixture fermented. The result is deep brown, rather dry with a burnt caramel flavour.

VIN DE CUVÉE

The term used in Champagne to describe the first 2050 litres of must pressed from a 4000 kilo *marc* of grapes which, after fermentation, *débourbage* and fining diminishes to 2000 litres, the equivalent of ten *pièces*. This juice comes from the central part of the grape pulp which is richest in sugar and trace elements and destined for the best champagnes.

VIN DÉLIMITÉ DE QUALITÉ SUPÉRIEURE

The second quality category in French wine law, below *Appellation Contrôlée*. The regulations cover similar aspects: vineyard area, grape varieties, yields, etc. VDQS may disappear as a category as many of the better wines are elevated to AC status.

VIN DOUX NATUREL

Translates literally as 'naturally sweet wine' a wine that is rich in natural sugar, as the fermentation has been stopped by the addition of alcohol. At 15°, it is higher in alcohol than a normal wine, with at least 125 grams of residual sugar. This is a particularly popular type of wine in the south of France; the best-known example is Muscat de Beaumes de Venise; there is also Banyuls, Rivesaltes, Muscat de Lunel, Maury, Muscat de Frontignan and Muscat de Mireval. V.D.N. is a common abbreviation.

VIN DE GARDE

Literally, 'a wine for keeping', the French term for a wine that is vinified so that it can then be laid down and aged in bottle, it will develop character and finesse with bottle age.

VIN DU GLACIER See Rèze.

VIN DE GOUTTE

The wine that is run out of the vat after fermentation before the grapes are pressed. The juice has come from the natural weight of the grapes. It was generally considered better quality than the pressed juice, but the combination of better presses and better techniques has improved the quality of the pressed juice.

VIN GRIS

A pale rosé wine, made from red grapes, vinified as white wine, such as in Gris de Toul.

VIN JAUNE

The most distinctive wine from the Jura; it is included in the appellations of Côtes du Jura, Arbois and L'Étoile, while Château Chalon is the finest example. *Vin jaune* is made from the white Savagnin grape; the wine is aged for a minimum of six years in small oak barrels, which are never topped up. The wine grows a kind of *flor*, like *fino* sherry, which gives it a very distinctive flavour. It is always sold in a *clavelin* bottle and can age for a considerable time.

VIN DE MÉDICIN

Was the term to describe a stronger heavier wine that was used to boost weaker, lighter wine. For instance the black wine of Cahors was often used in the 19th century as a *vin de médicin* for the lighter wines of the Gironde.

VIN DE MOSELLE   NORTHEAST FRANCE

As the name implies, this VDQS wine comes from the French *département* of the Moselle. The reds are made from Gamay and Pinot Noir grapes and the white from Pinot Blanc and Sylvaner. The wines are light and the production tiny.

VIN NATURE

In French, means a dry wine without any added sugar, or, in Champagne, it describes a still wine.

VIN NOBLE DU MINERVOIS
The Midi: FRANCE

A sweet white wine made from Muscat, Malvoisie, Grenache and Maccabéo. The grapes are picked when they are rich in sugar so that the wine reaches a natural 13° alcohol. In practice it is rarely made.

VIN NOIR   SOUTH WEST FRANCE

In the 19th century Cahors acquired a reputation for producing Vin Noir, supposedly a wine of immense longevity and rich in tannin. In reality it came from concentrated grape must and was often used in Bordeaux to boost weaker wines.

VIN ORDINAIRE

The everyday or ordinary wine that is legally defined as *vin de table*.

VIN DE L'ORLÉANAIS   *Loire:* FRANCE

A VDQS wine from vineyards around the city of Orléans in the Loire Valley. Production is small; the white is made from Chardonnay, called Auvernat Blanc locally; rosé is made from Cabernet and the most characteristic red is called Gris Meunier, and is a light fresh wine, made from Pinot Meunier. Auvernat Rouge, the local name for Pinot Noir, and Cabernet are other possible red grapes.

VIN DE PAILLE   *Jura:* FRANCE

Translates literally as straw wine. Although it is found in other parts of France, it is a speciality of the Jura. When the grapes are picked, they are left to dry, once on straw, but now in plastic trays, until January or February so that the juice concentrates and they become raisin-like. When they are pressed, they are left to ferment very slowly and aged in small oak barrels. The taste of *vin de paille* is sweet and concentrated.

VIN DE PAYS

Translates literally in French as country wine. It is the third and most recently introduced (1981) category of French wine law and denotes wine of more distinctive character and slightly better quality than ordinary anonymous table wine. The area may be as general as a *département* or even several *départements* such as Vin de Pays de l'Yonne or Vin de Pays d'Oc, or be a much smaller more precise zone such as Vin de Pays de Bigorre. Yields are larger, and the regulations, such as permitted grape varieties, more flexible than for *appellation contrôlée*.

VIN DE PAYS DE L'AGENAIS
SOUTH WEST FRANCE

The wines are mainly red from Bordeaux grape varieties as well as local grapes such as Abouriou, Tannat and Fer. The area of production covers the *département* of the Lot et Garonne.

VIN DE PAYS DE L'AIN   *Savoie:* FRANCE

The production of this white wine from the *département* of the Ain near Seyssel is minute. The wines are similar to Vin de Bugey.

VIN DE PAYS D'ALLOBROGIE
The Midi: FRANCE

A *vin de pays* that covers vineyards in the Ain, Savoie and Haute-Savoie, making mainly white wine from Jacquère, in a light Savoie style.

VIN DE PAYS DES ALPES DE HAUTE PROVENCE   *Provence:* FRANCE

Comes from the valley of the Durance in the *département* of the Alpes du Haute Provence. It is 70% red and 30% rosé, made from the usual Provençal grape varieties, mainly Grenache, Cinsaut, Mourvèdre and Carignan.

VIN DE PAYS DES ALPES MARITIMES   *The Midi:* FRANCE

Comes from the *département* of the Alpes Maritimes and is produced in tiny quantities from Carignan, Cinsaut, Grenache, Ugni Blanc and a local grape variety, Rolle. The production is two thirds red and one third rosé.

VIN DE PAYS DE L'ARDAILHOU
The Midi: FRANCE

One of the many *vins de pays* of the *département* of the Hérault, producing mainly red wine from Cinsaut, Grenache and Carignan grapes.

VIN DE PAYS DE L'ARDÈCHE
Rhône: FRANCE

This designation covers the *département* of the Ardèche to the east of the Rhône valley. The wines are very similar to Vin de Pays des Coteaux de l'Ardèche.

VIN DE PAYS D'ARGENS
Provence: FRANCE

Comes from the valley of the Argens river in the *département* of the Var and consists mainly of red wine, some rosé and a tiny amount of white. The grape varieties are the usual ones of Provence, mainly Grenache, Cinsaut, Mourvèdre and Carignan.

VIN DE PAYS DE L'AUDE
The Midi: FRANCE

A tricolour *vin de pays* covering the whole *département* of the Aude. There are 20 *vins de pays* within the *département*. The main grape varieties are Carignan, Grenache and Cinsaut. Bordelais grape varieties such as Cabernet Franc, Cabernet Sauvignon and Merlot, have also been introduced, as well as Sauvignon, Sémillon, and Chardonnay, to improve Clairette, Ugni Blanc and Bourboulenc. The production is very large, coming mostly from regional cooperatives, as well as two large companies, Nicolas and Chantovent, who have introduced some modern technology into the area.

VIN DE PAYS DES BALMES DAUPHINOISES
Savoie: FRANCE

A white wine, made from Jacquère and Chardonnay grapes, and a rosé and red wine from Gamay and Pinot Noir, grown in vineyards in the *département* of the Isère. The wines are light, resembling the wines of Savoie and produced only in small quantities. The term 'balme' is a local word to describe the valleys of the region.

VIN DE PAYS DE LA BÉNOVIE
The Midi: FRANCE

One of the many *vins de pays* of the *département* of the Hérault, producing mainly red and rosé wines from Cinsaut, Grenache and Carignan grapes around the town of Saint-Christol in the Coteaux du Languedoc. Bénovie is the name of a small stream which crosses the area.

VIN DE PAYS DU BERANGE
The Midi: FRANCE

One of the many *vins de pays* of the *département* of the Hérault, producing principally red and rosé wines from the grape varieties Cinsaut, Grenache, Carignan and some Syrah in the area of Lunel.

VIN DE PAYS DE BESSAN
The Midi: FRANCE

One of the many *vins de pays* of the *département* of the Hérault, making rosé, red and white wines in small quantities from the traditional grape varieties of the Midi, Cinsaut, Grenache and Carignan, around the town of Bessan.

VIN DE PAYS DE BIGORRE
SOUTH WEST FRANCE

This is a new creation, a red wine within the appellation of Madiran and designed to give the production from young vines in the appellation some identity. It is made predominantly from Tannat and Cabernet Franc grapes.

VIN DE PAYS DES BOUCHES DU RHÔNE
Rhône: FRANCE

Covers three main areas of vines in the *département* of the Bouches du Rhône, namely in the Coteaux d'Aix en Provence, in the Côtes de Provence and in the Camargue. The wine is predominantly red with some rosé, made from the usual grapes of the Midi.

VIN DE PAYS DE BOURBONNAIS
Loire: FRANCE

This *vin de pays* comes from the *departement* of Allier from the same grape varieties as St Pourgain, but in practice is rarely found.

VIN DE PAYS DE CASSAN
The Midi: FRANCE

One of the many *vins de pays* of the *département* of Hérault, taking its name from the old Abbey of Cassan. The production of red and rosé wines from the traditional grapes of the Midi (Cinsaut, Grenache and Carignan) is tiny.

VIN DE PAYS CATALAN
The Midi: FRANCE

One of the five *vins de pays* of the Pyrenées Orientales from vineyards south and west of Perpignan. There is a large production of mainly red wines, from Grenache, Cinsaut and Carignan, made mainly by the caves cooperatives.

VIN DE PAYS DE CAUX
The Midi: FRANCE

One of the many *vins de pays* of the *département* of the Hérault. There is a tradition for rosé which accounts for 60% of the production, made like the red, from the usual grapes of the Midi, Cinsaut, Grenache and Carignan. The cooperative of Caux is the main producer.

VIN DE PAYS DE CESSENON
The Midi: FRANCE

One of the many *vins de pays* of the *département* of Hérault. The wines are mainly red, from the traditional grape varieties of the area, Cinsaut, Grenache and Carignan, grown in the commune of Cessenon.

VIN DE PAYS CHARENTAIS
SOUTH WEST FRANCE

Vin de Pays Charentais covers the whole of the *départements* of the Charente and the Charente Maritime, including the Ile de Ré and the Ile d'Oléron. The wine is mainly white and comes from the same grapes as the base for Cognac, Ugni Blanc and Colombard. A very little red and rosé is produced from Merlot, Cabernet and Gamay grapes.

VIN DE PAYS DU CHER
Loire: FRANCE

One of the *départements* of the Loire that has the right to its own *vin de pays*. Whites are made principally from Sauvignon grapes and can resemble Sancerre; reds from Gamay are like a light Beaujolais; there is also some rosé and gris wine.

VIN DE PAYS DES COLLINES DE LA MOURE
The Midi: FRANCE

One of the many *vins de pays* of the *département* of the Hérault. The vineyards are on the hills between Montpellier and Sète; the wine is mainly red and rosé, made from the traditional grape varieties of the region, Cinsaut, Grenache and Carignan.

VIN DE PAYS DES COLLINES RHODANIENNES
Rhône: FRANCE

The hills of the Rhône Valley, as the name of this wine means, cover the northern part of the Rhône, stretching across the *départements* of the Isère, Loire, Ardèche, Rhône, and Drôme. The wine is mainly red from the grape varieties Syrah and Gamay, and also a little Pinot Noir in the Loire and Merlot and Cabernet Franc in the Isère. The white wine comes from Marsanne and Roussanne grapes with the introduction of some Aligoté, Chardonnay and Jacquère.

VIN DE PAYS DU COMTÉ DE GRIGNAN
Rhône: FRANCE

A tricolour wine from the *département* of the Drôme in the southern Rhône, named after the Château de Grignan at the centre of the area. The grape varieties are those common to the southern Rhône and the wine resembles a light Côtes du Rhône.

VIN DE PAYS DU COMTÉ TOLOSAN
SOUTH WEST FRANCE

A vin de pays covering several *départements*, namely the Haute Garonne, Gers, Pyrenées Atlantiques, Tarn, Tarn et Garonne, with the city of Toulouse at its centre, made in three colours from any of the possible grape varieties of the south west.

VIN DE PAYS DU CONDOMOIS
SOUTH WEST FRANCE

This is a red and white wine from around the town of Condom in the Gers. The grape varieties for the red wine are Tannat, Merlot and Cabernet and for the white, the Armagnac varieties of Colombard and Ugni Blanc.

VIN DE PAYS DES COTEAUX DE L'ARDÈCHE
Rhône: FRANCE

The Coteaux de l'Ardèche cover the rugged countryside of the southern half of the *département* of the Ardèche, limited by the Rhône in the east and the Cevennes in the west. The wines are mainly red, with a little rosé and white and can be either blends of Syrah, Grenache, Cinsaut and Carignan or single grapes, Syrah, Gamay, Cabernet Sauvignon, Merlot and Chardonnay. The main producers are the caves cooperatives and the Burgundian house of Louis Latour is creating a reputation for Chardonnay.

VIN DE PAYS DES COTEAUX DES BARONNIES
Rhône: FRANCE

A predominantly red wine, with a little rosé and negligible white, from the *département* of the Drôme in the southern Rhône. The red is made from the usual Rhône grape varieties, plus some Gamay, Merlot and Cabernet Sauvignon. Chardonnay is being introduced for white wine.

VIN DE PAYS DES COTEAUX DE BESSILLES   The Midi: FRANCE

One of the newer *vin de pays* coming from vineyards in the Hérault, near Montagnac.

VIN DE PAYS DES COTEAUX DE LA CABRERISSE   The Midi: FRANCE

One of the many *vins de pays* of the Aude, mainly red and some rosé wine coming from the Corbières area. The grape varieties are those of the Midi, Cinsaut, Grenache and Carignan, plus some improving grapes from the south west.

VIN DE PAYS DES COTEAUX CATHARES   The Midi: FRANCE

Was one of the many *vins de pays* of the Aude now replaced by Vin de Pays du Torgan; red and rosé wine is made to the north of the Corbières vineyards from the principal grape varieties of the Midi, Cinsaut, Grenache and Carignan.

VIN DE PAYS DES COTEAUX CEVENOLS   The Midi: FRANCE

A red and rosé wine from the foothills of the Cévennes north east of Alès in the *département* of the Gard. The principal grape variety is Carignan with some Cinsaut and Mourvèdre.

VIN DE PAYS DES COTEAUX DE CÈZE   The Midi: FRANCE

A tricolour wine from the north east part of the *département* of the Gard, from vineyards along the banks of the Rhône. The vineyards overlap with Côtes du Rhône from the village of Chusclan and the grape varieties are those of the southern Rhône, predominantly Carignan and Grenache.

VIN DE PAYS DES COTEAUX CHARITOIS   Loire: FRANCE

A *vin de pays* from the Nièvre, with white wines from Sauvignon and Chardonnay and reds mainly from Gamay.

VIN DE PAYS DES COTEAUX DU CHER ET DE L'ARNON   Loire: FRANCE

Red, dry white, gris and rosé wines are made in vineyards adjoining Quincy and Reuilly in the valley of the Cher and its tributary, the Arnon. The whites come from Chardonnay, Sauvignon and Pinot Gris grape varieties and the others from Gamay, Pinot Noir and Pinot Gris.

VIN DE PAYS DES COTEAUX DE LA CITÉ DE CARCASSONNE   The Midi: FRANCE

One of the many *vins de pays* of the *département* of the Aude, red and rosé wines from vineyards around the medieval city of Carcassonne. As well as the usual grape varieties of the Midi, (Cinsaut, Grenache and Carignan), Merlot and Cabernet Sauvignon are grown with some success.

VIN DE PAYS DES COTEAUX D'ENSERUNE   The Midi: FRANCE

One of the many *vins de pays* of the *département* of the Hérault. There is a large production of mainly red and rosé wines made from Grenache, Cinsaut and Carignan grapes, as well as some Syrah, Merlot and Cabernet Sauvignon grown in vineyards to the east of Béziers.

VIN DE PAYS DES COTEAUX DES FENOUILLÈDES   The Midi: FRANCE

One of the five *vins de pays* of the Pyrénées Orientales, from the north west of the *département*. It is principally a red wine from Cinsaut, Grenache and Carignan grapes.

VIN DE PAYS DES COTEAUX FLAVIENS   The Midi: FRANCE

Red, rosé and dry white, from vineyards along the Rhône-Sète canal to the south of Nimes. The grape varieties are Grenache, Carignan, Cinsaut and Syrah for red and rosé and Ugni Blanc, and Grenache Blanc for the white. Most of the wine is made by a central cooperative.

VIN DE PAYS DES COTEAUX DE FONTCAUDE   *The Midi:* FRANCE

One of the many *vins de pays* of the *département* of the Hérault. The wines are mainly red, with some rosé, from the traditional grape varieties of the Midi, Cinsaut, Grenache and Carignan, grown in vineyards to the west of Béziers, around the Abbey of Fontcaude.

VIN DE PAYS DES COTEAUX DE GLANES   SOUTH WEST FRANCE

Glanes is a tiny village near Saint Céré in the Lot where a group of *viticulteurs* produce very drinkable red wine from Gamay and Merlot in accordance with their pre-phylloxera tradition.

VIN DE PAYS DES COTEAUX DU GRESIVAUDAN   *Savoie:* FRANCE

A white wine made mainly from Jacquère and red and rosé wine made principally from Gamay and Pinot Noir grapes, produced in small quantities from vineyards in the *départements* of the Isère and Savoie near Grenoble.

VIN DE PAYS DES COTEAUX DE LAURENS   *The Midi:* FRANCE

One of the many *vins de pays* of the *département* of the Hérault. The wines are mainly red, with some rosé, made from Grenache, Cinsaut and Carignan grapes, as well as some Syrah, grown in vineyards to the north of Béziers.

VIN DE PAYS DES COTEAUX DU LÉZIGNANAIS   *The Midi:* FRANCE

One of the many *vins de pays* of the *département* of the Aude, mainly red and some rosé wines from vineyards around the town of Lézignan. Syrah improves the blend of Grenache, Cinsaut and Carignan grapes to make a full-bodied wine.

VIN DE PAYS DES COTEAUX DU LIBRON   *The Midi:* FRANCE

One of the many *vins de pays* of the *département* of the Hérault. There is a large production of mainly red wine from the traditional grape varieties of the Midi, Cinsaut, Grenache and Carignan, improved by some Cabernet and Merlot. The vineyards to the north of Béziers are crossed by the river Libron.

VIN DE PAYS DES COTEAUX DU LITTORAL AUDOIS   *The Midi:* FRANCE

One of the many *vins de pays* of the Aude, mainly red and a little rosé wine from the coastal region, made from Grenache, Cinsaut and Carignan grapes and not dissimilar to Corbières.

VIN DE PAYS DES COTEAUX DE MIRAMONT   *The Midi:* FRANCE

One of the many *vins de pays* of the *département* of the Aude, red and rosé wine from vineyards to the east of Carcassonne, made from the usual Midi grape varieties, of Cinsaut, Grenache and Carignan, as well as some Syrah, resulting in a lighter style of Minervois.

VIN DE PAYS DES COTEAUX DE MURVIEL   *The Midi:* FRANCE

One of the many *vins de pays* of the *département* of the Hérault, from around the town of Murviel-les-Béziers. The wines are mainly red, with some rosé from the traditional grape varieties of the Midi, Cinsaut, Grenache and Carignan.

VIN DE PAYS DES COTEAUX DE NARBONNE   *The Midi:* FRANCE

One of the many *vins de pays* of the *département* of the Aude, mainly red with some rosé and white wine from the usual Midi grapes, Cinsaut, Grenache and Carignan, grown in vineyards around the town of Narbonne.

VIN DE PAYS DES COTEAUX DE PEYRIAC   *The Midi:* FRANCE

From the Minervois area of the *département* of the Aude as well as from two communes in the Hérault. The large production is mainly red, from the traditional Midi grape varieties of Cinsaut, Grenache and Carignan and improved by some Syrah, Cabernet and Merlot.

VIN DE PAYS DES COTEAUX DU PONT DU GARD   *The Midi:* FRANCE

Comes from a small area around the famous Roman aqueduct between Côtes du Rhône and Costières du Gard. The wines are mainly red and rosé from the grape varieties Cinsaut, Grenache, Carignan and occasionally Syrah.

VIN DE PAYS DES COTEAUX DU QUERCY   SOUTH WEST FRANCE

A red wine from the southern part of the *département* of the Lot below Cahors and the northern part of the département of the Tarn et Garonne. Like Cahors, it is exclusively red, from Cabernet, Tannat, Malbec, Gamay and Jurançon Noir. The two main producers are the cave cooperatives at Parnac and Lavilledieu.

VIN DE PAYS DES COTEAUX DU SALAGOU   *The Midi*: FRANCE

One of the many *vins de pays* of the Hérault from near Lake Salagou. The production is very small, of mainly red wines from the traditional grape varieties of the Midi, Cinsaut, Grenache and Carignan, improved by some Syrah.

VIN DE PAYS DES COTEAUX DU SALAVÈS   *The Midi*: FRANCE

Red and rosé from vineyards to the east of Nimes in the *département* of the Gard. The grape varieties are the traditional Grenache, Cinsaut and Carignan to which a little Syrah and occasionally Merlot and Cabernet have been added. Most of the wine is made by a local cooperative.

VIN DE PAYS DES COTEAUX DU TERMENÈS   *The Midi*: FRANCE

One of the many *vins de pays* of the Aude, a tricolour wine in tiny quantities from the centre of the *département*.

VIN DE PAYS DES COTEAUX ET TERRASSES DE MONTAUBAN   SOUTH WEST FRANCE

As the name implies, this wine comes from the hills around the town of Montauban in the Tarn et Garonne. It is mainly red, from Cabernet, Gamay, Syrah, Tannat and Jurançon Noir and is produced by the cooperative of Lavilledieu.

VIN DE PAYS DES COTEAUX VIDOURLE   *The Midi*: FRANCE

Red, rosé and occasionally white from the valley of the Vidourle to the west of Nimes. The grape varieties are those of the Midi, Cinsaut, Carignan and Grenache. Most of the wine is made by a group of cooperatives.

VIN DE PAYS DES CÔTES DU BRIAN   *The Midi*: FRANCE

One of the many *vins de pays* of the Hérault, named after a small river in the south west of the *département*. The large production is of mainly red wine, made principally from the Carignan grape as well as some Syrah.

VIN DE PAYS DES CÔTES CATALANES   *The Midi*: FRANCE

One of the five *vins de pays* of the Pyrenées Atlantiques from the north east of the *département*. The production is mainly red, with some rosé and a little dry white from the usual grape varieties of the Midi.

VIN DE PAYS DES CÔTES DU CÉRÉSSOU   *The Midi*: FRANCE

One of the many *vins de pays* of the Hérault, taking its name from the mountain which overlooks the vineyards in the centre of the *département*. The red and rosé wines are made from the traditional grape varieties of the Midi, namely Cinsaut, Grenache and Carignan, improved by some Syrah, Merlot and Cabernet Sauvignon, and the small production of white comes from Clairette, Terret Blanc and Ugni Blanc.

VIN DE PAYS DES CÔTES DE GASCOGNE   SOUTH WEST FRANCE

This is a predominantly white wine from the *département* of the Gers in the heart of Gascony, made from the same grapes as the base for Armagnac, namely Ugni Blanc, and Colombard. Red wine comes mainly from Cabernet Sauvignon, Cabernet Franc, Merlot and Tannat grapes.

VIN DE PAYS DES CÔTES DE LASTOURS   *The Midi*: FRANCE

One of the many *vins de pays* of the Aude, a predominantly red wine produced in small quantities from Grenache, Cinsaut and Carignan grapes, as well as some improving Syrah, Cabernet Sauvignon and Merlot.

VIN DE PAYS DES CÔTES DE MONTESTRUC
SOUTH WEST FRANCE

This is a predominantly red wine from around the town of Auch in the Armagnac region of Gascony, produced mainly from Gamay, Cot, Fer and Jurançon Noir.

VIN DE PAYS DES CÔTES DE PÉRIGNAN
The Midi: FRANCE

One of the many *vins de pays* of the Aude from the same region as the appellation La Clape. It is mainly a red wine from the usual Midi grape varieties, Cinsaut, Grenache and Carignan, as well as a little rosé.

VIN DE PAYS DES CÔTES DE PROUILLE
The Midi: FRANCE

One of the many *vins de pays* of the *département* of Aude. A tiny production of mainly red, with some white and rosé wines from the traditional Midi grape varieties, Cinsaut, Grenache and Carignan, with some improving Cabernet Sauvignon and Merlot, sometimes as single grape varieties.

VIN DE PAYS DES CÔTES DE TARN
SOUTH WEST FRANCE

The area of production is synonymous with the production of Gaillac near Albi. The red wines include the grapes of Gaillac, Duras, Syrah, Cabernet, Merlot and Gamay, as well as Jurançon Noir and Portugais Bleu. The whites come from the Mauzac, Muscadelle and l'Enc de l'El grapes.

VIN DE PAYS DES CÔTES DE THAU
The Midi: FRANCE

One of the many *vins de pays* of the Hérault from the south of the *département* near the Etang de Thau. Whites (40%) are surprisingly important, coming from the Terret Gris and Blanc and Picpoul grapes, with reds (40%) and rosés (20%) from the three Midi grape varieties, Cinsaut, Grenache and Carignan.

VIN DE PAYS DES CÔTES DE THONGUE
The Midi: FRANCE

One of the many *vins de pays* of the Hérault, with a large production of mainly red, and some rosé and white wine from the centre of the *département*. As well as the usual Midi grape varieties of Cinsaut, Grenache and Carignan, there are wines made purely from Merlot, Syrah and Cabernet.

VIN DE PAYS DE CUCUGNAN
The Midi: FRANCE

One of the many *vins de pays* of the *département* of the Aude, with a tiny production of red and rosé wines from the usual Midi grape varieties, Carignan, Grenache and Cinsaut, by the cooperative of Cucugnan.

VIN DE PAYS DES DEUX SÈVRES
Loire: FRANCE

One of the *départements* of the Loire that has a right to its own *vin de pays*. The wine is mainly red from Gamay and Groslot grapes.

VIN DE PAYS DE LA DORDOGNE
SOUTH WEST FRANCE

This is a *vin de pays* whose area of production equates to the *départemental* limits of the Dordogne and is produced mainly in the region of Bergerac from the same grape varieties, Merlot and Cabernet for the red and Sémillon, and Sauvignon, as well as some Ugni Blanc for the white.

VIN DE PAYS DE LA DRÔME
Rhône: FRANCE

This designation covers part of the *département* of the Drôme on the east bank of the Rhône. The wine can be red, white or rosé; Syrah is the main grape for red, with some Grenache and Cinsaut. The white comes mainly from the Clairette grape.

VIN DE PAYS DE FRANCHE COMTE
Jura: FRANCE

Vin de Pays de Franche Comte in theory covers the *départements* of the Haute Savoie and the Jura. In practice the vineyards are concentrated around the towns of Champlitte, Charcenne and Offlanges. The wines are mainly white from Chardonnay and Auxerrois grapes, sold under the name of the grape. The small amount of red and rosé are made from Pinot Noir and Gamay grapes.

VIN DE PAYS DU GARD
The Midi: FRANCE

Produced all over the *département* of the Gard. Red and rosé are made from Carignan, Cinsaut, Grenache, Mourvèdre and Syrah grapes and the Bordelais grapes, Merlot and Cabernet, are being introduced with increasing success. The white wine is made from Clairette, Ugni Blanc, Bourboulenc and Grenache Blanc and some experimental plantings of Chardonnay and Sauvignon. Vinification methods have improved enormously in this area.

VIN DE PAYS DE GIRONDE
SOUTH WEST FRANCE

The tiny production of this *vin de pays* has more affinity with the wines of the adjoining *département* of the Charente than with Bordeaux itself for it is mainly white, from the Colombard and Ugni Blanc grapes grown in the northern part of the *département*.

VIN DE PAYS DES GORGES ET COTES DE MILLAU
SOUTH WEST FRANCE

This wine is produced solely by a cave cooperative in Aguessac on the banks of the Tarn above Millau. It is mainly red, made by primitive means principally from Gamay and Syrah grapes.

VIN DE PAYS DES GORGES DE L'HÉRAULT
The Midi: FRANCE

One of the many *vins de pays* of the *département* of the Hérault, with a small production of mainly red and rosé wines from the traditional grape varieties of Cinsaut, Grenache and Carignan, as well as some Syrah, Cabernet and Merlot.

VIN DE PAYS DES HAUTS DE BADENS
The Midi: FRANCE

One of the many *vins de pays* of the Aude. Small quantities of mainly red wine are made from Cinsaut, Carignan, Grenache and Syrah grapes grown in the commune of Badens.

VIN DE PAYS DE LA HAUTE GARONNE
SOUTH WEST FRANCE

The zone of production of this red wine corresponds to the *département* in south west France. The grape varieties are Négrette, Merlot, Cabernet Franc and Sauvignon and Jurançon Noir.

VIN DE PAYS DE LA HAUTE VALLÉE DE L'AUDE
The Midi: FRANCE

One of the many *vins de pays* of the *département* of the Aude. It is mainly red, coming from the Limoux region and, unusually, is not made from the Midi grape varieties, but those of the south west, such as Cabernet Sauvignon, Merlot, Malbec and Cabernet Franc, and therefore quite different from the other *vins de pays* of the *département*. The tiny amount of white wine is made from the Mauzac grape.

VIN DE PAYS DE LA HAUTE VALLÉE DE L'ORB
The Midi: FRANCE

One of the many *vins de pays* of the Hérault, from vineyards in the valley of the Orb. The production of mainly red wines from the three traditional grape varieties of the Midi, Cinsaut, Grenache and Carignan, is tiny.

VIN DE PAYS DE HAUTERIVE EN PAYS D'AUDE
The Midi: FRANCE

One of the many *vins de pays* of the Aude from an area near the coast to the south of Narbonne. The wines are mainly red from the usual grape varieties of the Midi, namely Cinsaut, Grenache and Carignan, and with some innovation from better producers.

VIN DE PAYS DE L'HÉRAULT
The Midi: FRANCE

A red, dry white and rosé wine coming from all over the Hérault, which is the largest wine producing *département* of France with 27 individual *vins de pays*. The principal grape variety is Carignan; Grenache, Cinsaut, Mourvèdre and Syrah are increasingly important, while Cabernet Sauvignon and Merlot are also contributing to an improvement in quality. *Macération carbonique* makes particularly successful fruity wines in this area. For white wines, which are of little importance compared to reds, Ugni Blanc and Clairette are the principal grape varieties, plus Picpoul, Marsanne, Maccabeo, Bourboulenc, Grenache Blanc and Muscat. Sauvignon has also been successfully introduced and white wines are improving with modern vinification techniques. The main producers are the caves cooperatives.

VIN DE PAYS DE L'ILE DE BEAUTÉ
CORSICA

Covers the whole of the island of Corsica for red, white and rosé wine. Grape varieties include the local Nielluccio and Sciacarello for reds and rosés and Malvoisie de Corse for white, as well as the more common grape varieties of the Midi, such as Carignan, Grenache, Cinsaut, occasionally Syrah and Ugni Blanc. Some more enterprising producers are experimenting successfully with Chardonnay, Chenin Blanc, Cabernet Sauvignon and Merlot.

VIN DE PAYS DE L'INDRE ET LOIRE
Loire: FRANCE

The Indre et Loire is the heart of Touraine and is one of the *départements* of the Loire that has the right to its own *vin de pays*. There are good whites from the Sauvignon grape as well as Chardonnay and Chenin Blanc; Gamay makes fresh fruity reds and rosés.

VIN DE PAYS DU JARDIN DE LA FRANCE
Loire: FRANCE

This *vin de pays* covers the whole of the Loire Valley, including the *départements* of the Cher, Indre, Indre et Loire, Loir et Cher, Loire Atlantique, Loiret, Maine et Loire, Deux Sèvres, Vendée, Vienne and Haut Vienne. All the grape varieties grown in the Loire valley can be used for this *vin de pays*, but Sauvignon and Gamay are the most successful.

VIN DE PAYS DES LANDES
SOUTH WEST FRANCE

The area of production of this wine covers a large part of south west France, equating to the extent of the pine forests of the Landes, as far as Tursan. The reds and rosés are made from Cabernet and Tannat and the whites from local grapes, Baroque, Raffiat de Moncade as well as Ugni Blanc, Colombard and Gros Manseng.

VIN DE PAYS DU LITTORAL ORB-HÉRAULT
The Midi: FRANCE

One of the many *vins de pays* of the Hérault, but its name has been changed to Vin de Pays d'Ardhailhou.

VIN DE PAYS DE LOIR-ET-CHER
Loire: FRANCE

The Loir-et-Cher is one of the *départements* of the Loire with the right to its own *vin de pays*. Red, dry white, gris and rosé are produced from vineyards around the châteaux of Blois and Chambord. The whites from the Chenin Blanc and Sauvignon grape varieties are crisp; the reds and rosés from Gamay, Malbec and Cabernet Sauvignon are light and fruity.

VIN DE PAYS DE LA LOIRE ATLANTIQUE
Loire: FRANCE

The Loire Atlantique is one of the Loire *départements* with the right to its own *vin de pays*. The wines are mostly white and very dry, coming from Folle Blanche and Muscadet grapes.

VIN DE PAYS DU LOIRET
Loire: FRANCE

The Loiret is one of the *départements* of the Loire valley with the right to its own *vin de pays*. The vineyards are mainly around the towns of Orléans and Gien and are planted with Gamay, Pinot Noir, Cabernet and Pinot Meunier for red, rosé and gris. A little white is made from Chardonnay and Sauvignon. These wines are rarely found outside the region.

VIN DE PAYS DU MAINE ET LOIRE
Loire: FRANCE

The Maine et Loire is one of the *départements* of the Loire with the right to its own *vin de pays*. The wines, red, dry white and rosé, are not dissimilar to the basic wines of Anjou and are made from the same grape varieties, namely, Cabernet Franc, Cabernet Sauvignon, Gamay, Cot, for red wines and for white, Chenin Blanc, Chardonnay and Sauvignon.

VIN DE PAYS DES MARCHES DE BRETAGNE
Loire: FRANCE

A predominantly white wine, from the Atlantic end of the Loire valley, south of Ancenis and Nantes. The white are made mainly from Muscadet, Folle Blanche, Sauvignon and Chenin Blanc grapes and the tiny amount of red and rosé from Gamay and Malbec.

VIN DE PAYS DES MAURES
Provence: FRANCE

Covers the south part of the *département* of the Var between St. Raphael and St. Tropez. Production is large and increasing, consisting of two thirds red and one third rosé wine and a very little white wine. Grape varieties are those common to Provence, mainly Grenache, Cinsaut, Mourvèdre and Carignan.

VIN DE PAYS DE LA MEUSE
NORTHEAST FRANCE

This is a wine from the Meuse *département* of northern France, both red and white, light, acidic and produced in tiny but growing quantities.

VIN DE PAYS DU MONT BAUDILE
The Midi: FRANCE

This *vin de pays* from the Hérault, takes its name from the mountain that dominates the skyline near Montpeyroux. The wine is mainly red from traditional Midi grape varieties.

VIN DE PAYS DU MONT BOUQUET
The Midi: FRANCE

Red and rosé from the northern part of the *département* of the Gard to the south east of Alès. Production has increased in recent years and as well as the traditional grape varieties of Cinsaut, Carignan and Grenache, there are some experimental plantings of Merlot and Cabernet.

VIN DE PAYS DU MONT CAUME
Provence: FRANCE

A tricolour wine from vineyards around Bandol in the Var, dominated by the hills of Mont Caume. Grape varieties are Grenache, Carignan, Cinsaut and Mourvèdre for red and rosé and Ugni Blanc and Clairette for the tiny amount of white wine.

VIN DE PAYS DES MONTS DE LA GRAGE
The Midi: FRANCE

One of the many vins de pays of the Hérault from the west of the *département* around Saint-Chinian. The production of mainly red wines from Cinsaut, Grenache, Carignan and Syrah grapes is tiny.

VIN DE PAYS DE LA NIÈVRE
Loire: FRANCE

The Nièvre is one of the *départements* of the Loire with the right to its own *vin de pays*. The production of red, dry white and rosé wines is tiny.

VIN DE PAYS D'OC
The Midi: FRANCE

Covers wines from all over the Midi, including the *départements* of the Aude, Gard, Hérault, Pyrénées Orientales, as well as the Ardèche, Bouches du Rhône, Var and Vaucluse. They are 75% red, 20% rosé and 5% white, from all the permitted grape varieties of the region. The red is from those traditional to the Midi such as Grenache, Cinsaut and Carignan, as well as improving varieties like Cabernet and Merlot from the south west. Local cooperatives are the main producers.

VIN DE PAYS DE PETITE CRAU
Provence: FRANCE

Comes from the northern part of the *département* of the Bouches du Rhône, from the region of St-Remy-en-Provence. The red (70%) and rosés (15%) are made from Grenache, Cinsaut, Syrah, Mourvèdre, Carignan and a little Cabernet Sauvignon and the whites (15%) mainly from Ugni Blanc and Clairette.

VIN DE PAYS DE PÉZANAS
The Midi: FRANCE

One of the many *vins de pays* of the Hérault from the commune of Pézanas in the centre of the *département*. The small production consists mainly of red, with some rosé wine, from the traditional grape varieties of the Midi, Cinsaut, Grenache and Carignan, as well as some Merlot and Cabernet Sauvignon.

VIN DE PAYS DE LA PRINCIPAUTE DE L'ORANGE
Rhône: FRANCE

A tricolour wine from the *département* of the Vaucluse in the southern Rhône. As the grape varieties are those of Côtes du Rhone, the wine resembles a lighter version of the appellation.

VIN DE PAYS DU PUY DE DÔME
Loire: FRANCE

Puy de Dôme is one of the *départements* of the Loire with the right to its own *vin de pays*, with vineyards in the Côtes d'Auvergne, near Clermont Ferrand. The production is tiny and mainly red from Gamay and Pinot Noir grape varieties.

VIN DE PAYS DES PYRENÉES ATLANTIQUES
SOUTH WEST FRANCE

The production area of this wine corresponds to the *département* of the Pyrenées Atlantiques, coming mainly from around Jurançon and Madiran. The wine is generally made from young vines, Tannat, Cabernet Franc and Cabernet Sauvignon for the red and Gros and Petit Manseng for the white.

VIN DE PAYS DES PYRENÉES ORIENTALES
The Midi: FRANCE

Comes from all over this *département* of the Midi, except the mountainous regions. The production is large, mainly of red wines from Carignan, Cinsaut, Grenache and a little Mourvèdre and Syrah, and occasionally some south western varieties. The white wine comes from Maccabéo, Ugni Blanc and Clairette. There is less experimentation here than in other parts of the Midi.

VIN DE PAYS DE RETZ
Loire: FRANCE

These wines come from vineyards south of the mouth of the Loire. Rosé is most important and made from the Groslot grape, with some reds from Cabernet Franc and a little Cabernet Sauvignon, Folle Blanche, Chenin Blanc and Sauvignon.

VIN DE PAYS DES SABLES DU GOLFE DU LION
The Midi: FRANCE

Comes from the coastal dunes of the Gulf of Lions which stretches across the *départements* of the Bouches du Rhône, Gard and Hérault. The wines are red, white, gris and rosé. The main producer, Les Salins du Midi have been responsible for many new developments in the area and for the introduction of grape varieties like Cabernet Sauvignon and Merlot for red wines and Sauvignon for white wines.

VIN DE PAYS DE SAINT-SARDOS
SOUTH WEST FRANCE

Produced by the cave cooperative of the village of the same name, near Montauban in the *départements* of the Tarn et Garonne and Haute Garonne. The wine is mainly red, from Syrah, Tannat, Cabernet Franc and Cabernet Sauvignon.

VIN DE PAYS DE LA SARTHE
Loire: FRANCE

The Sarthe is one of the *départements* of the Loire with the right to its own *vin de pays*. The production of mainly white wine from Chenin Blanc grapes is tiny.

VIN DE PAYS DU SERRE DU COIRAN
The Midi: FRANCE

Red and rosé wine from the *département* of the Gard to the south east of Nimes. The wines are made from the usual grapes of the Midi, Carignan, Cinsaut and Grenache and resemble Costières du Gard.

VIN DE PAYS DU TARN ET GARONNE
SOUTH WEST FRANCE

The area of production of this predominantly red wine corresponds to the *département* of the Tarn et Garonne in south west France. It is produced from a mixture of grape varieties, mainly Gamay, Syrah, Tannat, Cabernet Franc and Sauvignon.

VIN DE PAYS DES TERROIRS LANDAIS
SOUTH WEST FRANCE

A more precise version of Vin de Pays des Landes, covering vineyards in the valley of the Adour, on the Coteaux de Chalosse, the Sables Fauves and the Sables de l'Océan. The grape varieties are those of the south west.

VIN DE PAYS DE THÉZARD-PERRICARD
SOUTH WEST FRANCE

The newest *vin de pays*, from the Lot-et-Garonne near Agen. It is only red, from Cabernet, Merlot and Tannat.

VIN DE PAYS DU TORGAN
The Midi: FRANCE

One of the many *vins de pays* of the Aude; red and rosé wines are made to the north of the Corbières vineyards mainly from Carignan, Grenache and Cinsaut, replacing Vin de Pays des Coteaux Cathares.

VIN DE PAYS D'URFÉ
Loire: FRANCE

This is a relatively new *vin de pays* taking its name from the Château d'Urfé on the eastern edge of the Massif Central. The wines are mainly red, from the Gamay grape coinciding with the appellations of Côtes du Forez and Côtes Roannaises.

VIN DE PAYS DE L'UZÈGE
The Midi: FRANCE

Vin de Pays de l'Uzège is mainly red, with some rosé and dry white wine from the ancient duchy of Uzès to the north of Nimes. The wines come from the traditional grape varieties of the Midi, namely Grenache, Cinsaut and Carignan.

VIN DE PAYS DES VALS D'AGLY
The Midi: FRANCE

One of the five *vins de pays* of the Pyrenées Atlantiques from the north of the *département*. The wine is mainly red, from Carignan, Cinsaut and Grenache grapes, and is not unlike a Côtes du Roussillon.

VIN DE PAYS DU VAL DE CESSE
The Midi: FRANCE

One of the many *vins de pays* of the *département* of the Aude, mainly red wine from vineyards to the north of Narbonne. Both Midi (Cinsaut, Grenache and Carignan) and south west (Cabernet and Merlot) grape varieties are planted, making it one of the more successful *vins de pays* of the area.

VIN DE PAYS DU VAL DE DAGNE
The Midi: FRANCE

One of the many *vins de pays* of the *département* of the Aude, mainly red wine from vineyards to the south east of Carcassonne. The grape varieties are those of the Midi, Grenache, Cinsaut and Carignan, as well as those of the south west, Cabernet and Merlot.

VIN DE PAYS DU VAL DE MONTFERRAND
The Midi: FRANCE

One of the many *vins de pays* of the Hérault in the north of the *département*. There is a large production of mainly red wine from the traditional grape varieties of the Midi, Cinsaut, Grenache and Carignan, as well as some vin d'une nuit rosé.

VIN DE PAYS DU VAL D'ORBIEU
The Midi: FRANCE

One of the many *vins de pays* of the Aude coming from vineyards in the east of the *département*. It is mainly red, principally from Grenache grapes, plus Carignan and Cinsaut, making typical *vin de pays*.

VIN DE PAYS DE LA VALLÉE DU PARADIS
The Midi: FRANCE

One of the many *vin de pays* of the *département* of the Aude. This picturesque wine is mainly red from Carignan, Grenache and Cinsaut grapes, grown in a valley, otherwise called the Vallée de la Berre, in the Corbières area.

VIN DE PAYS DU VAR
Provence: FRANCE

Comes from the northern part of the *département* of the Var in south east France. The colour breakdown is 60% red, 30% rosé and 10% white. The grape varieties are those common to Provence, namely, Grenache, Cinsaut, Carignan, as well as Syrah, Mourvèdre and Cabernet Sauvignon for reds and rosés, and Ugni Blanc, Sémillon, Clairette and Rolle for whites.

VIN DE PAYS DE VAUCLUSE
Rhône: FRANCE

This designation covers the *département* of the Vaucluse to the east of Avignon and the Rhône Valley. The grape varieties are typical of Côtes du Rhône and the wines are mainly red, but also white and rosé. The local cooperatives are the main producers.

VIN DE PAYS DE LA VAUNAGE
The Midi: FRANCE

Vin de Pays de la Vaunage is principally a light red wine from a small area to the north west of Nimes. The grape varieties are those traditional to the Midi, Carignan, Cinsaut and Grenache and the main producer is a union of cooperatives at Saint Côme-et-Maruéjols.

VIN DE PAYS DE LA VENDÉE
Loire: FRANCE

The Vendée is one of the *départements* of the Loire with the right to its own *vin de pays*. The wine is very similar to the VDQS Fiefs Vendeéns and the name applies to the small amount of wine produced in the *département* that is not included in Fiefs Vendeéns.

VIN DE PAYS DE LA VICOMTÉ D'AUMELAS
The Midi: FRANCE

One of the many *vins de pays* of the Hérault from the thirteen communes which in the 12th century belonged to the Vicomte d'Aumelas. There is a large production of mainly red wines with some rosé from the traditional grape varieties of the Midi, Cinsaut, Grenache and Carignan, as well as some Merlot and Cabernet Sauvignon.

VIN DE PAYS DE VIENNE
Loire: FRANCE

The Vienne is one of the *départements* of the Loire with the right to its own *vin de pays*. A tiny amount of red, dry white and rosé wines are made from the same grape varieties as the wines of Haut Poitou, principally Sauvignon, Chardonnay, Cabernet and Gamay.

VIN DE PAYS DE LA VISTRENQUE
The Midi: FRANCE

Red and rosé wine from a tiny area on the plain of the Vistre in the north east of the *département* of the Gard. As the wine was only recognised in 1982, the production is tiny, but with the possibility of growth. It is made from the traditional grape varieties of the Midi, Carignan, Cinsaut and Grenache.

VIN DE PAYS DE L'YONNE
Burgundy: FRANCE

This is a white wine that, in theory, may be produced from young Chardonnay vines, destined for Chablis, but in practice the name rarely appears on a label.

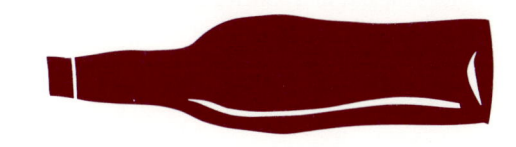

VIN PIERRE

The French term for a deposit of tartrate crystals.

VIN DE PRESSE

The wine that comes from pressing the grapes. It is tougher and more tannic than the *vin de goutte* and may not always be blended with it, depending on the winemaker's decision, based on the character of the year. If the *vin de presse* is included in the final blend, it gives backbone and tannin. If it is not used, it is sold as basic table wine or may be distilled.

VIN DE PRIMEUR

A French term for a young wine.

VIN RUSPO
Tuscany: ITALY

A non-DOC *rosato* produced within the DOC area of Carmignano and destined to become Carmignano Rosato.

VIN SANTO

VIN SANTO   Tuscany: ITALY

A dessert wine, sweet, semi-sweet or dry, traditionally made in Tuscany but also found in other parts of Italy such as Trentino where it is called Vino Santo and made from Nosiola grapes. The grapes, mainly Malvasia and Trebbiano in Tuscany, are picked, left to dry and then pressed. The juice is put into small barrels, called *caratelli* which already contain a *madre*, or mother, the lees of a previous wine. The barrels are sealed and then left to ferment and age. Purists do not touch the wine for six years while it is subjected to seasonal changes of temperature. Usually production is for family consumption.

VIN SUPÉRIEUR DE TUNISIE
TUNISIA

A general classification for Tunisian wines that was introduced in 1942 for vintage wines which are at least one year old and which have passed tasting and analysis tests. There is no appellation system in Tunisia, so geographical descriptions tend to be rather vague.

VIN DE TABLE

The fourth and last category as defined in French wine law. No precise provenance, apart from the country of origin, may be given on the label. The wines are often sold under a brand name.

VIN DE TAILLE

The second part of the pressing from a champagne *marc*, after the *vin de cuvée*. It is split into two, the *première taille* of 410 litres and the *deuxiéme taille* of 205 litres, comprising the final three *pièces* of the pressing. The vin de taille is of inferior quality to the *vin de cuvée*.

VIN DE TÊTE

A term used in Sauternes to describe a wine from the first, and therefore the best, pressing. The very best may be called a Crême de Tête, made from the ripest grapes, yielding very sweet rich wine.

VIN DU THOUARSAIS   Loire: FRANCE

A red, white and rosé wine from around the town of Bressuire in the département of the Deux Sèvres to the south of Angers. The whites are made from Chenin Blanc and the reds and rosés from Cabernet Sauvignon and Cabernet Franc. All are light and easy to drink.

VIN D'UNE NUIT

A poetic term to describe a rosé wine which has spent a few hours, over one short night, on the grape skins in order to obtain its colour.

VINA LINDEROS   CHILE

A small Chilean winery with wines coming exclusively from their own irrigated vineyards in the Maipo valley. Cabernet Linderos Pura Guarda is their best Cabernet Sauvignon.

VINA UNDERRAGA   CHILE

An old family firm founded a hundred years ago in the Maipo valley. Red wines are aged in old oak vats. Underraga continue to use the traditional Chilean bottle, the *caramoyole*.

VINAGE

The term for the addition of alcohol to wine to increase its strength and a process which is illegal in the EEC.

VINE

The plant which produces the grapes for wine. There are numerous species of vines; the most significant is *vitis vinifera*, which in turn comprises numerous different grape varieties.

VINEYARD

The place where vines are grown; it may consist of a few rows or several hectares and varies in soil, aspect and altitude.

VINHO

The Portuguese word for wine.

VINHO VERDE   PORTUGAL

Comes from the Minho region of northern Portugal. The green in its name is not a reference to its colour, but to its youthful freshness, for it can be red or white, and the term verde can be used to describe any young fresh table wine. *Vinho verde* is made from a variety of grapes, including white Loureiro, Trajadura, Alvarinho and red Vinhão. The vines are trained unusually high, traditionally on granite pillars and more commonly on *cruzetas*, T shaped wood or concrete posts so that the grapes have less sugar and more malic acid, which results in wines with a slight petillance. In Portugal red *vinho verde* is more common, while white is popular on the export market. A good *vinho verde* makes a refreshing summer drink.

VINICIDE

A dinner party term, an affectation describing the crime of drinking a fine wine too early, before its full potential of flavour has been realised.

VINIFERA WINE CELLARS   USA

As its name implies, this company concentrates on the production of *vitis vinifera* wines in New York State, where hybrid wines are more common. The founder of the company was a pioneer of *vitis vinifera* wines at Gold Seal Vineyards.

VINIFICATION

The all-embracing term describing the art of transforming freshly-pressed grape juice into wine, covering all aspects of this process from fermentation to ageing the wine.

VINO

The Italian and Spanish word for wine.

VINO DA ARROSTO

Literally means 'a wine to go with roast meat' in Italy, and implies a wine with quality and of an age that merits appreciation over a suitable meal.

VINO DE COLOR   SPAIN

A wine used to give colour to sherry, made by evaporating down unfermented must to form *arrope*, which is then mixed with more must before fermentation.

VINO DE DOBLE PASTO

A heavy red wine, with a very deep colour, rich in extract and at least 18° alcohol, made in the Levante, only for blending with lighter wines from other parts of Spain and elsewhere.

VINO DA MEDITAZIONE

Literally means 'a wine for meditation' in Italian; a great wine that should be drunk with due reverence and appreciation.

VINO NOBILE DI MONTEPULCIANO   Tuscany: ITALY

A red DOCG wine from the vineyards around the hill town of Montepulciano. The wine, made from Chianti grape varieties, Sangiovese, Canaiolo, Trebbiano and Malvasia, has had a good reputation for a long time but, nowadays, its nobility is sometimes uncertain although quality is improving again. Normal ageing is two years, *riserva* three years and *riserva speciale* four years.

VINO NOVELLO

Italian term for new wine. With the success of Beaujolais Nouveau and other *vins nouveaux*, some Italian winemakers, notably in Piedmont and Tuscany have followed their example and made wines that are ready for immediate drinking.

VINO DA PASTO

An Italian term to describe a wine that accompanies food, a simple uncomplicated wine.

VINO DE PASTO

The Spanish term for an ordinary light table wine for everyday drinking.

VINO DA PRANZO

An Italian term, like *vino da pasta*, a wine that needs to be drunk with food in order to be appreciated properly.

VINO DA TAVOLA

An Italian term for table wine and, by implication, the lowest category of Italian wine, without any distinguishing features. However, in practice some of the best Italian wines only merit *vino da tavola* status or, more precisely, *vino da tavola con indicazione geografica* which then allows the origin, grape variety and vintage to be given on the label but it is because Italians are individualistic, and wine makers, for one reason or another, choose not to conform to the DOC regulations of their region, so the resulting wine does not meet DOC standards. On paper, the wine merits the category of *vino da tavola* but, in the bottle, it may be a great wine like Tignanello or Fiorano.

VINO DA TAVOLA CON INDICAZIONE GEOGRAFICA

Italian table wine with a geographical definition. This is a more long-winded name for *vino tipico*. This category will contain the best table wines, including some of Italy's finest wines.

VINO TIPICO   See Indicazione Geografica.

VINÒT   Piedmont: ITALY

A red wine made from Nebbiolo grapes and first produced by Angelo Gaja of Barbaresco in 1975, modelled on Beaujolais Nouveau. Other *vini novelli* have followed Gaja's example.

VINOUS

Describes a pleasant smell of wine. The adjective also covers wine-related matters in general.

VINS DE LA MONTAGNE
Champagne: FRANCE

These wines come from the hilly part of the Montagne de Reims. The main villages in the *catégorie hors classe* are: Ambonnay, Beaumont sur Vesle, Bouzy, Louvois, Mailly, Sillery and Verzenay. These wines are said to give champagne its backbone.

VINS DE LA RIVIÈRE
Champagne: FRANCE

These wines come from the part of the Montagne de Reims that overlooks the Marne. The only village of *catégorie hors classe* is Ay. These wines contribute to the elegance of champagne, complementing the *vins de la montagne*.

VIN DES SABLES

A wine produced in the Landes near Capbreton. The vines were trained so low that the grapes actually rested on the sandy soil, so they ripened quickly to make heady alcoholic wine, which is now no more than a memory.

VINSANTERIA

A *vinsanteria* is the place, often a draughty attic, where the grapes for Vin Santo, the Italian dessert wine, are dried and the wine left to ferment and age, exposed to seasonal fluctuations of temperature.

VINSOBRES   Rhône: FRANCE

One of the villages of the appellation Côtes du Rhône Villages in the southern Rhône. The name translates literally as "sober wine" and seems rather incongruous for a wine village, but it is thought to have been making wine since the 4th century. Today its production is dominated by the two cave cooperatives, la Vinsobraise and la Cave du Prieuré plus a few private estates.

VINTAGE

The term used to describe the actual harvest of the grapes, in the sense that the vintage began on such a date and took place in beautiful weather.

In a second meaning it refers to the year of the wine, which may be a good or a bad vintage, as determined by the climatic conditions. For wines like port and champagne, which are usually sold without a vintage or year, a vintage may be declared only in the best years.

VINTAGE CHARACTER PORTUGAL

Good quality ruby port, almost as good as vintage port, that is matured in wood for four or five years. It is usually a blend of different years and provides an affordable way of drinking a wine that is not dissimilar to a vintage port in style.

VINTAGE CHART

A simplified means of reference as to the quality of the vintage in a particular region. Usually vintages are rated on a scale of 1 to 10. Such a chart is useful in giving an overall assessment of quality as a quick reference, but tends to generalise as it is unable to take into account the exceptions and it lacks details so this may confuse the rating of a vintage.

VINTAGE PORT PORTUGAL

Vintage port is the climax of fine port. The declaration of a vintage is each shipper's individual choice, although there is often a consensus of opinion about the quality of a year. A vintage is declared only in the best years, usually about three times in each decade. A vintage port is a blend of wine from a shipper's best vineyards, aged for two years in wood before bottling for further ageing in bottle. As from the 1975 vintage all vintage port must be bottled in the shippers' lodges in Vila Nova da Gaia, thus ending the tradition for British bottled vintage port.

VINTITULIST

A collector of wine labels, which for some wine enthusiasts is a popular hobby and a means of remembering enjoyable bottles.

VINTNER

An old-fashioned English term for a wine merchant who in the Middle Ages was a member of the Vintners Company. There are today members of the company who are Free Vintners, who have the right to sell wine by virtue of their position, and do not need to apply to a magistrate for a licence. 'Vintner grown' is a term sometimes found on a Californian wine label, indicating that a vintner may also be a winemaker. The term can be used by a winery when a wine does not meet the requirements for estate bottled.

VINTNERS' CLUB OF SAN FRANCISCO

An important wine society in California, with a membership comprising many of the state's winemakers.

THE VINTNERS' COMPANY

One of the twelve great livery companies in the City of London. In the Middle Ages, it controlled the trading of wine with Gascony and had extensive rights over wine merchants in England. Today, only a quarter of its membership comes from the wine trade; it now has an important social and charitable role and also coordinates the other associations of the wine trade.

VIOGNIER

The white grape that makes the most distinctive white wine of the Rhône, Condrieu and Château Grillet. A little can also be added to Côte Rôtie. The perfume and flavour of Viognier is unique, reminiscent of apricots. Production is tiny, for it is difficult to grow, giving only tiny yields. A little has also been introduced to California by Joseph Phelps.

LA VIOLETTE Bordeaux: FRANCE

A little-known Pomerol *château* next to Nenin.

VIPAVA YUGOSLAVIA

A white wine from the town of Vipava in Slovenia, made from a blend of grapes, mainly Laski Rizling and Rebula.

VIRÉ   See Mâcon Villages.

VIRGINIA USA

Virginia has a small pocket of *vitis vinifera* vines at Meredyth Vineyards, with Riesling and Chardonnay. Others have followed the example, but the health of the vines presents problems in the damp climate.

VIRIEU LE GRAND Savoie: FRANCE

One of the villages with the status of cru in the VDQS of Vin du Bugey. In practice the name is never used.

VISAN   Rhône: FRANCE

One of the villages of the appellation Côtes du Rhône Villages in the southern Rhône. Wine making here goes back to Roman times; today there is a village cooperative and a couple of good estates. Red, white and rosé wines are all entitled to the village appellation, but red is infinitely superior.

VISCOUS

Describes a heavy oily wine, almost unctuous, with weight on the palate and heavy tears.

VISPERTERMINE   SWITZERLAND

In the Valais region, this vineyard claims to be Europe's highest vineyard at 3700 feet.

VITE

The Italian word for vine.

VITICOLTORE

The Italian term for a grower of grapes.

VITICULTEUR

The French term for a grower of grapes; usually this is someone who has other crops as well as vines and is a member of the local cooperative so does not make wine on the property.

VITICULTURE

The science of cultivating vines and growing grapes, encompassing every aspect of work in the vineyard during the vine's annual cycle.

VITIGNO

The Italian word for a vine or vine type.

VITIS AMURENSIS

A vine species originating in Asia that is particularly resistant to cold and is being used for experimental purposes in Germany.

VITIS BERLANDIERI

A species of vine grown in North America. It is resistant to phylloxera and to chlorosis and has been used for rootstock for grafting *vitis vinifera*.

VITIS CINEREA

A vine variety of Middle America. It was used to develop Black Spanish, a grape of Madeira, but otherwise is of little importance.

VITIS LABRUSCA

One of the better-known American vines. It is not resistant enough to phylloxera to be used for rootstock. It features in America with varieties like Concord or hybrids like Catawba and Delaware and is responsible for the foxy flavour of these hybrids.

VITIS RIPARIA

A species of vine grown in North America. It is resistant to phylloxera and so is used for rootstock. Several hybrids have been developed from it as it is an early ripener and useful for cold climates.

VITIS ROTUNDIFOLIA

Part of the Muscadine family, a vine species originating in the Gulf of Mexico. Scuppernong is the best-known grape variety.

VITIS RUPESTRIS

A species of vine important for rootstock. Rupestris St. George and Rupestris du Lot are varieties of the species.

VITIS VINIFERA

The species of vine from which most of the world's wines are made. Some North American wine is made from other varieties.

VIURA

A synonym used in Rioja for the Maccabeo grape.

VOJVODINA   YUGOSLAVIA

A region of northern Yugoslavia with three main vineyard areas, Fruška Gora, Banat and Subotiča.

VOLATILE ACIDITY

In wine, this usually comes from acetic acid, normally associated with vinegar and caused by bacteria spoiling the wine when it is exposed to air. A common cause is the failure to top up the casks properly. A small amount of volatile acidity is necessary for the bouquet and flavour of a wine, but never more than 0.8 gms per litre.

A LA VOLEE   see dégorgement.

VOLNAY Burgundy: FRANCE

One of the great names of the Côte de Beaune with fine estates and vineyards and a long history. Some Meursault red wines can also be sold under the name of Volnay.

The Premier Cru vineyards are: en Cailleret, Cailleret Dessus, Champans, en Chevret, Fremiet, Bousse d'Or, la Barre or Clos de la Barre, Clos des Chênes (part), les Angles, Pointes d'Angles, les Mitans, en l'Ormeau, Taille-Pieds, en Verseuil, Carelle sous la Chapelle, Ronceret, Carelle Dessous (part), Robardelle (part), les Lurets (part), les Aussy (part), les Brouillards (part), Clos des Ducs, Pitures Dessus, Chanlin (part), les Santenots, les Petures (part) and Village de Volnay (part).

Growers and estates in Volnay include Marquis d'Angerville, Henri Boillot, Domaine Clerget, Mme Françoise de Montille, Michel Pont, Michel Lafarge and Domaine de la Pousse d'Or.

VON BUHL Rheinpfalz: GERMANY

Weingut Reichsrat von Buhl is one of the greatest family estates founded in 1849, with vineyards in the best sites of the region: Forst, Deidesheim and Ruppertsberg. They are planted with Riesling and other grapes. Barrel ageing is important; style ranges from very dry to extra sweet.

VON SCHUBERT Mosel-Saar-Ruwer: GERMANY

To give the estate its full title, C. von Schubert'sche Gutsverwaltung, one of the great estates of the region with origins dating back to 966. It was bought by the von Schubert family in 1882. They are the sole owners of three vineyards in the tiny village of Maximin-Grünhaus, Bruderberg (meaning 'for the brothers'), Herrenberg ('for the gentlemen') and Abtsberg ('for the abbot'), the best site of all, with deliciously subtle wines.

VORLESE

A German word for picking grapes in advance of the main harvest in order to remove rotten grapes or rescue a damaged crop.

VOROS

Describes red wine on a Hungarian wine label.

VOSGROS Burgundy: FRANCE

A Chablis Premier Cru vineyard. Part of the wine can also be sold under the name of Vaugiraut.

VÖSLAU AUSTRIA

A subdivision of Niederösterreich to the south of Vienna known for its red wine made from Blauer Portugieser grapes and also sparkling wine. Since the 1985 Austrian wine law, Vöslau has been renamed Thermenland.

VOSNE-ROMANÉE Burgundy: FRANCE

This village on the Côte de Nuits is known for its range of Grands Crus and also for some fine Premiers Crus. The Grands Crus are la Tâche, Richebourg, Romanée, Romanée-Conti and Romanée-St-Vivant.

The Premiers Crus are: aux Malconsorts, les Beaumonts, les Suchots, la Grande Rue, les Gaudichots, aux Brulées, les Chaumes, les Reignots, le Clos des Réas, les Petits Monts. Part of the vineyards lie in the neighbouring village of Flagey-Echézeaux, but have the right to the appellation of Vosne-Romanée.

The principal estates are Jean Grivot, Gros Père et Fils, Abbé Liger-Belair at the *château* of Vosne-Romanée, Jean Meó, Mongeard-Mugneret, Charles Noëllat and Domaine de la Romanée-Conti.

VOUGEOT Burgundy: FRANCE

The village of Vougeot on the Côte de Nuits owes its fame to its Grand Cru vineyard, Clos de Vougeot. It also boasts a few Premier Cru vineyards: le Clos Blanc, les Petits Vougeots, le Gras and Clos de la Perrière. There are two principal growers in the village: Ets. Bertagna and l'Héritier Guyot.

VOUVRAY Loire: FRANCE

The most versatile white wine of the Loire valley. Made from Chenin Blanc grown around the village of Vouvray on the north bank of the Loire, it can be very dry to very sweet, still or sparkling. The best Vouvray comes from over-ripe grapes so that it is demi-sec or even moelleux and in exceptional years *pourriture noble* is possible. Dry Vouvray also makes a very good base for sparkling wine. Vouvray Mousseux is made by the *méthode champenoise* and it is also possible to find Vouvray Pétillant. The best known producer is Marc Brédif.

VRAC

Means 'bulk' in French. A wine sold *en vrac*, in bulk, means that the bottling is the purchaser's responsibility.

VRANAC

A red Yugoslav grape variety accounting for some of the best wines of Macedonia and most of the wines of Montenegro. They are powerful and tannic.

VRAYE-CROIX-DE-GAY
Bordeaux: FRANCE

A little-known Pomerol *château*.

VUGAVA
YUGOSLAVIA

A heady aromatic white wine from the Dalmatian island of Vis.

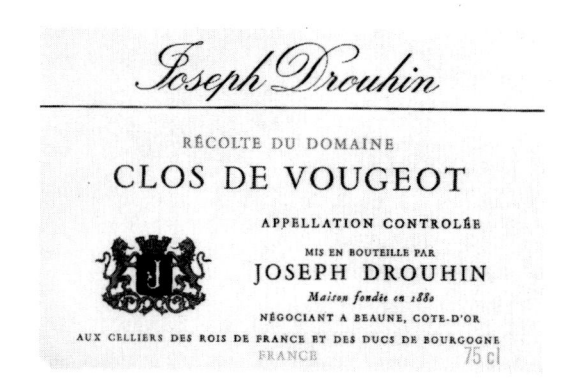

W

WACHENHEIM Rheinpfalz: GERMANY

One of the great villages of the Rheinpfalz. The principal *Grosslage* of the village is Mariengarten, which it also shares with Forst and Deidesheim, in addition to Schenkenböhl and Schnepfenflug. The best vineyards, or *Einzellagen*, are Goldbächel and Gerümpel. Other names include Böhlig, Rechbächel, Altenburg, Fuchsmantel, Mandelgarten and Luginsland. The leading producer of the village is Dr. Bürklin Wolf.

WAIKATO – BAY OF PLENTY
NEW ZEALAND

A wine region of New Zealand's North Island, about fifty miles south of Auckland. Its main importance is as the home of the Government Viticultural Research Station which was set up at Te Kauwhata in 1897. Cooks have vineyards here and see the area as a potentially fine red wine district with Cabernet Sauvignon, although it suffers from some climatic disadvantages of high rainfall, counterbalanced by higher than average temperatures.

WAIMAUKU see Kumeu.

WALDRACH Mosel-Saar-Ruwer: GERMANY

A wine village of the Ruwer within the *Grosslage* of Römerlay. The best known vineyards are Krone, Laurentiusberg, Jesuitengarten, Hubertusberg and Sonnenberg. Growers include the Bischöfliche Weinguter.

WALLUF Rheingau: GERMANY

A little known village on the Rheingau; its wines come within the *Grosslage* Steinmächer, or are sold locally under unknown *Einzellagen* names.

WÄLSCHRIZLING see Welschriesling

WARRE

The oldest English port house, founded in 1670 and now owned by the Symington family. Quinta da Cavadinha forms the basis of their vintage ports, while Warrior is their Vintage Character and Nimrod a fine tawny.

WASHINGTON STATE USA

One of the three wine producing states of the Pacific North West. It contrasts with Oregon in having a much drier, arid climate, with greater extremes of temperature. With the irrigation schemes of the Yakima Valley and ideal temperatures, the state produces healthy grapes in abundance. *Vitis Vinifera* vines were first planted in Washington State in the 1950s. As yet there are few wineries, so many grapes are blended with those from Oregon. Associated Vintners and Chateau Ste. Michelle are the two most important wineries.

WATERVALE See Clare-Watervale.

JIMMY WATSON AUSTRALIA

The Jimmy Watson Memorial Trophy is awarded annually to the best one year old red Australian wine at the Melbourne Show. Jimmy Watson was one of the great personalities of the Australian wine trade, who ran a wine bar in Melbourne, and the award in his memory is the most prestigious for an Australian wine to win.

WEEPER

A bottle of wine that is slightly leaking, or 'weeping' because of a faulty cork.

WEHLEN
Mosel-Saar-Ruwer: GERMANY

Thanks to the efforts of the Prüm family, this has become one of the most important Mittelmosel wine villages. An enormous white sundial gives Wehlen the name of its most famous vineyard, Sonnenuhr. Wines from this site command consistently high prices. Other vineyards are Klosterberg and Nonnenberg and the *Grosslage* is Münzlay. J. J. Prüm and Prüm Erben are leading producers.

WEIL
Rheingau: GERMANY

Weingut Dr. R. Weil is the leading estate of Kiedrich in the Rheingau. The family bought the property from an Englishman, Sir John Sutton, in 1868. The estate is planted with Riesling vines.

WEIN

The German word for wine.

WEINGUT

The German term for a wine estate or property. The term can only appear on a label if the wine comes exclusively from that estate.

WEINSTEIN

A German term for a deposit of tartrate crystals.

WEINSTRASSE

Literally means 'wine road', as in *Route du Vin* in France. It is the German term for a well signposted route through the vineyards. The best-known and oldest in Germany is the *Deutsche Weinstrasse* or Palatinate which even gives its name to the Bereich Mittelhaardt Deutsche Weinstrasse.

WEISSBURGUNDER see Pinot Blanc

WEISSER RIESLING see Riesling

WEISSHERBST

A German *rosé* wine, usually almost white in colour, and made from red grapes, often Spätburgunder. It comes especially from Baden but is also found in the Ahr, Franconia, Rheingau, Rheinhessen, Palatinate and Württemberg.

WELLOW
ENGLAND

One of the newer and largest English vineyards, with the first serious vintage in 1987. The owner Andy Vining aims to have 100 acres, planted with Germanic grape varieties, in production by 1992.

WELSCHRIESLING

Not to be confused with Rhine Riesling. Grown mainly in eastern Europe for fairly undistinguished but drinkable white wines. It is probably at its best in Austria, where it can develop noble rot with attractive results. It goes under a variety of names including Wälschriesling; Olaszrizling in Hungary; Laski Rizling in Yugoslavia, where it is responsible for the popular wines, Lutomer Laski Rizling and Riesling Italico, which has been anglicised as Italian Riesling. In a warm climate it is easy to grow and a prolific producer.

WENTE BROTHERS
California: USA

A Livermore winery founded in 1883. Wente are one of the great Californian wine families and the winery is now run by the fourth generation. Their reputation stands on their white wines, Arroyo Seco Riesling, Chardonnay and Sauvignon.

WESTBURY
ENGLAND

In Berkshire, this is one of the more controversial vineyards of England. The owner is fully convinced of the viability of Pinot Noir, despite the cool climate, and also grows more than two dozen different grape varieties, making four white and two red wines. The first vintage was in 1975.

WESTERN AUSTRALIA
AUSTRALIA

Western Australia has four wine regions, the Swan Valley, the South West Coastal plain, the Great Southern area and the Margaret River. See individual entries.

WESTSTEIERMARK AUSTRIA

The smallest of the Austrian wine regions, with the village of Stainz at the centre of the vineyards. The unusual Blauer Wilbacher is the main grape variety.

DE WETSHOF SOUTH AFRICA

One of the most important estates of the Robertson district of South Africa. The winemaker is Geisenheim trained and has made the estate one of the most influential and innovative of the Cape for the production of white wines, planting new grape varieties, Rhine Riesling, Chardonnay, Sauvignon Blanc and even Harslevelu, and making a botrytis wine Edeloes and an oak aged Chardonnay.

WHITE PORT PORTUGAL

Traditionally very sweet and designed as an after dinner drink. There has however been a recent trend to introduce dry white port made from grapes which have completely fermented before the addition of brandy, so that it makes an acceptable dry aperitif.

WHITE RIESLING

A Californian synonym for the grape variety Rhine Riesling.

WHITTAKER

One of the Englishmen who followed the example of John Woodhouse and began making Marsala. The original company is now incorporated with Florio and is part of the Italian Cinzano group.

WHOLESALE LICENCE

Used to allow for the sale of wine in quantities of not less than one dozen bottles. In practice, it is no longer necessary to hold such a licence in order to trade as a wholesale wine merchant.

WIDMERS WINE CELLARS USA

Widmers Wine Cellars is an important New York State winery, making a range of generic and hybrid wines.

WIESBADEN *Rheingau*: GERMANY

An attractive spa town and the capital of the State of Hessen, an important business centre and part of the Rheingau, coming within the *Grosslage* of Steinmächer. The one *Einzellage* of any note, Neroberg, is rarely found outside the town.

WILD YEAST see yeast.

WILLAMETTE VALLEY USA

One of the three designated wine areas of Oregon, covering nine counties from Portland 100 miles south to Eugene. Most of Washington's wineries are here at the northern end of the valley near Portland.

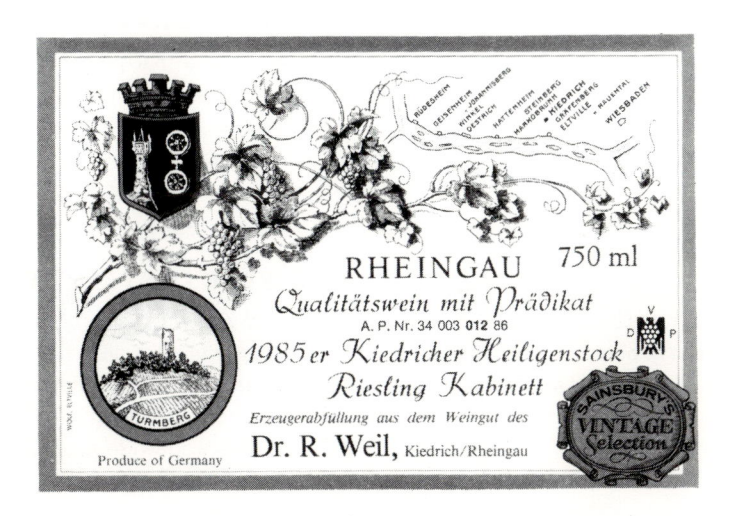

WILLIAMS & HUMBERT   SPAIN

The sherry company of Williams & Humbert was founded by Alexander Williams with his brother-in-law Arthur Humbert. Their offices used to house the British Consul in Jerez until it was discontinued in 1979. Dry Sack *amontillado* is their best known wine.

WILLMES

A common make of a pneumatic grape press.

WILTINGEN   Mosel-Saar-Ruwer: GERMANY

The finest village of the Saar and amongst the greatest of the whole Mosel. It comes within the *Grosslage* of Scharzberg and has a host of fine *Einzellagen*. Most notable of all is Scharzhofberg, which is always sold without the village name. The original vineyard, before the area was increased, was owned by Egon Müller and the Hohe Domkirche. Other vineyards include Braune Kupp, Rosenberg, Schlossberg, Sandberg, Hölle, Kupp, Gottesfuss, Klosterberg, Braunsfels and Schlangengraben. Several fine producers have property in the village including the Bischöfliche Weingüter, Kesselstatt, von Hövel and Le Gallais, which is administered by Egon Müller and has a 40% share of the Braune Kupp vineyard.

WIND

Can do considerable damage to vines, especially young vines, breaking shoots and harming vegetation. It also has a drying effect on the atmosphere and can prevent the development of rot. Growers in Provence appreciate the Mistral for this reason.

WINE

In the purest sense of the word, this is defined as the 'naturally fermented juice of grapes'. It should not include any of the so-called wines made from other fruits.

Wine can be divided into three broad categories: still table wines, which may be red, white or rosé, dry or sweet and all tastes in between; sparkling wines, of which champagne is the best, and fortified wine, to which some grape brandy has been added during the production process, such as madeira, port or sherry.

WINE AUCTION

Provides a way of buying wines such as older vintages and rare bottles, usually at a very fair price, which are no longer available on the usual commercial circuits. A wine may be offered at auction because its owner decides he or she does not like it or wants to raise money on the investment. Sometimes, entire cellars are sold on someone's death. The opportunity is sometimes offered to taste the wine beforehand, but the disadvantage of buying at auction is the lack of information, especially in the case of older wines, as to how they have been handled and stored. One maxim is to beware the eleven bottle lot.

WINE COOLER

As the name implies, this is a container for keeping a bottle of wine chilled. The most common modern ones are made from insulated plastic and work without using ice. The older, traditional wine cooler was much larger and more elaborate and ornate, allowing for ice and even glasses as well as the bottle and designed for presenting on an elegant dining table.

THE WINE DEVELOPMENT BOARD

The organisation that presents wine to the public, encouraging the consumption of wine, introducing it to the new wine drinker, and providing general information about it, without promoting any particular wine, company or country.

THE WINE INSTITUTE

Set up by Californian winemakers to reorganise their industry in 1934 after the end of Prohibition. The Institute laid down minimum quality standards and began a national education programme. Today it is still the worldwide promotional body of the Californian wine industry.

WINE LABEL

Provides information on the contents of a bottle of wine. There are various regulations to which a wine label must conform, giving some compulsory information and, depending on the quality of the wine, a certain amount of optional information. More is allowed for an appellation wine than a *vin de table*. However, all labels must give the country of origin, contents, alcoholic strength, colour and the bottler or producer. In addition, there can be more detailed information as to provenance, winemaker and so on. Back labels can also provide reams of technical information on vinification details, or can give advice on how to serve the wine. Design is important for a wine label. It must above all make the wine look tempting. The most esoteric of labels are those of Château Mouton Rothschild, where a famous artist is commissioned to design the label each year. Others have followed his example but on a less grandiose scale, and sometimes the plainest labels are the best.

WINE LAKE

The term for the excess production of wine in the Common Market, coming mainly from France and Italy. So many of the vineyards of the Midi were planted with high yielding vines producing wine of poor quality, for which there is no market. Most of this wine is ultimately distilled for industrial alcohol. Gradually viticulture in the region is changing as better grape varieties are planted and production methods improve.

WINE LIST

The means by which a wine merchant, restaurant or wine bar informs customers of their selection of wines. Information varies enormously. Some wine merchants give just the basic facts, such as the name of wine, the vintage and the producer; others write tasting notes, advise on drinkability and provide more detailed information about the winemaker and the wine. Restaurant wine lists vary in detail. Many are the restaurants which omit vital details such as vintage or producer. A good wine list is a delight to read and, if it is performing its function properly, it should have you eager to buy a bottle, or more.

WINE MERCHANT

Someone who trades in wine. Today the traditional image of the wine merchant who advises on purchases of port and claret is defunct. Such wine merchants do still exist, but with the greater diversity of the wine trade, a merchant, a purveyor of wine, may now be a supermarket, a wine warehouse, a High Street off-licence chain, or one person enthusing about a small vineyard area. The variations are infinite.

WINE MUSEUM

A museum dedicated to vinous artefacts. One of the finest is at Château Mouton-Rothschild, which was created by Pauline de Rothschild and is a wonderful collection of works of art all related to wine. Others that merit a visit include that at Torgiano in Umbria, run by the Lungarotti family, the wine museum at Villafranca del Penedés in Catalonia and, in England, the Harvey's of Bristol museum with its particularly fine collection of glasses.

WINE OF ORIGIN   SOUTH AFRICA

Wine of Origin is the South African equivalent of *Appellation Contrôlée*. The system was implemented in 1973 and defines 17 Regions of Origin, sometimes further divided into wards. The system also allows for estate status for certain producers, the extra qualification of Superior and the mention of a cultivar or grape variety. The application for the official seal depends upon the producer and is recognised by coloured bands on the neck of the bottle as follows:

blue band: origin, certifying that 100% of the wine comes from the indicated region, district or ward;

red band: vintage, that 75% of the wine comes from grapes harvested in the indicated year;

green band: cultivar, that the wine contains the legal minimum percentage of that particular cultivar and is characteristic of the cultivar;

estate – certifies that the wine is made on the estate from grapes grown on the estate. Bottling may be elsewhere.

Superior is an extra quality grading given after an extra tasting test.

WINE & SPIRIT ASSOCIATION

The official body of the wine and spirit trade, responsible for the trade's relationship with the Government and with the Common Market. It lobbies the Government on behalf of the wine trade and disseminates official information.

WINE STANDARDS BOARD

The body responsible for ensuring wine merchants' honest trading, for correct labelling of wines and saying they are indeed what they purport to be. English winemakers also come under their control.

WINE STONES

Another name for a deposit of tartrate crystals.

WINE TRADE

The general term for all aspects of wine commerce, beginning with the export of wine from a foreign producer through to its final sale to the general public. A member of the wine trade may be an importer, wholesaler, broker, retailer or wine merchant.

WINE WAREHOUSE

A relatively new phenomenon in the British wine trade. It is a wine shop, designed like a warehouse, with cases of wine stacked on palettes, rather than bottles on shelves. A minimum sale is a case of twelve bottles but not necessarily of the same wine.

WINE YEAST   see yeast.

WINERY

A New World term for the place where wine is made. Or it can describe a wine-making organisation or company.

WINKEL   Rheingau: GERMANY

Means 'a quiet corner' but is far from peaceful as the traffic on the main river road along the Rhine passes through this important Rheingau village, which merits its reputation as the home of Schloss Vollrads. Winkel comes mainly within the *Grosslage* of Honigsberg, apart from the Dachsberg vineyard which is in Erntebringer. Other fine sites include Hasenspring, Gutenberg, Jesuitengarten and Schlossberg, with Deinhard, Schloss Schönborn and Schloss Vollrads amongst the best producers.

WINTRICH   Mosel-Saar-Ruwer: GERMANY

A small wine village on the Mittelmosel within the *Grosslage* of Kurfürstlay. The best known vineyards are Ohligsberg, Grosser Herrgott, Sonnseite and Stefanslay.

WINZERGENOSSENSCHAFT

The German term for a growers' cooperative, it has the same functions and role as the French *cave coopérative* or Italian *cantina sociale*. It is larger than a *Winzerverein* which is the term for a smaller growers' cooperative.

WIRRA WIRRA   AUSTRALIA

An old winery in Langhorne Creek in South Australia. The name means 'amongst the gums' in Aborigine. The winery was revived in the early 1970s and makes some good red wine from Shiraz, Cabernet Sauvignon and Merlot.

WISCONSIN   USA

Wisconsin boasts one winery, the Wollersheim Winery, producing hybrid wines. The building dates back to the 1840s and was owned by Agoston Haraszthy, the pioneer of Californian viticulture.

WISDOM & WARTER   SPAIN

The sherry house of Wisdom & Warter was founded by two Englishmen in 1854. It was said once in Punch that 'Wisdom sells the wine; Warter makes it'. Their range today includes a variety of sherries such as Wisdom's Choice cream, Royal Palace *amontillado* and so on.

WONNEGAU
                              Rheinhessen: GERMANY

Meaning 'happy land' in German, one of the three *Bereich* of the Rheinhessen, covering the southern part of the region from Worms to Alzey.

WOOD PORT   PORTUGAL

A general term used to describe port that is blended and aged in cask until it is ready for drinking. Best of these is tawny port which may be aged for as long as forty years before bottling. Ruby and white port is also matured in wood.

WOODHOUSE

John Woodhouse takes credit as the instigator of Marsala, an English merchant who enjoyed the wines of western Sicily and fortified them to enable them to survive the journey home. His success at selling them encouraged him to start a winery. Nelson's fleet is said to have drunk his wine. The company is now incorporated with Florio under Cinzano.

WOODLEY WINES   AUSTRALIA

A historic winery in the Barossa Valley. The Queen Adelaide label is used for their best wines, including "claret", Riesling and "champagne".

WOODY

Describes a wine that has spent too long in barrel, so that all the fruit has disappeared and all that remains is a dry dull taste.

WOOTTON   ENGLAND

A small vineyard near Wells in Somerset, planted with Schönburger, Auxerrois, Müller-Thurgau and Seyval Blanc grapes. It has made award-winning wines since planting the first vines in 1971.

WORCESTER   SOUTH AFRICA

One of the Wine of Origin districts of the Breede River Valley, including the Wards of Nuy, Goudini, Slanghoek, Scherpenheuvel and Aan-de-Doorns. The region is delimited by mountain ranges; temperatures and rainfall vary considerably; irrigation is often necessary and dry white or fortified sweet wines are made, or wine for distillation.

WORMS   *Rheinhessen*: GERMANY

A cathedral city with the vineyard of the Liebfrauenkirche, that gave its name to Liebfraumilch. Today its wine is sold as Liebfrauenstift Kirchenstück; the property is split between two shippers and surrounded by tarmac and concrete in the middle of the city. Worms comes within the *Grosslage* of Liebfrauenmorgen.

WROTHAM PINOT

An English variation of Pinot Meunier and one of the few red grape varieties grown with any success in our cool climate.

WÜRTTEMBERG   GERMANY

A wine region of Germany which is not well-known as most of its production is drunk locally. The river Neckar gives the vineyards of Württemberg their shape, with southern slopes along its banks. Riesling is the best grape for white wine, with some Kerner and Müller-Thurgau, but the region's speciality is red wine and *rosé*, known as *Weissherbst*, made mainly from Trollinger and also other varieties such as Müllerrebe, Limberger, Portugieser and Spätburgunder. The grapes often lack sufficient colour for red wine and are made into *Weissherbst* or *Schillerwein* instead. Most of the production is in the hands of cooperatives; the main private estates are the Hofkammerkellerei of the Grand Dukes of Württemberg in Stuttgart, Graf Adelmann and Graf Neipperg. The region is divided into three *Bereichs*; Remstal-Stuttgart, Württembergisch Unterland and Kocher-Jagst-Tauber, with a total of 16 *Grosslagen*.

WÜRTTEMBERGISCH UNTERLAND   *Württemburg*: GERMANY

The largest of the three *Bereichs* of Württemberg, covering the Neckar valley north of Stuttgart.

WÜRTTEMBERGISCHE HOFKAMMER KELLEREI   *Württemberg*: GERMANY

One of the finest Württemberg estates. The wines are still made and aged in oak casks in the medieval ducal cellars in Stuttgart. Riesling is important, along with other grape varieties like Limberger and Trollinger.

WÜRZBURG STAATLICHER HOFKELLER   *Franconia*: GERMANY

One of the finest Franconian estates, founded in the 12th century and now the Bavarian State Domain. The cellars under the Baroque Princes Residence in Würzburg are magnificent. The wines live up to the surroundings with fine Rieslings, Müller-Thurgau, a little Spätburgunder and other varieties.

WÜRZER

A crossing of the Gewürztraminer and Müller Thurgau grape varieties, grown mainly in the Rheinhessen.

WYNDHAM ESTATE AUSTRALIA

A leading company in the Hunter Valley, owning the Hermitage Estate in the Lower Hunter, with vineyards at Hollydene and an association with Richmond Grove in the Upper Hunter. Dalwood was their original vineyard and now the base of their operations. Their wines include a full range of varietals.

WYNN WINEGROWERS AUSTRALIA

One of the largest wine producing companies of Australia. They own several estates, most notably in Coonawarra where they produce an excellent Coonawarra Cabernet Sauvignon, and also a Hermitage, a Hermitage-Cabernet blend, a Rhine Riesling and a Chardonnnay. In addition they own vineyards at the High Eden Estate between the Barossa and Eden Valleys, in Keppoch - Padthaway, in the Ovens Valley for Shiraz and they have a winery at Yenda in the M.I.A. They have a good reputation for consistency and quality.

X

XAREL-LO
One of the three grape varieties grown in Penedés for Cava, for blending with Parellada and Macabeo. By itself it would be uninteresting. It also contributes to still wine elsewhere in Catalonia.

XYNISTERI
The native white grape of Cyprus, used for Commandaria and for rather neutral white table wines.

XYNOMAVRO
One of the most widely planted red grape varieties of Greece, an indigenous variety. Xyno, meaning acid, and mavro, meaning black, describe the style of wine, of which Naoussa is the best.

Y

YAKIMA VALLEY — USA

The main grape growing area of Washington State although, until recently, most of the wineries were 150 miles away around Seattle. *Vitis vinifera* was not planted here until the 1950s. With only an average of 8 inches of rain per year, irrigation is essential.

YALUMBA — AUSTRALIA

The winery in the Barossa Valley belonging to the company S. Smith, run by the Hill Smith family. They own extensive vineyards, including Pewsey Vale and Heggies, cool climate sites on the Barossa ranges. Fortified wines like Yalumba Galway Pipe Port were once their best wines; today the reputation of this family firm stands on fragrant white wines and barrel aged red.

YAMAGATA — JAPAN

In northern Honshu, Japan's largest island, the country's second largest vineyard area.

YAMANASHI — JAPAN

The most important vineyard area of Japan, on the principal island of Honshu, southwest of Tokyo in the shadow of Fujiyama. The soil is volcanic and the microclimate temperate.

YARRA VALLEY — AUSTRALIA

A small, reviving wine area of Victoria just outside Melbourne. The climate is cool, with a long ripening period. Yields tend to be low and the vineyards small. The main grape varieties are Cabernet Sauvignon, Pinot Noir, Merlot and Chardonnay, producing some excellent wines.

YARRA YERING — AUSTRALIA

The first winery of the Yarra Valley, established in 1969 by Dr. Bailey Carrodus. Dry Red No. 1 is a blend of Cabernet Sauvignon, Merlot and Malbec, while No. 2 is based on Shiraz.

YEAST

Responsible for converting the sugar in grapes into ethyl alcohol. They are naturally present on the bloom of the grapes, but more technologically-advanced winemakers, especially in the New World, use cultured yeast. There are numerous varieties of yeast, which can be divided into wild yeast and wine yeast. The main wine yeast species is saccharomyces cerevisiae, of which the most important variety is saccharomyces ellipsoideus. If wild yeast, which far outnumber wine yeast, take over the fermentation, they can give the wine various off-tastes. Most wild yeast can be eliminated with a light dose of sulphur, but some winemakers prefer to destroy all the natural yeast and use instead cultured yeast, which are thoroughbred strains of natural yeast, raised in a laboratory for this specific purpose, and which have greater subtlety of flavour and resistance to a higher level of alcohol or sulphur dioxide.

YEAST AUTOLYSIS

Occurs after fermentation, when the yeast fall to the bottom of the container, be it tank or bottle, and begin to decay. The dead yeast give off certain flavours, which can be considered detrimental to still wines, but in the case of sparkling wine, most notably champagne, give it an essential character.

YEASTY

Describes the smell associated with fermentation. It should not be detected in wine in bottle, which would be an indication of yeast activity and a second fermentation.

YECLA   SPAIN

A D.O. of the Levante, producing similar wines to neighbouring D.O., Jumilla, mainly full-bodied reds from the Monastrell grape. The cooperative La Purisima is the main producer.

YELLOW GLEN   AUSTRALIA

The main wine producer of South Australia's Ballarat area, taking its name from an old gold mine. Champagne method wines from Pinot Noir and Chardonnay are their most important line, aspiring to be Australia's best sparkling wine. Cabernet Sauvignon and Shiraz are their successful table wines.

YERASSA   CYPRUS

One of the best villages for Commandaria, making a rich wine from Mavron and Ophthalmo grapes.

YESO   see gypsum.

YGREC   Bordeaux: FRANCE

The dry white wine of d'Yquem and the French for the letter Y. The *encépagement* is half Sauvignon grape and half Sémillon.

YIELD

The amount of grapes or wine produced at a vintage, measured in France in hectolitres per hectare, in Italy in quintales per hectare and in California as tons per acre. Yields are a factor of quality. A small yield will produce a better wine than an enormous yield from the same vineyard. In some countries, such as France, yields are strictly controlled in the *appellation contrôlée* regulations. In contrast, in Germany, it is left to the conscience of individual growers. In California, the better varietals produce much lower yields than those for jug wines.

YON-FIGEAC   Bordeaux: FRANCE

A large Grand Cru Classé of St-Émilion, once part of Figeac.

YORK MOUNTAIN   California: USA

An AVA in the northern part of San Luis Obispo County.

YOUNG

Describes an immature wine.

D'YQUEM   Bordeaux: FRANCE

The only first growth Sauternes and the epitome of great sweet white wine. It has belonged to the Lur Saluces family for 200 years and they run the property with meticulous care. Several pickings or *tries* are made at the vintage; the wine is fermented in new oak barrels and then aged in oak for three and a half years. The *château* is a fine medieval fortress with 80 hectares of vines in production. A dry wine is also made, Ygrec. 1847 was a legendary vintage; more recent great years include 1967, 1971, 1975 and 1983.

YUGOSLAV OAK   see Slavonic oak.

YUGOSLAVIA

Yugoslavia with its two alphabets, three religions, four languages, five nationalities, six republics and seven frontiers produces an enormous variety of different wines all over the country. The Laski Rizling is the most widely grown grape variety, accounting for the popular Lutomer Laski Rizling. Gewürztraminer, Sauvignon, Pinot Blanc are also enjoying some success, especially in Serbia, as are Cabernet and Merlot for reds. The more individual Yugoslav wines come from the Prokupac grape, grown widely in Serbia and the Plavac Mali grape which produces wines such as Dingac and Postup from the Dalmatian coast where the country's most traditional wines are made. Prŏsek is a characteristic dessert wine.

Z

Z.B.W. See Zentralkellerei Badischer Winzergenossenschaft.

ZACA MESA   California: USA

An important winery in the Santa Ynez Valley. The first vintage was in 1978. Cabernet Sauvignon, Pinot Noir and Johannisberg Riesling are considered their best wines.

ZAER See Rabat.

ZAGAROLO   Latium: ITALY

An unusual dry or sweet white wine from the town of Zagarolo, southeast of Rome. The dominant grape variety is Malvasia.

ZANDVLIET   SOUTH AFRICA

An important wine estate in the Robertson region of South Africa with an excellent reputation for Shiraz. Pinot Noir and Cabernet Sauvignon have also been planted.

ZAPATOS

Zapatos de pisar are the traditional studded cowhide boots that were worn in Jerez in Spain for treading the grapes.

ZELL   Mosel-Saar-Ruwer: GERMANY

A village and the name of a *Bereich* that covers the Mosel from Zell to the outskirts of Koblenz. The best-known vineyard of Zell is the *Grosslage* Zeller Schwarze Katz, known mainly because of the black cat on the label.

ZELTINGEN   Mosel-Saar-Ruwer: GERMANY

The village's full name is Zeltingen-Rachtig and it is the largest Mittelmosel wine commune. The *Grosslage* is Münzlay and important *Einzellagen* include Sonnenuhr, a continuation of the Wehlen vineyard, Schlossberg, Himmelreich and Deutschherrenberg. Good producers include von Schorlemer, J.J.Prüm and the Vereinigten Hospitien.

ZEMMOUR See Rabat.

ZENNATA See Casablanca.

ZENTRALKELLEREI BADISCHER WINZERGENOSSENSCHAFT   Baden: GERMANY

ZBW for short, this is a central cooperative which accounts for about 90% of the total wine production of Baden. It unites over 100 local cooperatives at one of Europe's largest and most modern wineries at Breisach. Over 400 different wines are produced each year from a mixture of grape varieties sold under the various *Bereich*, *Grosslage* and *Einzellage* names.

ZERKHOUN   MOROCCO

An *appellation d'origine garantie*, in the region of Meknès Fez.

ZIBIBBO

A synonym for the Muscat d'Alexandrie grape in Italy, notably on the island of Pantelleria. See Moscato di Pantelleria.

ZIERFÄNDLER   AUSTRIA

An Austrian white grape, grown in Niederösterreich, south of Vienna, notably for Gumpoldskirchen wine.

ŽILAVKA
YUGOSLAVIA

A white grape of Yugoslavia, grown notably in Bosnia-Herzegovina and making Žilavka, a pungent white wine from grapes grown around the city of Mostar. Žilavka is also grown in Kosmet.

ZIMBABWE

Viticulture in Zimbabwe received a tremendous boost with UDI, when it became impossible to obtain imported wines. The country looks to South Africa; the grape varieties are similar with Colombard, Bukettraube, Chenin Blanc, Pinotage, Muscat d'Alexandrie, Cabernet Sauvignon and so on, which are grown in favourable climatic conditions in vineyards at an altitude of 4000 feet. The main vineyard area is between Harare and Mutari in the north east of the country.

ZIND-HUMBRECHT
Alsace: FRANCE

One of the great names of Alsace and arguably the best grower. The family firm is owned and run by Leonard Humbrecht from the village of Wintzenheim. He has the exclusive ownership of the Grand Cru sites of Clos Saint Urbain, Clos Hauserer and Herrenweg as well as parts of Brand, Hengst and Rangen. Zind Humbrecht have bottled their wines since 1959 and make excellent *Vendange Tardive* wines.

ZINFANDEL

A peculiarly Californain grape variety. Its probable origins are in the Primitivo grape of southern Italy; it was introduced to California by Haraszathy where it is now widely grown to produce a variety of different wines, ranging from heady, raisiny Late Harvest Zinfandels, not unlike Recioto, as well as port style wines, through robust berry flavoured table wines from wineries like Ridge to light jug wines. It can even be vinified as a white wine. Vinification techniques vary from *nouveau* styles to serious oak ageing for long term drinking. It prefers cooler growing conditions, but is also extensively planted in the hot Central Valley for rather jammy jug wine. A little is planted in South Africa, but otherwise it rarely strays outside California.

ZITSA
GREECE

A semi-sparkling dry white wine made near Joannina in Epirus from Debina grapes.

ZÖLDSZILVÁNI

The Hungarian synonym for the Silvaner grape.

ZOOPIYI
CYPRUS

One of the best villages for Commandaria, making a rich wine from Mavron and Ophthalmo grapes.

ŽUPA
YUGOSLAVIA

An old vineyard area in the hills south of Belgrade, producing red and rosé wine mainly from the Prokupac grape.

ZÜRICH
SWITZERLAND

The most productive canton in German-speaking Switzerland, with Pinot Noir and Pinot Gris grapes grown in vineyards around Wädenswil and Winterthur.

ZWEIGELT BIEU

Grown in Austria, a crossing of Blaufrankisch and St. Laurent, developed by a Dr. Zweigelt.

ZWICKER

A term that was used in Alsace to denote a wine made from a blend of lesser grape varieties, which has now been abandoned in favour of Edelzwicker.

Suggested further reading:

Faber and Faber

Bordeaux – David Peppercorn (May '82)
The Wines of Portugal – Jan Read (Nov '87)
The Wines of Spain – Jan Read (Oct '86)
The Wines of Germany – Frank Schoonmaker (June '83)
Burgundy – Anthony Hanson (May '82)

Sotheby Publications

Wines of Chablis – Rosemary George (June '84)
Book of California Wine – edited by Doris Muscatine (Nov '84)
Champagne – Tom Stevenson (Sept '87)

Mitchell Beazley

Vines, Grapes and Wines – Jancis Robinson – (Sept '86)
The Wine Companion – Hugh Johnson (Oct '87)
Wine – Hugh Johnson (Oct '74)
World Atlas of Wine – Hugh Johnson (Oct '85)

For more detailed quick reference – the Mitchell Beazley pocket books

Sidgwick & Jackson

Life Beyond Lambrusco – Nick Belfrage (Sept '85)
Life Beyond Liebfraumilch – Stuart Piggott (Sept '88)

Little, Brown

Vino – Burton Anderson (June '81)

Gollancz

Champagne – Patrick Forbes (Sept '67)

Christopher Helm

Rich, Rare and Red, A Guide to Port – Ben Howkins (Aug '87)

Hamlyn

Wine Lore, Legends and Traditions – Pamela Vandyke Price (Oct '85)